RUNNING
Microsoft® Windows® 98

Craig Stinson

Microsoft Press

PUBLISHED BY
Microsoft Press
A Division of Microsoft Corporation
One Microsoft Way
Redmond, Washington 98052-6399

Library of Congress Cataloging-in-Publication Data
Stinson, Craig, 1943-
    Running Microsoft Windows 98 / Craig Stinson.
        p.   cm.
    Includes index.
    ISBN 1-57231-681-0
    1. Microsoft Windows (Computer file)   2. Operating systems
(Computers)   I. Title.
QA76.76.063S75555   1998
005.4'3769--dc21   98-11184
                                                        CIP

Printed and bound in the United States of America.

1 2 3 4 5 6 7 8 9   QMQM   3 2 1 0 9 8

Distributed in Canada by ITP Nelson, a division of Thomson Canada Limited.

A CIP catalogue record for this book is available from the British Library.

Microsoft Press books are available through booksellers and distributors worldwide. For further
information about international editions, contact your local Microsoft Corporation office or
contact Microsoft Press International directly at fax (425) 936-7329. Visit our Web site at
mspress.microsoft.com.

Acquisitions Editor: Kim Fryer
Project Editor: Saul Candib

Chapters at a Glance

iii

Table of Contents

Acknowledgments

I am indebted to many people for their contributions to the conception, management, production, and content of this book:

Scott Berkun and John Ross contributed material on Internet Explorer, FrontPage Express, Personal Web Server, and Outlook Express.

Kim Fryer and Saul Candib, of Microsoft Press, oversaw the project with grace and humor, despite the many delays and schedule revisions.

Greg Pickett, of CM Electronics in Littleton, CO, provided a great deal of hardware and other technical assistance at many different points in the project. And Alps America pitched in with the timely loan of an MD-4000 printer/scanner.

I am especially grateful to the team at Siechert and Wood Professional Documentation (Pasadena, California)—Blake Whittington, Paula Kausch, Thomas Williams, and Stan DeGulis—for combining the traditionally distinct functions of production and technical editing with unfailing skill and accuracy. In addition, as he has on so many previous versions of this book, Carl Siechert acted as my auxiliary eyes and ears on Microsoft's beta newsgroups, serving thereby as chief intelligence officer for the project.

And finally, once again, I thank my wife and children for their love and support. I'm sure it seemed like this one dragged on forever, but without their tolerance of my busy evenings and weekends, it would be dragging on even now.

Introduction

Welcome to Windows 98. If you're moving up from Windows 95, you'll find a host of new and improved features, all of which add up to a faster, more versatile, and more reliable operating system. Those new features can be grouped roughly under the following headings:

- Improved reliability and manageability

- Improved hardware support

- Better performance

- Better integration with the Internet

- Ease of use and convenience features

If you're leapfrogging from Windows 3.x to Windows 98, many more improvements await your discovery. In this introduction, we'll survey the features that are new since Windows 95 and provide a brief orientation for those who are moving up from Windows 3.x.

Improved Reliability and Manageability

If you open the Start menu, choose Programs, Accessories, and then open the System Tools submenu, you'll find a number of new and improved tools to help you keep your operating system running smoothly and efficiently.

System File Checker. System File Checker scans all critical components of Windows 98. If it finds a system file that appears to have become corrupted, the checker offers to restore it for you from your Windows 98 installation CD. You no longer have to reinstall the entire operating system to take care of a single file that may have become damaged.

Disk Cleanup. A cleanup utility helps you avoid overloading your hard disks with unneeded files. The program calculates how much space it could recover by getting rid of four kinds of potential clutter: temporary (cached) Internet files, ActiveX controls and Java applets downloaded from the Internet, the contents of the Recycle Bin, and temporary files. Then it offers to delete any or all of those elements.

Disk Defragmenter. In addition to rearranging all files so that they occupy contiguous disk sectors, Windows 98's improved defragmentation program can move the programs you run most often, along with any .DLL files used by those programs, to the outer tracks of your disk, so that they launch more quickly.

ScanDisk. If Windows 98 is shut down improperly, ScanDisk runs automatically at the next system startup, ensuring that any damage to the logical structure of your disk caused by files left open at shutdown is detected and repaired.

Maintenance Wizard. The new Maintenance Wizard lets you keep your system in tune by running ScanDisk, Disk Cleanup, and Disk Defragmenter automatically at scheduled intervals.

Registry Checker. A new utility scans your registry for errors and optionally backs it up. You can run this program from either the MS-DOS command line (in the event that you're unable to start Windows) or from within Windows.

Backup and system recovery. Windows 98's improved Backup program supports tape drives, floppy disks, hard disks, and removable media. It also includes a system recovery utility that you can use to restore a full system backup after a catastrophic event.

Automatic Skip Driver. Automatic Skip Driver identifies system components that are known to have caused Windows 98 to stop responding and marks them so they can be bypassed on subsequent startups.

System Information. Microsoft System Information, a new program included with Windows 98, provides detailed information about everything going on in your system—DMA and IRQ assignments, resource conflicts, memory use, the software environment, and much more. Problems are clearly flagged in red.

Troubleshooters. The new Help system includes fifteen interactive troubleshooters. If something goes wrong, you might be able to diagnose and repair the problem yourself with the help of one of these.

Windows Update. Microsoft's new Windows Update Internet site has two invaluable components: Update Wizard and Technical Support. The Update Wizard scans your system and offers to download any newer versions of its components that happen to be available. You can use the wizard to keep your system current with the latest operating system software and device drivers. The Technical Support section provides a search window into Microsoft's Knowledge Base.

Support for the Latest Hardware

Keeping up with the latest advances in hardware was a paramount design goal of Windows 98. The new operating system offers built-in support for all of the following:

- The Advanced Configuration and Power Interface (ACPI) standard
- DVD drives
- USB and IEEE 1394 ports
- AGP ports

In addition, Windows 98 supports television tuner cards with WebTV for Windows and WaveTop. WebTV for Windows lets you watch your favorite television programs on your computer screen, in either a full-screen or an intermediate-size window. If you also take advantage of Windows 98's support for multiple displays, you can have a television program going on one screen while you download your electronic mail or do some other work in the other screen. WaveTop, meanwhile, lets you download and cache selected Internet content free of charge and view it later in a browser much like Internet Explorer. The Internet content arrives over an unused portion of the television signal sent by PBS stations all across the United States. You need only a tuner card and a nearby PBS station to receive your personalized selection of news, weather reports, market information, and more.

Behind the new hardware support is a new driver model called WDM (Win32 Driver Model), which allows hardware developers to produce a single driver for both Windows 98 and Windows NT. Legacy drivers will continue to work as they have in the past, however.

Better Performance

Windows 98 offers system-wide performance improvements over Windows 95. You should notice, among other things, quicker boot times and shutdown times. If you take advantage of the new defragmentation utility, your programs will also load more quickly. In addition, Windows 98's support for DirectX enables developers to produce new kinds of high-performance graphics programs and games.

Most important, perhaps, Windows 98 offers FAT32, a new file system that makes much more efficient use of large hard disks. FAT32's smaller cluster size means that less of your valuable disk space will be wasted as "slack." You'll also be able to use large disks without partitioning them into smaller logical units.

If you're upgrading to Windows 98 from a system that uses the older FAT16 file system, you can use Windows 98's new FAT32 converter to switch to the new system. The conversion process does not alter existing files.

Better Integration with the Internet

If you choose, you can set up Windows 98 so that browsing your local and network-based disk resources is exactly like browsing resources on the Internet. You can, if you want, make your desktop look and behave like a page on the World Wide Web. Desktop shortcuts, made to act like Web links, can be launched with a single click. Live data from Internet sites can be fed to the desktop in the form of news tickers, weather maps, and so on. And developers can create HTML-encoded wallpaper to turn your desktop effectively into an Internet site.

To help you take advantage of the Internet itself, Windows 98 ships with Internet Explorer and a suite of related products, including a teleconferencing program (NetMeeting), an electronic mail client (Outlook Express), an IRC client (Chat), a Web-page development tool (FrontPage Express), and Personal Web Server, a tool that you can use to set up an intranet or small-scale Internet Web server.

Ease of Use and Convenience Features

If you have more than one PCI video adapter, you can spread your Windows desktop across multiple displays. With a multidisplay setup you can work in more than one maximized program at a time or put all your shortcuts on one display while you work at another.

Windows 98 also supports the aggregation of multiple modems. By using separate communication ports and telephone connections, you can combine multiple modems to achieve higher-bandwidth connectivity.

A new Scheduled Task facility lets you run maintenance tasks and other activities unattended at scheduled times. And a new scripting host allows VBScript and Jscript programs to be run from the Start menu's Run command.

Windows 95's Plus! add-on has been incorporated into Windows 98, making it easier for you to change standard desktop icons, apply font smoothing and full-window dragging, and take advantage of thematic wallpaper, cursors, and sound effects.

Additional usability enhancements include a brand new HTML-based help system (the Windows 3.x and Windows 95 help engines are still supported, of course, so earlier programs continue to work normally), the ability to add custom toolbars to the desktop (they can be docked on any edge or float in the middle), and the ability to rearrange the Start menu by dragging items and subfolders with the mouse.

Upgrading from Windows 3.x

If you're moving directly from Windows 3.x to Windows 98, you might feel a little disoriented on your first day "off the boat" in Windows 98. The following tips will help you master the new environment quickly:

- **Find everything you need on the Start menu.** The Start menu is Windows 98's replacement for Program Manager. You'll find almost every program and document you need on one of its branches. (For details, see "The Start Button and the Start Menu," page 8, and Chapter 2, "Using and Customizing the Start Menu.")

- **Switch programs with Alt+Tab or click the taskbar.** Alt+Tab works the way it always has, but now you can also switch by clicking a button on the taskbar. And you can make the taskbar "stay on top" or duck out of sight, as you prefer. (For details, see "Switching Between Windows," page 17, and "Personalizing the Taskbar," page 76.)

- **When in doubt, right-click.** Everywhere you go in Windows 98, a right-click provides either a properties dialog box (allowing you to see and change current settings), a menu of currently relevant commands, or both. Getting in the right-click habit will help you discover everything you can do in this operating system. (For details, see "Context ('Right-Click') Menus," page 24.)

- **Make shortcuts for the programs, documents, and folders you need every day.** Shortcuts save time and trouble by providing direct access to practically anything in your working environment. Shortcuts can be placed on the desktop for easy use. (For details, see "Adding Shortcuts to Your Desktop," page 83.)

■ **Check out Windows Explorer.** If outlines bring up painful memories of high-school English classes, use unadorned Windows Explorer windows to manage your disk resources. But if you *like* outlines, open Windows Explorer's All Folders Explorer Bar. This powerful browsing tool lets you take in all your local and networked file resources at a glance. (For details, see "'Open View' Versus 'Explore View,'" page 107.)

■ **Drop into your "nethood" to find the file server you need.** The Network Neighborhood icon is your entrée to all servers local and remote. Working with the network files and folders is exactly like working with items on your own hard disk. (For details, see "Using Network Neighborhood to Find Network Files," page 154.)

■ **If you're not sure what's in a document, take a *quick view*.** Windows 98 includes "quick viewers" for text documents, spreadsheets, graphics files, and other document types. If you're not sure a particular document is the one you want, right-click it and look for Quick View on the "context" menu that appears. A peek through the quick viewer is faster than opening the file in its parent application. (For details, see "Quick Viewing and Property Inspection," page 25.)

■ **Let the Find command be your skip-tracer.** It's easy to lose things on a large hard disk. It's easy to find them again with the Find command—which you'll find on the Start menu. (For details, see Chapter 6, "Using the Find Command.")

■ **Tailor the Recycle Bin to your comfort level.** Deleted files in Windows 98 ordinarily go to the Recycle Bin rather than directly into the ether. When the bin is full, the files that have been there longest are finally deleted for good. You can adjust the size of the bin in accordance with your hard-disk size and propensity toward accidental erasures. (For details, see "Restoring Deleted Folders, Files, and Shortcuts," page 138.)

■ **Work in whatever screen resolution you need for the task at hand.** In Windows 3.x, switching from one screen resolution to another might be more trouble than it is worth because you must close your programs and restart the operating system every time you want to switch. In Windows 98, a screen-res switch is as simple as a right-click and a dialog-box pick. No need to shut or restart anything. (For details, see "Changing Display Resolution," page 88.)

About This Book

This book has five parts. The first part, encompassing Chapters 1 through 4, provides a detailed guide to the Windows 98 user interface, covering everything you need to know to run programs, manage files and folders, and tailor the environment to your personal tastes.

Part II, Chapters 5 through 12, takes you beyond the basics and explains how to access network resources, share folders with other network users, install printers and fonts, and move information between documents and between programs.

Part III, Chapters 13 through 16, primarily addresses maintenance, optimization, and backup issues. We'll also look at the registry, Windows' central database of information about your system, and at simple procedures for installing and removing hardware and software.

Part IV, Chapters 17 through 23, covers several of the accessory programs shipped with Windows 98. Here you'll find chapters on WordPad, Paint, HyperTerminal, Phone Dialer, Imaging, and more.

Finally, Part V, Chapters 24 through 29, takes up mobile computing and the suite of Internet products included with Windows 98. We'll take a detailed look at Internet Explorer 4, Outlook Express, NetMeeting, Chat, FrontPage Express, and Personal Web Server.

Using the Companion CD

This book comes with a CD that includes the following software and book information:

- A powerful, searchable HTML version of the book that enables you to quickly locate specific information, such as a procedure or a definition, with only a click of the mouse

- A demonstration version of *Microsoft Windows 98 Starts Here,* a CD-based interactive training with video lesson introductions and step-by-step sequences to show you exactly how to accomplish important tasks

- One free month of Internet access to MSN, The Microsoft Network online service

Installing the Electronic Book

The CD-ROM includes an electronic version of *Running Microsoft Windows 98.* This is a powerful version of the book offering full-text search that enables you to locate specific information, such as a procedure or a definition, with only a click of the mouse.

Internet Explorer 4.0 or later is required to view the electronic book. As part of the installation process, the setup program automatically installs Microsoft Internet Explorer version 4.01 if it is not already installed on your system. Microsoft Internet Explorer 4.01 runs on Microsoft Windows 98, on Microsoft Windows 95, or on Microsoft Windows NT with Service Pack 3 installed.

If you're running Windows NT, you must install Service Pack 3 (not included) before you attempt to install the electronic book. For information about downloading the Microsoft Windows NT Service Pack 3, connect to http://backoffice.microsoft.com/downtrial/moreinfo/nt4sp3.asp.

To install the electronic version of the book, do the following:

1 Insert the CD into your CD-ROM drive.

2 Click Start on the Windows taskbar.

3 Choose Run from the Start menu.

4 Type *d:\ebook\setup.exe* (where *d* is the letter of your CD-ROM drive).

5 Click OK.

6 Follow the setup instructions that appear.

The Setup program for the electronic book installs a desktop icon and a Start menu item identified with the title. If it does not already exist, the

Setup program creates a Microsoft Press group for the item. To view the electronic book, you can either choose from the Start menu or double-click the desktop icon.

The first time you run Internet Explorer after installing it, the Internet Connection Wizard appears. This wizard helps you set up an account with an Internet service provider or establish a connection to your current service provider. (You do not have to be connected to a service provider to use the files on the CD.)

Installing Microsoft Windows 98 Starts Here (Demonstration Version)

To install the demonstration version of *Microsoft Windows 98 Starts Here*, choose Run from the Start menu, type *d:\WIN98SH\autorun.exe*, and then click OK. (If necessary, replace *d* with the letter of your CD-ROM drive; for example, use *f* if your CD-ROM is installed as drive F.)

Installing MSN

The companion CD also includes the client software for MSN, The Microsoft Network online service, along with one month of free access to MSN and the Internet. To take advantage of this offer, choose Run from the Start menu, type *d:\MSN\setup.exe*, and then click OK. (If necessary, replace *d* with the letter of your CD-ROM drive; for example, use *f* if your CD-ROM is installed as drive F.) Follow the installation instructions that appear on screen.

Additional Information

Every effort has been made to ensure the accuracy of the book and the contents of this companion disc. Microsoft Press provides corrections for books through the World Wide Web at

http://mspress.microsoft.com/mspress/support/

If you have comments, questions, or ideas regarding the book or this companion disc, please send them to Microsoft Press via e-mail at:

mspinput@microsoft.com

or via postal mail to:

Microsoft Press
Attn: Running Series Editor
One Microsoft Way
Redmond, WA 98052-6399

Please note that product support is not offered through the above addresses.

Microsoft Windows 98 Support

For support information regarding Microsoft Windows 98, you can connect to Microsoft Technical Support on the Web at:

http://www.microsoft.com/support/

In the United States, you can also call Microsoft Windows 98 technical support at (425) 635-7222, weekdays between 6 A.M. and 6 P.M. Pacific time.

For late-breaking information, look for the readme file on the companion CD.

PART I

Getting Started with Windows

Introducing Windows 98

Whether you're brand new to Windows or a veteran of many years, the screen that appears when you first start Windows 98 may include a few unfamiliar elements. You'll soon feel right at home in Windows 98, but to help you on your way, we'll begin this chapter with a brief survey of the landscape. We'll check out the Start menu, the taskbar, the My Computer and Network Neighborhood icons, the Recycle Bin, and the Windows desktop. Later in the chapter, we'll look at windows themselves (those rectangular frames that we spell with a lowercase *w*), menus, dialog boxes, and the Windows Help system.

If you've used Windows before, you will already be familiar with some of this territory. For example, your experience in working with Windows 3.x or Windows 95 menus and dialog boxes will continue to serve you in Windows 98. But we suggest you give the chapter a quick scan to be sure you don't overlook anything new and important.

Whether you're a rookie or a ten-year veteran, welcome to Windows 98!

Starting Windows

You don't need to type a command to get into Windows. Simply turn on your machine and you're there (in a moment or two). If your computer is part of a network, however, you will be invited to type your name and a password when Windows starts. This process is called "logging on." If your system has been set up to allow multiple users, each with his or her own set of customizing choices, you'll also be asked to identify yourself, even if your computer is not part of a network.

Also depending on how your system has been set up, once you're past the logon process, you may go directly into a program. (Windows 98 provides a means for starting selected programs automatically at the beginning of each session. For information about using "startup" programs see "The StartUp Submenu," page 50.) If you find yourself inside a program at startup, you'll want to make your electronic desktop completely visible before following along on this chapter's tour. You can do that in either of two ways. If you see an icon that looks like this:

along an edge of your screen, use your mouse to point to the icon and click the left mouse button. That icon redisplays your desktop, regardless of what windows may be lying atop it. Alternatively, use your mouse to point to the button in the upper right corner of your program's window that looks like this:

Click that button, along with the similar buttons of any other open windows, and your desktop will become completely visible.

Before beginning our tour, let's look for a moment at the logon process.

Mouse Terminology

To *click* an object, position the mouse pointer over that object and press the primary mouse button once. To *double-click*, position the pointer and press the primary mouse button twice in quick succession.

The *primary* mouse button is ordinarily the left button, the one that lies under the index finger of your right hand. If you're left-handed, you may want to make the right button your primary button. You can do that by choosing Settings from the Start menu, choosing Control Panel, and then double-clicking the Mouse icon. For details, see "Adjusting Mouse Behavior," page 260.

In this book, as in most other writing about Windows, to *right-click* means to press the secondary mouse button, whichever button that happens to be.

To *drag* an object, click it, and then while holding down the primary mouse button, move the mouse. When the object is where you want it to be, release the mouse button. Use the same method—except hold down the secondary mouse button—to *right-drag* an object.

To *select* a block of text with the mouse, click the beginning of the block, and hold down the mouse button while you move the mouse to the end of the block. Then release the mouse button.

Logging On for Networked Users

Figure 1-1 shows an example of a Windows 98 network logon dialog box. If your system requires you to log on to a network domain, the dialog box that confronts you at startup includes a third line, asking for the domain name. But at a minimum, you'll be asked for your name and password. With Windows NT networks, passwords are case sensitive, and you must type the password exactly as it was originally created. Some other networks are not as finicky about security, and you can enter the password in capital or lowercase letters, or any combination of the two. As you type, asterisks appear on the password line to protect your privacy.

FIGURE 1-1.
At startup, you'll be asked to enter your name and network password.

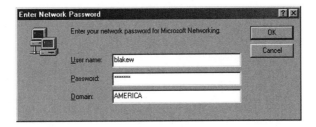

If you don't want to connect to the network, simply press Esc at the network password dialog box. You'll be able to use all your local disks and printers. By not logging on when you don't need network resources, you may be able to improve the performance of your system. Be aware, however, that any local resources you normally share will not be available to your fellow workers while you're disconnected from the network.

Logging On for Non-Networked Users

Even if your computer is not part of a network, you may still see a logon dialog box when you start Windows. That's because Windows 98 can create separate "user profiles" for each person who works at a particular computer. A user profile is a collection of information about a user's preferences regarding the appearance of the screen, programs that run automatically on startup, items that appear on the Start menu, and so on. If your system has been set up for profiles, Windows will ask you to log on so that it can set up the appropriate profile.

If your computer is not part of a network and you're the only one who uses it, you don't have to log on to start Windows. If the logon dialog box appears at startup, you can get rid of it. Run Control Panel, choose Passwords, click the User Profiles tab, and select the option button labeled "All users of this PC use the same preferences and desktop settings." You'll also need to delete your password, if any. Click the Passwords tab, click Change Windows Password, type your old password, and click OK. (Leave the New Password and Confirm New Password boxes empty.)

What to Do If You Forget Your Password

If you can't remember your password, there's no cause for alarm. Windows won't lock you out of the system. Simply press Esc or click Cancel when you see the logon dialog box. If your computer is normally part of a network, you'll begin your session disconnected from the network. Consult your network administrator to find out what your password is or have a new password established. If your computer is not part of a network, but Windows asks for a password so that it can restore your user profile, pressing Esc lets you work with default settings.

A Quick Tour

Figure 1-2 shows some of the elements of a typical Windows 98 desktop. Along the left edge of the screen are five *system icons*. These are objects that Windows 98 may create for you automatically when you install the operating system. Along the bottom edge is the *taskbar,* and within the taskbar are the *Start button,* the *Quick Launch toolbar,* two *task buttons,* and the *notification area.* Along the right edge of the screen is an *"Active Desktop" object.* Arrayed in a column to the left of the Active Desktop object are five *shortcut icons,* and to the left of those are three additional icons representing a folder, a program, and a document.

FIGURE 1-2.
A typical Windows 98 desktop includes these elements. Yours may have other kinds of objects as well.

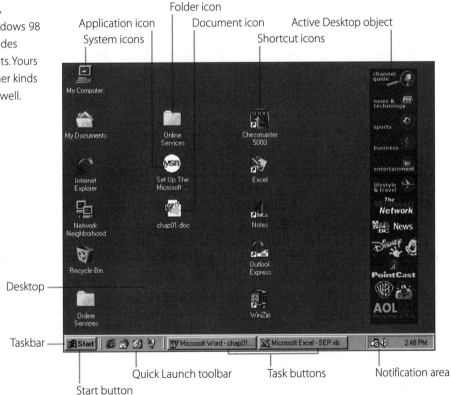

Your desktop may look similar to this, or it may look radically different. Some of the system icons shown in Figure 1-2, on the previous page, may not appear on your screen. Your taskbar may be taller than the one shown, it may lie against a different edge of your desktop, or it may be temporarily invisible. You may have a picture or a "wallpaper" pattern draped over your desktop, or your desktop may look like a page from the Internet's World Wide Web. Unlike the icons shown in the figure, yours may be underscored. And it's possible that your desktop has no visible icons at all.

? SEE ALSO

For information about customizing your desktop, see Chapter 3, "Using and Customizing the Desktop."

Windows 98 gives you great flexibility regarding the layout, content, and display style of your desktop. You can personalize it to suit your tastes and moods, and you can switch from one visual mode to another at will. For now, we'll concentrate on the objects shown in Figure 1-2, because these are important elements of the Windows user interface—elements that you're likely to see at one time or another as you work with this operating system.

The Start Button and Start Menu

The Start button's function in life is to open the Start menu. Click once on this all-important item, and a set of choices, similar to the one shown in Figure 1-3, emerges.

FIGURE 1-3.

The Start menu provides single-click access to the programs and documents you use most often.

The Start menu makes most of your programs, the documents you've most recently used, and even your favorite Internet sites, available with a single mouse click. It's also one of the simplest ways to accomplish several other important tasks, such as finding documents and programs on your own or a networked disk and accessing general help topics. The Start menu is also a "quit" menu; you may use its Shut Down or Log Off command whenever you need to end a Windows session, reboot your computer, or let another person use your computer.

⭐ **TIP**

> To get to the Start menu when it's covered by a program or other object, you can press Ctrl+Esc.

Toolbars

Toolbars encapsulate sets of related icons for easy mouse access, and you can use these icons to simplify commonplace tasks, such as launching programs or opening documents. The Quick Launch toolbar, shown in Figure 1-2 on page 7, provides icons for launching Internet Explorer and Outlook Express. It also includes a valuable Show Desktop icon, which makes your desktop completely visible, regardless of what may be lying upon it, and an icon for launching Internet Explorer's Channel Viewer.

❓ **SEE ALSO**

For information about toolbars, see "Using Toolbars," page 79.

Windows provides several toolbars that you can use or ignore as you please. To see which ones are available, right-click (click the right mouse button) while pointing to a blank area of your taskbar. Then choose Toolbars from the *context menu* (the menu that pops up when you right-click). You can add icons to or remove icons from the standard toolbars, and you can create new toolbars of your own. Toolbars can live on the taskbar, or they can "float" on the desktop.

⭐ **TIP**

> To change the width of a toolbar, drag the gray vertical bar that appears at the left edge of the toolbar. Before you begin dragging, your mouse pointer should change to a two-headed arrow. That way you know your pointer is in the right place. To move a toolbar away from the taskbar and out onto your desktop, drag that same gray vertical bar.

Task Buttons

In the center portion of the taskbar, you will see a button for each program you've started and each folder you've opened. (For information about folders, see "Working with Folders," page 21.) You can click these buttons to move from one open program or folder to another.

If you have a lot of programs or folders open, Windows may truncate some of the text on the task buttons. However, if you rest your mouse pointer for a moment on any button whose text is not completely visible, the full text will appear in a pop-up box.

TIP

> The taskbar with its task buttons replaces the Windows 3.x task list. If you're used to double-clicking the desktop to get the task list, you might be frustrated because that action does nothing in Windows 98. However, you can still get to the task buttons (even if they're hidden or covered by open windows) by pressing Ctrl+Esc.

The Notification Area

In the right corner of the taskbar (if the taskbar is displayed horizontally) or at the bottom (if it's displayed vertically), Windows provides information about the status of your system. When a local printer is active, for example, a printer icon appears in this *notification area.* When you're connected by modem to the Internet, an icon that looks like two connected computers appears. If you're running Windows on a laptop computer, icons in this area let you know whether your computer is currently draining or recharging its battery. Exactly what icons show up in your notification area depends on how you use your system and what programs you've installed. If you're not sure what an icon represents, hover your mouse pointer over it and read the pop-up description. (These pop-up descriptions are called *screen tips.*) In many cases, you can get additional information about a notification-area icon by double-clicking it.

The notification area also includes, by default, a clock. You can set the clock by double-clicking it and filling out the ensuing dialog box. The clock is also a calendar; hover the mouse pointer over the time, and the current date appears.

My Computer

② SEE ALSO

For information about Windows Explorer, see Chapter 4, "Using and Customizing Windows Explorer."

The My Computer icon lets you browse through all the resources attached to your own system. When you open My Computer, a Windows Explorer window similar to the one shown in Figure 1-4 appears. (Windows Explorer, more commonly known simply as Explorer, is the program that Windows uses to display folder contents.) This window includes icons for each of your computer's disk drives (floppy, hard, CD-ROM, or whatever) and any network directories that you have connected to your computer. It also shows additional *system folders*, providing access to the Windows Control Panel, your printers, Dial-Up Networking, and a folder that manages your scheduled tasks.

FIGURE 1-4.

The My Computer icon opens into a Windows Explorer window showing all resources attached to your own computer.

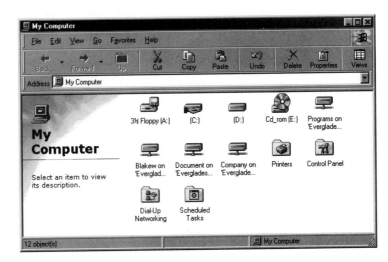

② TIP

You're not stuck with having it called My Computer. To change the name, right-click the icon. Choose Rename from the context menu. Type the name you want to use (or edit the one that's already there), and then press Enter.

② SEE ALSO

For more information, see "To Click or Double-Click?," page 66.

Double-clicking one of the icons in the My Computer window (or clicking it, depending on how you've set up your desktop) opens additional Explorer windows. For example, opening the icon labeled (C:) in Figure 1-4 would show you the contents of the C drive.

My Documents

Double-clicking (or clicking) the My Documents icon opens a folder that certain programs may use as a default location for storing documents. Not all programs use My Documents, but some of your newer ones (such as the accessory programs included with Windows 98) are likely to. Initially, the My Documents icon "points to" a folder whose path is, in fact, C:\My Documents (assuming you've installed Windows on your C drive.) But you can redirect it to some other folder if you want. For example, if you want programs that use My Documents to store their documents, by default, in D:\Writing\MSPress\Memphis\Chap01, you could make them do so by right-clicking My Documents, choosing Properties from the context menu, and then typing the desired path on the edit line next to the word Target. The icon would still say My Documents, but it would then open the folder whose path you just typed. (You can also rename the My Documents icon so that the text beneath the icon tells you exactly which folder the icon points to. To do this, right-click the icon, choose Rename from the context menu, and type.)

TIP

If you don't want the My Documents icon on your desktop, right-click it and choose Remove From Desktop. (If you change your mind later, right-click the My Documents folder in Windows Explorer and choose Add Item To The Desktop.)

Internet Explorer

The icon labeled Internet Explorer does what you probably expect; it launches Microsoft's Internet Explorer Web browser and (if you're currently offline) attempts to initiate an Internet connection.

TIP

If you don't want the Internet Explorer icon on your desktop, right-click it and choose Delete.

Network Neighborhood

Opening the Network Neighborhood icon provides a Windows Explorer window displaying the names of each server or computer in your own workgroup. In addition, the Network Neighborhood folder includes an Entire Network icon, which you can use to access other workgroups on

FIGURE 1-5.

The Network Neighborhood icon opens a folder showing all members of your own workgroup.

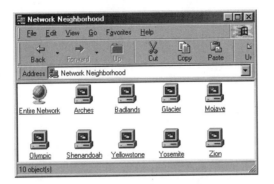

your network. Figure 1-5 shows how the Network Neighborhood folder might appear on a system that's part of a nine-member workgroup. In this illustration, the computer icons—Arches, Badlands, and Glacier, for example—represent computers in the workgroup.

 NOTE

If your computer isn't part of a network, the Network Neighborhood icon won't appear on your desktop.

The Recycle Bin

The Recycle Bin provides temporary storage for files and folders that you delete. If you change your mind after deleting a file, you may be able to recover the file by retrieving it from the bin. As Figure 1-6 on the next page shows, the Recycle Bin records the name, original location, deletion date, type, and size of each object you delete. A simple menu command lets you restore (undelete) any item.

Shortcut Icons

Icons with little arrows in their lower left corners (see the center of Figure 1-2, on page 7) represent *shortcuts*. A shortcut provides easy access to some object on your system, such as a program, a document, a printer, a local hard disk, or a network server. For example, clicking the icon labeled Excel in Figure 1-2 opens Microsoft Excel, a spreadsheet program.

It's important to recognize that a shortcut merely contains information about the location of some object. The shortcut is not the object itself,

FIGURE 1-6.

The Recycle Bin provides a safety net against accidental deletions.

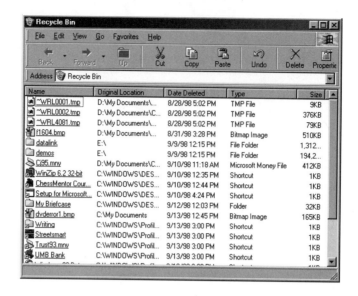

and deleting it does not delete the object. Shortcuts are a great convenience because they allow you to access frequently used programs, documents, or folders from many different places in Windows.

Program, Folder, and Document Icons

For more about the Desktop folder, see "The Desktop Is a Folder," page 65.

Non-system icons without arrows, such as the middle column of icons in Figure 1-2 on page 7, are not shortcuts but representations of the actual objects they describe. For example, the icon labeled Chap01.doc in Figure 1-2 represents an actual Microsoft Word document by that name. The document happens to be stored in a folder called Desktop, so it appears on the desktop.

Active Desktop Objects

SEE ALSO

For more information, see "Bringing the Internet to Your Active Desktop," page 69.

An Active Desktop object, such as the Channel Bar shown along the right edge of Figure 1-2 on page 7, lets you receive Internet content tailored to your interests.

Working with Windows

All Windows-based programs run within rectangular frames called windows. As shown in Figure 1-7, these features are common to nearly all windows:

FIGURE 1-7.
Nearly all Windows-based programs run in windows that include these elements.

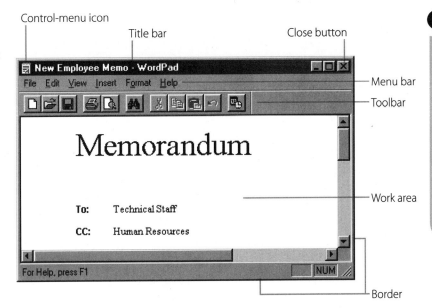

Control-menu icon

Title bar

Close button

Menu bar

Toolbar

Work area

Border

Borders. The four edges that define the perimeter of a window are called borders. You can drag the borders of most windows to change their size.

Title bar (caption). Directly below the top border is a region that includes the window's name. This is called the title bar, or caption. You can move a window by dragging its title bar.

Control-menu icon. At the left edge of the title bar is the Control-menu icon. You can click here to get a menu of basic commands for sizing and positioning the window. These commands all have mouse-action equivalents, so you may never need to use the Control menu.

Close button. At the right edge of the title bar is a square containing an *X*. You can click here to close a document or folder, or to terminate a program.

⭐ **TIP**

Another way to close a program window, folder window, or dialog box is to press Alt+F4.

Getting Started with Windows

Minimize, restore, and maximize buttons. To the left of the close button, you will find other buttons that look like this:

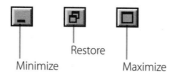

Minimize   Restore   Maximize

SEE ALSO

For information about Alt+Tab, see "Switching Between Windows," on the next page.

Clicking the minimize button causes a window to collapse into its taskbar button. The window is still open, and the program inside it continues to run. But the window no longer takes up space on your desktop. You can reopen a minimized window by clicking its taskbar button or by using the Alt+Tab task switcher.

Clicking the maximize button causes a window to occupy all of the desktop. While you're using a program, you may want to keep its window maximized most of the time, so that you have as much screen real estate as possible to work with.

Clicking the restore button causes a window to assume an intermediate size—neither maximized nor minimized. With windows restored, you can keep two or more programs in view at the same time. You can adjust the size of a restored window by dragging its borders. (See "Sizing and Moving Windows," below.)

TIP

> Another way to maximize a window is to double-click its title bar. If the window is already maximized, you can restore its intermediate size by double-clicking the title bar.

Menu bar. Directly below the title bar is the menu bar. The menu bar provides access to most of a program's commands.

Toolbar. Many windows include a toolbar, which is a row of icons and buttons that provide mouse-click shortcuts for a program's commonly used commands.

Work area. The inside of a window is called the work area or client area.

Sizing and Moving Windows

To change a window's size, drag its borders. For example, to make the window wider, drag either the left or right border. To make a window both wider and taller, you can drag one of the corners.

To move a window, drag its title bar.

TIP

Dialog boxes sometimes get in the way of underlying programs. To see what's under a dialog box, move it—by dragging its title bar.

Switching Between Windows

When two or more program windows are open at once, the one lying on top has what's called the *focus*. The window with the focus is the one that will respond to your next keystrokes. (The window that has the focus is sometimes also called the *foreground* or *active* window.) To switch the focus to another window, you can use any of the following techniques:

- Click anywhere on or in the window that you want to switch to.

- Click the taskbar button for the window you want to switch to.

- Press and hold the Alt key. Then press Tab to bring up the Windows task switcher. The task switcher displays an icon for each running program and draws a box around the icon whose window currently has the focus. Continue holding Alt and pressing Tab until the window you want to switch to has the focus.

TIP

If you're ever in doubt about which window has the focus, check your windows' title bars. The active window's title bar is normally displayed in one color, while the title bars of all inactive windows are displayed in another color. In addition, the taskbar button for the active window appears to be pressed in.

Arranging Windows on the Screen

If you have a lot of windows open at once, it may be hard to see what's going on. Windows provides some handy commands for making all your windows visible. To put all the windows in a neat stack, with each window's title bar visible, do the following:

1 Right-click an unoccupied area of the taskbar. (Press Ctrl+Esc first if you can't see the taskbar.)

2 Choose the Cascade Windows command.

With your windows in a cascade, you can easily switch focus by clicking any title bar—as well as by clicking the taskbar.

If you want to see a portion of the contents of each open window, choose one of the tiling commands. Right-click the taskbar and choose either Tile Windows Horizontally or Tile Windows Vertically.

 To minimize all open windows, right-click the taskbar and choose Minimize All Windows. Alternatively, if the Show Desktop tool is visible, simply click that tool. The Show Desktop tool is a standard element of the Quick Launch toolbar.

 TIP

After you've minimized all windows by clicking the Show Desktop tool, you can click that tool a second time to restore all windows to their former sizes and positions.

After cascading, tiling, or minimizing all windows, you can restore your windows to their previous positions by right-clicking the taskbar. The menu that appears includes a new command that reverses your previous action. For example, if you have just minimized all windows, the new command will read Undo Minimize All.

Keeping Windows on Top

Some windows are designed to stay on top, even when they don't have the focus. Windows that contain help information, for example, often behave this way, allowing you to read their helpful text even while you're working in a maximized program.

Most programs that stay on top give you the option of disabling this behavior. If a stay-on-topper becomes a visual nuisance, look in its menu system for a command such as "Always On Top" or "Stay On Top." Often you'll find it on the program's Control menu. (For information about the Control menu, see "The Control Menu and the Menu Bar," page 22.) These commands are usually *toggles;* you choose them once to turn the feature on and a second time to turn it off.

TIP

> The taskbar itself is a stay-on-top window. In its default display mode, it remains visible even when the foreground program is maximized. You can defeat this behavior by right-clicking an unoccupied part of the taskbar, choosing the Properties command, clicking the Taskbar Options tab, and deselecting the check box labeled Always On Top. (To get back to the taskbar when it's not visible, press Ctrl+Esc.)

Window Panes

Some programs use windows that are split vertically, horizontally, or even both vertically and horizontally. The resulting window divisions are called *panes.* Figure 1-8 shows an example of a window divided vertically into panes.

FIGURE 1-8.
This window is divided into a left pane and a right pane. You can change the size of the panes by dragging the pane divider.

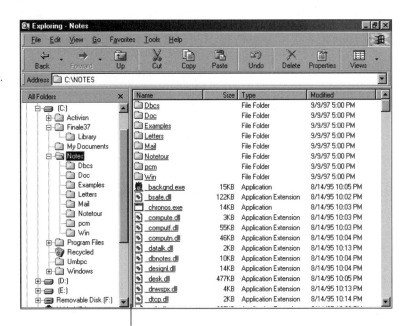

Pane divider

In most cases, when a window has been divided into panes, you can change the relative sizes of the panes by dragging the pane divider. In Figure 1-8 on the previous page, for example, you could make the left pane wider by dragging the divider to the right.

Working with Document Windows

Windows come in two varieties, called program windows and document windows. Program windows house programs or folders, can be moved freely around the desktop, and can be maximized to fill the screen or minimized to taskbar buttons. All the windows illustrated thus far in this chapter are examples of program windows.

Document windows live inside program windows. As their name implies, they are designed to hold documents, not programs. Document windows can be maximized, restored, minimized, moved, and sized, but they must remain within the confines of a program window. Figure 1-9 shows a program window containing four open and two minimized document windows.

FIGURE 1-9.

This program window contains four open document windows and two minimized document windows.

Open document windows

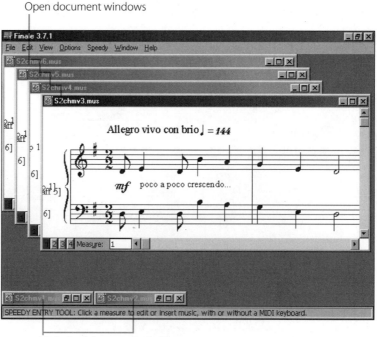

Minimized document windows

Notice that the title bar for one of the document windows (the one in the front of the cascade stack) is the same color as the title bar for the program window. That document window currently has the focus. Also notice that document windows, when minimized, become miniature title bars.

TIP

> You can close the current document window by pressing Ctrl+F4. In many programs, you can move from one document window to the next document window by pressing Ctrl+F6.

Working with Folders

A folder is a container for computers, disk drives, printer queues, other folders, and files. The most common kind of folder is exemplified by Figure 1-10. It's a place where programs, document files, and perhaps additional folders are kept. Such a folder is directly analogous to a directory in MS-DOS and in earlier versions of Windows. Your computer's hard disks, as well as those of your network's servers, are organized into hierarchies of folders.

FIGURE 1-10.
This Office folder contains the Binder program file, several folders, and numerous documents.

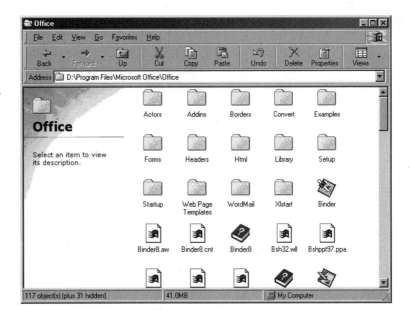

At the top of a disk hierarchy in MS-DOS is a directory called the root directory. The Windows folder corresponding to the root directory goes by the volume name assigned to the disk on which it lives. If you have named your C drive George, for example, its top-level directory is a folder named George.

Your computer itself is a folder called My Computer. Your network workgroup is a folder called Network Neighborhood.

? SEE ALSO

For more information about folders, see Chapter 4, "Using and Customizing Windows Explorer."

Windows uses *system folders* to hold items that are related to your computer system. For example, you can install and configure printers by opening a system folder called *Printers*, schedule programs to run automatically in a system folder called *Scheduled Tasks*, and customize Windows in a variety of ways using a system folder called *Control Panel*.

Working with Menus and Dialog Boxes

In virtually all Windows-based programs, commands are chosen from *drop-down menus*—sets of options that emerge from a menu bar at the top of the program window. When a program needs additional information from you before it can carry out your command, it presents a *dialog box*—a smaller window with places for you to fill in blanks or choose between preset options. These devices behave in a consistent and predictable way in all Windows-based programs.

The Control Menu and the Menu Bar

The two main elements of a Windows-based program's menu system are the Control menu and the menu bar. The Control menu emerges from the icon at the left side of the title bar. The menu bar is the row of commands directly below the title bar.

The Control menu provides a set of window-management commands common to all programs, such as commands to move, resize, or close a window. With few exceptions, each program's Control menu includes the same commands.

The menu bar includes commands specific to the current program. Each word on the menu bar opens a drop-down menu of related commands. For example, a program's File menu includes commands for opening and saving files, the Edit menu has commands for changing the contents of a document, and so on.

Choosing Commands with the Mouse

To get to the menu system with the mouse, click the desired word in the menu bar. To open the File menu, for example, click the word *File*. To open the Control menu, click the icon at the left edge of the title bar. To choose a command from a drop-down menu, move the mouse pointer down until you reach the desired command, and then click.

To get out of the menu system without choosing a command, click the mouse anywhere outside the drop-down menu.

Choosing Commands with the Keyboard

To choose any command with the keyboard, begin by pressing the Alt key. (You can also access the menu system by pressing F10.) When you do that, Windows highlights the first command on the menu bar. At this point, you can use the Left arrow and Right arrow keys to move around the menu bar. To open a particular menu, move to that menu and press the Down arrow or Up arrow key. To choose a command from a drop-down menu, use the Up arrow and Down arrow keys to highlight the command you want, and then press Enter.

To leave the menu system without choosing a command, press the Alt key, or click the mouse anywhere outside the menu system.

Accelerator Keys and Other Shortcuts

A more direct way to open a particular drop-down menu is to press Alt, followed by the menu's *accelerator key*—the underlined letter in the menu's name. The accelerator key is often, but not always, the first letter of the menu name. In Microsoft Word, for example, you can open the File menu by pressing Alt+F, but to get to the Format menu, you need to press Alt+O.

Some menu commands have shortcuts assigned to them. These are single keystrokes or simple keystroke combinations that execute a command directly. In many programs, for example, pressing Ctrl+S is equivalent to executing the File menu's Save command. When a keyboard shortcut is available, it usually appears to the right of the command name on the menu.

Context ("Right-Click") Menus

In many parts of Windows 98, as well as in many Windows-based programs, pressing the secondary mouse button brings up a small menu appropriate to the currently selected object (or the one the mouse is pointing to). For example, if you right-click the taskbar, you get a menu of commands relating only to the taskbar. If you select a block of text in Microsoft Word and then right-click, you get a menu that includes commands for formatting, moving, and copying the selected text. These right-click menus go by various names in various programs. Some programs call them "property inspectors," others call them "shortcut menus," still others identify them as "object menus." In this book, they're called *context menus*.

Whatever they're called, they often provide the quickest route to a needed menu command.

TIP

> When you right-click certain objects in Windows, the context menu includes one command in boldface type. The boldface command is the one that would have been executed had you simply double-clicked the object instead of right-clicking it.

Gray Commands, Checks, and Cascading Menus

Here are some other menu conventions observed by most Windows-based programs:

■ A command that appears in gray letters on a menu is one that's not available in the current context. In Microsoft Excel, for example, the Window menu's Unhide command remains gray until at least one window has been hidden.

■ A check mark beside a command indicates that a certain condition has been turned on. Choosing such a command turns the condition off and removes the check mark.

■ An arrowhead to the right of a command means that this command brings up a cascading submenu. The Start menu on the taskbar, for example, has five such commands: Programs, Favorites,

---

Quick Viewing and Property Inspection

Two commands that appear on many context menus are particularly important and useful. The Quick View command lets you look at the contents of a file
without opening the program that created the file. For example, by right-
clicking the icon for a text file, you can read the text without opening
WordPad or any other text editor. Not all files can be quick-viewed, but many
can. To see if a file can be quick-viewed, open the folder in which the file is
stored, and then right-click the file's icon or name. If a viewer is available for
this file type, the Quick View command appears on the context menu. (If Quick
View does not appear on any of your context menus, the Quick View facility
might not have been installed on your system. To add Quick View, if you don't
already have it, see "Adding or Removing Parts of Windows 98," page 326.)

Objects such as files and folders have properties, such as type, size, creation
date, and location. The Properties command, which appears at the bottom of an
object's context menu, lets you inspect those properties. For example, to find
out when a file was last changed, you can right-click that file's icon or name in a
folder window, choose Properties, and then read the "Modified" item in the
dialog box that appears. To find out how much space is taken up by all the files
in a folder, you can right-click the folder icon and choose Properties.

In some cases, you can not only inspect but also change an object's
properties by choosing the context menu's Properties command. For example,
right-clicking the taskbar and choosing Properties takes you to a dialog box in
which you can customize the appearance and behavior of the taskbar and the
Start menu. Right-clicking the desktop and choosing Properties lets you
customize the appearance of the desktop.

Documents, Settings, and Find. Choose any one of these
commands, and another menu unfurls.

Using Dialog Boxes

An ellipsis (...) is a punctuation symbol signifying an incomplete sentence
or quotation. In a Windows menu, an ellipsis following a command name
indicates an incomplete command. Such a command brings up a *dialog
box*, which is a device used by Windows to get more information from
you.

Dialog boxes come in all sizes and shapes. Some are simple, others quite complex. But nearly all dialog boxes have the following components:

- One or more places for you to enter information or choose options

- One or more command buttons

Most dialog boxes have a command button that you click after you've filled out the dialog box to your satisfaction and another that you click if you want to back out of the dialog box without making an entry. In many cases, these buttons are marked OK and Cancel, respectively. Many dialog boxes also have a button labeled Help or a button with a question mark on it; you can click this kind of button if you're not sure what some of the dialog-box options mean.

 TIP

Pressing Esc or Alt+F4 in a dialog box is usually equivalent to clicking the Cancel button. It dismisses the dialog box without taking any further action. Still another way to dismiss a dialog box is to click the Close button on its title bar.

Dialog Box Tabs

The dialog box shown in Figure 1-11 actually includes eight "pages" of options. You select the page you're interested in by clicking its tab at the top of the dialog box. For example, the portion of the dialog box shown in the figure offers viewing options; to select editing options, click the Edit tab—and so on. Press Ctrl+Tab to flip through the pages with the keyboard.

Accelerator Keys

Like menu commands, the names of dialog box elements often have under-lined letters that you can use for quick keyboard access. These accelerator keys provide a quick way to select dialog box options using the keyboard. In Figure 1-11, for example, F is the accelerator key for the Formula Bar check box; S is the accelerator key for the Status Bar check box, and so on.

To use accelerator keys in a dialog box, hold down the Alt key while you press the accelerator key.

FIGURE 1-11.

The tabs along the top of the dialog box let you shift from one set of options to another. The underlined letters in a dialog box, like those in a menu, provide keyboard shortcuts for selecting options.

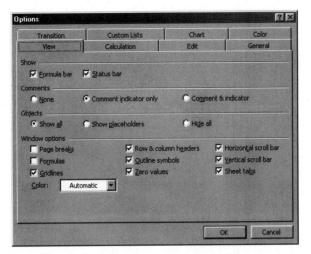

 TIP

If the current tab has a dotted marquee around it, as the View tab does in Figure 1-11, you can also move between tabs by pressing the arrow keys.

Dialog Box Elements

In the section of a dialog box where you enter information or select options, you'll encounter the following kinds of elements:

- Text boxes

- List boxes

- Drop-down list boxes

- Option buttons

- Check boxes

- Sliders

- Spinners

A *text box*, sometimes also called an *edit box*, is a place for you to type something. The rectangle containing the word *forest*, near the center of the dialog box shown in Figure 1-12 on the next page, is an example of a text box.

FIGURE 1-12.
A text box, such as the Containing Text text box shown here, provides a place to type.

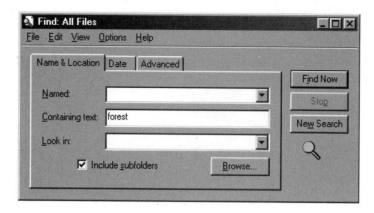

To fill out a text box, click in the box. You'll then see a flashing vertical line, which is called an *insertion point*. If the text box is empty, the insertion point appears at the left side of the box. If the box already contains text, the insertion point is located at the spot where you clicked the mouse. In either case, the insertion point marks the place where the characters you type will appear.

A *list box* presents a set of options in the form of a list, as shown in Figure 1-13.

FIGURE 1-13.
The Object Type list box displays a scrollable list of options.

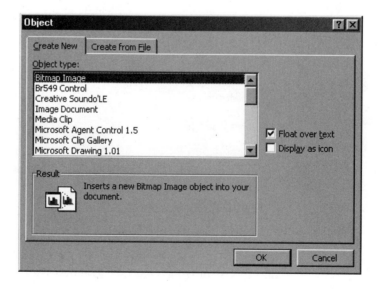

In most list boxes, you can choose only one item at a time, but in some you can choose two or more. If a list box allows you to choose more than one option at a time, hold down the Ctrl key while you click each item you want to choose.

If the list contains more items than can be displayed at once (as the list shown in Figure 1-13 does), you will find a *scroll bar* at the right side of the list box. The scroll bar helps you move quickly from one part of the list to another. (For more information about scroll bars, see "Using Scroll Bars," page 32.) You can also move through a list box by pressing the Up arrow or Down arrow key, or the Page Up or Page Down key.

⭐ **TIP**

> When you're scrolling through a list, the keyboard is often quicker than the mouse. In most newer programs, including the "applets" included with Windows 98, simply type the first few letters of a list item to move the highlight to that item. (If the highlight moves as you type each letter to the next item that *begins* with that letter, the program is using the older, Windows 3.x method of navigating through lists. Such programs consider only the first letter of each list item.)

A *drop-down list box* looks like a text box with a downward-pointing arrow to the right of it. The Of Type line in Figure 1-14 is an example.

FIGURE 1-14.
A drop-down list box initially displays only one option.

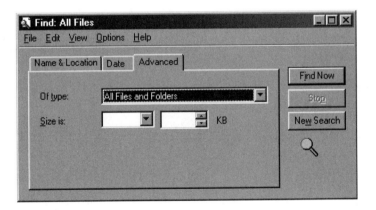

When you click the downward-pointing arrow (or press Alt+Down arrow), an ordinary-looking list box unfolds, as shown in Figure 1-15, on the next page.

FIGURE 1-15.

Clicking the arrow at the right of the drop-down list box expands the list.

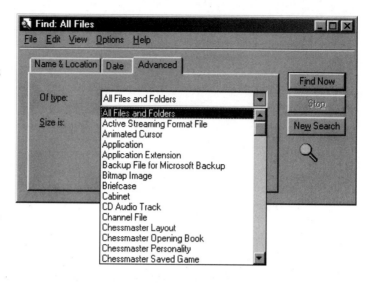

 TIP

> You can use the arrow keys to move through a drop-down list without first opening the list box. You can also type the first few letters of an item to move directly to that item. (In Windows 3.x–style programs, pressing a letter key moves to the next item that *begins* with that letter.)
>
> You can move from one item to another in a dialog box by pressing the Tab key (or Shift+Tab to go backwards).

Option buttons (sometimes called *radio buttons*) present a set of mutually exclusive options. In the dialog box shown in Figure 1-16, for example, the Coloring section has an option-button group with three buttons, labeled Checkerboard, Per Side, and One Color. You may select any option, but not more than one. To express your preference, click a button—or anywhere in the text next to a button.

Option buttons always come in groups of two or more. The buttons may be either round or diamond-shaped. Either way, they look quite different from check boxes, which are always square.

Check boxes come either in groups or one at a time. Each check box is independent of all others in the dialog box. Figure 1-16 includes three check-box items in the Coloring group, labeled Smooth, Slanted, and Cycle. You may select any combination of check boxes, or none at all. To select (place a check mark in) a check-box item, click the box or

FIGURE 1-16.

The white circles in this dialog box are option buttons, and the white squares are check boxes. Click one to select it.

anywhere in the text next to the box. To deselect (clear the check mark from) the item, click again. A "yes" vote for a check box may be marked by either an *X* or a check mark.

Some check boxes have three states—checked, unchecked, and partly checked. Usually, a gray (instead of black) check mark means that a certain condition applies to some of a selection but not all of it. For example, in Figure 1-17, some of the selected cells in a Microsoft Excel worksheet have been given the "strikethrough" effect. The rest have not.

FIGURE 1-17.

When the Strikethrough effect applies to part of the selected text, the check mark is gray.

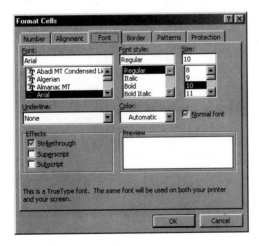

Getting Started with Windows

In the Format Cells dialog box, therefore, the Strikethrough check box has a gray check mark.

A *slider* works like the darkness setting on your toaster. Move it one direction to increase some value, move it the other to decrease the value. The Warp Speed setting in Figure 1-18 is an example of a slider.

FIGURE 1-18.

The Warp Speed slider lets you vary its setting along a continuous scale. The Density spinner lets you change a numeric value by clicking instead of typing.

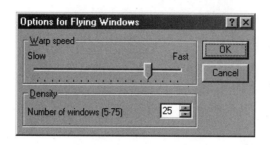

A *spinner* is a pair of arrows used to increment or decrement the value in a text box. In Figure 1-18, the Density box is an example of a spinner. To increase the value in the text box, click the up arrow; to decrease, click the down arrow.

Just because a text box has a spinner next to it doesn't mean you can't type directly into the text box. Typing may be quicker, particularly if you want to change the value by a significant amount.

Using Scroll Bars

If a window is not long enough to display its contents completely, Windows adds a *vertical scroll bar* to the right side of the window. If the window is not wide enough, Windows adds a *horizontal scroll bar*. If it's neither long enough nor wide enough, Windows adds both kinds of scroll bars. Figure 1-19 shows a window with vertical and horizontal scroll bars.

Scroll bars offer an easy way to navigate through a window with the mouse. They also provide useful information about the contents of the window.

In Figure 1-19, notice the rectangular *scroll box* in each scroll bar. The position of this box within the scroll bar tells you where you are in the window itself. In the vertical scroll bar, for example, the scroll box is situated about 20 percent of the way down the bar. That means that

FIGURE 1-19.

Scroll bars provide information about the contents of a window and allow you to move quickly from one part of the window to another.

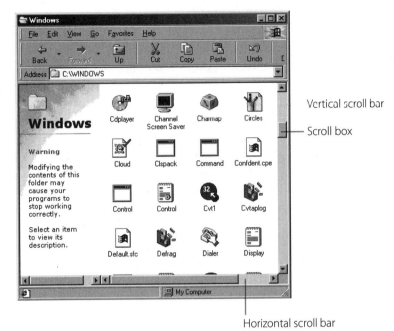

Vertical scroll bar

Scroll box

Horizontal scroll bar

roughly 20 percent of the window's contents lie above your current position in the window. In the horizontal bar, the scroll box is all the way at the left edge, telling you that there's nothing more to be seen to the left of your current position.

Now notice the size of the scroll boxes relative to the length of the scroll bars. The vertical box is about 5 percent of the length of the scroll bar itself. That means that about one twentieth of the window's vertical extent is currently visible within the window frame. The horizontal scroll box is about three-fourths as wide as the horizontal scroll bar, which means that about three-fourths of the window's horizontal extent is now visible.

For navigation purposes, you can use scroll bars in the following ways:

- To move up or down a line at a time, simply click the arrow at either end of the vertical scroll bar. To move side to side a character at a time (or by a small increment in a noncharacter display), click the arrow at either end of the horizontal bar.

- To move by approximately one windowful, click the mouse in the scroll bar itself, on either side of the scroll box.

- To continuously scroll a line at a time, click an arrow and hold down the mouse button. To continuously scroll a windowful at a time, click in the scroll bar itself and hold down the mouse button. When you arrive where you want to be, release the button.

- To move to a specific location, drag the scroll box. To move halfway down a long document, for example, you could move the vertical scroll box to about the midpoint of the vertical scroll bar.

Working with Outlines

The left pane in Figure 1-20 represents a set of folders as an outline. Looking at the figure, you can see a portion of a disk's folder structure at a glance. The horizontal positions of folder names, for example, tell you that Activisn, Finale37, My Documents, and Notes are some of the folders stored on drive C, that Library is a folder stored within the Finale37 folder, that the Notes folder contains eight folders, and so on.

FIGURE 1-20.
Windows Explorer displays the folder structure of a disk in outline form.

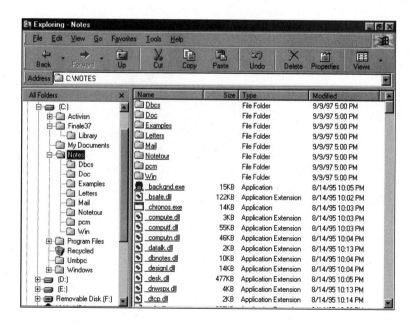

Outlines such as this are used in Windows Explorer, in the Windows help system, and in many programs. As a rule, double-clicking an outline entry expands that entry to show what subentries it contains. Or, if the entry is already expanded, double-clicking makes the entry collapse.

Many outlines, such as the one shown in Figure 1-20, use plus and minus signs to show you when an entry can be expanded or collapsed. A single click on a plus sign expands, and a single click on a minus sign collapses.

Entering and Editing Text in Documents

Unless you happen to be concerned only with visual images, you will probably spend much of your time in Windows entering and editing text. This is true whether your primary program is word processing, financial planning, database management, project management, or communications. Even though Windows is a graphical environment and uses your computer's graphics display modes, the information you work with consists primarily of letters and numbers—in other words, text.

Fortunately, a basic set of concepts and procedures applies to text in most programs for Windows.

The Insertion Point

The flashing vertical line that you see whenever you work with text in a Windows-based program is called the *insertion point*. It's analogous to the cursor in a character-based word processing program. The insertion point indicates where the next character you type will appear.

There's one difference between the insertion point and the cursor used in most MS-DOS–based programs. The insertion point is always positioned *between* two characters, *before* the first character in a block, or *after* the last character in a block. It never appears directly under a character. That's because characters are always *inserted* at the insertion point.

In the Figure 1-21 on the next page, for example, the insertion point is located between the *i* and the *n* in the word *tiny*.

To replace existing text with new characters that you type, Windows uses a different concept, called *selection*. More about that in a moment.

FIGURE 1-21.

The insertion point indicates the "cursor" position for typing text.

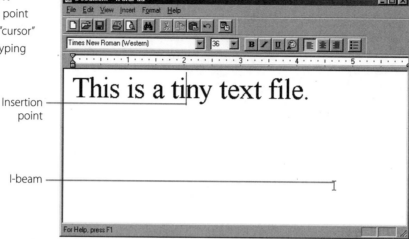

Insertion point

I-beam

The I-Beam

When you work with text, Windows changes your mouse pointer from an arrow to something that looks like a lanky capital *I*. The pointer is then usually called an *I-beam*. In Figure 1-21, you can see the I-beam in the lower right corner of the window.

The I-beam provides a way to relocate the insertion point. In the tiny text file in Figure 1-21, for example, if you want to move the insertion point to the beginning of the line, simply use the mouse to position the I-beam before the capital *T*, and then click. (You can also use the keyboard to move the insertion point, as we'll see in a moment.)

The Selection

To *select* something in Windows means to highlight it—with the keyboard or the mouse. In Figure 1-22, for example, the word *tiny* has been selected. The object that you select is called the *selection*.

You might select a block of text for any of several reasons:

- To apply a formatting change to the entire block (In Figure 1-22, for example, if you click WordPad's Underline tool after selecting the word *tiny*, the entire word is underlined.)

- To *copy*, *cut*, or *delete* the entire block

- To replace the entire block

FIGURE 1-22.

The selection is highlighted in a contrasting color.

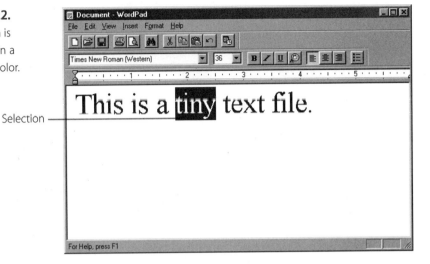

Selection

Notice that there's no insertion point in Figure 1-22. The insertion point disappears when you make a selection, because the next character you type *replaces* the entire selection.

Positioning the Insertion Point

As mentioned before, the easiest way to move the insertion point is with the mouse. Simply put the I-beam wherever you want the insertion point, and then click.

You can also use the keyboard. The following keystroke combinations apply to most Windows-based programs that work with text:

- The Right arrow and Left arrow keys move the insertion point forward or backward a character at a time. Ctrl+Right arrow and Ctrl+Left arrow move it forward or back a word at a time.

- End moves the insertion point to the end of the line. Home moves it to the beginning of the line.

- The Up arrow and Down arrow keys move the insertion point up or down a line at a time.

- Page Up and Page Down move up or down a windowful at a time.

- Ctrl+End moves to the end of the document. Ctrl+Home moves to the beginning of the document.

Some programs use additional keystroke combinations for moving the insertion point. In Microsoft Word, for example, pressing Ctrl+Down arrow takes you to the first word in the next paragraph, and Ctrl+Up arrow takes you to the beginning of the previous paragraph.

Selecting Text

To select text with the mouse, put the I-beam at one end of the block you want to select. Then hold down the mouse button, move to the other end, and release the mouse button. In other words, simply drag the mouse across the text you want to select. You can select a word by double-clicking anywhere in it.

To select text with the keyboard, first put the insertion point at one end of the block you want to select. Then hold down the Shift key and *extend* the selection to the other end of the block. The same keystrokes you use to move the insertion point extend the selection.

For example, to select three characters within a word, put the insertion point before the first character, and then hold down the Shift key while pressing the Right arrow key three times. To select an entire word, position the insertion point to the left of the word, hold down the Shift key, and press Ctrl+Right. To select from the insertion point position to the end of the line, hold down the Shift key and press End—and so on.

Deleting Characters

To delete a few characters, put the insertion point where you want to make the deletion. Then use the Backspace or Delete key to make your corrections. Backspace deletes characters to the left of the insertion point; Delete deletes characters to the right of the insertion point.

Deleting Blocks of Text

To delete a block of text, first select the block. Then do one of the following:

- Press Delete or Backspace.

- Choose the Edit menu's Delete or Clear command (if your program's menu has such a command).

- Choose the Edit menu's Cut command.

Pressing Delete or Backspace deletes the selected text. Choosing Delete or Clear from the Edit menu does exactly the same thing. Choosing the Cut command, however, does something quite different. It deletes the text from your document but stores it in an area of memory called the Clipboard. After the selection has been stored on the Clipboard, you can *paste* it somewhere else—in either the same or another document (even a document created by a different program).

Undoing a Deletion

Many programs include an Undo command on their Edit menus. This command gives you the opportunity to change your mind about a deletion. The Undo command usually can reverse only your most recent edit, however. So for example, if you delete a line of text, and then apply a formatting command to a different block of text, you won't be able to use the Undo command to reverse your deletion; at this point the Undo command is poised to undo the formatting change, not the deletion. (Some programs do have multiple-level Undo commands, however.)

Copying and Moving Text

SEE ALSO

For more information about using the Clipboard, see Chapter 9, "Exchanging Information Using the Clipboard and OLE."

The Clipboard makes it easy to copy or move text from one place to another. Follow these steps:

1 Select the text you want to move or copy.

2 To move, choose the Edit menu's Cut command. To copy, choose the Edit menu's Copy command.

3 Move the insertion point to the place where you want to move or copy your text.

4 Choose the Edit menu's Paste command.

This simple procedure can be used to move or copy text from one place to another in the same document, from one document to another created by the same program, or from one program to an entirely different program.

Getting Help

Most Windows programs include a Help menu as the rightmost item on the menu bar. Any time you're unsure how a feature or command works, you can pull down the Help menu and find useful information. In many cases, the help window stays on top of all other windows by default, so you can continue reading the help text as you work.

You'll also find an item named Help on your Start menu. The Help text that appears when you select this item provides a wealth of general information about Windows 98.

In your travels through Windows you are likely to find at least two and possibly three types of help systems. Your newest programs probably use the HTML-based help engine that was introduced with Windows 98. (HTML, which stands for *hypertext markup language*, is the language used to encode pages displayed on the World Wide Web. A help engine is a program, supplied by the operating system, that organizes and displays the help text supplied by your program vendors.) Other recent programs might use the Windows 95 help engine. Your oldest programs might use an earlier version of the Windows 95 help engine.

Figures 1-23 and 1-24 illustrate the Windows 98 and Windows 95 help engines. As you can see, the new HTML system displays an outline in one pane and help text in another. You can hide the outline pane by clicking the Hide tool in the toolbar. After you've hidden the outline, that tool changes to a Show tool, allowing you to redisplay the outline. The help engine offers three views, called Contents, Index, and Search. The Contents and Index views are comparable to the table of contents and index of a book. The Contents view lists general topics, while the Index view lists specific ones. The Search view, meanwhile, lets you hunt for any help topics that contain particular words or phrases. To switch between these three views, simply click the tabs below the toolbar.

The Windows 95 help engine offers a similar set of features in a single-pane window. Double-click the book icons in the Contents view to access deeper levels of the outline.

FIGURE 1-23.

The new HTML-based Windows 98 help engine displays an outline or list of index entries in the left pane and help text in the right pane.

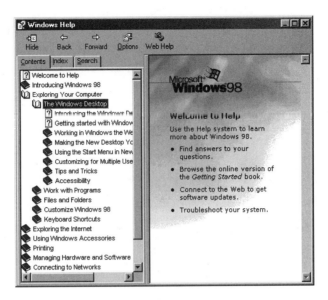

FIGURE 1-24.

Older programs are likely to use this Windows 95 help engine.

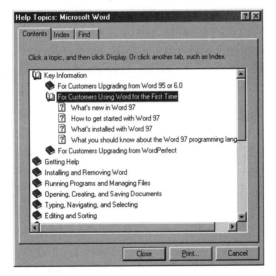

Getting Help in Dialog Boxes

In theory, all Windows dialog boxes are entirely self-explanatory, so you'll never pause in puzzlement over what a particular button or check box means. To accommodate the divergence between theory and reality, many programs include invaluable Help buttons in their dialog boxes. If you're stumped, call for help.

In many dialog boxes, you will also see a question-mark icon right beside the close box. That's the "What's This?" button. If you're not sure what some element of the dialog box means, click the What's This? button, and then click the element in question. An explanatory message will pop up. When you've finished reading, click inside the message box to make it go away.

Ending a Windows Session

Windows 98 provides various ways to quit. If your system is set up for user profiles or if it's connected to a network, a Log Off command appears near the bottom of your Start menu. Choosing this command shuts down all open programs and redisplays the logon dialog box, allowing another user to go to work at your system.

If your computer supports the Advanced Configuration and Power Interface (ACPI) specification, your Start menu's Shut Down command probably includes a Stand By option. Selecting this option puts your computer into a suspended state where it consumes very little power, but does not terminate your Windows session. When you return to work, all you have to do is press a key or a hardware button to bring your computer back to life.

The ability to suspend and reawaken your computer with simple software commands is part of Windows 98's support for the OnNow design initiative. OnNow is intended to make your computer behave more like other appliances in your house or office, allowing you to end and begin your interactions with it without lengthy delays.

 SEE ALSO

For more information about running MS-DOS–based programs, see Chapter 11, "Running MS-DOS–Based Programs."

As shown in Figure 1-25, other quitting options, all accessible via the Start menu's Shut Down command, are Restart, Restart in MS-DOS Mode, and Shut Down. Restart does exactly that; it ends the current session and reboots your computer. Restart in MS-DOS Mode begins an MS-DOS session in which almost all of Windows is removed from memory. In MS-DOS mode you may be able to run MS-DOS–based programs that are too large to fit in memory while Windows is running.

FIGURE 1-25.

At quitting time, use the Start menu's Shut Down command and choose the first option in this dialog box

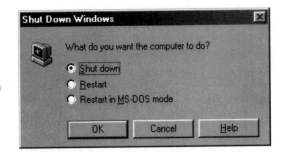

 TIP

When you choose Restart, your computer normally runs through all its power-on diagnostic tests before starting Windows again. You can bypass these tests and restart a bit more quickly by choosing Restart and then holding down the Shift key while you click OK.

To quit Windows and turn your machine off, choose the Shut Down option. In a moment or two, either your system will shut itself off or you will see a message saying that it's safe for you to shut the machine off.

If you choose any of the shut-down options and, for any reason, Windows is not ready to be shut down, you will be advised. For example, if you have unsaved work in a program, that program displays a prompt, giving you the opportunity to save before quitting. A program might also display a "can't quit" message if it objects to being closed for any other reason. This can happen, for example, if the program is in the middle of a communications session or if it's displaying a dialog box and waiting for you to respond.

If you respond promptly to a "can't quit" message, Windows stops trying to shut down your system. Then you can respond to your program or wait until it's no longer busy, and then use the Shut Down command again.

If you do not respond to the "can't quit" message within a certain period of time, however, Windows displays the message shown in Figure 1-26, on the next page. Your choices are spelled out in the text of the message. The safest thing to do is click Cancel, return to your program, and then either respond to its needs or wait until it has finished whatever it's doing.

Getting Started with Windows

FIGURE 1-26.

This message appears if you do not respond to a program's "can't quit" message or if a program is "hung."

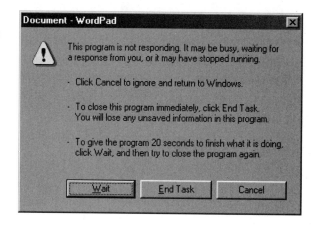

The message shown in Figure 1-26 also appears if a program has stopped responding to the operating system. You can use the End Task button to terminate such a "hung" program. You should not use this button capriciously, however. If a program is not hung but is simply busy, terminating it against its will may have adverse consequences—such as the loss of any work you've created since the last time you used the program's Save command.

Shutting Down If You Have Shared Resources

For information about sharing resources, see "Sharing Folders with Other Users," page 162, and "Sharing a Printer," page 205.

If you have made any of your computer's local resources—folders or printers, for example—available to other users on your network, you may see an advisory message when you shut down. The message tells you how many users are connected to your shared resources and warns you that shutting down will disconnect those users. If you know that no one will need the shared resources until you return to work, it's fine to go ahead and shut down. If you're not sure, or if you want to quit without disconnecting your colleagues, you can log off without quitting Windows.

CHAPTER 2

Using and Customizing the Start Menu

A s we saw in Chapter 1, the Start menu provides access to nearly everything you need to do in Windows 98. This invaluable command post pops up at a single click (or with the Ctrl+Esc keyboard shortcut) and lets you run programs, reopen recently used documents, visit favorite sites on the Internet's World Wide Web, and more. In this chapter we'll explore much of the Start menu in detail and look at the various ways you can tailor the Start menu to your own needs.

Taking Advantage of User Profiles

SEE ALSO

For details about user profiles, and for information about how to set up your own profile, see "Setting Up New User Profiles," page 269.

If you share your computer with other users—other members of your family, for example, or colleagues at the office—you might want to be sure that your system is set up for user profiles before you make any changes to your Start menu. User profiles allow multiple users to share a Windows system and maintain their own preferences. Depending on how you set up your profile, you can ensure that the following elements of the Start menu reflect your preferences:

- The top of the menu and the Programs menu

- The Favorites menu

- The Documents menu

You can also use profiles to preserve other aspects of the way you interact with Windows 98.

Changing the Overall Appearance of the Start Menu

The left side of Figure 2-1 shows the Start menu in its default state, with large icons next to menu items and a Windows 98 banner running up the left side of the menu. The right side of Figure 2-1 shows the same menu in an optional, more compact, presentation. The icons have been reduced in size and the banner has been removed. This small-icon version of the menu is particularly useful if you have a lot of commands at the top of your Start menu—so many that the menu is threatening to become taller than your screen.

To switch to a small-icon Start menu, follow these steps:

1 From the Start menu, choose Settings.

2 From the Settings menu, choose Taskbar & Start Menu.

3 In the Taskbar Properties dialog box, select the Show Small Icons In Start Menu check box.

4 Click OK.

Getting Started with Windows

FIGURE 2-1.

The "small-icon" version of the Start menu (right) helps keep the menu from overcrowding your screen.

The menus that cascade from the Start menu, such as the Programs menu or the Settings menu, are displayed by default in small-icon view, and there is no option to display them with large icons. Presumably, Windows doesn't give you a choice about these submenus because some of them—Programs, in particular—grow to large proportions on many users' systems.

SEE ALSO

For more about setting display properties, see "Changing Colors, Fonts, and Sizes," page 91.

There is one other setting that affects the appearance of your Start menu, however. That's the Menu setting, on the Appearance tab in the Display Properties dialog box. As Figure 2-2 on the next page shows, this dialog box lets you adjust the font, font size, color, style (bold, italic, bold italic, or normal), and line spacing ("size") of *all* menus in Windows 98. You can get to this portion of the Display Properties dialog box by right-clicking your desktop, choosing Properties, and clicking the Appearance tab.

You can also change the appearance of your menus by switching from one appearance "scheme" to another in the Display Properties dialog box—for example, from Windows Default to High Contrast #2 (extra large).

FIGURE 2-2.

If you want your Start menu items displayed in 18-point red Times New Roman bold italic, you can express that preference in the Display Properties dialog box. Be aware, though, that your choice here affects all menus, not just the Start menu.

Organization and Structure of the Start Menu

The Start menu consists of the following functional areas:

- The top of the menu (above the Programs menu)

- The Programs menu

- The Favorites menu

- The Documents menu

- The Settings menu

- The Find menu

- The Help command

- The Run command

- The Log Off and Shut Down commands

The Top of the Menu and the Programs Menu

The top of the Start menu and the Programs menu are primarily used for launching programs, but you can also put documents and folders in these areas. For example, if you frequently work with documents in a particular folder, you could create a menu item for that folder to make those documents more accessible.

Other than a Windows Upgrade item, which lets you obtain the latest upgrades to Windows via the Internet, the Windows Setup program does not ordinarily put anything in the top part of the Start menu because this area should be reserved for things you use every day and Windows doesn't presume to know what you do every day. Many programs (among them Microsoft Office and MSN, The Microsoft Network) are far less modest, however; their setup programs cheerfully populate this valuable Start-menu real estate. Fortunately, as we'll see, you can easily move any item onto or off the top part of the Start menu.

The bottom of the Programs menu is another area of prime real estate that you can get to easily without traversing a lengthy sequence of submenus. Here too, you'll probably find that many a brazen program has installed itself for your convenience. These elements, like those atop the main part of the Start menu, can be restationed with a wave of the mouse.

The remainder of the Programs menu consists of items that cascade into additional menus. If you've used Windows 3.x, or Windows for Workgroups, you'll recognize these as the functional equivalents of the old Program Manager's program groups.

All of this program-launching material—the top of the Start menu, the bottom of the Programs menu, and the various submenus within the Programs menu—is derived from the contents of a particular region of the local disk or server where your copy of Windows is installed. Exactly which region depends on whether your system is set up for user profiles. If you're not using profiles and Windows is installed locally on C:\Windows, this component of your Start menu lives in C:\Windows\Start Menu. If you are using profiles, these elements of each profile's Start menu reside in C:\Windows\Profiles*profilename*\Start Menu, where *profilename* is the name of a particular profile.

You can get to the folders that generate the top and Programs components of your Start menu by simply right-clicking the Start button and choosing either Open or Explore. As we'll see, certain customizing steps you might want to take require that you visit the underlying folders. Other modifications can be done directly on the menu, however.

The StartUp Submenu

The StartUp section of the Programs menu has a special purpose. It specifies programs that are to run and documents that are to be opened automatically whenever you begin a Windows session. Using customizing steps described later in this chapter, you can easily add programs and documents to the StartUp menu, or delete them from the StartUp menu, as needs dictate.

Starting Programs on Schedule

Windows 98 includes a Scheduled Tasks facility that you can use to launch programs at scheduled times. You can have a program run automatically at a certain time every day, every *n* days, once a week, on selected days of the week, once a month, on certain dates in certain months (for example, the second Tuesday of every other month), or at only one particular time in the future. You can also use the Scheduled Tasks facility as another means of launching a program at the start of a Windows session.

To schedule a launch, open the Start menu and choose Programs, Accessories, System Tools, Scheduled Tasks. In the Windows Explorer window that appears, launch Add Scheduled Task. A wizard then leads you through the process of specifying the program you want to run and the schedule on which you want to run it. On the wizard's last screen, the one on which the Finish button appears, select the "Open advanced properties ..." check box if you want to fine-tune your launch specifications. On the Settings tab in the dialog box that appears, you can add refinements such as not running the scheduled task on a laptop that's using battery power, waking up the computer if it's suspended at the scheduled launch time, and launching the scheduled task only if the computer is otherwise idle.

After you set up a scheduled task, an icon for it appears in the Scheduled Tasks folder (the folder that Windows Explorer displays when you choose Scheduled Tasks from the Start menu). To modify the settings for a scheduled task, right-click its icon and choose Properties from the context menu. To delete a scheduled task, select its icon and press the Delete key.

Other Ways That Programs May Start Automatically

You may find that certain programs or documents appear on your system at startup, even though they are not listed in the StartUp menu. That's because Windows 98 also supports two other startup-launch mechanisms. One of these is Win.ini, a vestigial configuration file used by Windows 3.1 and earlier versions of the operating system. The other is the system registry, a database of configuration settings that has largely supplanted Win.ini in Windows 95 and Windows 98.

You can find out whether Win.ini is causing anything to be run at startup—and eliminate any such startup items that you no longer need—by doing the following:

1 Click the Start button.

2 Choose Run.

3 Type *msconfig* and click OK.

In the System Configuration Utility program that appears, click the Win.ini tab. Click the plus sign next to the [windows] entry, and then look for the lines that begin with load= or run=.

Any program or document names that appear on the run= line are started as open windows whenever Windows starts. Any that appear on the load= line are started as minimized windows. To delete any startup items that you no longer need or want, simply select the load= line or the run= line and click Edit to modify the line. (If you don't want *any* of the load= or run= programs to run, deselect the line's check box.) Click OK to close System Configuration Utility.

The Win.ini startup mechanism is maintained in Windows 98 for the sake of compatibility with older programs. The registry mechanism, on the other hand, is provided for the benefit of programs that want to start automatically and don't want users to defeat that behavior. Presumably, a program that insinuates itself into the registry to ensure automatic startup has a good reason for doing so. But it's possible you may find an even better reason not to have it run automatically. To see what's running automatically at startup because of entries in your Registry, run System Configuration Utility and click the Startup tab. To remove an item, deselect its check box. CAUTION: Don't remove an item unless you're absolutely sure you don't need it!

The Favorites Menu

The Favorites menu presents the contents of a system folder called Favorites, which is stored in your Windows folder. (That is, its path is typically C:\Windows\Favorites.) You can open or run anything in that folder simply by clicking Start, navigating to the Favorites menu, and then selecting the item you're interested in.

Certain programs make it easy to store documents in the Favorites folder. The Save As dialog box in Microsoft Word, for example, includes a toolbar button that takes you directly to the Favorites folder, making it easy to store a Word document there. The program that uses the Favorites folder with particular gusto, however, is Internet Explorer. While you're browsing the Internet, if you tag a Web page with Internet Explorer's Add To Favorites command, the address of that page is stored as a shortcut in the Favorites folder, and the name of the page is added to the Favorites menu.

SEE ALSO

For information about browsing the Internet, see Chapter 25, "Using Internet Explorer."

Thus, the Favorites menu on most users' systems is a primarily a means for returning to beloved Web sites. When you pick an Internet-related item from this menu (or one of its submenus), Windows launches your Web browser (if it's not already running), reconnects to the Internet (if you're not already connected and have not set your browser to work off line), and transports you to the selected page.

Note that while browsers other than Internet Explorer might not directly populate the Favorites menu, those browsers can still create Internet shortcuts, which can still be used for rapid transit to favorite Web sites. For example, suppose your default Web browser is Netscape Navigator. Navigator's "bookmarks" are functionally comparable to Internet Explorer's "favorites," but they don't install Internet shortcuts in the Favorites section of the Start menu. If you right-click a link in a Navigator window, however, and choose Create Shortcut from the context menu, Navigator will deposit an Internet shortcut on your desktop. You can use that shortcut later to reawaken Navigator and return to the associated page. You can also move or copy the shortcut from your desktop to the Favorites menu, using simple mouse maneuvers described later in this chapter.

The Documents Menu

As you work with programs and create documents, Windows keeps track of your 15 most recently used documents and makes those files available on the Documents menu. You can reopen a recently used document by clicking Start, selecting Documents, and choosing the name of the document you want to work with. Windows restarts the program that created the document, and the program loads the document.

For example, suppose your Documents menu includes an item called Letter of Introduction, and that this item is the name of a file created in Microsoft Word. When you choose Letter of Introduction on the Documents menu, Windows runs Word and Word opens your letter.

Once your Documents menu contains 15 document names, newly arriving items replace least-recently-used items.

The Documents menu also includes one permanent item: My Documents. This menu entry is simply a copy of the My Documents icon on your desktop.

SEE ALSO

For more about My Documents, see "My Documents," page 12.

TIP

> Documents saved from programs written for versions of Windows prior to Windows 95 do not automatically appear on the Documents menu. For example, if the version of your word processor dates from Windows 3.x days, the files you save from that program will not automatically show up on the Documents menu. You can make them appear there, however. A document you open from a Windows Explorer window gets added to the Documents menu, regardless of its parent program.

Clearing or Pruning the Documents Menu

The Documents menu reflects the shortcut contents of a folder called Recent, which is stored either in your Windows folder or in a profile-specific location, depending on how you've set up your system. Windows normally gives this folder the hidden attribute, which means that Windows' designers thought it unwise for users to wander in. You can prune individual items from the Documents menu by setting Windows Explorer to show all files (even hidden ones), navigating to the Recent folder, and using the Delete key. But if you don't mind clearing the whole menu at once, there's a much simpler way:

1   From the Start menu, choose Settings.

2   From the Settings menu, choose Taskbar & Start Menu.

I

Getting Started with Windows

3 In the Taskbar Properties dialog box, click the Start Menu Programs tab.

4 Click the Clear button.

 TIP

Typically, a glance at the icon next to a Documents menu item is enough to tell you what the item's parent program is. If you want, though, you can also ensure that filename extensions appear along with document filenames. To do this, open the Start menu, choose Settings, and then choose Folder Options. In the Folder Options dialog box, click the View tab. Then deselect the check box labeled Hide File Extensions For Known File Types. After you do this, all new arrivals on the Documents menu will show their extensions. For more information, see "Options That Can Be Applied Only to All Folders," page 121.

SEE ALSO

For information about Control Panel, see Chapter 10, "Customizing Windows with Control Panel"; the Printers folder, see Chapter 7, "Installing, Configuring, and Using Your Printers"; the Taskbar & Start Menu command, see this chapter and "Personalizing the Taskbar," page 76; the Folder Options command, see "Folder Display Options," page 112; Active Desktop settings, see "To View or Not to View as a Web Page?," page 69. For information about the Windows Update command, see "Routine Maintenance for Your System," page 392. For information about the Find menu, see Chapter 6, "Using the Find Command." For information about the the Help command, see "Getting Help," page 40.

Note that you cannot add items to the Documents menu by making direct additions to the Recent folder. For the purposes of building this menu, Windows simply ignores anything in the Recent folder that it didn't put there itself. When you use the Clear command, however, *everything* in the Recent folder is deleted, no matter how it got there.

The Settings Menu, Find Menu, and Help Command

The Settings menu consists primarily of five items that let you specify preferences about the appearance and behavior of Windows 98. These items—Control Panel, Printers, Taskbar & Start Menu, Folder Options, and Active Desktop—are all described elsewhere in this book.

The Settings menu also includes a Windows Update command, which takes you to www.microsoft.com/windowsupdate/default.asp, an Internet site where you can download updates to your Windows system software and get technical support for problems you may be experiencing with your system.

The Find menu provides access to various forms of the invaluable Find command, which is described fully in Chapter 6.

The Help command invokes the Windows Help system, which displays help text concerning Windows 98.

Getting Started with Windows

The Run Command

The Run command provides a way to start programs, open documents or folders, or navigate to Web sites by entering a command string. Apart from its accommodation of users who actually prefer commands to menu picks, the Run command has two virtues: it allows you to specify command-line parameters along with the name of a program, and it remembers the command strings you enter.

Windows-based programs seldom need command-line parameters, but MS-DOS–based programs sometimes do. One way to run an MS-DOS–based program that needs a parameter is to open an MS-DOS Prompt window and type at the familiar C> prompt. Another is to use the Run command. For example, suppose you want to use the MS-DOS DiskCopy command to duplicate a floppy disk. You can do this by choosing Run from the Start menu and typing *diskcopy a: a: /v.*

If you're not sure of what to put on the Run command's command line, the Browse button can help. For example, if you want to run a particular program that's not on your Start menu, but you're not sure how to enter the path to the folder where that program is stored, you can choose Run, click Browse, and then use the Browse dialog box to navigate to the folder where the program is stored. (Alternatively, you can use the Find command to locate the program, and then run it from the Find window. See Chapter 6 for details.)

 SEE ALSO

For information about the Address toolbar, see "Using Toolbars," page 79.

Like the Address toolbar (one of the optional toolbars supplied with Windows 98), the Run command line accepts Internet addresses. If you type an Internet address, Run will invoke your browser, connect if necessary, and take you where you want to go.

⭐ **TIP**

> The Start menu's Run command and the Address toolbar function identically. Both can be used to run programs, open documents, open folders, or travel to Web sites. But the command and the toolbar maintain separate most-recently-used lists.

The Run command's most-recently-used list makes it easy to re-execute commands you've used before. To see what commands are available, simply click the arrow at the right side of the command line and scroll through the drop-down list. The commands you've used most recently appear nearest the top of the list.

The Log Off Command and Shut Down Command

SEE ALSO

For information about the Log Off command and the Shut Down command, see "Ending a Windows Session," page 42.

If your system is set up for user profiles or if it's connected to a network, a Log Off command appears near the bottom of your Start menu. Choosing this command shuts down all open programs and redisplays the logon dialog box, allowing another user to go to work at your system.

The Shut Down command lets you shut down your computer, place it in a standby condition, or restart your computer.

Customizing the Start Menu

Much of the Start menu is customizable. If you don't like the arrangement of your Programs submenu, for example, you can rearrange it. If items at the top of your Start menu are getting in your way, you can delete them or put them somewhere within the Programs submenu. You can reorganize the contents of your Favorites submenu, or move Favorites items onto other parts of the Start menu. You can even rearrange the Documents submenu or give Documents items permanent positions on your Favorites or Programs submenus. The only parts of the Start menu you cannot alter are Settings, Find, Help, Run, Log Off, and Shut Down.

We'll concentrate on the simplest customizing methods in the remainder of this chapter.

Adding Items to the Menu

The easiest way to add something to the Start menu is to drag it there. If you have a shortcut on your desktop, for example, that you'd like also to appear somewhere on the Start menu, simply click it, hold down the mouse button, and move your mouse pointer to the Start button. When the Start menu opens, after a moment's delay, you can drag the desktop shortcut to the top of the menu or to some other location within the

Programs or Favorites menus. As you move the mouse, a dark line shows where the new item will appear when you release the button.

Getting Started with Windows

> **NOTE**
>
> If you drag a shortcut to the Start button and release the mouse button before the Start menu opens, the new item will appear at the top of the menu.

You can use the same technique to drag items from Windows Explorer windows to the Start menu. Windows leaves the dragged item where you got it and plants a copy on the Start menu. If the dragged item isn't a shortcut to begin with, Windows creates a shortcut to it on the Start menu. Thus, for example, you can drag a folder to the Start menu without changing the folder structure of your disk in any way; Windows simply creates a pointer (a shortcut) to the folder on the menu.

If you're not sure how to get to a Windows Explorer window that displays the item you want on the Start menu, you can use the Find command to locate it—and then drag the item from the Find window to the menu. For example, suppose you want to put Notepad on the top of your Start menu, but you're not quite sure where Notepad lives. Open the Start menu and choose Find, Files Or Folders. Tell Find to find Notepad, and when Notepad.exe appears in the lower half of the Find window, simply drag it to the Start button.

In case you want to work a little harder than this, the following method is also available:

1. Choose Settings from the Start menu.

2. Choose Taskbar & Start Menu from the Settings menu.

3. Click the Start Menu Programs tab.

4. Click the Add button.

5. Type the path of the item you want to add to the menu, or use the Browse button to navigate to it.

6. Use the Select Program Folder dialog box to tell Windows where it should install the new item.

Removing Items from the Start Menu

To remove any item from the top of the Start menu or any part of the Programs menu, follow these steps:

1 Click the Start button, and then release the mouse button.

2 Move the mouse pointer to the item you want to delete.

3 Right-click the item you want to delete.

4 Choose Delete from the context menu.

Alternatively, you can open the Start menu and choose Settings, Taskbar & Start Menu. Click the Start Menu Programs tab, click Remove, and tell Windows what you want to remove.

Moving and Copying Items from One Part of the Menu to Another

To move an item from one part of the menu to another, simply grab it and drag it. Click the Start button, release the mouse button, move the mouse pointer to the item you want to move, and then click again and hold the mouse button down. Now move the mouse in the direction of the item's new destination. As you do, Windows draws a thick border around the item at its original location and a thick line to show where the item will land if you release the mouse button.

To copy an item into a new location, follow the same steps as for moving, but hold down the Ctrl key while you drag. A plus sign next to the mouse pointer confirms that you're copying, not moving.

Moving and Copying Items from the Menu to Other Locations

? SEE ALSO

For information about toolbars, see "Using Toolbars," page 79.

The drag-and-drop techniques that let you rearrange menu items also work for moving and copying items to off-menu locations. Thus, for example, if your menu gets crowded, you can move some items from the menu to your desktop, to a toolbar, or to a folder. In all cases, Windows creates a shortcut in the new location.

> **NOTE**
>
> Be aware that if you move or copy a program name or folder from one part of the Start menu to another and subsequently uninstall that program, the uninstall procedure might not be able to remove the item or folder from your Start menu. You might need to clean up the Start menu yourself after uninstalling.

Renaming Menu Items

If you click the Start button, move the mouse pointer to a Programs item, and right-click, you'll see that the resulting context menu offers some useful options but doesn't include a Rename command. Menu items are simply shortcuts stored in particular hard disk folders, however, and in their folder locations they can be renamed. To see how this can be done, right-click the Start button and choose the Open command. As Figure 2-3 shows, an Explorer window will appear, displaying shortcuts for each item at the top your Start menu as well as a folder icon labeled Programs.

FIGURE 2-3.

Right-clicking the Start button and choosing Open produces a Windows Explorer window displaying a Programs folder and shortcuts for each item at the top of the Start menu.

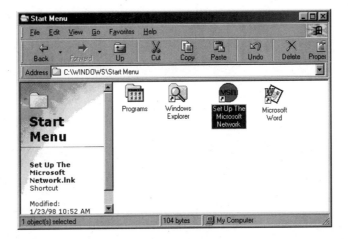

To rename an item at the top of the Start menu, right-click it, choose the Rename command, and type the new name. To rename an item somewhere within the Programs menu, click or double-click to open the Programs folder, and continue opening subfolders until you get to the item you want to rename. Then right-click, choose Rename, and type.

You can rename the Programs folder itself, but doing so simply creates a new cascading menu at the top of the Start menu. The Programs menu remains where it was and still bears the name Programs.

Assigning a Keyboard Shortcut to a Menu Item

Keyboard shortcuts are keystroke combinations that provide alternative ways to issue menu commands. For example, if you assign the shortcut Ctrl+Alt+P to the Paint program, then you can launch Paint by typing Ctrl+Alt+P, as an alternative to opening the Start menu, choosing Programs, choosing Accessories, and then locating the Paint item on the Accessories menu.

You can assign a keyboard shortcut to an item as follows:

1 Right-click the Start button.

2 Choose Open from the context menu.

3 In the Explorer window that appears (see Figure 2-3, on the previous page), navigate to the item you're interested in.

4 Right-click the item and choose Properties.

5 In the dialog box that appears, click the Shortcut tab.

You'll see a dialog box similar to the one shown in Figure 2-4.

6 On the Shortcut Key line, type the keystroke combination you want to use.

Shortcut keys assigned to menu items (or to shortcuts elsewhere in your system) take precedence over any shortcut keys used by programs. For example, all Windows-based programs use Alt+F4 as a shortcut for their Exit command. If you happen to assign Alt+F4 as a shortcut for launching Paint, you will no longer be able to quit programs by pressing this combination. Instead, no matter where you are, pressing Alt+F4 will get you another copy of Paint. Keep this in mind as you assign keyboard shortcuts.

FIGURE 2-4.

With this dialog box you can set a variety of properties for a Start menu item, including its shortcut key and the type of window the item should open.

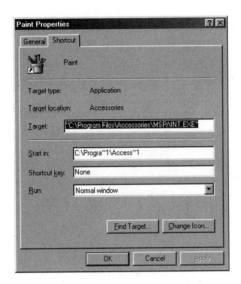

Specifying the Type of Window a Menu Item Opens

The Run line in the dialog box shown in Figure 2-4 lets you indicate what kind of a window you want your menu item to open—a maximized window, a "normal" window (one that's open but not maximized), or a minimized window. To specify a window type, simply select from the drop-down list on the Run line.

Changing a Menu Item's Icon

You can change the icons associated with programs and documents (but not folders) on the Start menu. To change an item's icon, follow the instructions on the previous page to get to the item's properties dialog box, as shown in Figure 2-4. Then click the Change Icon button. As Figure 2-5 on the next page shows, a dialog box showing all the icons available for the selected program (or for the program parent, if the item is a document) will appear. Choose the new icon you want, and then click OK twice to confirm your choice and leave the properties dialog box.

If you don't find an icon to your liking, you can specify a different filename on the top line in the dialog box shown in Figure 2-5. Or you can click the Browse button and navigate to a different file. Icons are stored in files with extensions .EXE, .DLL, .ICO, or .ICL. One excellent source of icons is the file C:\Windows\System\Shell32.dll. (Substitute

FIGURE 2-5.

The Change Icon dialog box initially presents all the icons that are stored in the file to which your menu item points.

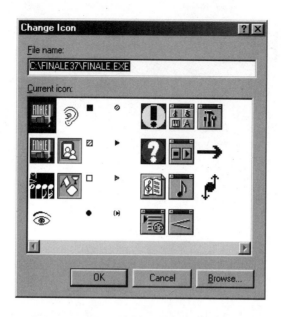

appropriately for C:\Windows\System if Windows is not installed in C:\Windows.)

Reorganizing the Programs Menu

You are by no means required to live with the current organization of submenus on your Programs menu. You can restructure the Programs menu in any way you see fit. For example, suppose your menu now includes submenus named Microsoft Internet Explorer, Microsoft CD Sampler, Microsoft NetShow, Microsoft Reference, Microsoft Money, and Microsoft Office 97. It's conceivable that it might make more sense to have one submenu called Microsoft, which would open into further submenus named Internet Explorer, CD Sampler, and so on.

? SEE ALSO

For information about creating folders, see "Creating New Folders," page 130. For information about moving objects between folders, see "Moving or Copying Folders, Files, and Shortcuts," page 131.

To reorganize the menu in the manner just described, you would right-click the Start button, choose Open, and then click or double-click the Programs folder in the ensuing Windows Explorer window. A new Windows Explorer window displaying the contents of Programs would appear. Here you would create a new folder called Microsoft. Within this folder, you would create additional folders called Internet Explorer, CD Sampler, and so on. Finally, you would move shortcuts from the Programs folder into the appropriate subfolders of the new folder named Microsoft.

CHAPTER 3

Using and Customizing the Desktop

The desktop is the backdrop to everything you do in Windows 98. It's the surface on which you run programs, a place where you can store documents and shortcuts, and, potentially, a kind of menu from which you can launch programs, open documents, and visit Web sites.

When you first install Windows, the Setup program provides a standard configuration for your desktop. You get a decent color arrangement, a serviceable screen resolution, appropriately sized buttons and icons, and so on. But because one size does not fit all, Windows gives you many choices about the appearance and behavior of your desktop. We'll explore those choices in this chapter.

Maintaining Individual Settings with User Profiles

? SEE ALSO

For information about setting up user profiles, see "Setting Up New User Profiles," page 269.

Before you begin customizing your desktop, you need to decide whether your system should be set up for user profiles. User profiles allow two or more users of a machine to establish individual settings that will be remembered and restored each time they log on. With profiles in place, you're free to paint your workspace purple without offending someone else who also needs to use your machine. Nearly all the customizing steps described in this chapter, including screen resolution and color depth, are profile-specific, which means that they affect only the current profile.

⭐ TIP

> Even if you're the only one that uses your machine, you might still find it convenient to use profiles. That way you can set up separate desktops for particular projects.

Activating the Active Desktop

Because the desktop in Windows 98 is capable of displaying Web pages and other content downloaded from the Internet, Microsoft's dialog boxes now refer to the desktop as the Active Desktop. You can choose just how "active" you want your desktop to be, however. Windows 98 provides two mechanisms for making your desktop look and act more or less like a page on the World Wide Web:

- You can set up your system so that you have to click an icon only once to launch or open the item represented by that icon. This makes desktop icons (and items in Windows Explorer) behave more like links on a Web page and less like icons in earlier versions of Windows, where double-clicking was required. If you place the mouse pointer on an icon in single-click mode, the pointer changes from an arrow to a hand, just as it does when you point to a link in your Web browser. And, of course, in this mode a single-click is all that's required to launch the object you're pointing at.

- You can choose to display your Active Desktop as a Web page. If you do this, your desktop can host objects such as stock or news

The Desktop Is a Folder

A *folder* in Windows 98 is a place to store things—programs, documents, shortcuts, and other folders. In most cases, a folder is also a chunk of disk space. The folder's *path* is an address that tells the operating system how to find the folder. So, for example, many of your Windows system files are probably stored in a folder whose path is C:\Windows. The C:\Windows folder, in addition to programs and documents, contains other folders. Their paths begin with C:\Windows and continue on from there, as C:\Windows\System, C:\Windows\Temp, C:\Windows\Media, and so on.

Windows Explorer, which we explore in Chapter 4, is the Windows program that lets you view and manipulate the contents of folders.

A few folders, such as Control Panel, Printers, and Dial-Up Networking, are special and don't represent disk storage units. Although you can't put files in these "system" folders, you can still view and manipulate their contents with Windows Explorer.

The desktop is also a special folder. Its specialness consists of the fact that you don't need Windows Explorer to see and work with it. It's just there all the time, lying beneath whatever else you happen to be using. It does, however, correspond to a piece of disk real estate, and you can use Windows Explorer to work with it if you want to. On a system that doesn't use profiles, the desktop's path is (typically) C:\Windows\Desktop. On a system with profiles, the path is C:\Windows\Profiles*profilename*\Desktop, where *profilename* is the name of the profile that's currently in use. (In addition, your Windows desktop displays the contents of a second folder—C:\Windows\All Users\Desktop—that you can use to store objects that are available to anyone who uses your system.)

Because the desktop is a folder, you can store programs, documents, shortcuts, and other folders in (on) it. Also because it's a folder, certain display options that you set in Windows Explorer affect the desktop, and certain options that you set on the desktop also affect appearances within Windows Explorer windows.

tickers that can be updated from the Internet automatically at scheduled times. An Active Desktop displayed as a Web page can also have, as its backdrop, an HTML document, complete with links to other HTML documents. (HTML, or *hypertext markup language*, is the programming language used to encode Web pages.) The View As Web Page option thus makes your desktop even more fundamentally Web-like than the single-click option.

These two options are independent. You can turn on the single-click option without displaying your Active Desktop as a Web page. And you can display your Active Desktop as a Web page but retain the classic (double-click) mode of launching programs and opening documents.

To Click or Double-Click?

Whether you want single-clicking or double-clicking is a matter of taste. Many users find that single-clicking makes life easier—but only after they have become used to it. The best way to find out which mode you prefer is to try both.

To do that, open the Start menu and choose Settings, Folder Options. This takes you to the General tab in the Folder Options dialog box, shown in Figure 3-1. In the Windows Desktop Update section on the General tab, select Web Style for single-clicking or Classic Style for double-clicking.

Selecting Web Style also turns on the View As Web Page option. If you want single-clicking but not Web-page view, select Custom in the Folder Options dialog box, and then click the Settings button. A second dialog box, shown in Figure 3-2, appears. In the top portion of this dialog box, select the second option button—Use Windows Classic Desktop. Down below, select Single-Click To Open An Item (Point To Select).

FIGURE 3-1.
Selecting Web Style in this dialog box turns on single-clicking and Web-page view. Selecting Classic Style turns off both options.

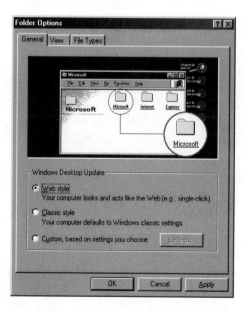

FIGURE 3-2.

To turn on single-clicking and turn off Web-page view, select Use Windows Classic Desktop and Single-Click To Open An Item.

Selecting Items in Single-Click and Double-Click Modes

In "classic" (double-click) mode, clicking an item once selects it, while clicking twice in rapid succession executes the item's default action. (An object's default action is the one that appears in bold type when you right-click the object.) In single-click mode, clicking once executes the default action; to select without executing, you have to remember not to click! Simply hover the mouse pointer over the object and wait for a moment. When the object becomes highlighted, you've selected it.

To select a contiguous group of objects in double-click mode, you can click the first and then Shift+click (hold down the Shift key while clicking) the last. To do the same in single-click mode, hover over the first item until Windows highlights it. Then hold down the Shift key while you hover over the last item.

To select a non-contiguous group of objects in double-click mode, hold down the Ctrl key while you click each item in turn. To do this in single-click mode, hold down the Ctrl key while you hover over each. Use the same technique to deselect an object that you've already selected.

All of the foregoing applies both to items on the desktop and items in a Windows Explorer window. To select a group of adjacent icons in

Windows Explorer with single-clicking in effect, for example, you'd point to the first one, wait a moment until Windows highlights it, hold down the Shift key, and then move the mouse to the last one and wait again. When the whole range of items is highlighted, you've made your selection.

Note that choosing single-click mode does not change the behavior of dialog boxes. As you may know, in many dialog boxes, double-clicking an item has the same effect as single-clicking it and then clicking the OK button. To bypass the OK button in a dialog box, you'll still need to double-click, even if you're single-clicking on the desktop and in Windows Explorer. If this dissonance disconcerts you, you might want to stick with double-clicking everywhere.

 TIP

> In either single-click or double-click mode, you can also select a group of adjacent items by drawing a "lasso" around the group. To select a group of icons, click just above and to the left of the upper left icon in the group. Then, while holding down the mouse button, drag the mouse to a point below and to the right of the lower right icon. When you release the button, the enclosed icons are all selected.

Turning Off the Underlining in Single-Click Mode

In single-click mode, the text associated with desktop icons and Windows Explorer items is normally underlined, the same way links on a Web page are underlined. You can turn off underlining by visiting the dialog box shown in Figure 3-2, on the previous page, and selecting Underline Icon Titles Only When I Point At Them. To turn underlining back on, select Underline Icon Titles Consistent With My Browser Setting.

NOTE

> If you've told Internet Explorer not to underline links until you point to them, the underlining will also be suppressed on your desktop and in Windows Explorer.

To View or Not to View as a Web Page?

Viewing your Active Desktop as a Web page lets the desktop host "live" objects from the World Wide Web and allows it to have an HTML document as its background.

If you don't need these features, there's no compelling reason to turn on Web-page view. On the other hand, unless you notice performance degradation, there's also no particular reason not to. If you do display live Internet objects on your desktop, however, you might find it convenient at times to turn off Web-page view. For example, suppose you have several stock-market-related objects on your desktop. When the market's closed, you might find those objects distracting. You can shut them down one by one, but turning off Web-page view suppresses the objects' display in one step instead of several. When the market reopens the next day, you can turn on Web-page view again to see what's happening.

The simplest way to toggle Web-page view on or off is by right-clicking a blank part of the desktop and choosing Active Desktop from the context menu. A submenu will appear, with View As Web Page at the top. If a check mark appears beside this command, choosing the command turns off Web-page view. If no check mark is there, choosing the command turns on Web-page view.

You can also turn on Web-page view by choosing Web Style in the Folder Options dialog box, shown in Figure 3-1 on page 66. Choosing Classic Style in the same dialog box turns off the feature. Be aware, though, that the Web Style option also turns on single-clicking. If you want Web-page view with double-clicking, in the Folder Options dialog box select Custom, Based On Settings You Choose. Then click the Settings button. In the Custom Settings dialog box, shown in Figure 3-2 on page 67, select the first option button (Enable All Web-Related Content On My Desktop) and the last (Double-Click To Open An Item).

Bringing the Internet to Your Active Desktop

Figure 3-3, on the next page, shows a desktop with two Internet objects—a stock market graph and a news ticker. These objects are updated periodically from the Internet.

FIGURE 3-3.

The stock market graph and news ticker on this desktop are Internet objects.

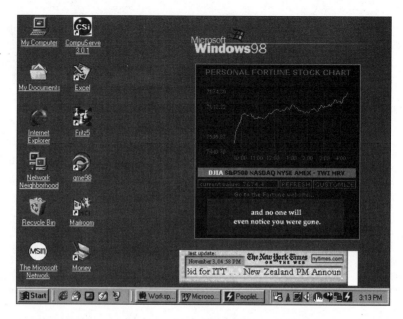

To add an Internet object to your Active Desktop, begin by right-clicking the desktop and choosing Properties from the context menu. In the Display Properties dialog box, click the Web tab. Make sure the View My Active Desktop As A Web Page check box is selected, and then click the New button. You will probably see the following dialog box, which offers to take you to Microsoft's Active Desktop Gallery Web site:

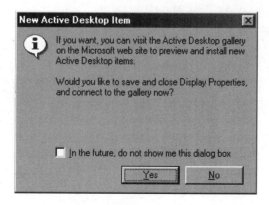

If you don't see this dialog box, it's because you or someone else has seen it before and selected its "In the future" check box. In that case, you can get to the Active Desktop Gallery Web site by directing your browser to www.microsoft.com/ie/ie40/gallery. (When you go to this page, you may see a "security warning" window asking if you want to download an ActiveX Control. Go ahead and click Yes if you see this message.)

The Active Desktop Gallery Web site provides access to Web sites that offer content designed expressly for display on your desktop. Figure 3-4 shows how that Web site appeared as this book was going to press. You're not limited to using the sites listed here, but these will give you a good idea of what's possible.

FIGURE 3-4.

The Active Desktop Gallery Web site (www.microsoft.com/ie/ie40/gallery) provides access to vendors who offer Web content designed for display on the desktop.

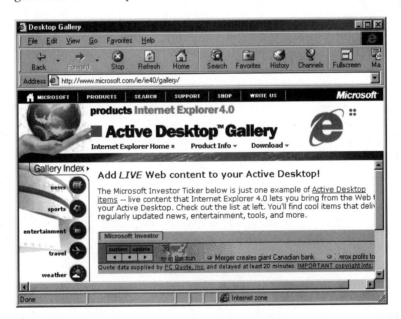

To add an object to your desktop, first visit its site. Supply any information and perform any downloads required by the site, and then look for a button or link that looks like this or offers the equivalent option:

When you click that button, you'll be asked to confirm that you want to add the item to your desktop. After you confirm, you'll see a new dialog box that looks something like this:

To add the item to your Active Desktop and accept the vendor's default update schedule, simply click OK. If you want to set up your own schedule, click Customize Subscription. A scheduling dialog box will appear, as shown in Figure 3-5.

To specify a schedule other than the publisher's recommended schedule, click New and fill out the ensuing dialog box. To change a schedule you've already set up, click Edit. To turn off automatic updating, select the Manually check box. If you do this, your object will be updated only when you choose Update All Subscriptions from Internet Explorer's Favorites menu.

FIGURE 3-5.

The Subscription Wizard dialog box lets you specify the schedule for updating the content of an Active Desktop item.

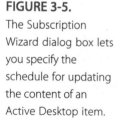
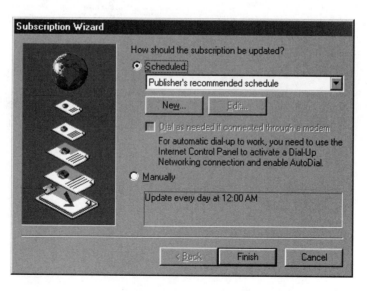

Once your Internet object has arrived on your desktop, you can interact with it exactly as you would if you were working within a Web browser. When you click a link, Windows activates your browser, connects to the Internet if you're not already online, and then performs the action stipulated by that link.

 TIP

> Some Web sites give you the option of displaying content via the Channel Screen Saver. To use this content, subscribe to one or more channels, and then select Channel Screen Saver as your screen saver.

Displaying the Channel Bar

One Internet-related object that you can display on your Active Desktop without having to fetch it from the Internet is the Channel Bar. The Channel Bar provides easy access to channels—Internet sites that can deliver news and other timely information to your desktop. You can click a channel's icon on the Channel Bar to activate Internet Explorer, initiate an Internet connection (if you aren't already connected), and visit a channel's Web site.

To display the Channel Bar on your desktop, first be sure you have displayed your Active Desktop as a Web page. Then right-click the desktop, choose Active Desktop, Customize My Desktop, and select Internet Explorer Channel Bar.

Adding "Non-Gallery" Internet Objects to Your Desktop

When you add an Internet object to your Active Desktop, what you're doing is entering a subscription to the Web site that generates that object, and stipulating that downloaded content from the subscription be displayed on your desktop. The Web sites made available via Microsoft's Active Desktop Gallery are good ones to try, because their content has been tailored for desktop display. But you can subscribe to any Web site and display that site's contents on your Active Desktop.

To turn a "non-Gallery" Web site into an Active Desktop object, right-click the desktop, choose Properties, and click the Web tab. Click the

New button, click No (if you see the dialog box that asks whether you want to go to the Active Desktop Gallery), and then either type the address for the site you're interested in, or (if the site is already listed in your Favorites folder) click Browse and navigate to the site.

After you've specified the address for your site, click Customize Subscriptions, supply a password if one is needed, and specify the updating schedule you want to follow.

 TIP

You can also turn any Web link into an Active Desktop object. Simply right-drag the link (the underlined word or words) from your browser window to the desktop, and then choose Create Active Desktop Item(s) Here from the context menu.

Displaying a Folder as an Active Desktop Object

 SEE ALSO

For information about toolbars, see "Using Toolbars," page 79. For information about folder views, see "Folder Display Options," page 112.

You can display a folder as an Active Desktop object. Like displaying a folder as a toolbar, doing so provides convenient access to a folder's contents because it's always on the desktop. But displaying a folder as an Active Desktop object has the additional advantage of displaying the folder using any view available in Windows Explorer. And the Active Desktop object displays any folder customization you've created, such as folder backgrounds, HTML pages, and so on.

To add a folder to your Active Desktop:

1   Right-click the desktop, choose Properties, and click the Web tab.

2   Click New. If the dialog box that asks whether you want to go to the Active Desktop Gallery appears, click No.

3   In the Location text box, type *file://* followed by the complete path of the folder you want to display. For example, to display your My Documents folder, type:

```
file://c:\my documents
```

4   Click OK in the New Active Desktop Item dialog box and in the Display Properties dialog box. The folder appears on the desktop.

5   If you want to view the folder as a Web page, right-click in the new object, click View, and choose As Web Page.

Moving and Sizing Internet Objects

Internet objects displayed on your Active Desktop are windows, albeit unconventional ones. You can move them around, change their sizes, and close them. You can't maximize or minimize them, however.

To move one of these windows, start by hovering your mouse pointer somewhere near the window's top edge. After a moment, a gray border pops up from the top edge. To move the window, drag this gray border. To close a window, click the X in the upper right corner of the gray border. (You can also close the window by choosing Close from the Control menu that appears when you click the down arrow in the upper left corner of the border.)

To change a window's size, point to one of the window's borders. When your mouse pointer changes shape, drag.

Changing an Object's Update Schedule

To change an object's update schedule, visit its properties dialog box. Here are some ways to get there:

- Point to the top edge of the object, click the down arrow that appears in the upper left corner to open the Control menu, and choose Properties.

- Right-click the desktop, choose Properties, click the Web tab, select the item whose schedule you want to change, and click the Properties button.

- Use Windows Explorer to display the Subscriptions folder, whose path is typically C:\Windows\Subscriptions. Then right-click the item whose schedule you want to change, and choose Properties from the context menu.

- Choose Manage Subscriptions from Internet Explorer's Favorites menu. In the Subscriptions folder that appears, right-click the item whose schedule you want to change, and then choose Properties from the context menu.

Figure 3-6, on the next page, shows an example of a subscription properties dialog box. To change the update schedule, click the Schedule tab. You'll see a dialog box similar to the one you filled out when you set up the object's initial schedule.

Getting Started with Windows

FIGURE 3-6.

The subscription properties dialog box lets you modify an object's update schedule or cancel your subscription.

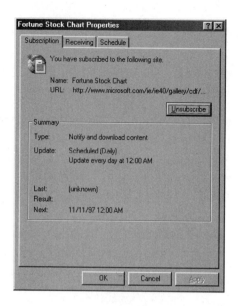

To see when an Internet object was last updated, display your Subscriptions folder (it's typically C:\Windows\Subscriptions, but you can also get to it by choosing the Manage Subscriptions command from Internet Explorer's Favorites menu). Once the folder is displayed, choose Details from the View menu. In the column headed Last Update, you'll find the date and time of the most recent update for each subscription.

Getting Rid of an Internet Desktop Object

What do you do when you're tired of looking at that news ticker, weather map, or other desktop object? You can suppress its display by simply closing it. (Point to the top edge, and then click the *X* icon in the upper right corner.) But Windows will continue to update it even if it's not being displayed. To remove it altogether, you need to "unsubscribe." To do that, display the object's properties dialog box (as described in the preceding section), and then click the Unsubscribe button on the Subscription tab.

Personalizing the Taskbar

The taskbar houses the Start menu, the notification area, and buttons for each running program. You can use these "task buttons" to switch from one running program to another. You can also click a task button to minimize an open window or reopen a minimized one. Your taskbar may also hold one or more toolbars—collections of icons that let you start programs quickly. As we'll see later in this chapter, though, toolbars can live in other desktop locations as well as on the the taskbar.

The default location of the taskbar is along the bottom edge of the desktop. If you're a veteran of Windows 3.x, which put icons for minimized programs at the bottom of the screen, you may be quite at home with this arrangement. But you can move the taskbar to any other edge of the screen if you want to try something a little different.

By default, the taskbar shows one row of buttons (or one column, if your taskbar is docked against the left or right edge of the desktop). If you keep toolbars on the taskbar, you might find it convenient to expand the taskbar to two or even three rows. Simply position the mouse along the inner boundary of the taskbar (the edge closest to the center of the screen). When the mouse pointer becomes a two-headed arrow, drag toward the center of the screen to expand the taskbar.

Other Ways to Make More Room on the Taskbar

You can also increase button space by removing the clock from the taskbar. If you don't need Windows to tell you the time of day, you can probably squeeze at least one more button onto the bar by unloading the clock. Right-click an unoccupied space on the taskbar and choose Properties from the context menu. On the Taskbar Options tab in the Taskbar Properties dialog box (see Figure 3-7, on the next page), deselect the Show Clock check box.

TIP

> You can also make room for more buttons by switching to a higher-resolution display. See "Changing Display Resolution," page 88.

SEE ALSO

For more information about the Appearance tab, see "Changing Colors, Fonts, and Sizes," page 91.

You can make room for more text on each taskbar button by reducing the point size of the text. You can do this by choosing a smaller size for the Inactive Title Bar item on the Appearance tab in the Display Properties dialog box. To get there, right-click the desktop, choose Properties, and click the Appearance tab.

FIGURE 3-7.

The Always On Top and Auto Hide check boxes in this dialog box provide ways to keep the taskbar out of your hair.

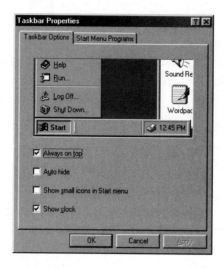

To decode an overcrowded taskbar, rest your mouse pointer for about a half second on each button. If a button's caption is truncated, Windows displays its full text in a pop-up window. If you rest your pointer on the clock, Windows displays the date in a pop-up window.

If the Taskbar Gets in Your Way

By default, your taskbar is a stay-on-top window. That means it remains visible even when you're working in a maximized program. If that's inconvenient for any reason, you can tell it to get out of the way. Simply right-click any unoccupied part of the taskbar, choose Properties from the context menu, and click the Taskbar Options tab. Windows displays the Taskbar Properties dialog box shown in Figure 3-7.

Deselect the Always On Top check box and click OK. Now you'll be able to see the taskbar at all times *except* when a window is maximized.

> Regardless of how you set options in the Taskbar Properties dialog box, you can make the taskbar visible at any time by pressing Ctrl+Esc.

Another way to make the taskbar less obtrusive is to select the Auto Hide check box shown in Figure 3-7. With this option on, Windows hides the taskbar as soon as you open any window. To get back to the taskbar, you can press Ctrl+Esc or move the mouse pointer to the edge of the screen where the taskbar is located.

Using Toolbars

A toolbar is a collection of icons that simplify commonplace tasks. The standard Windows setup process installs one toolbar on your taskbar. That toolbar, called Quick Launch, includes the following icons: Internet Explorer, Outlook Express, WebTV, Show Desktop, and View Channels. (If you haven't installed the WebTV program, your Quick Launch toolbar does not include the WebTV icon.) The first three of these icons simply launch their corresponding programs. The Show Desktop icon displays the desktop, in the process minimizing whatever windows may be open, and the View Channels icon displays Internet Explorer's channel viewer.

TIP

The Show Desktop tool is particularly useful, because it lets you see your desktop even when a system-modal dialog box (one that you must fill out before you can select another window) is blocking your view. Click this tool to reveal the desktop; click a second time to restore all the windows that were open when you clicked the first time.

The following other toolbars are also available (see Figure 3-8, on the next page):

- Address

- Links

- Desktop

SEE ALSO

For information about the Run command, see "The Run Command," page 55. For information about the Address toolbar in Windows Explorer, see "Navigating Through Folders," page 110.

The Address toolbar provides a place where you can enter an Internet address, the name of a program or document, or the name and path of a folder. When you press Enter, Windows takes you to the Internet address, launches the program, opens the document, or displays the folder in a Windows Explorer window. The Address toolbar is functionally equivalent to the Start menu's Run command or the Address bar in Windows Explorer or Internet Explorer.

The Links toolbar provides a set of shortcuts to selected Internet sites. It's equivalent to the Links toolbar that you can display in Internet Explorer or Windows Explorer.

FIGURE 3-8.

You can customize these four standard toolbars and create your own new toolbars.

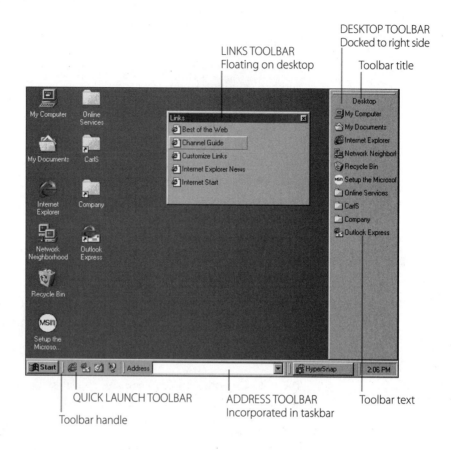

The Desktop toolbar provides copies of all the icons currently displayed on your desktop. You might find this toolbar handy if you're using an HTML page as background for your desktop and your normal desktop icons are getting in the way.

You can customize any of the supplied toolbars except for Address. So, for example, you can add icons for your own programs or shortcuts to the Quick Launch toolbar, remove from the Links toolbar links that you don't find useful (or add links to your own favorite sites), and so on. You can also create entirely new toolbars.

Toolbars appear initially on the taskbar, but you can "float" them on the desktop or "dock" them against any side of the desktop. Thus, for example, you can have your taskbar docked against the bottom edge of the screen and line the other three edges with toolbars.

Installing and Removing Toolbars

To install a new toolbar or remove one you're currently using, right-click any unoccupied part of the taskbar. (If you're having trouble finding an unoccupied place, first drag the inside border of the taskbar to enlarge it.) Choose Toolbars from the context menu that appears, and then choose from the ensuing submenu. A check beside a toolbar's name means that toolbar is already displayed. Choosing a checked toolbar name removes that toolbar.

 TIP

The Desktop toolbar displays miniature versions of all the icons on your desktop. If you're covering your entire desktop with an Internet object or an HTML background, you might find it convenient to suppress the desktop display of icons and show the Desktop toolbar instead. To suppress icon display, right-click the desktop, choose Properties, and click the Effects tab in the Display Properties dialog box. Then select Hide Icons When The Desktop Is Viewed As A Web Page.

Sizing and Positioning Toolbars

There's a thin vertical bar at the left edge of every toolbar positioned on the taskbar. (If the taskbar is displayed vertically against the left or right edge of the desktop, the bar is horizontal and appears at the top of the toolbar.) This is the toolbar's handle. (See Figure 3-8.) To move a toolbar out onto the desktop, position the mouse pointer on the handle. When the pointer changes shape, drag the toolbar. To dock a toolbar against a different edge of the screen, drag it all the way to that edge. When you release the mouse button, the toolbar will dock.

On the desktop, the toolbar will take the form of a simple window, with a title bar and a close button. You can move the toolbar around by dragging its title bar or close it by clicking the close button.

To reposition a toolbar on the taskbar, simply drag its title bar to the taskbar.

You can also use the handle to change a toolbar's size or position on the taskbar. Assuming your taskbar is horizontal, dragging the handle to the right decreases the width of the toolbar and makes more room for the toolbar on the left. Dragging to the left has the opposite effect.

To change the size of a desktop toolbar, simply drag one of its borders.

> A toolbar that's too large to fit in its taskbar space will scroll if you click the arrow that appears at its left or right edge.

Customizing Toolbar Contents

To remove an icon from a toolbar, right-click the icon, choose Delete from the context menu, and answer the confirmation prompt. To add an icon to a toolbar, drag the icon from the desktop or a Windows Explorer window and deposit it wherever you want it to appear on the toolbar.

Customizing the Appearance of a Toolbar

Toolbars can be displayed with either large or small icons, with or without their titles, and with or without text identifying each tool. To avail yourself of any of these customizing options, right-click the toolbar you want to modify. Choose View, followed by Large or Small to change the icon size, Show Text to suppress or display tool descriptions, or Show Title to suppress or display the toolbar title.

Note that if you don't display tool descriptions, you can still see the name of any tool simply by hovering your mouse pointer over it.

Creating a New Toolbar

Any folder in your system can become a toolbar. This includes Windows system folders, such as Printers or Control Panel. To create a new toolbar, right-click an existing toolbar or a spot on the taskbar, choose Toolbars, and then choose New Toolbar. In the next dialog box, navigate to a folder and click OK.

The folder's name will become the name of the new toolbar, and each item within the folder will become a tool.

Opening and Refreshing Toolbars

With the exception of the Address toolbar, every toolbar is a representation of a folder that exists somewhere within your system. To see a toolbar's underlying folder in a Windows Explorer window, right-click the toolbar and choose Open. If the folder is on a network server, you can refresh it (that is, make sure it reflects the current state of the server) by right-clicking it and choosing Refresh.

Adding Shortcuts to Your Desktop

A shortcut is a tiny file that's linked to a program, document, folder, or Internet address. The file is represented by an icon that includes a black arrow in its lower left corner, like this:

Outlook
Express

If the shortcut is linked to a file or folder, that file or folder can be anywhere—on a local hard disk or CD-ROM drive, on a floppy disk, or on a network server. The item to which the shortcut is linked can even be a local hard disk or CD-ROM drive, a floppy drive, or a network server.

Like any other kind of file, a shortcut may be stored in any folder, including your desktop. If you store shortcuts for programs and documents on your desktop, you can get to them easily at any time. For example, if you use a half dozen or so programs nearly every day, why not simply add shortcuts for them to your desktop? Particularly if the items in question are buried several levels deep in the Start menu, it can be easier to get to them via desktop shortcuts.

A shortcut is a pointer to an object, not the object itself. That means that you can create and delete shortcuts without in any way affecting the underlying object. It also means you can create a shortcut to a major program without duplicating the large file that actually runs that program. Shortcuts themselves use less than 2 KB of disk storage, so a proliferation of shortcuts is not likely to run you out of hard-disk space.

Creating a Shortcut

There are three easy ways to create a shortcut: by dragging and dropping, by using cut and paste, and by visiting the Create Shortcut wizard.

Creating a Shortcut Using Drag and Drop

If the item for which you want to create a shortcut is visible in a Windows Explorer window, right-drag that item to wherever you want the shortcut to appear. Then, from the context menu, choose Create Shortcut(s).

You can also drag an item from the Start menu to create a shortcut on the desktop. Click the Start button to open the menu. Move your mouse pointer to the menu item you're interested in. Then drag the item to your desktop.

All the procedures described here for creating shortcuts on the desktop work for creating shortcuts in other folders as well.

You can turn any Web link into a desktop shortcut by simply dragging the link (the underlined text) and dropping it on the desktop. Clicking or double-clicking that shortcut later will activate your browser, connect you to the Internet (if you're not already there) and take your browser to the appropriate URL.

You can also create a shortcut by dragging an item from a Find window. Thus, if you want to create a shortcut to a program and you're not sure where that program resides, you can use Find to locate it. Then right-drag the found item to the desktop to create the shortcut. For information about Find windows, see Chapter 6, "Using the Find Command."

Some shortcuts can be used as targets for drag and drop. For example, if you put a shortcut for a printer on your desktop, you can print files by dragging them from Windows Explorer windows to the printer shortcut. If you create a shortcut for a floppy disk drive or the top-level folder on a hard disk, you can copy files by dragging them from Windows Explorer windows to the shortcut. For more information, see "Drag-and-Drop Printing," page 191, and "Moving or Copying Folders, Files, and Shortcuts," page 131.

Creating a Shortcut Using Copy and Paste

Right-dragging an item from a Windows Explorer window to the desktop is not convenient when the Windows Explorer window is maximized. In that situation, the easiest way to build your shortcut is to right-click the item and choose Copy from the context menu. Then display the desktop, right-click anywhere on it, and choose Paste Shortcut from the context menu.

Creating a Shortcut Using the Create Shortcut Wizard

To use the Create Shortcut wizard, start by right-clicking the desktop. From the context menu, choose New, and then choose Shortcut. The Create Shortcut wizard appears, as shown in Figure 3-9.

FIGURE 3-9.
The Create Shortcut wizard makes it easy to populate your desktop—or any other folder—with shortcuts.

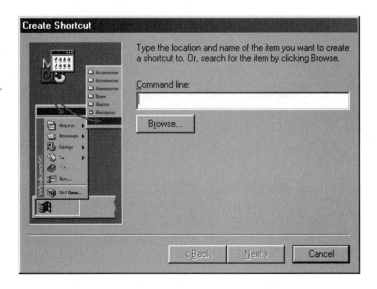

If you know the command line required to run your program or open your document, simply type it and click the Next button. (The command line is whatever you would type to run your program or open your document if you were using the Start menu's Run command.) If you don't know the command line, or if Windows gives an error message when you click Next, click the Browse button. In the Browse dialog box, locate the item for which you want to create a shortcut. Then click the Open button. After you click Open, the wizard returns you to its initial dialog box, with the command line filled in.

Click Next, type a name for your shortcut, click Finish, and your shortcut will appear.

Renaming a Shortcut

When you first create a shortcut, Windows gives it a default name based on the underlying object. You can change that to any other name you want, as follows:

1 Right-click the shortcut.

2 From the context menu, choose Rename.

3 Type the name you want to use.

TIP

You can also rename any object by selecting it, pressing F2, and typing the new name.

Assigning Other Properties to a Shortcut

SEE ALSO

For details about shortcut properties, see "Customizing the Start Menu," page 56.

You can assign a keyboard shortcut to a shortcut, allowing you to activate the shortcut with a combination of keyboard characters, (For example, you might assign Ctrl+Alt+P to the Paint program.) You can also change the icon displayed by a shortcut, specify what kind of window the shortcut should open (maximized, minimized, or "normal") and assign an initial data folder to be used by whatever program the shortcut opens. All these customizing steps involve modifying the shortcut's properties, just as you would to customize items on the Start menu.

Repositioning Shortcuts on the Desktop

You can change the positions of your desktop shortcuts at any time. Simply drag them. You can also get Windows to help you keep your shortcuts neatly aligned. Follow these steps:

1 Use your mouse to bring your shortcut icons into approximate alignment.

2 Right-click the desktop.

3 From the context menu that appears, choose Line Up Icons.

If you want all your desktop shortcuts organized in columns starting at the left side of the desktop, right-click the desktop, choose Arrange Icons, and then choose Auto Arrange. With Auto Arrange turned on, your icons always stay neatly aligned, even if you try to drag them out of place.

Whether you choose Line Up Icons or Auto Arrange to tidy up your desktop, Windows aligns the icons to an invisible grid that evenly spaces the icons. If you want the icons to be closer together or farther apart, you can adjust the grid spacing. To do so, follow these steps:

1 Right-click the desktop.

2 From the context menu, choose Properties.

3 In the Display Properties dialog box, click the Appearance tab.

4 Open the Item drop-down list and select Icon Spacing (Horizontal) or Icon Spacing (Vertical).

5 Adjust the setting in the Size box. (A larger number increases the space between icons.)

> **NOTE**

In addition to controlling the desktop icons, changing the icon spacing affects the spacing of icons in folders when you use large-icons view.

Deleting a Shortcut

To remove a shortcut, simply select it and press the Delete key. Or right-click it and choose Delete from the context menu. Either way, Windows asks you to confirm your intention—thereby protecting you from an accidental deletion. Note that deleting a shortcut does not delete the program or document that the shortcut points to; doing so deletes only the shortcut itself.

Changing Your Desktop's Display Properties

Like just about everything else in Windows, your desktop has a properties dialog box, and that properties dialog box allows you to change many aspects of your desktop's appearance. You can modify the display resolution (so that more or less information fits on screen), modify the color depth (the richness of color that Windows uses to display everything you see), add a background pattern or "wallpaper" (a background image, optionally displayed as a repeating pattern), change colors and fonts used for various components of the Windows user interface, install a screen saver, and change the icons assigned to standard desktop elements (such as My Computer and Network Neighborhood). You can also use the Display Properties dialog box to get to an additional dialog box that governs your video hardware.

To see and work with the Display Properties dialog box, right-click your desktop and choose Properties. Or launch Display in Control Panel.

Changing Display Resolution

Resolution is a measure of the amount of information that Windows can fit on your screen. It's measured in pixels horizontal by pixels vertical, where a pixel (a contraction of the words *picture element*) is the smallest point of light that can be displayed. Common resolutions include 640×480 (also known as VGA resolution), 800×600 (sometimes called Super VGA or SVGA resolution), 1024×768, 1152×864, 1280×1024, and 1600×1200. The range of resolutions available to you depends on your display hardware.

The higher your resolution, the more data you can work with at once. A spreadsheet that shows 17 rows and 9 columns in 640×480, for example, might show 33 rows and 15 columns at 1024×768. High resolutions also allow you to keep many windows visible at once without their overlapping one another.

The tradeoff for increasing the number of pixels on screen is that each pixel must be smaller. Smaller pixels means smaller images. A 10-point font that is easy to read at 800×600 might become illegible at 1240×1024 (depending, of course, on your visual acuity and the size of your monitor).

To change your display resolution, follow these steps:

1 Click the Settings tab in the Display Properties dialog box, shown in Figure 3-10.

FIGURE 3-10.

In this dialog box, you can change the resolution and color depth of your display.

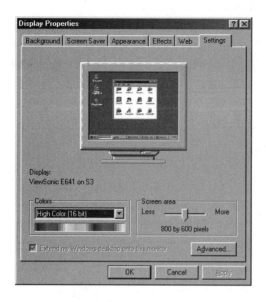

2 Drag the Screen Area slider to the right to increase resolution or to the left to decrease it.

3 Click OK.

4 Click OK again to answer the confirmation prompt.

5 Click OK again when Windows asks if you want to keep the new screen resolution.

Windows asks for the confirmation in step 5 because it's possible (but unlikely) that the Display Properties dialog box will offer you a resolution choice that doesn't work on your hardware. If you happen to choose an unworkable resolution, your screen would probably go blank and you wouldn't see that final confirmation prompt. After waiting 15 seconds for your okay, Windows simply restores your prior resolution.

 TIP

Many Windows-based programs include a Zoom command that lets you magnify or reduce the size of on-screen text and graphics. For example, if you like working with graphics programs at 1024×768 but find writing impossible at this resolution, check to see if your word processor has a Zoom command. Zooming the word processor to about 150 percent makes it emulate a lower resolution, allowing you to work with text at one level and graphics at another.

A Quicker Way to Change Resolution

You can make changes to your resolution or color depth more quickly by adding an icon to the notification area of your taskbar and then using this icon instead of the Display Properties dialog box. Here's how to add the icon:

1 Click the Settings tab in the Display Properties dialog box, shown in Figure 3-10, on the previous page.

2 Click the Advanced button.

3 On the General tab in the dialog box that appears, select the check box labeled Show Settings Icon On Task Bar.

4 Click OK twice to close the Display Properties dialog box.

To change resolution or color depth, click the icon and make your choice from the pop-up menu. When you make your changes this way, Windows does not ask you to confirm the new settings.

WARNING

Because the resolution-settings icon does not prompt for confirmation, it's possible you'll select a setting that does not work on your hardware. In that event, you'll be facing a blank screen. Before you choose any untried setting from the resolution-settings icon's pop-up menu, make sure it works by selecting it from the Display Properties dialog box. If you ignore this advice and get a blank screen from the pop-up menu, you'll have to quit Windows and restart in Safe Mode. You may lose unsaved work in the process. To quit Windows when you can't see the screen, press Ctrl+Esc to open the Start menu, type *u* to choose Shut Down, and then press Enter. As soon as Windows begins its restart, press the F8 key. From the menu that appears, choose Safe Mode. In Safe Mode (which always uses 640×480 resolution), use the Display Properties dialog box to switch to a resolution setting that you know is good. Then restart Windows again.

Changing Color Depth

The term *color depth* denotes the number of distinct colors that your system can display. The higher the color depth, the more realistic images appear. As with display resolution, the available color depth choices depend on your hardware. The common options are 16 colors, 256 colors, 16-bit "high color" (65,536 colors), and 24-bit and 32-bit "true color" (approximately 16 million and 4 billion colors, respectively).

Choosing the highest possible color depth makes things look as good as they possibly can on your screen, but it may also cause images to be displayed somewhat more slowly. That's because the greater the number of colors your system can display, the more video memory it has to manage. You might want to experiment to see what color depth seems optimal on your equipment.

To change color depth, visit the Settings tab in the Display Properties dialog box. As Figure 3-10 on page 89 shows, that dialog box includes a Colors drop-down list. Simply select the option you want from this list.

Unlike earlier versions of Windows, Windows 98 does not require you to restart Windows after changing color depth. Because some programs may not perform correctly after a change in color depth, however, Windows might issue a prompt asking if you want to restart anyway, even though it isn't strictly necessary. Or your system may have been set up so that Windows automatically restarts after a change in color depth, just to preclude any problems with programs that don't know how to adjust. In any case, you should be able to tell by simple experimentation whether a restart is necessary for the programs that you run. And if your system is set up to restart automatically, you can change that behavior by clicking the Advanced button on the Display Properties dialog box's Settings tab (see Figure 3-10), and then selecting an option from the Compatibility section on the following dialog box's General or Performance tab.

Changing Colors, Fonts, and Sizes

When you first install Windows 98, it uses a combination of colors, fonts, and sizes called Windows Standard. It's a fine arrangement, but you can also choose from a number of alternative schemes. And if you don't like any of the appearance combinations that Windows offers, you can design your own. Once you've found a pleasing arrangement of colors, fonts, and sizes, you can name and save the arrangement. You can design as many custom appearance schemes as you want, adding each to the menu that Windows supplies. As mood or necessity dictates, you can switch from one scheme to another by choosing from a simple drop-down list.

To see what the supplied appearance schemes look like, choose Properties from the context menu that appears when you right-click the desktop, and click the Appearance tab. Windows presents the dialog box shown in Figure 3-11. The upper part of this dialog box is a preview window, showing you a sample of each screen element whose color, font, or size you can modify.

FIGURE 3-11.

As you select from the supplied appearance schemes or create your own, the upper part of this dialog box provides a preview of your selections.

Click the drop-down list labeled Scheme, and then use the Up arrow and Down arrow keys to scroll through the list of named appearance schemes. As you highlight the name of each scheme, Windows displays a sample of that scheme in the upper part of the dialog box. You can apply any appearance scheme to your Windows environment by highlighting its name and clicking OK.

You can get a larger sample of the current color, font, and size settings without leaving the dialog box. Simply make your selections and then click Apply.

Modifying the Supplied Appearance Schemes

To modify one of the supplied appearance schemes, select its name in the Scheme drop-down list. In the sample window, click the screen element you want to change. Then use the drop-down lists and buttons at the bottom of the dialog box to make your color, font, and size selections.

For example, suppose you want to modify the Windows Standard color scheme, making the active window's title bar gradated from yellow to red, with black text in 12-point bold italic MS Serif. To assign this admittedly garish combination, you would do as follows:

1 Select Windows Standard in the Scheme list.

2 In the preview area of the dialog box, click the title bar labeled Active Window. (Or select Active Title Bar in the Item list.)

3 In the Font list, select MS Serif.

4 In the Size list directly to the right of the Font list, select 12.

5 Click the *I* button to the right of the font-size list.

6 Open the Color drop-down list to the right of the Item list and select yellow.

7 Open the Color 2 drop-down list and select red.

8 Open the Color drop-down list to the right of the Font list and select black.

If You Don't See the Color You Want

The drop-down lists for Item Color and Font Color offer a selection of 20 colors. If you don't see the one you're looking for, click the button labeled Other. Windows then displays a larger menu, consisting of 48 colors. Should you fail to find exactly the shade you want in this expanded offering, you can define your own custom colors.

Defining Custom Colors

To add your own colors to the ones offered by Windows, open the Color drop-down list for the screen element you want to change. (That is, if you want to customize a text element, open the Font Color drop-down list. If you want to customize a nontext element, open the Item Color drop-down list.) Then click the Other button. Windows opens the custom color selector, shown in Figure 3-12.

The cross hair adjusts hue and saturation.

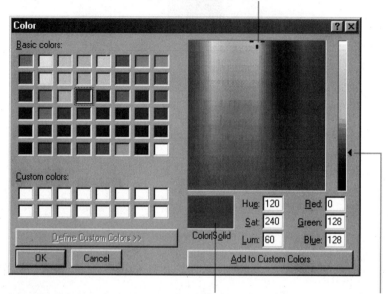

A sample of the current settings appears here.   The arrow adjusts luminosity.

To set a custom color with the mouse, adjust the position of two pointers—the cross hair in the big square grid and the arrow to the right of the vertical scale. As you move these pointers, Windows displays a sample of the selected color in the box near the center of the dialog box. If you prefer using your keyboard, you can enter numbers for either or both of the two scales in the boxes at the lower right corner of the dialog box.

The sample box actually comprises two halves because your system might not be capable of displaying every possible color. For colors that your system can't display directly, Windows creates a patterned mixture of two or more colors that it can display directly—a process called *dithering*. The left half of the sample box (the one marked Color) displays the dithered color; the right half (marked Solid) displays a closely related color that your system can display without dithering. (For information about color parameters, see "How Colors Are Defined," below.)

How Colors Are Defined

Colors in Windows are recorded as a combination of three parameters: hue, saturation, and luminosity. Roughly speaking, the basic quality of a color—its redness, blueness, or whatever—is defined by its *hue*. The purity of a color is defined by its *saturation*; a lower saturation value means more gray is mixed in. The brightness or dullness of a color is defined by its *luminosity*.

Hue, saturation, and luminosity are the parameters that Windows uses internally, but your video display hardware lives by a different set of numbers. Images on a color monitor are formed by a combination of dots, or *pixels*. To make each pixel visible, a beam of electrons is fired at three tiny spots of phosphor—one red, one green, and one blue. The result is three points of distinctly colored light so close together that they're perceived as a single light source. The apparent color of that light source is determined by the relative intensities of its red, green, and blue components.

Every combination of hue, saturation, and luminosity, therefore, is translated by Windows into varying levels of energy directed at those spots of red, green, and blue phosphor.

Thus there are two sets of boxes in the lower right corner of the custom color dialog box—one for the parameters used by Windows, the other for the relative red, green, and blue intensities. You can define a custom color by modifying the numbers in either set of boxes—or by simply dragging the mouse pointers until you see the color you're looking for.

Experimenting with Color

In the Color dialog box, the vertical scale on the right controls luminosity (brightness). As you move its pointer higher, the color becomes lighter. Putting the pointer at the top of the scale creates pure white, no matter where the cross-hair pointer may be in the grid; putting the pointer at the bottom of the luminosity scale produces black.

The square grid controls hue and saturation. Moving the cross hair from side to side changes the hue; moving it higher increases the saturation.

To see the range of "pure" colors available, start by putting the luminosity pointer about halfway up the vertical scale. Then put the cross hair at the upper left corner of the square grid. This combination gives you a fully saturated red of medium luminosity. Now slowly drag the cross hair across the top of the grid; as you do so, you'll move from red through yellow, green, blue, violet, and back to red again. (Alternatively, you can enter a value in the Hue box to step the Hue parameter from 0 to 239.)

To see the effect of luminosity on color, double-click the Solid half of the sample box or press Alt+O. This moves the cross-hair pointer to the nearest position where you see a pure color in both sample boxes. Then move the luminosity pointer up and down the scale (or change the value in the Lum box).

To see the effect of saturation, put the luminosity pointer back in the middle of the scale and drag the cross hair straight up and down in the square grid (or change the value in the Sat box).

Adding Custom Colors to Your Palette

When you find a color you like, you can add it to your Custom Colors palette by clicking Add To Custom Colors. (If you prefer to add the solid color, double-click the Solid half of the sample box or press Alt+O first.) Windows adds the color to the first available Custom Colors box. If you want to add it to a specific box in your custom palette (for example, if you want to replace a custom color), select that box before clicking Add To Custom Colors.

When you've filled out the custom palette to your satisfaction, click OK. Now you can assign your custom colors to the screen elements exactly as you did the basic colors.

Changing the Size of Particular Display Elements

You can make certain elements of the Windows user interface—such as title bars, caption (title bar) buttons, and window borders—larger or smaller by using the Size box to the right of the Item list. If a number appears in this box, the element shown in the Item list can be sized.

Windows automatically adjusts the size of elements that contain text. For example, if you increase the font size for your active title bars, Windows adjusts the size of the title bar itself to accommodate the larger text. But you can override Windows' judgment by manipulating the spinners next to the Size box.

Saving an Appearance Scheme

If you hit upon a pleasing new combination of colors, fonts, and sizes, it's a good idea to name and save it before leaving the dialog box. That way, you'll be able to switch back and forth between your own custom formats and the ones supplied by Windows—or between several of your own making.

To save a scheme, simply click the Save As button and supply a name. Windows adds the name you provide to the list.

If you tire of your new scheme, you can easily remove it. Simply select its name, and then click the Delete button.

Using Wallpaper

The term *wallpaper* refers to any background image displayed on the desktop, whether a small image repeated to fill (as in conventional wallpaper), a centered image, or a large image that covers the entire desktop. If you're not using Web-page view, your wallpaper can be supplied by any graphics file with the extension .BMP, .DIB, or .RLE. On a desktop that's viewed as a Web page, you can also use GIF and JPEG files (graphics formats commonly used on Web pages), or you can drape your desktop with an HTML file stored on your computer or on a network drive, complete with live links.

To make a wallpaper choice, right-click the desktop, choose Properties from the context menu, and click the Background tab. This takes you to the dialog box shown in Figure 3-13, on the next page. Note that the default choice, (None), appears at the top of the list. You'll want to return to (None) if you get tired of having wallpaper.

Select an image file from the Wallpaper list, or click the Browse button to find one that's not on the list. Note that if you choose a GIF or JPEG image, or an HTML file, Windows offers to turn on the View As Web Page option if it's not already on.

After choosing a wallpaper file, you can choose either Center, Tile, or Stretch from the Display drop-down list. If you choose Tile, your image is

FIGURE 3-13.
The Background tab in the Display Properties dialog box lets you add a pattern, picture, or HTML page to your desktop.

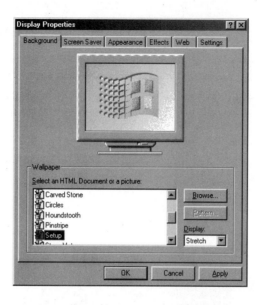

repeated as often as needed to fill the screen. If you choose Stretch, Windows enlarges your image to fill the screen (in the process possibly distorting it beyond recognition).

Using a Background Pattern

A pattern is an eight-pixel by eight-pixel "picture" that can be used like tiled wallpaper. You can either fill your entire desktop with a pattern, or, if you have a centered wallpaper image, you can fill the space around that image with a pattern. Windows supplies 19 patterns to choose from, and you can edit any of these to create your own patterns.

To apply a pattern, first visit the dialog box shown in Figure 3-13. Then click Pattern to get to the dialog box shown in Figure 3-14. Note that the Pattern button is unavailable unless your current wallpaper is centered or you have no wallpaper.

Editing an Existing Pattern

To edit one of the Windows-supplied patterns, select its name in the Pattern list and click the Edit Pattern button. The Pattern Editor, shown in Figure 3-15, will appear.

FIGURE 3-14.

A pattern can be used alone or with centered wallpaper.

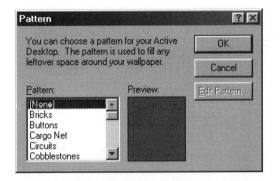

FIGURE 3-15.

The Pattern Editor lets you modify or create background patterns for your desktop.

The Pattern Editor shows two boxes. The Sample box, on the right, shows a swatch of the current pattern. The Pattern box, on the left, shows a magnified image of the eight-pixel by eight-pixel cell that produces the pattern. To edit the pattern, you'll work with the Pattern box. You can see the effects of your work by watching the Sample box.

Each pixel in the Pattern box is displayed in either black or the current background color of your desktop. Clicking a pixel inverts it from black to color or vice versa. When you're satisfied with your editing, click Change to save the revised pattern. Then click OK to select it.

Creating a New Pattern

To create a new pattern, simply edit an existing one. Then give your work a new name by replacing the text in the Name text box. Windows grays out the Change button and activates the Add button. Click Add, and your new pattern joins the list of existing patterns.

Using a Screen Saver

Cathode-ray-tube (CRT) displays used by desktop computers create images by firing electron beams at phosphor-coated screens. If the same picture or text remains on a screen for a long period of time, the phosphor coating can be damaged, leaving a faint but permanent image on the screen. Screen savers reduce this hazard by monitoring screen activity. Whenever your screen remains unchanged for a specific length of time, the screen saver displays its own constantly varying image. As soon as you press a key or (with most savers) move the mouse, the screen saver restores the original image.

That's the ostensible purpose of a screen saver, at any rate. In truth, with current display technology, the probability that you'll damage your screen with a burned-in image is remote. But screen savers have other virtues, as well. They're fun to watch, and they're one way to prevent others in your office from prying while you're away from your machine. Many screen savers have "save now" and password options. The save-now option lets you display the saver pattern on demand, either by pressing a certain keyboard combination or by moving the mouse to a particular corner of the screen. The password option ensures that only you are able to restore the original image. If your screen saver has these features, you can display the saver image any time you walk away from your computer and be reasonably confident that no one will invade your privacy.

To install one of the Windows-supplied screen savers, right-click the desktop and choose Properties from the context menu. Then click the Screen Saver tab to get to the dialog box shown in Figure 3-16.

To apply a screen saver, select from the drop-down list. Then use the Wait spinners to specify how long a period of inactivity Windows should allow before displaying the screen saver.

All the Windows-supplied screen savers (except for Blank Screen) include options that you can set. These options let you adjust colors, speed, and other display preferences. Figure 3-17 shows the settings dialog box for the 3D Flower Box screen saver.

FIGURE 3-16.

The Screen Saver tab in the Display Properties dialog box offers a choice of customizable screen savers.

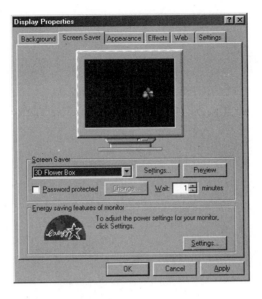

FIGURE 3-17.

After selecting a screen saver, you can click the Settings button to specify display options.

Changing Icon Appearance

Tired of looking at the same old My Computer and Recycle Bin icons? As Figure 3-18 on the next page shows, you can go to the Effects tab in the Display Properties dialog box to change them. Simply select the icon you want to change, and then click Change Icon. You'll see a dialog box similar to the one shown in Figure 3-19, on the next page. Select a new icon from the ones displayed, or click Browse to point to a different icon file.

FIGURE 3-18.

The Effects tab in the Display Properties dialog box lets you change the content, size, and color depth of system icons, among other things.

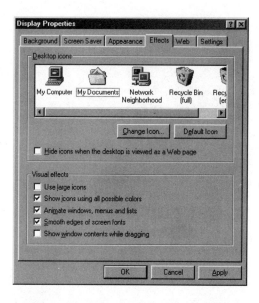

FIGURE 3-19.

Select an icon to replace the default icon. Click Browse to view the icons from another file.

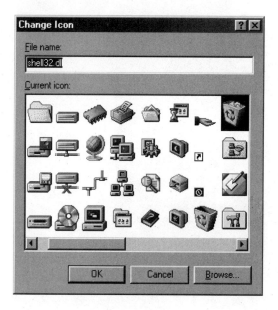

You can also use check boxes on the lower part of the Effects tab (see Figure 3-18) to enlarge your system icons and change their color depth. If you're running your system at 16-bit or higher color depth, selecting Show Icons Using All Possible Colors will get you a prettier icon display— but you'll have to restart your system for the change to take effect.

When you're using an HTML page as a background for your Active Desktop, some of your desktop icons might clash visually with some of your HTML links. In that case, you might want the desktop icons to disappear altogether. To perform this vanishing act, select the Hide Icons When The Desktop Is Viewed As A Web Page check box on the Effects tab. (If you need the icons, you can deploy them in a more compact and out-of-the-way manner by displaying the Desktop toolbar. For details, see "Using Toolbars," page 79.)

Controlling Menu Animations, Font Smoothing, and Window-Drag Display

The last three check boxes on the Effects tab in the Display Properties dialog box, shown in Figure 3-18, control miscellaneous visual effects.

Selecting Animate Windows, Menus And Lists causes the Start menu and its submenus to unfurl somewhat less than instantaneously. Deselect this check box if you want the menus to appear more quickly.

Selecting Smooth Edges Of Screen Fonts causes Windows to fill in the jagged edges of large fonts, giving large-point-size typography a more natural appearance. It also slows down your display slightly, but with a fast processor you may not notice the performance hit.

With Show Window Contents While Dragging selected, Windows displays the full contents of a window as you drag it. If you turn off this option, Windows displays only a ghost border while you drag and updates the window position when you release the mouse button. Turn off this option if your performance drags while you drag.

4

Using and Customizing Windows Explorer

Windows Explorer is the program that lets you work with the contents of folders, both ordinary disk folders (places on disk where you store your programs and documents) and "system folders," such as Printers or Network Neighborhood. With Windows Explorer, you can run programs and open documents, move and copy files from one place to another on your hard disks and servers, format and copy floppy disks, and even view pages on the World Wide Web. As we'll see in this chapter, Windows Explorer can take on many different appearances, but its underlying functionality remains the same, regardless of how you have set it up to look.

Is It Windows Explorer or Internet Explorer?

In Windows 98, it's both. Microsoft has merged its Web browser (Internet Explorer) and its tool for browsing local and LAN resources (Windows Explorer). While you're looking at the contents of a hard-disk folder via what is ostensibly Windows Explorer, you can type an Internet address in Explorer's Address Bar, and—voilà—you're in Internet Explorer. Conversely, while viewing a Web page, you can type the path of a local (or network) folder in Internet Explorer's Address Bar to get back to Windows Explorer.

Menus change slightly, depending on the context you're working in. While you're viewing Web pages, for example, the View menu offers a Fonts command and other items appropriate to the Internet context. While you're working with local resources, the same menu changes to include a Folder Options command and other commands appropriate to folders. For practical purposes, however, there is no longer any difference between Internet Explorer and Windows Explorer. Hence, in many contexts, this book refers to the blended browser as, simply, Explorer.

In this chapter, we'll concentrate on the use of Explorer for displaying and manipulating local resources. To learn more about using Explorer to travel the Internet, see Chapter 25, "Using Internet Explorer."

The Basic Layout

Figure 4-1 shows a Windows Explorer view of the My Computer folder. The window displays an icon for each local disk drive, an icon for each network folder that has been mapped to appear as a local drive, and icons for four system folders: Printers, Control Panel, Dial-Up Networking, and Scheduled Tasks. Double-clicking the desktop My Computer icon was all that was required to open this Windows Explorer window.

The Windows Explorer window shown in Figure 4-1 also includes two toolbars, the one that Windows Explorer calls Standard Buttons and, below that, the one that Windows Explorer calls Address Bar. At the bottom of the window is Windows Explorer's status bar. Both toolbars and the status bar are optional elements of the display. You can remove any

FIGURE 4-1.

A Windows Explorer view of My Computer shows your computer's resources.

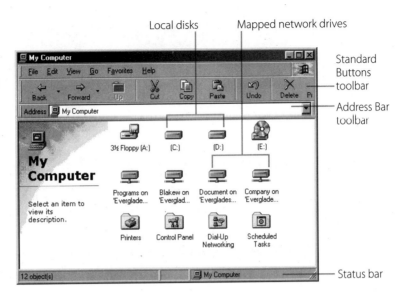

Local disks

Mapped network drives

Standard Buttons toolbar

Address Bar toolbar

Status bar

of them by visiting the View menu. (To remove a toolbar, open the View menu, select Toolbars, and then find the bar you want to remove on the cascading submenu.)

A third toolbar, called Links, is also available but not shown by default. This one is useful for Internet exploration and does appear by default when you display a Web page.

SEE ALSO

For information about clicking versus double-clicking, see "To Click or Double-Click?," page 66.

Each of the icons in Figure 4-1 represents a folder, and launching (that is, double-clicking or clicking, depending on how your system is set up) any of these folders causes Windows Explorer to display the contents of that folder. You can use folder icons, as well as tools on the Standard Buttons toolbar, to navigate through your entire set of local and network resources.

In Figure 4-1, the contents of My Computer are shown in large-icons view, and the View As Web Page option is on. These settings produce only one of many possible kinds of Windows Explorer displays.

"Open View" Versus "Explore View"

Figure 4-2, on the next page, shows a different sort of Windows Explorer window. Its title bar includes the word *Exploring*, and its menu bar includes a Tools menu. At the left side of the window, an "All Folders"

FIGURE 4-2.

In "explore view," Windows Explorer includes a Tools menu and an "All Folders" pane. The latter outlines all local resources.

Click minus signs to hide subordinate entries.

Click plus signs to see subordinate entries.

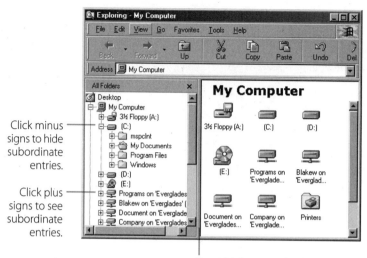

Drag this bar to make the All Folders pane wider or narrower.

pane provides an outline of all local resources. Each icon displayed in the main part of the window appears in the outline as an item subordinate to the My Computer item, which, in turn, is subordinate to an item named Desktop. The C: item, meanwhile, has been opened to reveal the names of all folders stored within the C: folder. Plus signs and minus signs in the outline denote entries that can be expanded or collapsed, respectively.

Windows calls the views shown in Figures 4-1 (on the previous page) and 4-2 "open view" and "explore view," respectively. By default, you get open view when you launch Windows Explorer by double-clicking or clicking a folder icon or shortcut. You get explore view when you launch Windows Explorer from the Start menu, or when you right-click a folder icon or shortcut and choose Explore from the context menu.

⭐ **TIP**

A folder's default action (the one that happens automatically when you click or double-click the folder's icon) is normally Open. This action generates a Windows Explorer window in open view. If you prefer explore view, you can switch things around so that Explore is the default action. For the steps required to do this, see "Changing a File Type's Default Action," page 147.

SEE ALSO

For information about mapping network drives, see "Mapping a Network Folder to a Drive Letter," page 159.

The Tools menu in explore view includes three commands: Find, Map Network Drive, and Disconnect Network Drive. (The latter two appear only if your computer is connected to a network.) Choosing Find here is equivalent to choosing Find from the Start menu, except that, by default, the command focuses its search on the current folder and its subfolders. The Map Network Drive command allows you to make a network server appear to be a local hard disk, and the Disconnect Network Drive command reverses that action.

The Tools menu might prove handy from time to time, but the most significant difference between explore view and open view is the All Folders pane. The All Folders pane gives you an overview of your disk structure, and it's also useful as a navigational tool (you can jump from one folder to another by clicking outline entries) and for moving or copying objects between folders.

TIP

> The Tools menu's commands are still available in open view. You can summon the Find command by pressing F3, and you can get the two networking commands by adding them to your Standard Buttons toolbar. To do the latter, choose Folder Options from the View menu, click the View tab, and select the check box labeled "Show Map Network Drive button in toolbar."

You can't move directly from an open view of a folder to the same folder in explore view. But if you're in open view you can display the current folder in a new explore-view window by right-clicking Windows Explorer's Control menu and choosing Explore.

You can, however, remove the All Folders pane from a window that's currently displaying it. Simply click the *X* (the Close button) to the right of the words *All Folders* at the top of the pane. (Or open the View menu, choose Explorer Bars, and then choose All Folders.)

TIP

> **Other Ways to Open Windows That Have an All Folders Pane**
> You can also display a folder in a view that includes the All Folders pane by selecting a folder icon and then holding down the Shift key while double-clicking the icon or pressing Enter.
> Easier yet, open the Start menu and choose Programs, Windows Explorer.

Navigating Through Folders

Double-clicking (or clicking) a folder icon anywhere, on the desktop, in a Windows Explorer window, or in the All Folders pane, opens that folder in a Windows Explorer window. Thus, to display the contents of C:\Windows\System, you could double-click the My Computer icon on your desktop, double-click the C: icon in the Windows Explorer window that appears, double-click the Windows icon, and then double-click the System icon.

 **TIP**

You can go directly to a deeply nested folder by using the Start menu's Run command. For example, to get to C:\Windows\System, you could choose the Run command, type *c:\windows\system*, and then click OK.

 To move the other direction in your folder hierarchy—from a folder to its containing folder, click the Up button on the Standard Buttons toolbar. If that toolbar isn't visible, choose Up One Level from the Go menu.

 **TIP**

You can also press Backspace to move upward in the folder hierarchy. Pressing Backspace while looking at C:\Windows, for example, takes you to C:.

 You can also move about with the help of the Standard Buttons toolbar's Back and Forward buttons. If you've spent any time on the Internet, the operation of these buttons will probably be familiar to you already. The Back button returns you to where you last were; the Forward button allows you to reverse your steps after you've used the Back button. Both buttons have drop-down arrows beside them. These allow you to retrace several steps at once. For example, if you've gone from My Computer to C: to Windows to System, clicking the Back button's drop-down arrow will give you the choice of going directly to My Computer or C:, as well as moving back a single step to Windows.

The Address Bar toolbar gives you yet another way to navigate. You can type the name of the folder you want to see directly into the Address Bar. Or you can click the Address Bar's own drop-down arrow and choose from a list of potential destinations. Figure 4-3 shows an opened Address

FIGURE 4-3.

Opening the Address Bar's drop-down list lets you choose from many destinations but does not give you an expandable outline of your entire folder structure.

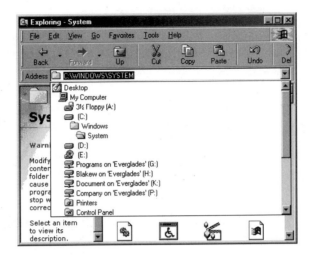

Bar drop-down list. Notice that, while the list includes all stations on the path to your current folder, as well as other top-level folders, it does not provide an expandable outline of your folder structure. For that, you need to display the All Folders pane.

Running Programs and Opening Documents

 SEE ALSO

For information about clicking versus double-clicking, see "To Click or Double-Click?," page 66.

Icons for programs, documents, and shortcuts in a Windows Explorer window behave exactly as they do on the desktop. Double-click them (or click them, depending on how you've set up your system), and they perform their default actions. Generally speaking, that means that programs open, documents open within their parent programs, and shortcuts activate the objects to which they're linked.

Nondefault actions are available via the context menu—the menu that appears when you right-click an object. The choices on that menu vary depending on the kind of object you right-click. You might want to experiment with documents you use regularly to see what commands appear on their context menus.

TIP

Opening Documents in Different Programs

To open a document in a program other than its parent (that is, other than the program in which the document was created), hold down the Shift key and right-click the object's icon or entry in a Windows Explorer window. Choose Open With from the context menu. In the Open With dialog box that appears, select the name of the program you want to open the document.

Folder Display Options

Windows Explorer gives you many ways to view the contents of your folders. You can choose from five display styles, sort folder entries in a number of ways, and decide whether to keep your folder icons in tidy columns or not. You can also choose whether filename extensions should be included with all Windows Explorer icons, decide whether the complete path of the current folder should appear in Windows Explorer's title bar, command Windows Explorer to display one of its Explorer Bars alongside your folder contents, and express preferences on various other display matters.

Some of Windows Explorer's display options can be applied either to the current folder only or to all folders at once. Others can be applied only to the current folder, and still others can be applied only to all folders at once.

Options That Can Be Applied to the Current Folder or All Folders

The following display options can be applied either to the current folder or to every folder. To apply the options to all folders, first apply them to the current folder. Then choose the Folder Options command on Windows Explorer's View menu, click the View tab, and click the Like Current Folder Button. To return all these display options to their original settings (those that were in place when you installed Windows), choose Folder Options from the View menu, click the View tab, and then click the Reset All Folders button.

Big Icons or Small?

By default, Windows Explorer displays a folder's contents as a set of "large icons." Other display styles are available, and you can choose the style you prefer with commands on the View menu or by clicking the drop-down arrow next to the Views tool on the Standard Buttons toolbar. The alternatives to large-icons display are small icons, list, details, and thumbnails. (See Figure 4-4.)

FIGURE 4-4.

The View menu lets you choose between five display options. One option, thumbnails, requires that you set a folder property.

Large Icons view

Small Icons view

List view

Details view

Thumbnail view

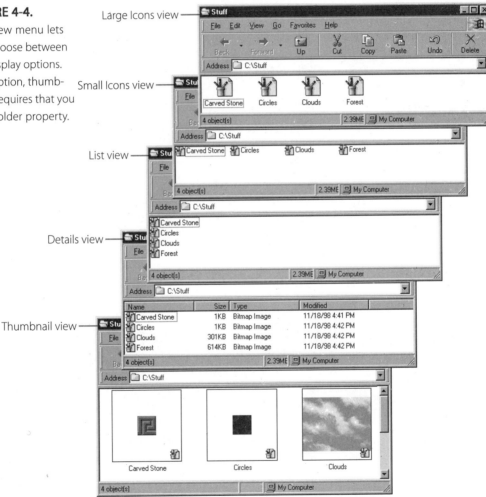

> **NOTE**
>
> The thumbnails option requires that you set a folder property, and thus can be applied to only one folder at a time. For details, see "Enabling Thumbnails View," page 120.

The small-icons view has the virtue of letting you see more file and subfolder names without enlarging the window. The list view is identical to the small-icons view except that the folder's contents are arranged vertically instead of horizontally. In the details view, the folder's contents are also arranged vertically, but Windows Explorer includes useful information about each entry. In most disk folders, details view shows each entry's size, type, and the date of the most recent edit.

> **TIP**
>
> A details view of My Computer shows the total size and available free space for each disk on your system.

> **TIP**
>
> **Adjusting Column Width in Details View**
> To change the width of a column in details view, drag the boundary between column headings. To adjust a column's width automatically, so that it's just wide enough for the column's widest entry, double-click the right boundary of the column heading.

> **TIP**
>
> The details view tells you when a file was last edited. To find out when it was created and when it was last accessed, right-click the filename or icon and choose Properties from the context menu.

The View As Web Page Command

The View menu's As Web Page command turns your Windows Explorer window into an HTML document. When you turn on this feature, Windows Explorer by default displays the current folder contents with the help of an HTML template called Folder.htt, which is stored as a hidden file in C:\Windows\Web. Using the Customize This Folder command, described later in this chapter, you can edit Folder.htt or replace it with your own HTML template file.

If you keep the Windows-supplied Folder.htt, your folder contents take on the appearance of Figure 4-5. In a frame on the left side of the window, Windows Explorer displays a folder icon and the name of the folder. Below that, when possible, Windows Explorer displays a thumbnail image of the item currently selected on the right. Thus you can use View As Web Page as an alternative to the thumbnails view option.

FIGURE 4-5.

By default, the View As Web Page feature shows a thumbnail image of the current folder item.

Sorting Options

In details view, you can sort the contents of a folder by clicking a column heading. For example, to arrange a folder's contents by file size (smallest to largest), click the Size heading. Click the column heading again to reverse the sort order (largest to smallest).

In the other views, you can sort the contents by choosing Arrange Icons from the View menu, and then selecting a sort key (name, file type, file size, or date) from the submenu. You can also choose the Arrange Icons command from the context menu that appears when you right-click any unoccupied area of the Windows Explorer window.

Neatly Arranged or Casual?

In large-icons and small-icons views, you can have Windows Explorer automatically preserve an orderly arrangement of folder contents. To do this, open the View menu and choose Arrange Icons. If the Auto Arrange command, at the bottom of the Arrange Icons submenu, is not checked, select it. With Auto Arrange on, any icon you add to a folder (by creating a new file, for example) automatically falls in line with the rest of the folder's contents. If you delete an icon, the remaining icons automatically close ranks. If you drag an icon out of position, Windows Explorer snaps it back into place.

If you don't like this regimentation, you can turn it off—by opening the View menu, choosing Arrange Icons, and then choosing the Auto Arrange command again. With Auto Arrange off, you can drag your icons anywhere you please. (See Figure 4-6.)

FIGURE 4-6.

Turning off Auto Arrange gives you the freedom to drag icons out of their orderly rows and columns.

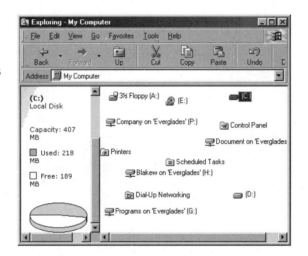

The Auto Arrange option applies only to the current folder, so you can use it for some of your folders and not for the rest.

Turning off Auto Arrange has the advantage of letting you create ad hoc groupings. For example, you can put all the items that you're currently working with together at the top of the folder. But with this freedom comes some hazard: if you're too casual with your ad hoc arrangements, you can lose track of items. For example, if you drag an icon so far from its comrades that you have to scroll a long distance to see it, you might forget you have it.

TIP

When Auto Arrange is off, you can choose any of the sorting commands (By Name, By Type, By Size, or By Date) to return your icons to orderly rows·and columns.

 TIP

To turn Auto Arrange on or off for your desktop icons, right-click anywhere on the desktop and choose Arrange Icons.

 **TIP**

If your folder icons are lined up neatly in rows and columns, but they don't use the full width of the window, check to see if Auto Arrange is on. With Auto Arrange off, icon positions are not adjusted when a window's size changes.

Displaying Explorer Bars

The View menu's Explorer Bar command lets you split your Explorer window into two panes. In Figure 4-2, on page 108, we've seen one example of an Explorer Bar, the All Folders pane. This particular Explorer Bar is available only when you open Windows Explorer in explore view. Four other Explorer Bars are available in all contexts. They are called Search, Favorites, History, and Channels. Figure 4-7 shows a Windows Explorer window with the History Explorer Bar.

FIGURE 4-7.
The History pane at the left side of this Windows Explorer window is an example of an Explorer Bar.

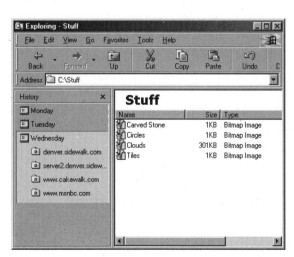

SEE ALSO

For more information about Explorer Bars, see "Displaying and Hiding Explorer Bars," page 610.

With the exception of All Folders, the Explorer Bars are useful primarily for Internet exploration. For example, the History bar lets you redisplay Web pages that you have recently visited, and the Favorites bar (a duplicate of the Favorites section of your Start menu) lets you select one of the Web sites that you have designated as a favorite.

TIP

While it was presumably intended primarily as a repository for Internet shortcuts, the Favorites bar and Favorites menu can also be used for other purposes. Any folder, document, or shortcut stored in your Favorites folder (C:\Windows\Favorites on most systems) appears on your Favorites bar and Favorites menu. So, for example, by creating shortcuts to disk folders that you use frequently and storing those shortcuts in C:\Windows\Favorites, you can give yourself yet another handy navigational tool.

Options That Can Be Applied Only to the Current Folder

Some display options can be applied only to the current folder. With these options, you can:

- Apply a background image or an HTML template

- Change the color of icon text

- Enable thumbnails view

Applying a Background Image or an HTML Template

Like the desktop, a Windows Explorer window can be decorated with a background image or an HTML page. To modify the background of a Windows Explorer window, choose the Customize This Folder command from Windows Explorer's View menu. You'll see the dialog box shown in Figure 4-8.

NOTE

The Customize This Folder command is available only for folders; you won't find it on the menu if My Computer is selected.

FIGURE 4-8.

The Customize This Folder command lets you apply a background image or an HTML page to the current folder.

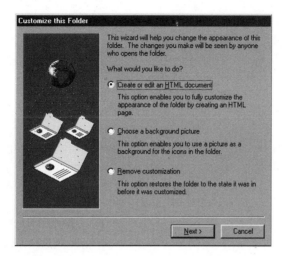

To add a background image to your folder, select the second option button and click Next. As Figure 4-9 shows, a new dialog box appears, in which you'll be able to choose from files in the BMP, GIF, and JPEG formats. A preview of your selection appears at the left side of this dialog box.

To add an HTML page as your folder's background, or to edit the default Folder.htt file that Windows provides, select the first option button in the dialog box shown in Figure 4-8. Windows Explorer starts your HTML source code editor and opens the current version of Folder.htt. There you can edit or start over completely.

FIGURE 4-9.

A folder's background image can be a BMP, GIF, or JPEG file. You can also use this dialog box to change the appearance of a folder's text.

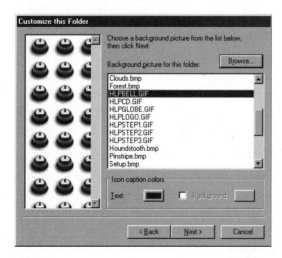

If you change your mind about changes you've made via the Customize This Folder command, revisit the command and select the Remove Customization option. Windows Explorer then reverts to its default appearance.

Changing the Color of Icon Text

You can also use the Customize This Folder command to change the foreground and background colors of the text that appears with each folder item. To do this, start by choosing Customize This Folder, selecting the Choose A Background Picture option button, and clicking Next. To change the foreground color, click the color box that appears next to the word Text. To change the background color, first select the Background check box. Then click the color box that appears to the right of the word Background. Figure 4-10 shows one possible modification.

FIGURE 4-10.

Simply applying Bubbles.bmp as a background image and changing icon caption text to yellow creates a distinctive, though admittedly gaudy, folder view.

Enabling Thumbnails View

Thumbnails view shows, where possible, a picture of each file's contents. (See Figure 4-4, on page 113.) You might find thumbnails view handy for folders that contain mostly graphics files. To use thumbnails view, you must first enable it, as follows:

1   Use Windows Explorer to display the folder that contains the folder for which you want to enable thumbnails view.

2   Right-click the folder for which you want to enable thumbnails view, and choose Properties from the context menu.

3 Select the Enable Thumbnail View check box and then click OK.

4 Display the folder in which you want thumbnails view.

5 Choose Thumbnails from the View menu.

Options That Can Be Applied Only to All Folders

The View tab in the View menu's Folder Options command, shown in Figure 4-11, includes a list of "Advanced" Settings that govern global display options—options that apply to all folders, including the desktop. Here is a summary of those options:

- **Remember each folder's view settings.** If you leave this option on (its default state), the display settings you assign to a folder persist. The next time you open a folder, it will look the same way it did the last time you opened it. If you turn the option off, closing a folder restores the settings that were in place when you installed Windows.

FIGURE 4-11.

The View tab in the Folder Options dialog box gives you choices about what should be included in Windows Explorer windows.

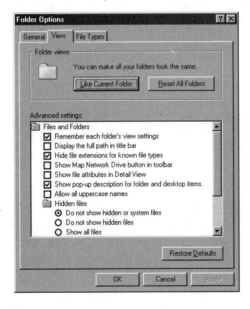

- **Display the full path in title bar.** If you leave this option off (its default state), Windows Explorer's title bar shows only the name of the current folder. If you turn on the option, the title bar shows the folder's full path. Overriding the default here can help you keep track of where your folders live within your overall folder hierarchy.

- **Hide file extensions for known file types.** This option, on by default, causes Windows Explorer to display the names of registered file types without their filename extensions. In most cases, you can recognize what kind of file each Windows Explorer entry represents by looking at its icon. If you're not sure what the icons signify, you can turn off this option. Alternatively, you can switch to details view. The third column in details view (see Figure 4-4, on page 113) shows the file type of each entry.

 TIP

When the Hide File Extensions For Known File Types option is turned off, Windows Explorer displays extensions for *all* files, not just unregistered file types. You can also display the extensions for only a particular registered file type. To do this, use the File Types tab in the Folder Options dialog box. Select the file type you're interested in, click the Edit button, and then select the Always Show Extension check box.

SEE ALSO

For information about mapping network drives, see "Mapping a Network Folder to a Drive Letter," page 159.

- **Show Map Network Drive button in toolbar.** Off by default, this option places the Map Drive and Disconnect buttons on the Standard Buttons toolbar. These buttons, which are shortcuts to the Tools menu's Map Network Drive and Disconnect Network Drive commands, provide a quick way to assign a drive letter to a network drive and to subsequently reclaim that drive letter.

SEE ALSO

For information about attributes, see "Setting Attributes for Folders, Files, and Shortcuts," page 142.

- **Show file attributes in Detail view.** File attributes are markers that indicate whether a file is hidden, restricted to read-only access, a system file, or one that needs to be backed up. You can view (and set) a file's attributes by looking at its properties dialog box. Or you can turn on this option to include file attributes in Windows Explorer's details view. The option is off by default.

What Is a Filename Extension?

A *filename extension* is any group of characters that appears after the final period in a filename. As you may know, versions of Windows prior to Windows 95, as well as the versions of MS-DOS on which they were built, allowed filenames to have extensions of up to three characters. Such extensions provided a means of categorizing files. All batch files, for example, had the extension .BAT; all graphics files in the Windows bitmap format had the extension .BMP, and so on.

Windows 95 did away with the three-character extension limit—as well as the onerous eight-character limit that applied to the main part of a file's name. Windows 98 filenames can consist of up to 255 characters, including as many periods as you like and as many characters as needed after the final period.

These emancipations notwithstanding, Windows 98 and Windows-based programs still use filename extensions to categorize files. Many programs, for example, automatically append an extension to any filename you supply, even though you might not see the extensions in the entries that appear in your Windows Explorer windows.

Windows 98 uses the *registry*—its central depository of information about programs, their documents, and your system—to determine what kind of icon to display next to names in Windows Explorer windows. Excel documents get Excel-style icons, text files get icons that look like notepads, and so on.

Document files for which no registry entry exists get a "miscellaneous" icon—something that looks like a Windows logo on a page with a dog-ear in its upper right corner. By default, only files of such unregistered types have their extensions displayed in Windows Explorer windows.

If you'd like to see extensions for all filenames, choose the View menu's Folder Options command and click the View tab. In the dialog box that appears (see Figure 4-11, on page 121), deselect the check box labeled "Hide file extensions for known file types." You might want to make this change if you're having difficulty determining which icon represents which kind of file. You can, of course, switch back to the default display mode at any time.

■ **Show pop-up description for folder and desktop items.** On by default, this option causes Windows Explorer to display descriptions of certain Windows Explorer and desktop items when you hover the mouse pointer over those items.

- **Allow all uppercase names.** By default, Windows displays filenames expressed in all capital letters as initial cap only. For example, HOHO.PFT becomes Hoho.pft. You can preserve your all-uppercase filenames by turning on this option.

- **Hidden files.** By default, Windows Explorer shows all files and folders except the following:

  - Files with the hidden attribute

  - Dynamic-link libraries (.DLL files)

  - Files with the extension .SYS

  - Device drivers (.VXD, .386, or .DRV files)

The .DLL, .SYS, and device-driver files are crucial to the operation of programs and of Windows itself. They're not normally included in Windows Explorer's displays because accidental deletion or relocation of one of them can have serious adverse consequences—possibly requiring you to reinstall a program or even Windows itself. Therefore, unless you need to work with these types of files, it's a good idea to leave them out of sight.

Files with the hidden attribute that are not also .DLL, .SYS, or device-driver files are potentially another story. You might occasionally want to create a hidden file, or even an entire hidden directory, to keep it invisible to others using your computer. (To do this, see "Setting Attributes for Folders, Files, and Shortcuts," page 142.) If you hide some of your files, there will undoubtedly be times when you'll want to be able to find those files. By toggling on and off Windows Explorer's option to display the names of hidden files and directories, you can keep sensitive material out of sight except at those times when you need to work with that material.

As Figure 4-11 on page 121 shows, Windows Explorer offers three "Hidden files" option buttons. Select the first to keep all hidden and critical items invisible. Select the second to hide only those files with the hidden attribute. Or select the third to show everything.

> **NOTE**

Be aware that in the context of the Folder Options dialog box, the term "system files" does not mean files that have the system attribute. It means files with the extension .DLL, .SYS, .VXD, .386, or .DRV.

> **TIP**

File types not shown in Windows Explorer windows are also invisible to the Find command. If you want to be able to search for particular types of files with the Find command, be sure to make those file types visible in your folders.

The options shown under the Visual Settings heading—Hide icons when desktop is viewed as Web page, Smooth edges of screen fonts, and Show window contents while dragging—provide an alternative way to set options on the Effects tab in the Display Properties dialog box. For details about these options, see "Changing Icon Appearance," page 101, and "Controlling Menu Animations, Font Smoothing, and Window-Drag Display," page 103.

Restoring Default Settings

If you change your mind after tinkering with the Folder Options command's "advanced settings," simply click the Restore Defaults button at the bottom of the dialog box shown in Figure 4-11, on page 121.

Refreshing the Contents of a Windows Explorer Window

The Refresh command, on Windows Explorer's View menu, ensures that a Windows Explorer window's display reflects any changes to the folder's contents that might have taken place since you opened the window. For example, if you're looking at a folder on a network server, other users might be adding, deleting, or renaming files on that folder while your window is open. To be sure that what you see matches what's out there, choose the View menu's Refresh command—or type its keyboard shortcut, F5.

Working with Folders, Files, and Shortcuts in Windows Explorer

Now that you know how to work with all of Windows Explorer's display and viewing options, you probably want to do some work with your own folders, files, and shortcuts. Windows Explorer is a complete file-management tool. In the pages that follow, we explore the many ways in which Windows Explorer allows you to organize and reorganize your local disk resources.

Selecting Folders and Files in a Windows Explorer Window

 SEE ALSO

For information about clicking versus double-clicking, see "To Click or Double-Click?," page 66.

The first step in many operations in Windows—opening, copying, or moving a document, for example—is to *select* the folder or file you want to use. When a folder or file is selected, its icon and title appear in a color that's different from unselected items. You can select a folder or file in a Windows Explorer window in any of the following ways:

- If you're using double-click mode, click its icon or title; if you're using single-click mode, hover the mouse pointer over its icon or title. (Note that in details view, you must click or hover over the icon or title to select an object—not the other parts of the description line.)

- Type the first few letters of the title.

- Use the arrow keys to move the highlight.

You'll often want to select more than one item at a time. Here are some ways to select a group of objects:

- "Lasso" them. Hold down the mouse button while you drag a rectangle around all members of the group.

- Hold down the Ctrl key while you click (or, in single-click mode, hover the mouse pointer over) each item in the group.

- If the items are next to one another in the window, click (or hover over) the first. Then hold down the Shift key while you click (or hover over) the last.

- Choose Select All from the Edit menu—or use its keyboard shortcut, Ctrl+A—to select all the items in the window.

Two commands on Windows Explorer's Edit menu can be useful when you need to select groups. If you need to select everything in a folder, choose Select All (or press Ctrl+A). If you want to select nearly all items, select those that you do *not* want to select. Then choose the Invert Selection command. This action deselects what you've already selected and selects everything else.

Inspecting Folder and File Properties

Windows provides you with a simple way to learn a folder or file's size, creation date, and other vital statistics. Simply right-click a folder or file and choose Properties from the context menu. (If the Standard Buttons toolbar is visible, you can click the Properties button to get to the properties dialog box directly.) Figure 4-12 and Figure 4-13 (on the next page) illustrate the dialog box for a folder and a file.

FIGURE 4-12.

This folder's properties dialog box shows that the folder includes 8,811 files and 310 subfolders, occupying a total of 343 MB (megabytes).

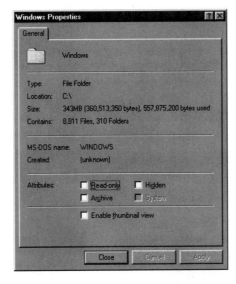

FIGURE 4-13.

Along with other details, the properties dialog box for this Microsoft Office document shows when the file was created, last modified, and last accessed. Not all file properties dialog boxes have the additional tabs that this one has.

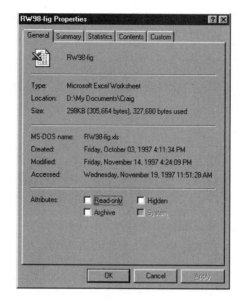

 TIP

To read the properties dialog box for an open folder, right-click anywhere within the folder's unoccupied space. Then choose the Properties command.

Notice that the folder properties dialog box shows how many subfolders the folder contains as well as the number of files. The number of folders and files, along with their cumulative size, includes the contents of the folder and all its subfolders. (The statistics in Windows Explorer's status bar do not take into account the contents of subfolders.)

SEE ALSO

For information about sharing folders, see "Sharing Folders with Other Users," page 162. For information about setting properties for MS-DOS–based programs, see "Working with Program Properties," page 287.

If your computer is part of a network and your system has been set up to allow file sharing, the folder properties dialog box includes a Sharing tab. By clicking here, you can make the folder available to others on your network (or stop making it available).

The file properties dialog box (see Figure 4-13) includes three dates—the date the file was created, the date it was most recently changed, and the date that it was most recently opened. If the file is a document created by a program that uses OLE, it might include additional information. Properties dialog boxes for Excel 97 documents, for example, include the additional tabs shown in Figure 4-13. If the file is an MS-DOS–based program, the properties dialog box includes tabs that let you set operating parameters for the program.

TIP

The Accessed date on a file's properties dialog box can help you determine whether a file might be a good candidate for deletion. If it hasn't been accessed any time during the last two years, perhaps you no longer need it.

Inspecting Properties for Groups of Objects

By selecting two or more folders or files, and then right-clicking, you can inspect properties for groups of objects. The resulting properties dialog box tells you the total size of the selected objects, whether they're all of the same type, and whether they're all located in the same folder. Figure 4-14 shows a properties dialog box for a group of files.

FIGURE 4-14.
This properties dialog box indicates that the 41 selected files are all Finale binary files stored in the D:\My Documents\Russell folder, and that together they occupy 3.77 MB (megabytes).

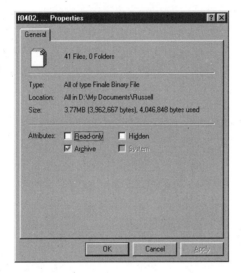

 TIP

To select a group of folders or files that are not all in the same folder, use the Find command to collect the objects in a Find window. Then select each object you're interested in.

Inspecting a Disk's Properties

The properties dialog box for a disk's top-level folder is different from all others. It uses a large pie graph to show how much of the disk is in use and how much remains available. Figure 4-15, on the next page, shows an example.

FIGURE 4-15.

The properties dialog box for a disk's top-level folder lets you see how much space is available.

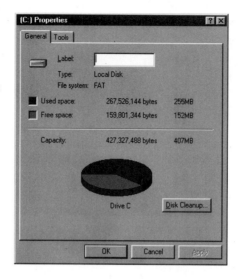

To get to the top-level folder for a disk, begin by opening My Computer. Then right-click the icon for the disk you're interested in. That icon might look like a disk instead of a folder, but the object it represents is still a folder—as you can see by opening it.

Creating New Folders

Folders in Windows can be nested to any level. That is, you can have folders within folders within folders—to whatever degree of complexity you want.

To create a new folder, begin by displaying the folder in which you want the new folder to reside. Right-click anywhere within this parent folder's unoccupied space, and then choose New from the context menu. When the submenu appears, choose Folder. (Alternatively, you can choose New from the folder window's File menu, and then choose Folder from the submenu.)

 SEE ALSO

For more information about renaming folders, see "Renaming Folders, Files, and Shortcuts," page 135.

Your new folder begins with a default name, such as "New Folder" or "New Folder #2." To rename it, type the name you want and press Enter.

If you click away from the new folder before renaming it, simply right-click it and choose Rename from the context menu. (Alternatively, choose Rename from the folder window's File menu.)

Moving or Copying Folders, Files, and Shortcuts

To move or copy an object in a Windows Explorer window, right-drag it from its current position to its destination. When you release the mouse button, a context menu appears. From this context menu, you can choose Copy Here, Move Here, or Create Shortcut(s) Here. Make the appropriate selection, and you're done.

To move or copy an entire folder, simply display the folder's parent folder. Then right-drag the folder icon (or the folder entry, if you're working in list or details view). Be aware that this action moves or replicates not only the folder but everything within the folder as well.

If you copy an object to a new destination in the same folder, Windows gives the copy a default name, such as "Copy of Myfile." While the object is still selected, you can give it a new name by typing and pressing Enter. Alternatively, right-click it and choose Rename.

If you prefer to drag with the left mouse button, you can do so, but in this case you need to know the following:

- If you left-drag a program file from one folder to another or to the desktop, Windows leaves the program in its source folder and creates a shortcut to the program in the destination folder. (Note that Windows ignores this "rule" if more than one file is selected and at least one selected file is not a program.)

- If you left-drag any other file type from one folder to another on the same disk, Windows performs a move.

- If you left-drag from a folder on one disk to a folder on a different disk, Windows performs a copy.

- If you left-drag a folder or any file other than a program file from a folder to the desktop, Windows performs a move—provided the source folder resides on the disk where you installed Windows. If the source folder is on a different disk, Windows performs a copy instead of a move.

TIP

> You can force Windows to *copy* the selected objects—regardless of file type and destination—by holding down the Ctrl key as you drag. You can force Windows to *move* objects by holding down the Shift key as you drag. You can force Windows to create a shortcut by holding down Ctrl and Shift as you drag.

TIP

> If you display the All Folders pane, you can use it as a target for moves and copies. Simply drag files or folders from the right side of your Windows Explorer window and drop them on the appropriate entry in the All Folders pane. You can also move entire folders by dragging and dropping within the All Folders pane.

Moving or Copying Objects to Unopened Folders

In many cases, you can move or copy an object to a new folder without opening the destination folder. For example, suppose the file Rough Draft is stored in the folder PMFeature and you want to move it to the folder Outtakes, which is also stored in PMFeature. Simply grab Rough Draft with your mouse, drag it to the folder icon for Outtakes, and then release the mouse button.

TIP

> As you drag an object from one folder to another or to the desktop, Windows displays a ghost image of the object you're dragging. If you're dragging with the left mouse button, you can look at the lower right corner of this image to see what action Windows will perform when you release the button. If Windows is going to create a copy, you'll see a plus sign in the lower right corner. If Windows is going to create a shortcut, you'll see a shortcut arrow. If Windows is going to move the object, you won't see anything in the lower right corner.
>
>   If you don't like the proposed action, click the right mouse button before you drop the object on the destination to cancel the drag operation in process.

If the destination folder is minimized, you can move or copy an object to it by dragging the object to the folder's taskbar button. Hold the object over the button for a moment while holding down the mouse button, and the Windows Explorer window will open.

> If you have a shortcut for a folder on your desktop, you can move or copy items to that folder by dragging them to the shortcut.

Moving or Copying Objects with Menu Commands

If dragging and dropping is not convenient, you can move or copy objects using the Edit menu's Cut, Copy, and Paste commands (or their toolbar shortcuts).

> It's often quicker to use the keyboard shortcuts for Cut, Copy, and Paste than it is to visit the Edit menu. Press Ctrl+X to cut or Ctrl+C to copy, and then press Ctrl+V to paste.

- To move an object, select it and choose Cut from the source folder's Edit menu. Then choose Paste from the destination folder's Edit menu. (If the desktop is your destination, right-click the desktop and choose Paste from the context menu.)

- To copy an object, select it and choose Copy from the source folder's Edit menu. Then choose Paste from the destination folder's Edit menu. (If the desktop is your destination, right-click the desktop and choose Paste from the context menu.)

TIP

> When you cut an item, that item is not removed from its source folder until you paste it somewhere. If you change your mind in midstream, simply press Esc.

Moving or Copying Groups of Folders and Files

SEE ALSO

For more information about selecting a group of folders or files, see "Selecting Folders and Files in a Windows Explorer Window," page 126.

To move or copy a group of folders or files, select all members of the group, and then follow the same procedure you would use to move or copy a single item. To select a group, hold down the Ctrl key while you select each member. Alternatively, if the items are located next to one another in the Windows Explorer window, you can select the first, and then hold down the Shift key while you select the last.

Moving or Copying Objects with the Send To Command

When you right-click a folder or file, the context menu includes a Send To command. In response to this command, Windows displays a submenu of destinations, typically including any floppy-disk drives on your system, as well as various other destinations. You can use the Send To command as a quick and easy way to copy or move a folder or file to any destination. You can also customize the Send To menu so that it includes destinations you frequently use.

> When you use the Send To command with a folder destination, Windows treats the object just as if you dragged the object to the folder using the left mouse button. That is, if the destination and source folders are on the same disk, Windows performs a move; if the destination and source folders are on different disks, Windows performs a copy.

Customizing the Send To Menu

The contents of the Send To menu are determined by the contents of a folder named SendTo. On a system that does not use profiles, the SendTo folder is located within the Windows folder. On a system that uses profiles, each user has his or her own SendTo folder. To locate yours, use the Find command.

To add destinations to the Send To menu, simply create shortcuts for those destinations and store the shortcuts in the SendTo folder. For example, suppose you want to create a Send To menu item for a folder named Budgets, which is a subfolder of C:\My Documents. Here is one way you can accomplish this addition:

1 Choose Run from the Start menu, type *c:\windows\sendto*, and click OK.

2 Right-click any unoccupied space in the SendTo folder, choose New from the context menu, and choose Shortcut.

3 In the Command Line text box in the Create Shortcut wizard, type *"c:\my documents\budgets"* (including the quotation marks, which are necessitated by the space in the folder name). Then click Next.

4 In the wizard's next dialog box, accept or modify the wizard's proposed name for your new shortcut. Then click Finish.

Of course, you can also use any other technique for creating a shortcut to your new destination folder.

SEE ALSO

For more information about creating shortcuts, see "Creating a Shortcut," page 83.

Using Programs and Other Kinds of Destinations on the Send To Menu

Your Send To menu can include programs, printers, and other types of "destinations," as well as folders. If you select a document and then choose a program from the Send To menu, Windows launches the program and attempts to open the selected document. If you select a document and choose a printer, Windows tries to print your document using that printer. In all cases, Windows does what it would have done had you dragged the selected document to a shortcut for the destination object. In other words, the Send To command is a menu alternative for a drag-and-drop operation.

NOTE

If you select a folder and try to send it to a program on the Send To menu, you'll get an error message. You'll also get an error message (a different one) if you try to send multiple documents to a program that can't handle multiple documents. No harm is done in either case.

TIP

Putting a shortcut for Notepad in your SendTo folder gives you a way to inspect plain text files that may not be identified in the registry as quick-viewable. For example, suppose you have a file named READ.ME, and your registry knows nothing about .ME files. With Notepad on your Send To menu, you can simply right-click and send the file to Notepad for easy viewing and printing.

To add a program to the Send To menu, simply create a shortcut for that program in your SendTo folder, in the same way as you would add a folder destination to the Send To menu.

Renaming Folders, Files, and Shortcuts

The simplest way to rename an object is to right-click it, choose Rename from the context menu, and then type a new name. But other methods are also available:

- Select the object and choose Rename from Windows Explorer's File menu.

- Select the object. Then click the object's name. When a rectangle appears around the object's name, type a new name or edit the current name.

  When you use this method, you need to pause a moment between selecting the object and clicking the object's name. Otherwise, Windows interprets your action as a double-click and opens the selected object. (And this method won't work at all if your computer is set up for single-click launching.)

- Select the object and press F2. Then type a new name or edit the current name.

TIP

If you make a mistake while changing a name, simply press Esc to cancel the process.

Windows 98 Filename Restrictions

Names of folders and files used by programs written for Windows 98 can include as many as 255 characters. Thus, there's no need to be cryptic or overly compact in your choice of a filename. Instead of naming that departmental budget worksheet EBUD99-1, you can call it Editorial Budget for 1999—First Draft.

Programs designed for Windows 3.x and not yet updated for Windows 95 or Windows 98 still adhere to the old limit of eight characters plus an optional three-character extension. If a program you're using rejects long filenames, check with the vendor to see if an updated version is available.

In any filename, long or short, certain characters are prohibited. These characters are:

* | \ < > ? / " :

Spaces and the following additional characters are prohibited in MS-DOS (short) filenames:

+ , . ; = [ ]

These prohibited characters are reserved for use by the operating system.

Reversing Moves, Copies, and Name Changes with the Undo Command

 If you change your mind after moving or copying something, you can reverse your action by choosing the Undo command from any Windows Explorer window's Edit menu. (If the Standard Buttons toolbar is visible, you can simply click the Undo button.) Be aware, however, that you must use the Undo command right away. As soon as you perform some other action, Undo will reverse that action, not your move or copy.

 TIP

> If you've chosen not to display extensions for registered files, be careful not to type the extension when you rename a file. For example, suppose you have a file named My Picture.bmp, and your Windows Explorer window displays that file's name as simply My Picture. If you change the name to Your Picture, be sure to type *Your Picture*, not *Your Picture.bmp*. Otherwise, the file's name will be recorded as Your Picture.bmp.bmp.

Deleting Folders, Files, and Shortcuts

 To delete an object or a group of objects, select what you want to delete and press the Delete key or click the Delete button. If you prefer a more complicated method, try one of these:

- Right-click an object and choose Delete from the context menu.

- Select an object or group of objects, pull down Windows Explorer's File menu, and then choose Delete.

> **Sharing Windows 98 Files with Systems That Don't Allow Long Filenames**
>
> If you need to share documents with users of Windows 3.x or MS-DOS, you might be concerned that those users will not be able to read files with long names. Fortunately, there is no need to worry. When you save a file with a long filename, Windows 98 also records an alternative short name. You can find out what the short version of any filename is by inspecting the file's properties. (See "Inspecting Folder and File Properties," page 127.) In the properties dialog box, the short name is identified as the "MS-DOS Name." Thus, you don't need to constrain your filenames for the sake of other users.

■ Select an object or a group of objects, and then drag it to the Recycle Bin icon on your desktop—or to a shortcut for Recycle Bin.

However you do the deed, Windows presents a prompt and asks you to confirm your intent. This protects you from accidental deletions.

 TIP

If you don't want Windows to prompt for confirmation when you delete folders or files, clear the Display Delete Confirmation Dialog Box check box at the bottom of the Recycle Bin Properties dialog box.

As further protection, items you delete from hard disk folders or the desktop are automatically transferred to the Recycle Bin, from whence you can retrieve them if you change your mind.

 TIP

If you change your mind right away about a deletion, you can restore whatever you deleted by choosing the Undo Delete command from Windows Explorer's Edit menu.

Restoring Deleted Folders, Files, and Shortcuts

Have you ever deleted one file when you really meant to delete a different one? Wiped out a whole directory by mistake? Or simply trashed a document you thought you were finished with, only to discover the following week that you desperately needed it back?

Windows provides a way to recover gracefully from accidents such as these. For a period of time after you delete an object, that object remains accessible via the Recycle Bin. If you change your mind, a simple menu command or mouse action restores selected items to the folders from which they were deleted.

The Recycle Bin is like that large trash barrel outside your house or the dumpster in the alley behind your office. Until the big truck comes to empty that container, anything you've tossed out can still be retrieved. (For information about when the big truck arrives in Windows, see "Setting Your Recycle Bin's Capacity," on page 140.)

When you open the Recycle Bin, Windows displays the names of recently deleted items in an ordinary Windows Explorer window. (See Figure 4-16.) Displaying the window in details view includes columns that show when each item was deleted and which folder it was deleted from. As in other Windows Explorer windows, you can click column headings to change the sort order, and you can use toolbar icons or commands on the View menu to switch to list view or large- or small-icons view.

FIGURE 4-16.
Opening the Recycle Bin reveals an ordinary Windows Explorer window. Displaying the contents in details view lets you see when each item was deleted.

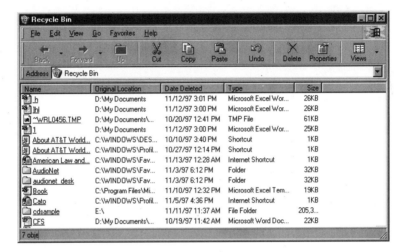

To restore an item from the Recycle Bin, simply select it and choose the File menu's Restore command (or right-click the item and choose Restore from the context menu). The Restore command puts the item back in the folder from which it was deleted. If that folder doesn't currently exist, Windows asks your permission to re-create it.

You also have the option of restoring a deleted item and putting it in a different folder. To do this, select the item and choose Cut from the File menu or context menu. Go to the folder in which you want the item to be restored, and then choose the Paste command on that Windows Explorer window's Edit menu.

Here are three other important things to know about the Recycle Bin:

- Items deleted from floppy disks or network servers are not stored in the Recycle Bin. When you delete such an item, Windows asks you to confirm the deletion.

- Some programs provide their own commands for deleting files. If you use a program's delete command your deleted file might not be transferred to the Recycle Bin.

- If you delete a folder, the Recycle Bin shows the deleted folder but does not record separate entries for the folder's files and subfolders. If you restore the folder, however, Windows re-creates the folder and its contents.

The Find command cannot be used to locate items in the Recycle Bin. To search for items in the Recycle Bin, sort the Recycle Bin display on the column heading of interest. For example, to find an item when you know its name, click the Name heading so that all deleted items' names appear in alphabetical order. To find items that were deleted on a particular day, click the Date Deleted column heading.

Setting Your Recycle Bin's Capacity

Although you have only one Recycle Bin icon (plus any shortcuts to that icon that you've created), Windows actually maintains a separate recycle bin for each hard disk on your system. The default size of each recycle bin is 10 percent of the capacity of the hard disk on which it's stored. When a recycle bin exceeds that limit, Windows begins removing files permanently, starting with the files that have been in the Recycle Bin the longest.

You can make your recycle bins larger or smaller by right-clicking the Recycle Bin icon and choosing Properties. (If the Recycle Bin is already open, you can get to the context menu by right-clicking the window's Control-menu icon.) You'll see a dialog box similar to the one shown in Figure 4-17, with a tab for each of your system's hard disks.

To adjust the size of all recycle bins on your system, select the Use One Setting For All Drives option button, and then adjust the slider on the Global tab. To adjust the size of recycle bins individually, select the Configure Drives Independently option button, and then adjust the sliders on each disk drive tab. To turn off recycle bin functionality globally, select the check box labeled "Do not move files to the Recycle Bin; remove files immediately when deleted." To do this only for a

FIGURE 4-17.

The Properties command lets you configure each hard disk's recycle bin.

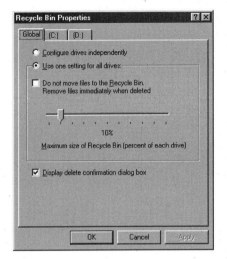

particular hard disk, select the Configure Drives Independently option button, and then select the "remove files immediately" check box on the appropriate disk tab.

> To delete a file without moving it to the Recycle Bin, hold down the Shift key while you press Delete.

Purging the Recycle Bin

A deleted file sitting in your Recycle Bin takes up just as much space as it did before it was deleted. If you're deleting files in order to free up room for new programs and documents, simply transferring them from ordinary disk folders to the Recycle Bin folder won't do you much good. You need to get the old files off your system permanently. The safest way to do this, of course, is to move the files to a removable medium, such as a floppy disk. That way, you can always get your files back if you change your mind.

If you're sure you'll never need a particular file again, however, you can delete it in the normal way, and then purge it from the Recycle Bin. To delete an item from the Recycle Bin, simply display the Recycle Bin, select the item, and then press the Delete key. Be aware as you answer the confirmation prompt that this deletion removes your selection permanently.

To delete a group of items from the Recycle Bin, hold down the Ctrl key while you select each one, and then press the Delete key. (If the files are located next to one another in the Recycle Bin window, you can select the first member of the group, and then hold down the Shift key while you select the last member.)

⊕ TIP

You can check the properties of a file before deleting it by double-clicking the file's icon in the Recycle Bin window.

To empty the Recycle Bin in one fell swoop, simply right-click the Recycle Bin icon and choose Empty Recycle Bin from the context menu. Or, if you're already in the Recycle Bin window, choose this command from the File menu.

Setting Attributes for Folders, Files, and Shortcuts

Attributes are markers that file systems employ to identify certain characteristics of files. In the Windows 98 file system, folders, files, and shortcuts can have no attributes or any combination of the following attributes: archive, hidden, read only, and system. The properties dialog box (see Figure 4-12, on page 127, and Figure 4-13, on page 128) lets you see an item's current attributes and change them if necessary.

The *archive* attribute indicates that an item has been modified since it was last backed up. Each time you create a new file or change an old one, Windows assigns the archive attribute to that file. Backup programs typically remove the archive attribute when they back up a file. If you change the file after backing it up, the file again gets the archive attribute so your backup program can recognize it as needing to be backed up again.

A few programs use the *hidden* and *system* attributes (either, but usually both) to mark important files that must not be modified or deleted because they are critical components of the program or Windows.

You can open a file with the *read-only* attribute, but you can't save it unless you first rename it. Some programs—and many users—set this attribute to prevent accidental changes to a file.

In many contexts, the read-only attribute not only prevents an item from being altered, but also keeps it from being deleted. For example, the MS-DOS Erase and Del commands refuse to delete files that are marked read-only. (You'll get the error message "Access denied" if you try.) If you select a read-only file in a Windows Explorer window and press the Delete key, Windows presents a confirmation prompt, reminding you that the file is read-only.

⭐ **TIP**

Assigning the read-only attribute to important files makes it less likely that you will delete those files accidentally. To assign this attribute, right-click the file, choose Properties from the context menu, and then select the Read Only check box. Note, however, that you will need to remove this attribute (by deselecting the check box) if you want to edit the file without changing its name.

You can assign attributes to entire folders as well as to individual files. Making a folder read-only does not alter the attributes of files or folders contained within the read-only folder, but it does afford some protection against accidental deletion of the folder.

Working with the File Types List

If you choose Folder Options on Windows Explorer's View menu, and then click the File Types tab, Windows displays a list of all registered file types. A sample of this list is shown in Figure 4-18, on the next page.

Working with this list, you can do a number of things:

- Decode the icons in your Windows Explorer windows

- Change a file type's icon

- Add or remove quick-view capability for a file type

- Change the registered name of a file type

- Specify whether the file type's extension should be displayed in Windows Explorer windows

- Remove a file type from the registry

FIGURE 4-18.

The File Types tab in the View menu's Folder Options dialog box lists all file types known to the registry, provides details about how they're associated, and allows you to change document icons or add quick-view capability. Stepping through the File Types list may help you sort out what all those icons in your Windows Explorer windows represent.

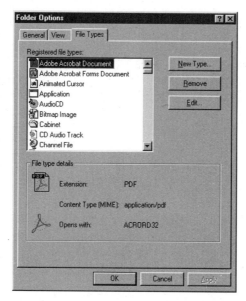

- Change the actions carried out by commands on the file type's context menu

- Add or delete commands on the file type's context menu

- Create new file types

Decoding Document Icons

As you've undoubtedly noticed, document files are marked by icons shaped like pages with a dog-ear in the upper right corner. Icons for registered documents resemble those of their parent programs, and icons for unregistered documents bear the generic Windows emblem. But if you open your Windows folder or its System subfolder, you'll probably find dozens of files with icons that may not be familiar. What do all these icons signify?

One way you can find out is by stepping through the File Types list. As you select each file type in the list, a full-size version of the file type's icon appears in the bottom of the dialog box along with the file type's extension and the icon used by its parent program (if it has one). You will learn, for example, that an icon that looks like a folder window with a big gear stands for an MS-DOS batch file, that .COM files are marked by plain window icons without the big gear, and so on.

Changing a File Type's Icon

Just as you can change the icons used by your programs (see "Changing a Menu Item's Icon," page 61), you can also reassign document icons. To do this, open Windows Explorer's View menu, choose Folder Options, and click the File Types tab. In the Registered File Types list, find the file type you want to modify, and then click Edit. Click the Change Icon button at the top of the ensuing dialog box, and then choose a new icon from the Change Icon gallery.

If you don't see a suitable icon in the Change Icon gallery, you can specify a different program in the File Name text box—and then "borrow" an icon from that program.

Adding or Removing Quick-View Capability

The Quick View facility lets you look at many types of files, including both text and graphics files, without invoking the programs that created them. If a file type's context menu does not include the Quick View command, you can add it as follows:

1   Select the file type in the File Types list.

2   Click the Edit button.

3   Select the Enable Quick View check box and click OK.

SEE ALSO

For information about Quick View, see "Quick Viewing and Property Inspection," page 25.

If Windows doesn't have a viewer specific to the selected file type, it uses the plain-text viewer. This may or may not produce an edifying display. If it doesn't, no harm is done. You can go back to the File Types list and deselect the Enable Quick View check box.

Changing the Registered Name of a File Type

The names that appear in the File Types list may show up in menus used by your programs. For example, if you use the Insert Object command in WordPad (or in another program that supports OLE), you'll see a list of embeddable objects. This list is derived from the File Types list. You can change what you see on the menus by changing the names in the File Types list. There's probably no compelling reason to do this, unless you simply object to the length of some of the names.

For example, suppose you tire of seeing the name *Microsoft* before every file type created by a Microsoft program. To reduce Microsoft Access Blank Database Template to something a bit simpler, such as Access Database Template, you could do as follows:

1 In the File Types list, select the Microsoft Access Blank Database Template entry.

2 Click the Edit button.

3 In the Description Of Type box, type the short name you prefer, and then click OK.

Specifying Display of Extensions

SEE ALSO

For more information about enabling or suppressing filename-extension display, see "Options That Can Be Applied Only to All Folders," page 121.

By default, Windows Explorer windows do not show extensions for registered file types. You can turn on the extension display for all file types using Windows Explorer's Folder Options command. Using the File Types list, you can also show extensions for a particular file type, while suppressing the extensions for other registered file types. Here's how:

1 Select the file type in the File Types list.

2 Click the Edit button.

3 Select the Always Show Extension check box and click OK.

Removing a File Type from the Registry

SEE ALSO

For information about the Add/Remove Programs wizard, see "Installing Programs," page 328.

If you use the Add/Remove Programs wizard to uninstall Windows-based programs that you no longer need, you should not have to "unregister" the file types used by those programs. The wizard should take care of that detail for you. But if the wizard lets you down, or if you remove a program without the wizard's assistance, you might want to visit the File Types list to clean up. You can remove a file type from the registry as follows:

1 Select the file type in the File Types list.

2 Click the Remove button and reply to the confirmation prompt. Then click OK.

Modifying a File Type's Context Menu

If you know what you're doing, you can change the contents of a file type's context menu or modify the behavior of commands on the menu. To see what commands are on the context menu, select a file type and click the Edit button. To see what a particular command does, select that command in the Actions section of the ensuing dialog box, and then click Edit in that dialog box. To make changes, modify the next dialog box that appears.

Changing a File Type's Default Action

A file type's default action is the one that appears in boldface type in the Actions list. To make a different action the default, select it and then click the Set Default button. For example, to make Windows Explorer include the All Folders pane by default, follow these steps:

1 Choose Folder Options from Windows Explorer's View menu.

2 Click the File Types tab.

3 Select Folder (not File Folder) in the list of Registered File Types.

4 Click the Edit button.

5 Select Explore in the Actions list.

6 Click the Set Default button.

7 Click Close twice.

Creating New File Types

The New Type button in the File Types list allows you to add new file types to the registry. Normally, you should have no reason to use this button. Instead, if you want to create an association between an unregistered file type and a program, simply launch an instance of that file type in a Windows Explorer window. Then fill out the Open With dialog box.

Formatting Disks

To format a disk, right-click the disk's icon in Windows Explorer, and then choose Format from the context menu. Windows displays a dialog box similar to the one shown in Figure 4-19, on the next page.

FIGURE 4-19.

To format a disk, right-click its icon and choose Format from the context menu.

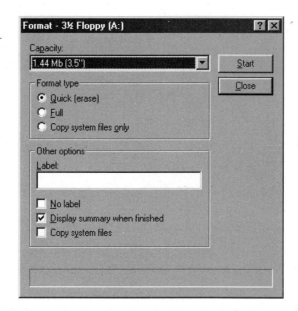

First choose the capacity of the disk you're about to format. Next choose the type of format you want. If you choose a full format, Windows checks the disk for bad sectors after completing the format. If you go for a quick format, Windows skips the media check and simply erases everything on the disk. This option can't be used with disks that have never been formatted.

The Copy System Files Only option turns a floppy disk that's already been formatted into a "boot disk"—a disk that you can use to boot your computer. If you want to format a disk *and* make it a boot disk, choose Full or Quick in the Format Type section of the dialog box, and also select the Copy System Files check box.

 TIP

Windows can also make a "startup disk" that is not only a boot disk, but also includes several utility and diagnostic programs. To make a startup disk, launch Add/Remove Programs in Control Panel. Click the Startup Disk tab, and then click Create Disk. For more information, see "Being Prepared with Startup Disks and Backup Tapes," page 397.

You cannot use the Format command to format the hard disk on which your Windows files are stored. You can use it to format other hard disks, though.

Copying Floppy Disks

To copy a floppy disk, right-click its icon in Windows Explorer and choose Copy Disk from the context menu. Make sure the Copy To and Copy From sections of the dialog box are correctly filled out, and then click Start. When the copy is complete, the dialog box remains on screen. If you want to copy another disk, insert it and then click Start again.

Using Command Lines to Open Windows Explorer

With command-line expressions you can open Windows Explorer and make it display a particular folder, display a folder and select a particular object in that folder, or limit its display to a subset of your namespace. (*Namespace* is Windows' term for your system's entire collection of navigable resources, including Network Neighborhood, the desktop, and all of your local disks.) You can use these command lines with the Start menu's Run command, assign them to a shortcut, or store them in an MS-DOS batch file. (By entering command strings in an MS-DOS batch file, you can open two or more Windows Explorer windows with a single command.)

The syntax is as follows:

```
explorer [/n][/e][,/root,object][[,/select],subobject]
```

/n	always opens a new window, even if the specified folder is already open.
/e	opens the folder in explore view (that is, a window that includes the All Folders Explorer Bar). If you omit /e, Windows Explorer opens in open view.
/root,*object*	restricts Windows Explorer to *object* and all folders contained within *object*.

SEE ALSO
For information about explore view and open view, see "'Open View' Versus 'Explore View,'" page 107.

| /select,*subobject* | gives initial focus to the parent folder of *subobject* and selects *subobject*. If /select is omitted, *subobject* specifies the folder that gets the initial focus. |

 NOTE

> The square brackets in the syntax statement indicate optional items.

Here are some examples:

```
explorer /e,/root,C:\Windows
```

opens an explore view restricted to C:\Windows (and all folders contained in C:\Windows). The window includes the All Folders Explorer Bar.

```
explorer /e,/select,C:\Windows\Win.ini
```

opens an explore view of C:\Windows, with the Win.ini file selected. The window includes the All Folders Explorer Bar.

```
explorer C:\Windows
```

opens an open view of C:\Windows.

```
explorer
```

opens an explore view of C:\ (or the disk on which your Windows files are stored). Note that when no arguments are given, you don't need to include /e to include the All Folders Explorer Bar.

PART II

Further Explorations

Using and Sharing Files on the Network

W indows 98 was designed from the start as a networking operating system. In many other
networking environments, the networking functionality is superimposed on a single-user-oriented operating
system. In Windows 98, networking features are fully integrated into every aspect of the system.

Windows 98 provides support for networks from a number of
vendors, including Microsoft, Novell, Artisoft, Banyan, Digital
Equipment Corporation, and IBM. In addition, the system
supports the simultaneous use of multiple networking protocols.
This means that, assuming your network administrator has set up
your system properly, you should be able to work successfully in
a heterogeneous network environment, making use of servers
that run Windows NT, Windows 98, Windows 95, Windows for
Workgroups, Novell NetWare, and other operating systems.

Best of all, using network resources and sharing your own
resources with other network users is almost as simple and
straightforward as using your own local resources. Browsing a
network folder is just like browsing a folder on your own hard
disk. Sending a document to a network printer is just like
printing at your own machine. The procedures for interacting

SEE ALSO

For information about using network printers, see "Printing to a Network Printer," page 192. For information about remote access, see "Using Dial-Up Networking," page 578.

with one kind of server (say, a Windows NT server) are identical to the procedures for working with another kind (for example, a NetWare server). You don't have to learn network commands to use your network's resources.

In this chapter, we'll look at the steps involved in working with programs and documents stored on network servers, as well as at what you need to do to share your own folders and files. Other networking topics can be found in other parts of this book.

Using Network Neighborhood to Find Network Files

Network Neighborhood is your gateway to all available network resources, just as My Computer is the gateway to resources stored on your own system. Launching Network Neighborhood opens a Windows Explorer window that contains icons for all workstations and servers in your immediate workgroup (as defined and configured by your network administrator). Figure 5-1 shows the Network Neighborhood folder for a typical small local-area network.

FIGURE 5-1.
The icons in the Network Neighborhood folder represent workstations in your workgroup.

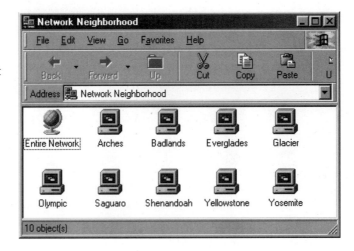

TIP

To include an All Folders pane in Windows Explorer, which lets you browse your network hierarchy, right-click the Network Neighborhood icon and then choose Explore from the context menu.

TIP

If you're not sure what kind of files are contained on a server, use details view. You might find a comment (entered by the person who shared the folder) that describes the contents of the server or folder.

In addition to entries for each workstation in your workgroup, the Network Neighborhood folder includes an entry labeled Entire Network. Launching Entire Network opens a folder that displays a top-level view of your entire corporate network. If your network is particularly complex, you might find it helpful to view its structure in an All Folders pane. To do that, right-click the Entire Network icon and choose Explore. Figure 5-2 uses Windows Explorer to show the "entire-network" view of the network shown in Figure 5-1.

II

Further Explorations

FIGURE 5-2.

The Documentation icon in this window represents the workgroup shown in Figure 5-1.

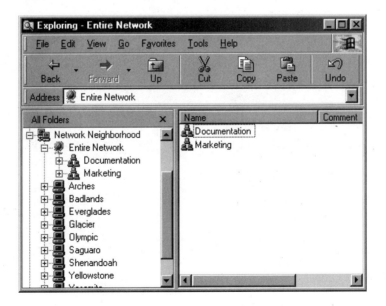

If you frequently need access to a network server that isn't included in your Network Neighborhood, create a shortcut for it, and put the shortcut in your Network Neighborhood folder. To do this, simply open Entire Network, find the server you need, right-drag it to the Network Neighborhood icon, and then choose Create Shortcut(s) Here from the context menu.

Connecting to a Network Server

A *server* is a remote source of shared resources. Because the Microsoft networking services are "peer-based," a server can be a computer that acts solely as a repository for shared files (a "dedicated" server), or it can simply be a shared folder on a computer used by one of your colleagues.

In either case, to interact with a server, simply open that server in your Network Neighborhood window. This opens a new Windows Explorer window, in which you can see all the folders and printers on the selected server to which you have been granted access. Figure 5-3 shows such a window. Opening a folder reveals all folders and files stored in that folder, and so on.

FIGURE 5-3.
The details view of a Windows Explorer window can include a comment for each server or shared resource. The comment is provided by the person who set up the server or shared the resource.

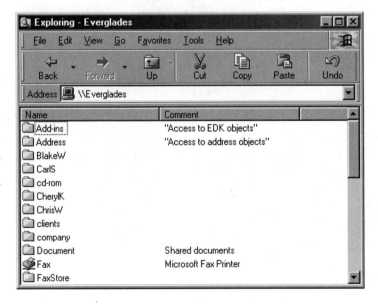

Your Network Neighborhood folder also includes an icon for your own computer. By launching this icon, you can see the names of all folders and printers on your own system that have been made available to other network users.

When you open a server-based folder, you may be asked to supply a password. If so, you will see a dialog box similar to the one shown in Figure 5-4. Before typing in your password, you might want to make sure the check box at the bottom of the dialog box is selected. That way Windows will add your password to a list of passwords associated with your name, and you won't have to reenter the password the next time you open this folder.

FIGURE 5-4.
If you select the check box, you won't have to reenter the password the next time you open the folder.

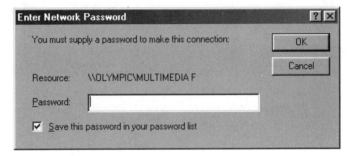

TIP

Create desktop shortcuts for the network folders you use regularly. That way, you won't have to travel through the Network Neighborhood each time you want to read or save a server-based file. To create a desktop shortcut for a network folder, simply right-drag its icon to the desktop, and then choose Create Shortcut(s) Here.

If you don't want to clutter your desktop, but you still want to avoid traveling down the Network Neighborhood path to find a folder, you can drag its icon to the Network Neighborhood folder (or any other convenient folder) instead of to the desktop.

TIP

You can use the Find command to locate network servers, server-based folders, and individual server-based files. For details, see Chapter 6, "Using the Find Command."

II

Further Explorations

Access Rights

What you can do with a network resource depends on your access rights to that resource. If you have *read-only access*, you can work with the folder's programs and documents, but you can't save documents to that folder. To save a document that you retrieved from a read-only network folder, specify a local folder (or a network folder for which you have full-access rights) as the document's destination.

If you have *full access* to a network folder, you can do anything with its documents and programs that you can do with files stored in local folders. In the absence of file-specific restrictions, you can read, write, rename, delete, move, and copy files in full-access folders, just as though they were on your own computer. (Individual files can also have access restrictions, such as password protection or the read-only attribute.)

(?) SEE ALSO

For information about assigning access rights, see "Assigning Access Rights with Share-Level Access Control" and "Assigning Access Rights with User-Level Access Control," page 165.

In some cases, you might have *either* full access or read-only access, depending on the password you supply. For example, a network administrator might want to give some users unrestricted access while limiting others to read-only use. In such cases, if you've been entrusted with both passwords, you might want to limit your full-access use to times when you actually need to change files on the server. Operating with read-only access rights at other times will protect you against accidental changes to or deletions of critical documents.

Connecting to a Server from the Common Dialog Boxes

If the program you're working with uses the Windows 98 common File Open, File Save, and File Save As dialog boxes, you can retrieve or save files on servers without going through your Network Neighborhood icon. Simply open the Look In or Save In drop-down list at the top of the dialog box and then select Network Neighborhood. As shown in Figure 5-5, the big window in the center of the dialog box then displays the names of your servers, allowing you to navigate to the folder of your choice.

FIGURE 5-5.

In the common Open dialog box, select Network Neighborhood when you want to navigate to shared resources.

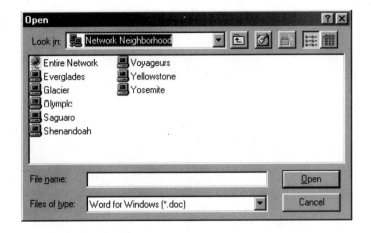

Mapping a Network Folder to a Drive Letter

"Mapping" a network folder makes it appear to Windows as though the folder is part of your own computer. Windows assigns the mapped folder a drive letter, just as if it was an additional local hard disk. You can still access a mapped folder in the conventional manner, by navigating to it through Windows Explorer. But mapping gives the folder an alias—the assigned drive letter—that provides an alternative means of access.

Folder mapping offers the following benefits:

- It makes the network folder available to programs that don't use the Windows 98 common dialog boxes.

   With programs that use the common dialog boxes, you can navigate to network folders just as you would with Network Neighborhood. But to read a document from or save a document to a network folder using other programs (older Windows-based programs, for example, or MS-DOS–based programs), you will probably need to map the folder to a drive letter.

- It makes the network folder accessible from the My Computer icon.

   Because a mapped folder becomes a "virtual" disk on your local computer, an icon for the folder appears in the My Computer folder, right alongside your real local disks. If you do most of your work with files stored locally but occasionally need access to particular servers, you might find it convenient to map them. That way, you won't have to bother opening the Network Neighborhood icon to find the servers you need.

■ Windows can automatically reconnect to your mapped network folders at startup.

When you navigate to a server using Network Neighborhood, you might experience momentary delays while Windows locates and opens a channel to the selected server. If you map the folder and choose the Reconnect At Logon option, any connection delays will occur at the beginning of your work session, and you'll be less likely to find them intrusive.

■ Mapped folders become part of My Computer for file-search purposes.

When you use the Find command to search for files stored on My Computer, the search encompasses not only your real local disks but also any mapped network folders. If you sometimes need to search for items that may be stored *either* locally or in a particular network folder, you can save yourself a search step by mapping the network folder.

To map a network folder, follow these steps:

1 Navigate to the folder in Network Neighborhood.

2 Right-click the folder icon and choose Map Network Drive from the context menu.

The dialog box shown in Figure 5-6 appears.

3 Choose a drive letter in the Drive drop-down.

Windows proposes the first available drive letter, but you can choose any letter that's not already in use. You might want to pick one that's mnemonically related to the content of the folder—for example, R for Reports.

FIGURE 5-6.

Right-clicking a network folder icon and choosing Map Network Drive lets you turn the folder into a virtual local hard disk.

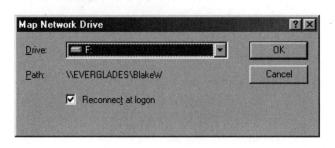

4 Select the Reconnect At Logon check box if you want Windows to connect to this server automatically at the start of each session.

"Unmapping" a Mapped Network Folder

If you change your mind about mapping a network folder, simply right-click the folder's icon in your My Computer folder. As Figure 5-7 shows, you'll see a Disconnect command in the resulting context menu. Choose this command, and the tie will be severed.

FIGURE 5-7.
To "unmap" a network folder, right-click the folder's icon in My Computer and choose Disconnect from the context menu.

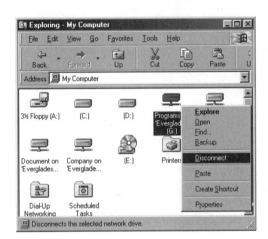

Using Path Specifications to Open Network Folders

In Windows 98, you do not have to memorize path specifications to use network folders. Instead, you can simply navigate to the folders you need using Windows Explorer. But every network folder does, in fact, have a path specification, and you're welcome to use those path specifications wherever you find it convenient.

A network folder's path consists of two backslash characters, followed by a server name, another backslash, and a *share* name. The share name is the name assigned to the folder by the person who made the folder available on the network. (For more information about share names, see "Sharing Folders with Other Users," on the next page.) So, for example, the network path for the folder selected in Figure 5-7 is

\\EVERGLADES\PROGRAMS

because this folder's share name is Programs and it's stored on a server named Everglades.

If the server in question is part of a Windows NT *domain* (a collection of computers that share a common domain database and security policy), you may need to include the domain name in the path. For example, a folder named Fafner, stored on the Budgets server in the Marketing domain would have the following path:

```
\\MARKETING\BUDGETS\FAFNER
```

Additionally, a network path may include subfolder names. To get to the December folder on Fafner, for example, you could specify

```
\\MARKETING\BUDGETS\FAFNER\DECEMBER
```

You can specify a shared folder's path in the Address Bar of a Windows Explorer window, in the Address toolbar, or via the Start menu's Run command. For example, when you want to get to a network folder quickly, without traversing a sequence of Windows Explorer windows, you can simply pop up the Start menu, choose Run, and type the path for the folder you need.

Note that you can also use this technique to open a window for the server itself, from which you can then choose any available subfolder. For example, to display all the shared folders on the server named Wotan, you can type *wotan* in the Address Bar of any Windows Explorer window.

The Run command and the Address toolbar each keep a list of your most recently used entries. Thus, if you often need to use a particular server or network folder, you can type its path once in the Address toolbar, and then choose its path from the drop-down list the next time you need it.

Sharing Folders with Other Users

When it comes to sharing your own local folders with other users, Windows 98 provides two types of access control, called share-level and user-level. With share-level access control, you can assign passwords to shared folders, so that only those users who know the passwords can access your files. You also have the option of sharing folders with read-only access rights, so that users cannot add, change, or delete files.

With user-level access control, you have more control, but your computer must be part of a Windows NT domain. User-level access control lets you assign specific kinds of access rights to specific users or groups of users.

To share folders using either form of access control, you first need to enable file sharing. You do this by launching Network in Control Panel. (Open the Start menu, choose Settings, Control Panel, and then click or double-click Network.) On the Configuration tab, click the File And Print Sharing button. Select the check box labeled "I want to be able to give others access to my files" (if it's not already selected), and click OK.

Next click the Access Control tab and select either the Share-Level Access Control or User-Level Access Control option button. As Figure 5-8 shows, if you select User-Level Access Control, a text box labeled "Obtain list of users and groups from" becomes available. Usually, this box is already filled out with the name of the Windows NT domain where you logged on.

After you make these changes in the Network dialog box, you must restart your computer before you can begin sharing folders.

FIGURE 5-8.

The Access Control tab in the Network dialog box lets you choose between share-level access control and user-level access control.

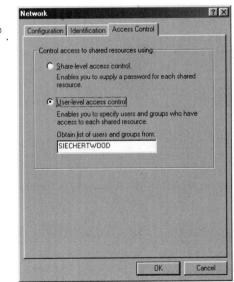

Once you've enabled file sharing, you can share a folder by right-clicking it in a Windows Explorer window and choosing Sharing from the context menu. This takes you to the Sharing tab in the folder's properties dialog box. This looks like Figure 5-9, if you're using share-level access control, or like Figure 5-10, if you're using user-level access control.

FIGURE 5-9.

If you're using share-level access control, your folders' Sharing tabs look like this.

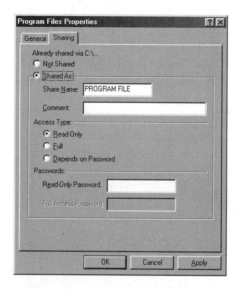

FIGURE 5-10.

If you're using user-level access control, you'll see this style of Sharing tab.

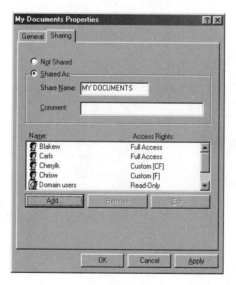

CAUTION

When you share a folder, you also make that folder's subfolders available on the network. If the access rights you give for the folder are not appropriate for any of its subfolders, either reconsider your choice of access rights or restructure your folders to avoid the problem.

TIP

In either case, select the Shared As option button, and then accept or amend the proposed share name. The share name is the name that will appear by the folder icon when others access this folder via their own Network Neighborhood icons. It's also the name that will be used in the folder's network path specification. By default, the share name is the same as the folder name. In most cases that's an ideal name, but you're not obliged to use it. You might want to change it, for example, if your workgroup already is using a shared folder with the same name.

In the Comment line, you can type a description of the folder's contents. Other users will see this description when they use details view in their Network Neighborhood folders.

> You can separately share a subfolder of a folder that you've already shared. When you do that, the Sharing tab in the folder's properties dialog box indicates that the folder is already shared, by way of its parent (or another ancestor further removed). For example, the line "Already shared via C:\...," near the top of Figure 5-9, indicates that the Program Files folder is already available to network users. Sharing Program Files in this case might still be a good idea, however, because it gives network users a way to go directly to a folder of interest without having to drill down through layers of folders and subfolders.

Assigning Access Rights with Share-Level Access Control

SEE ALSO

For more information about access, see "Access Rights," page 158.

With share-level access control, a folder can be shared with any of three types of access rights—Read Only, Full, and Depends On Password. If you select either Read Only or Full, you can specify a password, but you are not required to do so. If you select Depends On Password, you *must* specify two passwords, one for read-only access and one for full access.

Assigning Access Rights with User-Level Access Control

To assign access rights with user-level access control, begin by clicking the Add button in the dialog box shown in Figure 5-10. This takes you to the Add Users dialog box, shown in Figure 5-11, on the next page. In the left side of this dialog box, you'll see a list of all users and user groups known to the domain controller for the domain identified in the upper right corner.

II

Further Explorations

FIGURE 5-11.

You can use this dialog box to assign read-only, full, and custom access rights to specific users and groups of users.

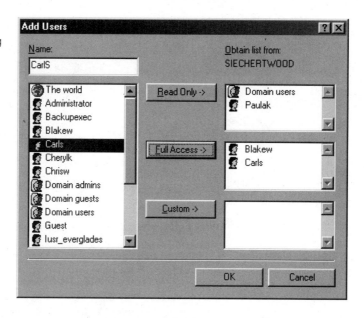

To assign access rights to a user or group, select the appropriate name in this list and then click one of the three buttons in the center of the dialog box. Click OK when you've finished making assignments.

If you have assigned custom access rights to any users or groups, clicking OK takes you to the dialog box shown in Figure 5-12. By selecting check boxes in the lower part of this dialog box, you can specify exactly what kind of custom rights you want to assign.

FIGURE 5-12.

By choosing custom access rights, you can get quite specific about what users may and may not do with your shared files.

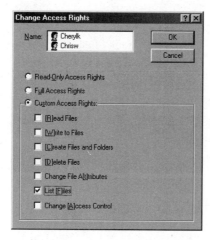

Changing Access Right Assignments

To change the access rights associated with a shared folder, revisit that folder's properties dialog box (right-click it and choose Properties from the context menu) and click the Sharing tab. If you're using user-level access control, select the user or group whose assignment you want to change, and then click the Edit button. This action returns you to the dialog box shown in Figure 5-12, allowing you either to change the user's (or group's) custom access rights or to switch to read-only or full access.

Monitoring the Use of Shared Resources

One potential disadvantage of sharing local resources is that if many users happen to be accessing files on your system at the same time, your system's performance may degrade significantly. At such times, you might find it helpful to know who's doing what with your shared resources. Windows supplies a tool called Net Watcher for this purpose. Net Watcher not only shows you who's connected to what, it also lets you add shares, delete shares, and disconnect users. Clearly, you don't want to disconnect someone who has a valid reason to access one of your shared folders, but you might want to sever a connection that has been left open inadvertently.

If Net Watcher has been installed, launch it by opening the Start menu and choosing Programs, Accessories, System Tools, Net Watcher. Figure 5-13, on the next page, shows a sample of Net Watcher's display.

NOTE

If Net Watcher has not been installed on your computer, launch Add/Remove Programs in Control Panel, click the Windows Setup tab, select System Tools, and click the Details button. Select Net Watcher and click OK.

Net Watcher's "by Connections" view, shown in Figure 5-13, organizes the connection information by connected user. Alternative views present the same information sorted by shared folder and by open file. You can switch between these views by choosing commands on the View menu or clicking tools on Net Watcher's toolbar.

To disconnect a user, select that user's name while viewing by connections. Then choose Disconnect User from the Administration menu. Net

FIGURE 5-13.

Net Watcher lets you see which of your shared resources is being used by whom. The Connected Time column shows how long a connection has been open.

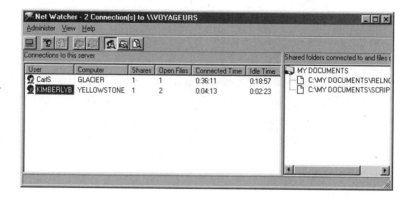

Watcher asks you to confirm your intention, because disconnection might cause the user to lose information in any open files. To break a connection to a particular file, so that all users are shut out from that file but no user is disconnected from the share to which that file belongs, switch to "by Open Files" view, select the file in question, and choose Close File from the Administration menu.

To create a new share, choose Add Shared Folder from the Administration menu. Net Watcher then asks for the path to the folder you want to begin sharing. When you've supplied it, a dialog box identical to the Sharing tab in the folder's properties dialog box appears. Here you can specify passwords and access rights.

To stop sharing a folder, choose By Shared Folders from Net Watcher's View menu. Then select the folder name and choose Stop Sharing Folder from the Administration menu. Although Net Watcher asks you to confirm your intention, its message box doesn't make it clear that users who are currently using files in the folder might lose information when you stop sharing.

Using Net Watcher to Monitor Use of Remote Resources

You can use Net Watcher to monitor the use of resources on servers other than your own, provided those servers have been set up to allow remote administration. To see what's happening on another server, choose Select Server from the Administration menu. Then browse to the server you're interested in or type its network path. (Alternatively, you can right-click a server in the Network Neighborhood folder, choose Properties from the context menu, and then click the Tools tab. On the Tools tab, click Net Watcher.) If the remote server uses share-level access control, you'll need to supply a password to administer the server.

TIP

> If you have remote administration privileges for a server, you can view all of that server's local resources (even those that aren't shared); start and stop sharing its folders; and create, modify, move, and delete files and folders on the server—just about all the file-related tasks you can do on your own computer. To perform any of these tasks, right-click the server in the Network Neighborhood folder, choose Properties, click the Tools tab, and click the Administer button. This opens a Windows Explorer window that shows all of the server's resources.

NOTE

> When you use Windows Explorer to view a server for which you have remote administration privileges, you'll see additional "administrative shares" that are hidden from users without administration privileges. These share names end with a dollar sign ($). For example, an administrative share appears for each hard drive on the system, and the share name is the drive letter followed by a dollar sign, such as c$.

Allowing Remote Administration of Your System

SEE ALSO

For information about changing the user list, see "Assigning Access Rights with User-Level Access Control," page 165.

To make your own system accessible to others via Net Watcher, launch Passwords in Control Panel, click the Remote Administration tab, and select the Enable Remote Administration Of This Server check box. Then, if you're using share-level access control, supply and confirm a password. If your computer is part of a Windows NT domain and you're using user-level access control, the list of users with administrative access rights

II

Further Explorations

initially includes the Domain Admins group; you can add or remove users and user groups from this list just as you can with access lists for shared folders.

WARNING

As mentioned in the previous tip, users who know your administrative password (or who are on the list of administrative users) have nearly total control of the files on your computer. Therefore, you must be very selective about who you allow to remotely administer your computer.

Using the Find Command

S cooting around your hard disk or network with Windows Explorer is dandy when you know where you're going. But it's less dandy when all you know about the item you need is that it's "out there somewhere." In that all-too-common circumstance, you'll want to use Windows 98's versatile Find command.

The Find command can quickly locate documents, programs, folders, and even entire computers, anywhere on your own computer or amongst the shared resources of your network. You can find what you're looking for by name, creation date, size, file type, content, or any combination of these. For example, you can ask the Find command to locate all 1-2-3 for Windows documents created within the last month that are at least 30 MB in size and contain the word "xenon." Or you can use it to generate a list of all programs on a particular server. Or to find all files that are larger than 100 KB and haven't been modified during the last six months. And so on.

For information about finding Web sites and other information on the Internet, see "Using Search to Find New Sites," page 621.

Find's integration with the Internet can also help you locate Web sites and people. If you choose On The Internet from Find's menu, Find connects you with an Internet search service. If you choose People, Find transfers you to your choice of several Internet-based LDAP (Lightweight Directory Access Protocol) servers. These servers can help you track down e-mail addresses and phone numbers for people you need to contact.

Certain of your programs may also attach themselves to the Find command. If you use Microsoft Outlook or MSN, The Microsoft Network online service, for example, you will see entries in the Find menu that are tailored for those programs. You can use the On The Microsoft Network command to help you locate other MSN members or the Using Microsoft Outlook command to find items in one of your Outlook folders. (Be aware that program-specific entries in the Find menu invoke program-specific search engines. These may or may not work the same way as the generic search tools described in this chapter.)

After you've found an item or group of items that you're looking for, you can work with the search results directly in the Find window, just as if it was an ordinary folder window. Alternatively, you can select any item in the Find window and use a File-menu command to go directly to the item's containing folder.

After you have performed a Find operation, if you leave the Find window open, Find continues rechecking the disks or folders it searched originally, to see if any new items have appeared that match your search criteria. Thus, you can use it to keep a more or less constant eye on a network server and alert you when particular files have arrived on that server. You can also take advantage of a Save Search command to make a set of search criteria easily reusable. When you do this, you can either save the criteria as well as the current search results, or simply save the criteria without the current results.

Finding the Find Command

The Find command is a permanent fixture of the Start menu, so you can always invoke it there. Alternatively, you can choose Find from the Tools menu that appears when you launch Windows Explorer in explore view or by right-clicking any folder icon or folder shortcut and choosing Find from the context menu.

TIP

In Windows Explorer, you can press F3 to invoke Find and limit the search to the current folder and its subfolders. F3 is a shortcut for the Find command that appears on Windows Explorer's Tools menu. This shortcut works even when you're using Explorer in open view—in which case, you don't have a Tools menu.

When you choose Find from a folder's context menu, Find proposes to conduct its search beginning at the current folder. Thus, if you know that the items you're looking for are in a particular folder (or one of its subfolders), and if that folder is at hand, it's more efficient to choose Find from the folder's context menu, saving you the effort of specifying a starting point for the search. Otherwise, it's probably simpler to open the Start menu.

Finding Files and Folders

When you choose Find from the Start menu, a submenu similar to the one shown in Figure 6-1 appears. (Depending on what software you have installed, your submenu might include more or fewer items.) Because most of the time you're likely to be hunting for files and folders, we begin with an overview of that branch of the Find facility.

FIGURE 6-1.

When you choose Find from the Start menu, it first asks you to tell it what kind of object you're looking for.

Telling Find Where to Search

After you choose Files Or Folders from the submenu shown in Figure 6-1, the dialog box shown in Figure 6-2 appears. Notice the two text boxes with associated drop-down arrows in this dialog box. The second of these, Look In, is already filled out with whatever area you last searched.

FIGURE 6-2.

Find can look for files and folders on all local hard disks, a particular local or remote disk, or a particular local or remote folder.

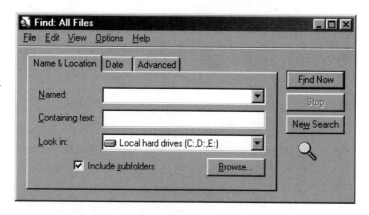

? SEE ALSO

For information about mapping network drives, see "Mapping a Network Folder to a Drive Letter," page 159.

To change the contents of the Look In line, click the drop-down arrow. The list that emerges includes My Computer, as well as entries for each local hard disk, all local hard disks, each local floppy disk, each local CD-ROM or DVD drive, each network drive that you have mapped to a local drive letter, and the last specific folder that you have searched.

If you want to search an unmapped network server or restrict the search to a particular folder (that isn't already listed in the Look In drop-down), click the Browse button instead of the Look In drop-down arrow. Find then displays an outline of all resources available to your system, exactly as you might see in the All Folders pane of a Windows Explorer window. Select the folder where you want to begin the search, and then click OK.

By default, Find searches the disk or folder specified on the Look In line, plus all the subfolders of that disk or folder. If you don't want to search the subfolders, deselect the Include Subfolders check box.

Telling Find What to Search For

You can use any of the following criteria, singly or in combination, when searching for files and folders:

- Name

- File content

- Creation, most recent modification, or access date

- File type

- File size

If you use a combination of criteria, Find ferrets out only those items that meet *all* criteria.

 TIP

> When you finish a search, Find retains your search criteria in case you want to perform another search based on similar criteria. If you want to start a brand new search, it's a good idea to click the New Search button. That way you won't inadvertently reuse a criterion from your previous search.

Searching by Name

To specify a search by name, click the Name & Location tab (if this tab isn't already displayed) and enter the appropriate text on the Named line. If the name you're looking for is one you've recently used in a search, you can save yourself some typing by clicking the drop-down arrow at the right side of the Named line and selecting the text from the ensuing list.

You can search by name without knowing exactly how the item you want is spelled. If you know any part of it, enter that part on the Named line. Find locates all items whose names include the letters you type. For example, if you simply type *Sales* on the Named line, Find locates items with names such as Quarter 1 Sales, Quarter 2 Sales, Sales Forecast, Salespersons, and Sales Tax.

Using Wildcards

A *wildcard* is a character used as a proxy for one or more other characters. If you're an MS-DOS veteran, you might be accustomed to using wildcards in directory searches. You'll be glad to know the same wildcards also work with filename searches conducted by the Find command. The two wildcards recognized by Find are ? and *.

The question mark represents any single character. For example, specifying

    199?

returns any file or folder that includes any year from 1990 to 1999 in its name, as well as files and folders that include 199 followed by any other character. You can use as many question-mark wildcards in a specification as you want.

The asterisk represents any single character or combination of characters. For example, searching for

    1*4

might turn up 123r4, 1994, 1024, and so on. The most common use for the asterisk wildcard is to find all files with a common extension. For example, to find all files with the extension .XLS, you can enter

    *.xls

on the Named line. If you simply enter *xls* without the wildcard and period, you get, in addition to all the files with the extension .XLS, all files with "xls" anywhere else in their names. An alternative way to find all files with a certain extension is to use the search-by-file-type option. But the search-by-file-type option is useful only for file types that are recorded in your Windows registry. For extensions that are not in the registry, the wildcard approach is ideal.

 SEE ALSO

For information about the search-by-file-type option, see "Searching by File Type," page 178. For information about extensions in the registry, see "Working with the File Types List," page 143.

Interrupting a Search

Once the item or items you're looking for appear in the Find window, there's no need to sit on your hands while Find continues searching. You can halt the search at any time by clicking the Stop button.

Alternatively, you can begin working with an item in the Find window while the search goes on. Simply select any item in the window and use it any way you like. You can right-click the item to get its context menu, double-click it to open it (if it's a document) or run it (if it's a program), drag it somewhere if you want to copy it or make a shortcut from it, and so on.

Searching by File Content

To search for files containing some particular text, click the Name & Location tab. Then type the text you're looking for on the Containing

Text line. Note that the text you type is treated literally—that is, you cannot use wildcards on the Containing Text line. Also be aware that searching for files by their content takes much longer than searching by name, modification date, type, or size. To avoid unnecessarily lengthy searches, restrict the search as much as is practical. For example, if you're looking for a Microsoft Excel spreadsheet with a particular number or phrase in it, restrict the file type to Excel documents and, if all the likely possibilities are stored in a certain folder, enter that folder name on the Look In line.

Making a Search Case Sensitive

Content searches ignore case by default. If you're sure how the text you're looking for is capitalized, you might want to make the search case sensitive. To do that, simply open the Options menu and choose Case Sensitive. A check mark will appear beside the command name, indicating that the next search will be case sensitive.

If you turn on the case-sensitive option, all your searches will be case sensitive until you turn off the option. Also be aware that, although you can turn this option on or off while Find is searching, your change doesn't take effect until the next search.

Searching by Date

To use a date or timeframe as a search criterion, click the Date tab in the Find dialog box. That takes you to the dialog box shown in Figure 6-3. You can search by creation date, last modification date, and most-recent-access date. Note that a file's most recent modification or access may have been performed by the operating system or a program, not directly

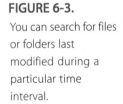

FIGURE 6-3.
You can search for files or folders last modified during a particular time interval.

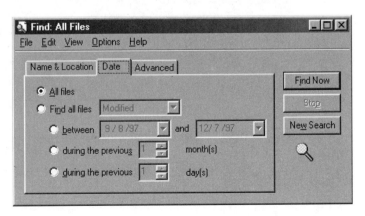

by you. (You might be surprised to discover how many files get accessed by the operating system in the course of a day.)

The date options are commonly used in conjunction with other specifications. For example, if you want to locate all Microsoft Word documents that were modified within the last seven days, you can select the Find All Files option button, select Modified from the drop-down list, select the second "during the previous" option button, and type 7 in its associated text box. Then, on the Advanced tab, select Microsoft Word Document (see "Searching by File Type," below).

Note that when you tell Find to locate all objects created, modified, or accessed during the previous n days, that means the previous n days plus all of today. For example, if you ask Find to locate all files modified during the previous 1 day, it finds everything that was changed yesterday plus anything that was changed today. (And, unfortunately, you cannot enter 0 to search only for those items created, modified, or accessed today.)

Searching by File Type

To search for a particular kind of file, or to restrict the search to folders only, click the Advanced tab. That brings up the dialog box shown in Figure 6-4.

The default type specification, shown in Figure 6-4, is All Files And Folders. To narrow the search to a particular type, click the drop-down arrow on the Of Type line, and select from the ensuing list. Note that the

FIGURE 6-4.

Using the Advanced tab, you can search for a particular type of file, for folders only, or for files of a minimum or maximum size.

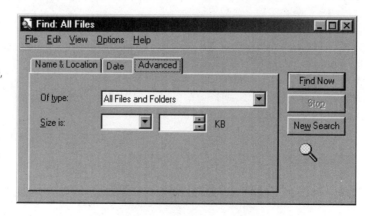

drop-down list includes some general categories, as well as the various document types known to your system's registry. For example, to search for programs, choose Application. To search for folders, excluding documents and programs, choose Folders, and so on.

Searching by File Size

To search for files and folders that are larger than or smaller than a particular size, click the Advanced tab. Then, in the dialog box shown in Figure 6-4, click the drop-down arrow on the Size Is line. A two-item list unfolds, giving a choice of At Least and At Most. If you're looking for files smaller than some threshold amount, choose At Most. Otherwise, choose At Least. Finally, type the size threshold in the KB text box, or manipulate its spinner to indicate the size you're interested in.

Saving Search Results

To preserve the criteria used in a Find operation for reuse after you close the Find dialog box, open the File menu and choose Save Search. To preserve the current search results as well as the criteria, first choose Save Results from the Options menu. Then choose Save Search from the File menu. With results or without, Find creates an icon on your desktop and assigns that icon a default name. For example, if you ask Find to locate all folders whose names include the word *personal*, and then save the results of that search, your new desktop icon will be called something like *Files of type Folder named personal*. Because the default name is long and not always completely descriptive (it will not, for example, include date specifications), you'll probably want to assign your own name to the new icon. You can do that by right-clicking and choosing Rename.

The Save Search command puts an icon on your desktop, regardless of whether you invoked the Find command from the Start menu or from the context menu of a folder. But the icon itself represents an ordinary document file, and you may copy it, move it, or create a shortcut to it, just as you can any other document file.

To reuse a saved set of search criteria, launch the desktop icon and click Find Now.

II

Further Explorations

Finding a Network Server

To look for a particular computer on the network, right-click the Network Neighborhood icon and choose Find Computer. Or open the Start menu and choose Find, Computer. Either way, you'll come to the dialog box shown in Figure 6-5.

FIGURE 6-5.
The Find command can help you locate a server in the vast expanse of your network.

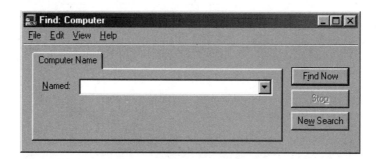

Note that the Find Computer dialog box does not include a Look In line. That's because Find assumes that when you're looking for a particular server, you want to scan your entire network.

 TIP

> To get a list of all servers in your workgroup or domain, choose Find Computer and leave the Named line blank.

Working with Search Results

SEE ALSO

For information about working with items in an Explorer window, see "Running Programs and Opening Documents," page 111, and "Working with Folders, Files, and Shortcuts in Windows Explorer," page 126. For information about Quick View, see "Quick Viewing and Property Inspection," page 25.

As the Find command searches, it presents its findings in the bottom half of an expanded window, as shown in Figure 6-6. Here you can work with found items exactly as though they were in an ordinary Windows Explorer window. For example, you can click the column headings (Name, In Folder, Size, and so on) to change the sorting order of the found items, or use commands on the View menu to switch from the default details view to an icon or list view. You can also right-click any item and then choose Properties to inspect the item's properties dialog box or choose Quick View to take a peek at the item without opening its parent program (if a quick viewer is available for that file type). You can open an item, or right-drag an item to the desktop or to another folder to copy, move, or create a shortcut for the selected item.

FIGURE 6-6.

You can work with found items exactly as you would work with items in an Explorer window.

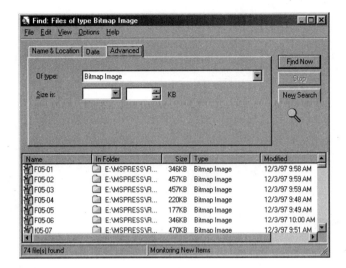

In addition, the Find command's File menu includes one handy command not found in Windows Explorer windows: Open Containing Folder. By selecting an item and choosing this command, Windows opens the selected item's folder, allowing you to navigate immediately to the folder in which the item is stored.

Finding People

Looking for the e-mail address, phone number, or physical address of a colleague, author, or old flame? One of the LDAP services and other directories accessible via the Find People command might be able to provide you with that information. Figure 6-7, on the next page, shows a sample of the Find People command.

In the drop-down list at the top of the Find People dialog box, you can select one of several available directory services, as well as your own local address book. In the remainder of the dialog box, specify a name or an e-mail address (or both), and then click Find Now. The Find command activates your Internet connection if appropriate, and passes your search specification to the selected service. In a moment or two, you might be rewarded with some information about the person you seek. If the service you selected doesn't return any useful information, you can pull down the Look In drop-down list and try again with another service.

FIGURE 6-7.

You can use the Find People command to reconnect with a long-lost friend or to find out who owns a particular e-mail address.

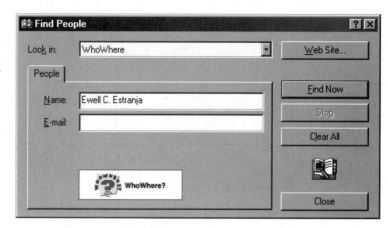

It's possible that the search facility you choose might turn up more than one match for your search criteria. (See Figure 6-8.) If that happens, you might not be sure which person—if any—is the one you want. To learn more about a person whose name appears in the results section of the Find dialog box, select that person's name and click the Properties button. You might want to do this even if only one name is returned, just to make sure you don't try to reestablish contact with someone who's never heard of you. When you're sure you've located that someone you seek, you can click Add To Address Book to create a new entry in your local address book.

FIGURE 6-8.

The Find People command might find more people than you want. You can select a name and click Properties to get additional details about a found person.

TIP

Depending on which directory service you use, the results section of the Find People dialog box might include Business Phone and Home Phone columns, in addition to names and e-mail addresses. If you don't see the phone columns, widen the dialog box.

Directory services vary considerably in the kind of information they provide. To learn more about a service, select its name in the Look In drop-down list, and then click the Web Site button. By going to the search facility's own Web site, you might be able to do other useful things as well, such as adding geographic or other parameters to your search criteria.

II

Further Explorations

Installing, Configuring, and Using Your Printers

W hen it comes to translating your work from the computer screen to the printed page, Windows provides a wealth of support. The operating system's printing features let you (or your system administrator) do the following things, among others:

- Print in the background to any local or shared network printer

- Print in the background from MS-DOS–based programs as well as from Windows-based programs

- Examine the print queues for any local or shared network printer so that you can choose the printer that's likely to get your job done soonest

- Control the position of documents in print queues, or remove documents from queues

- Create multiple logical printers for any physical output device, assigning different characteristics to each logical printer

Goodbye Print Manager, Hello Printers Folder

Unlike Windows 3.x, Windows 98 does not include a Print Manager. In its place is a system folder called *Printers*. All the functionality that was provided by the Windows 3.x Print Manager is now available via the Printers folder.

To get to the Printers folder, open the Start menu and choose Settings, Printers. Alternatively, open the Printers item in My Computer. Figure 7-1 shows an example of a typical Printers folder.

FIGURE 7-1.

You can find out anything you need to know about your printing resources by opening the Printers folder.

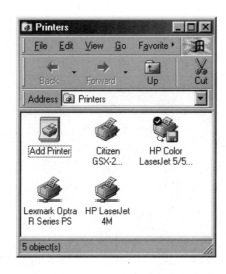

 SEE ALSO

For information about folders, see Chapter 4, "Using and Customizing Windows Explorer."

Although it's a system folder, Printers looks and acts in most respects like an ordinary disk folder. You can choose to display or not display the toolbar and status bar, display printers as icons or list entries, select browsing and viewing options from the View menu, and use standard navigation techniques to move from this folder to any other folder on your system.

TIP

Display the Printers folder in details view to see the number of queued documents and the current status of each local and network printer available to your system. If a descriptive comment has been associated with a printer, that comment also appears in details view.

Within the Printers folder, you'll find entries for each printer you've installed, including local printers and printers attached to network servers. The Printers folder also includes an icon labeled Add Printer, which you can use to install new printers.

Windows uses the following icons to distinguish various kinds of printers from one another:

 A printer attached to your own computer

 A printer set as your default printer

 A printer attached to a network server

 A printer attached to your computer but made available to other network users

 A printer attached to your computer but set up to redirect output to a disk file

For information about printer properties, see "Inspecting and Setting Printer Properties," page 201. For information about print queues, see "Inspecting and Managing a Print Queue," page 194.

To view or change the properties of any printer, right-click its icon and choose Properties.

To inspect or modify the contents of a printer's queue, launch the printer, or right-click its icon and choose Open.

How Do I Print Thee? (Let Me Count the Ways)

In Windows, there is nearly always more than one way to accomplish a task. Printing is no exception. Here are three ways to transport information from a program to your printer:

- Use your program's Print command.

- Drag a file and drop it on a printer icon.

- Right-click a file and use the Send To command (if the SendTo folder includes one or more shortcuts to printers).

Printing from a Program

If the document you want to print is already open, the simplest way to print it is to open the File menu and choose Print. Or simply click the Print button on the program's toolbar—if it has a toolbar with a Print button. The toolbar approach typically bypasses all dialog boxes and sends your entire document to the current default printer. The *default printer*, as its name suggests, is the one that Windows uses unless you tell it to do otherwise.

What if you want to print to a different printer? In that case, you have a couple of choices. You can change the default printer, or you can use a menu command to select a different device.

> In the Printers folder, a check mark appears above the icon for the default printer. To make a different printer the default, right-click its icon in the Printers folder and choose Set As Default from the context menu.

Selecting a Printer

Figure 7-2 shows the dialog box for the Print command used by many programs. This dialog box, or something similar to it, is what you are most likely to see when you print from a newer Windows-based program. The Name drop-down list near the top indicates the name of the current default printer—the printer that will be used when you click OK. Opening the drop-down list reveals the names of all installed printers, allowing you to select a different printer if you don't want to use the default device. The

FIGURE 7-2.

The Print dialog box in most programs lets you select a printer and set options without changing system defaults.

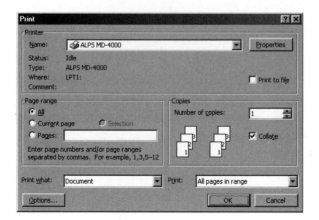

Properties button provides access to settings options associated with the default printer (or the alternative printer you select), and the Status line below the drop-down tells you how busy that printer is.

TIP

> The Status line in the Print dialog box provides useful information about the printer selected in the Name list. In Figure 7-2, for example, the Status line reports that the printer named ALPS MD-400 is idle. If ALPS MD-400 were busy, the Status line would tell you how many jobs were currently in its queue. By scrolling through the Name list and checking the status of each printer, you can determine which one has the shortest queue.

In some programs, you might find the list of printers in a dialog box labeled Choose Printer, Printer Setup, or something similar. Sometimes this dialog box is accessible via a button in the Print dialog box; in other cases, you get to it via a separate File-menu command. In any event, most Windows programs provide some mechanism for selecting a printer other than the default printer.

A few programs, particularly simple programs that handle unformatted text only, do not allow you to select a printer. To print to a different device from a program such as this, you'll need to visit the Printers folder and change the default.

TIP

> While a print job that you initiate remains in a print queue, a printer icon is displayed in the taskbar notification area, just to the left of the clock. When that icon disappears, you know that all your print jobs have finished. If you want to check the status of your print jobs, you can launch that printer icon to open the folder for the printer you're using and inspect that printer's queue. For more information about print queues, see "Inspecting and Managing a Print Queue," page 194.

How Much to Print?

In addition to letting you select a printer, the Print dialog box in most programs lets you set options for that printer. For example, you can specify whether you want to print all of your document, only a range of pages, or only the portion of your document that's currently selected.

II

Further Explorations

Printing Multiple Copies

The Print dialog box also lets you indicate the number of copies you want and whether you want multiple copies collated. If you don't collate, Windows prints all copies of your first page, followed by all copies of your second, and so on. If you collate, you'll get all pages of your first copy, followed by all pages of your next copy, and so on.

> Some programs and drivers for some printers do not support multiple copies and collating.

Switching Between Portrait and Landscape Orientation

The Print dialog box in most programs does not include an orientation option. In many programs you can switch between portrait orientation (in which the printed sheet is taller than it is wide) and landscape orientation (the opposite) by choosing a Page Setup command from the File menu. This command (or something similarly named) also typically allows you to set margins and choose paper size and source.

For more information about properties, see "Inspecting and Setting Printer Properties," page 201.

You can also change orientation by modifying your printer's properties. You can view the properties dialog box by clicking the Properties button in the Print dialog box. When you change orientation in the properties dialog box, however, your change affects all subsequent printouts. If you want just a particular document printed in landscape instead of portrait orientation, it's better to use your program's Page Setup command.

Changing Resolution

Resolution is a measure of the density at which a printer puts dots on paper. High resolutions, such as 600 or 1200 dpi (dots per inch), produce smoother, higher-quality output but require longer printing times. Lower-resolution settings, such as 75 dpi, produce draft-quality output. Generally speaking, resolution is an issue associated with graphics printing; therefore, you probably won't find an option for setting resolution anywhere within your word processor's printing and page-layout dialog boxes. Your graphics programs may offer such an option, however.

You can also change resolution by modifying your printer's properties. A change in the properties dialog box affects all future printouts.

Drag-and-Drop Printing

 SEE ALSO

For information about the registry and associating documents with programs, see "Working with the File Types List," page 143.

If the document you want to print is not open, you can launch its icon in a Windows Explorer window, and then use the Print command in its parent program. But you don't need to do this. Another way to print that document is to grab its icon and then drag it to a printer icon. However, this method works only with documents that are associated with their parent program in your Windows registry. If you try it with an unregistered document type, you'll get an error message.

To print a document, you can drag it to the printer icon with either mouse button. As you reach the drop zone, the printer icon darkens and your document icon sprouts a plus sign to indicate that you are copying data to the printer (as opposed to moving it there permanently).

When you drop a document onto a printer icon, Windows loads the parent program and executes its print command. Depending on the program, you may or may not have to respond to a dialog box before printing begins. As soon as the information has been transferred to the print queue, the program closes.

⭐ **TIP**

Although you can print by dragging a document icon to a printer icon in your Printers folder, you'll probably find it more convenient to create a desktop or toolbar shortcut for each printer you plan to use this way. To create a printer shortcut, open your Printers folder, right-drag the printer's icon, and release the mouse button on your desktop or a toolbar (such as the Quick Launch toolbar, for example). From the context menu, choose Create Shortcut(s) Here.

Printing with the Send To Command

If you don't like cluttering your desktop with printer icons, or if you find it inconvenient to make those icons visible when you want to print, try using the Send To command. Simply right-click the icon for the document you want to print, choose Send To from the context menu, and then choose the name of the printer you want from the Send To menu. If the printer's name isn't on the Send To menu, you can put it there as follows:

1 Open your Printers folder.

2 Open your SendTo folder.

SEE ALSO

For more information about the SendTo folder, see "Customizing the Send To Menu," page 134.

3 Right-drag the printer's icon from the Printers folder to the SendTo folder.

4 Choose Create Shortcut(s) Here from the context menu.

5 Right-click the new icon in the SendTo folder and choose Rename. Delete "Shortcut to" and then press Enter.

When you print with Send To, Windows first opens your document's parent program, just as it does when you drag the document to a printer icon.

Printing from MS-DOS–Based Programs

 SEE ALSO

For information about MS-DOS mode, see "Running a Program in MS-DOS Mode," page 291.

To print from an MS-DOS–based program running under Windows, simply use that program's normal print procedures. Unless you are running your program in MS-DOS mode, Windows prints your document in the background, just as it would print any Windows document.

Printing to a Network Printer

Printing to a network printer is just like printing to a local printer, provided the network printer has been shared (your network administrator should do that for you), you have been given access to it (also a task for your network administrator), and a copy of the printer's driver has been installed on your own computer (something you may need to do yourself). If access to the printer requires a password, you will be prompted for that password when you initiate the print job.

Once the network printer's driver is installed locally, you can print an open document to a network printer using your program's Print command, just as you would for a local printer.

Installing a Local Copy of a Network Printer Driver

If a network printer's driver hasn't been installed on your own system, the printer will not appear in your program's list of available printers. You have to install the driver before you can print an open document to that printer. You can do this with the Add Printer icon in your Printers folder. Or you can use drag and drop.

TIP

If your network printer is down, or if you just want to avoid traffic jams during times of peak usage, you can tell Windows to print offline. All your print jobs will then be stored locally. When rush hour is over, you can go back online and have your print jobs transferred to the printer. To print offline, open your Printers folder, right-click the icon for your network printer, and choose Use Printer Offline. While the printer is offline, its icon in your Printers folder is dimmed. To go back online, right-click the printer again and choose Use Printer Offline a second time. (You might need to press F5 to refresh the window for the icon to brighten again.)

Getting Notification from WinPopup

WinPopup is a little utility that enables network administrators to broadcast messages to network users. It also provides automatic notification to users when network printing jobs are complete. If you have WinPopup running on your system and you send a job to a network printer, WinPopup pops up to let you know when you can fetch your printout. (Note that WinPopup does not have to be running on the print server—only on your own machine.)

If you've installed WinPopup, you can run it by using the Start menu's Run command and typing *winpopup*. If you haven't installed it, use Add/Remove Programs in Control Panel, click the Windows Setup tab, select System Tools, and click the Details button. You'll find WinPopup among the optional programs.

Drag-and-Drop Installation of a Network Printer

Here are two ways to install a network printer using drag and drop:

- Find the printer's icon in your Network Neighborhood folder. Then drag that icon to your own Printers folder.

- Find the printer's icon in your Network Neighborhood folder. Then drag a document icon (for a document you want to print) and drop it on the printer icon.

 SEE ALSO

For more information about installing printer drivers, see "Installing a New Printer," page 196.

Either way, you'll be greeted by the Add Printer wizard and walked through the steps involved in setting up a local copy of the printer driver. If the computer to which the printer is connected is running Windows 95 or Windows 98, these steps are very simple because Windows copies the driver across the network to your own computer. You still need to supply a few details (such as the name by which the printer will be known on your own computer), but most of the information Windows needs is transferred automatically from the network server.

If the computer to which the printer is connected is running Windows NT, Windows for Workgroups, or another operating system, the steps are almost as simple. But you might be prompted to insert one or more floppy disks or a CD containing the necessary printer-driver files.

Inspecting and Managing a Print Queue

When you print a document, Windows creates a temporary file, called a *spool file,* on your hard disk (if the printer is local) or the hard disk of the computer to which your network printer is attached. While this file is being created, your program is temporarily busy and unavailable. After the spool file has been created, the print job enters a print queue and you can return to your program while printing continues in the background. If no other jobs are in the queue, your document's spool file is "despooled" to the printer. Otherwise, it waits its turn.

You can check the status of a printer's queue by launching the printer's icon in your Printers folder. Windows displays the print queue in a folder window similar to that shown in Figure 7-3.

Using commands on this folder window's Printer and Document menus, you can do the following:

- Pause and resume printing the entire queue

- Pause and resume individual documents in the queue

- Remove individual documents from the queue

- Purge the entire queue

FIGURE 7-3.

Launching a printer icon displays the printer's queue, allowing you to manipulate the flow of jobs to the printer.

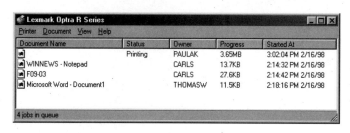

NOTE

If you're viewing the print queue of a network printer, you might not have permission to alter the queue (an "access denied" message stops you), depending on the type of network and the restrictions imposed by the network administrator.

Pausing and Resuming the Print Queue

To pause an entire print queue, choose the Pause Printing command on the Printer menu. The folder window's title bar then changes to include the word *Paused*, and a check mark appears beside the Pause Printing command. Choose the Pause Printing command a second time to resume printing.

Pausing a Particular Document

To suspend temporarily the printing of a particular document, select that document in the print queue window. Then choose Pause Printing from the Document menu. To resume printing, select the paused document and choose Pause Printing a second time.

If the paused document is at the top of the queue (that is, if Windows was actually printing it when you chose the Pause Printing command), the printer itself will be effectively paused until you resume printing of the document. If the paused document is somewhere else in the queue, lower-priority jobs will be printed ahead of it as long as the document remains paused.

Removing a Document from the Queue

To remove a document from the print queue, select it. Then choose Cancel Printing from the Document menu. Be aware that the print queue has no Undo command. If you change your mind, you'll have to begin the printing process anew.

Removing All Documents from the Queue

To remove all documents from a print queue, simply choose the Purge Print Documents command from the Printer menu. Use this command with caution! The queue window has no Undo command!

II

Further Explorations

TIP

You can pause a local printer or remove all documents from its queue without opening its queue window. Simply right-click the printer's icon in the Printers folder, and then choose Pause Printing or Purge Print Documents.

Installing a New Printer

What Windows calls a *printer* is more precisely a constellation of settings applied to an output device. That device may be a traditional printer, a fax modem, a disk file, or perhaps something else altogether. Each combination of settings and output device constitutes a *logical* printer. Each logical printer is treated as a separate device, and is displayed as a separate icon or list entry in your Printers folder. You can install as many logical printers as you like, and you can install multiple logical printers for the same physical output device.

The settings that make up a logical printer include the following:

- The name of the printer

- A *share* name, if the printer is available to other network users

- For shared printers, a description that network users will see when they browse Network Neighborhood in search of a printer (if they use details view)

- The *printer driver*—a software component that enables Windows to translate output into the language used by the physical printer

- Various properties, including the paper tray to be used, the paper size, the amount of memory in the printer, any font cartridges or soft fonts in use, and so on; the available properties vary from printer to printer

- Certain other defaults, such as orientation and resolution

- The port to which the printer is connected

- The name of a separator-page file, if one is to be used

- The length of time Windows should wait before notifying you in case of an error

You might find it useful to set up several logical printers for a single physical printer if you frequently switch among groups of settings. If you often switch between portrait and landscape orientations, upper and lower paper trays, or duplex and single-sided printing, for example, you can set up a logical printer for each. This way, you can simply select a different "printer" to change settings.

Installing a Plug and Play Printer

SEE ALSO

For more information about Plug and Play, see "Plug and Play: The End of the Hardware Blues?," page 333.

If the physical printer you want to install conforms to the Plug and Play standard, Windows should recognize it and know automatically what kind of printer it is, how much memory it has, what font cartridges are installed, what paper tray it's set up to use, and possibly other details.

If you connect a Plug and Play printer to your computer while Windows is not running, you might see a message similar to Figure 7-4 at the beginning of your next Windows session. You will then be placed in the benevolent hands of the Add Printer wizard, who will have only a few more questions to ask you.

FIGURE 7-4.

If you attach a Plug and Play printer to your computer while Windows is not running, you'll see a message similar to this one the next time you start Windows.

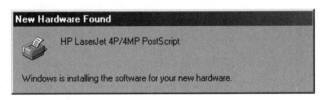

Installing a Non–Plug and Play Printer

To begin installing a printer that does not support the Plug and Play standard, or to create a new logical printer using a physical output device that's already installed, start by doing the following:

1 Open your Printers folder and launch Add Printer. This brings you to the Add Printer wizard.

2 Click Next to get to the wizard's second screen.

This brings you to the screen shown in Figure 7-5, on the next page. At this point, if the printer you're installing is physically connected to your own computer, choose the Local Printer option. Otherwise, choose Network Printer. Then click Next again.

FIGURE 7-5.
Windows provides a
wizard to assist you
with printer installa-
tion.

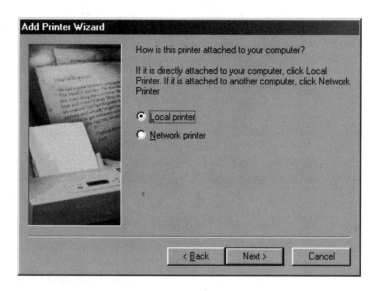

> **NOTE**
>
> The term *network printer* means a printer attached to some other computer.
> If the printer is attached to the machine you're typing at, that's a local
> printer—even if the printer is to be shared with others.

If your choice was Local Printer, the next thing you see will be the screen
shown in Figure 7-6.

FIGURE 7-6.
Windows supports
hundreds of printers.
Odds are you'll find
your make and model
in these two list boxes.

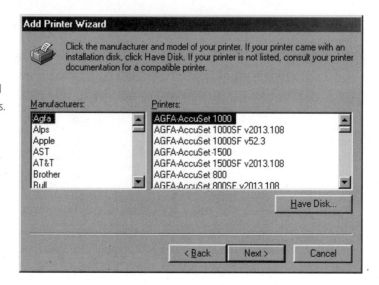

If your choice was Network Printer, you will be asked for the location of your network printer and whether you intend to use this printer with MS-DOS–based programs as well as Windows-based programs. (If you answer Yes, the wizard lets you assign a port to this printer, something required by most MS-DOS–based programs.) For the printer location, you can either supply a network path specification or click the Browse button and find the printer server in a hierarchical diagram of your network. After you've supplied this information, if the printer server is a machine running Windows 95, Windows 98, or Windows NT, the appropriate printer driver will be copied from the server to your own computer. Otherwise, you will arrive at the screen shown in Figure 7-6.

Choosing a Printer Driver

In the screen shown in Figure 7-6, you indicate the make and model of your printer so that Windows can install the appropriate driver for your printer.

After you've made your selections in the list boxes shown in Figure 7-6, Windows might prompt you to insert the Windows CD so that it can copy the necessary files to your system. If the required driver is already present on your hard disk, the wizard asks your permission to use it. (Knowing that your intention may be to install an updated version of the driver, the wizard does not assume it should use the existing driver.)

What to Do If Your Printer Isn't on the List

If your printer isn't on the list of supported printers shown in Figure 7-6, you might want to contact the printer vendor to see if a driver for Windows 98 is available. If you can obtain a driver, repeat the steps that brought you to Figure 7-6. Then click Have Disk and follow the prompts to direct the Add Printer wizard to your driver file.

If no driver is available, check your printer documentation to see if your printer emulates another printer make and model—one for which a Windows 98 driver is available. If your printer can emulate a supported printer, use the emulation mode and select the supported driver in the dialog box shown in Figure 7-6.

Specifying a Port for Your Printer

After you select a driver and supply the necessary source media, click Next. This takes you to the screen shown in Figure 7-7, on the next page.

II

Further Explorations

FIGURE 7-7.

After you select a printer driver, the wizard needs to know which port your printer is connected to.

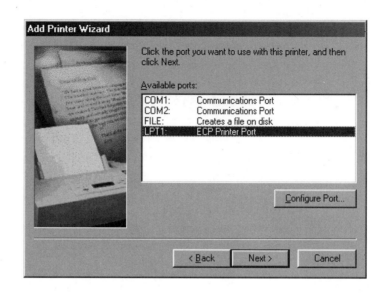

Here you tell Windows what port to use. (The *port* provides the physical link between your computer and your printer.)

If you're installing a network printer, you won't see the screen shown in Figure 7-7. Instead, you'll skip ahead to the printer-naming screen. See "Name That Printer," on the next page.

The ports most commonly used for printing are LPT1: (or LPT with some other number) for a printer that uses a parallel cable and COM1: (or COM with some other number) for a printer that uses a serial cable. If you select a COM port, you should also click the Configure Port button and make sure the communications settings (bits per second, data bits, parity, stop bits, and flow control) are correct for your printer. Consult your printer's documentation if you're not sure what settings to use. (Note: *bits per second* might be called *baud rate* in your printer's documentation.)

Printing to a Disk File

To send your output to a disk file, select FILE: as your printer port. Windows will prompt for a filename whenever you print. You can copy the resulting disk file to a physical printer at a later time by running MS-DOS Prompt. For example, if you have a physical printer attached to

LPT1:, you can copy a print file to that printer by choosing MS-DOS Prompt from the Start menu's Programs submenu. Then, at the MS-DOS command prompt, type

```
copy filename lpt1:
```

where "filename" is the name of the file you want to print. The print-to-file option is also useful if the machine on which you ultimately intend to print is not attached to your network—for example, if you plan to use a service bureau to generate high-resolution PostScript output.

 TIP

> If you sometimes want to print to a physical printer and sometimes to a file, you can change the port setting as needed by visiting the properties dialog box for your printer. (See "Inspecting and Setting Printer Properties," below). Alternatively, you can set up two printers using the same driver. Assign one printer to a physical port and one to FILE:.

Name That Printer

After you choose a port and click Next, the wizard asks you to name your new printer. The name you choose here will appear under the printer icon in your Printers folder, as well as in your programs' Print dialog boxes.

Printing a Test Page

As a final step in the installation process, you can ask the wizard to send a test page to your new printer. This is a good idea. If you've made any incorrect choices in the wizard's dialog boxes (such as choosing the wrong port), it's better to find out now rather than when you're trying to generate some real output.

Inspecting and Setting Printer Properties

The most crucial questions regarding printer setup—the printer driver and the port to be used—get resolved at the time the printer is installed. The decisions you make in these matters are recorded in your printer's properties dialog box, which you can inspect by right-clicking the printer's icon in your Printers folder and choosing Properties. They're also recorded in the Windows registry so the information is available to inquiring programs.

The properties dialog box stores many additional choices, however, that affect the behavior of your printer. It's a good idea to visit the properties dialog box after installing a new printer to make sure all options are set as you want them. You might also have occasion to change properties as you work.

Many of the property options, such as the choice between portrait and landscape orientation, are merely defaults that you can override from within your programs. For example, if you normally print in portrait mode but occasionally need to generate a report in landscape, you don't need to change the property setting; you can simply select landscape mode using your program's Page Setup (or equivalent) command. Other matters, however, such as whether to use separator pages, can only be specified via the properties dialog box.

Property options vary from printer to printer. In the next several pages we survey some of the most important options you're likely to find in your printer's properties dialog box.

Providing a Comment

On the General tab in most printer properties dialog boxes, you can enter a comment describing the printer. This information appears in the Print dialog box, shown in Figure 7-2, on page 188. Figure 7-8 shows an example of the General tab.

Using Separator Pages

A separator page is like a fax cover sheet. It separates one print job from the next and identifies the person who sent the job, the time it was sent, and the name of the document printed. On the General tab in a printer's properties dialog box, you can choose between two styles of separator pages: full and simple. The full page uses large type and is adorned with the Windows logo. The simple page provides the same information in humble 12-point Courier New. If you don't fancy either of these built-in separator pages, you can click the Browse button and choose your own. Any file in the Windows metafile format (.WMF) can serve as a separator page.

Separator pages can be assigned only to local printers. If you're the only one using the printer, you probably don't need separator pages. But if you plan to share the printer, and particularly if you anticipate a high

FIGURE 7-8.
On the General tab in
a printer's properties
dialog box, you can
describe the printer,
choose a separator
page, and print a test
page.

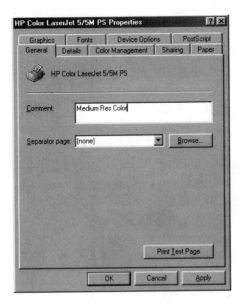

volume of network use, those with whom you share it will probably
appreciate having separator pages.

> Separator pages are printed *before* each print job. If you're printing a special
> form, such as a sheet of checks, be sure your printer has a blank sheet of paper
> on top of the form.

Changing the Port

Should you ever need to change the port for a printer, you can do that
on the Details tab in the printer's properties dialog box. (See Figure 7-9,
on the next page.) Simply open the drop-down list labeled "Print to the
following port," and select a different port. If you want to add a new port
(such as a network port), click Add Port.

Changing Drivers

If by any chance you've installed the wrong driver for your printer, you
can fix the problem by going to the Details tab in the printer's properties
dialog box. Click the New Driver button, and Windows displays the list of
printer manufacturers and models shown in Figure 7-6, on page 198.

II

Further Explorations

FIGURE 7-9.
The Details tab in a printer's properties dialog box lets you change ports, drivers, and timeout settings.

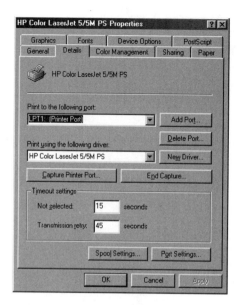

Printer vendors often update their printer drivers. To get the maximum functionality from your printer, be sure you're using the latest version of the driver. If you acquire a later version, install it by going to the Details tab in your printer's properties dialog box. Click the New Driver button, and then click Have Disk when the list of printer manufacturers and models appears.

Changing Timeout Settings

The Details tab in a printer's properties dialog box includes two timeout settings. These affect the behavior of your system when, for some reason, Windows is unable to communicate with your printer.

The Not Selected value sets the length of time that Windows waits before notifying you that your printer is unplugged, turned off, or offline. The default value of 15 seconds is reasonable; it gives you a chance to switch the printer on if you notice after issuing a Print command that it's turned off.

The Transmission Retry value sets the length of time Windows waits if the printer is online but "busy." Printers can't handle information as fast as computers can send it to them. They store data in memory buffers while they print, and when the buffer gets full, they send a signal to the computer to hold up until further notice. When they're ready for more, they send another signal, telling the computer to resume. The default Transmission Retry setting of 45 seconds means that Windows will give up and issue an error message if it doesn't get a resume signal from the printer after 45 seconds of waiting. This should be ample, except possibly under one of the following conditions:

- If you're using a serial port; serial ports don't transmit data as quickly as parallel ports

- If you're printing to a network printer and there's a lot of network traffic

- If you're printing complex graphics, which take longer to process than text

If you find yourself getting timeout error messages when nothing is wrong, try increasing the Transmission Retry setting.

NOTE

PostScript printers have a different set of timeout defaults. To adjust those timeout settings, click the PostScript tab in the properties dialog box.

Sharing a Printer

The Sharing tab in a printer's properties dialog box lets you make a printer available to other network users. If you want, you can include a comment and a password on this part of the properties dialog box. The comment appears in details view when you use Windows Explorer or Network Neighborhood to view the printer. You can use the password to limit access to particular users.

TIP

You can get directly to the Sharing tab by right-clicking the printer's icon in the Printers folder. Then choose Sharing.

II

Further Explorations

> You can share only printers that are connected to your computer. You can't share a network printer that you've installed, nor can you share a printer that's connected to FILE:.
>
> If the properties dialog box for your local printer doesn't have a Sharing tab, you need to enable printer sharing. Launch Network in Control Panel. On the Configuration tab in the Network dialog box, click File And Print Sharing. In the dialog box that appears, select the check box labeled "I want to be able to allow others to print to my printer(s)." Click OK in each dialog box and then restart your computer.

Changing the Default Paper Size, Paper Source, Orientation, and Number of Copies

Most printers print 8½-inch by 11-inch sheets of paper by default but can accommodate a variety of other sizes as well. To change paper size, go to the Paper tab in the printer's properties dialog box.

On the Paper tab, you can also specify the default paper source (upper tray or lower tray, for example) and the default orientation—portrait or landscape. Depending on the printer you use, you might find additional options here—such as the number of copies printed by default, duplexing (two-sided printing) control, and even the ability to shrink images to fit two or four pages on a single sheet of paper.

TIP

> Don't change the Copies option in your printer's properties dialog box unless you want multiple copies for all printouts. If you want only certain reports printed in multiple copies, use your program to specify the number you want.

Changing Default Resolution, Dithering Options, and Intensity

Most printers allow you to choose between two or more resolutions for printing graphics. These options are expressed in terms of the number of dots per inch the printer creates. To change resolution, go to the Graphics tab in the printer's property sheet. (See Figure 7-10.)

II

Further Explorations

FIGURE 7-10.
The Graphics tab in a printer's properties dialog box lets you change resolution, dithering style, and intensity.

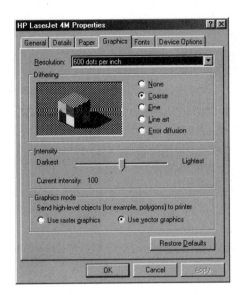

Some printers include a set of dithering options labeled None, Coarse, Fine, Line Art, and Error Diffusion. These settings govern the way Windows prints bitmap images on black-and-white printers.

Dithering is a process by which a device, such as a printer or video display, approximates colors that it cannot generate directly. When you print a color bitmap on a monochromatic printer, the printer driver uses dithering to translate colors other than black and white into shades of gray. The dithering options available with certain drivers govern the method by which these drivers do their dithering. The Rubik's cube in the center of the properties dialog box shows you what effect different options have.

In general, you'll probably want to avoid the None and Line Art choices, except in special circumstances. (You might choose None if you want to emphasize contrast in a printout at the expense of shades of gray.) When a bitmap image has closely related colors, those colors will usually be easiest to distinguish if you print with the Coarse setting. But the best policy is to experiment. Try all the options to see what generates the most satisfactory results with your images and your printer.

Specifying Font Cartridges

If your printer supports font cartridges, you can indicate which ones you're using by going to the Fonts tab in the printer's properties dialog box.

Printing TrueType Fonts as Graphics

The Fonts tab in the properties dialog box for many printers includes an option that lets you print TrueType fonts as graphics. Normally, Windows downloads TrueType font information to your printer's memory. This default setting lets your printer print documents in the shortest possible time. Under one circumstance, however, you might want to override the default and have your text printed as a page of bitmap graphics.

If your document includes graphic objects overlying text, downloading the fonts might cause the text to "bleed through" the graphics, producing a document that doesn't match what you see on screen. For example, if you print a Microsoft Excel document that includes a chart embedded on the worksheet, text that is not visible on screen might appear in your printout.

To correct this problem, select the Print TrueType As Graphics option on the Fonts tab in the printer's properties dialog box. Note that printing TrueType fonts as graphics slows your printer down considerably because Windows must compute a bitmap for the entire printed page (instead of relying on your printer's intelligence to render the text).

Specifying the Amount of Memory in Your Printer

If your printer supports different amounts of memory, it's important for Windows to know how much memory is installed. Otherwise, you might get unnecessary out-of-memory error messages when printing complex graphics. You can check, and change if necessary, the memory setting by visiting the Device Options tab in your printer's properties dialog box.

CHAPTER 8

Installing and Using Fonts

One of the great advantages of creating text documents in a graphical operating environment such as Windows is that you can employ a variety of fonts and typographical styles and judge their impact before committing your work to paper. Within limits, and with some exceptions, what you see on screen is what you'll get from any output device, whether it be a dot-matrix printer, a laser printer, a plotter, or a fax machine.

Windows puts typography at your disposal. Using it well, however, can be a challenge. To help you meet this challenge, this chapter begins with an overview of basic terminology. Then we'll look at the procedures for adding and deleting fonts, getting better acquainted with the fonts you have, using them in your documents, and using some of the special characters—accented letters, commercial symbols, and so on—that are included with most fonts but can't be accessed with normal typewriter keystrokes.

Terminology

A *font* is a complete set of characters in one typeface design. For example, all the letters, numbers, punctuation marks, and other symbols available in Courier New constitute one font.

Text is further identified by its font size, weight, and style. In the name "12-point Courier New bold italic," for example, 12-point is the font size, Courier New is the font, bold is the weight, and italic is the style. When the weight is "normal" and the style is "roman," these terms are usually omitted.

Font Size

A font's size is usually measured in points and expressed as a "point size." A *point* is a printer's measurement, equal to 1/12 of a *pica*. (A pica, in turn, is 1/6 of an inch, so there are 72 points in an inch.) A font's point size is approximately the distance in points from the top of its highest character to the bottom of its lowest character, as shown in Figure 8-1. (This definition applies to a font's printed size only. On screen, point size has no absolute significance at all because of the differences in screen size and resolution. For example, a 10-point font on a 17-inch screen at 640×480 resolution will probably be larger than a 12-point font on a 14-inch screen at 800×600 resolution.)

FIGURE 8-1.
A font's point size is a measure of its height—from the top of its highest character to the bottom of its lowest.

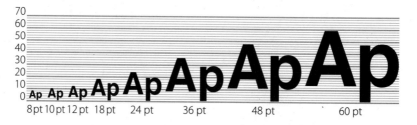

Point size is a rough measure of a font's height but says nothing about its width. Many font families come in *compressed* and *expanded* variants, as well as normal width. Some programs, such as desktop publishing programs and sophisticated word processors, allow you to squeeze characters closer together without changing their individual widths. This process, called *kerning*, can change the apparent width of a font, creating a denser look and allowing you to put more words on a line. Some programs also allow you to add extra increments of space between characters, a process called *letterspacing*.

Style and Weight

The most common *style* variants for fonts are roman and italic. Roman characters are the "normal" kind, with vertical strokes predominating. Italic characters, which are forward slanting and often more rounded, are used for emphasis, for book titles, and so on.

The term *weight* refers to the thickness of a font's strokes. The most common weights are normal (also called regular) and bold, but some font families also include other weights, such as thin, light, heavy, ultra, and black.

Serif and Sans Serif Fonts

Most fonts fall into one of two categories—*serif* or *sans serif*. Serif fonts have fine lines that finish off the main strokes—for example, at the bottom of a capital *T* and at the ends of the *T*'s crossbar. These "finishing strokes," called serifs, are absent in sans serif fonts, such as the font used for the headings in this book. Serif fonts, such as Times New Roman, are generally considered more suitable for conventional text, such as that in a newspaper or book. Sans serif fonts, such as Helvetica and Arial, have a more modern appearance and are often used in headlines, tabular material (such as spreadsheet reports), and advertising.

Monospaced and Proportionally Spaced Fonts

Fonts in which every character takes up the same amount of space are called *monospaced*. Fonts in which some characters (such as *m* and *w*) are wider than others (*i* and *t*, for example) are called *proportionally spaced*. (See Figure 8-2, on the next page.) Proportionally spaced fonts produce a more typeset appearance and are generally considered easier to read. Monospaced fonts are often preferred for such things as legal documents, which have traditionally been produced on typewriters.

II

Further Explorations

FIGURE 8-2.

In proportionally spaced fonts, characters have different widths. In monospaced fonts, all characters have the same width.

Microsoft Windows 98

Proportionally spaced

Microsoft Windows 98

Monospaced

Arial and Times New Roman are examples of proportionally spaced fonts. Windows 98 includes two monospaced fonts: Courier New and Lucida Console.

Keep in mind that although the widths of letters in a proportionally spaced font vary, the widths of numerals are usually all the same so that numbers can be aligned in tables.

Scalable and Nonscalable Fonts

Fonts can also be described as *scalable* or *nonscalable*. Scalable fonts are those for which a single master can produce any point size. Nonscalable fonts are designed for use at particular sizes; enlarging or reducing them generally produces unattractive distortions, such as serrated diagonal lines and jagged curves.

Nonscalable fonts are also sometimes called *bitmap fonts* because the form in which they're stored on your hard disk (or in a printer's read-only memory) records the relative position of each dot comprising each character. For example, a capital *I* might be stored as a column of 12 dots plus two 6-dot crossbars. To generate a character from a bitmap font, your screen or printer simply reproduces the bitmap at the desired location.

Scalable fonts are sometimes called *outline fonts* because they are stored as a collection of outlines; an outline is a mathematical description of each character. To generate a character from an outline font, font-management software uses a process called *scan conversion* to convert the outlines to bitmaps, which are then reproduced on your screen or printer. To avoid jagged lines and other distortions in the final rendering, particularly at smaller point sizes, the font-management software employs *hints*—algorithms that modify the scan-conversion process to produce optimal-looking characters.

Because outline fonts are stored as mathematical descriptions, they can be scaled to a wide range of point sizes. They can also be slanted, rotated, compressed, extended, inverted, and otherwise manipulated.

Their *metrics* (character-width specifications) can also be modified to produce kerned or letterspaced typography. The one small disadvantage of outline fonts is that the scan-conversion process takes a modest amount of processing time. The first time you use an outline font at a given point size, therefore, you might encounter a slight delay while your system performs the calculation required to convert the font's outline into the appropriate set of bitmaps. After the bitmaps have been rendered, however, they're stored in an area of memory called a *cache*. When you need to reuse the font, Windows simply grabs the bitmaps out of the cache, thereby avoiding the original calculation delay.

Fonts Supplied with Windows

Incorporated into Windows 98 is a scalable font technology called TrueType. Along with this font-management technology, Windows includes several TrueType font families, including the ones shown below.

Arial	No one should drive a hard bargain with an
Comic Sans MS	No one should drive a hard bargain with
Impact	No one should drive a hard bargain with an artist
Lucida Console	No one should drive a hard
Tahoma	No one should drive a hard bargain with an
Verdana	No one should drive a hard bargain
Times New Roman	No one should drive a hard bargain with an artist.
Courier New	No one should drive a hard
Symbol	Νο ονε σηουλδ δριϖε α ηαρδ βαργαιν ωιτη
Webdings	👁 ⚓ 🏖 ?🚍 📧✈ 🛡 ✗ⓘ🚍 🏢 ✔
Wingdings	♟□ □■♏ ♦〰□◆●♌ ♌□✴✦♏ ♋

In addition to the TrueType families, Windows also includes five bitmap fonts—MS Serif, MS Sans Serif, Courier, Symbol, and Small Fonts—to provide compatibility with earlier versions of Windows. (MS Serif was previously known as Helv, and MS Serif is the former TmsRmn.) They're available only in certain point sizes, and you can't use them with laser printers.

Along with this assortment of font resources, you might find additional fonts on your system, courtesy of particular programs that you have installed. Any font installed by a program is available not only in that program but also in any other Windows-based program you run.

Your Printer's Own Font Resources

? SEE ALSO

For information about printer drivers, see "Installing a New Printer," page 196.

In addition to the fonts that Windows supplies and any additional fonts that you install in Windows, you can use your printer's internal fonts. Your printer driver tells Windows which fonts the printer provides, and those fonts appear in the Font dialog boxes used by your programs.

When you use your printer's internal fonts, Windows doesn't have to download font information or turn each page of your document into a bitmap (a time-consuming process), so printing is likely to be quicker. In exchange for this speed increase, however, you might have to sacrifice some degree of correspondence between the appearance of your document on screen and its appearance on paper.

When you format a document with an internal printer font, Windows displays the same font on screen if it can. If Windows does not have a screen font to match the printer font you select, it gives you the closest match that it can. For example, if you choose the Courier font that's built into your printer, Windows formats your text on screen using its own TrueType Courier font (Courier New). If you select your PostScript printer's Avant Garde font (and you have not installed Adobe Type Manager and the Avant Garde screen font), Windows uses Arial, the nearest TrueType equivalent, on screen.

Even when the screen font used by Windows doesn't exactly match the printer font you select, Windows-based programs attempt to show you where your lines will break on the printed page. The correspondence of line endings on screen to line endings on paper might not always be perfect, however, and some programs do a better job of this than others. If precise text positioning is critical, it's always best to avoid printer fonts that don't have equivalent screen fonts.

Viewing and Printing Font Samples

To see samples of the fonts installed in your system, start by opening the Fonts folder, which is stored in your Windows folder. The easiest way to open the folder is to launch its shortcut in Control Panel. To open Control

Panel, choose Settings from the Start menu, and then choose Control
Panel. Figure 8-3 shows an example of a Fonts folder.

FIGURE 8-3.

To see samples of your
fonts, install new fonts,
or delete fonts, open
your Fonts folder.

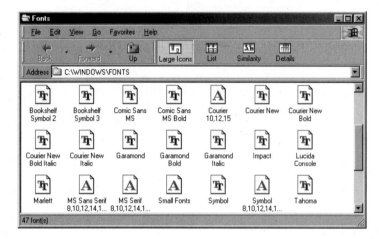

NOTE

PostScript fonts rendered by Adobe Type Manager do not appear in your
Fonts folder. To see samples of these fonts, use Adobe Type Manager.

The icons with two *T*s represent TrueType fonts; those with an *A*
represent nonscalable fonts. The point sizes for which these nonscalable
fonts were designed are usually included with the font name.

To see a sample of any font, simply double-click its icon—or right-click the
icon and choose Open from the context menu. As Figure 8-4 on the next
page shows, the ensuing window displays the font at various point sizes.

To print the font sample, click the Print button.

Viewing Options in the Fonts Folder

Like an ordinary file folder window, the Fonts folder offers icon, list, and
details views of your font library. You can choose these options from the
Standard Buttons toolbar or the View menu. In addition, the Fonts folder
offers two other viewing options: List Fonts By Similarity and Hide
Variations. These options are also available on the View menu.

Further Explorations

FIGURE 8-4.

Double-clicking a font icon produces a printable sample of the font at various point sizes.

The List Fonts By Similarity option lets you find all the fonts in your library that are similar to some other font. As Figure 8-5 shows, when you choose this option, a drop-down list of your fonts appears below the toolbar. Your font library appears in the window listed in order of decreasing similarity to the font selected in the drop-down list.

FIGURE 8-5.

In this "similarity" view, fonts are listed in order of decreasing similarity to Arial.

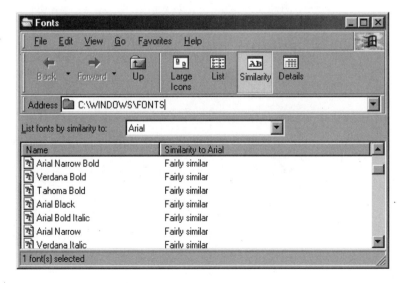

If you choose Hide Variations, Windows displays only one font from each font family. For example, suppose your Fonts folder includes Arial, Arial Bold, Arial Italic, and Arial Bold Italic. If you choose Hide Variations, the list shows only Arial. This option, which you may use in any viewing mode, is particularly handy when you have a large font library

Adding Fonts

Scalable TrueType fonts, in addition to the ones supplied with Windows, are available from Microsoft and numerous other vendors. When you acquire an additional font, you need to install it so that Windows knows it's available.

To install a new font, simply open the Fonts folder and choose Install New Font from the File menu. You'll be greeted by the Add Fonts dialog box, shown in Figure 8-6.

FIGURE 8-6.

The Add Fonts dialog box makes it easy to expand your font library.

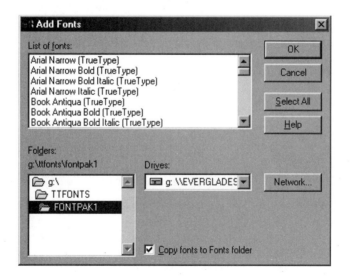

Use the Drives and Folders sections of this dialog box to indicate where the fonts you want to install are currently stored. For example, if your new fonts are on a floppy disk in drive A, select drive A in the Drives list. The names of all fonts available for installation will then appear in the top section of the dialog box. Choose Select All if you want to install the whole lot. To install particular fonts, hold down the Ctrl key while you select the fonts you want.

When you're finished selecting fonts, click OK. In a moment your new fonts will appear in your Fonts folder and will be available for use in your programs.

 TIP

Drag and Drop to Install

You can also use drag and drop to add fonts to your system. For example, if you have a new font stored in a folder named Download, you can install that font as follows: Display both the Download folder and the Fonts folder. Then drag the font icon from the Download folder to the Fonts folder.

To Copy or Not to Copy?

If you're installing fonts from a floppy disk, be sure to select the Copy Fonts To Fonts Folder check box in the Add Fonts dialog box. Windows then copies your font files to the Fonts folder, a subfolder of your Windows folder. If the fonts you're installing are already stored in another folder on your hard disk, Windows duplicates the font files in the Fonts folder.

If you prefer to keep your fonts in other folders (for example, in a folder that you use for downloading files from the Internet), you can do so. Simply deselect the Copy Fonts To Fonts Folder check box. Windows will remember which folder you installed your fonts from, and, provided you don't rename or move that folder, your fonts will still be available to your programs.

 TIP

It's always a good idea to select the Copy Fonts To Fonts Folder check box. That way, you're unlikely to delete font files inadvertently.

Deleting Fonts

To "deinstall" a font, simply remove it from your Fonts folder. You can do that by deleting the font icon or by moving the icon to another folder. If you delete a font icon, Windows stores the font in your Recycle Bin, so you can restore it if you change your mind.

Using Fonts in Documents

 SEE ALSO

For information about the Script drop-down in the Font dialog box, see "Installing Language Support and Using Keyboard Layouts," page 256.

To use fonts in your documents, simply follow standard Windows editing procedures: select the text you want to format, and then choose your program's Font command. (You'll find it on the Format menu in most programs.) In many programs you can also select fonts by right-clicking the selected text and choosing Font from the context menu that appears, or by clicking icons on a toolbar.

In many programs, choosing the Font command brings you to a dialog box similar to the one shown in Figure 8-7. This dialog box, shown here in the form used by WordPad, is one of the Windows "common dialogs," so you can expect to see close approximations of it in many Windows-based programs. Notice that you can use it to choose color and two special effects, strikeout and underlining, in addition to font, style, and size.

FIGURE 8-7.

The standard Font dialog box lets you choose font, style, size, color, and special effects.

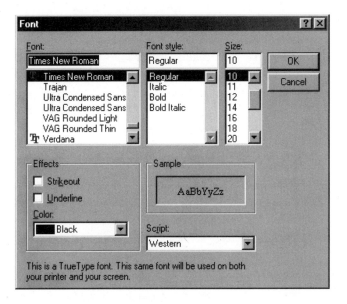

Embedding TrueType Fonts

If you create documents that will be read on other computers, it's a good idea to stick with fonts that all your readers are likely to have. The safest ones to use are Arial, Courier New, and Times New Roman—the sans serif, monospaced, and serif faces shipped with all versions of Windows since 1992.

What happens if a reader's system does not have one of the fonts used by your document? For example, suppose you've formatted your entire report in Bozo Bold, but you're the only one in your company who's installed the Bozo family? In that case, Windows substitutes a closely related font on your reader's system. For example, assuming Bozo is a serif face, your reader will probably see Times New Roman on his or her computer. (You can get an idea what fonts Windows considers "similar" by opening your Fonts folder and using the View menu's List Fonts By Similarity command.)

If it's crucial that all readers see your document in the exact fonts you've used, check to see if the program you used to create the document supports TrueType font embedding. If the program can embed the TrueType fonts your document uses, your document will include a copy of the font file for each TrueType font you use. Your readers will then see your document with its original fonts. And, unless the document has read-only status, they'll be able to edit with those fonts as well.

Note that embedding TrueType fonts adds greatly to the size of your document. A 5-KB report, for example, might easily grow to 50 KB with only one font embedded. If you use italic and bold, along with regular roman, your document could swell another 100 KB or so. Although most TrueType fonts can be embedded, font manufacturers can disable that capability. Therefore, always check to make sure a font is embeddable before you do any work that depends on this capability. (You can tell if your font is being embedded by comparing the size of the same document saved with and without embedding.)

TIP

Embedding Fonts in Microsoft Word Documents

If you're using Microsoft Word 6.0 or later, you can turn on embedding by choosing the Options command from the Tools menu, clicking the Save tab, and selecting the Embed TrueType Fonts check box. Note that this setting is file-specific—that is, changing it for one document does not affect other documents.

TIP

> **Embedding Fonts in Other Programs**
> To see if a program offers TrueType embedding, use the program's Help facility's Search command to search for "TrueType."

Note that TrueType embedding has nothing to do with OLE. A program that supports OLE may or may not offer TrueType embedding, and one that offers TrueType embedding may or may not support OLE.

Fonts and Character Sets

Most Windows fonts use a common character layout known as the eight-bit American National Standards Institute (ANSI) character set. This is simply a table in which each character in the font is mapped to a particular number from 0 through 255. Because characters in your documents are recorded using their ANSI numbers, and because most fonts use the ANSI scheme, switching text from one font to another usually produces no change in the identity of the characters.

You should be aware, however, that the ANSI character set used by most Windows fonts is not the same as the "extended ASCII" character set used by most MS-DOS–based programs. The letters *A* through *Z* in uppercase and lowercase, the numerals 0 through 9, and the common punctuation symbols are mapped to the same values in both ANSI and extended ASCII. But the two systems diverge widely for accented letters and other special symbols.

SEE ALSO

For more information about using the Clipboard to copy text, see "What the Cut, Copy, Paste, and Paste Special Commands Do," page 228.

When you copy text to the Clipboard from most Windows-based programs, the text is stored on the Clipboard in at least two formats, called Text and OEM Text. The inclusion of the OEM Text format, in most cases, allows you to copy symbols from a Windows-based program to the Clipboard, and then to paste those symbols (unchanged) into an MS-DOS–based program.

For example, if you copy the letter *a* with a circumflex accent from Word for Windows to the Clipboard, and then paste this character into an MS-DOS–based program, you will still get an *â* in your MS-DOS–based program—even though this character is mapped to the value 226 in the ANSI character set and the value 131 in the extended ASCII set. Windows takes care of the translation for you. A similar conversion process takes place automatically when you copy text via the Clipboard from an MS-DOS–based program to a Windows-based program.

Using Character Map

Character Map, one of the accessory programs included with Windows, is a utility that shows you the character set of each of your fonts. You'll find Character Map invaluable when you need to work with a non-ANSI font (such as Symbol or Wingdings), and when you need accented letters, commercial symbols, and other characters that are not available on the standard typewriter keys of your keyboard. Character Map's initial display is shown in Figure 8-8.

FIGURE 8-8.

Character Map helps you find and use special characters in any font.

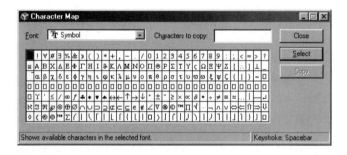

> **NOTE**
>
> If Character Map has not been set up on your computer, launch Add/Remove Programs in Control Panel, click the Windows Setup tab, select System Tools, and click the Details button. Select Character Map and click OK two times.

In the top left corner of the window is a drop-down list in which you can select any font available on your system. Below the list is a table displaying all the characters available in the selected font. You can't change the size of the Character Map window (other than to minimize it), but you can get an enlarged view of any character by selecting it with the mouse or the keyboard.

To select a character with the mouse, simply click the character. To select a character with the keyboard, press Tab until the highlight is in the character grid. Then use the arrow keys to move the highlight. Figure 8-9 shows how Character Map looks when the copyright symbol in the TrueType font Times New Roman is selected.

FIGURE 8-9.

To get an enlarged view of any character, simply select it.

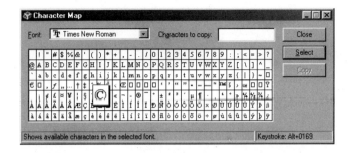

The panel in the lower right corner of the Character Map window tells you how you can produce any character using the keyboard. For example, in Figure 8-9, the panel reads "Keystroke: Alt+0169." This means that in most Windows-based programs, you can get a copyright symbol in Times New Roman by doing the following:

1 Use your program's formatting commands to specify Times New Roman as your font.

2 Hold down the Alt key.

3 Type *0169* on the numeric keypad (not on the row of numbers at the top of your keyboard).

4 Release the Alt key.

If you don't want to type Alt-key sequences, you can generate special characters with the help of Character Map's Select and Copy commands. For example, you can enter a copyright symbol or another character in your document by doing the following:

1 Be sure the Characters To Copy box (in the upper right corner of the Character Map window) is blank. If it is not blank, clear it by selecting whatever is currently there and pressing the Delete key.

2 Use the mouse or keyboard to select the copyright symbol or other character in the main part of the Character Map window.

3 Click the Select button or press Enter.

As an alternative to steps 2 and 3, you can simply double-click the copyright symbol.

4 Click the Copy button to copy the contents of the Characters To Copy box to the Clipboard.

II

Further Explorations

5 Activate your word processor or other program and use its Paste command.

You can use this method to copy more than one character at a time. Each time you click the Select button, Character Map adds the current character to the end of the character sequence in the Characters To Copy text box.

Exchanging Information Using the Clipboard and OLE

I n the bad old early days of desktop computing, transferring information from one program to another was a process beset with difficulties. In that time before Windows, users who wanted to build "compound documents"—documents with elements derived from two or more programs—often had to rely on clumsy TSR (terminate-and-stay-resident) utilities to act as data-moving intermediaries between programs. The dearth of file-format standards and the absence of treaties governing relations among programs that shared memory made the exchange of information frustrating and perilous. Single-program documents were the norm, and a compound document was usually something assembled by a pasteup artist.

Nowadays, compound documents have become so normal that the term itself has fallen into disuse. Windows users expect to be able to move text, graphics, sound, and video freely within and between documents and are seldom disappointed. In Windows 98, the process of generating what used to be called a compound document is easier than ever, thanks both to improvements in the Windows user interface and the growing prevalence of a standard called OLE (pronounced *olay*, with the stress on the second syllable) object technology.

In this chapter, we'll examine the methods and mechanisms for moving information between and within programs.

Servers, Clients, Sources, Destinations, Objects, Containers (and All That Jazz)

There are two parties to any OLE transaction. One party supplies the goods, the other receives them. For example, if you take a range from an Excel spreadsheet and embed it in a PowerPoint presentation, you have a supplying document (the Excel spreadsheet) and a receiving document (the PowerPoint presentation).

In OLE parlance, the supplying document is called the *OLE server*, or the *source*. The receiving document is known as the *OLE client*, the *destination*, or the *container*. The goods, whatever they may be, are known simply as the *object*.

The terms *server* and *client*, of course, are also used in the context of networking. A server is a shared resource, typically a hard disk on a computer dedicated to storing files needed by many different users. A client is a computer that connects to a server. To minimize confusion in this book, we'll stick with *source* and *destination* when the subject is OLE, reserving *server* and *client* for their more traditional networking meanings.

Data Exchange: A Symphony with Three Movements

Three forms of data exchange are common in Windows:

- Static moving and copying

- Embedding

- Linking

A *static* move or copy is a one-time transaction with a no-return policy. If you copy or cut a range of numbers from your spreadsheet and paste them statically into your word processor document, your word processor handles those numbers exactly as though you had typed them directly at the keyboard. You can format them, edit them, delete them, or stand them on their heads (if your word processor does that sort of thing), but they have no further relationship to the document and program in which they originated.

? SEE ALSO

For more information about embedding, see "How to Embed," page 233.

When you *embed* one document's data in a second document, the data remembers where it came from. If you want to edit that data, Windows lets you work in the data's original context. For example, suppose you copy a block of numbers from a spreadsheet and embed them in a word processing document. When you want to edit those numbers, the original spreadsheet program reappears, allowing you to use its commands, instead of your word processor's, to do your editing.

? SEE ALSO

For more information about linking, see "How to Link," page 236.

When you *link* one document's data to a second document, the data you link is not actually stored in the receiving document. Instead, the receiving program stores a visual representation of the data plus information about where the data came from. Continuing with our spreadsheet–word processor example, if you use a linking command to paste the spreadsheet numbers into your word processor document, the numbers look exactly as if you typed them in at the keyboard. But when you save that document to a disk file, the file does not include the numbers. Instead, it includes everything Windows needs to know in order to find those numbers again the next time you open the file. If you change the numbers in the spreadsheet, your changes also appear in your word processor document.

Embedding and linking also have one other important virtue: they allow you to incorporate material into your documents that your documents cannot render directly. For example, you can embed or link a sound annotation or a video clip into documents created by most word processors, database managers, and spreadsheet programs. Those programs display an icon to indicate where the sound or video has been embedded

II

Further Explorations

or linked. When you want to hear the sound or see the video, you simply double-click the icon. Windows then renders the object, using the sound or video program in which the object originated. (For more information about working with sound and video, see Chapter 20, "Using the Multimedia Accessories.")

 TIP

Many programs give you the option of displaying embedded or linked data as an icon, even if the program *can* render the data. For example, your word processor might permit you to embed a block of text but display it as an icon. The readers of your document can then skip over the embedded material if they're not interested in it. If they are interested, they can double-click the icon and read the embedded text.

What the Cut, Copy, Paste, and Paste Special Commands Do

As you probably know, the universal method for moving or copying an item from one place to another is as follows:

 SEE ALSO

For information about selecting part of a document, see "Selecting Text," page 38. For information about selecting files and folders, see "Selecting Folders and Files in a Windows Explorer Window," page 126.

1 Select whatever it is you want to move or copy—a block of text, a region within a graphical image, a range of spreadsheet cells, a file in a folder window, or whatever.

2 Choose the Cut command if you want to move the selected object. Choose the Copy command if you want to copy it. In virtually all Windows-based programs, these commands can be found on the Edit menu. In many programs, you can right-click and choose these commands from the context menu.

3 Move to the place where you want the data transferred and choose Paste or Paste Special. Like Cut and Copy, these commands can be found on programs' Edit menus. If you're pasting something onto the desktop or into a folder window, right-click and choose Paste from the context menu.

TIP

> You can save a lot of time by using keyboard shortcuts for Cut, Copy, and Paste. Use Ctrl+X for Cut, Ctrl+C for Copy, and Ctrl+V for Paste.

Now that many programs support moving and copying via drag and drop, this cut-and-paste (or copy-and-paste) sequence is no longer the only way to relocate data in Windows documents. But it's probably still the most commonly used method, so let's take a look at what happens when you use these commands.

 TIP

> You can use Copy and Paste with MS-DOS–based programs as well as Windows-based programs. For more information, see "Using Copy and Paste," page 284.

The Clipboard, Windows' Invisible Transfer Agent

When you select data and use a program's Cut or Copy command, the selected data is stored on the Clipboard, an area of memory used to hold data in transit. When you use a program's Paste command, the Clipboard's data is copied into the program.

 CAUTION

Some programs clear the Clipboard "behind the scenes." Microsoft Excel, for example, often removes its own data from the Clipboard, on its own initiative, after you paste it or execute another command. This is uncommon behavior, however, and you're not likely to see it in most programs you use.

Data on the Clipboard usually remains there until new data arrives to replace it. That means that you can copy or cut something to the Clipboard, and then paste it as many times in as many places as you please. But as soon as you use another Cut or Copy command, the data you were previously pasting disappears from the Clipboard.

Be careful with the Cut command. In most programs, the data you cut disappears from its source document as soon as you use this command. If you get distracted between cutting and pasting and happen to put another item on the Clipboard before pasting the first, you might lose the first item. If you change your mind between cutting something and pasting it, simply paste it back where you cut it. (If the cut item is one or more files or folders in a Windows Explorer window, the selected files or folders remain in place until you paste them in another folder.)

II

Further Explorations

TIP

To move information without disturbing the current Clipboard contents, drag it with the mouse. (Or hold down the Ctrl key as you drag to copy information.) Many Windows-based programs offer some level of drag-and-drop support (within a document, between documents, or even between programs), and this form of data movement bypasses the Clipboard.

Controlling the Outcome with Paste Special

When you cut or copy information from a program, the program supplies the information to the Clipboard in as many formats as it can. If you cut a paragraph in a Microsoft Word document, for example, Word transfers that paragraph to the Clipboard in both text and graphics formats. If you copy a spreadsheet range from Microsoft Excel, the Clipboard receives your selection in a large assortment of formats, including some that allow the data to be exported to other spreadsheet programs.

This multiple-format arrangement allows a program to receive Clipboard data in whichever format best suits it. For example, the fact that a Microsoft Word paragraph is stored on the Clipboard in both graphics and text formats means that you can paste it into Notepad, a program that accepts only text, as well as into other programs that accept only graphics.

The multiple-format arrangement also means that you often have choices about how to paste your data. When you use a program's Paste command, you get whatever format the program thinks you're most likely to want. But in many programs, you can use a Paste Special command and choose an alternative format. Figure 9-1 shows an example of a Paste Special dialog box. In this example, the source data is a range of spreadsheet cells. If you want to paste an image of those cells, rather than the text contained in the cells, you can choose one of the available graphic formats: Picture, Bitmap, or Picture (Enhanced Metafile).

 TIP

The Result section of the Paste Special dialog box often contains information about each available format. This information can help you decide which format to paste.

FIGURE 9-1.

The Paste Special command lets you choose what format to paste, as well as whether to embed, link, or paste statically.

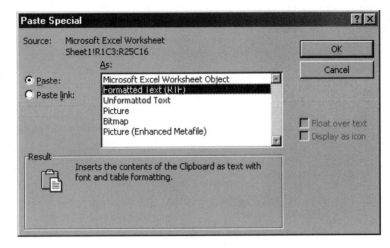

Table 9-1, on the next page, describes some of the data formats you might encounter in your programs' Paste Special dialog boxes.

As we'll see, Paste Special also can be used to control whether Clipboard data is embedded, linked, or pasted statically.

TIP

To view the current contents of the Clipboard, you can use a program called Clipboard Viewer. With commands on Clipboard Viewer's Display menu, you can see what the current Clipboard contents look like in various display formats. To launch Clipboard Viewer, open the Start menu and choose Programs, Accessories, System Tools, Clipboard Viewer. (If Clipboard Viewer has not been installed on your system, launch Add/Remove Programs in Control Panel, click the Windows Setup tab, select System Tools, and click Details.)

NOTE

The ClipBook Viewer program that was included with Windows for Workgroups and Windows NT is not part of Windows 98. To create and share files of Clipboard objects ("clipbook pages," in Windows for Workgroup parlance), use the "scrap" feature. For details, see "Creating Scrap Files," page 243.

II

Further Explorations

TABLE 9-1. **Common Formats for Clipboard Data**

Data Format	Description
Text	Unformatted character information (without style attributes, such as boldface and italics), using the ANSI standard character set used by all Windows-based programs.
Formatted Text (RTF)	A text format that uses embedded codes to store style information, such as bold and italic. Microsoft Excel, Microsoft Word, and a growing number of other programs support rich text format.
Unicode Text	A 16-bit text-encoding format that allows for both Latin and non-Latin alphanumeric characters, plus an assortment of commercial, mathematical, and scientific symbols.
Bitmap	A graphic format in which each pixel in an image is represented by one or more data bits. Unlike a picture or metafile, bitmap data is specific for a given output device. If you display a bitmap on a device with resolution or color capability different from the one on which it was created, you're not likely to be pleased with the result. Also, although bitmap images can be resized or reshaped, this process generally introduces gross distortions.
Picture	A graphic format in which image elements are stored as a sequence of commands. An image in picture format can be reproduced without gross distortion at different sizes or shapes, as well as on different kinds of output devices. But a bitmap image might display more quickly because it doesn't have to be re-created from programmatic instructions. An image in picture format is also sometimes called a metafile (although the terms are not precisely equivalent).
DIB	A device-independent bitmap. This bitmap format eliminates some, but not all, of the device specificity of the standard bitmap format by including information about the color palette and resolution of the originating device.
Link, OwnerLink, ObjectLink	Formats used to establish OLE links between documents.

To Embed, to Link, or Merely to Paste?

Should you embed, should you link, or should you do neither? Here are a few guidelines:

Embedding's advantages are permanence and portability. Because the embedded object actually resides in the receiving program, you don't have to worry about what will happen if the source document becomes unavailable. Thus, for example, you'll want to choose embedding, not linking, if you plan to move the receiving document somewhere where it won't have access to the source document.

Linking's advantages over embedding are two. First, the resulting compound document is smaller because it stores "pointers" only, not the actual source data. Second, changes in the source data can be reflected automatically in the receiving document. You should use linking when you want your compound document to stay current with its component sources over time.

What about plain old-fashioned static pasting? If the documents involved do not support OLE, of course, that is your only choice. For example, if you paste a paragraph from a Notepad document into your word processor, that paragraph arrives as static text because Notepad is a simple program that does not support OLE. Even with OLE source programs, though, there might be occasions when a straightforward static paste is more suitable than a fancy embedded object. Offsetting the convenience of editing an object in its source program, for example, is the time required for Windows to launch that program. If that delay is vexing, don't embed. OLE is a service, not an obligation.

II

Further Explorations

How to Embed

In most cases you can embed an object simply by selecting it in its source document and pasting it into its destination document. That's because, when multiple formats are available on the Clipboard, the format that produces an embedded object is usually the default. It is not *always* the default, however. So if you want to be certain that you're embedding something and not simply pasting it statically, it's a good idea to use the Paste Special command. In the list of available formats presented by the Paste Special dialog box, the one that does the embedding will typically have the word *object* somewhere in its name. When you select that option, the explanatory text at the bottom of the dialog box will probably include words such as "so that you can edit it using," followed by the name of the source program.

Embedding a New Object

The previous paragraph assumes that the object you want to embed already exists somewhere in its source document. But what if it doesn't? Suppose, for example, that you're working in a WordPad document and you want to embed a graphic that doesn't exist yet. In that case, you can go to the Start menu, launch your graphics program, create the object, copy it to the Clipboard, and so on. Alternatively, you can simply use the Object command on WordPad's Insert menu. Figure 9-2 shows the dialog box you will see.

FIGURE 9-2.

To embed an object that doesn't exist yet, you can use the Insert Object command.

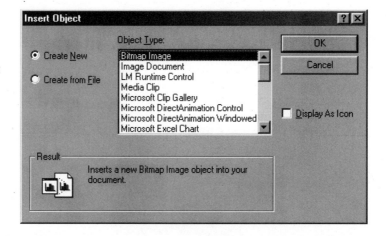

The Object Type list in this dialog box enumerates all the embeddable data types known to the Windows registry. Select the type of object you want to embed, select the Display As Icon check box if you want the embedded object to appear as an icon, and click OK. Windows then either starts the program that's appropriate for the object type you selected or simply displays that program's menus and toolbars. At that point, you can create the object you want to embed. For example, if you are working in WordPad and select Bitmap Image as the object type,

Windows replaces WordPad's menus with those of Paint, the program with which the Bitmap Image object type is associated. Figure 9-3 shows what you would see.

FIGURE 9-3.

If you use the Object command on WordPad's Insert menu, and then choose the Bitmap Image object type, Windows replaces WordPad's menus and toolbars with those of Paint, allowing you to create a new object.

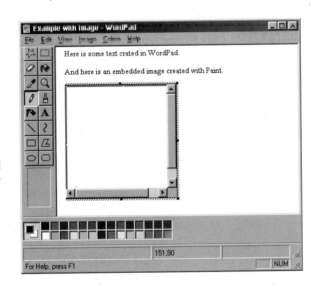

The menus and tools shown in Figure 9-3 are those of Paint. The frame below the text is a Paint frame, embedded within a WordPad document. As long as the frame is selected, you can use Paint's menus and tools to create a bitmap image. When you finish, you can return to WordPad by simply selecting any part of the document outside the Paint frame.

If you choose to have the embedded object displayed as an icon, or if the program you're working with does not support in-place editing, clicking OK in the Insert Object dialog box causes Windows to launch the program that creates the object, rather than simply displaying that program's menus and toolbars within the destination program. In that case, when you finish creating the object, you can embed it by choosing the Exit & Return To Document command, at the bottom of the File menu. Figure 9-4, on the next page, shows what you see if you choose WordPad's Insert Object command, select Bitmap Image as the object type, and also select the Display As Icon check box.

The copy of Paint shown in Figure 9-4 is exactly like what you get by running Paint directly from your Start menu, except for its title bar and File menu. The title bar reveals the fact that this instance of Paint was

FIGURE 9-4.

If you choose to display a new embedded object as an icon, or if your program does not support in-place editing, Windows launches a full copy of the program with which the object type is associated.

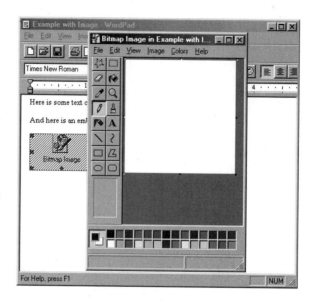

launched for the purpose of creating (or editing) an embedded object, and the File menu includes two new commands—one to quit Paint and update the containing document and one to update the containing document without leaving Paint.

How to Link

To link an object, follow these steps:

1 Select the object in its source document and copy it to the Clipboard.

2 Activate the destination document and place the insertion point where you want the linked object to go.

3 Choose the Edit menu's Paste Link command.

This creates a link to the source document and displays the source object in the default format. If you prefer a different format, choose Paste Special instead of Paste Link. In the Paste Special dialog box, select the format you want and then choose Paste Link.

Two Linking Hazards to Avoid

When you create a link, a visible change occurs in the destination document: new data arrives. At the same time, Windows makes a change in the source document, but this change is not visible. The reason for the change in the source document is that the source document now has a new "responsibility": it must notify the destination document whenever the linked object changes.

If you close the source document immediately after performing a paste link, you will be prompted to save your changes, even though you might not have done any editing in that document since your most recent save. Windows wants you to save your changes because the document has assumed the responsibility of supplying a link. If you ignore the prompt, the data in the destination document will be correct (for the time being), but the link might be broken. To avoid this mishap, be sure to save the source document after paste-linking an object into a destination document.

Another hazard arises when the source document is a spreadsheet. In a typical spreadsheet link, the source data is identified in the destination document by its cell coordinates. However, what happens to the link in this situation if someone working with the source document decides to add a few new rows or columns? Any such worksheet rearrangement can change the cell coordinates of the linked object and thereby invalidate the link—or worse, the link can remain valid as far as Windows is concerned, but it no longer contains the data you're interested in.

To avoid this trap, do the following:

1 In the source document, name the cell or range you want to link.

2 After you paste-link the object into your destination document, use the destination program's Edit Links command to verify that the link is recorded by your worksheet range name, not by absolute cell coordinates.

3 If the link is not identified by the range name, edit the link, replacing the cell coordinates with the range name.

II

Further Explorations

The exact procedure for editing the link depends on the destination program. In WordPad, for example, the Edit Links dialog box includes a Change Source command button. Clicking this button brings up a "browser" dialog box, in which you can change the name of the source file or the description of the source object. As Figure 9-5 shows, the source object is described on a line marked Item Name. To replace cell coordinates with a range name, simply edit the Item Name line.

FIGURE 9-5.

In WordPad, by choosing Links from the Edit menu and then clicking the Change Source button, you can change the description of the linked object. In other programs, the procedure might be slightly different.

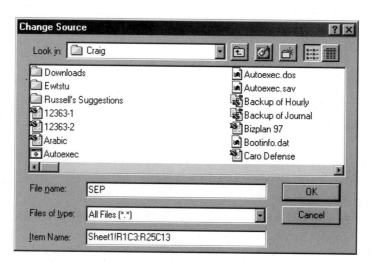

Embedding or Linking a File

In all our examples so far, the source object to be linked or embedded has been a part of a file—for example, a range of spreadsheet cells, a paragraph in a word processing document, or a selection from a graphic image. You can also link or embed entire files. Depending on the type of file involved and your preferences, the destination document either displays the contents of the file or an icon representing the file.

To embed or link a file, choose the Object command (in many programs it's called New Object) from the containing program's Insert menu, and then select the Create From File option button. The object type list in the center of the dialog box is replaced by a File text box and a Browse button, as shown in Figure 9-6.

FIGURE 9-6.

If you select the Create From File option button in the dialog box shown in Figure 9-2 on page 234, the dialog box changes to let you type a filename or browse through your folders to find the file you want to embed or link.

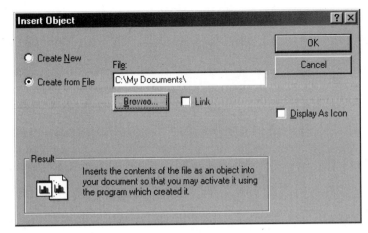

Working with Embedded Objects

The simplest way to edit an embedded object is to double-click it. Depending on whether the object is fully visible or shown as an icon, and depending on the level of OLE support provided by your programs, either you are transported to a copy of the object's source program or the source program's menus and toolbars appear at the top of your document. In either case, you edit the object using the facilities of the object's source program.

If you're editing in a copy of the source program, choose the last command in that program's File menu when you are finished editing. This command closes the source program and returns you to the document in which the object is embedded.

If the menus and toolbars of the object's source program have replaced those of the destination program (that is, you are editing in place), simply select another part of the destination document when you are finished editing the object. The original menus and toolbars then reappear.

Alternatively, you can edit an embedded object by selecting it and looking for an editing command at or near the bottom of the Edit menu. Figure 9-7, on the next page, shows what you see on WordPad's Edit menu when you select an embedded bitmap image.

FIGURE 9-7.

To edit an embedded object, simply double-click it. Or select it and look for an editing command on the Edit menu.

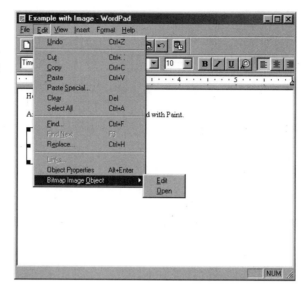

Playing an Embedded Sound or Video Object

To play an embedded sound or video object, select the embedded object and choose the "Object" command on your program's Edit menu. This command identifies the type of object you selected. If you select a sound clip created in Sound Recorder, for example, the command says *Sound Recorder Document Object.* When you choose this command, a submenu appears. Choose Play from the submenu to play the embedded object.

Modifying the Properties of an Embedded Object

Like just about everything else in Windows 98, embedded objects have properties that can be inspected and modified. To get to the properties dialog box for an embedded object, you can do any of the following:

- Right-click the object and choose Object Properties from the context menu.

- Select the object and press Alt+Enter.

- Select the object and choose Object Properties from the Edit menu (if you're working in a context where there is an Edit menu).

In the properties dialog box, you might be able to do such things as switch between a rendered and an iconic display of the object or change the object's display size.

⭐ **TIP**

> If the selected object is displayed as an icon, you can use the object's properties dialog box to change the icon, the icon's caption, or both. Even if you're content with the default icon, you might want to replace the default caption with something descriptive. "Picture of Mom," for example, might serve your needs better than "Bitmap Image." To do so, click the Change Icon button in the properties dialog box, and then modify the Label text.

Working with Links

When a data object is linked to a document, changes to the object are reflected in the destination document. Whether they're reflected automatically or only on demand is up to you. Most (but not all) programs create automatic links by default. In any case, you can switch between automatic and manual linking by opening the properties dialog box for the link in question. To open the properties dialog box, select the linked object and choose Object Properties from the containing program's Edit menu. Figure 9-8 shows an example of a linked object's properties dialog box.

FIGURE 9-8.
On the Link tab in a linked object's properties dialog box, you can switch between automatic and manual linking, open the object's source document for editing, sever the object from its source document, or specify a different source document.

II

Further Explorations

TIP

> If your destination program does not include an Object Properties command, look for a Links command on the Edit menu. That command displays a list of all links in the current document. By selecting an item in the list and choosing command buttons in the Links dialog box, you can switch between automatic and manual linking, open the source document for editing, break the link, or respecify the source document.

To switch between automatic and manual linking, go to the Link tab in the properties dialog box and choose the appropriate option button in the Update group. If you choose Manually, you can refresh the containing document by clicking the Update Now button. If you choose Automatically, the containing document is refreshed any time the source document changes.

Another Linking Hazard

Under certain circumstances, it is possible for an automatic link *not* to reflect the current state of the source document. Here's how it can happen:

1 You double-click the linked object to edit its source document.

2 You change the object in the source document, and the link is updated appropriately.

3 You close the source document without saving changes.

After this sequence, the source document reverts to its former state (because you didn't save your changes), but the destination document does not. The two documents are now out of step with one another.

To be absolutely sure that all links in a destination document, both automatic and manual, are up-to-date, follow these steps:

1 In the destination document, choose the Links command from the Edit menu.

2 In the Links dialog box, select the first link listed. Then scroll to the bottom of the list and hold down the Shift key while selecting the last link listed. (This selects all links in the list.)

3 Click the Update Now button.

Breaking a Link

If you no longer want a linked object to reflect changes in the object's source, visit the Link tab in the object's properties dialog box, and then click the Break Link button. If it can, Windows converts the item to an embedded object.

What to Do If the Source Document Is Moved or Renamed

If the source document for a link is renamed or relocated, the link becomes invalid. When you open a destination document containing such an invalid link, you might or might not receive a warning from the destination program. (It depends on the program.) If you know the link has become invalid, choose Links from the Edit menu. Then click the Change Source (or equivalent) button and follow your program's procedures for editing the link.

If you're not sure whether or not the link is valid, choose the Edit menu's Links command. Select the link in question (or all links) and click the Update Now (or equivalent) button. The destination program should then tell you if any source object is unavailable. If you have invalid links, you can click the Change Source (or equivalent) button to edit them.

Creating Scrap Files

Windows Explorer is an OLE program. That means you can embed data objects in folders or on your desktop. So, for example, if there's a particular image you want to use repeatedly, you can drag it out of a Paint window and drop it onto your desktop. To reuse it in your word processor, simply drag it again and drop it into the receiving document.

OLE objects in folders or on the desktop are called *scrap files*. When you create such an object, Windows gives it a default name based on its contents or source, such as "WordPad Document Scrap 'Now is the time ...'" You can assign your own name by pressing F2 and typing.

A scrap file must originate in a program that supports OLE as a source. If the program also supports OLE drag and drop, you can create the scrap by simply dragging the object. If not, select the object in its source program, choose the Copy command, and then move to your folder or to the desktop and choose Paste.

TIP

> ### Picking Up Where You Left Off
> You can use a scrap to create a pointer to the spot in a document where you last worked (without actually changing the document in any noticeable way), allowing you to close the document and then later resume working in the same place. Simply select some text at the point you want to mark, right-drag it to the desktop (or to a folder), and choose Create Document Shortcut Here from the context menu. This creates a shortcut, which you can double-click to reopen the document. The document scrolls to your previous location, and the same text is highlighted.

Sharing and Using OLE Objects Across the Network

SEE ALSO

For information about using shared folders, see Chapter 5, "Using and Sharing Files on the Network."

By storing scrap files in a shared folder, you can make OLE objects on your system available to other network users. Similarly, by opening a shared folder on a server, you can access OLE objects stored on that server. To embed a server-based scrap file, for example, simply open the network folder in which the scrap resides, using Network Neighborhood or a mapped folder. Then drag the object to wherever you want it to go. Alternatively, select the object in the network folder, and then paste it into a program or local folder.

To activate a network scrap object's parent program, either for editing purposes or to render an object that's embedded as an icon, you must have a local copy of the parent program.

Customizing Windows with Control Panel

The Control Panel system folder contains a variety of icons to display dialog boxes (sometimes called *property sheets*) or folders that help you customize and configure different aspects of your Windows system. We've already seen a few of these dialog boxes and folders—Display Properties, Printers, and Fonts—in earlier chapters of this book. Others will be taken up in later chapters. In the present chapter, we'll look at Control Panel itself, and at most of the Control Panel items that don't fall neatly into other chapters. Specifically, we'll look into procedures for doing the following:

- Resetting the date, time, or time zone

- Applying desktop themes—combinations of thematically related sounds, backgrounds, custom mouse pointers, fonts, and screen savers

- Extending your desktop across two or more monitors

- Installing, testing, and configuring a game controller

- Adjusting keyboard repeat parameters

- Setting up different keyboard layouts, such as the Dvorak layout or a layout for a different language

- Using Windows' support for multiple languages

- Installing, configuring, and testing a modem

- Adjusting the behavior of your mouse

- Choosing alternative mouse pointers

- Changing a network configuration

- Changing your network computer name, computer description, and workgroup name

- Changing your network and other passwords

- Specifying "regional" settings, such as date and time formats, the default symbol for currency, and the symbols used for decimal points and thousands separators

- Adding new user profiles

Most of the icons in Control Panel represent generic operating system tools. But programs and hardware devices may add their own icons as well. Microsoft Office, for example, installs a Find Fast icon in Control Panel. The Intel EtherExpress Pro network adapters add a testing and configuration icon specific for those adapters. Hardware- or program-specific items such as these are not covered in this book.

How to Get to Control Panel

Figure 10-1 shows the Control Panel folder for one of the systems used to create this book. Your own Control Panel may differ.

You can get to Control Panel by choosing Settings from the Start menu, and then choosing Control Panel from the Settings submenu. Alternatively, you can double-click (or click) the Control Panel icon in your My Computer folder.

Each item in Control Panel is a file with the extension .CPL. You can create a shortcut for any of these items, just as you would create a shortcut to a document, folder, program, or Internet site. If you find yourself using particular Control Panel items regularly, you might want to put shortcuts for those items on your desktop, on a toolbar, or on the

FIGURE 10-1.

The Control Panel folder contains icons to launch dialog boxes and folders that help you customize and configure your system.

Start menu. You can also create a desktop or toolbar shortcut for the entire Control Panel folder by right-dragging it out of My Computer and choosing Create Shortcut(s) Here from the context menu.

As Figure 10-2 on the next page shows, it's also possible to create a handy Control Panel submenu on your Start menu. Such a submenu allows you to pick just the Control Panel item you need directly from the Start menu without having to display the entire Control Panel folder. Creating a Control Panel submenu gives you an opportunity to exercise your typing skills. Here are the steps:

1   Right-click the Start button and choose either Open or Explore.

2   In the Windows Explorer window that appears, right-click an empty space, choose New, and then choose Folder.

3   Rename the new folder Control Panel.{21EC2020-3AEA-1069-A2DD-08002B30309D}

4   Close the Windows Explorer window.

If you type that monstrous name correctly (be sure to include the period between "Panel" and the opening brace!), you're rewarded with a

FIGURE 10-2.
With a bit of careful
typing, you can create
a Control Panel
submenu for your
Start menu.

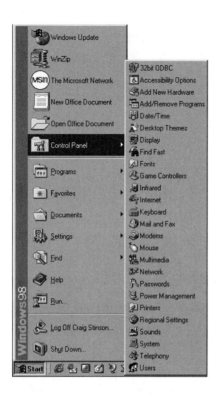

cascading Control Panel menu. (You can tell you did it correctly because
only the words *Control Panel* appear as the new folder's name; everything from the period to the closing brace disappears.) If you make any
mistakes, you don't get the menu item you want, but you do get a folder
with a funny name. In that case, press F2 and edit.

> **TIP**
>
> You can use the same trick to create submenus for your Printers and Dial-Up
> Networking folders. The names to type are:
>   Printers.{2227A280-3AEA-1069-A2DE-08002B30309D}
>   Dial-Up Networking.{992CFFA0-F557-101A-88EC-00DD010CCC48}

Once you get into a dialog box launched from a Control Panel item, you
can make your selections and click OK. Alternatively, you can make
changes and click the Apply button. The Apply button lets you see the
effect of your changes without leaving the dialog box. If you don't like
what you see, you can try something else.

Resetting the Date, Time, and Time Zone

To change your computer's date or time setting, launch Date/Time in Control Panel. You'll see the Date/Time Properties dialog box, shown in Figure 10-3.

FIGURE 10-3.

To change your system's date or time, launch Date/Time in Control Panel.

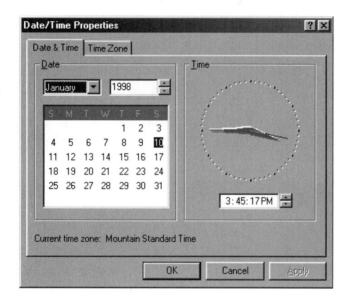

The Date/Time Properties dialog box has two tabs. Use the Date & Time tab to adjust your system's clock or calendar. Use the Time Zone tab if you're moving to a different time zone, or to enable or disable Windows' automatic adjustment for daylight saving time.

 TIP

You can also get to the Date/Time Properties dialog box by double-clicking the clock on your taskbar.

On the Date & Time tab, you can adjust the day of the month by clicking the calendar. To choose a different month or year, select from the drop-down list and spinner above the calendar. To change the time of day, click the appropriate portion of the time edit box, and then use the spinners to the right of the edit box. For example, if the clock says 2:36 P.M., but it's really only 2:31, select the 36 and then click the downward arrow five times. (Unfortunately, you can't adjust the time by dragging the hands on the clock.) If the clock says A.M., but it's actually P.M., click on or beside the "AM" and then click either spinner arrow once.

While you make time-of-day adjustments, your clock stops. After you've made your changes, click Apply or OK to start the clock running again.

 TIP

> To change the display format used by the clock—for example, to change AM and PM to am and pm—use the Time tab in the Regional Settings Properties dialog box. For more information, see "Specifying Regional (International) Settings," page 267.

You can also adjust the date and time by running MS-DOS Prompt and using the Date command or the Time command. Changes made this way have exactly the same effect as changes made via the Date/Time Properties dialog box.

On the Time Zone tab, select a time zone from the drop-down list at the top of the dialog box. (Unlike in Windows 95, you can't simply click your location on the world map.) Windows uses this information to track time information for files saved on a network that operates across multiple time zones.

Windows can automatically adjust your system's clock when daylight saving time begins or ends. If you want to use this feature, select the Automatically Adjust Clock For Daylight Saving Changes check box, on the Time Zone tab in the Date/Time Properties dialog box.

TIP

> If your computer is connected to a Windows NT, Windows 98, Windows 95, or Windows for Workgroups network, you can set your computer's clock to match the time on another computer in your network. To do so, choose the Run command from the Start menu, and type *net time \\computer /set /yes*, where *computer* is the name of the computer you want to synchronize with. To synchronize your clock automatically each time you start Windows, create a shortcut with this command and place it in your StartUp folder.

Applying Desktop Themes

Desktop themes add thematically consistent sounds and sights to your system, using wallpaper, specially designed icons, sound schemes, color schemes, fonts, animated mouse pointers, and screen savers. If you choose the Travel theme, for example, you get a train station for wallpaper, assorted propellers and clocks for mouse pointers, an airplane for a screen saver, and various toots, honks, beeps, and a-oogas to enliven your day. You can install any of these thematic elements separately (just the horns, without the propellers, for example), or accept the whole package.

> **NOTE**
>
> If your Control Panel does not include a Desktop Themes icon, launch Add/Remove Programs in Control Panel, click the Windows Setup tab, select Desktop Themes, and click OK.

Windows 98 supplies 16 themes. Some of these require 16-bit or better color depth (high color); the others look fine in 256 colors. To see what's available, launch Desktop Themes and open the Theme drop-down list. As you scroll through the list, Windows shows a preview of each theme in the center of the dialog box, shown in Figure 10-4. You can sample the sounds, the mouse pointers, and the screen saver associated with

FIGURE 10-4.

In one fell swoop, Desktop Themes lets you change your screen saver, sound scheme, mouse pointer scheme, wallpaper, desktop icons, and appearance scheme.

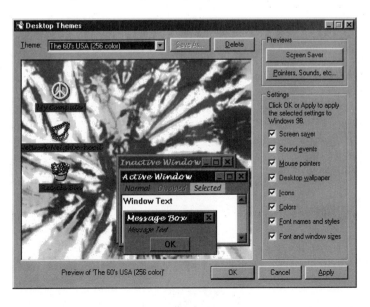

each theme by clicking the two buttons in the Previews area of the dialog box. If you want to omit certain parts of the themes (the mouse pointers and fonts, for example), you can do so by deselecting check boxes along the right side of the dialog box.

If you decide that thematic madness isn't your cup of latte, you can restore sobriety by returning to the Desktop Themes dialog box and choosing Windows Default from the Theme drop-down list.

Creating and Modifying Desktop Themes

You can modify the supplied themes or create your own from scratch. To change an existing theme, first apply that theme. Then, using other Control Panel icons, modify whatever elements you want to change. For example, to use a different wallpaper, go to the Background tab in the Display Properties dialog box. To change a mouse pointer, launch Mouse and click the Pointers tab. When you have everything the way you want it, go back to the Desktop Themes dialog box. Select Current Windows Settings in the Theme drop-down list (it's the first item in the list), click the Save As button, and supply a filename.

To create your own theme from scratch, simply use Control Panel to set up all the elements of your theme. Then go to Desktop Themes, select Current Windows Settings, click Save As, and name your theme.

Extending Your Desktop Across Two or More Monitors

If you have a computer with a PCI bus, you may be able to extend your desktop across two or more monitors. You need a separate PCI or AGP display adapter for each monitor you want to use. Windows 98 supports up to nine monitors.

Extending your desktop across multiple monitors gives you much more display real estate, allowing you, for example, to have more than one maximized program visible at the same time. You can assign separate resolutions and color depths to each monitor. So, for example, if you have a 19-inch monitor and a 15-inch monitor, you could run the larger display at 1024×768 and the smaller one at 800×600.

To configure your monitors, launch Display in Control Panel. Once you've installed more than one supported display adapter, the Settings tab in the Display Properties dialog box changes to show the current physical arrangement of your monitors. Figure 10-5 shows an example of how that dialog box might appear. Note that a number appears on the screen of each monitor shown in the dialog box. These numbers correspond to entries in the Display drop-down list.

FIGURE 10-5.

When you have multiple display adapters installed, the Settings tab in the Display Properties dialog box lets you specify the physical arrangement of your monitors.

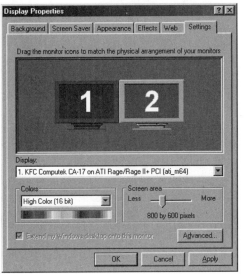

In order to allow you to move display objects from one monitor to another, Windows needs to know how your monitors are physically arranged. To give Windows this information, go to the Settings tab in the Display Properties dialog box and simply drag the monitors until they assume the correct positions.

Once you've shown Windows the layout of your displays, you can drag icons and windows from one monitor to the other. If your secondary display is to the left of your primary, for example, you can move an icon from primary to secondary by dragging it off the left edge of the primary display.

If you maximize a window, it fills only the screen on which it currently resides. If a window is currently split across two or more screens, Windows maximizes it on whichever screen currently displays its largest portion.

II

Further Explorations

NOTE

> MS-DOS–based programs can be displayed in full-screen windows only on the primary monitor.

To change the resolution or color depth for one of your displays, go to the Settings tab in the Display Properties dialog box. Select the display you want to modify from the Display drop-down list. Then make your resolution and color-depth choices from the Screen Area and Colors sections of the dialog box.

 NOTE

> Screen savers act only on the primary monitor.

Installing, Configuring, and Testing a Game Controller

To install, configure, or test joysticks and other game controllers, launch Game Controllers in Control Panel. Normally, if you're installing a game controller that conforms to the Plug and Play standard, you don't need to use the Game Controllers dialog box for installation purposes. (If you do need to, click Add on the General tab in the Game Controllers dialog box, and follow the prompts.) But you might want to use it for configuration or testing.

The General tab in the Game Controllers dialog box presents a list of installed controllers and an indication of their status (okay or otherwise). Selecting a device and clicking the Properties button takes you to a new dialog box specific to that device. Figure 10-6 shows an example of this dialog box. The Test tab in this case lets you test the operation of specific buttons and other controls. The Settings tab lets you turn the rudder on and off, and the Diagnostic tab provides information that might be useful to technicians if a malfunction prompts you to call for help. The properties dialog box for your own joystick may differ from this one.

The Advanced tab in the Game Controllers dialog box allows you to change the Controller ID values for individual devices if you have more than one game controller installed.

FIGURE 10-6.

From the Game Controllers dialog box, you can get to a property dialog box specific for your joystick.

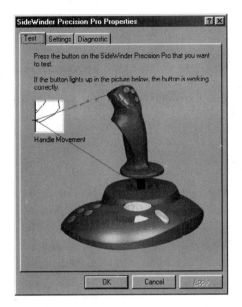

Adjusting Keyboard Repeat Parameters

Unless you have disabled the "typematic" behavior of your keyboard to take advantage of the accessibility features in Windows, Windows repeats a character after you have held its key down for a certain length of time. You can adjust both the repeat speed and the interval that Windows waits before beginning to repeat. To do this, launch Keyboard in Control Panel to get to the dialog box shown in Figure 10-7, on the next page.

SEE ALSO

For more information about controlling or disabling the keyboard repeat rate, see "Controlling the Keyboard Repeat Rate with BounceKeys (FilterKeys)," page 310.

To shorten the delay before repeating begins, drag the Repeat Delay slider to the right. To increase the repeat speed, drag the Repeat Rate slider to the right. Putting both these sliders as far as they'll go to the right makes your keyboard as responsive as Windows will allow. If you find yourself occasionally getting unwanted repeated characters, move the Repeat Delay slider, or both sliders, to the left. You can use the text box to test your settings before clicking OK.

In the lower part of the dialog box shown in Figure 10-7, you'll find another slider, for adjusting the rate at which the cursor blinks. If you're not happy with the default blink rate, you might want to experiment with moving this slider. The blinking line to the left of the slider shows your new cursor blink rate.

Further Explorations

FIGURE 10-7.

The Keyboard Properties dialog box lets you adjust your keyboard's repeat speed and the speed at which the cursor blinks.

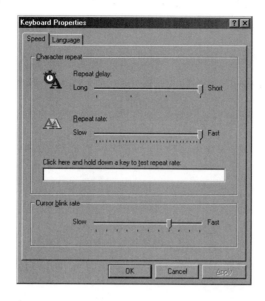

The Keyboard Properties dialog box also allows you to install keyboard support for a variety of languages.

Installing Language Support and Using Keyboard Layouts

Windows comes with support for a multitude of languages and keyboard layouts. If you work in more than one language or communicate with speakers of other languages, you might find it convenient to have two or more languages installed simultaneously. Then you can use simple mouse and keyboard procedures to switch from one language to another.

Languages and layouts are separate but related issues. When you activate another language, programs that have been written with language support in mind can provide appropriate services, such as using a different spelling checker or using special characters in TrueType fonts. For example, if you switch from English to Russian, WordPad automatically uses Cyrillic characters.

When you switch to a different language, you get the default keyboard layout for that language, but you can choose alternative layouts. For German, for example, Windows supplies a standard layout and an IBM layout. For Russian, there's a standard layout and a typewriter layout—and so on.

Even if you work only in English, you might want to check out alternative layouts. Typing letters with accents, for example, might be simpler if you use the United States–International layout. And if the standard QWERTY system of typing isn't your preference, you can opt for the United States–Dvorak layout.

Installing a New Language

You can install support for a new language as follows:

1   Launch Keyboard in Control Panel.

2   Click the Language tab.

These steps take you to the Language tab in the Keyboard Properties dialog box, as shown in Figure 10-8.

FIGURE 10-8.

In the Keyboard Properties dialog box, you can add support for other languages or switch keyboard layouts.

3 Click the Add button and select the language you want from the drop-down list.

Windows might prompt you to insert your Windows CD.

> If the language you're looking for isn't in the drop-down list, launch Add/ Remove Programs in Control Panel. Click the Windows Setup tab, select the Multilanguage Support check box, and click OK. After you complete this process, return to the Keyboard item in Control Panel.

Before leaving the Keyboard Properties dialog box, select one of the option buttons for switching languages. By default, you can switch from one language to another by holding down the Alt key on the left side of your keyboard and pressing the Shift key. If you prefer, you can opt for the combination of Ctrl and Shift instead. Or you can turn off switching-by-keystroke altogether.

By default, Windows displays a two-letter symbol in the notification area of your taskbar whenever you have more than one language installed. You can use this symbol both as a reminder and as a switching mechanism. To switch languages, click the language symbol and then choose from the list that pops up. If, for some reason, you don't want this convenience, deselect the Enable Indicator On Taskbar check box at the bottom of the Keyboard Properties dialog box.

> By right-clicking the language symbol in the notification area of your taskbar and choosing Properties from the context menu, you can go directly to the Keyboard Properties dialog box without opening Control Panel.

Switching Keyboard Layouts

To switch keyboard layouts, first go to the Language tab in the Keyboard Properties dialog box, following steps 1 and 2 on the previous page. Select the language for which you want to switch layouts, and then click the Properties button. Then select the layout you want from the drop-down list that appears.

Installing, Configuring, and Testing a Modem

To install, configure, or test a modem, launch Modems in Control Panel. Normally, if you're installing a modem that conforms to the Plug and Play standard, you don't need to use the Modems Properties dialog box for installation purposes. (If you do need to, click Add on the General tab in the Modems Properties dialog box, and follow the prompts.) But you might want to use it to change a modem's settings or ensure that the modem is working properly. For example, you might decide that you don't need to hear the modem's speaker every time it dials, or that you'd rather hear it at a lower volume. You can make these and other adjustments via the Modems Properties dialog box.

 NOTE

If you launch Modems and you don't already have a modem installed, Windows automatically launches the Install New Modem wizard.

To make sure your modem is connected and functioning properly, you can click the Diagnostics tab. Select the modem you want to test from the list that appears, and then click the More Info button. Windows will commune with your modem and return a table showing the state of each of your modem's registers, along with other potentially useful information.

Setting Up Dialing Locations

 SEE ALSO

For information about dialing properties, see "Setting Dialing Properties," page 576.

You can use the Dialing Properties button on the General tab in the Modems Properties dialog box to set up "dialing locations." For example, if you regularly pick up your e-mail while traveling in New York, Denver, and Monte Carlo, you can set up dialing parameters for each locale. Then, whenever you're on the road, you can choose from the list of locations to ensure that your modem dials the appropriate access and area codes.

 NOTE

You can also set dialing properties by launching Telephony in Control Panel. The My Locations tab in the dialog box that appears is identical to the dialog box that appears when you click Dialing Properties on the General tab in the Modems Properties dialog box.

II

Further Explorations

Adjusting Mouse Behavior

Windows lets you tailor the behavior of your mouse or other pointing device to suit your tastes. The options available depend on what kind of device you're using, but for most pointing devices you can adjust the pointer-movement and double-click speeds, as well as swap the functionality of the left and right mouse buttons. You might find it handy to swap mouse button functions if you're left-handed, so you can put the mouse on the left side of your keyboard and still use your index finger for most mouse commands.

To make mouse adjustments, launch Mouse in Control Panel. If you're using a Microsoft IntelliMouse, you'll see a dialog box similar to the one shown in Figure 10-9.

FIGURE 10-9.

The Mouse Properties dialog box lets you swap mouse-button functionality, adjust double-click speed, and set other mouse preferences.

In the top part of this dialog box, you can swap mouse-button functionality. In the lower part, you can adjust the double-click speed. (The double-click speed specifies the time interval within which two mouse clicks in the same location are interpreted as a double-click.)

The Motion tab in this dialog box allows you to adjust the pointer speed. Pointer speed refers to the relationship between movement of the mouse on your desk and movement of the pointer on screen. If you often find your mouse pointer overshooting its target as you select commands or objects in Windows, you might find it helpful to decrease the pointer speed. On the other hand, if you find yourself "rowing"— picking up the mouse, bringing it back through the air, and then sliding it over the mouse pad again merely to get the pointer from one side of the screen to the other—try increasing the pointer speed.

Your Mouse applet might also include a Pointer Trail option. If selected, this option causes your mouse to leave a temporary trail of pointer images as it moves across the screen. This trail can help you keep track of the pointer's location on your display.

Changing Mouse Pointer Shapes

Tired of the same old arrows and hourglasses? You can use the Pointers tab in the Mouse Properties dialog box to try on a different set of pointer shapes. Figure 10-10 shows a sample of what you'll find on the Pointers tab.

FIGURE 10-10.

You can substitute a variety of alternative static and animated pointer shapes for the standard arrows and hourglasses.

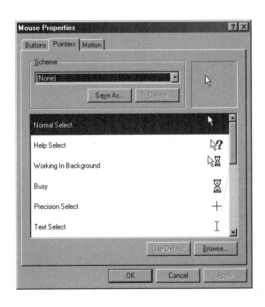

The lower part of this dialog box shows all the different kinds of mouse actions recognized by Windows and the pointer shape currently assigned to each action. To make a substitution, select an entry in this list and click the Browse button. The Browse dialog box that appears shows available shapes, each stored in a separate file with the extension .CUR or .ANI. The

.CUR files are static shapes, while the .ANI files are animated. (To see only the static or animated offerings, open the Files Of Type drop-down list and select the type you're interested in.) When you select a filename in the Browse dialog box, a Preview window shows what you've selected. Once you've selected an alternative shape, you can return to the default shape by selecting it in the list and clicking the Use Default button.

In the Scheme drop-down list at the top of the Pointers tab, you'll find nearly a dozen named combinations of pointer shapes. You can install one of these by selecting it from the list. Or, after you select the pointers you want, you can click the Save As button to create your own scheme.

NOTE

> If your Scheme drop-down list offers only a few choices, visit Add/Remove Programs in Control Panel to install additional cursors and schemes. Launch Add/Remove Programs, click the Windows Setup tab, select Accessories, and click Details. Then select Mouse Pointers and click OK two times.

To restore all the default shapes at once, choose Windows Standard from the Scheme list.

Changing Network Settings

The Configuration tab in the Network dialog box, shown in Figure 10-11, lets you modify the components that define your network configuration. The currently installed components are listed in the center of this dialog box, and, as the figure shows, when you select an item in the list, a description of the selected item appears at the bottom of the dialog box. The installed component list may include four categories of components, each identified by a distinctive icon: client software, adapters, protocols, and services. The meanings of those terms are as follows:

- Client software allows your system to connect to shared resources on dedicated servers or other network computers.

- An adapter is the hardware component that sits in one of your computer's slots and physically connects your computer to the network.

FIGURE 10-11.

The Configuration tab in the Network dialog box lets you change the components that define your network.

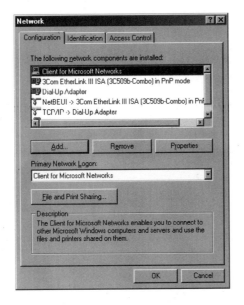

- A protocol is the language that allows your computer to communicate with other computers. You can have more than one protocol installed, but your computer and the computer you're communicating with must use the same protocol.

- A service allows your computer to perform some specific network task, such as sharing files or a printer, performing automatic backups across the network, or administering other network computers.

TIP

As an alternative to launching Network in Control Panel, you can right-click the Network Neighborhood icon and choose Properties to display the Network dialog box.

To read the properties associated with any installed component, double-click its entry in the list, or select the entry and click the Properties button. If you're using Client for Microsoft Networks as your client software, you might want to familiarize yourself with that item's properties dialog box. There you can specify or change the name of the Windows NT domain that you log onto (if you log onto a Windows NT domain), or choose between quick and full logon options. The full logon, selected by default, restores all your network connections and verifies that each mapped network drive is available for use. The quick option makes the network available to you but does not restore connections to mapped drives; in this case, connections are restored the first time you try to access the network drive.

To add a network component, click the Add button. In the next dialog box that appears, choose a component type—Client, Adapter, Protocol, or Service—and then click Add again.

Changing Your Computer's Network ID

The Identification tab in the Network dialog box, shown in Figure 10-12, records the name by which your computer is known to the network. This is the name that another network user would click in Network Neighborhood (or type as part of a network path specification) to access a folder or printer that you are sharing. To change this name, type the new name on the top line of the dialog box. A computer name can be up to 15 characters long (spaces are not allowed), and it must not be the same as the name of any other computer in your workgroup or domain.

FIGURE 10-12.

Should you need to change the name of your computer, this is the place to do it.

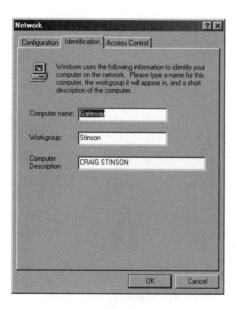

The Identification tab also records your workgroup name, if any, and a description of your computer. The workgroup is a unit consisting of one or more computers that appears as a separate entity in users' Network Neighborhood folders. The description is what users see in the Comment column when displaying Network Neighborhood in Details view. (The description also appears in your computer's properties dialog box, which users can display by right-clicking your computer in their Network Neighborhood folders.)

Switching Between Share-Level and User-Level Access Control

? SEE ALSO

For information about access control, see "Sharing Folders with Other Users," page 162.

You can share your system's folders using either of two access-control methods: share-level access and user-level access. The latter requires that you be connected to a Windows NT domain. To switch from one method to the other, use the Access Control tab in the Network dialog box.

Changing Passwords

The Passwords Properties dialog box, which appears when you launch Passwords in Control Panel, lets you change the password you use to log on to a Windows network, a Windows NT network, or your user profile. The Change Passwords tab, shown in Figure 10-13, includes two buttons, Change Windows Password and Change Other Passwords. Use the first button to change the password you use to log on to a Windows network or your own user profile. Use the second to change the password you use to log on to a Windows NT network. Certain other passwords you use, such as for unlocking a screen saver, may also be modifiable via the Change Other Passwords button.

FIGURE 10-13.

The Passwords Properties dialog box lets you change your logon password.

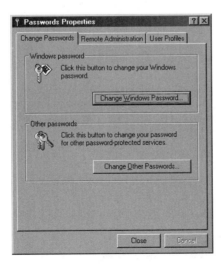

NOTE

> Passwords you've assigned to local shared resources—that is, passwords that other users must supply when connecting to your shares—cannot be changed via the Passwords Properties dialog box. To change these, right-click the shared folder in Windows Explorer and choose Sharing from the context menu.

Windows keeps track of additional passwords you use, such as passwords for logging onto password-protected Internet sites, in a file with the extension .PWL, stored in your Windows folder. This is an encrypted file, so you can't read it with a conventional text editor. The Windows 98 CD includes a program called Password List Editor, however, which sounds as if it might be a tool for editing your password list. (To run Password List Editor, use the Find command to locate and run a file named Pwledit.exe.) Unfortunately, its services are limited to showing you the list of passwords it maintains and allowing you to delete selected items. Password List Editor is illustrated in Figure 10-14.

FIGURE 10-14.
The Password List Editor program, included on the Windows 98 CD, lets you prune, but not otherwise modify, a miscellaneous list of passwords maintained by Windows.

Allowing Remote Administration

 SEE ALSO

For more information about remote administration, see "Monitoring the Use of Shared Resources," page 167.

The Remote Administration tab in the Passwords Properties dialog box lets you allow other users on your network—those who know the password you require—to monitor the usage of your shared folders and printers. Those who have remote-administration access to your system can also create or change your shared resources—and nearly any file on your computer. To enable remote administration, click the Remote

Administration tab, select the single check box there, and then supply and confirm a password.

NOTE

> The Remote Administration tab appears in the Passwords Properties dialog box only if the File And Printer Sharing service has been installed in the Network dialog box.

Enabling User Profiles

The User Profiles tab in the Passwords Properties dialog box allows you to enable or disable user profiles. With user profiles enabled, multiple users can run Windows on your computer, and each user can maintain his or her own customized desktop, Start menu, My Documents folder, and downloaded Web pages. Any time a new user logs on, Windows offers to create a new profile for that user.

SEE ALSO

For information about Users, see "Setting Up New User Profiles," page 269.

A better way to enable profiles in general and set up profiles for particular users is to go back to Control Panel and launch Users, which is new in Windows 98.

Specifying Regional (International) Settings

The Regional Settings icon in Control Panel allows you to adjust the way Windows displays dates, times, currency amounts, large numbers, and numbers with decimal fractions, as well as whether Windows should employ the metric or "imperial" system of measurement. This section of Control Panel corresponds to what was called International in Windows 3.x.

To modify any of Windows' regional settings, start by launching Regional Settings in Control Panel. You will see the five-tabbed dialog box shown in Figure 10-15, on the next page.

On the first tab in the Regional Settings Properties dialog box, you'll find a map of the world. If you're adjusting your system for a new country—for example, if you've just taken your portable computer overseas—start by selecting the new language and country from the drop-down list above this map. In response, Windows applies the default settings for all

II

Further Explorations

FIGURE 10-15.

You can change many regional settings at once, simply by selecting a language and a country on the Regional Settings tab in the Regional Settings Properties dialog box.

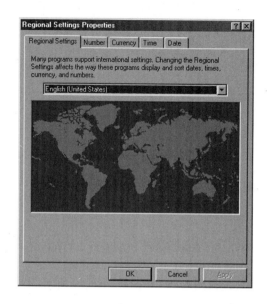

adjustable items—numbers, currency, times, and dates—all at once. In most cases, you won't need to make any further changes.

? SEE ALSO

For information about keyboard layouts, see "Installing Language Support and Using Keyboard Layouts," page 256.

Windows does not change the keyboard layout when you choose a different country in the Regional Settings Properties dialog box. To specify a different keyboard layout, use the Keyboard Properties dialog box.

To override one or more default settings for a country, click the appropriate tab in the Regional Settings Properties dialog box and make your changes. Figure 10-16 shows the dialog box you'll see if you click the Number tab. Note that the Measurement System drop-down list, near the bottom of this dialog box, lets you switch between the metric and "imperial" measurement systems. (The latter is called U.S. in the dialog box.)

Be aware that all the settings in the Regional Settings Properties dialog box are merely defaults. Windows makes your choices available to programs, but the programs are not required to use them. Some programs ignore the Windows default settings and instead maintain their own formatting defaults. If you ask for a particular display format style via Control Panel, but a program uses a different style, consult the documentation or help file for that program.

FIGURE 10-16.

On the Number tab, you can choose the display formats to be used for decimal points and large numbers, as well as choose a default system of measurement.

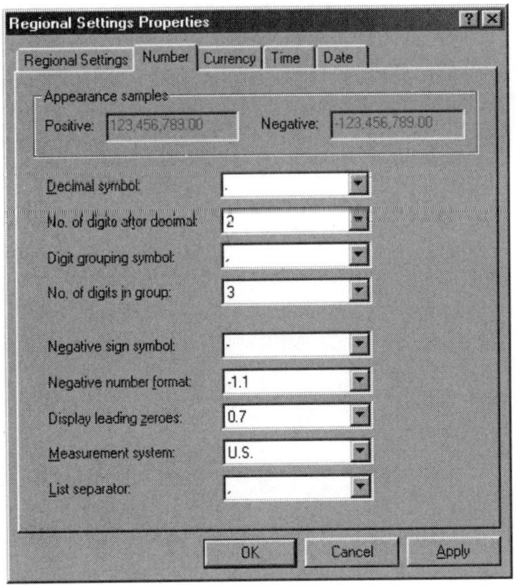

Setting Up New User Profiles

The Users icon—a new feature of Windows 98—lets you enable user profiles, set up a profile for each user, and modify or delete those profiles. The first time you launch Users (if no user profiles have been set up), a wizard steps you through the process of setting up a new user profile. And if you aren't already using profiles, the wizard also enables profiles in general (an action equivalent to selecting the "Users can customize their preferences . . ." option button on the User Profiles tab in the Passwords Properties dialog box), as well as setting up parameters for a particular new user.

The wizard prompts for a user name and password, and then offers the dialog box shown in Figure 10-17, on the next page, where you can select the items you want to personalize.

With the five check boxes in this dialog box, you can get quite specific about how much of the new user's profile should be unique to that user. Selecting a check box causes Windows to create a separate set of the specified folders for the new profile.

■ The Desktop folder is the folder whose contents determine the appearance of the desktop. The Documents menu is a component of the Start menu.

II

Further Explorations

FIGURE 10-17.

In this dialog box, you can specify which components of a new user's environment should be unique to that user's profile.

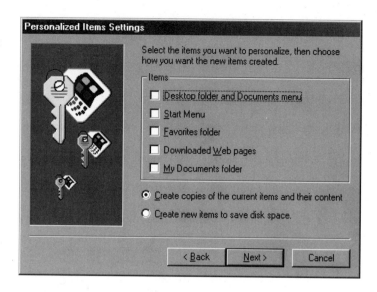

- The item labeled Start Menu refers to the Programs submenu of the Start menu and to the items that appear above Programs, at the top of the Start menu.

- The Favorites folder determines the contents of the Start menu's Favorites submenu, as well as the Favorites menu that appears in Windows Explorer and Internet Explorer.

- Downloaded Web pages are maintained in several special cache folders.

- The My Documents folder is the folder pointed to by the My Documents desktop icon.

The two option buttons at the bottom of the dialog box allow you to specify whether the new profile should be based on current settings (that is, the settings in use by the user who is currently logged on) or default settings. Using default settings (the choice labeled "Create new items . . .") saves disk space, because Windows doesn't have to copy all the current settings into a new collection of folders; instead, Windows creates new, empty folders.

After the wizard finishes setting up the new user, the User Settings dialog box appears, as shown in Figure 10-18. (After you have enabled user profiles and set up at least one user, launching Users in Control Panel takes you directly to this dialog box.) In the User Settings dialog box, you can:

FIGURE 10-18.

From the User Settings dialog box, you can add, delete, or modify user profiles.

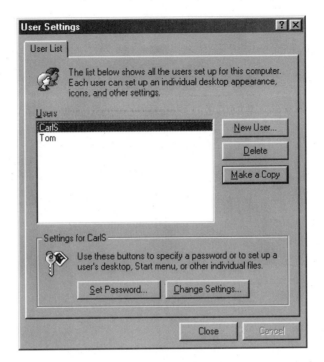

■ Add another user profile. Click New User, which invokes the now-familiar Add New User wizard. Alternatively, you can select a user and click Make A Copy. This also invokes the wizard, but the selections in the Personalized Items Settings dialog box match those of the selected user, perhaps saving you a few clicks.

■ Delete a user profile. Select a profile and click Delete.

■ Change the Windows logon password for a user. Select a profile and click Set Password.

■ Change the selections you made when you added a user profile. Select a profile and click Change Settings.

Running MS-DOS–Based Programs

L ike earlier versions of Windows, Windows 98 lets you run MS-DOS–based programs without leaving Windows. Subject to constraints imposed by the overall memory capacity of your system, you can run as many MS-DOS "sessions" (programs) simultaneously as you please. You can run most of your MS-DOS–based programs in windows that look and behave much like those of Windows-based programs. Or you can run MS-DOS–based programs in "full-screen" mode, so that they look the way they did when you ran them outside of Windows.

Windows provides multitasking services for MS-DOS–based programs, just as it does for Windows-based programs. That means, for example, that a lengthy macro in an MS-DOS–based spreadsheet program or a script in an MS-DOS–based communications program can continue to run while you focus your attention on another program. (You can disable the background processing of any MS-DOS–based program if you want.) Windows also manages resource contention among MS-DOS–based programs and between MS-DOS–based programs and Windows-based programs. So, for example, if you print a document from an MS-DOS–based word processor and your printer is busy, your document joins the printer queue just as though it had come from a Windows-based program.

If you were unable to run certain large MS-DOS–based programs under Windows 3.x, you may be pleasantly surprised to discover that your programs run fine under Windows 98. That's because Windows 98 stores more of its own essential "driver" files in extended memory, thereby making a smaller demand on the memory range used by MS-DOS–based programs. Unless your particular hardware requires one or more "real-mode" drivers, each of your MS-DOS sessions should be able to access considerably more memory than it could when running under earlier versions of Windows.

Having a smaller footprint in conventional memory is only one of the ways in which Windows 98 provides improved support for MS-DOS–based programs. Other improvements include a streamlined interface for tailoring the way individual programs use memory and other resources (eliminating the need for the PIF Editor program supplied with Windows 3.x), the ability to run MS-DOS–based programs in scalable windows, the ability to tailor the MS-DOS environment on a program-by-program basis, and better support for graphics-intensive programs such as games.

In this chapter we'll survey the ins and outs of running MS-DOS–based programs under Windows 98. We'll also spend a few paragraphs looking at the MS-DOS prompt itself. If you're accustomed to using MS-DOS commands for tasks such as copying files, creating directories (folders), or running commands in batch mode, there's no requirement to change your ways. Fortunately, thanks to support for UNC pathnames at the MS-DOS prompt, even these kinds of housekeeping chores should be easier to perform under Windows 98 than under previous versions of Windows.

Launching an MS-DOS–Based Program

You can start an MS-DOS–based program using any of the techniques you use to start Windows-based programs. To start a program, you can do any of the following:

- Choose the MS-DOS–based program from the Start menu, if it's there.

- Click or double-click the icon for the MS-DOS–based program in a folder or Windows Explorer window.

- Choose the Start menu's Run command, and then type the name of the program in the Open text box.

- Run MS-DOS Prompt and then type the name of the program at the MS-DOS command prompt.

If you start the program from either the Run dialog box or the MS-DOS command prompt, you might need to include the program's path as well as its name. In other words, starting the program using either of these techniques is exactly like starting it from the MS-DOS prompt in earlier versions of MS-DOS.

 TIP

> To maximize the amount of memory available to an MS-DOS–based program, launch it from within Windows, rather than from an MS-DOS prompt. Running MS-DOS Prompt itself consumes some memory that would otherwise be available to the program.

 SEE ALSO

For more information about creating shortcuts, see "Creating a Shortcut," page 83.

In addition to all these methods, you can, of course, create a shortcut for any MS-DOS–based program and then run the program by launching its shortcut. Creating a shortcut for an MS-DOS–based program is exactly like creating a shortcut for a Windows-based program.

 TIP

> To work exclusively in MS-DOS, without going into Windows, press F8 as your computer is booting. That is, turn on your computer. After the computer checks out its memory and other components, and after it finishes running whatever commands you have have in your Autoexec.bat and Config.sys files, you'll hear a beep and Windows will begin to load. At that moment, press the F8 key. (You'll have about two seconds in which to do this.) A menu will appear on your screen. Choose Command Prompt Only to begin an MS-DOS session. Later, if you want to go into Windows, you can either reboot or type *win* at the MS-DOS command prompt.
>
> If you're already running Windows and you want to work exclusively in MS-DOS, choose Shut Down from the Start menu. Then select Restart In MS-DOS Mode. To quit your MS-DOS–only session and restart Windows, type *exit* at the MS-DOS prompt. If you're quitting for the day, you can safely turn your computer off; Windows will then start normally at your next session.

Of PIFs and Properties

If you have installed Windows 98 as an upgrade to an earlier version of Windows, you may already have created Program Information Files (PIFs) for some of your MS-DOS–based programs. If so, Windows 98 will continue to use the settings in your PIFs as you run your programs in the new environment.

> **NOTE**

In a folder window's details view, the file type for a PIF is shown as "Shortcut to MS-DOS Program."

> **SEE ALSO**
>
> For information about program properties, see "Working with Program Properties," page 287.

Windows also maintains information about popular MS-DOS–based programs in a file called Apps.inf. If you run a program for which no PIF exists, Windows looks for information about the program in Apps.inf. Windows uses any information it finds there to create a PIF for the program. If Windows finds no PIF for the program, and the program is not included in Apps.inf, Windows runs the program with default settings. In the majority of cases, these defaults allow the program to run effectively, so you don't need to concern yourself with property settings. If you want, however, you can adjust the program's settings by working with its properties dialog box. When you make any changes to the properties, Windows records your choices in a newly created PIF.

Terminating an MS-DOS Session

The best way to end any MS-DOS–based program is to use the program's normal Quit or Exit command. Doing so ensures that the program is terminated in an orderly manner and that you're given the option to save any work created in the program.

If you're running an MS-DOS–based program in a window, however, you can also close it by clicking the Close button at the right edge of the title bar, by choosing Close from the Control menu, or by double-clicking the Control-menu icon. Normally, it's not a good idea to use any of these methods for shutting down the program, however, because Windows cannot ensure that the program is ready to be terminated. You can lose work or damage open data files by using a Windows procedure to shut down an MS-DOS–based program.

By default, when you use a Windows procedure to close an MS-DOS–based program, Windows displays a warning. You can then ignore the warning and go ahead with the program's termination, or you can go back to the program and use its own shut-down procedure. Normally, Windows also requires you to close all MS-DOS–based programs before shutting down Windows itself. (By changing a property, you can disable these safeguards for particular programs. For details, see "Allowing Windows to Close an MS-DOS–Based Program," page 299.)

Depending on how another option on the MS-DOS–based program's properties dialog box is set, the program can remain visible in a window after you shut it down. If it does, the title bar for the closed program's window will include the word *Finished*. A program marked *Finished* has already shut itself down, so it's perfectly safe to close its window by clicking the Close button or pressing Alt+F4. (The option to keep a closed program visible in a *Finished* window is handy at times because it allows you to see the program's final output, including any messages displayed by the program if it happens to terminate abnormally. For information about using this option, see "Keeping a Program's Final Screen Visible at Close," page 291.)

Full Screen or Window?

With few exceptions, you can run any MS-DOS–based program either in a full screen or in a window. (The principal exceptions are graphics programs that use resolutions higher than 640×480.) If you run a program in a full screen, it looks exactly as it does in a pre–Windows 95 version of MS-DOS. If you run it in a window, it has a title bar, a Control menu, and all the other standard window paraphernalia. Figure 11-1, on the next page, illustrates an MS-DOS–based program running in a window.

Full Screen Advantages

One advantage of running a program in a full screen is that it gets the maximum amount of screen real estate—the same amount of display space it would have if it were running outside of Windows. If you run a program in a window, you can maximize the window but the presence of a window title bar means you'll still have something less than the full screen to work with.

FIGURE 11-1.

In a window, an MS-DOS–based program has all the standard window equipment—a title bar, sizing buttons, a Control-menu icon, and so on.

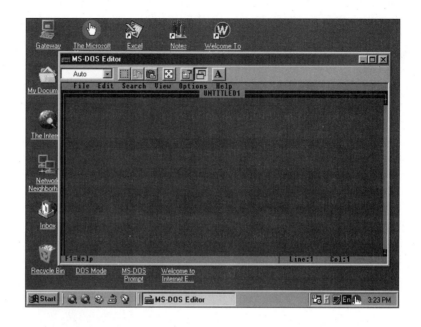

NOTE

"Maximizing" an MS-DOS window does not necessarily fill the screen, as it does with most Windows-based programs. The portion of the screen that the maximized window occupies depends on your Windows display resolution, the display mode used by the MS-DOS–based program, and the font size you select. (For information about changing the Windows display resolution, see "Changing Display Resolution," page 88. For information about font-size options, see "Font Options in a Window," page 281.)

Depending on the speed of your hardware, you might also enjoy faster screen performance in a full screen. Particularly with graphics programs, this could be a compelling reason to choose full-screen mode.

If you're running in a full screen, you can switch to a different program by pressing Alt+Tab to invoke the "task switcher," by pressing Ctrl+Esc to invoke the Start menu, or by first switching the program back to a window. When you switch away from a full-screen MS-DOS–based program, a button for the program appears on the taskbar. You can switch back to the full-screen program by clicking its taskbar button.

TIP

If you have more than one full-screen MS-DOS session running and you want to switch from a full-screen MS-DOS session to the desktop, press Alt+Tab to invoke the task switcher. This lets you switch between programs, but not to the desktop—unless you *click* somewhere while the task switcher is displayed. Clicking anywhere on the screen takes you to the desktop.

You can also switch to the desktop by pressing Ctrl+Esc, which displays the desktop and opens the Start menu.

Window Advantages

Running MS-DOS–based programs in windows, on the other hand, confers several benefits:

- You can keep several programs in view at the same time.

- You can more easily switch between programs.

- You can copy (but not cut) material from one program and paste it into another.

- You can read or modify a program's properties.

Switching Between a Full Screen and a Window

 Provided your MS-DOS–based program is not one of the few that run only in a full screen, and provided you have not disabled the Alt+Enter shortcut key, you can switch from a full screen to a window by pressing Alt+Enter. If you're running a program in a window, you can use Alt+Enter to switch to a full screen. Or, if the toolbar is visible, you can click the Full Screen button—the fourth icon from the right.

 TIP

If you want to switch from a full screen to a window but you've forgotten which keystroke combination to use (Alt+Enter), press Alt+Tab or Ctrl+Esc to switch to another program. Then right-click the taskbar button for the program you switched away from. Choose Properties from the context menu, click the Screen tab in the properties dialog box, and select the Window option button.

Using the Toolbar

 SEE ALSO

For information about controlling the appearance of the toolbar whenever you start a program, see "Displaying or Hiding the Toolbar," page 296.

Like a folder window, the window that displays an MS-DOS–based program includes an optional toolbar. You can toggle this toolbar on or off by right-clicking anywhere on the window's title bar and choosing the Toolbar command from the ensuing Control menu. The toolbar slightly reduces the maximum amount of space that your program can use, but in return it offers the handy commands shown in Table 11-1.

All of these commands are also available via the Control menu, the menu that appears when you right-click the window's title bar (or click with either button on the icon at the left edge of the title bar), but you might find them more accessible with the toolbar in view.

TABLE 11-1.   MS-DOS Window Toolbar

Toolbar Icon	Description
Auto ▼	Lets you choose between preset font options and an automatic mode in which the display font automatically adjusts as the program's window is resized
⬚	Allows you to select text or graphics prior to copying (If you have turned on QuickEdit, you do not need to use this command before selecting. For details, see "Mouse Options in a Window," page 282.)
🖺	Copies the selection to the Clipboard
📋	Pastes the Clipboard's contents into the MS-DOS–based program
✛	Switches from a window to a full screen
🖳	Displays the program's properties dialog box
🗗	Allows a process in the program to continue running when you switch to other programs; background processing is on if the toolbar icon appears to be pushed in
A	Displays the Font tab in the program's properties dialog box

Font Options in a Window

When you run an MS-DOS–based program in a window, Windows always displays its text in a monospaced font. That's because MS-DOS–based programs typically depend on uniform character spacing. You have choices about the size of the font to be used, however. To exercise your options, right-click the program's title bar, choose Properties from the Control menu, and then click the Font tab. You'll see the dialog box shown in Figure 11-2. The list box in the upper right quadrant of this dialog box presents the available font-size choices, while the two preview boxes below show the relative space occupied by the program's window and a sample of the selected font.

FIGURE 11-2.

Text in a windowed MS-DOS–based program is always displayed in a monospaced font of Windows' choosing, but you have options about font size.

If you choose Auto (the default option), Windows automatically picks the optimal font and size whenever you change the dimensions of the program's window. If you select any of the other size options, Windows adjusts the dimensions of the window to fit the selected font size. With any size other than Auto in effect, you can't increase the size of the window. (You can click the Maximize button, but its only effect is to move the window to the upper left corner of the screen—without enlarging it.) You can decrease the window's size, but Windows then "clips" (truncates) the window's contents rather than adjusting the size of the text.

Note that the available font sizes (see Figure 11-2, on the previous page) are not listed as conventional point sizes. Instead, they're listed by the pixel dimensions of the font's character matrix. For example, 4 × 7 denotes a font in which each character occupies some portion of a box measuring four pixels wide by seven pixels tall. Some of the character matrix, of course, is actually "white" space. If you experiment with the various size options, you'll find several in which the vertical dimension is double or nearly double the horizontal dimension. These are not tall and skinny fonts; rather, they're options in which text lines are more widely spaced. If you find the text in a windowed display hard to read, you might want to sample some of these options.

Fonts available for use in windowed MS-DOS–based programs come in two flavors: bitmap and TrueType. In the properties dialog box (see Figure 11-2, on the previous page), you can restrict the font choices to one type or the other, but it's unlikely you'll find a compelling reason to do so. For performance reasons, Windows uses a bitmap font when one happens to be available at the optimal size. Otherwise, it uses TrueType for scalability.

As you've seen, the toolbar includes a font-size drop-down list as well as a button that summons the properties dialog box. When all you want to do is make a size selection, and you don't care about seeing a preview of the selected size, the drop-down is a more direct way to get the job done.

Mouse Options in a Window

If an MS-DOS–based program supports a mouse, and you run the program in a full screen, the MS-DOS–based program "owns" the mouse. That is, you can choose commands, make selections, or do anything else with the mouse that you would be able to do if you were running the program outside of Windows.

If you run the program in a window, you have a choice about mouse ownership. You can continue to let the MS-DOS–based program own the mouse, or you can let Windows own it. If the program owns the mouse, you will need to use the Mark command (on the toolbar or the Control menu) before copying anything to the Clipboard. If you let Windows own it, you can use your mouse to select information and copy it to the

Clipboard, exactly as you would do in a Windows-based program. But you won't be able to use the mouse for choosing commands in the MS-DOS–based program.

Whichever mouse mode you elect to use, you can use the mouse to change the window's size or position, to choose commands from the toolbar, or to choose commands from the Control menu. In other words, the issue of who owns the mouse arises only when the mouse pointer lies within the client area of the program's window. On the borders, the toolbar, or the title bar, Windows always retains control of the mouse.

 To switch from one mouse mode to the other, first display the program's properties dialog box—by clicking the Properties button on the toolbar or by right-clicking the title bar and choosing Properties from the Control menu. Then click the Misc tab in the properties dialog box. You'll see the dialog box shown in Figure 11-3.

FIGURE 11-3.

On the Misc tab in the properties dialog box, you can tell Windows how your mouse should behave when its pointer lies within the MS-DOS–based program's client area.

For information about the other Misc-tab options, see "Options on the Misc Tab," page 297.

In the Mouse section, near the upper right corner of this dialog box, select the QuickEdit check box if you want to be able to select and copy window contents without first choosing the Mark command—that is, if you want Windows to have full control over your mouse. Leave this check box deselected if you want to be able to use your mouse to interact with the MS-DOS–based program.

Further Explorations

The Mouse section of the Misc tab in the properties dialog box also includes an Exclusive Mode option. If you select this option, the MS-DOS–based program will have sole dominion over the mouse as long as the MS-DOS–based program has the focus. That is, in exclusive mode, the mouse pointer will appear to be trapped within the client area of the MS-DOS–based program's window.

 TIP

If you turn exclusive mode on and then change your mind, you can return mouse control to Windows by pressing Alt+Spacebar to open the Control menu. Then click the Properties icon on the toolbar or choose Properties from the Control menu. Then you can click the Misc tab and deselect the Exclusive Mode check box.

Using Copy and Paste

 SEE ALSO

For more information about copying and pasting, see Chapter 9, "Exchanging Information Using the Clipboard and OLE."

Windows provides basic copy-and-paste services (without OLE) for MS-DOS–based programs, just as it does for Windows-based programs. The procedures for copying and pasting are nearly the same in both kinds of programs.

Copying from an MS-DOS–Based Program

To copy a block of data from a windowed MS-DOS–based program:

1 Click the Mark button on the toolbar. Or right-click the title bar, choose Edit from the Control menu, and then choose Mark on the submenu that appears.

2 Drag the mouse to select the data you want to copy.

3 Press Enter or click the Copy button on the toolbar.

4 Activate the document into which you want to paste, position the insertion point where you want the copied material to appear, and choose the Paste command.

If you have turned on the QuickEdit option for your MS-DOS–based program, you can omit step 1. (For more information about the QuickEdit option, see "Mouse Options in a Window," page 282.) How do you know if the QuickEdit option is on? You can go to the Misc tab in the properties dialog box and look at the QuickEdit check box. Or, more simply, you can drag with the mouse and see what happens. If QuickEdit is on, the word *Select* appears in the program's title bar as soon as you start dragging. If it does not, you are not in QuickEdit mode, and you need to click the Mark button before making your selection.

Note one important difference between selecting text in an MS-DOS–based program and selecting text in a Windows-based program: in an MS-DOS–based program, a selection is always rectangular, even if that means that lines of text are truncated on the left side, the right side, or both. Figure 11-4, on the next page, shows an example of a text selection in an MS-DOS window. In contrast, when you select text in a Windows-based program, the selection follows the flow of the text, whether or not that produces a rectangular block.

 TIP

You can also select data in an MS-DOS–based program using the keyboard. Open the Control menu by holding down the Alt key while you press the Spacebar. Press E to open the Edit submenu, followed by K to choose the Mark command. You will see a rectangular cursor in the upper left corner of the program's window. This is your (unexpanded) selection. Use the Up, Down, Left, and Right arrow keys to position this cursor in one corner of the area you want to select. Then hold down the Shift key while you use arrow keys to expand the selection. When you have made your selection, press Enter to copy it to the Clipboard.

Pasting into an MS-DOS–Based Program

 To paste data into an MS-DOS–based program, simply position the cursor where you want the pasted data to appear. Then open the Control menu, choose Edit, and choose Paste. Or click the Paste button on the toolbar.

FIGURE 11-4.

When you select text in an MS-DOS–based program, your selection is rectangular, even if that means that lines are truncated.

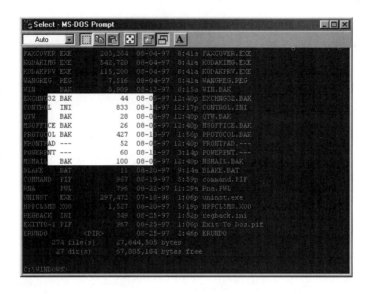

Note that the Paste command in an MS-DOS–based program is always active, even if the Clipboard is empty or contains data in a format that's not appropriate for the program. If you try to paste graphics data into a text-based program, you'll get an error message when you paste. A different error message appears if the Clipboard is empty when you try to paste.

Also be aware that when you paste text into an MS-DOS–based program, Windows feeds characters to the program exactly as if you had typed them yourself at the keyboard. That is, the program itself cannot tell that the characters aren't coming directly from the keyboard. If you paste into a program that performs some kind of syntax checking—for example, a spreadsheet that checks cell entries for correct formulation, or a program editor that verifies correct programming code—your paste may be interrupted by error messages from the program.

If you experience other kinds of problems pasting into an MS-DOS–based program, try disabling the Fast Pasting option. With this option on (as it normally is), Windows feeds character data to the program as fast as it can. Most, but not all, programs can accept this fast transfer. If yours cannot, open the Misc tab in the program's properties dialog box and deselect the Fast Pasting check box.

Working with Program Properties

Every MS-DOS–based program has a properties dialog box that spells out everything Windows needs to know to run the program. (As mentioned, Windows records property settings in a Program Information File, or PIF.) You can use the properties dialog box to adjust such things as the amount of memory allocated to the program, the program's initial display mode (window or full screen), the behavior of your mouse when the program is running in a window, and so on.

To get to a program's properties dialog box, do any of the following:

- If the program is already running, right-click its title bar or its taskbar button and choose Properties from the Control menu. (If the program is running in a full screen, first press Alt+Enter to switch to a window.)

- If the program is already running and the toolbar is visible, click the Properties button.

- If the program is not running, right-click its entry in a folder or Windows Explorer window. Then choose Properties from the context menu.

? SEE ALSO

For more information about the General tab, see "Inspecting Folder and File Properties," page 127.

If you open its properties dialog box while a program is not running, you'll see a tab called General that does not otherwise appear. This tab includes information about the size of the program, its creation and most-recent-access dates, and so on.

Options on the Program Tab

Figure 11-5, on the next page, shows the Program tab in an MS-DOS–based program's properties dialog box. Here you can do any of the following:

- Change the name that appears on the program's title bar when the program is running in a window.

- Add command-line parameters or otherwise modify the MS-DOS command line used to execute the program.

- Specify a startup data folder.

FIGURE 11-5.

The Program tab lets you specify basic information about a program, such as its name and location.

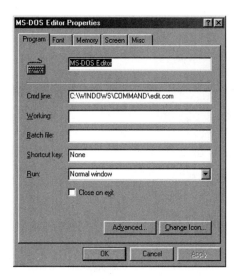

- Specify the name of a batch file that Windows will run prior to launching the program.

- Specify a shortcut key that you can use to launch the program.

- Indicate whether you want the program to start running in a maximized window, in a restored window, or as a minimized taskbar button.

- Elect to keep the program's final display visible in a window after you quit the program.

- Change the icon that appears on the program's title bar, on its taskbar button, and in folder and Windows Explorer windows.

- "Hide" the program from Windows, so the program won't be able to detect the fact that you're running it under Windows.

- Run the program in MS-DOS mode.

- Have Windows recommend MS-DOS mode if Windows doesn't have enough resources to run the program normally.

If you decide to run the program in MS-DOS mode, the properties dialog box offers some additional options, discussed below.

Changing a Program's Title Bar Caption

To change the text that appears on a program's title bar, simply modify whatever appears in the first text box on the Program tab. For example, entering *DOS Editor* in the first text box in the dialog box shown in Figure 11-5 changes the title bar from "MS-DOS Editor" to "DOS Editor."

Adding Command-Line Parameters

The second text box on the Program tab, the one marked Cmd Line, specifies the command line that MS-DOS uses to run the program. Many programs allow you to specify one or more command-line parameters following the name of the program's executable file. Depending on the program involved, parameters can be used for such things as loading a data file at the same time the executable file is launched, modifying some aspect of the program's behavior, and so on. If you regularly want an MS-DOS–based program to use a particular command-line parameter, you can specify that parameter in the Cmd Line text box. Be sure to include a space character immediately after the name of the executable file, just as you would if you were entering the parameter at the MS-DOS command prompt.

TIP

Prompting for Parameters

If you enter a question mark as the program's parameter (that is, you follow the program name in the Cmd Line box with a space and a question mark), Windows pauses to ask for any command-line parameters whenever you start the program. This is useful, for example, for programs that use the name of the file you want to open as a command-line parameter.

Specifying a Startup Folder

The Working text box on the Program tab lets you specify an initial data folder ("directory" in MS-DOS parlance) to be used by the MS-DOS–based program. For example, if you enter *c:\mystuff* on the Working line for the MS-DOS Editor Properties dialog box, MS-DOS Editor will initially be set to read files from and save files to the folder C:\MyStuff. This line is blank by default, which means the program makes its own choice about what default data folder to use. In most programs, the default data folder is the folder in which the program's executable file is stored.

Specifying the Name of a Batch File

If you enter the name of a batch file on the Batch File line on the Program tab, Windows always runs that batch file prior to launching the MS-DOS–based program. You can use this technique to launch a terminate-and-stay-resident (TSR) program that will share an MS-DOS session with the MS-DOS–based program. (If you run the TSR directly, instead of using this batch-file approach, the TSR will run in its own separate MS-DOS session, and the program will not have access to its services.) You can also use a batch file to modify some aspect of the MS-DOS environment. For example, when you run MS-DOS Prompt from the Start menu, you are running an MS-DOS session whose executable file is Command.com. If you want your MS-DOS Prompt sessions to use something other than the default pg (C:\>) prompt string, you can enter a Prompt command in a batch file and then specify the name of that batch file on the Batch File line of the Program tab for the Command.com properties dialog box. (For another way to modify the MS-DOS environment, see "Running a Program in MS-DOS Mode," on the next page.)

Specifying a Shortcut Key

SEE ALSO

For information about assigning a shortcut key to a Windows-based program, see "Assigning Other Properties to a Shortcut," page 86.

On the Shortcut Key line, you can specify a keyboard shortcut for switching to the MS-DOS–based program. For example, if you run the MS-DOS–based version of Systat 6.0 under Windows 98, you might want to supply Systat with the shortcut Ctrl+Alt+S. Note, though, that unlike a shortcut key assigned to a Windows-based program, the shortcut you give to an MS-DOS–based program cannot be used to launch the program. It works only for switching to the program after the program is already running.

Specifying the Initial Window State

SEE ALSO

For information about full-screen display, see "Full Screen or Window?" page 277.

You can use the Run line on the Program tab to indicate whether you want the program to open initially in a maximized window, in a restored window, or minimized. You might, for example, want to have the program open minimized if you include it with one or more other programs in your StartUp folder. That way, it will be unobtrusively available at the beginning of each Windows session.

Note that if you choose Minimized, the program will always start minimized, even if you also choose full-screen display on the Screen tab.

Keeping a Program's Final Screen Visible at Close

If an MS-DOS–based program terminates abnormally, it might be useful to keep the program's final screen output visible in a window after the program closes. That way you can read any error messages that the program might have displayed.

To exercise this option, deselect the Close On Exit check box on the Program tab in the properties dialog box.

Changing a Program's Icon

Windows assigns a default MS-DOS icon to all MS-DOS–based programs. This icon appears on the program's title bar, on its taskbar button, and in your folder and Windows Explorer windows. If you'd like to choose a different icon, click the Change Icon button, near the bottom of the Program tab. A selection of alternative icons appears in the ensuing dialog box. If none of those suit you, specify an .ICO file (or the name of a .DLL or .EXE file containing icon resources) on the File Name line of that dialog box. Or click the Browse button and navigate to a file containing icon resources.

Preventing a Program from Knowing That It's Running Under Windows

Given adequate memory, nearly all MS-DOS–based programs are fully functional when running under Windows. In rare cases, however, a program might not run or might not run normally if it detects the presence of Windows. Should your program be one of those exceptional few, you can use a "stealth" feature to keep it from knowing that Windows is running. To do this, click the Advanced button near the bottom of the Program tab. Then select the check box labeled Prevent MS-DOS–Based Programs From Detecting Windows.

Running a Program in MS-DOS Mode

If an MS-DOS–based program won't run satisfactorily under Windows, no matter how you tweak its properties, you'll want to run it in MS-DOS mode. Before launching a program in MS-DOS mode, Windows closes all running programs and then removes most of itself from memory. The only part of Windows that remains is a stub that Windows uses to reload itself after you quit the MS-DOS–based program. In this mode, you can run only a single MS-DOS session; all other programs—whether Windows-based or MS-DOS–based—are closed before entering MS-DOS mode.

To set a program so that it always runs in MS-DOS mode, click the Advanced button on the Program tab. Then select the MS-DOS Mode check box. If you're not sure whether the program requires MS-DOS mode, click Advanced on the Program tab, and then select the check box labeled Suggest MS-DOS Mode As Necessary. Windows will then recommend MS-DOS mode if it appears that the program will not run without it.

Whether you run a program in MS-DOS mode by your own insistence or at Windows' recommendation, you also have the option of specifying Config.sys and Autoexec.bat settings tailored for the program you're planning to run. In other words, you can have default Config.sys and Autoexec.bat files that are applied to all your normal (non-MS-DOS-mode) MS-DOS sessions and different versions of Config.sys and Autoexec.bat for each program that you run in MS-DOS mode.

To modify the Config.sys and Autoexec.bat files used by a particular program running in MS-DOS mode, first click the Advanced button on the Program tab in the program's properties dialog box. Select the MS-DOS Mode check box on the Advanced page, and then click the option button labeled Specify A New MS-DOS Configuration. In the windows below this option button, you can edit the current Config.sys and Autoexec.bat files.

Going into MS-DOS mode can be disruptive because Windows has to shut down all running programs before it can do this. Therefore, by default, Windows displays a confirmation prompt before launching any program in MS-DOS mode. If you want to disable this prompt, click the Advanced button on the Program tab in the program's properties dialog box and deselect the check box labeled Warn Before Entering MS-DOS Mode.

Options on the Font Tab

The Font tab allows you to choose alternative display fonts to be used when an MS-DOS–based program is running in a window. For more information about the Font tab, see "Font Options in a Window," page 281.

Options on the Memory Tab

The Memory tab, depicted in Figure 11-6, allows you to allocate to your programs particular amounts of memory in various categories. Those categories are as follows:

Conventional	Memory in the 0–640 KB range
Expanded (EMS)	Physical memory above 1024 KB that is "mapped" into ranges between 640 KB and 1024 KB
Extended (XMS)	Memory above 1024 KB
DOS Protected-Mode (DPMI)	Extended memory that is managed by the DOS Protected Mode Interface specification

FIGURE 11-6.

Options on the Memory tab let you limit the amount of memory available to a program.

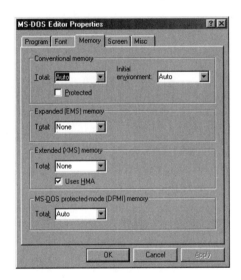

NOTE

If your Config.sys file invokes Emm386.exe with the *noems* option, the EMS drop-down will not be available.

In all four cases, the default setting, Auto, should work for most programs.

For conventional memory, Auto means that Windows supplies your program with as much memory as it can. Unless you're running a particularly small-scale MS-DOS–based program and you need to conserve memory for other programs, it's unlikely you'll find a good reason not to choose Auto.

Auto also means "as much as possible" in the EMS and XMS drop-downs. In rare cases, an MS-DOS–based program may have trouble handling an unlimited amount of EMS or XMS memory. If your program is one of the exceptional few, use these drop-downs to reduce the available EMS or XMS memory.

In the case of DPMI, the Auto setting causes Windows to allocate an amount of memory based on your current configuration. Here, too, it's unlikely that you'll need to choose a different setting.

The Memory tab also provides a drop-down in which you can specify the size of your program's MS-DOS environment. The environment is an area of memory used by the MS-DOS command interpreter, Command.com, to store information about the current *path* (the set of directories that MS-DOS searches when you issue a command that does not include a path specification), the current prompt string, the location of a TEMP directory, and other similar variables. If you leave the Auto setting in place here, Windows allocates the amount of memory specified by the Shell statement in your Config.sys file (or the default amount, if there is no Shell statement). If you ever see "Out of environment space" errors in your MS-DOS sessions, try increasing this memory allocation.

Options on the Screen Tab

Options on the Screen tab in the properties dialog box allow you to do the following:

- Choose between a full screen and a window.

- Stipulate that a session should start with a 25-line, 43-line, or 50-line display.

- Display or hide the toolbar.

- Indicate whether Windows should remember your screen size, window position, and font at the end of the current session and restore it at the beginning of the next session.

- Disable a technique that Windows uses by default to achieve faster screen performance, in case that technique causes problems with your program.

- Disable a technique that Windows uses to allocate memory more efficiently, in case that technique causes problems with your program.

Figure 11-7 shows an example of the Screen tab.

FIGURE 11-7.

On the Screen tab you can choose between a full screen and a window, opt for a 43-line or 50-line display, and override two of Windows' performance defaults.

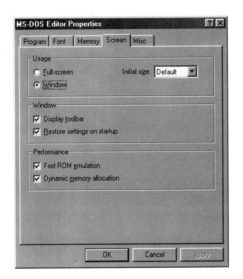

Choosing Between a Full Screen and a Window

You can switch between a full screen and a window at any time simply by pressing Alt+Enter. Should you want to change the default display mode, you can do so by visiting the Screen tab and selecting the Full-Screen or Window option button.

Specifying a 43-Line or 50-Line Display

Most MS-DOS–based programs display 25 lines of text per screen. Some also allow you to choose a 43-line or 50-line display. If your program supports these alternative display modes, you can use its properties dialog box to make either the default mode on startup. Click the Screen tab and select from the options listed in the Initial Size drop-down.

To let an MS-DOS–based program make its own decision about how many lines per screen to display, choose Default from the Initial Size drop-down.

Displaying or Hiding the Toolbar

SEE ALSO

For information about the toolbar, see "Using the Toolbar," page 280.

The toolbar makes it easier to choose commands when an MS-DOS–based program is running in a window. In return for the favor, it slightly reduces the amount of screen real estate available for the program's display. You can suppress the toolbar (or reenable it) by means of the Display Toolbar check box on the Screen tab.

Remembering or Forgetting Window Settings

By default, when you end a windowed MS-DOS session, Windows records the size and position of the window, as well as the current font size. At the start of your next session, those settings are restored. If for any reason you'd rather have Windows forget the current window settings, visit the Screen tab in the properties dialog box and deselect the check box labeled Restore Settings On StartUp.

NOTE

Windows always records whether a program is running in a full screen or a window when you close the program—whether or not the Restore Settings On StartUp check box is selected. The next time you run the program (unless you edit its properties in the meantime), it will start the same way it was when you last closed it—in a full screen or in a window.

TIP

If you want to ensure that a program always starts in a particular display mode, regardless of its condition when you last closed the program, open the properties dialog box for its PIF from a Windows Explorer window. (You can use the Find command to find the PIF. On the Name & Location tab, enter the name of the program. On the Advanced tab, in the Of Type drop-down, select Shortcut To MS-DOS Program.) Make all the settings you need, including the selection of Full-Screen or Window on the Screen tab. Then switch to the General tab and select the Read-Only check box. This prevents Windows from updating the PIF when you close the program.

Turning Off Video ROM Emulation

To achieve faster screen performance, Windows normally uses volatile memory (RAM) to emulate video routines that are stored in read-only memory (ROM). If you experience any abnormal screen behavior in an MS-DOS–based program, try turning this emulation off. Deselect the Fast ROM Emulation check box on the Screen tab.

Turning Off Dynamic Memory Allocation

Programs use considerably less video memory when displaying text than when displaying graphics. When an MS-DOS–based program switches from a graphics display to a text display, Windows normally takes advantage of the "memory dividend" so that more memory will be available for other programs. When an MS-DOS–based program switches back to a graphics display, Windows reallocates memory to the MS-DOS session. If you experience any problems switching from text mode to graphics mode in an MS-DOS–based program, try turning off this "dynamic memory allocation." Deselect the Dynamic Memory Allocation check box on the Screen tab in the properties dialog box.

Options on the Misc Tab

Figure 11-8, on the next page, illustrates the Misc tab in the properties dialog box. Using the options on the Misc tab you can do the following:

- Disable your screen saver when an MS-DOS–based program has the focus.

- Specify how you want your mouse to behave when an MS-DOS–based program has the focus. (For information about QuickEdit and exclusive mode, see "Mouse Options in a Window," page 282.)

- Allow or disallow background processing of an MS-DOS–based program.

- Disable the warning that Windows normally displays when you use the Close icon to terminate an MS-DOS–based program, as well as the requirement that you close the MS-DOS–based program before quitting Windows.

II

Further Explorations

FIGURE 11-8.

The Misc tab in an MS-DOS–based program's properties dialog box provides control over mouse behavior and several other matters.

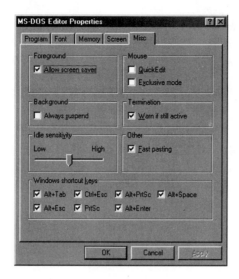

- Adjust the "idle sensitivity"—the amount of time Windows will wait before reducing the resources allocated to an idle MS-DOS–based program that has the focus.

- Adopt a slower pasting mode for an MS-DOS–based program that cannot accept data from the Clipboard as quickly as Windows normally supplies it.

- Disable certain keystroke combinations (such as Alt+Tab) that are normally used by Windows so that those combinations can be used by an MS-DOS–based program.

Disabling the Windows Screen Saver

Normally, Windows starts the current screen saver after a specified amount of idle time has elapsed, regardless of what program has the focus. If an MS-DOS–based program has its own screen saver (and you want to use it instead of the Windows screen saver), or if for any reason the Windows screen saver interferes with an MS-DOS–based program's functionality, visit the Misc tab in the program's properties dialog box and deselect the Allow Screen Saver check box.

Allowing an MS-DOS–Based Program to Run in the Background

If you want processing in an MS-DOS–based program to continue while you work in another program, deselect the Always Suspend check box on the Misc tab. If the program doesn't need background processing, it's best to leave this check box selected.

Allowing Windows to Close an MS-DOS–Based Program

By default, Windows displays a warning if you try to quit a windowed MS-DOS–based program by using a Windows procedure—clicking the Close icon, double-clicking the Control-menu icon, or choosing Close from the Control menu. Windows also normally requires you to close all MS-DOS sessions before shutting down Windows itself. These safeguards protect you against accidental loss of data.

If your MS-DOS–based program is one that never creates data files, you can safely disable Windows' normal safety measures. To do this, deselect the Warn If Still Active check box on the Misc tab in the program's properties dialog box.

Adjusting the Idle Sensitivity

When an MS-DOS–based program running in the foreground sits idle—for example, while it's waiting for your next keystroke—Windows makes some of the resources it normally allocates to that program available to other running programs. The Idle Sensitivity slider on the Misc tab gives you some control over how much idle time Windows tolerates before reallocating resources. If the program seems less responsive than you want it to be, move the slider to the left. If you want other programs to run more quickly while the MS-DOS–based program has the focus, move the slider to the right.

Slowing the Paste

? SEE ALSO

For more information about pasting, see "Using Copy and Paste," page 284.

If Windows doesn't correctly paste data from the Clipboard into an MS-DOS–based program, try deselecting the Fast Pasting check box on the Misc tab in the properties dialog box. This will slow the rate at which Windows feeds Clipboard data to the program.

II

Further Explorations

Disabling Windows Shortcut Keys

Windows normally reserves certain keystroke combinations for itself, even while an MS-DOS–based program has the focus. For example, if you press Alt+Enter while working in an MS-DOS–based program, Windows assumes that keystroke combination is intended for *it*, rather than for the MS-DOS–based program. The reserved keystroke combinations and their normal effects are as follows:

Alt+Tab	Lets you switch to a different program
Ctrl+Esc	Displays the Start menu
Alt+Print Screen	Copies the current window, as a bitmap, to the Clipboard
Alt+Spacebar	Displays the current program's Control menu
Alt+Esc	Switches the focus directly to another program
Print Screen	Copies the desktop, as a bitmap, to the Clipboard
Alt+Enter	Switches between a full screen and a window

To make any of these shortcuts available to your MS-DOS–based program, deselect the appropriate check box in the Windows Shortcut Keys section on the Misc tab in the program's properties dialog box.

Entering Commands at the MS-DOS Prompt

Like previous versions of Windows, Windows 98 allows you to enter commands, run batch files, and run programs by typing commands at the MS-DOS prompt. If you're accustomed to performing file-management and disk-management operations at the command line, there's no need to change your ways in Windows 98.

To get to the MS-DOS prompt, do any of the following:

- Choose MS-DOS Prompt from the Start menu.

- Choose the Run command from the Start menu and type *command*.

- Launch the Command icon in your Windows folder, or any shortcut for Command.com.

To close an MS-DOS Prompt session, type *exit* at the MS-DOS prompt.

TIP

You can run Windows-based programs as well as MS-DOS based programs from the MS-DOS prompt. To run a Windows-based program, simply type its name (along with its path, if needed), just as you would if you were running an MS-DOS–based program. Or use the Start command. (For information about the Start command, see "Running Programs with the Start Command," page 303.)

The MS-DOS Prompt Versus the Run Command

SEE ALSO

For information about the Run command, see "The Run Command," page 55.

The MS-DOS prompt and the Run command are similar in that they both accept traditional operating-system commands, with or without command-line parameters. The principal differences are the following:

- The MS-DOS prompt runs in a separate "virtual machine," and that virtual machine remains open after any MS-DOS command (other than Exit) is executed, allowing you to view the command's output or execute additional commands. The Run command does not maintain an open virtual machine after your command is executed. (A virtual machine is a session running in a processor mode that emulates a 640-KB computer running MS-DOS. Most processes running in a virtual machine cannot distinguish the virtual machine from a computer that is running *only* MS-DOS.)

- You cannot use the Run command to execute internal MS-DOS commands directly. To execute internal MS-DOS commands, you must use the MS-DOS prompt or precede the command in the Run dialog with *command /c.*

  The majority of MS-DOS commands are programs stored in files with the extension .EXE or .COM. These are the *external* commands of MS-DOS. A few commands are intrinsic, or *internal* to the operating system. (They're built into Command.com.) These commands can be run only from the MS-DOS prompt. The following commands are internal: Break, Call, CD, Chcp, ChDir, Cls, Copy,

II

Further Explorations

Ctty, Date, Del, Dir, Echo, Erase, Exit, For, LH, LoadHigh, MD, MkDir, More, Path, Prompt, RD, Ren, Rename, RmDir, Set, Time, Type, Ver, Verify, and Vol.

 TIP

Help for MS-DOS Commands

To display help for any MS-DOS command, run MS-DOS Prompt. Then type the command, followed by a space, followed by a slash and a question mark. For example, to read about all the ways in which you can use the Dir command, type *dir /?* at the MS-DOS prompt.

MS-DOS in Windows 98 Versus MS-DOS in Windows 3.x

The version of MS-DOS that is available in Windows 98 has been designed for maximum compatibility with previous versions. Much of the operating system has been rewritten in 32-bit code, and MS-DOS has been incorporated into Windows so that the two are now a single operating system. (Earlier versions of Windows were essentially an extension of MS-DOS. To run Windows 3.x, for example, you started MS-DOS and then executed an MS-DOS program called WIN.COM, which in turn loaded the rest of Windows.) But to your programs, nothing will appear to have been changed.

As you work at the MS-DOS command prompt, however, you will notice a few improvements:

- MS-DOS now supports long filenames.

- MS-DOS now supports hard drives formatted with the FAT32 file system.

- MS-DOS now lets you access network resources using UNC path specifications.

- You can now run Windows-based programs as well as MS-DOS–based programs at the MS-DOS command prompt, as well as incorporate commands to launch Windows-based programs in MS-DOS batch files.

■ You can use a new Start command to launch one virtual-machine session from within another and to specify a program's initial window state.

To see long filenames in action, type *dir* at the MS-DOS prompt. MS-DOS displays traditional filenames (eight characters plus an optional three-character extension) on the left side of the directory listing and long filenames on the right side.

To access a network directory or file using a UNC path specification, type two backslashes, followed by a server name, another backslash, and a share name. Follow the share name by another backslash and the remainder of the path specification. For example, to display a directory listing for the Msoffice\Clipart directory, which is a subdirectory of the Programs share on the Acadia server, type:

```
dir \\acadia\programs\msoffice\clipart
```

If you map a network folder to a drive letter using Windows 98 commands, you can use that drive letter at the MS-DOS prompt. For information about mapping drives, see "Mapping a Network Folder to a Drive Letter," page 159.

Running Programs with the Start Command

You can run both Windows-based and MS-DOS–based programs simply by typing their names, with path specifications if necessary, at the MS-DOS prompt. You can also run them using the Start command.

The principal advantage of using Start is that it provides a way to run an MS-DOS–based program in a new virtual machine, separate from the one in which you issue the Start command. For example, if you type

```
Start MyDOSPrg
```

at the MS-DOS prompt, you can continue working at the MS-DOS prompt and also use MyDOSPrg.

II

Further Explorations

Start also allows you to specify a program's initial state—maximized, restored, or minimized. The syntax is as follows:

Start /m *MyProgram*	Starts *MyProgram* minimized
Start /max *MyProgram*	Starts *MyProgram* maximized
Start /r *MyProgram*	Starts *MyProgram* restored

If you do not include /m, /max, or /r, the program starts in a restored window.

CHAPTER 12

Using the Accessibility Features

Windows 98 offers a wide range of features to make computer use more accessible for people with disabilities. Whether the issue is impaired vision or hearing or an inability to use both hands for typing, Windows has a solution.

And you'll find that these features are not only for the "disabled." If you work in a noisy environment or it's not convenient to use the mouse, for example, the accessibility features can help. Following are some of the available options. You can:

- Turn on "StickyKeys," which enables you to use Ctrl, Alt, and Shift key combinations without having to hold down more than one key at a time.

- Use visual cues instead of sounds to alert you to system events.

- Use a special high-contrast appearance scheme throughout your Windows-based programs.

- Increase the size of icons, system text, scroll bars, and your mouse pointer.

- Use Microsoft Magnifier to increase the size of everything in the current window.

- Use the keyboard instead of the mouse to click, double-click, and drag.

- Attach an alternate "SerialKey" input device to your serial port if you are unable to use a standard mouse or keyboard.

This chapter covers these and other accessibility features. You'll learn how to use each option, in what situations it might be appropriate, and tips for effective use.

 TIP

> If more than one person uses your computer, but not all users require the accessibility features, set up a different profile for each user. For information about user profiles, see "Setting Up New User Profiles," page 269.

Getting to the Accessibility Features

Windows 98 includes an Accessibility Wizard that simplifies your selection of accessibility features. To get to the wizard, open the Start menu and choose Programs, Accessories, Accessibility, Accessibility Wizard. You can also make accessibility-feature choices by opening Accessibility Options in Control Panel. To get to Control Panel, choose Settings, Control Panel from the Start menu.

NOTE

> If you don't find any accessibility features on your system, open Control Panel and launch Add/Remove Programs. Then click the Windows Setup tab and select Accessibility in the Components list. Click OK to begin installation. You'll then need to restart your computer.

Some options that affect the behavior of accessibility features are available only via Accessibility Options in Control Panel. For example, using Accessibility Options, you can specify that, with StickyKeys on, pressing the Shift key twice in a row turns on Shift Lock. Accessibility Options also lets you enable support for SerialKey devices, an option not provided by the wizard.

Other options that are provided by the wizard do not appear in Accessibility Options in Control Panel. For example, the wizard gives you more choices regarding visual enhancement than Accessibility Options does.

It's best, therefore, to take a walk through both the Accessibility Wizard and Accessibility Options. You might want to start with the wizard, and then do any necessary fine-tuning with the help of Control Panel.

Some keyboard accessibility features can be turned on and off via special keyboard toggles. For example, pressing the Shift key five times in a row can turn on StickyKeys—or turn it off if it's already on. You'll find these keyboard shortcuts handy if it's difficult for you to get to the wizard or Control Panel. You must first enable the shortcut keys, however, and that task does require a visit to Control Panel.

Setting Keyboard Options

The following options allow you to control how Windows handles keyboard input:

- StickyKeys allows you to type keystroke combinations without the need to hold down one key while you press another.

- BounceKeys can be set to ignore accidentally repeated keystrokes or brief keystrokes that are made by touching a key in error.

- ToggleKeys provides an audible notification whenever you press the Num Lock, Caps Lock, or Scroll Lock key.

Facilitating Entry of Keystroke Combinations with StickyKeys

Windows makes extensive use of keyboard shortcuts, which generally require you to press more than one key at a time. For example, to use the keystroke combination Ctrl+Alt+Del, a user must hold down the Ctrl and Alt keys while pressing the Del key. In cases where a user is limited to one hand or a mouthstick, pressing multiple keys at the same time might not be possible.

II

Further Explorations

StickyKeys enables users to input key combinations by pressing the applicable keys in sequence rather than simultaneously. This option causes the Ctrl, Alt, and Shift keys to become *sticky*—when a user presses one of these *modifier keys*, the key is locked down until any other key (except for Ctrl, Alt, or Shift) or a mouse button is pressed and released. Pressing the modifier key twice locks it "permanently"—until you press that modifier key a third time.

While a key is locked, that key's space in the notification area of the taskbar is shaded.

To turn on StickyKeys using the Accessibility Wizard, step through the wizard until you come to the screen shown in Figure 12-1. Select I Have Difficulty Using The Keyboard Or Mouse, and then click Next (or press Enter). Depending on what else in Figure 12-1 you have selected, you will come either immediately or eventually to a screen in which you'll be given the option to turn on StickyKeys.

FIGURE 12-1.

The Set Wizard Options screen provides a set of check boxes in which you can specify the particular kinds of disabilities you're seeking to remedy.

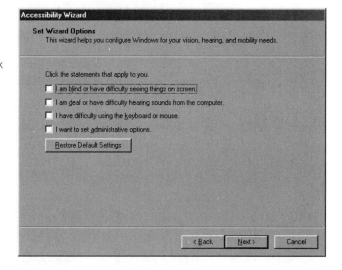

To turn on StickyKeys using Accessibility Options in Control Panel, select the first check box on the Keyboard tab in the Accessibility Properties dialog box. (See Figure 12-2.) Then click Settings to make sure that options affecting the StickyKeys feature are set as you want them. Figure 12-3 shows the Settings For StickyKeys dialog box.

FIGURE 12-2.

The Keyboard tab in the Accessibility Properties dialog box (accessible via Control Panel) lets you turn on or off the StickyKeys, FilterKeys, and ToggleKeys features.

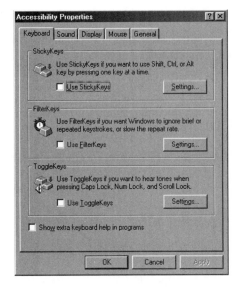

FIGURE 12-3.

The Settings For StickyKeys dialog box lets you customize StickyKeys behavior.

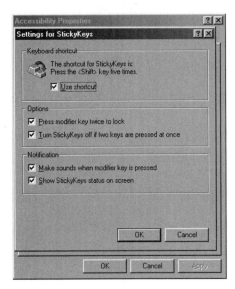

The following settings are available for StickyKeys:

■ To enable the keyboard shortcut, select the Use Shortcut check box. Once you've done this, you can turn StickyKeys on or off by pressing the Shift key five times in succession.

- The StickyKeys feature allows users to lock a modifier key (Ctrl, Alt, or Shift) by pressing a modifier key twice. The key remains locked until you press it a third time. As a general rule, if you have a need for the StickyKeys feature at all, you should leave this option enabled. You can, however, disable it by deselecting Press Modifier Key Twice To Lock.

- If several people use the same computer, keep Turn StickyKeys Off If Two Keys Are Pressed At Once selected (as it is by default). With this option selected, users who don't require StickyKeys can turn off the feature simply by pressing a modifier key and any other key at the same time. This option is great for multiple users; the StickyKeys feature can be kept on for those who need it, and users who don't need it can use standard key combinations.

- Make Sounds When Modifier Key Is Pressed can provide useful auditory feedback each time a Ctrl, Alt, or Shift key is pressed. It's a handy reminder that StickyKeys is active. If, however, you're the only user and have no need to be reminded, deselect this option.

- You shouldn't need to change the default setting for Show StickyKeys Status On Screen, which displays an icon in the taskbar's notification area. In addition to alerting you that the feature is active (and which modifier keys are currently locked), you can right-click the icon for quick access to StickyKeys settings. Right-clicking the taskbar icon also offers a command that displays an enlarged StickyKeys icon in a movable window.

Controlling the Keyboard Repeat Rate with BounceKeys (FilterKeys)

The BounceKeys options provide precise control over the keyboard repeat rate. These options are particularly useful if involuntary hand movements cause accidental key presses.

For reasons unknown, the feature that is called BounceKeys in the Accessibility Wizard is called FilterKeys in the Accessibility Properties dialog box. FilterKeys in the Accessibility Properties dialog box offers some additional settings that you can't make using the wizard.

SEE ALSO

For information about setting the keyboard repeat rate, see "Adjusting Keyboard Repeat Parameters," page 255.

To activate this feature using the Accessibility Wizard, step through the wizard until you come to the screen shown in Figure 12-1, on page 308. Select I Have Difficulty Using The Keyboard Or Mouse, and then click Next (or press Enter). Keep moving through wizard screens until you come to the BounceKeys screen. Select Yes and then click Next. The next screen allows you to set the minimum time before which repeated keystrokes are ignored and to test your settings. When you are satisfied, exit the wizard.

TIP

You don't have to click Next repeatedly until you reach a Finish button to exit the wizard. After you've made the settings you want, click Cancel. The wizard then asks if you want to save the changes you've made; click Yes.

To activate FilterKeys using Accessibility Options in Control Panel, click the Keyboard tab, select the Use FilterKeys check box, and then click the Settings button and make sure the options are set as you want them. Figure 12-4 shows the Settings For FilterKeys dialog box.

To enable the keyboard shortcut, select the Use Shortcut check box. Once you've done this, you can turn FilterKeys on or off by holding down the right Shift key for eight seconds.

FIGURE 12-4.

The Settings For FilterKeys dialog box lets you ignore repeated keystrokes or brief keystrokes.

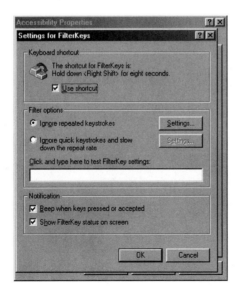

Use the Ignore Repeated Keystrokes option button to instruct Windows to ignore all but the first keystroke when a key press is rapidly repeated. The dialog box shown in Figure 12-5 allows you to set the minimum time before which repeated keystrokes are ignored. Test your settings in the test area provided before you accept them.

FIGURE 12-5.

With FilterKeys (or BounceKeys) enabled, key presses repeated more rapidly than the time shown in the Advanced Settings For FilterKeys dialog box are ignored.

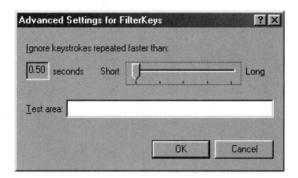

The Ignore Quick Keystrokes And Slow Down The Repeat Rate option causes the computer to ignore keys that are pressed only briefly. When FilterKeys is active, these settings override Control Panel's Keyboard repeat settings. Figure 12-6 shows the Advanced Settings dialog box for this option.

Select No Keyboard Repeat to turn off the keyboard repeat feature altogether. With this option selected, it doesn't matter how long you hold down a key; it won't repeat under any circumstances.

FIGURE 12-6.

Adjust keyboard speed and repeat rates here.

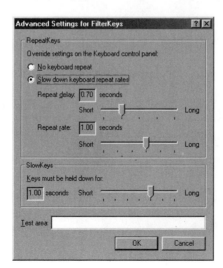

Select Slow Down Keyboard Repeat Rates and adjust the Repeat Delay and Repeat Rate settings if you want to retain the ability to repeat keystrokes.

Using ToggleKeys to Indicate Keyboard Status Changes

The ToggleKeys option causes Windows to sound a tone each time the Caps Lock, Num Lock, or Scroll Lock key is pressed. To activate this feature using the Accessibility Wizard, step through the wizard until you come to the screen shown in Figure 12-1, on page 308. Select I Have Difficulty Using The Keyboard Or Mouse, and then click Next (or press Enter). Keep moving through wizard screens until you come to the ToggleKeys screen. Select Yes and exit the wizard. To activate ToggleKeys using Accessibility Options in Control Panel, click the Keyboard tab, select the Use ToggleKeys check box, and then click Settings to make sure the shortcut key option is set as you want it. If you activate the shortcut key, holding down Num Lock for five seconds toggles the ToggleKeys feature on or off.

Setting Sound Options

The following options are designed for users who are hearing-impaired:

- SoundSentry causes Windows to display a visual cue whenever your computer beeps. Separate options let you customize the visual cues for windowed and full-screen programs.

- ShowSounds is the Windows 98 equivalent of closed-captioned television. In programs that use digitized speech or other audible cues, ShowSounds instructs the program to provide visible feedback, such as text captions. Not all programs have this capability.

> **NOTE**
>
> The SoundSentry actions take place only when your system plays a sound through its internal speaker. (Most programs that beep through the internal speaker are MS-DOS–based programs.) Sounds played through external speakers via a sound card do not invoke SoundSentry.

II

Further Explorations

The accessibility features designed for hearing-impaired users can also be used effectively in situations in which the computer's speakers must be turned off or in extremely noisy workplaces.

To turn on either SoundSentry or ShowSounds via the wizard, select I Am Deaf Or Have Difficulty Hearing Sounds From The Computer in the screen shown in Figure 12-1, on page 308. Then work your way through whatever screens appear next until you come to the SoundSentry and ShowSounds screens. Select Yes on the appropriate screens and then exit the wizard.

To turn on these features via Accessibility Options in Control Panel, click the Sound tab. You'll see the screen shown in Figure 12-7. Select the option buttons for either or both features, and then click Settings to specify what kind of visual cues you want.

FIGURE 12-7.

SoundSentry and ShowSounds cause Windows to augment some of its normal sounds with visual cues.

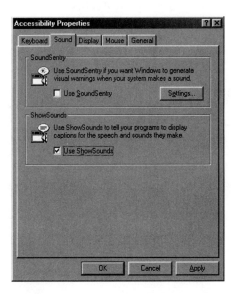

Setting Display Options

The Accessibility Wizard provides a number of options for making your display easier to read. Most of these options are not available in Control Panel's Accessibility Options, but you can get to them via Display in Control Panel. With the wizard, you can do the following:

- Increase the size of all text.

- Increase the size of window title-bar text and menus.

- Use Microsoft Magnifier to open a floating window at the top of your screen that presents a magnified display of everything appearing in the lower part of your screen.

- Switch to a lower screen resolution (which makes text appear larger).

- Increase the size of window borders and scroll bars.

- Increase icon size.

- Choose one of four available high-contrast appearance schemes.

To take advantage of Windows display accessibility options, start up the Accessibility Wizard. In the first screen, use the Up arrow and Down arrow keys to select the smallest type size you can read comfortably. Then click Next. This brings you to the screen shown in Figure 12-8. Windows proposes to select one of more of the check boxes shown in the figure, depending on which type size you selected in the wizard's initial screen. Make any changes to Windows' proposal that you think are appropriate, and then click Next again. This time, you'll arrive at the screen shown in Figure 12-1, on page 308.

FIGURE 12-8.

The choices made by the Accessibility Wizard on this screen depend on the smallest type size you say you can read. You can override the wizard's selections if you want.

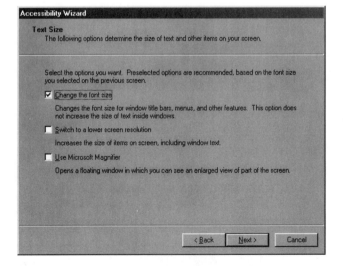

II

Further Explorations

SEE ALSO

For information about appearance schemes, see "Changing Colors, Fonts, and Sizes," page 91.

In this next dialog box, select I Am Blind Or Have Difficulty Seeing Things On Screen. Then click Next. Depending on what other check boxes (if any) you have selected, you'll come either immediately or eventually to a screen in which you can choose enlarged window borders and scroll bars. This is the first of three additional screens that provide display options.

 TIP

> Because you can have one appearance scheme set in the Display Properties dialog box and another one in the Settings For High Contrast dialog box, you can easily toggle between two appearance schemes by pressing the keyboard shortcut for High Contrast: press the left Alt key, the left Shift key, and the Print Screen key—all at the same time. To enable the keyboard shortcut, go to the Display tab in the Accessibility Properties dialog box, click Settings, and select the Use Shortcut check box.

Using Microsoft Magnifier

Microsoft Magnifier splits your screen into two parts, with the upper part showing a magnified image of the lower part. (See Figure 12-9.) By default, you see a magnified image of your mouse pointer as well as every other screen detail.

FIGURE 12-9.
Microsoft Magnifier devotes the upper part of your screen to a magnified image of the lower part.

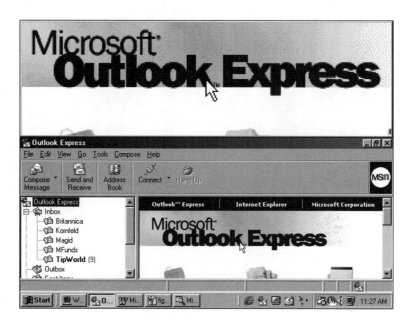

When you first start Magnifier, the following small dialog box appears:

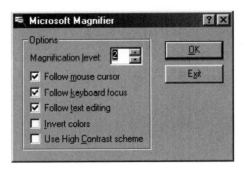

With the Magnification Level spinner, you can adjust the degree of magnification—from a useless 1 to a gigantic 9. With the check boxes, you can control other aspects of Magnifier's behavior. Chances are you want to leave the first three boxes selected. That way, the image on top always stays in sync with your activity below. Try selecting the Invert Colors and Use High Contrast Scheme check boxes to see if they improve the legibility of the magnified image.

If you want, you can leave the Microsoft Magnifier dialog box open on screen while you work. That way, you can adjust the magnification level up or down as situations require. Alternatively, if you click the OK button in the dialog box, the dialog box simply minimizes itself, remaining on your task bar for easy reuse. (You can press Alt+Tab to reopen it.) Click Exit in the dialog box when you're ready to leave Magnifier.

TIP

To allocate more or less space to the magnified part of the screen, drag the border that separates the two parts.

You can start Magnifier in either of two ways—by choosing it from the Accessibility section of your Start menu or by using the Accessibility Wizard. You'll find a check box for activating Magnifier on the wizard's second screen.

II

Further Explorations

TIP

> You might want to assign a keyboard shortcut to the menu command that launches Magnifier. That way you won't have to hunt for it on the menu. For more information, see "Assigning a Keyboard Shortcut to a Menu Item," page 60.

Using the Keyboard Instead of the Mouse

MouseKeys lets you use Windows 98 without a mouse. Normally, despite programs' implementation of keyboard shortcuts, there are some tasks that can be performed only by moving the mouse pointer, clicking, and dragging. But with MouseKeys on you can use the keys on the numeric keypad to simulate mouse actions, as follows:

- To move the mouse pointer, press any number key except 5. The arrows in Figure 12-10 show the direction in which each key moves the pointer. If you hold down a directional number key, the mouse pointer begins moving slowly and then accelerates to its maximum speed.

- To select which mouse button to use for clicking and dragging, press the slash (/) key to select the left button, the minus (–) key to select the right button, or the asterisk (*) key to select both buttons. Your selection stays in effect until you select another; you don't need to select a button before each click or drag.

FIGURE 12-10.
Use the numeric keypad to imitate mouse actions.

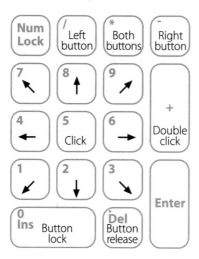

- To click the selected button, press the 5 key.

- To double-click the selected button, press the plus (+) key.

- To drag with the selected button, position the mouse pointer on the object and press the 0 key (Ins). Then use the directional number keys to move the mouse pointer. Press the period (.) key (Del) to "release" the mouse button, which completes the drag operation.

- To move the mouse pointer in larger increments, hold down the Ctrl key while you use the direction keys.

To turn on MouseKeys with the Accessibility Wizard, select I Have Difficulty Using The Keyboard Or Mouse in the screen shown in Figure 12-1, on page 308. Then click Next. After several screens relating to keyboard options, you'll come to the MouseKeys screen. Select Yes here and click Next again to get to the MouseKeys option screen, shown in Figure 12-11. In this dialog box, you can adjust the speed at which your mouse moves and accelerates. You can also tell the system whether you want MouseKeys to work with Num Lock on or off.

To activate MouseKeys with Accessibility Options in Control Panel, click the Mouse tab and select Use MouseKeys. Then click the Settings button to adjust the speed and acceleration of your mouse. The Settings dialog

FIGURE 12-11.

You can use this dialog box to change the speed and accelera-tion characteristics of your MouseKeys mouse.

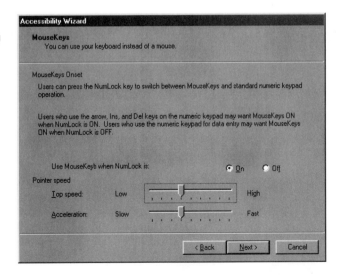

box that you reach via Control Panel is organized somewhat differently from the wizard screen shown in Figure 12-11, on the previous page, but it includes all the wizard's options.

The Settings dialog box reached via Control Panel also offers two options not provided by the wizard. The first option, on by default, activates a Ctrl-key and Shift-key throttle system. With the throttle on, if you hold down a direction key, the mouse pointer begins moving slowly and then accelerates to its maximum speed. If you hold down Shift while you hold down a direction key, the mouse pointer moves at a slow, steady rate. The second option, off by default, turns on the shortcut key for MouseKeys. With the shortcut key on, pressing the left Shift key, the left Alt key, and Num Lock at the same time toggles MouseKeys on or off.

Making the Mouse Pointer Easier to See

 SEE ALSO

For information about Mouse in Control Panel, see "Adjusting Mouse Behavior," page 260.

The Accessibility Wizard offers some additional options for making the mouse pointer more visible. You can change the size and color of the pointer, switch the primary and secondary mouse buttons, change the pointer speed, and add a trail of mouse-cursor shapes to help you track the position of your mouse pointer as you move it across the screen. These options are presented in a series of wizard screens that appear if you select I Have Difficulty Using The Keyboard Or Mouse in the screen shown in Figure 12-1, on page 308. These choices do not appear in Control Panel's Accessibility Options, but you can get to them via Mouse in Control Panel.

Setting Administrative Options

The Accessibility Wizard also offers the following administrative settings:

- You can have StickyKeys, FilterKeys, ToggleKeys, and high-contrast display turn off automatically whenever the computer has been idle for a period of time you specify (five minutes, by default).

- You can make your accessibility settings apply automatically to any new profiles ("user accounts") created on your system.

■ You can save your accessibility settings in a file, and then use that file to set up another system with the same settings. (To set up another system, copy the file you create to the new system. Then simply launch the file in Windows Explorer to apply the settings.)

To avail yourself of any of these options, choose I Want To Set Administrative Options in the dialog box shown in Figure 12-1, on page 308.

Two other administrative settings are provided only by the General tab of Accessibility Options in Control Panel:

■ You can cause a warning message to appear whenever an accessibility feature is turned on or off.

■ You can cause the system to make a sound whenever an accessibility feature is turned on or off.

These options are both on by default.

Installing Support for SerialKey Devices

A SerialKey device is a device that plugs into one of your computer's serial ports and provides alternative access to keyboard and mouse features. To use one of these devices, you must enable its support by going to the General tab of Accessibility Options in Control Panel. Select Support Serialkey Devices in that dialog box. Then click the Settings button and specify the serial port you'll be using and the baud rate (speed).

II

Further Explorations

PART III

Maintaining Your Windows System

CHAPTER 13

Installing and Uninstalling Software and Hardware

Windows 98 has taken major strides toward making it easy for you to change components of your systems. The Add/Remove Programs item in Control Panel, for example, simplifies the task of bringing new programs on board or helping old ones disembark. And thanks to Windows 98's implementation of Plug and Play technology, many of the potential frustrations and bewilderments associated with hardware changes have been eliminated. In many cases, adding a new peripheral is truly as simple as hooking up the device and getting on with your work.

In this chapter, we'll survey the tools and wizards that Windows 98 supplies to help you keep your system current as your hardware and software needs change.

325

Adding or Removing Parts of Windows 98

Windows 98 includes both essential and optional components. Among the latter are such things as screen savers, wallpaper images, accessory programs, and The Microsoft Network. When your system was first set up, chances are the person doing the setup installed many, but not all, of the optional components. As time passes you might find you need certain items that aren't currently installed. Alternatively, you might discover that some of the Windows accessories are merely taking up space on your hard disks without serving any useful purpose. In either case, it's easy to make the appropriate adjustments.

To add or remove an optional component of Windows 98, start as follows:

1 Choose Settings from the Start menu.

2 Choose Control Panel.

3 Launch Add/Remove Programs.

4 Click the Windows Setup tab.

These steps bring you to the Windows Setup tab in the Add/Remove Programs Properties dialog box, shown in Figure 13-1.

FIGURE 13-1.

To add or remove components of Windows, click the Windows Setup tab in the Add/Remove Programs Properties dialog box.

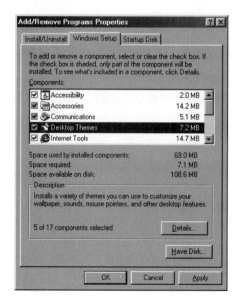

In this dialog box, optional components of Windows are listed by category. To the right of each category heading, you see the amount of disk space used by the elements within that category that are currently installed. Below, to the left of the Details button, the dialog box tells you how many items in the selected category are currently installed. So, for example, on the system depicted in Figure 13-1, 5 of 17 Desktop Themes components are currently installed, and those 5 items consume a total of 7.2 megabytes of disk space.

Categories with all components installed are marked with a check mark in a white check box. Categories in which some, but not all, components are installed are marked with a check mark in a gray check box. Figure 13-1 shows a system on which all components in the Accessibility and Internet Tools categories, but only some components in the Accessories, Communications, and Desktop Themes categories, are installed.

To add or remove a component, first select the component's category, and then click the Details button. This reveals a list of the items that make up the selected category, as shown in Figure 13-2.

Here again, installed items are flagged with check marks. Figure 13-2 shows that the Inside Your Computer and Jungle themes are not installed.

To install a component, select its check box. To remove a component, deselect its check box. Then click OK twice—once to return to the dialog box shown in Figure 13-1, and a second time to close the dialog box.

FIGURE 13-2.
To find out what's in a category, select it and click the Details button.

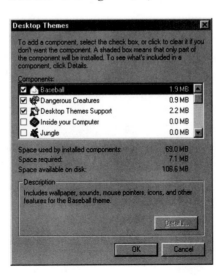

III

Maintaining Your System

In most Windows dialog boxes, clicking the text next to a check box has the same effect as clicking the check box itself. This is not the case in the Windows Setup dialog box. Here selecting the text simply gives you an opportunity to read a description of the selected item. To change the state of the check box, you have to click the check box itself.

If you're installing an item, Windows might prompt you to insert a floppy disk or the Windows CD. (If you installed Windows initially from a network server, Windows looks on that server for the components it needs; be sure the network is available.)

If your Windows installation files are not in the place where Add/Remove Programs expects to find them, click the Browse button and select the drive or folder that contains the files. The folder you point to will then be available on the Copy Files From drop-down list the next time you use Add/Remove Programs. You can also make a permanent change to the folder where Windows expects to find installation files. To do this, you need to modify the registry. For details, see "Changing the Source Path Used by the Windows Setup Program," page 369.

Installing Programs

Windows 98 includes a wizard for installing programs. When you're installing, the wizard scans your floppy-disk drives and CD-ROM drives for installation programs. You don't have to use this wizard to install programs—you could locate and launch the installation program yourself—but you might find it convenient to do so.

Many CD-ROM–based programs automatically launch their installation program when you insert the CD in your CD-ROM drive. For these programs, you don't need to consult the wizard; just follow the on-screen messages. How do you find out if a program has this feature? Just insert the CD and wait a few seconds.

To install a program using the wizard, follow these steps:

1 Choose Settings from the Start menu.

2 Choose Control Panel.

3 Launch Add/Remove Programs.

4 Insert the first disk in a floppy-disk drive or the CD in your CD-ROM drive.

5 Click the Install button.

6 Click the Next button.

 NOTE

> You can use this procedure for both Windows-based and MS-DOS–based programs.

Most original program disks include a program called Setup or Install. This program takes care of all the details of getting a program copied to your hard disk, updating the Windows registry, creating a new Start-menu item, and so on. When you click the Install button in Control Panel's Add/Remove Programs, the install wizard scans each of your floppy-disk drives in turn, followed by any CD-ROM drives, until it finds a program called Setup or Install. As soon as it locates such a program, the wizard presents a screen similar to the one shown in Figure 13-3, on the next page. If the name of the installation program shown on the command line of this screen is correct, simply click the Finish button. In the unlikely event that the wizard has proposed the wrong installation program, you can click Browse instead of Finish, and then find the correct program from the ensuing dialog box.

When you click Finish, Windows runs the installation program. At that point, the new program's installation program will probably ask you some questions about where you want the program installed, what optional components you want to install, and so on. If you're installing from floppy disks, you'll also be prompted to change disks from time to time.

III

Maintaining Your System

FIGURE 13-3.
The install wizard automatically finds a program named Setup or Install and then asks you to confirm that it has found the correct installation program.

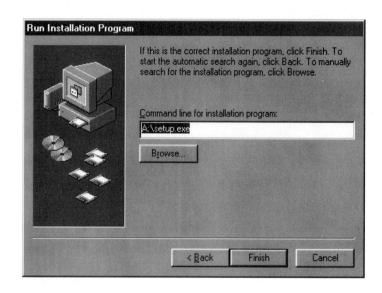

Uninstalling Programs

If you've ever tried to remove a Windows-based program from your system "by hand," you probably know that the task is anything but trivial. Getting rid of an unneeded program by simply deleting files is complex for the following reasons:

■ Many Windows-based programs use .DLL files in addition to .EXE files. DLLs, *dynamic-link libraries*, are components that can be shared by two or more programs. Such components might or might not be stored in the same folder as the program's .EXE files. Even if you know exactly which DLLs a program uses, deleting them all might damage another program that relies on some of the same DLLs.

■ Most Windows-based programs create entries in the registry, the database in which Windows records all vital information concerning your hardware and software. Even if you safely delete all executable components of your Windows-based program, if you don't also correctly modify the registry, the registry will no longer accurately describe your system.

■ Some Windows-based programs (in particular, many older ones) either create their own "private" configuration (.INI) files or create entries in a Windows configuration file called Win.ini. Private .INI files might or might not be stored in the same folder as the rest of a program's files. Completely eradicating a Windows-based program means getting rid of its .INI files (or its entries in Win.ini) as well as removing all of its other components.

For all of these reasons, but particularly because of the possibility of inadvertently deleting a DLL needed by some other program, it's best not to try removing Windows-based programs by simply going into a folder and deep-sixing its files. Instead, try the following steps (in order):

1 Check to see if Add/Remove Programs knows how to uninstall the program for you.

   If the program you want to uninstall has registered an uninstall utility, you'll be able to run that utility by selecting the program on the Install/Uninstall tab in Add/Remove Programs. (See Figure 13-4.)

2 If Control Panel's Add/Remove Programs doesn't show your program as being uninstallable, check to see if there's an uninstall utility in the folder where your program itself is stored.

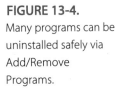

FIGURE 13-4.

Many programs can be uninstalled safely via Add/Remove Programs.

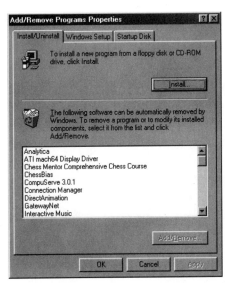

III

Maintaining Your System

It's possible your program has an uninstall utility, but Add/Remove Programs doesn't know about it. Look for something labeled "Remove" or "Uninstall." With most Microsoft programs, the Setup program also serves to uninstall the program. If you don't find an obvious uninstall utility, check your program's documentation to see if it provides any useful information.

3 If you're still not sure how to remove the program, give the program vendor's tech-support service a call. Ask them exactly what files you should and should not delete.

TIP

If Add/Remove Programs' list of uninstallable programs includes items that are no longer on your system, you can remove those items from the list by modifying the registry. The names of uninstallable programs are stored in the registry key HKEY_LOCAL_MACHINE\Software\Microsoft\Windows\CurrentVersion\Uninstall. To remove an item, run Registry Editor, navigate to this heading, and then delete the item from Registry Editor's left pane. As always, back up the registry before making changes to it, and exercise caution when making your changes. For more information, see Chapter 15, "Understanding the Registry."

Moving Programs

The task of moving a Windows-based program from one disk or folder to another, like that of deleting a program, is seldom simple. The Windows-based program you want to move might rely on dynamic-link libraries (DLLs), which might or might not be stored in the same folder as the rest of the program's executable files. And it might use a configuration (.INI) file in which (among other things) its current disk and folder are recorded. Simply packing up all the files in a program's folder and shipping them off to some other folder might work for the most rudimentary Windows-based programs, but more often than not it will fail.

If you must relocate a Windows-based program, the safest way to do it is to uninstall the program first, using whatever removal services the program provides. After you've uninstalled it, reinstall it in the appropriate folder.

Plug and Play: The End of the Hardware Blues?

Removing or relocating programs may be a pain sometimes, but it's a walk in the park compared to the travails that, until recently, have attended the installation of new hardware. Traditionally, the act of adding a new peripheral has been an exercise in frustration for many personal computer users, as well as a heavy expense for corporate support departments.

Hardware devices typically compete for a limited number of input-output (I/O) addresses, memory addresses, interrupt request (IRQ) lines, and direct memory access (DMA) channels. In order for your system to work properly, all of its pieces have to dance together without stepping on each other's toes. If your new sound card wants the same interrupt request line as your existing network adapter, something's got to give (in this case, the new sound card). Until recently, resolving a conflict of this kind has entailed some combination of the following: determining which resource is in contention, finding a nonconflicting alternative setting for the new peripheral, making a physical adjustment to the hardware (moving a jumper, for example), and modifying some aspect of the software that uses the new peripheral.

To alleviate these difficulties, Microsoft and other computer-industry firms developed the Plug and Play specification. Plug and Play, as its name implies, is intended to make adding a new peripheral to your computer as painless as installing a new toaster in your kitchen.

The full realization of this goal requires Plug and Play support from three elements of your system:

- The BIOS (*basic input-output system*)

- The operating system

- Any new peripherals you want to install

III

Maintaining Your System

Because Windows 98 is a Plug and Play operating system, one of these elements is already in place on your computer. If your computer is fairly new, it will most likely have a Plug and Play BIOS. (The BIOS, routines that manage the transfer of information between system components, is built into the computer's read-only memory, or ROM.) And most peripherals sold these days are also Plug and Play compliant.

With all three elements in place, a newly installed hardware device announces its presence and resource requirements to the operating system. If necessary, the operating system restructures resource assignments on the fly (without requiring you to turn your computer off) to eliminate conflicts. The operating system then broadcasts a message to any running programs, letting them know about the change in your hardware setup so that they can take advantage of any new features. If a device is removed, the operating system hears about it from the BIOS and informs programs so that they can make any appropriate adjustments.

So, for example, a Plug and Play laptop computer that supports "hot-docking" can be connected to or disconnected from the docking station without first being turned off. If the docking station has access to a local or network printer, your programs will immediately know about any fonts or other resources offered by the printer, and Windows will begin despooling any print jobs that you have accumulated offline.

⚠ WARNING

> Even if your computer has a Plug and Play BIOS, always turn the computer off before adding or removing any device *inside* the system.

Provided a new device does not present an unresolvable resource conflict, the act of adding Plug and Play hardware to a Plug and Play BIOS computer running Windows 98 should indeed be toaster-transparent. And if an unresolvable conflict does arise, Windows identifies it for you, so that at least you'll know what options you have.

With a "legacy" computer (one that does not use a Plug and Play BIOS), Plug and Play still offers significant benefits, particularly if you're installing or removing a Plug and Play peripheral. By using the Add New Hardware Wizard (see "Installing a Legacy Peripheral," on the next page), you can make Windows aware that a new device is present. If the device supports Plug and Play, Windows can determine what type of device it is and what resources it requires. By consulting the registry (where current resource assignments for all your hardware are recorded), Windows can determine if the new device's default assignments create any conflicts. If a conflict exists, Windows can make adjustments to the new device (or another Plug and Play device already attached) to avoid the conflict.

When you attach a legacy peripheral, Windows 98 cannot adjust the new device's chosen settings, but if other of your peripherals support Plug and Play, it may be able to adjust their settings to eliminate conflicts. If not, and if conflicts exist, Windows advises you. You may then have to reset one or more jumpers on the peripheral yourself.

Installing a Plug and Play Peripheral

After attaching a Plug and Play peripheral, you might see a message indicating that Windows has recognized the new device. (If you have installed the device while your computer was turned off, this message appears at the start of your next Windows session. If your computer was on at the time you connected the device, the message simply pops up on your desktop.) If Windows needs a driver that it doesn't currently have, you may be prompted to insert a disk or the Windows CD.

If you don't see a message and your new device is working fine, assume that all is well. If you don't see a message and your device does not seem to be working, use the Add New Hardware Wizard to let Windows know you've installed something new.

Installing a Legacy Peripheral

After you install a new legacy peripheral (one that is not Plug and Play–compatible), use the Add New Hardware Wizard to let Windows know what you've done. Choose Settings from the Start menu and Control Panel from the Settings submenu. Then launch Add New Hardware in Control Panel. After passing the wizard's introductory screens, you'll come to a screen similar to the one shown in Figure 13-5, on the next page.

III

Maintaining Your System

FIGURE 13-5.
The Add New Hardware Wizard lets you tell Windows what's new on your system.

The wizard can detect many types of devices, even if they don't support Plug and Play. If you want the wizard to try to determine what you've added, select the Yes (Recommended) option button and click Next. You'll see a warning that the detection process might take several minutes and might cause your system to lock up. If you still want to go ahead, close all your programs (for safety's sake) and click Next again. If Windows succeeds in identifying one or more new devices, it presents you with a list of all devices found. Select the first member of the list and click Next. You'll then receive instructions about what to do next. (For example, you might be asked to insert a disk or the Windows CD so that Windows can get one or more driver files.) If the wizard is unable to detect the new device, click Next after the wizard informs you of this result. You'll then see a screen similar to the one shown in Figure 13-6, where you can identify the device yourself.

If you prefer to skip Windows' automatic-detection services, select the No option button in the screen shown in Figure 13-5. In the screen shown in Figure 13-6, select the type of hardware you're installing and click the Next button. Make-and-model options appear in the next screen. (See Figure 13-7.) Select the vendor of your new hardware on the left side of this dialog box and the specific model on the right. Then click Next once more and follow the ensuing instructions.

FIGURE 13-6.

If you decide not to let the wizard detect your new hardware (or it's unable to), you must tell it what type of hardware you want to install.

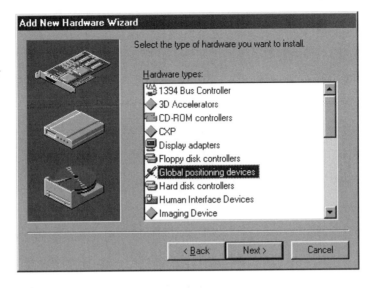

FIGURE 13-7.

After telling the wizard what kind of hardware you're installing, you'll be asked to identify the hardware's make and model.

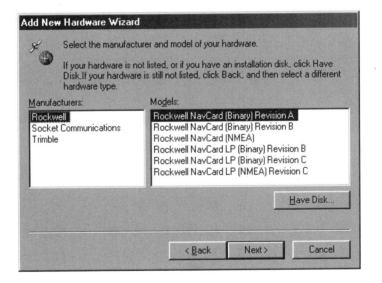

Alternative Ways to Install Certain Legacy Devices

You can use the Add Hardware wizard to install any type of new device. For a new display, modem, or printer, however, you can also use other Control Panel items to let Windows know what you've done.

III

Maintaining Your System

For more information about setting up a modem, see "Installing, Configuring, and Testing a Modem," page 259.
For more information about setting up a printer, see "Installing a New Printer," page 196.

- To install a new monitor or display adapter, launch Display in Control Panel or right-click the desktop and choose Properties. Click the Settings tab in the Display Properties dialog box. Click Advanced Properties, and then choose either the Monitor or Adapter tab in the Advanced Properties dialog box. Click Change.

- To install a new modem, launch Modems in Control Panel, and then click the Add button in the Modems Properties dialog box.

- To install a new printer, launch Printers in Control Panel. (Or launch Printers in the My Computer folder.) Then, in the Printers folder, launch Add Printer.

Uninstalling a Legacy Peripheral

After permanently removing a legacy peripheral from your system, you should let Windows know the device is gone so that the resources it used can be reassigned as needed. To inform Windows that a device is no longer present, follow these steps:

1 Right-click My Computer, and then choose Properties from the context menu.
   Alternatively, you can launch System in Control Panel.

2 Click the Device Manager tab.

3 Select the View Devices By Type option button.
   The Device Manager presents a list of your hardware devices organized by type, as shown in Figure 13-8. Like the All Folders Explorer Bar in a Windows Explorer window, this list is organized as an outline. Plus signs indicate outline headings that can be expanded. Minus signs indicate entries that can be collapsed back into their headings.

4 Click the plus sign beside the category heading that describes the hardware you have removed.

5 Select the name of the item you have removed.

6 Click the Remove button.

FIGURE 13-8.

To remove a device, click the plus sign to expand the device's category display. Then select the device and click Remove.

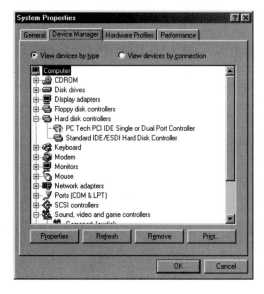

CHAPTER 14

Protecting Your Data with Microsoft Backup

You don't have to use computers for long to know the frustration of losing data. It happens to everyone. Although Windows 98 can't prevent mistakes and accidents from occurring, Microsoft Backup, the backup program included with Windows 98, provides a form of insurance to help you deal with such misfortunes.

With Backup, you can back up files from your own hard disks or from network drives to a tape drive attached to your computer. You can use either a SCSI tape drive, such as a 4-mm DAT drive, or a QIC (quarter-inch cartridge) drive. You can also back up to a file on a hard disk, a network drive, or removable disks (such as floppy disks or Zip disks).

You can select individual files, folders, or entire disks to back up. And you can specify whether to include all files or only those that haven't already been backed up. You can include or exclude the Windows registry, as you choose. When you need to restore files, you can view a catalog of backup sets that includes file and folder information, so you can select the files you want to restore.

To help you automate backup routines, Backup lets you create "backup jobs"—named constellations of backup settings. You can reuse a backup job by simply selecting its name.

341

The Windows 98 CD includes a system recovery utility. With this utility, a current full-system backup, and a startup disk, you can probably recover your system in the event of a catastrophic system failure.

Backup Types and Strategies

Microsoft Backup can perform three common types of backup: full, incremental, and differential.

- A full backup copies all selected files to the backup medium, regardless of when the files were last changed, and clears the archive attribute for each file to mark it as backed up.

- An incremental backup copies only selected files that have changed since the most recent full or incremental backup, and clears the archive attribute for each file. Therefore, the first incremental backup after a full backup copies all files that have changed since the full backup, the second incremental backup copies only those files that have changed since the first incremental backup, and so on.

- A differential backup copies only those selected files that have changed since the most recent full or incremental backup. Unlike incremental backups, however, a differential backup does not clear the archive attributes for the files it copies. Therefore, successive differential backups copy all the files that have changed since the last full (or incremental) backup, not just the ones that have changed since the last differential backup.

Selecting a backup type involves evaluating tradeoffs between safety on the one hand, and time and media space on the other. If safety were your only concern, you could back up your entire hard drive every day. But the time required to do this would be burdensome, and you'd spend a fortune on backup tapes. If spending minimal time and money on backups were your only concern, you might back up only a few crucial files once a month. Common sense suggests there must be a happy medium.

A common strategy combines full and differential backups as follows:

- At some regular interval, such as once a week, perform a full backup.

- At regular intervals between full backups—for example, at the end of each work day—perform a differential backup.

With this strategy, if the unthinkable happens and you need to restore one or more files, you need to look in only two places to find the most recent version of any file: the most recent full backup and the most recent differential backup.

Differential backups take longer than incremental backups (and require more tape), so some users prefer to use an incremental backup as their daily backup. If you follow this strategy, don't collect more than a half-dozen or so incremental backups between full backups. Otherwise, you might have to search through a lot of backup sets to find particular files in the event that you need to restore them from the backup tape.

 TIP

> For extra security, it's a good idea to rotate backup tapes. For example, if you do a full backup once a week and differential backups on the intervening days, you might want to keep one week's worth of backups on one tape and then use a different tape the following week. If disaster strikes twice—your original storage medium and your backup tape are both damaged—you'll still be able to restore files from the previous time period's backup tape. The files you restore probably won't be the most current versions, but you'll be better off than if you had to re-create everything from scratch.

How Does Backup Know Which Files to Back Up?

Like most operating systems, Windows 98 maintains an *archive attribute* for each file. Every file is either marked as needing to be archived (backed up), or it isn't marked.

Whenever a program creates or modifies a file, the operating system marks the file as needing to be archived by setting the archive attribute, which indicates that the file has changed since the last archive. When Backup sees a file with the archive attribute set, it backs up the file and, if you're performing a full or incremental backup, clears the attribute. The next time Backup runs, the archive attribute is gone (unless you've modified the file again) and Backup knows that it doesn't need to back up the file.

You can view (and set or clear) the archive attribute for a file by viewing the file's properties dialog box.

TIP

> If possible, store your backup tapes away from your computers. Otherwise, if you experience a fire or theft you may lose both your originals and your backups.

What Should You Back Up?

Exactly what you need to back up depends on your circumstances, of course, but here's a general principle worth observing: don't make your backup routine so onerous and time-consuming that you lose the motivation to adhere to it.

In practice, what this means for many users is the following:

- Exclude from your regular full and differential backup routine program files and DLLs that you have installed from a CD, floppy disks, or a network server. Keep programs and data in separate folders so you can easily exclude programs from backups.

- Include all data files (documents) in your full and differential backups. These are the files that change the most and that would be the most difficult to replace.

- If you don't have a regular full and differential backup routine, at least perform ad hoc backups of the files you're currently working with. If you don't have a tape drive, use Microsoft Backup to back up these files to another hard disk. If you don't have another hard disk, back them up to floppy disks or other removable media.

Creating a Backup Job

To perform a backup, you must first create a *backup job*. A backup job is simply a named constellation of backup settings. You can create a backup job in either of two ways: by using the Backup Wizard or by making your settings manually. The manual method is preferable, because some options are not offered by the wizard.

When you first run Backup—by opening the Start menu and choosing Programs, Accessories, System Tools, Backup—you may see a welcome dialog box that offers three options: Create A New Backup Job, Open An Existing Backup Job, and Restore Backed Up Files. Choosing the first option summons the Backup Wizard. Click Close to leave the welcome dialog box without choosing any of its options. This action brings you to the main Backup window, shown below. Follow these steps to create a backup job without the help of the Backup Wizard:

2 To copy an entire folder, including its subfolders, select the associated check box. To copy only some files in a folder, click the folder names in the left pane and check boxes for the files you want in the right pane.

1 Choose full or partial backup here.

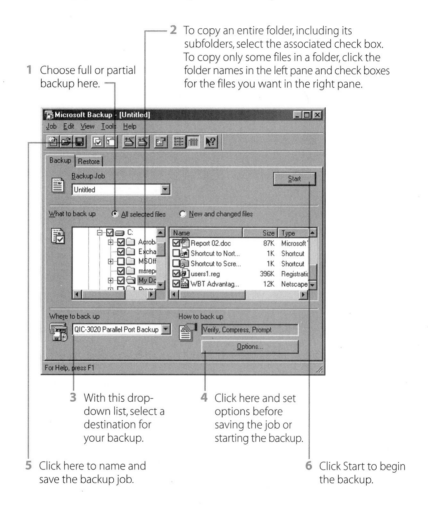

3 With this drop-down list, select a destination for your backup.

4 Click here and set options before saving the job or starting the backup.

5 Click here to name and save the backup job.

6 Click Start to begin the backup.

The following paragraphs explain these steps in greater detail.

If you want to start Backup without seeing the welcome dialog box, choose Preferences from the Tools menu and deselect Show Startup Dialog When Microsoft Backup Is Started.

III

Maintaining Your System

Choosing a Full or Partial Backup Type

With the Backup tab displayed, use the What To Back Up option buttons to tell Backup whether your job is to be a backup of all selected files (a full backup) or only of new and changed files (a differential or incremental backup). If you select New And Changed Files, you'll have the opportunity momentarily to tell the program whether you want a differential or an incremental backup.

Marking Disks, Folders, and Files for Backup

Your next step is to tell Backup what to back up, using the two list panes in the center of the main Backup window. The left pane lets you specify disks and folders; the right pane lets you specify certain files within folders.

To specify all files within a folder, simply click the open check box next to a folder name. For example, to back up all files in C: (including all files in subfolders of C:\), click the check box to the left of C:. A check mark appears when you click a folder's check box. If you change your mind, click the check box a second time to remove the check mark.

If the folder you want to back up is not at the top level of your disk hierarchy, click the plus sign beside the disk name to show the disk's top-level subfolders. Continue clicking plus signs until you come to the folder you want to back up. For example, to back up only the C:\Windows folder, click the plus sign next to C:. Then click the check box beside Windows.

To back up most of a disk but exclude particular subfolders, first click the check box associated with the disk. Then click the disk's plus sign to reveal its top-level subfolders. You'll find that each top-level subfolder is already checked, because selecting a disk automatically selects all of its subfolders. Click the check boxes next to the folders you do not want to back up to deselect those folders.

To back up only particular files within a folder, first display the folder by clicking plus signs in the left pane. Next, click the folder name in the left pane, which causes the folder's filenames to appear in the right pane. Now, make your file selections by clicking check boxes in the right pane.

To back up most of a folder but exclude particular files in that folder, first click the check box associated with the folder name in the left pane. Then click the folder name so that the folder's filenames appear in the right pane. Now click check boxes to deselect files in the right pane.

> One of the choices available via the Options button lets you exclude particular categories of files, such as files with the extension .EXE, from selected disks and folders. For details, see "Excluding Particular File Types," page 349.

Specifying Where to Back Up

Having chosen a full or partial backup type and told the program what you want to back up, you're ready to indicate where you want the backup to go. Do this by selecting from the Where To Back Up drop-down list. In this list, you'll find the names of any tape devices attached to your system, as well as the word *File*.

Backing Up to a Disk File

If you select File in the Where To Back Up drop-down list, a new text box appears directly below the drop-down list, as shown in Figure 14-1. Here you can specify the path and name of a disk file.

FIGURE 14-1.

To back up to a file, select File in the Where To Back Up drop-down list, and then name or point to your file in the new text box that appears.

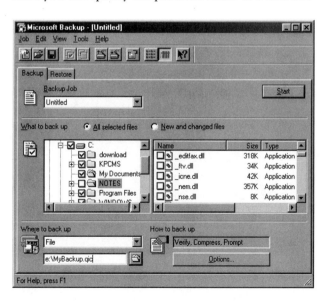

Maintaining Your System

If you're not sure how to specify the path to your backup file, click the folder icon to the right of this new text box. A new dialog box will appear, in which you can navigate to the file of your choice.

Note that when you back up to a file, all the disks, files, and folders you back up go into a single file—the file whose name and path your specify. By default, Backup gives this file the extension .QIC.

> If you use removable media (such as floppy disks or Zip disks) for your backup file destination and the files you're backing up won't fit in that media's remaining free space, that's okay. When you run the backup job, Backup asks you to insert another disk when a disk becomes full; the backup can span an unlimited number of disks.

Telling Backup How to Back Up

Your next step is to choose Backup options. Clicking the Options button takes you to the dialog box shown in Figure 14-2.

FIGURE 14-2.
The Backup Job Options dialog box offers a large number of choices about how your backup is to be carried out.

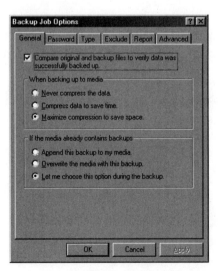

Compare? Compress? Append?

On the General tab in the Backup Job Options dialog box, you can tell Backup whether you want to include a compare (verify) step in your backups, what kind of compression (if any) you want to apply to your backed-up data, and whether you want to keep multiple backups on the same backup medium.

The defaults are compare on, maximum compression, and prompt before appending. Be aware that the compare operation effectively doubles the time required to complete a backup. If you trust your backup media, you can save a great deal of time by omitting this step. On the other hand, it's a good idea to leave compare on at least occasionally, just to ensure that your backup device is working correctly.

Require a Password to Restore?

To assign a password to your backup, click the Password tab in the Backup Job Options dialog box, and then enter and confirm your password. Be careful; if you forget your password, you won't be able to restore files from your backup.

Full, Differential, or Incremental?

SEE ALSO

For information about backup types, see "Backup Types and Strategies," page 342.

The Type tab in the Backup Job Options dialog box should already be filled out to indicate whether your job is for a full or partial backup. If you're doing a partial backup, however, you'll need to use the option buttons on this tab to tell Backup whether you want a differential or an incremental backup.

Excluding Particular File Types

On the Exclude tab in the Backup Job Options dialog box, you can tell Backup not to back up particular types of files, even if those files are stored on selected disks or within selected folders. To build a list of excluded file types, click the Exclude tab in the Backup Job Options dialog box, and then click the Add button. You'll see a dialog box similar to the one shown in Figure 14-3, on the next page.

The top half of the dialog box lists registered file types. If the file type you want to exclude doesn't appear on this list, click the Custom Type option button. Then type your file type's extension without a period (for example, XYZ).

What to Include in Backup's Reports

After every backup, Backup creates a text file detailing its most recent operation. You can view this report on screen or print it. (The report is a plain text file, suitable for printing via Notepad.) You can use the Report

III

Maintaining Your System

FIGURE 14-3.

This dialog box, which you reach by clicking Options, Exclude, and then Add, lets you specify which files in selected folders you don't want to back up.

tab in the Backup Job Options dialog box to tell Backup what it should and should not include in the report. By default, reports list all files that were scheduled to be backed up but were not backed up (for example, scheduled files that were in use when Backup tried to copy them), any errors encountered by Backup during the backup process, any warnings issued by the program during the backup, any messages and prompts it would have displayed had you not requested an "unattended" backup (more about that in a moment), and a summary of the entire operation. By default, reports do not include a list of every file backed up.

Requesting an "Unattended" Backup

Buried at the bottom of the Report tab in the Backup Job Options dialog box is a check box that lets you request an "unattended" backup. If this check box is selected (as it is by default), Backup suppresses any messages it would otherwise issue during the backup. If you deselect this check box and Backup feels inclined to prompt or warn, the program will suspend the remainder of the backup job until you respond to the message. Therefore, unless you intend to sit in front of your computer while Backup is at work, it's best to leave this box selected. As long as the List Unattended Messages And Prompts check box is also selected, you can find out what prompts you missed by reading Backup's report after the job is done.

Back Up the Registry?

The Advanced tab in the Backup Job Options dialog box offers a single option: Back Up Windows Registry. This one is selected by default, meaning that the registry will be included in all full backups (even if you don't include your Windows folder and subfolders in the backup) and, if it has changed, in all partial backups as well. Unless you must minimize time and media use, it's a good idea to leave this option selected.

Saving the Backup Job

Your final task in creating a backup job is to name it and save it. This you do by means of the Job menu's Save or Save As command or, more simply, by clicking the Save button on the toolbar. The name you choose will appear in the Backup Job drop-down list, making it easy to reuse the job in the future.

Creating a Backup Job with the Backup Wizard

If you prefer to use the Backup Wizard, you can get to it in either of two ways. If the welcome dialog box appears when you start Backup, select Create A New Backup Job and click OK. If this dialog box does not appear, choose Backup Wizard from the Tools menu.

Executing a Backup

If you've just finished creating your backup job, you can run it by clicking the Start button.

If you're returning to Backup on another occasion, you can reopen a backup job by selecting Open An Existing Backup Job from the welcome dialog box (if the welcome dialog box appears) or by selecting the name of the job you want from the Backup Job drop-down list. Alternatively, you can open the job with the Job menu's Open command. Then click Start to begin the backup.

While the backup is underway, the program displays a progress dialog box, showing you what operation it's performing (a backup or a verify, for example), what file it's working on, how long it's been working, and how much longer it expects to be busy. You can continue to work or

III

Maintaining Your System

have automated tasks run while Backup is backing up, but any files that are in use when Backup tries to copy them will not be backed up. The names of such files appear in Backup's report unless you deselect List Files That Were Not Backed Up on the Report tab in the Backup Job Options dialog box.

Viewing and Printing the Backup Report

Backup automatically creates a plain-text report summarizing each backup you create. You can view this report by clicking the Report button in the dialog box that Backup displays upon finishing a job. Or you can choose Report from the Tools menu, and then choose View from the cascading submenu. Backup opens the report file in Notepad. To print the report after viewing it, simply use Notepad's Print command. Alternatively, you can print the report directly by choosing Report from the Tools menu, and then choosing Print from the cascading submenu.

Restoring Files

Like backing up, restoring is a matter of specifying what, whence, whither, and how. You can do this by invoking the Restore Wizard (choose Restore Wizard from the Tools menu) or by pointing and clicking in the Restore tab of the Backup window. Working directly in the Restore tab of the Backup window gives you slightly more control over the process. You do not have to create a named restore job to carry out a restore operation.

To restore files by working directly in the Restore tab of the Backup window, start Backup and click the Restore tab. When you do, the program issues a prompt asking if you want to "refresh the current view." It does this because, before you can restore anything, Backup needs to build a "temporary catalog" of the files available for restoration. A temporary catalog is a temporary disk file that lists the contents of one backup set. A backup set, not to be confused with a backup job, is the collection of files that were copied during one backup operation. (A single backup job can be reused many times to produce many different backup sets.)

Insert the backup medium (tape or disk) from which you plan to restore, and then click Yes to refresh the view. Backup will scan the medium, present a list of the backup sets it finds, and then ask you to choose the one from which you want to restore. Then it will build a temporary catalog of that backup set and show its findings in the Restore tab of the Backup window.

After you have refreshed the view, make your choices by clicking various parts of the restore window, following these steps:

3 Select filenames here to restore only particular files in a folder.

1 Select your backup device or filename from this drop-down list.

2 Select check boxes here to restore entire folders with their subfolders.

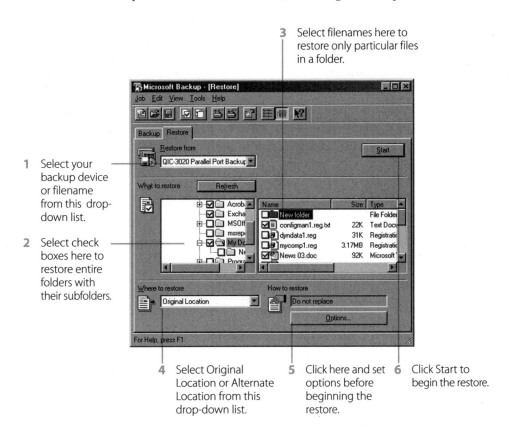

4 Select Original Location or Alternate Location from this drop-down list.

5 Click here and set options before beginning the restore.

6 Click Start to begin the restore.

Setting Restore Options

To set restore options, click the Options button at the bottom of the Restore tab. Alternatively, go to the Restore tab and choose Options from the Job menu. The Restore Options dialog box, shown in Figure 14-4, on the next page, lets you specify what Backup should do when a file to be restored already exists on the target disk, what details should be included in the restore report, and whether Backup should restore the registry.

FIGURE 14-4.

The Restore Options dialog box is simpler than the Backup Options dialog box, but just as important.

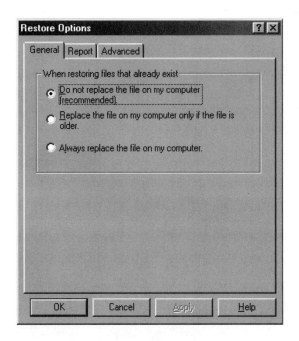

Overwrite Options

When a file that Backup is about to restore already exists on the disk to which you're restoring, Backup needs to know what you want it to do. The default and recommended choice is not to restore any file that's already on the target disk. But you can opt to have the program restore when the backed-up copy is newer than the existing copy. Or you can have the program always restore. What you can't do is ask for a yes/no prompt every time the question arises. If you want some files always to be overwritten and some files never to be overwritten, you'll need to perform separate restore operations for each category of file.

Report Options

For more information about backing up and restoring the registry, see "How Windows Backs Up the Registry," page 359, and "Other Ways to Back Up and Restore the Registry," page 360.

The Report tab in the Restore Options dialog box lets you decide what details to include in a restore report. Your choices here are analogous to the ones offered in the Backup Job Options dialog box.

Restore the Registry?

The Advanced tab in the Restore Options dialog box lets you indicate whether you want Backup to restore your registry—assuming you backed up the registry.

> Unless you know your registry has been corrupted and you want to restore an earlier, uncorrupted version, do not restore the registry. Otherwise, the restored registry may not accurately reflect the current state of your hardware and software.

Insuring Your System Against a Catastrophic Failure

Your Windows 98 CD includes a system recovery utility that may be able to rebuild your system in the event of a catastrophic failure. Provided you have a recent full-system backup on hand, as well as a startup disk, the odds are good that this utility will get your system running again when all else has failed.

To give yourself some disaster insurance, start by finding that startup disk that the Windows Setup program made for you when you first installed Windows 98. If that disk isn't handy, here's how to make one:

1 In Control Panel, launch Add/Remove Programs.

2 Click the Startup Disk tab.

3 Click Create Disk and follow the prompts.

Next, make sure your Windows CD is handy! The system recovery utility lives there, and even if you copied it to your hard disk, you might not be able to get to it in your time of need.

Finally, make a complete backup of your system, including the Windows registry. Repeat this step regularly and frequently!

Running the System Recovery Utility

To recover your system, first boot your computer from the startup disk. (Put the disk in drive A and start your computer.) A startup menu will appear. Choose option 1, Start Computer with CD-ROM Support. This action installs a generic CD-ROM driver, allowing you to run the system recovery utility from your CD-ROM drive.

Insert your Windows 98 CD in the CD-ROM drive. At the A> prompt, type the drive letter of your CD-ROM drive, followed by a colon.

III

Maintaining Your System

Now that you're logged onto your CD-ROM drive, type:

```
cd \tools\sysrec
```

Finally, type *pcrestor* and follow the prompts.

The system recovery utility first runs an automated setup script to reinstall portions of Windows 98. This process takes between a half hour and an hour, depending on the speed of your hardware. You will not be required to answer any prompts during this process. Once this much of Windows has been reinstalled, a System Recovery Wizard appears. The wizard might install additional drivers if needed. Finally, a Backup Restore Wizard appears to finish the job for you.

During this last phase of the recovery, you will have choices. Among other things, you'll be asked whether you want to restore everything from your backup, or only particular files. You'll also have the opportunity to forgo restoring your hardware's registry settings. This option can prove useful if you have changed your hardware since your system crashed.

Understanding the Registry

Just about everything Windows 98 needs to know about your system—about your hardware, your software, and any restrictive policies that may have been set by a system administrator—is stored in a database called the registry. This centralized information repository essentially replaces the myriad configuration files that had been used in earlier versions of Windows (prior to Windows 95) and in MS-DOS. If you've used Windows 3.0 or 3.1, you may have had occasion to examine or modify files named Win.ini and System.ini. These files still exist in Windows 98 (and you must not delete them!), but only for the sake of compatibility with older programs. For nearly all newer programs, as well as for the operating system itself, the registry has taken over the role once played by Win.ini and System.ini.

The registry has also eliminated the need for many of the "private" .INI files used by some programs. Under Windows 3.x, many programs stored configuration details and information about your preferences in their own .INI files. With the advent of the registry in Windows 95, software developers have been able to store this kind of information in the registry instead. You'll almost certainly still find an assortment of miscellaneous

.INI files on your hard disk, because older programs still use them and some newer ones do despite the registry. (Even Windows 98 creates a few.) But more and more, the crucial data that makes your system and your software go, as you want it to go, is held in the registry, not in .INI files.

In this chapter we'll take a cursory look at the organization of the registry. More important, we'll explore the various means by which you can protect yourself against registry corruption. Windows automatically creates backups of the registry files, but it's important to know how to restore those backups should something go amiss. Finally, we'll look at Registry Editor, the program that Windows supplies for direct editing of registry contents, and at some of the customizing steps you can take by using Registry Editor to modify certain registry entries.

One Database, Two (or Three) Files

When you look at the registry through Registry Editor, all the data appears in one place. But on disk it's actually stored in two, or sometimes three, separate files. These files are called System.dat, User.dat, and Policy.pol. System.dat, the largest of the three, records information about your hardware. User.dat records everything you've done to personalize your Windows environment. And Policy.pol records any restrictive policies that have been established for your system. Policy.pol is an optional component. (Restrictive policies are set via the Windows Policy Editor, Poledit.exe, which is stored on the Windows CD and not installed by default. The use of Policy Editor is not covered in this book. For information, consult the Windows 98 Resource Kit or the help file for Policy Editor, Poledit.hlp.)

? SEE ALSO

For more information about profiles, see "Setting Up New User Profiles," page 269.

If you use profiles on your system (to allow different users to operate the same computer, each with his or her own set of customizations), each profile has its own User.dat. The registry incorporates only the User.dat for the current user, and it swaps out one User.dat for another when one user logs off and another logs on.

Your registry files may or may not be stored on a local hard disk. Your system administrator may, for example, have set Windows up with your User.dat on a network server. Such an arrangement allows you to have your customized version of Windows at any computer with access to that server. If your administrator has established policies governing several networked computers, the controlling Policy.pol file is almost certainly stored on a server.

Windows gives your registry files read-only and hidden attributes, to make it less likely that you will accidentally delete or modify them. By default, such files do not appear in Windows Explorer windows. (You can make them appear by choosing Folder Options from Explorer's View menu, clicking the View tab, and then selecting the Show All Files option button.) The files are also excluded from the list that appears when you choose Folder Options from Explorer's View menu and click the File Types tab. (An entry for .REG files, another kind of registry file that we will encounter later in this chapter, does appear in the File Types list, and you may have occasion to modify the default action associated with this file type.)

How Windows Backs Up the Registry

By default, every time you start Windows successfully, Windows backs up your registry files, as well as Win.ini and System.ini. Each set of backups is combined and compressed into a single "cabinet" (.CAB) file, which is stored, by default, in the Sysbckup subfolder of your Windows folder. The Sysbckup folder is hidden, by default. The number of backup files maintained, the names of any additional files backed up in this process, and the storage location of the resulting cabinet files are all determined by settings in a file called Scanreg.ini, which is kept in your Windows folder.

Each time you boot Windows, Windows scans the registry to make sure it hasn't been corrupted. If problems are found, the system restores the most recent backup. If no backups are available, the system attempts to fix whatever problems it has found.

TIP

You can use Registry Checker to manually scan the registry and make a backup. To run Registry Checker, open the Start menu and choose Run. In the Run dialog box, type *scanregw* and click OK.

III

Maintaining Your System

Restoring Registry Backups Manually

As mentioned, Windows always restores the most recent registry backup if problems are discovered at logon. Should you ever want to perform that restoration yourself, or should you ever want to restore an earlier backup, you can do so as follows:

1 Open your Sysbckup folder in Windows Explorer. (If you don't find the folder, choose Folder Options from Explorer's View menu, and then on the View tab, select Show All Files.)

2 Look for files named rb*nnn*.cab, where *nnn* is a three-digit number. Use the files' creation dates to find the backup you want to restore.

3 Click or double-click the .CAB file to open it in an Explorer window.

4 Click or double-click the icon for the file you want to extract from the cabinet.

5 Tell Windows which folder it should extract the selected file to. Use a folder on a floppy drive or a hard drive that you can access from MS-DOS.

6 Restart Windows in MS-DOS mode.

7 Copy the extracted file to your Windows folder.

Other Ways to Back Up and Restore the Registry

For an extra measure of security, you can make your own backups of the registry. You can copy the .DAT files with MS-DOS commands, with Microsoft Backup (a program supplied with Windows) or a third-party backup program, or with one of the two configuration-backup utilities that are available from Microsoft. The Registry Editor program, discussed later in this chapter, also has an Export command that you can use to back up all or a portion of your registry.

Backing Up with MS-DOS Commands

The following sequence of steps copies User.dat and System.dat from C:\Windows to a removable storage medium (a Zip drive, perhaps) in drive F. If you're copying to a different location, substitute the appropriate drive and/or directory name for F.

1 Choose Shut Down from the Start menu, and then select Restart In MS-DOS Mode.

2 At the MS-DOS prompt, type *cd c:\windows* and press Enter.

3 Type the following commands (press Enter after each):

```
attrib -h -r -s system.dat
copy system.dat f:
attrib +h +r +s system.dat
attrib -h -r -s user.dat
copy user.dat f:
attrib +h +r +s user.dat
```

4 Restart the computer.

Backing Up with Microsoft Backup

SEE ALSO

For information about Backup, see Chapter 14, "Protecting Your Data with Microsoft Backup."

Microsoft Backup, the backup program supplied with Windows 98, includes an option to back up registry files. This option is selected by default when you do a complete backup of your system. If you have a recent backup that includes the registry files, you can use Microsoft Backup to restore your registry.

Backing Up with Configuration Backup and Emergency Recovery Utility

Microsoft has created two other utility programs that you can use to back up your registry. Configuration Backup lets you create as many as nine compressed backups of your registry files. Emergency Recovery Utility maintains only one backup at a time, but that backup can include a number of other vital files, along with the registry. You can download these programs from Microsoft's Web site, www.microsoft.com.

To use either program, search the Web site for Cfgback.exe (the executable file for Configuration Backup) or Eru.exe (Emergency Recovery Utility).

III

Maintaining Your System

Using Configuration Backup

When you run Configuration Backup, the first thing you see is a sequence of messages describing the program. You can select a check box below each message if you don't want the messages to appear on subsequent runs. If you ignore the messages altogether, however, you will miss two important details about Configuration Backup:

■ Although you can copy the .RBK files created by Configuration Backup from your Windows folder (where they initially land) to other media, you can restore these files only from the Windows folder.

■ If your system is set up for multiple users (that is, if you have profiles turned on), the User.dat file is not included in Configuration Backup's backups. (In that case, use another backup method.)

Finally, you arrive at a screen that looks like the one shown in Figure 15-1. Here you can supply a name for the backup you want to create, and then click the Backup button to proceed. You'll get a confirmation prompt, a couple of progress screens, and then a message confirming a successful backup.

If you have already created nine backups with Configuration Backup, you'll need to delete at least one before creating another. At the screen

FIGURE 15-1.
Configuration Backup can maintain up to nine compressed backups of your registry files.

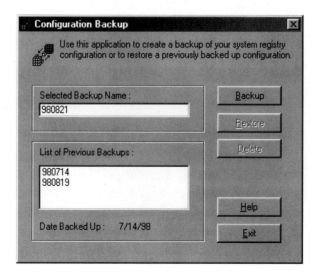

shown in Figure 15-1, simply select the one you want to remove, and then click the Delete button.

To restore a backup using Configuration Backup, select its name in the list at the bottom of the screen shown in Figure 15-1. Then click the Restore button.

Using Emergency Recovery Utility

The Emergency Recovery Utility can create uncompressed copies of any or all of the files listed in Figure 15-2. You can send these copies either to the root directory of a floppy disk or some other fixed or removable directory of your choosing. The program recommends that you store the backups on a blank system floppy disk (one that you can boot from in the event that Windows does not start), but, unfortunately, System.dat is too large to fit on an uncompressed 1.44-MB system disk alongside all the other files that Emergency Recovery Utility wants to back up. Thus, if you select the default (floppy disk) option, the program proposes to copy all the files shown in Figure 15-2 except System.dat.

In addition to copying system files, Emergency Recovery Utility stores files named Erd.exe and Erd.inf on the target medium. To restore the backups, you run Erd.exe from the directory (or floppy disk) where the backups are located. You cannot run Erd.exe while Windows is running.

FIGURE 15-2.

Emergency Recovery Utility copies all the files listed here.

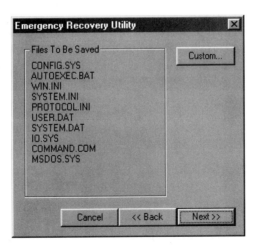

III

Maintaining Your System

Given the fact that Emergency Recovery Utility cannot back up all of your system files to a floppy disk, the best way to use this utility appears to be one of the following:

- Back up to a floppy disk but exclude all the .INI files. If you do this, it's possible you will have room for your SYSTEM.DAT. To change the list of files that Emergency Recovery Utility will back up, click the Custom button in the screen shown in Figure 15-2, on the previous page.

- Alternatively, back up everything to a hard disk. Create a Windows startup disk. In the event that Windows doesn't start, boot from the startup disk. Then log onto the hard disk directory to which you backed up using Emergency Recovery Utility. From there, run Erd.exe.

Introducing Registry Editor

The Windows 98 Setup procedure normally installs Registry Editor in your Windows directory, but it does not create a Start menu item for it. To run Registry Editor, assuming it's already on your hard disk in the usual place, choose the Start menu's Run command and type *regedit*. This launches Regedit.exe, Registry Editor's executable file.

Be aware that Registry Editor was designed for programmers, and it offers few convenience or safety features. More luxurious registry editors are available from third-party software vendors.

Precautions to Take When Using Registry Editor

When you edit text in a word processor, your changes don't become permanent (that is, they are not stored on disk) until you use the word processor's Save command. Such is not the case in Registry Editor, which has no Save command! Any changes you make to the registry via Registry Editor occur *immediately*. Therefore, the rules to observe are:

- Be alert when using Registry Editor!

- Back up at least that part of the registry that you plan to work with.

- Write down (or remember) any values you're about to change. If something goes haywire, you'll need to restore those original values.

- Close Registry Editor as soon as you're finished with it.

WARNING

> Making the wrong changes to your registry can render your entire system inoperable, forcing you to reinstall Windows 98.

Registry Editor's Export and Import Commands

The Export Registry File and Import Registry File commands, on Registry Editor's Registry menu, provide yet another way to back up and restore portions of or all of your registry. When you select one of the "hkeys" in Registry Editor's left pane (see Figure 15-3) and choose Export Registry File, Registry Editor saves that hkey as a plain text file. If you select My Computer and choose Export Registry File, Registry Editor saves the entire registry. If you select a key (an entry subordinate to one of the hkeys) and export, you get only that key. Before you modify any part of the registry, you might want to export either that part alone or the entire registry.

To restore a saved registry file, choose Import Registry File. Registry Editor merges the saved file into the current registry. Incoming values replace existing values. Keys in the saved file that don't exist in the current registry are added to the current registry.

FIGURE 15-3.

Registry Editor's left pane displays the structure of your registry as an outline, much the way Explorer can show the folder structure of your hard disk.

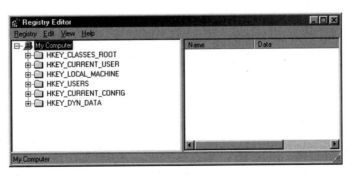

If the saved registry file has the extension .REG (the default) and you haven't changed the default action associated with this extension, you can also merge the saved registry file by simply launching its entry in a Windows Explorer window. You might find this convenience a hazard, however. With a single click (or a double-click, depending on how you've set up your Windows environment), you can easily merge a saved file *whether you intend to or not*.

TIP

> To avoid accidental merging of an exported registry file, save the file with an extension other than .REG. Alternatively, change the default action associated with .REG files. To do the latter, choose Folder Options from the View menu in any Windows Explorer window. Click the File Types tab, scroll through the file-type list, and select Registration Entries. Click the Edit button, select Edit in the Actions list, and then click Set Default. Now, launching a .REG file opens the file in Notepad (or WordPad, if the file is too large for Notepad). If you want to merge the exported file, you can use Registry Editor's Import Registry File command.

Hkeys and Keys

The registry is organized into six main units called (for reasons best known to the designers of Windows) *hkeys*. As Figure 15-3 on the previous page shows, Registry Editor initially displays these six hkeys as second-level outline entries, subordinate to My Computer.

Below the hkeys in the registry hierarchy are *keys*, which are shown with folder icons in Registry Editor's left pane. The contents of these folders are called *values*. Values always appear in the right pane. Each value has a name and contains data. Data can be one of several types.

Like filenames with a full path specification in Windows, registry values can be uniquely identified by listing the hierarchy leading to the value, separating each element with a backslash. In Figure 15-4, for example, we've navigated to HKEY_CURRENT_USER\Control Panel\Accessibility\HighContrast. In the right pane, we see the values that comprise the High Contrast key: Default, Available, ConfirmHotKey, HotKeyActive, On, and OnOffFeedback. Each value has data associated with it, and to the left of each setting name is an icon indicating the value's data type.

FIGURE 15-4.
Registry Editor's right pane shows the values that comprise the key selected in the left pane.

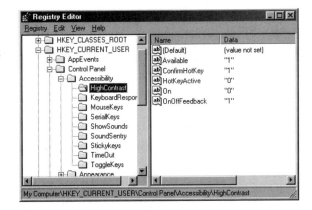

The "ab" symbols in Figure 15-4 show that the High Contrast settings all use text values.

To change a value's data, simply double-click the value's name, and an edit dialog box appears. As Figure 15-5 shows, double-clicking brings up a dialog box in which you can enter a new value.

FIGURE 15-5.
Double-clicking a value brings up an edit dialog box, like this one, where you may alter the current data.

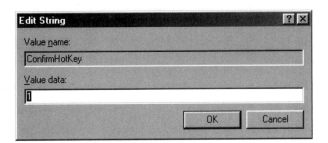

To add a new key or value, select the key that will contain the new element and then choose New from the Edit menu. From the submenu that appears, choose Key or choose the data type of the new value you want to add.

If you explore the registry via Registry Editor, you'll see that there is redundancy among the various limbs of the six hkeys. The contents of HKEY_CLASSES_ROOT, for example, are identical to those of HKEY_LOCAL_MACHINE\SOFTWARE\Classes. This redundancy serves the cause of efficiency.

III

Maintaining Your System

A Few Useful Registry Modifications

The designers of Windows intended that the registry would be modified only by the operating system itself, by choices that you make via the Windows user interface (that is, by the preferences you express in Control Panel and elsewhere), and by your software. They achieved this goal almost, but not quite, completely. The remainder of this chapter presents a few customizing changes that you can make only by direct modification of the registry.

Changing the Registered Owner and Registered Organization

If your computer came from its vendor with Windows 98 preinstalled, you might find that certain of your programs insist that your name is something like Preferred Customer of XYZ Inc. No matter how you log on and what you do via the Windows user interface, you can't seem to remove that irritating moniker. With the help of Registry Editor, you can do it:

1 Navigate down the left pane to HKEY_LOCAL_MACHINE\ SOFTWARE\Microsoft\Windows\CurrentVersion. Click the word *CurrentVersion*, so that you get the open folder icon.

2 In the right pane, double-click RegisteredOwner.

3 In the dialog box, type your name and click OK.

4 Back in the right pane, double-click RegisteredOrganization.

5 In the dialog box, type the name of your company and click OK.

You can use the Find command on Registry Editor's Edit menu (shortcut: Ctrl+F) to help you navigate. But because of all the similarly named keys in your registry, Find is not as convenient as it may first appear. However you navigate, you can use the status bar at the bottom of Registry Editor's window to confirm that you're in the right place before you change any values.

Changing the Source Path Used by the Windows Setup Program

When you install a new Windows component, or when Windows needs to get a new driver file from disk, Windows always searches a particular directory, perhaps on your CD-ROM drive or a network server. If it habitually goes to the wrong place, you can alter its behavior by changing a registry value:

1 Navigate to HKEY_LOCAL_MACHINE\SOFTWARE\Microsoft\ Windows\CurrentVersion\Setup. Click the word *Setup* so that you get the open folder icon.

2 In the right pane, double-click the word *SourcePath*.

3 In the dialog box, type the correct source path and click OK.

> Be sure you include a backslash at the end of the source path. For example, if you want to default to the CD-ROM in drive F, type *F:\WIN98* in the Value Data box.

Pruning the Run MRU

The Start menu's Run command maintains an "MRU"—a list of your most-recently-used entries. Should you ever wish to delete an item on that list, here's how:

1 Navigate to HKEY_CURRENT_USER\Software\Microsoft\ Windows\CurrentVersion\Explorer\RunMRU.

2 In the right pane, select the letter associated with the item you want to delete. Then choose Delete from the Edit menu.

Adding an Open With Command for Every File Type

As you may know, if you want to open a document in a program other than the one with which the document's file type is associated, you can right-click the document while holding down the Shift key. The context menu that appears when you Shift+right-click always includes an Open With command, and that command lets you specify the program in which

III

Maintaining Your System

you want to open your document. If you find it hard to remember to Shift+right-click, however, you can add the Open With command to every file type's normal context menu, by following these steps:

1   Navigate to HKEY_CLASSES_ROOT\Unknown\Shell\openas\ command.

2   In the right pane, double-click the Default entry.

3   In the dialog box, a long command string appears. Press Ctrl+C to copy this command string to the Clipboard.

4   Click Cancel to leave this dialog box.

5   Navigate back up to the first entry under HKEY_CLASSES_ROOT, which should be *.

6   In the left pane, right-click the asterisk. Point to New, and then choose Key.

7   Name the key Shell.

8   Right-click Shell, point to New, choose Key, and name the key openas.

9   Right-click openas, point to New, choose Key, and name the key command.

10   In the right pane, double-click the Default entry.

11   In the dialog box, press Ctrl+V to paste the command string from the Clipboard. Then click OK.

The foregoing are just a smattering of the kinds of things you can do by tweaking the registry. If you read computer magazines, you'll probably encounter other similar ideas. Just remember to proceed with caution, back up before you dive in, and get out of Registry Editor as soon as you've finished!

Optimizing, Maintaining, and Troubleshooting

This chapter takes up three interrelated topics: how to get your system running as well as it can, how to perform routine maintenance on your system so that it always hums along happily, and what to do when things go awry. Windows 98 provides several new or improved tools to help you keep your system in good order. If you have adequate hardware to begin with and you use these maintenance tools regularly, the odds are good that you'll never have serious problems. In case you do run into trouble, however, Windows 98 also provides direct links to Microsoft's Internet-based support services, as well as better diagnostic information to assist support personnel.

Getting Optimal Performance from Windows 98

Aside from the speed of your microprocessor, the elements of your system that have the most bearing on Windows' performance are memory (RAM) and available hard disk space. Windows *loves* memory. No matter what you run, but particularly if you run large, computation-intensive programs such as graphics editors and computer-aided design programs, you can scarcely have too much RAM on board. In any event, you shouldn't even try to run Windows 98 with less than 16 MB (megabytes), and if you're getting unsatisfactory performance on a system with less than 64 MB, one of the first things to consider is plugging in some additional memory.

Windows uses your hard disk as "virtual memory"—that is, as an extension of main memory. When things get overloaded in memory, Windows automatically writes some data from memory to a "swap file" on your disk—a process called *paging*. When Windows needs that information again, it reads it back from the swap file, at the same time (if necessary) swapping something else out.

Because disk access is far slower than memory access, paging impedes performance. Increasing the amount of memory on your system improves performance by minimizing paging.

In earlier versions of Windows (prior to Windows 95), users could choose between a permanent swap file and a temporary one. The permanent swap file provided faster access, but walled off a sizable block of disk space that could no longer be used for program and document storage. A temporary swap file provided flexibility at the cost of slower paging.

The permanent/temporary tradeoff is no longer available in Windows, and indeed is no longer necessary. Windows normally manages the paging process in the most efficient manner, without requiring you to make any decisions or intervene in any way.

The only time it might make sense to get involved in setting paging parameters is if you have two or more hard disks and one of them is significantly faster than the one on which Windows is installed. Windows normally pages to the drive on which it's installed, and if you think you can gain performance by pointing it to a different drive, you can do so as follows:

1   Right-click My Computer and choose Properties from the context menu. (Alternatively, launch System in Control Panel.)

2   Click the Performance tab, and then click the Virtual Memory button.

3   In the Virtual Memory dialog box (see Figure 16-1), select the Let Me Specify My Own Virtual Memory Settings option button, and then select the disk where you want paging to occur. Then click OK.

FIGURE 16-1.
You can use this dialog box to override Windows' default paging parameters, but usually there's no reason to do so.

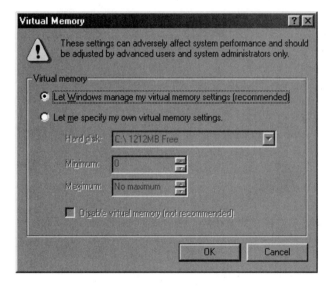

A better solution, if you happen to have a drive that's dramatically faster than the one where Windows installed, is to reinstall Windows on the faster drive.

The dialog box shown in Figure 16-1 also lets you specify a minimum and a maximum size for your swap file. Unless your hard disk space is severely limited, there's no good reason to change these parameters. And if your disk space is severely limited, it's far better to address the disk-space problem than to constrain Windows' page file.

Freeing Up Hard Disk Space

If available hard-disk space falls too low, you will begin seeing error messages from programs and from Windows itself. You may see these even when you have 100 MB or so of free space, simply because Windows is running out of room to page. Here are some ways to reduce the population density of your hard disk:

- Uninstall programs that you don't need.

- Uninstall Windows components that you don't need.

- Delete or move documents that you don't need.

- Switch to the FAT32 file system, if you aren't already using it.

- Use DriveSpace 3 to compress your disk (an option not available on drives that are already using FAT32).

- Use third-party compression tools to compress particular files.

Cleaning Up with Disk Cleanup

The easiest way to take most of these steps is to run Disk Cleanup, a utility program supplied with Windows. Figure 16-2 shows a sample of the work that Disk Cleanup can do. The program lists several categories of potentially expendable disk files and shows you how much space you could recover by deleting each category. The More Options tab, meanwhile, provides access to the Windows Setup program (so you can delete unneeded components of Windows), Add/Remove Programs (so you can get rid of programs you aren't using), and the FAT32 Drive Converter (if your disk isn't already using the FAT32 file system).

To run Disk Cleanup, open the Start menu and choose Programs, Accessories, System Tools, Disk Cleanup. Disk Cleanup begins by asking which drive you want to clean up. Select a drive and click OK.

 TIP

A Faster Way to Launch Disk Cleanup
In a Windows Explorer window, right-click the icon for the drive you want to clean up and choose Properties. On the General tab in the properties dialog box, click Disk Cleanup.

FIGURE 16-2.

The easiest way to recover disk space is to use Disk Cleanup, a utility supplied with Windows.

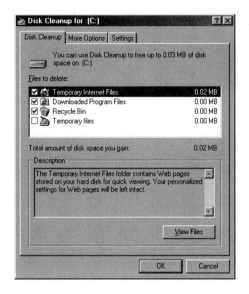

Uninstalling Unneeded Programs and Windows Components

To see a list of programs that can easily be uninstalled, launch Add/Remove Programs in Control Panel. To uninstall a program, select its name and click the Add/Remove button.

To uninstall Windows components that you don't need, launch Add/Remove Programs and click the Windows Setup tab. You can uninstall a whole category of components (Desktop Themes, for example) by deselecting the associated check box. Or you can uninstall some of a category's elements by selecting the category name and then clicking Details. In the Details display, deselect the check boxes for any items you want to uninstall.

You might also want to consider uninstalling unneeded components of some of your programs. Perhaps you don't need 3000 clip-art images, a French dictionary (assuming you don't write in French), or the help files for a programming language in which you don't program. Try launching Add/Remove Programs in Control Panel and running the uninstall routine for your largest programs. Many uninstall programs let you remove particular components without getting rid of the entire program. If your program doesn't have this capability, you can simply back out of the uninstaller without removing anything.

III

Maintaining Your System

Deleting or Moving Unneeded Documents

When looking around for document files that are good candidates for deletion, be sure to include the following:

- The contents of your Recycle Bin
- Old files with the extension .TMP
- Files with the extension .CHK

 TIP

The Maintenance Wizard can help you get rid of files that you don't need. (See "Automating Maintenance with the Maintenance Wizard," page 398.)

 SEE ALSO
For more information about the Recycle Bin, see "Restoring Deleted Folders, Files, and Shortcuts," page 138.

To get rid of everything in your Recycle Bin, right-click the Recycle Bin icon and choose Empty Recycle Bin. To remove items selectively, launch Recycle Bin. If necessary, choose Details from Explorer's View menu to see the date on which each file was deleted. Click the Date Deleted column heading twice to sort the files by deletion date, with the oldest files at the top. These oldest files are probably your best candidates for removal.

 NOTE

When you delete files from your Recycle Bin, they're gone for good, and they can't be easily or reliably recovered.

Many programs create temporary files while you work. These files, which commonly have the extension .TMP, are normally deleted when you quit the program. If you have any kind of irregular shutdown, however (for example, if the program crashes, or if you turn off your computer without going through the normal shutdown procedure), the temporary files linger until you ferret them out and remove them by hand.

The Start menu's Find command can help you do the ferreting. If Find turns up .TMP files whose creation dates lie before your most recent system shutdown (see Figure 16-3), you can be reasonably sure that it's safe to delete those files.

FIGURE 16-3.

On August 28, a search of local hard drives for files with extension .TMP produced this list. The first five items are good candidates for deletion.

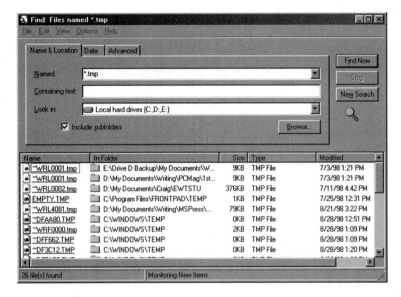

Files with the extension .CHK are sometimes created by the ScanDisk utility, described later in this chapter. After you verify that that your .CHK files don't include any data that you want to salvage, it's safe to delete these files.

TIP

> Hold down the Shift key while you delete .TMP and .CHK files. Otherwise, those files will merely move to the Recycle Bin, and your deletion won't free up any disk space.

After deleting unneeded Recycle Bin contents, .TMP files, and .CHK files, wander through your hard disk and see if you can find ordinary documents that can safely be archived onto removable media or a server. This will give your system a little room to breathe, allowing more efficient paging and forestalling the day when you have to face those low-disk-space error messages again.

Switching to the FAT32 File System

FAT32 (the letters stand for File Allocation Table) is an improved version of the file system that's been around since the first version of MS-DOS. From the standpoint of disk-space conservation, FAT32's principal advantage over FAT (the old system) is that it can use smaller "allocation units" on large disks. An *allocation unit*, also known as a *cluster*, is the smallest amount of disk space that the operating system can allocate to a file. If you create a 100-byte file on a disk whose allocation units are 32,768 bytes, that file will consume 32,768 bytes, of which 32,668 bytes will be wasted. On such a disk, you'll also waste a huge amount of space if you create a file that's 32,868 bytes long, because the operating system will have to give that file two entire allocation units. In short, large allocation units almost invariably waste large amounts of disk space. By switching from FAT to FAT32, you can usually increase the effective capacity of a disk by a significant amount.

The disadvantages and limitations of FAT32 are as follows:

- You can't access a FAT32 disk from operating systems that do not use FAT32, including older versions of Windows and Windows NT.

- You can't use DriveSpace 3 compression on a FAT32 disk.

- Some disk-utility programs written for FAT drives won't work with FAT32 disks.

- You can't use FAT32 on disks smaller than 512 MB.

The first point applies only to systems that "dual boot" Windows 98 and another, pre-FAT32 operating system. If, for example, you have both Windows 98 and Windows NT 4.0 on the same computer, Windows NT will not be able to access your FAT32 disk. Note that the inaccessibility of FAT32 drives to older operating systems does not mean that you cannot access your FAT32 disks across a network from an older operating system. You can still get to your FAT32 files from other computers on your network, regardless of which version of which operating system those other computers are running.

As for the inability to apply DriveSpace compression to a FAT32 disk, the increased storage efficiency of FAT32 means that you may not miss DriveSpace.

To find out whether a hard disk is currently using FAT32, launch My Computer, right-click the entry for the disk in question, and choose Properties from the ensuing context menu. Near the top of the General tab in the disk's properties dialog box, you'll see either FAT or FAT32.

To convert a FAT disk to FAT32, run Drive Converter (FAT32). If your Start menu hasn't been dramatically rearranged, you'll probably find that item by choosing Start, Programs, Accessories, System Tools.

NOTE

If Drive Converter (FAT32) has not been set up on your system, launch Add/ Remove Programs in Control Panel, click the Windows Setup tab, select System Tools, and click the Details button. Select Drive Converter (FAT32) and click OK.

The Drive Converter (FAT32) wizard first asks you to save all open documents and close all running programs so that it can reboot your system in MS-DOS mode. Before it does that, it scans your system for any programs that appear to be incompatible with FAT32. If it finds any, it gives you the opportunity to decide whether or not to go ahead with the conversion. The wizard also invites you to back up your disk before you proceed. This is an optional step, of course, but a last-minute backup will probably enhance your comfort level. Finally, after completing the conversion (which takes only a few minutes), the wizard offers to defragment your new FAT32 disk. This step, too, is optional—but in most cases extremely time-consuming. The defragmentation process is described later in this chapter.

Using DriveSpace 3 to Compress a FAT Disk

DriveSpace 3 is a program that increases the effective capacity of hard and floppy disks. It does this by creating a "compressed volume file" (CVF) on a disk. When you save a file to a CVF, DriveSpace compresses the file on the fly—that is, without requiring any special action by you. When you read a file from a compressed disk, the file is automatically expanded. The net result is that, while you continue to work with your files the way you always have, your disk has much more room than it ever had before.

How much extra room you get depends on what kind of data your files hold. DriveSpace achieves its compression by identifying patterns in your data. Files that are highly structured—for example, a bitmap graphics file, in which certain pixel patterns appear over and over—can be compressed more than files whose contents are essentially random. Executable files and DLLs are usually less compressible than documents. In the

III

Maintaining Your System

typical case in which both executable files and documents are involved, you can expect the effective size of your disk to nearly double.

What about performance? Your computer's processor has to do extra work when reading files from or saving files to a CVF. On the other hand, the smaller size of your compressed files means that your system has to perform fewer disk reads. Because the hard disk is a relatively slow component of your system, you may experience no performance penalty at all when using DriveSpace. And if your uncompressed disk doesn't have room for an adequate swap file, you'll undoubtedly get better performance by using DriveSpace.

The important tradeoff for using DriveSpace is not performance but data security. When DriveSpace compresses a disk, it combines all the compressed files on that disk into a single file. Under ordinary circumstances you never see that file, because DriveSpace gives it hidden and system attributes. What you see instead is a virtualized disk that looks exactly the same as your disk looked before you ran DriveSpace, except that it's much larger.

For example, suppose your C drive has a capacity of 400 MB and you currently have files filling all but 60 MB of that space. After running DriveSpace on this disk, you'll still have a C drive, and your files will have the same size properties that they had before. That is, Windows will still report that drive C contains 340 MB of data. But drive C will now appear to be an 800-MB drive (or something close to 800 MB).

DriveSpace 3, DriveSpace, and DoubleSpace

DriveSpace 3 is an improved version of DriveSpace, which was introduced with Windows 95. DriveSpace, in turn, was an improved version of an MS-DOS–based tool called DoubleSpace. DriveSpace 3 can compress larger disks than DriveSpace could, and it offers a choice of two compression methods. One method gives you higher compression than the other, at a small performance cost.

With DriveSpace 3, you also get Compression Agent, a utility that can change the compression method applied to particular files, or even decompress particular files.

If you've installed Windows 98 on a system that has one or more drives compressed with the original DriveSpace or DoubleSpace, you don't need to recompress those drives with DriveSpace 3—but you can if you want to.

To achieve the illusion that your files are the same size as before but your disk has ingested a packet of growth hormone, DriveSpace creates a new (uncompressed) "host" drive on your disk. It assigns this drive an unused drive letter, such as H. Then it compresses all your files and combines them into a single file on the host drive. That single file is your CVF. When you read or save a document, you're actually interacting with some piece of the CVF, but DriveSpace deploys its smoke and mirrors to make it look as if you're working with ordinary files on the original drive.

The only hazard in all of this is that corruption or accidental deletion of the CVF can wipe out a whole disk's worth of data. Because the CVF does not ordinarily show up in Explorer windows, or in directory listings generated at the MS-DOS prompt, it's unlikely that you would ever delete it accidentally. But the consequences would be severe if you did. Therefore, if you use DriveSpace, it's more important than ever that you back up your data regularly.

Compressing a Disk

Compressing a hard disk with DriveSpace may take several hours, depending on the size of your disk. During this time, you will not be able to use your computer for any other purpose. You might therefore want to begin the compression process at the end of a work day.

To compress a disk, open the Start menu and choose Programs, Accessories, System Tools. On the System Tools menu, choose DriveSpace.

NOTE

If you don't find DriveSpace there, launch Add/Remove Programs in Control Panel, click the Windows Setup tab, select System Tools, and click the Details button. Select Disk Compression Tools and click OK. (If Disk Compression Tools doesn't appear in the Disk Tools list, DriveSpace has already been installed. Unlike most Windows components, once installed you can't remove DriveSpace, so it doesn't appear in the list. In this case, use the Find command to locate and run a program named Drvspace.exe.)

III

Maintaining Your System

DriveSpace's initial display lists the drives on your system, including any that you have already compressed. Before applying one of DriveSpace's commands, select the drive that you want the command to affect.

TIP

As a quicker alternative for compressing a particular drive, you can right-click the drive's icon in a Windows Explorer window. Choose Properties from the context menu and then click the Compression tab. (This tab appears only on uncompressed drives.)

Before starting the compression process, be sure to visit the Settings command on DriveSpace's Advanced menu. (See Figure 16-4.) Here you can select from the following compression options:

- **HiPack compression.** This option gives you the highest compression ratio, thereby giving you the maximum possible disk space. As a tradeoff, you have to put up with slower disk reads and writes. As the dialog box says, this one is not a good choice on 486-based machines.

- **Standard compression.** This option gives you less effective disk space than HiPack but provides faster access to your files.

- **No compression, unless...** This means that files written to your disk remain uncompressed, unless your hard disk reaches a capacity threshold that you set. At that point, DriveSpace begins compressing anything you save.

- **No compression.** This option allows you to save new files uncompressed to a drive that has previously been compressed. (Old files on this drive remain compressed.) The new files will

FIGURE 16-4.

The Settings command on DriveSpace's Advanced menu lets you choose the degree of compression you want.

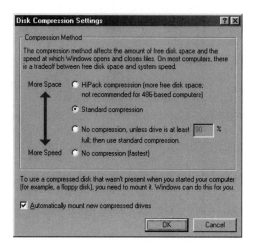

probably take up less space on the DriveSpace disk than they would on an ordinary disk, even though they're not compressed. That's because, as part of the CVF, they don't have to occupy integral multiples of the disk's allocation unit size.

> **NOTE**
>
> Compression Agent, described below, offers an even higher-compression option called UltraPack. After you've compressed a disk with DriveSpace, you can run Compression Agent to increase the compression of particular files or all files.

After choosing a compression option, click OK and then choose Compress from the Drive menu. In the Compress A Drive dialog box, DriveSpace displays before-and-after pie charts showing you how much additional disk space you can expect to achieve by compressing this disk, as shown in Figure 16-5.

If the uncompressed size of your drive is larger than 1 GB (gigabyte), the Compress A Drive dialog box also presents a message to this effect. DriveSpace 3 has a maximum CVF size of a little over 1 GB. When you run DriveSpace on a large disk, therefore, the system compresses only as much of your original disk as it can. Then it moves the remainder of the disk, uncompressed, to the newly created host drive. The host drive, in this case, remains visible in Windows Explorer windows.

FIGURE 16-5.

These diagrams illustrate the estimated effect of running DriveSpace on a 503-MB hard disk.

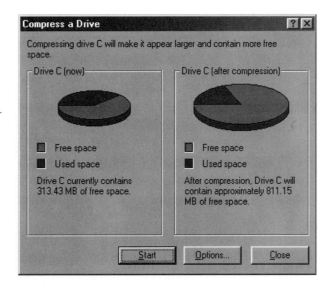

Compress a Drive

Compressing drive C will make it appear larger and contain more free space.

Drive C (now)

Drive C (after compression)

■ Free space
■ Used space

Drive C currently contains 313.43 MB of free space.

■ Free space
■ Used space

After compression, Drive C will contain approximately 811.15 MB of free space.

Start   Options...   Close

When you're ready, click Start to begin the compression process. If you're compressing a hard disk, DriveSpace first suggests that you create a Windows startup disk (a good idea). Then it checks your drive for errors. After getting a clean bill of disk health, it suggests you perform a backup (a splendid idea). Finally, it restarts Windows in a special mode and goes to work on your disk. If you're compressing a floppy disk, DriveSpace goes about its business in Windows' normal operating mode, but it slows down your system so dramatically that you won't want to try to work until it's finished.

Compressing Only the Free Space on a Disk

As an alternative to compressing an entire disk, you can ask DriveSpace to compress only the space that's currently unused. DriveSpace turns this free space into a new compressed drive and assigns that drive an unused drive letter.

To compress the free space only, select the drive whose free space you want to compress, and then choose Create Empty from the Advanced menu. You'll see a dialog box similar to the one shown in Figure 16-6.

This dialog box reports the drive letter that DriveSpace plans to use, the amount of space that will be compressed, the estimated capacity of the new compressed volume, and the amount of free space that will remain on your uncompressed volume. (The program leaves a small amount so that your uncompressed files have room to grow.) You can change any of these settings before beginning the compression process.

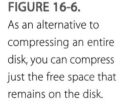

FIGURE 16-6.

As an alternative to compressing an entire disk, you can compress just the free space that remains on the disk.

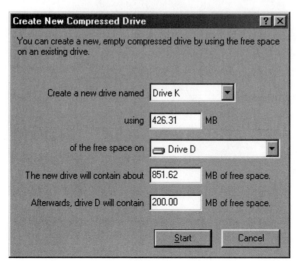

Compressing Floppy Disks

You can use the Compress command to compress an entire floppy disk. You cannot, however, compress only the free space on a floppy.

Compressed floppy disks are "mounted" by default. That simply means they're made available to the system as soon as you've finished compressing them or whenever you insert such a disk in the drive. DriveSpace includes an Unmount command (on the Advanced menu) that lets you make a floppy's CVF unavailable, but there's no particular reason to use this command.

Formatting a Compressed Floppy Disk

To format a compressed floppy disk, select the disk in DriveSpace's main dialog box. Then choose Format from the Drive menu. Note that the disk must be compressed before you can use this command and that you cannot use the standard Format command with a compressed disk. (To turn a compressed disk back into an uncompressed one, use the Uncompress command, discussed next.)

Decompressing a Compressed Volume

If you no longer want a drive to use DriveSpace's compression services, you can "uncompress" it—provided enough room remains to accommodate all the files in their uncompressed state. If the drive does not have enough room, you'll first need to move some of its files from the compressed volume to another drive.

To restore a compressed drive to its normal state, select the drive in DriveSpace's main window. Then choose Uncompress from the Drive menu.

Using Compression Agent to Change the Compression Parameters of a DriveSpace Disk

? SEE ALSO

For information about scheduling Compression Agent to run automatically, see "Automating Maintenance with the Maintenance Wizard," page 398.

Once you've compressed a disk with DriveSpace, you can use a program called Compression Agent to modify the way in which some or all of that disk's files are compressed. Compression Agent lets you balance speed with performance in an optimal way by applying high-compression techniques to particular files. Compression Agent can squeeze your files using either the HiPack method or an ultra-high-compression algorithm called UltraPack. (You can also use Compression Agent to remove compression from particular files.) You can tell Compression Agent to use

III

Maintaining Your System

its UltraPack method only on files meeting a particular description, such as files that you haven't worked with during the most recent 30 days.

To run Compression Agent, open the Start menu and choose Programs, Accessories, System Tools. If you don't find Compression Agent on the System Tools menu, use the Find command to locate and launch a program named Cmpagent.exe.

? SEE ALSO

For information about Scheduled Tasks, see "Starting Programs on Schedule," page 50.

You can work while Compression Agent is active, but you probably won't want to. To automate Compression Agent, so that it works while you don't, use Scheduled Tasks.

Using Third-Party Compression Tools to Compress Particular Files

If applying DriveSpace to an entire disk seems like a drastic solution to a storage problem, you might want to consider using a third-party compression tool such as Niko Mak Computing's WinZip. These tools are somewhat less convenient than DriveSpace, because they don't compress and expand files on the fly. Their advantages are that they can easily be applied to particular files (files that you don't use often, for example) and they don't radically alter the structure of your disk.

Optimizing Disk Performance with Disk Defragmenter

When you store files on a freshly formatted disk, Windows writes each file's data in a set of adjacent disk clusters. One file might use clusters 3 through 24, for example, the next 25 through 31, a third 32 through 34, and so on. As soon as you begin deleting files, however, this neat pattern is likely to be broken.

For example, if you delete the file that occupies clusters 25 through 31, and then create a new file 20 clusters in length, Windows stores the new file's first 7 clusters in 25 through 31 and the remaining 13 somewhere else. This new file, in other words, would be *fragmented;* it would occupy at least two noncontiguous blocks of clusters. As time went on and you added and deleted more files, the odds are good that more and more of your files would become fragmented.

Fragmentation does not affect data integrity, but it does reduce the efficiency of your hard disk. Fragmented files take longer to read and write than contiguous ones.

You can eliminate disk fragmentation and enhance Windows' performance by using the Disk Defragmenter program that's included with Windows 98. This program rearranges files, storing each file in a block of contiguous sectors. Disk Defragmenter can also move the programs that you use most often to a disk location that minimizes access time, thereby making your programs launch more quickly.

You can use Disk Defragmenter with any uncompressed local hard disk (including FAT32 drives) or floppy disk, or with any local disk that has been compressed with DoubleSpace, DriveSpace, or DriveSpace 3. You cannot use Disk Defragmenter with network drives, disks that have been compressed with programs other than DriveSpace and DoubleSpace, read-only disks, or locked drives.

SEE ALSO

For information about scheduling Disk Defragmenter to run automatically, see "Automating Maintenance with the Maintenance Wizard," page 398.

It's a good idea to use Disk Defragmenter regularly. The Maintenance Wizard, described later in this chapter, can automatically run Disk Defragmenter at prescribed times.

To run Disk Defragmenter, open the Start menu, and then choose Programs, Accessories, System Tools, Disk Defragmenter. If you don't find Disk Defragmenter there, use the Find command to locate and run a program named Defrag.exe.

TIP

> You can also run Disk Defragmenter for a particular disk by right-clicking that disk's icon in a Windows Explorer window. Choose Properties from the disk's context menu, and then click the Tools tab in the disk's properties dialog box. Finally, click Defragment Now. This method does not let you change defragmentation settings, however.

Disk Defragmenter begins by displaying the Select Drive dialog box, asking you to choose the drive you want to optimize. Make your selection in the drop-down list and then click the Settings button. In the Settings dialog box, you'll find two check boxes. With the first, you can tell Disk Defragmenter to rearrange your program files so that your programs start more quickly. With the second, you can have your disk

III

Maintaining Your System

checked for errors before the defragmenting begins. It's a good idea to vote yes on both these propositions.

> While Disk Defragmenter is working, you can click a Show Details button to see a real-time diagram of the program's progress. It's a pretty display, but it slows down the defragmentation process. To get the fastest performance from Disk Defragmenter, skip the details display and don't use the disk that's being defragmented.

Other Optimizing Steps

Once you've ensured that your system has enough memory and an ample, defragmented hard disk, here are some additional optimizing steps to consider:

- Eliminate real-mode (MS-DOS compatibility) drivers.

- Disable background processing of MS-DOS–based programs.

- Watch out for MS-DOS–based programs that hog extended memory.

- Evaluate printing performance tradeoffs.

- Evaluate video performance tradeoffs.

Eliminate Real-Mode (MS-DOS Compatibility) Drivers

Windows 98 supplies 32-bit drivers that run in your computer's protected mode. These drivers provide better performance and security than the 16-bit, real-mode drivers that were used by Windows 3.x and MS-DOS. If you have installed Windows 98 on a system that previously used an earlier operating system, however, it is possible that Windows is continuing to use some of your earlier drivers. You can find out whether this is the case by doing the following:

1 Right-click My Computer and choose Properties from the context menu. (Alternatively, launch System in Control Panel.)

2 Click the Performance tab.

If your system is using any real-mode drivers, you will see some indication of that fact on the Performance tab in the System Properties dialog box.

Figure 16-7, for example, depicts a system whose performance is impaired by the presence of a real-mode driver for several CD-ROM drives.

FIGURE 16-7.
Check the Performance tab in the System Properties dialog box to see if your system is using any real-mode drivers.

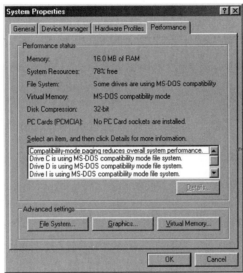

If you see the words "compatibility mode" anywhere on this tab, your system is not giving you optimal performance. You can learn more about what's going on by selecting each item in the list box in turn and then clicking the Details button. If your system *requires* a real-mode driver for some reason, you might need to live with less than ideal performance. In many cases, however, real-mode drivers can easily be eliminated. In the system shown in Figure 16-7, for example, a single statement in the Autoexec.bat file was slowing down all activity of the hard disks. Removing that statement restored the system to optimal performance.

TIP

> To inspect or edit your Autoexec.bat or Config.sys file, use the Start menu's Run command and run SysEdit.

Disable Background Processing of MS-DOS–Based Programs

When you run an MS-DOS–based program and then switch away to a different program, Windows continues to allocate some of your computer's processing time to that MS-DOS–based program, even though

III

Maintaining Your System

it's no longer running in the foreground. Letting an MS-DOS–based program run in the background may degrade your system's overall performance unnecessarily. Unless you really need background processing, it's a good idea to turn it off. You can do that as follows:

1 Right-click the icon for the MS-DOS–based program, and then choose Properties from the context menu.

2 Click the Misc tab.

3 Select the Always Suspend check box.

Certain MS-DOS–based programs—for example, communications programs—might not function reliably without background processing. And with some programs (language compilers, for example), background processing provides a benefit that compensates for any performance degradation it may cause. You'll need to decide on a case-by-case basis whether it makes sense to leave background processing on. But, as a rule, if you don't need it, don't use it.

Watch Out for MS-DOS–Based Programs That Hog Extended Memory

? **SEE ALSO**

For more information about memory settings for MS-DOS–based programs, see "Options on the Memory Tab," page 293.

The default extended-memory setting for an MS-DOS–based program is "Auto," which means that Windows imposes no limit on the amount of extended memory the program can have. Generally, that works out fine. Windows allocates as much extended memory to the MS-DOS–based program as it thinks it needs, subject to overall system constraints. But a few ill-behaved programs, when offered a large helping of extended memory, take every byte and hoard it, whether they need a large amount or none at all. If you find your system slowing down markedly whenever a particular MS-DOS–based program is running, try limiting the amount of extended memory that program may use, as follows:

1 Right-click the icon for the MS-DOS–based program, and then choose Properties from the context menu.

2 Click the Memory tab.

3 Open the Extended (XMS) Memory drop-down list and choose an amount other than "Auto."

Evaluate Printing Performance Tradeoffs

When you send a document to a non-PostScript printer, Windows first creates an intermediate disk file, called a *spool file* or *enhanced metafile* (EMF). While the EMF is being created, you cannot work in the program that's printing the document. (During this time, the program normally displays a dialog box that monitors the progress of the printing process.) As soon as Windows has finished creating the EMF, you can go on working in your program. At that point, if the print job is at the head of its print queue, Windows *despools* the EMF. That is, it converts the EMF to language specific for your printer and sends the printer-specific commands to the printer.

Exactly where each of the steps takes place depends on whether the printer is attached to your computer, to a server running Windows 95 or Windows 98, or to a server running another operating system (such as Novell NetWare or Windows NT).

If the printer is attached to a server running Windows 95 or Windows 98, the conversion of the EMF to your printer's language takes place on the server. If the printer is attached locally or to a server running another operating system, the EMF-to-printer-language conversion occurs on your own computer. This process takes place in the background but still has some temporary effect on the overall performance on your system. Therefore, all other things being equal, you might want to give preference to printers attached to servers that are running Windows 95 or Windows 98.

Assuming a print job does not have to wait behind other jobs in a print queue, Windows normally begins despooling it as soon as the first page has been rendered into EMF form. Windows continues despooling pages as they become EMF-ready. This overlapping of the EMF-building and despooling processes gives you the shortest possible time from when you click OK until the last page drops into the tray. It also minimizes the size of the temporary disk files that Windows has to use. But it makes you wait a little longer until you can resume working in your program.

If you want to be able to get to work more quickly, you can tell Windows *not* to despool until the entire EMF has been created. To do this:

1 Open the Start menu, choose Settings, and then choose Printers.

Maintaining Your System

2 Right-click the printer you're going to use, and then choose Properties from the context menu.

3 Click the Details tab.

4 Click Spool Settings.

5 Select the option button labeled "Start printing after last page is spooled."

SEE ALSO

For information about changing the resolution, see "Changing Display Resolution," page 88. For information about changing color depth, see "Changing Color Depth," page 90.

Note that this option requires Windows to create a larger temporary disk file and produces a somewhat later finish time for the entire print job.

Evaluate Video Performance Tradeoffs

High screen resolutions and high color depths make your processor work harder than low screen resolutions and low color depths. If you work primarily with text, or if your video system is less snappy than you'd like, consider switching to a lower resolution or color depth. (Of the two factors, color depth has the greater impact on performance.)

Routine Maintenance for Your System

Just as you perform regularly scheduled maintenance on your car, so should you take some simple maintenance steps at regular intervals to keep your Windows system running smoothly. In particular, it's wise to run ScanDisk and Disk Defragmenter regularly. ScanDisk, described below, finds and corrects any damage to the logical structure of your disks. If you want, you can also have it check the integrity of your disk media. Disk Defragmenter, described earlier in this chapter, keeps your files in contiguous blocks and moves your programs to locations from which they can be launched most quickly.

In addition to ScanDisk and Disk Defragmenter, you might want to run Windows Update periodically. Assuming you have an Internet connection, the Windows Update command takes you to www.microsoft.com/windowsupdate/default.asp, a Web page where you can determine whether newer drivers are available for any component of your system. If your system isn't using the latest available drivers, this Web site can download and install them for you. The Windows Setup program normally adds the Windows Update command to the top section of your Start menu.

An important part of a routine maintenance schedule is backing up your data, and having the necessary tools on hand to restore your data if the worst should happen. One of these tools is a startup disk.

SEE ALSO

For information about Scheduled Tasks, see "Starting Programs on Schedule," page 50.

You can use Scheduled Tasks to automate a maintenance routine. Or you can use the Maintenance Wizard, described later in this chapter.

Ensuring Disk Integrity with ScanDisk

ScanDisk can be used with any hard disk or floppy disk, including disks compressed with DriveSpace or DoubleSpace. ScanDisk cannot be used with CD-ROM disks. The program finds and fixes the following kinds of logical errors (errors involving the organization of files and other data structures):

- Problems with the file allocation table (FAT)

- Problems involving long filenames

- Lost clusters

- Cross-linked files

- Problems involving the directory structure

- On disks compressed with DriveSpace or DoubleSpace, problems involving the volume header, volume file structure, compression structure, or volume signature

(The *file allocation table* is a data structure that keeps track of the physical location and file ownership of each cluster on a disk. A *cluster*, also known as an *allocation unit*, is the smallest group of sectors that the operating system can allocate to a file. A *lost cluster* is one that's not used by any file but that the FAT hasn't marked as available for new data. A *cross-linked file* is a file containing clusters that have been erroneously allocated to more than one file.)

ScanDisk can also be used to find physical disk errors (bad sectors). The program doesn't physically repair your media, but it moves data away from any bad sectors it finds.

To run ScanDisk, open the Start menu and choose Programs, Accessories, System Tools, ScanDisk. If you don't find ScanDisk there, use the Find command to locate and launch a program named Scandskw.exe.

III

Maintaining Your System

? SEE ALSO

For information about scheduling ScanDisk to run automatically, see "Automating Maintenance with the Maintenance Wizard," page 398.

In the ScanDisk dialog box (see Figure 16-8), select the disk you want to check. (You can select more than one disk for checking by holding down the Ctrl key as you click each disk name.) To perform only a logical test, choose the Standard option button. To check the media as well as the logical structure, choose Thorough. If you want errors fixed automatically, select the Automatically Fix Errors check box. (After it finishes, ScanDisk can display a message indicating whether it found any errors. It can also create a log file on disk, detailing the errors it found and the steps it took to correct them.) If you want to decide, case-by-case, whether ScanDisk should fix errors, deselect this check box. ScanDisk will then stop and display a dialog box each time it finds an error. (See Figure 16-9.) Click Start when you're ready to begin the test.

Testing the physical integrity of every disk cluster takes time, particularly with large disks. While ScanDisk is testing, you can continue to work, but

FIGURE 16-8.
Choose Standard if you want ScanDisk to check logical structures only. Choose Thorough if you also want to check for bad sectors.

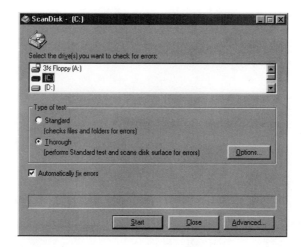

FIGURE 16-9.
When ScanDisk finds an error, it displays a dialog box that explains the error and, in some cases, offers choices about correcting the problem.

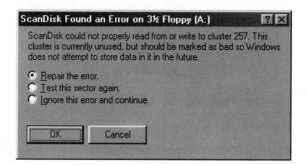

you may find your system rather sluggish, and if any data is written to the disk that's being tested, ScanDisk must start over. You can simplify the thorough test somewhat by clicking the Options button in the dialog box shown in Figure 16-8. As Figure 16-10 shows, your options include restricting the test to the system or data area and eliminating write-testing. (When testing thoroughly, ScanDisk normally reads each disk sector and then writes the same data back into the sector. If you skip the write-testing, ScanDisk still finds sectors whose data cannot be read, but it won't find any problems that might arise only during the writing process.)

FIGURE 16-10.
The thorough test takes awhile. You can make it quicker—if somewhat less thorough—by eliminating write-testing.

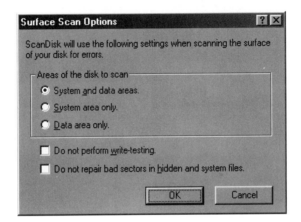

You can also use the Options dialog box (see Figure 16-10) to restrict ScanDisk's test to the system area of your hard disk. This makes the test go much more quickly because the system data structures occupy a relatively small portion of any disk. A system-only test also turns up the most disastrous kinds of media errors—those that involve the boot sector, the partition table, or the file allocation table.

WARNING

If you use copy-protected software, don't let ScanDisk repair bad sectors in hidden and system files. ScanDisk "repairs" bad sectors by relocating data to good sectors. Some copy-protected programs record the absolute physical location of particular hidden or system files. If they find such files in new locations, they assume your program has been illegally copied. To prevent this from happening, select the check box labeled "Do not repair bad sectors in hidden and system files," in the dialog box shown in Figure 16-10.

III

Maintaining Your System

Other ScanDisk Options

The Advanced button in ScanDisk's dialog box provides additional options, as shown in Figure 16-11.

FIGURE 16-11.

Among other things, ScanDisk's "advanced" options let you tell it what to do with lost clusters and cross-linked files.

By default, ScanDisk finishes its work by displaying its findings on screen and recording them in a log file called Scandisk.log. The log file is stored in the top-level folder (root directory) of the tested disk and, by default, replaces the log file from any previous test. You can override all these defaults by using the Display Summary and Log File option-button groups.

If ScanDisk finds any cross-linked clusters, its default procedure is to create a new copy of the cross-linked data in each affected file and, in the process, eliminate the cross-links from your file allocation table. In most cases, the cross-linked data belongs to only one of the affected files. After ScanDisk has done its work, you may be able to use ordinary editing procedures to eliminate the data from the file to which it does not belong. Thus, the Make Copies option button in the Advanced Options dialog box is usually the appropriate setting. But if you'd rather, you can have ScanDisk simply delete or ignore cross-linked data.

By default, ScanDisk organizes any chains of lost clusters it finds into new disk files, storing the files in the top-level folder (root directory) of the disk on which the lost clusters were located and giving them names such as File0000.chk. If ScanDisk's summary report indicates that lost clusters were found, you can then open the top-level folder and read the lost-cluster files with Notepad or another editor. If you find anything you want to keep, you can copy and save it. Otherwise, you'll probably want to send the whole file to the Recycle Bin. If you'd rather skip this process and have ScanDisk simply free up any lost clusters it finds, select the Free option button in the Advanced Options dialog box.

By default, ScanDisk ensures that files have valid filenames, but it doesn't bother checking for valid dates and times. That's because an invalid filename is a serious error and may prevent a program from opening the affected file. An invalid date or time may affect file-sorting operations or the operation of backup programs, but it does not prevent you from using the file. To override either default setting, use the check boxes in the Check Files For section of the Advanced Options dialog box.

Finally, when testing disks compressed via DoubleSpace or DriveSpace, ScanDisk normally checks the host drive first. That's because apparent errors in a compressed volume can result from errors in the host drive. There's probably no good reason to change this default, but ScanDisk will let you change it if you want. (Deselect the Check Host Drive First check box.)

Being Prepared with Startup Disks and Backup Tapes

As part of your routine maintenance, you should always keep a startup disk and a recent full-system backup handy. A startup disk is a floppy disk that you can use to boot your system if you're unable to start Windows. As described in Chapter 14, "Protecting Your Data with Microsoft Backup," a startup disk in conjunction with a full-system backup and the Windows 98 system recovery utility (on your Windows 98 CD) can be used to restore a system after a catastrophic failure.

The startup disk also provides generic support for IDE and SCSI CD-ROM drives. Most users therefore will be able to access their CD-ROM drives after booting with the startup disk. You will probably not need to load real-mode drivers for your CD-ROM.

? SEE ALSO

For information about system recovery, see "Running the System Recovery Utility," page 355.

III

Maintaining Your System

The startup disk also creates a 2-MB RAM drive (a portion of memory made to act like a disk drive) and copies useful diagnostic programs and files to this RAM drive. Table 16-1 lists these files and their functions. To learn more about any of these programs, at the command prompt, type the command name followed by a space and /?.

TABLE 16-1. RAM Disk Files Created by a Startup Disk

File	Function
Attrib.exe	A tool that lets you read and change file attributes
Chkdsk.exe	A simple tool for testing disk integrity
Debug.exe	A tool for debugging programs
Edit.com	The real-mode MS-DOS editor, which is good for viewing and changing Autoexec.bat, Config.sys, and other text files
Ext.exe	A tool for extracting files from Windows .CAB files
Format.com	A tool for formatting disks
Mscdex.exe	Microsoft CD-ROM extension for MS-DOS
Scandisk.exe	A more complex tool for testing disk integrity
Scandisk.ini	A configuration file used by Scandisk.exe
Sys.com	A command for transferring MS-DOS system files to disks, making disks bootable
Uninstal.exe	A tool for removing Windows 98

To create a startup disk, launch Add/Remove Programs in Control Panel. Click the Startup Disk tab, and then click Create Disk.

Automating Maintenance with the Maintenance Wizard

The Maintenance Wizard provides a simple means of scheduling four kinds of maintenance tasks:

- Running Compression Agent (if you have one or more DriveSpace volumes)

- Running Disk Defragmenter

- Running ScanDisk

- Running Disk Cleanup

In addition to scheduling these maintenance tasks, the Maintenance Wizard can remove any programs it finds in the Startup section of your Programs menu, thereby making Windows start more quickly. If you opt to remove programs from your Startup menu, you can still run those programs, of course, but they won't start automatically when you begin a Windows session. (The Maintenance Wizard also maintains a list of the programs it removes from the Startup menu, making it easy for you to put them back in the Startup menu.)

To activate the Maintenance Wizard, open the Start menu and choose Programs, Accessories, System Tools, Maintenance Wizard. If you don't find this item on the System Tools menu, use the Find command to locate and launch a program named Tuneup.exe.

NOTE

> Be aware that the option described by the Maintenance Wizard as "Optimize Hard Disk" invokes Compression Agent, not Disk Defragmenter. The option called "Speed Up Programs" is the one that schedules Disk Defragmenter.

The first time you run it, the wizard offers a choice between an Express mode and a Custom mode. The Express mode uses default settings. To see your full range of choices, select Custom mode.

Next the wizard asks what time of day you want maintenance activities to occur, proposing midnight to 3:00 A.M. as a default. After you make your decision here, subsequent screens will still give you the opportunity to alter the schedule for particular activities.

For each of its scheduled maintenance options (that is, all of its options except for removal of Startup-menu items, which is a one-time, rather than scheduled, event), the wizard proposes an initial run time and a repeat interval. For example, it might offer to run Disk Defragmenter at 11 P.M. on "every Tuesday of every week" (not just some of the Tuesdays of every week), beginning on August 11, 1998. You can express your own scheduling preferences by clicking the Reschedule button. This summons a simple dialog box that provides a wealth of scheduling

III

Maintaining Your System

options. Be sure to click the Advanced button in the Reschedule dialog box to see all the options at your disposal.

For each scheduled activity, you'll be able to click a Settings button and set options. For example, by clicking Settings on the "Speed Up Programs" screen, you'll be able to tell the wizard which of your disks you want it to optimize and whether you want it to move program files to optimal locations.

② SEE ALSO

For information about Scheduled Tasks, see "Starting Programs on Schedule," page 50.

Once you've given marching orders to the Maintenance Wizard, the wizard passes your instructions to the Scheduled Tasks facility. You can examine or modify the maintenance schedule by revisiting the Maintenance Wizard or by opening your Scheduled Tasks folder.

Backing Up and Restoring System Files with System Configuration Utility

Windows 98 includes a handy System Configuration Utility that you can use to make backups of your Config.sys, Autoexec.bat, System.ini, and Win.ini files. You can also use this utility to restore the most recent backups of these files. To run System Configuration Utility, choose Run from the Start menu and type *msconfig*. You'll find the Create Backup and Restore Backup buttons on the program's General tab.

What To Do When Things Go Awry

Given the complexity of Windows, the ambitious scope of current programs, and the multitude of potentially conflicting hardware devices that Windows has to support, it's almost inevitable that some component of your system, at some time, will not work exactly the way you expect or intend. When that moment of perplexity arrives, you'll need to know a few basic troubleshooting procedures.

Using the Help File's Troubleshooters

The help text supplied with Windows 98 includes troubleshooters for a number of common problems, including problems with networks, modems, printers, and memory. To see what troubleshooters are available, choose Help from the Start menu. Click the Contents tab in the main help document that appears, click the book icon next to the word *Troubleshooting*, and then click the book icon next to Windows 98 Troubleshooters.

Each of the help file's troubleshooters presents a branching series of questions about your current problem. At each step in the process, the troubleshooter suggests a remedy you can try. If the suggested remedy doesn't solve your problem, the troubleshooter asks another question or offers another suggestion.

The troubleshooters won't solve every problem that might arise, but they are a good place to start your search for help.

Using the Windows Knowledge Base and Other Online Resources

If your cry for help isn't answered by the help file's troubleshooters or other local help documents, the next place to shout is online. Choosing Help from the Start menu and then clicking the Web Help button displays a page that describes Windows Update Technical Support. Clicking the link on this page activates your browser and takes you to Microsoft's WindowsUpdate Web site. Here you will find, among many other resources, additional troubleshooters and a huge problem-solving database called the Knowledge Base. The Knowledge Base, compiled and frequently updated by Microsoft support personnel, provides a simple interface for building a query about your problem, as shown in Figure 16-12. Help is returned in the form of articles that you can print or

FIGURE 16-12.

The Microsoft Knowledge Base is an encyclopedia of current technical support information regarding all Microsoft products. To get there, choose Help from the Start menu, and then click Web Help.

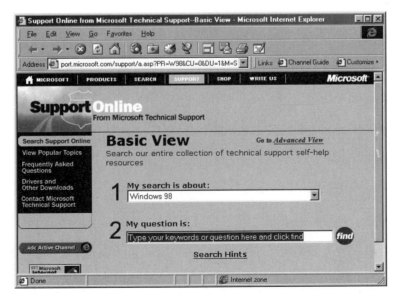

Maintaining Your System

download. The Knowledge Base covers all Microsoft operating systems and programs.

If your problem concerns a specific non-Microsoft program, you should also consult your program vendor's Web site. In most cases, that Web site's URL consists simply of www followed by a period, the vendor's name, another period, and com.

If a Program Stops Running

If your immediate problem is that a program appears to have hung—that is, it no longer responds to anything you do—you'll want to "kill" that program (metaphorically speaking) so that you can either try running it again or get on with something else. Windows provides a "local reboot" mechanism that lets you "terminate" an errant program without affecting other running programs or Windows itself. To remove a hung program, hold down the Ctrl and Alt keys and then press Delete. Windows responds with the Close Program dialog box, which list all current processes. (See Figure 16-13.)

FIGURE 16-13.
This dialog box, which appears when you press Ctrl+Alt+Delete, gives you a safe way to close a misbehaving program.

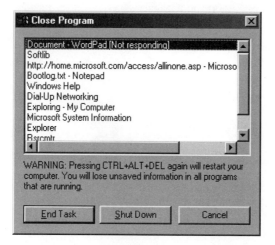

The programs that you've been working with most recently appear at the top of this list. To close a misbehaving program safely, simply select it in this list and then click the End Task button. Be aware that the terminated program will not go through its usual shutdown maneuvers; that is, you will not be given the opportunity to save any work in progress.

If a Program Crashes Sporadically

If your program crashes every time you run it, no matter what else is running, and particularly if it always crashes in the same way (for example, any time you take a particular action), you almost certainly have a defective program or program component. Try reinstalling the program. If that doesn't help, you will probably want to discuss the problem with your software vendor.

If, however, the program crashes only when several other programs are also running, the trouble may be due to insufficient RAM or system resources. You can see how much memory Windows thinks your system has by right-clicking My Computer and choosing Properties from the context menu. Near the bottom of the General tab in the properties dialog box, you'll find the amount of your computer's installed memory (RAM). If the number is less than 16 MB, adding memory might solve your problem. If the number reported in the dialog box appears to be incorrect, consult the Memory troubleshooter in the Windows help text.

Even if you have plenty of main memory, your problem may be caused by a shortage of a particular kind of memory, called system resources. Windows reserves two small regions of memory for particular purposes. Because these regions are limited in size, they can get used up, even if a huge amount of general-purpose memory is still available. To check the status of your system resources, right-click My Computer, choose Properties from the context menu, and then click the Performance tab. Near the top of the dialog box, you'll find your available system resources, reported as a percentage. If that percentage figure is less than 50, your program might be crashing because of inadequate resources. The system-resource shortage could be caused by any program currently running (or a combination of programs), not just the one that happens to be crashing.

If you suspect a system-resource shortage, it's a good idea to try to find out which program is eating all the resources. Resource Meter, a utility included with Windows 98, can help. To run Resource Meter, open the Start menu and choose Programs, Accessories, System Tools, Resource Meter.

NOTE

> If Resource Meter has not been set up on your system, launch Add/Remove Programs in Control Panel, click the Windows Setup tab, select System Tools, and click the Details button. Select System Resource Meter and click OK.

III

Maintaining Your System

Resource Meter sits in your notification area and shows two color-coded bars in an iconic beaker. Those bars represent the two kinds of system resources. As Figure 16-14 shows, double-clicking the Resource Meter icon reveals separate percentages for each type of resource as well as a third gauge ("System Resources") that simply reports the lower of the two other figures.

FIGURE 16-14.

When you suspect a shortage of system resources, the Resource Meter can help you pinpoint the problem.

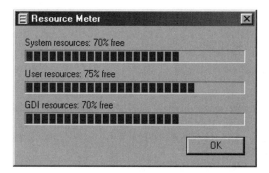

Ideally, both bars in your Resource Meter icon should remain green. If either turns red, you have a problem. Keeping Resource Meter running all the time may slow your system down slightly, but it can flag a resource shortage as soon as it occurs and help you figure what process is causing the problem.

Verifying that System Files Have Not Changed

If a system that has been functioning flawlessly suddenly begins to misbehave, it's possible that one or more of your system's essential files have either been corrupted somehow or have been overwritten by an out-of-date version. The latter misfortune can sometimes occur when an older program is installed.

System File Checker, a utility supplied with Windows 98, can record a snapshot of all your system files and subsequently tell you if any of those files have been changed or deleted. It does this by creating a "verification data file" containing checksum information about each critical file that it inspects as part of its initial snapshot. On subsequent runs, then, it compares current data against the verification data file, and adds information about any new system files. System File Checker also can restore the original copy of a corrupted or modified system file.

Windows does not create a Start-menu item to launch System File Checker directly. To launch it, open the Start menu and choose Programs, Accessories, System Tools, System Information. In the System Information window, open the Tools menu and choose System File Checker. Alternatively, use the Find command to locate and launch a program named SFC.exe.

When you run System File Checker the first time, click the Settings button in the program's initial dialog box. You'll see a dialog box similar to the one shown in Figure 16-15.

FIGURE 16-15.

Use the System File Checker Settings dialog box to set log-file and backup parameters, as well as to tell System File Checker what kinds of files it should check.

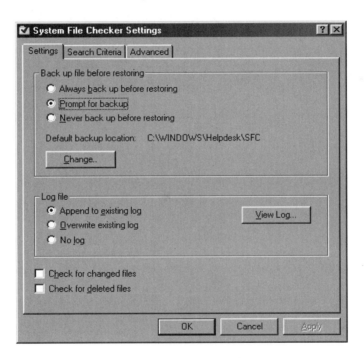

On the Settings tab in this dialog box, you can tell the utility whether and where to back up any system files that you choose to restore from the Windows 98 CD. It's a very good idea to select one of the first two option buttons here. That way, if you change your mind after overwriting a changed file with its original version, you'll still have the modified copy. In the lower part of this dialog box you can tell System File Checker whether and how it should keep a log file recording its activities. Here, too, it's wise to select one of the first two option buttons.

On the Search Criteria tab, you can tell System File Checker what kinds of files it should check and where it should look for them. The defaults

III

Maintaining Your System

here are dandy, but you can add file types to the checklist if you want. Finally, on the Advanced tab, you can create a new verification data file or restore the settings in the verification data file to the original ones that came with Windows.

If System File Checker finds a file that has changed, it displays a dialog box similar to the one shown in Figure 16-16. If you're not sure whether you should restore the original version of the file, it's best to select the Ignore option button. Then find the file in an Explorer window, right-click it, and look at its properties dialog box. By looking at the Created date on the General tab in the properties dialog box, you can determine when this file was installed on your system. This information might help you figure out why and by whom it was installed, so you can inquire about whether the change was necessary and whether it's likely to cause any problems. Also, if the properties dialog box has a Version tab, you might be able to use that to determine the company that supplied the new file.

FIGURE 16-16.

If System File Checker finds a changed file, it notifies you with a dialog box like this one.

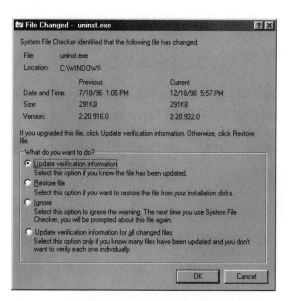

The remaining options in this dialog box are probably self-explanatory. Choose the first option if you're sure you want to keep the modified file and you want that to be the standard against which System File Checker checks in the future. Choose the second option if you're positive you want to restore the original version (but don't neglect to back up before restoring), and choose the fourth option if you don't want to be bothered with further change notifications during this run of System File Checker.

Using Device Manager and Microsoft System Information to Track Hardware Conflicts

If two hardware devices are both trying to make use of the same I/O address, DMA channel, or IRQ level, odds are one of those devices isn't going to work. If you suspect that a resource conflict of this kind is causing some component of your system to malfunction, you can follow up on your suspicion with the help of Device Manager or Microsoft System Information.

To run Device Manager, right-click My Computer, choose Properties from the context menu, and then click the Device Manager tab. As Figure 16-17 shows, Device Manager displays an exclamation point next to any device that isn't working properly.

FIGURE 16-17.

The Device Manager flags problem devices with exclamation points.

To learn more about a device problem, select its entry in the Device Manager list, and then click the Properties button. The Device Status box in your device's properties dialog box might tell you everything you need to know. (See Figure 16-18.) If the problem involves a resource conflict, click the Resources tab in the device's properties dialog box to see what resources—interrupt request (IRQ) lines or direct memory access (DMA) channels, for example—your device is using.

FIGURE 16-18.

To learn more about a device problem, select the device name, click the Properties button, and read the device's properties dialog box.

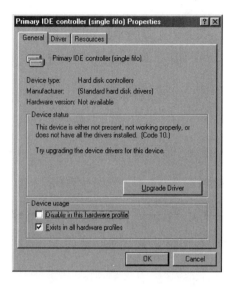

For a complete summary of the devices in your system and the resources they use, right-click My Computer, choose Properties, click the Device Manager tab, click the Print button, and then choose the All Devices And System Summary option. The resulting report summarizes IRQ and DMA commitments; shows what I/O addresses are in use and what devices are using them; lists drivers by filename, size, and version number; and more.

Microsoft System Information provides the same information as Device Manager, plus a good deal more. To run it, open the Start menu and choose Programs, Accessories, System Tools, System Information. Alternatively, use the Find command to locate and launch a program named MSInfo32.exe.

To pinpoint resource conflicts, open the Hardware Resources heading in Microsoft System Information's outline pane. Then click the Conflicts/Sharing subheading. Information about conflicts will appear in the right pane.

Unless you're an expert at working with hardware resource conflicts, it's best to use Device Manager and Microsoft System Information as diagnostic tools. Leave the conflict resolution to someone in your company who gets paid for doing that sort of thing, or call your hardware vendor to get instructions on how to proceed. Be aware that careless changes in Device Manager have the potential to bring down your whole system.

Using Microsoft System Information to Check Your Registry

You can use Microsoft System Information to determine whether your registry has been corrupted. To do this, choose Registry Checker from System Information's Tools menu. You can also use this command to back up an intact registry.

Starting Windows in Safe Mode

Some circumstances—a resource conflict between peripherals, a problem with network settings, or a problem with display settings—may prevent Windows from starting in its normal mode. You may, however, be able to start Windows in Safe Mode. In Safe Mode, the operating system disables the network and peripherals and starts up in a 640×480 16-color display. You can then open Control Panel, change display settings, check Device Manager for resource conflicts, and so on. After making changes of this sort, you can try again to start Windows normally.

To start Windows in Safe Mode, turn off your machine. Then turn it back on, and, after your system has performed its initial self-check, press F8. From the menu that appears, choose option 3, Safe Mode.

Diagnostic Startups

If you suspect that a "bad apple" in one of your startup files—Config.sys, Autoexec.bat, Win.ini, System.ini, or Winstart.bat—is preventing Windows from starting normally, you can try a logged startup. When you do this, Windows creates a file, C:\Bootlog.txt, that records the name of every process involved in the startup, along with a notation about whether or not that process was carried out successfully. After you've started Windows (or attempted to start Windows) in this manner, you can use a text editor (such as Notepad or MS-DOS Editor) to read the log file. To see where problems were encountered, use the editor's search command to look for the word *Failed.*

III

Maintaining Your System

To create a log file at startup, turn off your machine. Then turn it back on, and, after the system has performed its initial self-check, press F8. From the menu that appears, choose option 2, Logged.

It's also possible to try starting Windows without some of its normal startup components. To do this, press F8 after your system has performed its initial self-check, and then choose option 4 (Step-By-Step Confirmation) from the menu that appears. You'll get a confirmation prompt for each instruction in your Config.sys and Autoexec.bat files, as well as for each component that Windows normally loads on startup. You can then bypass any element that you suspect is causing trouble.

If Windows is already running in some fashion, you can use the System Configuration Utility to order a diagnostic restart. Choose Run from the Start menu, and type *msconfig*. On System Configuration Utility's General tab, choose Diagnostic Startup to restart with confirmation for each startup component. Select Selective Startup and use the check boxes to have Windows restart without processing a particular startup file, such as Autoexec.bat or Config.sys.

PART IV

Using the Windows Accessories

Writing with WordPad

This chapter introduces WordPad, the word processor that comes with Windows 98. Is it a full-featured word processor that will take care of all your writing needs? No. But it does give you a lot to play with as you explore the power of Windows word processing. Your WordPad documents can include basic text and paragraph formatting—font changes, indents, tabs, and so on. WordPad also supports OLE, so you can add graphical images and even sound and video clips to your documents.

WordPad can read .WRI files—documents that were created in Write, a simple word processor that was included with Windows 3.x. In the past, many programs have used Write documents for documentation, for licensing information, and as last-minute "read me" files. You can still read those files in Windows 98, even though Write itself is no more. Simply launch a Write document to read it in WordPad. WordPad can also read and save documents in any of five file formats: Word 6.0, Rich Text Format (RTF), text, text (MS-DOS format), and Unicode text. The Word 6 format, which can be read by all recent versions of Microsoft Word as well as many other popular word processors, is WordPad's default file format.

NOTE

> The version of WordPad included with Windows 98 can read files created in Microsoft Word 97's native format. But the Word format it uses for saving is that of Word 6.

Notepad, the plain-text editor of earlier Windows days, is also included in the Windows 98 package. Notepad differs from WordPad in that it offers practically no formatting capability (you can choose which font you want to use, for example, but you can't change fonts within a Notepad document) and can't handle large documents. Notepad's virtue is speed. It's fast to load and supremely easy to use—because it doesn't do much. Text files (files with the extension .TXT) are Notepad's registered document type. If you launch one of these, you'll be transported to Notepad. If the file is too large for Notepad, you'll be given the option of opening it in WordPad.

Windows 98 also includes FrontPage Express, an editor for generating HTML documents. FrontPage Express is described in Chapter 29.

Starting WordPad

To get WordPad running, click its icon, which can be found in the Accessories folder within the Start menu's Programs folder.

NOTE

> If WordPad has not been set up on your computer, launch Add/Remove Programs in Control Panel, click the Windows Setup tab, select Accessories, and click the Details button. Select WordPad and click OK.

WordPad's opening screen looks like the one shown in Figure 17-1.

The following elements make up the WordPad window:

Toolbar. WordPad's toolbar, like the toolbar in most other programs, contains buttons for issuing commonly used commands. To see what a particular button does, simply move your mouse pointer over the button. A short description appears just below the mouse pointer, and a more detailed description appears on the status bar. Table 17-1 describes the buttons on the toolbar.

IV

Using the Windows Accessories

FIGURE 17-1.
WordPad opens with a
blank editing area.

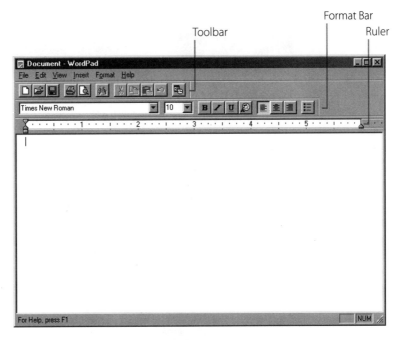

TABLE 17-1.   WordPad Toolbar

Toolbar Icon	Description
	Creates a new, blank document
	Opens an existing document
	Saves the current document to disk
	Prints the current document
	Displays a preview of the printed page—without committing it to paper
	Finds text that you specify
	Cuts (deletes) the selection and places it on the Clipboard
	Copies the selection to the Clipboard

(continued)

TABLE 17-1. *continued*

Toolbar Icon	Description
	Pastes (inserts) the Clipboard's contents at the insertion point
	Undoes your last editing or formatting action
	Inserts the date and time in your document

Format bar. Like the toolbar, the format bar provides one-click access to commands. Most of WordPad's formatting options are available on the format bar. Table 17-2 describes the buttons on the format bar.

Ruler. The ruler provides an easy way to change tab and margin settings.

TABLE 17-2.   WordPad Format Bar

Format Bar Icon	Description
Times New Roman	Changes the font (typeface) of the selection
10	Changes the font size of the selection
B	Changes the selection to boldface (or, if the selection is already boldface, changes it back to normal)
I	Changes the selection to italic (or, if the selection is already italic, changes it back to normal)
U	Underlines the selection (or, if the selection is already underlined, removes the underline)
	Changes the color of the selection
	Left aligns the selected paragraphs
	Center aligns the selected paragraphs

(continued)

IV

Using the Windows Accessories

TABLE 17-2. *continued*

Format Bar Icon	Description
	Right aligns the selected paragraphs
	Changes the selected paragraphs to an indented, bulleted list (or, if the selection is already bulleted, removes the bullets and indents)

Creating a WordPad Document

Creating a basic WordPad document couldn't be easier. There are only two essential steps:

1 Type.

2 Save.

 When you start WordPad, all you have to do is type the text you want, pressing Enter twice when you want a blank line between paragraphs. To save a document for the first time, click the Save button on the toolbar (or choose Save from the File menu). Give the document a name, and choose a document type from the Save As Type drop-down list box.

Inserting the Date or Time

 You can easily add the date or time to a WordPad document. Just click the Date/Time toolbar button, select a format from the Date And Time dialog box shown in Figure 17-2, and choose OK. The current date or time appears at the insertion point location in the format you selected.

FIGURE 17-2.
WordPad allows you to choose from many date and time formats.

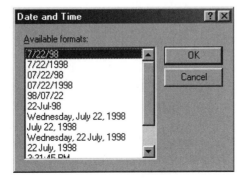

Starting a New Document

When you click the New button on the toolbar or choose New from the File menu, WordPad opens the New dialog box shown in Figure 17-3.

FIGURE 17-3.

The New dialog box lets you specify a document type.

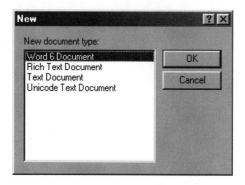

? SEE ALSO

For information about view options, see "Changing View Options," page 440.

When you select a document type and choose OK, WordPad closes the current document (prompting you to save if necessary) and presents a blank document window. The document window uses the view options for the document type you selected.

Editing Text

As you may recall, the insertion point in Windows documents always lies *between* characters. To insert text into an existing document, simply position the insertion point where you want the new material to go. Whatever you type is inserted to the left of the insertion point, and the existing text moves to the right to accommodate the new text.

To replace existing text, start by selecting the text you want to replace. (The following sections review the procedures for moving around in a document and selecting text.) When a block of text is selected, whatever you type replaces the text in the selection.

To erase a small amount of text, position the insertion point either before or after the text you want to erase. Then press Backspace or Delete. Backspace erases the character to the left of the insertion point; Delete erases text to the right of the insertion point. Careful! The Backspace and Delete keys both repeat—if you hold down either key it continues to erase text until you release the key.

To erase a large amount of text, start by selecting the text. Then press Delete. If you want to delete a block of text but preserve it on the Clipboard, select the text and choose Cut from the Edit menu (or press Ctrl+X). Keeping the deleted text on the Clipboard gives you the option of putting it right back in the place you removed it from (if you should change your mind) or of reusing it somewhere else. Keep in mind, though, that the Clipboard stores only the last item you cut or copied. So any text you place on the Clipboard can be reused only until you cut or copy something else.

Navigating in a Document

You can use the mouse or the keyboard to move around in WordPad documents. The keystrokes you use in WordPad for moving the insertion point are listed in Table 17-3, on the next page.

NOTE

Don't use Tab, Spacebar, or Backspace when all you want to do is move the insertion point. The Tab key and Spacebar add blank space to your document, and the Backspace key erases the character to the left of the insertion point.

Selecting Text

WordPad uses the same methods for selecting text as virtually all other Windows-based word processors and text editors. You can do any of the following:

- Position the mouse pointer at one end of the area you want to select, press and hold down the left mouse button as you drag the mouse to the other end of the area to be selected, and then release the mouse button.

- Place the insertion point at one end of the area you want to select, move the mouse pointer to the other end of the area to be selected (without clicking), and then hold down the Shift key while you click.

TABLE 17-3. Navigation Keystrokes in WordPad

Keystroke	Moves the Insertion Point
Right arrow	To the next character
Left arrow	To the previous character
Down arrow	To the next line
Up arrow	To the previous line
Ctrl+Right arrow	To the beginning of the next word
Ctrl+Left arrow	To the beginning of the previous word if the insertion point is between words or to the beginning of the current word if the insertion point is in a word
Ctrl+Down arrow	To the beginning of the next paragraph
Ctrl+Up arrow	To the beginning of the current paragraph or to the beginning of the previous paragraph if the insertion point is at the beginning of a paragraph
PgDn	Down one windowful
PgUp	Up one windowful
Ctrl+PgDn	To the end of the last line in the current window
Ctrl+PgUp	To the beginning of the first line in the current window
Home	To the first character in the current line
End	To the last character in the current line
Ctrl+Home	To the beginning of the document
Ctrl+End	To the end of the document

■ Hold down the Shift key while you press any of the arrow keys or other navigation keys. You can also select text by using the Shift key with any of the navigation keystroke combinations described in Table 17-3. For example, to select text and spaces to the beginning of the next word, hold down the Shift key while you press Ctrl+Right arrow.

If you extend the selection so that it includes more than one word, WordPad selects whole words automatically, so you needn't be so precise in cursor positioning. If you prefer to make selections by character, choose Options from the View menu, click the Options tab, and deselect Automatic Word Selection.

Additional techniques, specific to WordPad, allow mouse users to quickly select the current word, the current line, the current paragraph, or the entire document:

- Double-click to select the current word.

- Triple-click to select the current paragraph.

To use the following techniques, start by positioning the mouse pointer in the margin area to the left of your text. You can tell you're in the correct place when the mouse pointer changes from an I-beam to a "northeast"-pointing arrow.

Now you can do any of the following:

- Click once to select the current line.

- Double-click to select the current paragraph.

- Triple-click or hold down the Ctrl key and click once to select the entire document.

Press Ctrl+A to quickly select the entire document. For this shortcut, it makes no difference where the insertion point or mouse pointer is located.

Undoing Mistakes

WordPad's Edit menu includes a valuable Undo command that enables you to recover from many mishaps—unwanted deletions, formatting changes that don't produce the desired effect, and even search-and-replace operations of which you immediately repent.

As a keyboard shortcut for the Undo command, press Ctrl+Z.

The Undo command can reverse more than one editing action. The first time you use it, it undoes your most recent action. The second time, it reverses your next-to-most-recent action, and so on. Note, however, that the command doesn't tell you what it's about to undo, and that, unlike more sophisticated word processors, WordPad does not offer a Redo command.

Copying and Moving Text

For more information about copying and moving text, see "Copying and Moving Text," page 39.

You can use the standard Clipboard procedures to copy or move text from one place to another within a WordPad document, from one WordPad document to another WordPad document, or from a WordPad document to a document created in a different program.

Finding Text

WordPad's Find command helps you locate a particular combination of text (letters, numbers, or words and spaces).

To open the Find dialog box shown in Figure 17-4, choose Find from the Edit menu or click the Find button on the toolbar. As a keyboard shortcut for the Find command, press Ctrl+F. Type the text you're looking for in the Find What text box.

FIGURE 17-4.

Enter the text you want to search for in this dialog box.

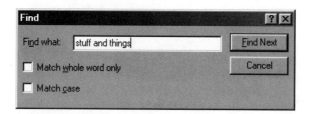

Select Match Whole Word Only if you want WordPad to find the search text only if it's a whole word. With this option checked, a search for *and* would find only the word *and*, but not *band, android,* or *salamander.* Select Match Case if you want WordPad to find instances of the search text only if the capitalization is an exact match. With this option checked, a search for *Microsoft* would not find *MICROSOFT.*

Starting a Search

After you have filled out the Find What text box and chosen your search options, you can start the search by clicking the Find Next button or pressing Enter. WordPad searches from the insertion point forward; if it reaches the end of your document without finding your search text, it continues the search starting at the top of the document.

As soon as WordPad finds an occurrence of your search text, it selects the text and stops searching, but the dialog box remains on screen. At this point, you have several options:

- If you have found what you're looking for and don't want to do any more searching, close the dialog box by pressing Esc or by clicking Cancel or the dialog box's Close button.

- If you want to search for the next occurrence of the same search text, click Find Next again.

- If you want to search for different text, replace the text that's currently in the Find What text box with the new text, and then click Find Next.

Repeating a Search

If you want to resume working on your document but you think you might need to search for the same text again, you can do either of the following:

- Move the Find dialog box to a position on your screen where it won't be in your way. Then click outside the dialog box (or press Alt+F6) to return to the document. When you're ready to repeat the search, simply click the Find Next button again, or press Alt+F6 to return to the Find dialog box and then press Alt+F to choose the Find Next command.

- Close the dialog box. When you want to repeat the search, press F3 (or choose Find Next from the Edit menu).

Replacing Text

The Edit menu's Replace command lets you replace one set of characters or words with another. As a keyboard shortcut for Replace, press Ctrl+H. The Replace dialog appears, as shown in Figure 17-5. You can confirm each replacement, or you can have WordPad replace every occurrence of the search text automatically.

FIGURE 17-5.
When you choose the Replace command, this dialog box opens.

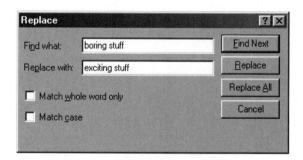

Telling WordPad What to Replace

To specify the text you want to replace, fill out the Find What text box. (This box works exactly the same way as the Find What text box in the Find dialog box.) Enter the new text in the Replace With text box.

Replacing What You Want to Replace

When you've filled out the Replace dialog box, you can start the Replace operation in either of two ways:

- To replace all occurrences of the search text automatically, click Replace All.

- To have WordPad pause for confirmation before making each replacement, click Find Next.

If you click the Find Next button, WordPad stops as soon as it finds an occurrence of your search text. At that point, you can do any of the following:

- If you do *not* want WordPad to replace this occurrence of the search text, click Find Next.

- If you want WordPad to replace this occurrence and continue searching for further occurrences, click Replace.

- If you want WordPad to replace all occurrences of the search text, click Replace All.

- To stop the Replace operation without making any further replacements, press Esc or Alt+F4, click the dialog box's Close button, press Alt+F6, or click anywhere outside the dialog box.

If you press Alt+F6 or click outside the dialog box, the dialog box remains on screen. You can use it at any time by pressing Alt+F6 again or clicking within the dialog box.

Changing Your Document's Appearance

WordPad provides several options for formatting documents, including options that can be applied to characters, to paragraphs, or to the entire document.

The following options can be applied either to a selection of existing text or to new text that you're about to enter. If you select a character or group of characters before choosing one of these options, the option is applied to the selection only. If you do not select text before choosing the option, the option is applied to everything new that you type at the current insertion point position, but not to existing text. You can:

- Choose fonts and point sizes

- Apply boldface, italics, strikeout, or underlining

- Change text color

The following options apply to individual paragraphs or selections of consecutive paragraphs. You can:

- Create bulleted lists (such as the one you're looking at right now)

- Apply indents

- Set a paragraph alignment style (flush left, flush right, or centered)

- Define tab stops

The File menu's Page Setup command contains several more formatting options that apply to the entire document. You can:

- Specify paper size

- Specify left, right, top, and bottom margins

> You can use the ruler to apply left and right margin settings to selected paragraphs (or to all paragraphs from the insertion point onward, if the insertion point is at the end of the document).

- Select a page orientation: portrait (vertical, like a portrait painting) or landscape (sideways, like a landscape painting).

Changing Fonts

The easiest way to choose a font or point size is by making selections from the format bar. Simply pull down the Font list to select a new font, or pull down the Font Size list to select a new size.

Adding Font Attributes

WordPad's font attribute options include Bold, Italic, Underline, Text Color, and Strikeout. Buttons for all of these except Strikeout are located on the format bar. (Strikeout must be accessed through the Font dialog box, as described on the next page.) All of these options can be used singly or in combination with one another.

> You can press Ctrl+B, Ctrl+I, or Ctrl+U as keyboard shortcuts for bold, italic, or underline.

Changing Text Color

To change the color of your text, click the Color button on the format bar and pick the color you want. (See Figure 17-6.)

FIGURE 17-6.
You can open the Color drop-down list by clicking its format bar button.

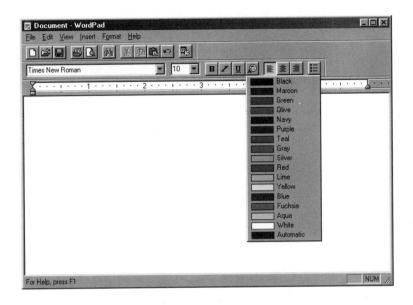

IV

Using the Windows Accessories

You might have noticed the color named Automatic at the bottom of Figure 17-6. "Automatic" applies no color attribute at all. Instead, text formatted as Automatic is displayed in the Window font color defined in the Display Properties dialog box. For most color schemes, the Window font color (and, therefore, the Automatic color in WordPad) is black. If you select any color other than Automatic, WordPad uses that color regardless of the settings in the Display property sheet.

Using the Font Dialog Box

All of the character formatting options just covered can be accessed from the Font dialog box shown in Figure 17-7, on the next page. (Choose Font from the Format menu.) If you plan to make several changes at once, it can be easier to use the Font dialog box than to click several buttons on the format bar.

 TIP

Remember to Right-Click
The context menu that appears when you right-click a selection provides a handy set of formatting commands that might save you a trip to the menu bar.

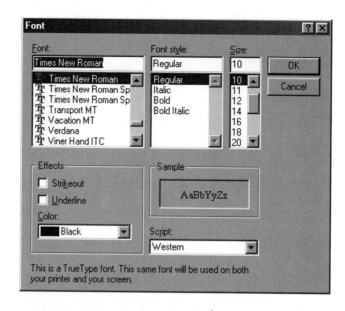

Adding Bullets

With WordPad, it's easy to add a bullet in front of a paragraph. With the insertion point anywhere in the paragraph, simply click the Bullets button on the format bar (or choose Bullet Style from the Format menu.) To add bullets to several consecutive paragraphs, select the paragraphs before choosing the bullet style.

Indenting Text

You can use three kinds of indents in WordPad paragraphs:

- An indent from the left margin that applies to all lines in a paragraph

- An indent from the right margin that applies to all lines in a paragraph

- An indent from the left margin that applies only to the first line in a paragraph

The last of these options can be used to set up automatic paragraph indenting or to create a paragraph with hanging indentation. (For details, see "Using Hanging Indents," on the next page.)

Choose Paragraph from the Format menu to open the dialog box shown in Figure 17-8.

FIGURE 17-8.
The Paragraph dialog box lets you set indents and alignment.

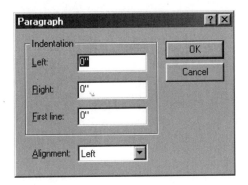

Left and right indents are measured from the left and right margins, respectively. The first-line indent is measured from the left indent. Simply fill out the appropriate boxes and click OK.

 TIP

> You can also set indents by dragging the ruler's indent markers. For details, see "Using the Ruler," page 431.

Using Hanging Indents

A paragraph is said to have *hanging indentation* when all of its lines except the first are indented. This style is useful for such things as bibliographies and bulleted or numbered lists. To set up a hanging indent, simply specify a positive left indent and a negative first-line indent.

With a left indent of 2 inches and a first-line indent of –2 inches, for example, all lines except the first will appear two inches from the left margins. The first line will start at the left margin.

Aligning Text

WordPad offers three paragraph-alignment styles:

- Flush left (left margin straight, right margin ragged)

- Centered (both margins ragged, each line centered between the margins)

- Flush right (left margin ragged, right margin straight)

To specify the alignment for the paragraph that contains the insertion point, select an option from the drop-down list in the Paragraph dialog box (see Figure 17-8, on the previous page), or click one of the alignment buttons on the format bar.

Setting and Using Tab Stops

By default, WordPad documents have tab stops every 0.5 inch. You can replace those default stops with tab stops of your own wherever you like. You can do this by filling out a dialog box or by using the ruler. When you set your own tab stops by either method, WordPad removes its 0.5-inch tab stops to the left of your tab stops. All of the WordPad tab stops to the right of your rightmost tab stop remain in place.

Tab stops apply to the entire paragraph in which the insertion point is positioned when you set them. You can set different tab stops in each paragraph if you like.

To set tab stops with a dialog box (shown in Figure 17-9), choose Tabs from the Format menu. In the text box, type the distance from the left margin to where you want a tab stop to be, and then click Set to add the setting to the Tab Stop Position list. Repeat this procedure for each tab stop you want to add. When you're finished adding tab stops, click OK.

FIGURE 17-9.

Use the Tabs dialog box to set tab stops.

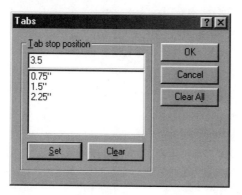

To remove a tab stop from the Tabs dialog box, select the tab stop you want to remove and click Clear. To remove all tab stops at once, click Clear All.

Setting Margins

WordPad's default top and bottom margins are 1 inch. The default left and right margins are 1.25 inches. To override any of these settings, choose Page Setup from the File menu and make changes in the appropriate margin text boxes.

Note that the margin settings in the Page Setup dialog box apply to the entire document. If you want to change left or right margins for particular paragraphs, set indents. (See "Indenting Text," page 428.)

Using the Ruler

The ruler (shown in Figure 17-10) provides an easy way to set tabs and indents. If the ruler isn't displayed, choose Ruler from the View menu to display it.

FIGURE 17-10.

WordPad's ruler shows the space between a document's margins, as well as the indents and tab stops for a paragraph.

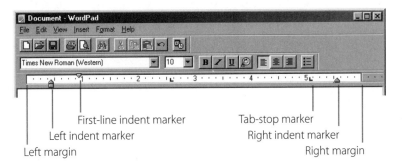

First-line indent marker   Tab-stop marker
Left indent marker   Right indent marker
Left margin   Right margin

The white area of the ruler indicates the space between the left and right margins of the page. Markers on the ruler indicate the indent and tab-stop settings for the paragraph that contains the insertion point.

 NOTE

You can change the units used by the ruler. To do so, choose Options from the View menu, and then click the Options tab. In the Measurement Units section, select Inches, Centimeters, Points, or Picas.

Setting Indents with the Ruler

To set left or right indents with the ruler, simply drag the left or right indent marker to a new location. Note that if you drag the triangular left indent marker, only the left indent changes. If you instead drag the rectangular box below the left indent marker, the left indent and the first-line indent markers move in unison.

Setting Tab Stops with the Ruler

To set tab stops with the ruler, just position the mouse pointer where you want the tab stop and then click.

To adjust the position of any tab stop, drag the tab-stop marker along the ruler.

To remove a tab stop, simply drag the tab-stop marker off the ruler and release the mouse button.

Putting Pictures in WordPad Documents

WordPad documents can include pictures as well as text. You can use ready-made clip art or create your own images in Paint or other programs. Pictures (as well as other objects such as documents and sound or video) can be copied, embedded, or linked into WordPad documents.

To incorporate a picture in a WordPad document, do the following:

1   Create the picture in a graphics program, such as Paint (or load an image from disk into a program such as Paint).

2   Select the picture (or portion of it) that you want to use in your WordPad document.

3   Use the program's Copy or Cut command to put the picture on the Windows Clipboard.

4   Open (or switch to) WordPad and place the insertion point where you want the picture to appear.

5   Use the Paste command to insert the picture.

If your source program has put the picture on the Clipboard in more than one format, the Paste Special command (on WordPad's Edit menu) will also be available. You can use this command to choose among the available formats. (See "Controlling a Pasted Object's Format," on the next page.)

Sizing or Moving a Picture

To change the size of a picture, simply select the picture and then drag one of its handles. (To select a picture or other object, click it.) Release the mouse button when the picture is the size you want.

To move a picture, start by selecting the picture. Then, with the mouse pointer anywhere inside the picture, drag the picture to a new location.

Using Data from Other Programs

WordPad is capable of acting as an OLE destination and source program. This means that you can embed or store links to the following kinds of data, among others, in your WordPad documents:

- Graphical images copied to the Clipboard from OLE source programs, such as Paint or Microsoft Word

- Charts or worksheet ranges copied from Microsoft Excel

- Sound annotations copied from Sound Recorder

? SEE ALSO

For information about embedding and linking, see Chapter 9, "Exchanging Information Using the Clipboard and OLE."

To embed data from the Clipboard, simply use WordPad's Paste command. If the data's source program is an OLE source, the data will automatically be embedded. To link the data instead of embedding it, choose Paste Special instead of Paste from the Edit menu.

Alternatively, you can embed or link data by choosing the Paste Special command. (See "Controlling a Pasted Object's Format," below.) If the data on the Clipboard came from an OLE source, the Paste Special dialog box indicates what type of data it is and which program it came from, as you can see in Figure 17-11, on the next page.

To edit an embedded or linked object, double-click anywhere within the object.

Controlling a Pasted Object's Format

Sometimes when you copy a graphical image to the Clipboard, the source program puts the image on the Clipboard in more than one

FIGURE 17-11.

Here's the Paste Special dialog box with more than one format available.

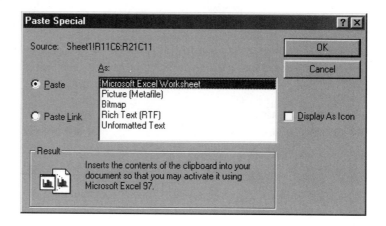

format. It might, for example, store the image on the Clipboard in both *picture* format and *bitmap* format. Whenever the data to be pasted is available in more than one format, WordPad's Paste command uses the most information-rich format. But in these cases WordPad also enables the Paste Special command (also on the Edit menu), allowing you to make your own choice about which format to use. Simply select the format you prefer, and then click the Paste button.

Usually, WordPad's Paste command makes the best choice for you automatically. For example, when the available formats are picture and bitmap, it chooses picture—and, generally speaking, the picture format gives you more satisfactory results. (In particular, because the picture format is not tied to the resolution of a specific output device, it usually gives you a much better printed image than the bitmap format.) However, the Paste Special command is there, just in case you want to override the default choice.

SEE ALSO

For more information about data formats and the Clipboard, see "Controlling the Outcome with Paste Special," page 230.

When the source program happens to be an OLE source, WordPad's Paste command normally embeds the data stored on the Clipboard. If you want to control whether WordPad copies the Clipboard data to your document as a static object rather than embedding it, you need to use the Paste Special command instead of Paste.

Embedding an image doesn't add any more bulk to your file than pasting the image in as a picture, and it allows you to edit the image quickly and easily.

TIP

Save Your Source Document First
To maintain a link to OLE source data, you must save that data in a disk file.
Therefore, if you are creating a link to data in a new document, you must save
the source document before you create a link to it.

Moving and Sizing Embedded or Linked Objects

For display purposes, WordPad handles embedded and linked objects the
same way it handles static graphical images. You can move and size such
objects using the same procedures you would use with static objects. For
more information, see "Sizing or Moving a Picture," page 433.

TIP

If you edit an embedded image after changing its size in WordPad, don't
worry when the image appears at its original size in the source program.
When you update the WordPad document after making your edits, the image
will reappear at the modified size.

Activating, Playing, and Editing Embedded or Linked Objects

When you select an object in a WordPad document that was embedded
or linked from an OLE source, the Object command at the bottom of
WordPad's Edit menu becomes available. It also changes to reflect the
kind of object you select. Figure 17-12, on the next page, shows how the
Object command appears if you select a chart embedded from a
Microsoft Excel worksheet.

The cascading menu for most object types offers two choices, Edit and
Open. Choosing the Edit command activates the object's source program—Microsoft Excel in this example—and allows you to edit the object
in place. The Open command opens the object in a separate window.

TIP

The simplest way to edit a graphical object, such as a picture or chart, is to
double-click it.

FIGURE 17-12.

The Edit Object command tells you what kind of object is selected.

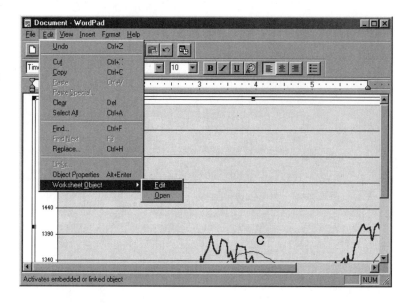

If the embedded or linked object is an iconic representation of a nongraphical data type, such as a sound annotation, the Object command presents a small cascading submenu like the one shown in Figure 17-13.

FIGURE 17-13.

You can choose to Play or Edit a sound object.

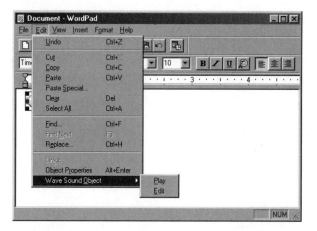

Choosing Play "renders" the object (lets you hear the sound annotation, for example), whereas choosing Edit invokes the object's source program so that you can make changes. Double-clicking a nongraphical object is a shortcut for the Play command. If you want to edit the object, you have to choose the Edit command from the menu.

IV

Using the Windows Accessories

Embedding with the Insert Object Command

The Object command on the Insert menu lets you initiate the embedding or linking process from within your WordPad document, instead of from within an object's source program. When you choose this command, WordPad displays a dialog box that lists the embeddable and linkable object types available to Windows on your system. (See Figure 17-14.)

FIGURE 17-14.

The Insert Object dialog box lets you create an object from within WordPad.

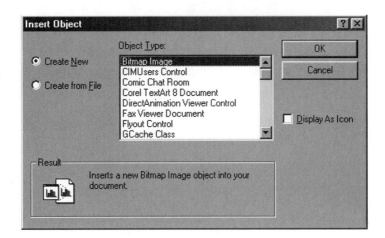

Choose the kind of object you want to embed or link, and then click OK. WordPad activates the object type's source program, allowing you to create an object (if you select the Create New option button) or load one from a disk file (if you select Create From File).

Modifying Links with the Links Command

When you link an object, as opposed to embedding it, WordPad does not store the object in your file. Instead, it stores a "pointer" to the object's source, such as the name of the source program and the file in which the object is stored. If you subsequently rename or move the object's source file, the stored link will no longer be valid. In that case, you can repair the link with the help of WordPad's Links command.

The Links command, on WordPad's Edit menu, displays the Links dialog box, shown in Figure 17-15, on the next page. The Links dialog box lists all objects linked to the current WordPad document.

FIGURE 17-15.
Use the Links dialog box to change or update links.

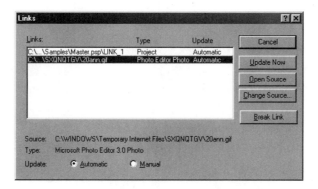

To change the source file for a link, select the link you want to modify, and then click the Change Source button. WordPad presents a file-browser dialog box, allowing you to pick the file you need.

The Links dialog box also allows you to change a link from automatic to manual, or vice versa. Links are always automatic by default, which means that any changes in the source data are reflected as soon as possible in your WordPad document. If you prefer to have them updated only on demand, choose the Links command, select the link you want to change, and then click the Manual option button. After you do this, your links will be updated only when you choose Update Now from the Links dialog box.

Viewing and Modifying Link Data for a Single Object

The Link tab in a linked object's property sheet contains, for that object, all the commands that appear in the Links dialog box. You can view an object's property sheet by right-clicking the object and choosing Object Properties.

Saving and Retrieving Documents

WordPad uses the same procedures for saving and retrieving documents as most other Windows-based programs. Use the following File menu commands (all of them except Save As have toolbar counterparts):

- Save, to save the current document

- Save As, to save the current document under a new name or to choose different file-saving options

■ New, to remove the current document from memory and begin creating a new one

 ■ Open, to load an existing document from disk into memory

By default, WordPad is set up to save new documents in Word for Windows 6.0 format with an extension of .DOC. To save a file as a different type, choose Save As, open the Save As Type drop-down list, and choose the type you want. If you don't specify an extension, WordPad automatically uses .DOC for Word for Windows 6.0 files, .TXT for text files, and .RTF for Rich Text Format files.

Choosing a File Type

When you save a document with Save As or begin a new document, WordPad gives you the opportunity to choose a different file format. The following file format descriptions will help you make an informed choice:

■ **Word for Windows 6.0:** This is the same file format used in Microsoft Word for Windows 6.0. If you use a document saved in this format with any recent version of Word, or with another word processor that accepts Word for Windows 6.0 documents, all of your formatting will remain intact.

■ **Rich Text Format (RTF):** RTF is a compromise between the Word for Windows 6.0 and Text Document formats. It's a format that was designed for transferring formatted text between diverse programs. Most word processors have an option for saving documents in Rich Text Format. If you want to use a WordPad document in a word processor that does not support the Word 6.0 format, try RTF.

■ **Text Document:** This option saves documents as plain (unformatted) text. WordPad saves the words in your document but removes all character, paragraph, and document formatting. Your document also loses any embedded or linked data and any pictures pasted in as static objects. The main reason to use the Text Document format is if you need to transmit the document over a modem to a system that cannot accept a binary file transfer. (For information about binary and text file transfers, see "Transferring Files," page 494.) This format can also be used to create or edit MS-DOS batch files, Windows configuration files, and HTML code.

- **Text Document–MS-DOS Format:** This option is like Text Document in every respect except one: it saves documents using the extended ASCII character set instead of the Windows-standard ANSI character set. (For more information about character sets, see "Fonts and Character Sets," page 221.) Use this format if you plan to reopen the document in an MS-DOS–based program.

- **Unicode Text Document:** This option is like Text Document in every respect, except that it saves documents using the Unicode character set instead of the Windows-standard ANSI character set.

Changing View Options

Each document type has its own default options that determine whether the ruler, toolbars, and status bar are displayed and how word wrap behaves when you open or start a new document in that format. You can choose separate settings for regular and embedded text.

To look at or change the view options, choose Options from the View menu. The Options dialog box appears, as shown in Figure 17-16.

FIGURE 17-16.

Change text viewing options here.

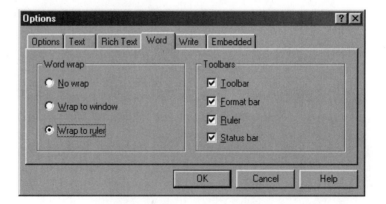

Click the tab for the document format you want and make the changes you desire.

Word wrap, which is the default action in most word processors, means that when the text you type reaches the right margin, the rest of the text automatically moves to the next line. Here's what the different options mean:

- The No Wrap option disables word wrap altogether. By default, word wrap is turned off (No Wrap is selected) for text files. That's because text format is often used for entering program codes, for which you don't want text to move around on you.

- If you select Wrap To Window, when the text you type reaches the right edge of the document window, the text wraps to the next line. This is the default setting for RTF.

- If you select Wrap To Ruler, when the text you type reaches the right margin as defined on the ruler, the text wraps to the next line. This is the default setting for Word 6 and Write documents.

In the Toolbars section of the Options dialog box, you can select which options you want displayed; deselect the ones you don't. You can always override these selections by choosing View menu commands.

Putting It on Paper

To print your document, choose Print from the File menu. As a keyboard shortcut, press Ctrl+P. The Print dialog box appears, as shown in Figure 17-17.

FIGURE 17-17.
The Print dialog box allows you to choose printing options and send your document to the printer.

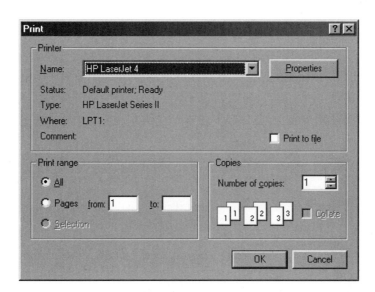

- To switch to a different printer, open the Name drop-down list and make a selection.

- To change the settings for your selected printer, click Properties.

- To print more than one copy, change the number in the Number Of Copies box.

- To print a range of pages instead of the entire document, fill in the page numbers you want in the From and To boxes.

When you've made all your selections in the Print dialog box, choose OK to send your document to the printer.

> **Use the Toolbar to Print**
> If you want to print your document and don't plan to change any options in the Print dialog box, simply click the Print toolbar button. This sends the document directly to the printer, bypassing the Print dialog box. If you choose Print from the File menu or press Ctrl+P, the dialog box opens.

Saving Paper with Print Preview

 If you want to see what your document looks like before you print it, click the Print Preview button (or choose Print Preview from the File menu).

Print Preview, shown in Figure 17-18, allows you to do the following things:

- Move from page to page to see where WordPad has placed page breaks. To do this, click Next Page or Prev Page.

- View two pages of your document at once by clicking Two Page.

- Zoom in to get a closer look at the document, or zoom out to get back to the default full-page view. Click Zoom In or Zoom Out.

- Open the Print dialog box by clicking Print. You can easily preview a document and then print it in one procedure.

FIGURE 17-18.
Use the Print Preview window to preview your printed output.

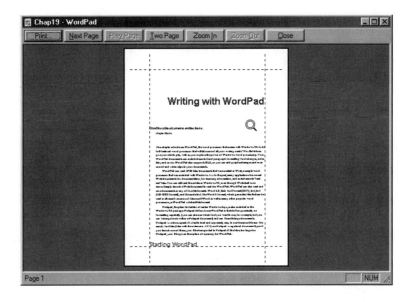

 TIP

In Figure 17-18, notice that the mouse pointer has changed to a magnifying glass. When the magnifying glass is visible, click anywhere in the document to zoom in one level, and then click again to zoom in to the second level. When the mouse pointer turns back to an arrow, clicking zooms you back out to full-page view.

Drawing with Paint

This chapter introduces Paint, the painting program included with Windows 98 that lets you create and edit graphics images. You can use Paint to produce anything from simple text-oriented flyers and line diagrams to complex works of art. You can start from scratch on a blank canvas, or you can modify existing images. Any graphics information that can be copied to the Clipboard can be pasted into Paint and modified—everything from clip art images to images created in other Windows-based programs (like Microsoft Excel charts) to scanned images.

The Windows 98 version of Paint is nearly identical to the one that was included in Windows 95. The most significant difference is that, if programs with appropriate graphics filters are installed on your system, Paint now supports some additional file formats. With Microsoft Office 97 installed, for example, Paint can read TIFF, JPEG, GIF, PCX, Targa, and Kodak Photo CD files, in addition to the standard Windows BMP files. The filters supplied via Office 97 also enable Paint to save GIF and JPEG files. You'll find the GIF and JPEG options useful if you use Paint to prepare or edit images for use in Web pages.

Starting Paint

To get Paint running, click its icon, which you can find on the Accessories menu within the Start menu's Programs submenu. Paint's opening screen looks like the one shown in Figure 18-1.

FIGURE 18-1.

When you start Paint, you get a blank drawing area.

Mouse pointer

Tool box

Drawing area

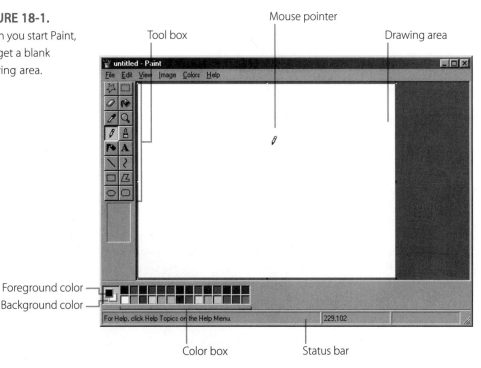

Foreground color
Background color

Color box

Status bar

> **NOTE**
>
> If Paint has not been installed on your computer, launch Add/Remove Programs in Control Panel, click the Windows Setup tab, select Accessories, and click the Details button. Select Paint and click OK.

The blank area that makes up most of Paint's window is the *drawing area*. The icons to the left of the drawing area make up the *tool box*. These icons represent the drawing and editing tools that you use to draw and edit images in the drawing area.

At the left side of the *color box*, Paint displays the current foreground and background color selections. When you start Paint, the foreground color is black and the background color is white.

In Figure 18-1, notice that the Pencil tool in the tool box appears pushed in and the mouse pointer in the drawing area is in the shape of a pencil. The pointer changes shape depending on which tool is active. Like the insertion point in a word processing program, the pointer indicates where your next drawing action will take place.

Painting 101

When you use Paint to create a picture, you use tools to apply various elements to the drawing area—your canvas in Paint. This works much like painting in real life. If you were creating a real painting on a real canvas, you might use a variety of paintbrushes. If you were painting a house, you might use rollers, spray cans, and so on. The Paint program provides the tools to make it easy to create exactly what you have in mind.

The general steps for creating a picture are:

1 Select a drawing tool.

To select a tool, just click it.

Each drawing tool is specialized for a particular kind of object. To draw a straight line, for example, select the Line tool; to draw a rectangle, select the Rectangle tool—and so on.

It's easy to figure out what many of the tools do just by looking at their icons. If that doesn't give you enough of a clue, remember that you can position the mouse pointer over a tool to display a screen tip that tells you what the tool is. For information about each of the tools and its properties, see "Exploring the Tool Box," page 457.

2 Select a line width, brush shape, or rectangle type from the group of choices below the tool box. (Notice that the choices change depending on which tool you have selected.)

You can draw lines from one pixel to five pixels wide, and you can select from several different brush shapes and rectangle types.

3 Select a foreground color.

To select a foreground color, click a color or pattern in the color box.

If you don't find the color or pattern you want in the color box, you can create it with the Edit Colors command on the Colors menu. For more information, see "Editing Colors," page 474.

4 Select a background color.

Some tools, such as Rectangle and Ellipse, can use the current background color to fill the shape they draw in the foreground color. Other tools, such as Line, use the foreground color if you use the left mouse button and the background color if you use the right button. You need to concern yourself with this step only if you're using a tool that uses the background color.

To select a background color, point to the color or pattern you want to use and click the right mouse button.

5 Draw.

After drawing the new object on the canvas, it's not too late to change your mind, thanks to the Undo command. For more information, see "Using the Undo Command," page 450.

Saving and Opening Paint Documents

To save a Paint document for the first time, choose Save or Save As from the File menu. The Save As dialog box appears.

You can select from several bitmap formats. To pick one, open the Save As Type drop-down list, as shown in Figure 18-2. Click the format of your choice and then click the Save button.

- Select Monochrome Bitmap to store the picture as a black-and-white image.

- Select 16 Color Bitmap to store the picture in color but without the full spectrum of colors. This is an efficient way to store images in which you haven't used more than 16 colors because it uses less disk space than the 256-color and 24-bit color options.

- Select 256 Color Bitmap to include more of the color spectrum. This takes more disk space and is usually a good compromise format.

FIGURE 18-2.

The Save As dialog box lets you specify the name, format, and location of the file.

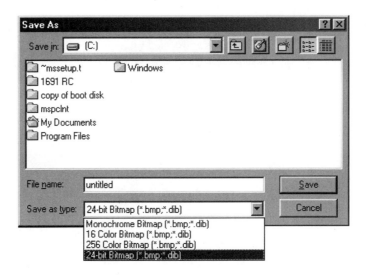

■ Select 24-bit Bitmap to save the picture with the full spectrum of colors. You'll generally want to use this option for photographic quality images, such as scanned images or those imported from a high quality clip art collection. The 24-bit format takes the largest amount of disk space, but it retains the highest degree of picture accuracy.

> **NOTE**

There's usually no reason to save an image using more colors than your system can display (unless you're going to use the image on a system that can display more colors or print it on a color printer). If you use a 16-color display driver, for example, you'll never see the additional colors stored by a 256-color or 24-bit color image. By default, Paint proposes to save the image using the maximum number of colors your system can display. To find out how many colors are in your system's palette, or for information about changing this setting, see "Changing Color Depth," page 90.

To open a saved Paint document when the Paint program is already running, choose Open from the File menu and double-click the name of the file you want.

TIP

Opening Recently Used Documents

Paint lists the last four documents you used at the bottom of the File menu. To open one of these recent documents, just select the name of the file you want to open from the File menu.

Quick Fixes: The Undo and Repeat Commands

Mistakes happen. When you draw something you didn't mean to or change your mind after an editing procedure, Paint lets you gracefully take one, two, or even three steps back.

Using the Undo Command

To undo your last Paint action, choose Undo from the Edit menu. To undo your second-to-last action, choose Undo again. Choose Undo a third time to undo your third-to-last action.

Using the Repeat Command

Paint is so forgiving, it even lets you change your mind after you use Undo. You can restore any actions you changed with Undo by choosing Repeat from the Edit menu.

Just as with Undo, you can repeat up to three actions.

 TIP

The keyboard shortcut for Undo is Ctrl+Z. Just like choosing Undo from the Edit menu, you can press Ctrl+Z up to three times to undo up to three actions.

The keyboard shortcut for Repeat is F4.

Setting Up for a New Picture

Although you can start a new picture without any planning, taking a few minutes to prepare your "canvas" can save time later. You should consider these items when setting up for a new picture:

- The background color or pattern that will be used for your picture

- The dimensions of the picture

- Whether you want to work in color or black and white

Choosing a Background Color or Pattern

A new Paint document always uses white as its background color. (This is a change from previous versions of Paint, which allowed you to choose a different background color for a new document.) To make the background anything other than white, click your selection in the color palette. Then click the Fill With Color tool and click the canvas.

Establishing the Size and Shape of Your Picture

Just as a word processing document can extend beyond a single screen, the actual size of your picture may be larger or smaller than what you see in Paint's drawing area.

To specify the dimensions of your picture, choose Attributes from the Image menu. You'll see a dialog box like the one shown in Figure 18-3.

Specify the width and height you want for your picture, in whatever units you find most convenient to work with. You can use inches, centimeters, or pixels. (A *pixel* is a single "dot" on your display.)

FIGURE 18-3.

The Attributes dialog box sets the size and colors for your picture.

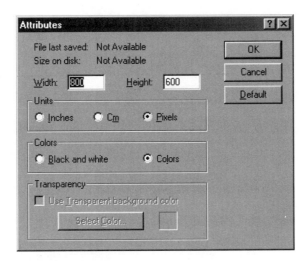

To revert to the default size for your screen's resolution, click the Default button.

Paint allows you to change the image size at any time—even after you've begun painting. However, if you reduce the picture size so that part of the image gets cropped, that part of the image won't be restored if you later enlarge the picture. (You can recover it by using the Undo command. See "Using the Undo Command," page 450.)

Choosing Color or Black and White

The Attributes dialog box is also the place where you decide whether your image will be in black and white or color.

When making this choice, it's a good idea to consider the medium in which you're most likely to output your new image. Color is unquestionably more interesting to work with than black and white, but if you're going to print your image on a black-and-white printer, you'll get better control of the final product by working in black and white.

You can change the setting of the Colors section of the Attributes dialog box at any time—even after you've begun painting. If you switch from Colors to Black And White, all colors in your image change to black or white. Be sure this is what you want before you proceed, for the Undo command does *not* restore colors that have been converted this way.

Seeing the Larger Picture

Figure 18-4 shows a picture that's considerably larger than the drawing area of Paint's window. Paint offers three ways to see more of a large picture. You can:

- Use the View Bitmap command
- Remove the tool box, color box, and status bar
- Use the scroll bars to bring other parts of the picture into view

FIGURE 18-4.

Paint can create and edit a picture that's larger than the drawing area.

Using the View Bitmap Command

The View Bitmap command, on the View menu, temporarily removes all elements from the screen except your picture, giving it the maximum possible space, as you can see in Figure 18-5. If your picture is smaller

FIGURE 18-5.

The View Bitmap command removes all extraneous screen clutter.

than your screen, Paint centers the picture on the screen. If your picture is larger than the screen, Paint places the upper left corner of the image from the drawing area in the upper left corner of the screen.

After you use this command, your very next keystroke or mouse click returns the display to its previous state, so you can't do any work with your picture in this mode. It's a useful command, though, when you want to see those parts of your picture that lie just off screen.

TIP

> The keyboard shortcut to the View Bitmap command is Ctrl+F. After pressing Ctrl+F, press any key to return to the normal display.

Removing the Tool Box, Color Box, and Status Bar

To give your picture as much breathing room as possible and still be able to work with the picture, use the Tool Box, Color Box, and Status Bar commands on the View menu. Removing the tool box extends the drawing area to the left edge of Paint's program window. Removing the color box extends the drawing area to just above the status bar. Removing the status bar extends the drawing area to the bottom of Paint's program window.

All three commands are toggles. Choose Tool Box once, for example, to make the tool box go away. Choose it again to make it reappear.

TIP

> The keyboard shortcut for toggling the tool box on or off is Ctrl+T. To toggle the color box on or off, press Ctrl+L.

Navigating on a Large Canvas

Paint displays scroll bars whenever the entire picture won't fit in the drawing area. Use the scroll bars to move to a different part of a large picture. For example, the right side of a large picture comes into view with just a couple of clicks on the horizontal scroll bar, as you can see in Figure 18-6.

FIGURE 18-6.

By scrolling to the right, you can see that this picture has more people than first appeared.

Precise Pointer Positioning

For certain kinds of work in Paint, it's helpful to know precisely where the mouse pointer is or how large an object is as you're drawing it. This information could be useful if, for example, you're trying to draw two vertical lines of exactly the same length. The numbers that are displayed toward the right side of Paint's status bar whenever the mouse pointer is in the drawing area give you pointer position information, which you can use for that purpose.

In Figure 18-7, on the next page, the numbers on the far right end of the status bar indicate the size of the object being drawn. The first of the two size numbers shows how much horizontal space the object occupies. The second number shows the vertical space.

While you're drawing an object, the numbers just to the left of the size numbers (the pointer position numbers) indicate the mouse pointer position where you began. After you release the mouse button, those numbers show the location of the pointer.

These numbers are expressed in *pixels*. A pixel is the smallest dot your screen can display and the smallest increment by which you can move the mouse pointer. So if the size numbers are, for example, 2×40, the object occupies 2 horizontal pixels and 40 vertical pixels.

FIGURE 18-7.

The size and position of the rectangle are shown on the right side of the status bar.

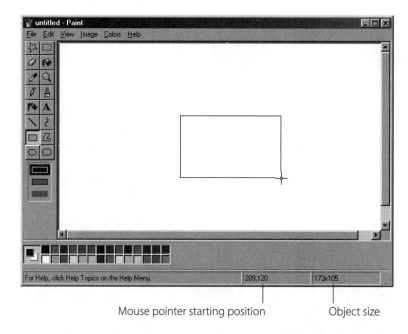

Mouse pointer starting position   Object size

The pointer position numbers to the left of the size numbers represent the offset from the upper left edge of the picture. For example, 200,100 means 200 pixels from the left and 100 pixels from the top edge of the picture.

> The position numbers are always visible on the status bar as you move the mouse pointer over the drawing area. The size numbers, however, are visible only while you're drawing an object.

What the Pointer Shapes Mean

The drawing or editing tool you use determines the mouse pointer's shape. Paint's default tool is the Pencil, and the pointer shape corresponding to that tool is the pencil shape. At other times during your work in Paint, it won't be quite so clear from the pointer shape what tool you've selected. Table 18-1 shows the variety of pointer shapes Paint uses.

TABLE 18-1.   Mouse Pointer Shapes Used in Paint

Pointer	Used with These Tools
╪	Free-Form Select, Select, Text, Line, Curve, Rectangle, Polygon, Ellipse, Rounded Rectangle
▢	Eraser
▨	Fill With Color
⌇	Pick Color
⚲	Magnifier
✎	Pencil
╪	Brush
▨	Airbrush

When you work with text in Paint, the mouse pointer is replaced by an insertion point and an I-beam. These look and function exactly like the insertion point and I-beam in WordPad and other text-processing programs. (For information about the insertion point and the I-beam, see "Entering and Editing Text in Documents," page 35.)

Exploring the Tool Box

To use a tool in Paint, you simply click its icon in the tool box. Paint's tool box includes the sixteen tools shown in Table 18-2.

TABLE 18-2.   Paint Tools

Tool Icon	Description
▨	The Free-Form Select tool selects an irregularly shaped cutout. (A cutout is a selection that can be cut, copied, moved, and manipulated in a variety of other ways. See "Working with Cutouts," page 467.)
▢	The Select tool selects a rectangular cutout.

(continued)

TABLE 18-2. *continued*

Tool Icon	Description
	The Eraser tool erases portions of an object from a picture.
	The Fill With Color tool fills enclosed shapes with the foreground or background color.
	The Pick Color tool changes the foreground or background color to match the color in another part of the picture.
	The Magnifier tool zooms in on portions of the picture.
	The Pencil tool draws free-form lines.
	The Brush tool draws free-form lines using a variety of brush shapes.
	The Airbrush tool creates "spray-paint" effects.
	The Text tool adds text to a picture.
	The Line tool draws straight lines.
	The Curve tool draws smooth curves.
	The Rectangle tool draws rectangles and squares.
	The Polygon tool draws irregular closed shapes.
	The Ellipse tool draws ellipses and circles.
	The Rounded Rectangle tool draws rectangles and squares with rounded corners.

You might think of the Free-Form Select, Select, Eraser, Pick Color, and Magnifier tools as editing tools and the rest as drawing tools. We'll look at the drawing tools first, and then examine the editing tools.

Using Paint's Drawing Tools

Paint provides 11 drawing tools that let you apply paint to your canvas.

Free-Form Drawing with the Pencil Tool

 The Pencil tool is the default drawing tool when you start Paint. To draw using the foreground color with the Pencil, move the mouse pointer into the drawing area, press the left mouse button, and drag. (To draw using the background color, use the right mouse button.)

 TIP

> **Drawing Straight Lines**
> If you want to draw perfectly straight vertical, horizontal, or diagonal lines with the Pencil tool, hold down the Shift key while you draw. (For more information about drawing straight lines, see "Drawing Straight Lines with the Line Tool," on the next page.)

Free-Form Drawing with the Brush Tool

 The Brush tool works like the Pencil tool except that you can choose from a variety of brush shapes.

To use the Brush tool, click the Brush icon in the tool box. The available brush shapes appear in the box just below the tool box, as shown in Figure 18-8. Click the brush shape you want to select it. The mouse pointer shape changes to reflect the brush shape you choose.

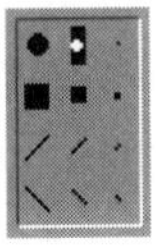

FIGURE 18-8.
The palette of brush shapes appears when you select the Brush tool.

If you're adept at calligraphy, try one of the diagonal shapes. They allow you to paint with thick and thin brush strokes.

To draw with the Brush, hold down the left mouse button (to draw using the foreground color) or the right mouse button (to draw using the background color) and drag.

The Brush tool is primarily intended for free-form drawing. If you want to draw straight lines, it's best to use the Line or Pencil tool.

Drawing with Spray Paint: The Airbrush Tool

 The Airbrush tool deposits a circular pattern of dots. To draw with the Airbrush tool, click the Airbrush icon in the tool box, and then click one of the three spray sizes that appear below the tool box. Finally, move the mouse pointer to the drawing area, hold down the left mouse button (to draw using the foreground color) or the right mouse button (to draw using the background color) and drag.

Like a real can of spray paint, the slower you drag the mouse, the denser the spray; the faster you drag, the lighter the spray.

Drawing Straight Lines with the Line Tool

 The Line tool creates straight lines. To draw a line, click the Line tool, and then choose the line width from the choices that appear below the tool box. Move the mouse pointer to the drawing area and hold down the left mouse button (to draw using the foreground color) or the right mouse button (to draw using the background color) and drag.

> **Drawing at 90-Degree or 45-Degree Angles**
> To draw perfectly straight vertical, horizontal, or diagonal lines, hold down the Shift key while you drag. Using the Shift key to create lines will eliminate—or at least reduce—the jagged edges that lines at other angles sometimes have.

Drawing Curved Lines with the Curve Tool

 The Curve tool lets you create a line with two curves in it. To use the Curve tool, follow these steps:

1 Click the Curve tool in the tool box.

2 Click one of the line width choices that appear below the tool box.

3 Position the mouse pointer in the drawing area at the place where you want the curve to begin, hold down either mouse button and drag to where you want the curved line to end, and then release the mouse button.

At this point you have a straight line.

4 Move the mouse pointer near the part of the line you want to bend. Hold down either mouse button and drag in the direction you want the line to curve.

Now you have a line with one curve.

5 To add a second bend, repeat step 4. Use the left mouse button if you want the curve to appear in the foreground color or the right mouse button if you want it to appear in the background color.

It might take some practice to get used to the behavior of the Curve tool. If your curve isn't shaping up the way you want, click both mouse buttons (or the Curve tool in the tool box) any time before finishing the second bend to delete the line, and then start over.

Drawing Rectangles and Squares with the Rectangle Tool

To create rectangles and squares, use the Rectangle tool. Click the Rectangle tool, and then choose the rectangle type from the three choices below the tool box.

The first rectangle type lets you draw the outline of the rectangle using the foreground or background color. The second type lets you draw the outline in either the foreground or background color with the interior filled in with the other color. The third type lets you draw a rectangle filled with the background or foreground color, but without a border.

After choosing the rectangle type, move to the drawing area, and then hold down the left mouse button (to use the foreground color for the rectangle's outline) or the right button (to use the background color) and drag diagonally to create the rectangle.

⭐ **TIP**

Drawing Perfect Squares
You can create a perfect square by holding down the Shift key while you drag.

Drawing Rectangles with Rounded Corners

To draw rectangles with rounded corners, use the Rounded Rectangle tool. The Rounded Rectangle tool works exactly the same as the regular Rectangle tool except that it produces rounded corners.

Drawing Ellipses and Circles with the Ellipse Tool

 To create ellipses (ovals) or circles, use the Ellipse tool. The Ellipse tool works much like the Rectangle tool described on the previous page. After selecting the tool, you choose a type—unfilled border, filled with border, or filled without border, just as with the rectangles. Then put the mouse pointer where you want the corner of an imaginary rectangle that will contain your figure. Hold down the left mouse button (to use the foreground color for the ellipse's outline) or the right mouse button (to use the background color) and drag to expand the figure. When the figure reaches the desired size, release the mouse button.

> **Drawing Perfect Circles**
> To create a perfect circle, hold down the Shift key while dragging.

Drawing Irregular Closed Shapes with the Polygon Tool

 To create any kind of closed shape other than a rectangle, square, ellipse, or circle, use the Polygon tool. With this tool you can draw as many straight line segments as you want. Each segment begins where the last one ended. When you double-click, Paint closes the polygon by connecting the end of your last line segment with the beginning of your first.

You can create anything from simple triangles to complex shapes with overlapping lines. To create a polygon, follow these steps:

1 Click the Polygon tool.

2 Choose the polygon type from the three choices below the tool box: unfilled, filled with border, or filled without border.

3 Move the mouse pointer to the beginning of the first line segment. Hold down the left mouse button (to use the foreground color for the polygon's outline) or the right mouse button (to use the background color) and drag to the end of the first line segment.

4 Move the mouse pointer to the place where you want the next line segment to end and click using the same mouse button.
    Paint draws a new line segment from the end of the first line.

IV

5 Repeat step 4 until the mouse pointer is at the end of the next-to-last line segment you want, and then double-click.

 TIP

To create perfect vertical, horizontal, or diagonal line segments, hold down the Shift key while creating each segment.

Using the Fill With Color Tool to Fill an Enclosed Shape

 The Fill With Color tool allows you to fill any enclosed portion of your picture with the current foreground or background color.

To use the Fill With Color tool, click it in the tool box, and then position the mouse pointer over the area in the picture you want to fill. Click the left mouse button to fill the area with the foreground color, or click the right mouse button to fill the area with the background color.

Note that if the area you want to fill has any gaps—even a gap of a single pixel—the color will leak through the gap. If that happens, use the Undo command, and then patch the leak and try again. To patch a very small leak, you might want to use the Zoom command. (For information about the Zoom command, see "Fine Tuning Your Image with Zoom," page 473.)

Adding Text with the Text Tool

 Paint's Text tool is a special kind of implement. You don't really *draw* with this tool; instead you choose a typeface, style, and point size, and then type characters from the keyboard (or paste them from the Clipboard). Nevertheless, after you've completed your text entry, the text behaves just like any other part of your picture.

The general procedure for adding text is as follows:

1 Select the Text tool.

2 Drag diagonally to create a rectangular text frame about the size you want for your text.

An insertion point—like the one in a word processing program—appears inside the frame to let you know where your text will appear.

TIP

Placing Text Over an Opaque Background

By default, text frames are "transparent"—which means that text appears in the foreground color and the frame's background is "clear," allowing the image underneath to show through. This can be a problem if you're adding text on top of a colored background. Black text on a black background, for example, isn't legible. To use the color box's background color for your text frame's background color, click the icon for the opaque option (just below the tool box). The text frame is filled with the selected background color.

3 Type your text or choose Paste from the Edit menu.

 SEE ALSO

For more information about formatting text, see Chapter 8, "Installing and Using Fonts."

4 Change text attributes using Paint's Fonts toolbar, shown below, which automatically appears when you create a text frame. (If the Fonts toolbar isn't visible, choose Text Toolbar from the View menu.) You can select a font, size, and style (bold, italic, underlined, or a combination).

5 Click outside the text frame or select another tool from the tool box to confirm the text entry.

 NOTE

Until you confirm the text entry by clicking outside the frame or by choosing another tool, you can edit the text or change the font, size, or style of the text. However, once you confirm the text entry, you can't do any text editing other than erasing or using the Undo command and starting over.

 TIP

Moving the Text Frame

Before you confirm the text entry, you can move the text frame. To do so, move the mouse pointer to any edge of the frame; the pointer changes to a standard pointer arrow. Then drag the frame where you want it. You can also resize the frame. Point to one of the resizing handles (the solid boxes along each side of the frame) and drag.

Using Paint's Editing Tools

The editing tools in Paint's tool box let you clean up your drawing as well as select or view part of it for further manipulation.

Using the Eraser Tool to Clean Up Mistakes

 The Eraser tool lets you "erase" anything in the drawing area by simply dragging the mouse over the portion of the object you want to remove. What the eraser is really doing, however, is painting with the current background color. So, if you have a black object—text, rectangle, whatever—on a white background, dragging the Eraser tool over any of the black portions of the object appears to erase them, but it's really just "whitewashing" them to match the white background.

 SEE ALSO

For information about erasing a large area of your drawing, see "Erasing a Cutout," page 472.

To use the Eraser tool, click the Eraser icon in the tool box, and then select from one of the four eraser sizes that appear below the tool box. Finally, position the mouse pointer where you want to start erasing, hold down the left mouse button, and drag.

 TIP

> **Erasing a Single Color**
> Dragging the Eraser tool while holding down the right mouse button erases (applies the current background color to) only the portions of the drawing area that are in the current foreground color. Set the foreground color to match the color of the object you want to erase and nothing else in the drawing will be disturbed.

Selecting a Color with the Pick Color Tool

 The Pick Color tool lets you change the foreground or background in the color box to the color of any object in your drawing. To change the foreground color, click the Pick Color tool, and then click the object or area in your drawing that's drawn in the color you want to use as your new foreground color. To change the background color, click the Pick Color tool, and then right-click the object or area in your drawing that's drawn in the color you want to use as your new background color.

Using the Magnifier Tool

Using the Magnifier tool, you can zoom in to a specific portion of your drawing or magnify the entire image. To magnify a particular area of the drawing, click the Magnifier tool. Move the pointer—which assumes the shape of a large rectangle—over the portion of the drawing you want to enlarge, and then click. Paint magnifies the drawing and places the portion of the drawing area that the rectangle pointer was over at the center of the drawing area. To return to normal, unmagnified view, click the Magnifier tool again, and then click anywhere in the drawing area.

If you want to enlarge the image by a factor of 2, 6, or 8, click the Magnifier tool, and then click 2×, 6×, or 8× just below the tool box. You can return the drawing area to normal size by clicking the Magnifier tool, and then clicking the 1× choice just below the tool box.

Paint remembers the last magnification you used and uses that factor as its default the next time you use the Magnifier tool to select an area to be enlarged.

? SEE ALSO

For more information about magnified views, see "Fine Tuning Your Image with Zoom," page 473.

Defining Cutouts with the Free-Form Select Tool and the Select Tool

The Free-Form Select and Select tools at the top of the tool box are used for specifying *cutouts*—selected areas of the drawing that can be manipulated in various ways. (See "Working with Cutouts," on the next page.)

Using the Select tool, you can define a rectangular-shaped cutout. Using the Free-Form Select tool, you can define any portion of any shape in the drawing area as a cutout. The Free-Form Select tool is particularly useful when you want to select an irregularly shaped object and don't want to include any of the surrounding canvas.

 To use the Free-Form Select tool, start by clicking the Free-Form Select tool icon. Then position the mouse pointer somewhere along the edge of the object you want to select. Hold down the left mouse button and then drag around the object. You draw a solid line as you drag the mouse. When you have the object completely surrounded, release the mouse button. (You don't actually have to close the selection. When you release the mouse button, Paint connects the current pointer position to the place where you started.) When you release the mouse button, Paint displays a dotted rectangular line around the object you've selected.

When the object you want to select is rectangular, or when it doesn't matter if you select a bit of background canvas along with the object, the Select tool is the best way to go.

To use the Select tool, position the mouse pointer at one corner of the object you want to select, and then drag to the opposite corner.

Working with Cutouts

SEE ALSO

For information about defining a cutout, see "Defining Cutouts with the Free-Form Select Tool and the Select Tool," on the previous page.

After you've defined a cutout, you can do any of the following with it:

- Cut it to the Clipboard

- Copy it to the Clipboard

- Copy it to a separate disk file

- Move it to another place within the current picture

- Copy it to another place within the current picture

- "Sweep" it across your picture, leaving a trail of copies in its wake

- Change its size or shape

- Stretch (distort) or skew (slant) it

- Flip or rotate it

- Reverse its colors

- Erase it

TIP

The easiest way to perform most cutout operations is to select a command from the cutout's context menu. After you define a cutout, right-click it to display its context menu.

Cutting or Copying a Cutout to the Clipboard

To put your cutout on the Clipboard, choose Cut or Copy from the Edit menu (or from the context menu that appears when you right-click the selection). If you choose Cut, Paint removes it from the current picture and transfers it to the Clipboard. If you choose Copy, Paint puts a copy of the cutout on the Clipboard and leaves the current picture unchanged.

Linking and Embedding Cutouts

Paint is an OLE server program. That means that pictures created or edited in Paint can be linked or embedded in documents created by OLE client programs, such as WordPad, Microsoft Excel, or Microsoft Word. For information about OLE, see Chapter 9, "Exchanging Information Using the Clipboard and OLE."

When you use the Cut command to put the cutout on the Clipboard, the area of the picture that was occupied by the cutout assumes the current background color. If you want the area to look like the blank canvas after the cutout is removed, be sure the current background matches your initial background color.

Copying a Cutout to a Disk File

② SEE ALSO

For information about the Save As dialog box, see "Saving and Opening Paint Documents," page 448.

You can copy a cutout to a separate disk file, thereby creating a new Paint document. It's a good idea to do this if you want to use the cutout in different pictures.

To save the cutout to a new document, choose Copy To from the Edit menu or the cutout's context menu and fill out the Save As dialog box that appears.

Pasting a Cutout from the Clipboard

To paste a cutout from the Clipboard, choose Paste from the Edit menu. Your cutout appears in the upper left corner of the drawing area surrounded by a dotted line. At this point you can drag it to any part of the drawing area, or you can manipulate it in any of the other ways described in the following sections.

Note that pasting in Paint is a bit different from pasting in other programs. In a word processor, for example, you first position the insertion point where you want the contents of the Clipboard pasted, and then choose Paste. In Paint, you paste first, and then you position the pasted object.

NOTE

Paint handles Clipboard text differently from graphics. When you paste text from the Clipboard, you must position the insertion point first, and then choose the Paste command.

Pasting from a Disk File

To paste a cutout that was saved as a separate disk file, choose Paste From from the Edit menu, and then choose the file you want from the Open dialog box that appears. This is the same dialog box as the one that appears when you choose Open from the File menu.

When you choose Paste From, the cutout appears in the upper left corner of the drawing area, just as when you paste from the Clipboard.

TIP

If you want to place the contents of a saved cutout somewhere other than the drawing area's upper left corner, you can drag it after you choose Paste From. But there's an easier way: use the Select tool to define a cutout *before* you choose Paste From, and the saved cutout is then pasted into the upper left corner of the selected cutout.

Moving a Cutout

To move a cutout from one place to another, position the mouse pointer anywhere within the dotted line (the pointer changes to a four-headed arrow), and then drag. When you move a cutout, the portion of the picture you move the cutout onto is obscured by the cutout object.

Copying a Cutout Within a Picture

To make a duplicate of a cutout, position the cursor within the dotted area surrounding the cutout and hold down the Ctrl key while dragging the mouse. The original cutout remains where it was and a duplicate appears where you release the mouse button.

Sweeping a Cutout

To "sweep" a cutout means to create a trail of copies with it as you pass the mouse across the canvas. Figure 18-9, on the next page, shows an object that has been swept across the canvas.

This Ought to Clear Things Up

Cutouts can be moved, copied, or swept either opaquely or transparently. When you move, copy, or sweep a cutout opaquely (the default), any background portions of the cutout are moved, copied, or swept along with the foreground material and can obscure another object that the cutout lands on. If you move, copy, or sweep a cutout transparently, any parts of the cutout that are in the current background color disappear, allowing the underlying image to show through. To select transparent operations so the background won't obscure other parts of the drawing, choose Draw Opaque from the Options menu to remove the check mark, or click the draw transparent icon below the tool box.

The opaque and transparent options also control the background of a text box when you use the Text tool.

FIGURE 18-9.
Sweeping can be useful, or it can just make a mess.

Draw opaque ——
Draw transparent ——

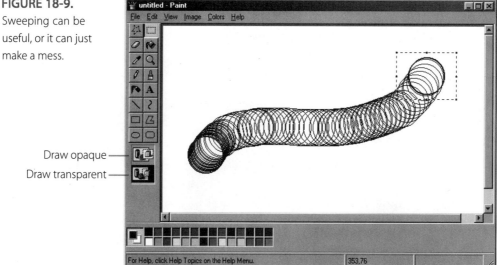

To sweep a cutout, first move the cutout where you want to begin the sweep. Then position the cursor within the dotted area and hold down the Shift key while dragging.

The speed at which you drag the mouse determines the number of copies that result from the sweep.

TIP

Most often you will want to select the draw transparent icon below the tool box. Otherwise, each new image in the sweep obscures part of the image that preceded it.

Resizing a Cutout

You can change the size of a cutout horizontally, vertically, or both. To change the size of a cutout, position the mouse pointer over one of the handles in the dotted rectangle surrounding the cutout. There are eight handles—one in each corner and one in the middle of each side.

When the mouse pointer is correctly positioned, it assumes the shape of a double-headed arrow. If it's on a corner handle, the arrow is diagonal and you can size vertically and horizontally at the same time.

Stretching and Skewing a Cutout

To adjust a cutout with absolute precision, choose Stretch/Skew from the Image menu to display the Stretch And Skew dialog box, as shown in Figure 18-10. Using this dialog box you can alter the size of the cutout either horizontally or vertically by specifying a percentage greater or smaller than its original 100 percent. You can skew the cutout horizontally or vertically by specifying the number of degrees to skew.

FIGURE 18-10.
With the Stretch And Skew dialog box, you can precisely control the image's size and shape.

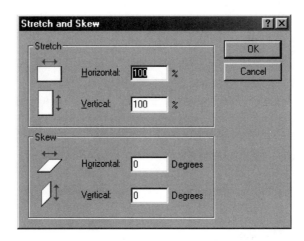

To change the size of a cutout, enter the percentage in the appropriate text box. For example, to double the vertical size of a cutout enter 200 in the Vertical text box.

To skew the cutout, enter the number of degrees to skew. Use a positive number to skew the cutout in the direction of the sample icon in the dialog box, or a negative number to skew the cutout in the opposite direction.

Flipping or Rotating a Cutout

Using the Image menu's Flip/Rotate command, you can flip any image vertically or horizontally, or rotate it 90, 180, or 270 degrees. To flip or rotate a cutout, choose Flip/Rotate from the Image menu; the Flip And Rotate dialog box appears. Click the Flip Horizontal, Flip Vertical, or Rotate By Angle option button. If you choose Rotate By Angle, you must also select one of the angle option buttons. Finally, click OK.

Reversing the Colors of a Cutout

The Image menu's Invert Colors command "reverses" the colors of your cutout. Black becomes white, white becomes black, and colors switch to their complementary color on the red-green-blue color wheel.

Inverting color can give unexpected, and sometimes unwanted, results. Just remember that you can use the Undo command if the new colors aren't what you had in mind.

Erasing a Cutout

You can erase a large area by defining it as a cutout and then choosing the Clear Selection command from the Edit menu or the cutout's context menu. Like the Cut command (see "Cutting or Copying a Cutout to the Clipboard," page 467), this command removes the cutout and replaces it with the current background color. However, it does not move the cutout to the Clipboard, so if you want to leave the Clipboard contents unchanged, use the Clear Selection command.

Fine Tuning Your Image with Zoom

Paint stores images you create as *bitmaps*, which record the position and color of each dot in the picture. The individual dots on the screen are known as *pixels*.

You might not normally be aware of separate pixels as you create and modify your Paint images. But, when you want to see and edit the image pixel by pixel, Paint can accommodate you.

Simply choose Zoom from the View menu, and then choose Large Size from the Zoom submenu. The image appears enlarged with a small section of the picture shown in "real size" in a small window in the upper left corner of the drawing area, as shown in Figure 18-11. The small window is called a *thumbnail*. (If the thumbnail doesn't appear, choose Show Thumbnail from the Zoom submenu.)

FIGURE 18-11.

In Zoom view, every pixel is visible.

 TIP

> To make it easier to edit in the zoomed-in view, choose Show Grid from the Zoom submenu. This shows each pixel in its own square, as you can see in Figure 18-11.

To specify a zoom percentage, choose Zoom from the View menu, and then choose Custom to display the Custom Zoom dialog box. The dialog box lets you choose zoom percentages of 100%, 200%, 400%, 600%, or 800%. Click the option button next to the desired zoom percentage, and then click the OK button.

You can also specify a zoom percentage using the Magnifier tool. Click the Magnifier tool in the tool box, and then click 1×, 2×, 6×, or 8× just below the tool box.

SEE ALSO

For information about Paint's drawing and editing tools, see "Exploring the Tool Box," page 457.

You can perform any of the normal picture creation and editing maneuvers while you're zoomed in. One of the more useful tools is the Pencil because you can manipulate one pixel at a time. You can click to paint a single pixel, or drag to draw in the usual way.

Editing Colors

For most of your day-to-day painting needs, the standard set of 28 colors or patterns that appear in the default color box are more than adequate. However, when the creative need arises, Paint lets you replace any of the standard colors by choosing from a group of 48 predefined colors or by creating almost any custom colors you can imagine.

Choosing Predefined Colors

To replace one of the colors in the color box with any of the 48 predefined colors, click the color you want to replace, and then choose Edit Colors from the Colors menu to display the Edit Colors dialog box shown in Figure 18-12.

In the Basic Colors group, click the color you want to use as the selected color's replacement, and then click the OK button. The color you originally selected is replaced in the color box with the new color. Repeat the process to replace as many of the default colors as you want.

The default color set will reappear the next time you start Paint.

FIGURE 18-12.

The Edit Colors dialog box gives you additional colors to splash on your palette.

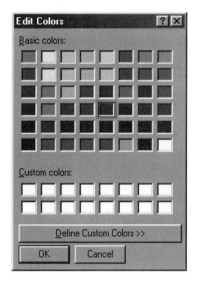

Adding Custom Colors

SEE ALSO

For more information about using the Edit Colors dialog box, see "Defining Custom Colors," page 93.

When none of the 48 predefined colors will do, you can create virtually any color in the rainbow and add it to your color palette. To create a custom color, click the color in the color box that you want to replace with the custom color, and then choose Edit Colors from the Colors menu. When the Edit Colors dialog box appears, click the Define Custom Colors button to expand the dialog box, as shown in Figure 18-13.

FIGURE 18-13.

The expanded Edit Colors dialog box lets you create custom colors.

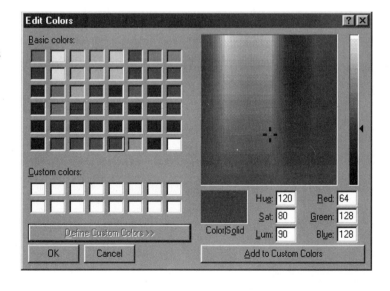

Drag the cross-hair pointer and the luminosity pointer until the color you want to use as a new color appears in the Color|Solid box. (Or you can enter numeric values in the Hue, Sat, and Lum or Red, Green, and Blue text boxes.) Then click the Add To Custom Colors button. The new color is added to the first empty square in the Custom Colors portion of the dialog box. The new color replaces the original color you selected in the color box when you click the OK button.

> **NOTE**
>
> Before leaving the Edit Colors dialog box, you can create as many as 16 custom colors, which you can use to replace colors in the color box, as described in the previous section.

Printing Your Paint Image

To print your Paint image, choose Print from the File menu.

Specify which pages to print in the Print Range portion of the dialog box, and the number of copies to print in the Copies box. When all the settings are as desired, click the OK button.

Changing Page Settings

If you want to change paper size, orientation (direction), or margins, choose Page Setup from the File menu before you choose the Print command. In the Page Setup dialog box, choose the paper size from the Size drop-down list, and, if the option is available for your printer, the source from the Source drop-down list. To change the print orientation, click the appropriate option button in the Orientation portion of the dialog box.

To change the margins—the white space surrounding your picture—select the entry in the text box for the margin you want to change (Left, Right, Top, or Bottom) and enter the new value.

When the settings are correct, click the OK button and then print the document.

IV

Using the Windows Accessories

Printing Color Images to Black-and-White Printers

You don't have to make any special accommodations to print color Paint images to your black-and-white printer. However, the results might not be what you expect—or want. When color images are sent to a black-and-white printer, the colors are converted to black-and-white dot patterns (called dithering) to simulate gray shades.

You can adjust the way colors are dithered by clicking Properties in the Print dialog box. Then click the Graphics tab of your printer's properties dialog box, and experiment with different dithering options.

 TIP

You can use Print Preview to see what your printout will look like before sending it to the printer. Choose Print Preview from the File menu. If you like what you see, click the Print button in the Print Preview window. If you don't, click Close to return to the main Paint window for further editing.

Making Wallpaper

Printing your pictures on paper isn't the only way to use your Paint creations. You can also use them as Windows wallpaper—the background for your desktop. If you already have a Paint image saved on your computer's hard disk, you can use the Display properties dialog box to choose it as your wallpaper. However, there's an easier way to use the current Paint image as wallpaper without using the Display properties dialog box at all.

 NOTE

You can use a Paint image as your desktop wallpaper only if you're *not* displaying the desktop as a Web page. To disable Web-page view so you can display wallpaper, right-click the desktop, choose Active Desktop, and choose View As Web Page if it's checked. (If View As Web Page is not checked, simply click anywhere else to close the context menu; your desktop is ready to be wallpapered.)

SEE ALSO

For information about using the Display properties dialog box to apply wallpaper, see "Using Wallpaper," page 97.

Before you can use a Paint image as wallpaper, you must save it. Once the image is saved, choose Set As Wallpaper (Tiled) or Set As Wallpaper (Centered) from the File menu. The Tiled option displays as many copies of the picture as required to fill the screen. Centered uses one copy of the image—centered on the screen.

As soon as you choose one of the Set As Wallpaper commands, the image immediately becomes your wallpaper, although you won't be able to see it if Paint is maximized or if your desktop is covered with other programs.

 TIP

Before you use a Set As Wallpaper command, you might want to move the wallpaper file to the directory in which your other wallpaper files are stored. This makes the file easier to find in case you ever change to another wallpaper file and then want to switch back. The default folder for wallpaper files is C:\Windows.

Making Connections with Phone Dialer and HyperTerminal

In this chapter we'll look at two simple Windows accessory programs designed to facilitate communications via your computer's modem. Phone Dialer is a utility that uses your modem to dial the phone, thereby helping you make voice connections. You can use it to set up eight speed-dial numbers that can be dialed with the click of a button. HyperTerminal is a program that can help you connect with bulletin board services (BBS's) or exchange files with another computer.

NOTE

> To use either Phone Dialer or HyperTerminal, a modem must be properly installed in your computer and configured in Windows 98. If you haven't done so already, install the modem, and then launch Modems in Control Panel. Click the Add button to start the Install New Modem Wizard, which leads you through the configuration process.

Using Phone Dialer

To start Phone Dialer, open the Start menu, and then choose Programs, Accessories, Communications, Phone Dialer. Phone Dialer appears, as shown in Figure 19-1.

FIGURE 19-1.

Phone Dialer includes eight speed-dial buttons.

 NOTE

> If Phone Dialer has not been set up on your computer, launch Add/Remove Programs in Control Panel, click the Windows Setup tab, select Communications, and click the Details button. Select Phone Dialer and click OK.

Setting Up the Speed-Dial Numbers

You can enter the eight speed-dial numbers in two ways. If you want to enter them all at one sitting, or edit existing numbers as a group, choose Speed Dial from the Edit menu. The Edit Speed Dial dialog box appears, as shown in Figure 19-2.

FIGURE 19-2.
The Edit Speed Dial dialog box is for entering a group of speed-dial numbers at once.

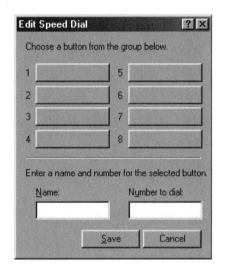

Click the button for the first speed-dial button you want to set up or edit, and then, in the Name text box, enter or edit the text you want to appear on the button. Then, in the Number To Dial text box, enter the phone number (or edit the existing number). After completing all the entries, click the Save button.

To set up numbers one at a time, click one of the blank speed-dial buttons in the main Phone Dialer window. The Program Speed Dial dialog box for that button appears, as shown in Figure 19-3.

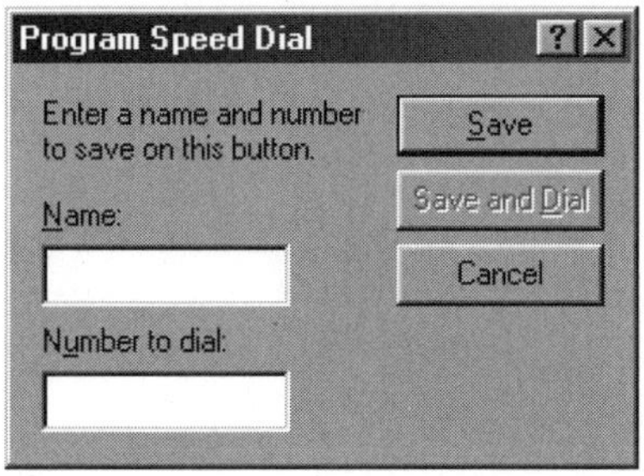

FIGURE 19-3.
The Program Speed Dial dialog box lets you program a single speed-dial button.

After entering the name and number in the appropriate text boxes, you can click the Save button to save the entry, or click the Save And Dial button to save the entry and dial it immediately.

Making a Call

To use Phone Dialer to place a call, you must have a modem installed in your computer. Unless you're using a voice modem, you must also have a telephone connected to the modem. If you try to make a call without a modem installed, Phone Dialer prompts you to install one. (If you try to make a call without a voice modem or a telephone connected to the modem, you'll have no way to talk with the person who answers!)

To make a call, click the speed-dial button for the number you want to call. The Dialing dialog box appears while the connection is being made, and it becomes an Active Call dialog box when the other party answers. If you're not using a voice modem, a Call Status dialog box appears; pick up your telephone's handset and click the Talk button to start the conversation, or click the Hang Up button to disconnect.

After the call is completed, you simply click the Hang Up button in the Active Call dialog box, or hang up the handset to terminate the call.

Although you can use Phone Dialer to dial phone numbers by typing them into the Number To Dial text box or clicking the numbers on Phone Dialer's number pad, it's usually more efficient to just dial your telephone without using Phone Dialer. However, if you must precede each phone number with a lengthy calling card code or long distance access code, you might find Phone Dialer convenient. Another possible advantage to using Phone Dialer even for manually dialed calls is to have them included in Phone Dialer's history log. See the next section for details.

Viewing a Log of Your Calls

To see a list of the calls you've made using Phone Dialer, choose Show Log from the Tools menu. The Call Log window appears, as shown in Figure 19-4.

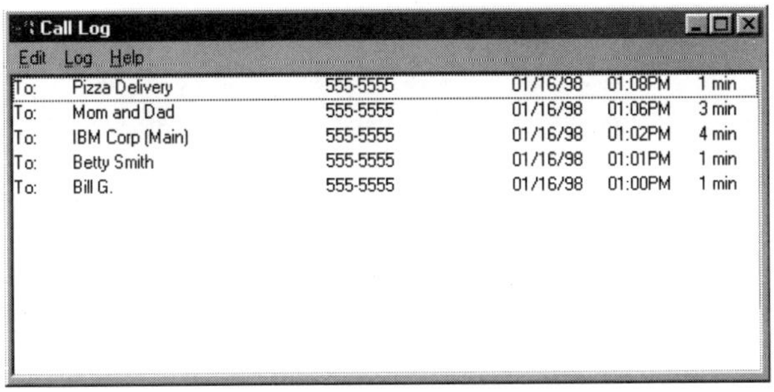

FIGURE 19-4.

The Call Log window shows your call activity.

To delete an entry in the call log, click the entry and choose Delete from the Edit menu.

To call one of the numbers in the call log, click the entry and choose Dial from the Log menu, or double-click the entry.

To hide the log, choose Hide Log from the Tools menu.

? SEE ALSO

For information about dialing properties, see "Setting Dialing Properties," page 576.

Changing the Dialing Properties

You can change several dialing properties to make Phone Dialer more useful. To change the dialing properties, choose Dialing Properties from the Tools menu.

Why HyperTerminal?

? SEE ALSO

For information about using a modem to connect to a network, see "Using Dial-Up Networking," page 578.

You don't have to get involved with HyperTerminal to have your computer cruising the information superhighway. In fact, most of the popular online services, such as The Microsoft Network and America Online, require their own specialized software to make the connection.

HyperTerminal's principal use is for connecting to bulletin board services (BBS's), electronic mail services (such as MCI Mail) that don't supply or require proprietary software, and Telnet. HyperTerminal is the default Telnet terminal for Internet Explorer 4. If you enter a Telnet URL in Internet Explorer's address bar, the browser automatically starts your Telnet session in HyperTerminal.

⊛ **TIP**

Even when connecting to services that don't need special software, you're often better off using special software. For example, although you can connect to CompuServe with HyperTerminal, you'll find it more efficient to use the software that comes with your CompuServe account.

A Typical HyperTerminal Session

A typical communications session using HyperTerminal goes something like this:

1 Start HyperTerminal. For details, see "Starting HyperTerminal," page 486.

2 Open or create a connection file.

Before establishing a communications link, you have to supply HyperTerminal with the phone number and some additional information about how to communicate with the service you're calling. For details, see "Making New Connections," page 487.

 3 Choose Connect from the Call menu or click the Connect toolbar button, and then click the Dial button in the Dial dialog box. (Table 19-1 describes the toolbar buttons.)

HyperTerminal uses your modem's built-in dialing capabilities to establish a telephone connection with the remote computer, which is often called the *host computer* (or simply the *host*). After a connection has been established, whatever you type in HyperTerminal's window is sent across the phone line to the host computer. If the person or computer at the other end of the line sends information back, it appears in HyperTerminal's window as though someone behind the screen were typing.

4 Log on to the host computer or service.

If you're communicating with a mainframe or information service, you'll probably be required to enter your name and password as soon as the connection is established. This process is called *logging on.*

TABLE 19-1. **HyperTerminal Toolbar**

Toolbar Icon	Description
	Creates a new connection file
	Opens an existing connection file
	Connects to a remote system (dials the modem)
	Disconnects from a remote system (hangs up the modem)
	Sends a file to the remote system
	Receives a file from the remote system
	Displays the property sheet for the current connection file

5 Interact with the party you're connected to.

Your conversation might consist of nothing more than messages typed at the keyboard. Or you might transmit a great deal of information stored on the Clipboard by choosing Paste To Host from HyperTerminal's Edit menu. You can also exchange files with the host computer. For details, see "Transferring Files," page 494.

6 Log off the host computer or service.

The procedure for logging off depends on the service you use. Typically, you type *quit, exit, bye,* or a similar command at the service's command prompt or main menu.

7 Choose the Disconnect command from HyperTerminal's Call menu.

When you log off, the host computer might end the telephone connection itself. HyperTerminal might not recognize that, however, so it's best to use the Disconnect command regardless of what the other party does.

8 Close HyperTerminal.

If the telephone connection is still open (or if HyperTerminal thinks it is), HyperTerminal prompts you to disconnect from the host computer before quitting.

Starting HyperTerminal

To start HyperTerminal, open the Start menu, and then choose Programs, Accessories, Communications, HyperTerminal. This opens a folder that contains an icon for the HyperTerminal program and for each Hyper-Terminal connection you have created and saved. To open an existing connection, simply launch the connection. Otherwise, launch the Hyper-Terminal program. HyperTerminal's opening screen appears, followed by the Connection Description dialog box, as shown in Figure 19-5.

FIGURE 19-5.

The Connection Description dialog box is the place to enter specifications for a new terminal connection.

NOTE

If HyperTerminal has not been set up on your computer, launch Add/Remove Programs in Control Panel, click the Windows Setup tab, select Communications, and click the Details button. Select HyperTerminal and click OK. Click OK again in the Add/Remove Programs Properties dialog box.

If you've already specified connection settings—perhaps to dial up a company's support bulletin board or the local library's online research service—click the Cancel button to close the Connection Description dialog box. Otherwise, follow the instructions below to create settings for a new connection.

Making New Connections

The first time you use HyperTerminal, or when you want to connect to a new computer service, HyperTerminal doesn't have a clue about what you want to connect to, so you'll have to supply the details it needs to get hooked up.

To create a new connection, follow these steps:

1 Type a descriptive name for the connection in the Name text box.

 The name doesn't have to be the actual name of the service you're connecting to, just something that will be descriptive enough for you. For example, you might call your connection to the local bicycle club BBS "Bike BBS" instead of using its official name, "UWBIKECLUB."

2 Select an icon to represent the new connection.

 You can use the horizontal scroll bar to view the available connection icons.

3 Click OK.

 HyperTerminal displays the Connect To dialog box, as shown in Figure 19-6.

FIGURE 19-6.

Use the Connect To dialog box to enter the number for the new connection.

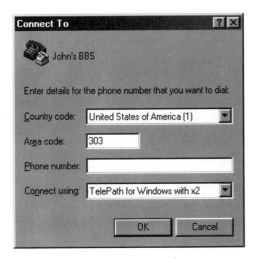

4 Fill in the phone number and area code.

If you have more than one modem connected to your computer, use the Connect Using drop-down list to select the modem you want to use for this connection.

If you're connecting to a Telnet site, choose TCP/IP (Winsock) from the Connect Using drop-down. You will also then need to supply the Telnet URL (without the Telnet://) and your port number.

5 Click the OK button.

Unless you're using the TCP/IP (Winsock) device, the Connect dialog box appears, as shown in Figure 19-7.

FIGURE 19-7.
The Connect dialog box shows the current primary settings for the new connection.

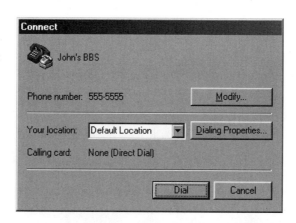

6 Click Dial to connect to the service now or Cancel if you want to connect to the service later.

7 After you log off or after choosing Cancel without logging on, choose Save from the File menu to retain the connection settings you just created.

Opening Existing Connections

 To open a connection that has already been defined, launch the connection in the HyperTerminal folder. If HyperTerminal is already running, choose Open from the File menu, or click the Open toolbar button. The Open dialog box appears, as shown in Figure 19-8.

FIGURE 19-8.

The Open dialog box lets you choose the predefined connection you want to use.

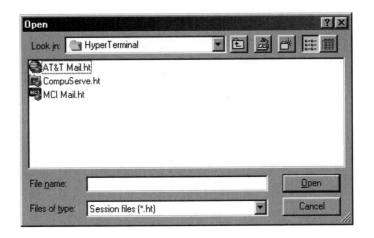

Click the name of the file you want to use in the list box, and then click Open. Like other programs for Windows, the HyperTerminal title bar displays the name of the connection you've chosen.

If you open a file for a modem connection (such as to a BBS), the Connect dialog box appears. (See Figure 19-7.) Click Dial to make the connection.

If you open a file for a TCP/IP connection (such as a Telnet connection), HyperTerminal immediately connects to the connection's host address. (If you have a dial-up connection to the Internet, HyperTerminal first launches your Internet dialer.)

Modifying Connection Settings

In most cases, the basic connection information you enter in the Connection Description (see Figure 19-5 on page 486) and Connect To (Figure 19-6 on page 487) dialog boxes is sufficient. You can, however, customize the settings in a number of ways to suit your needs. This can be done as you create a new connection or after the connection has been defined.

 To modify a connection's properties after it has been defined, open the connection as described in the previous section. Then choose Properties from the File menu. The Properties dialog box for the open connection appears, as shown in Figure 19-9, on the next page.

FIGURE 19-9.

The Connect To tab in the Properties dialog box provides access to several basic settings.

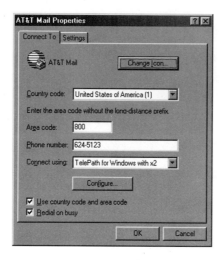

The Connect To tab in the Properties dialog box includes the following controls for changing options:

■ The Change Icon button lets you pick an icon from the group of icons that was presented when you created the connection. You can also change the connection name via the Change Icon button.

■ The Country Code lists the part of the world where the host computer is located.

■ The entries in the Area Code and Phone Number text boxes need to be changed only if the number for your connection changes or if you made a mistake when you entered them initially.

■ Use the Connect Using drop-down list to specify a different modem if your computer has more than one modem attached. If you're connecting to a Telnet site, choose TCP/IP in the Connect Using drop-down list, and then specify the host address and port number. The host address should be the URL of the Telnet site.

The Connect Using drop-down list also provides for direct connection to each of your computer's serial (Com) ports. Although you can use this method to connect two nearby computers with HyperTerminal (and no modems), a better solution in that case is to use Direct Cable Connection. For details, see "Transferring Files with Direct Cable Connection," page 592.

- To change the modem settings for this connection, click the Configure button. HyperTerminal displays the properties dialog box for your modem. The modem properties dialog box lets you select a port, baud rate (modem speed), and other communications parameters and dialing settings. For details, see "Installing, Configuring, and Testing a Modem," page 259.

TIP

If you're connecting to a service that charges by the minute—or it's a long distance call—you can set up your modem to disconnect automatically if you don't use it for a period of time. In the properties dialog box for the connection, click Configure to display the modem properties dialog box. Click the Connection tab, and then select the Disconnect A Call If Idle For More Than check box. Enter a reasonably short time (perhaps 10 or 15 minutes) so you won't be paying for a lot of connect time while you're not using the system. (Unfortunately, this check box is not available in the Properties dialog box for all brands and types of modems.)

The Settings tab in the Properties dialog box for the connection includes the following additional options, as shown in Figure 19-10.

- Select Terminal Keys (the default) or Windows Keys to specify how function keys, arrow keys, and Ctrl-key combinations are used during connections. If you select Terminal Keys, these keystrokes are sent to the host computer; if you select Windows Keys, Windows processes these keystrokes as it does in other programs.

FIGURE 19-10.
The Settings tab in the connection's Properties dialog box controls the appearance of transmitted data, among other functions.

For example, with some services, pressing Ctrl+C stops the transmission of a file. If you have selected Windows Keys, however, pressing Ctrl+C copies the current selection (if any) to the Clipboard. It's usually best to leave this option set to Terminal Keys so these keystrokes will be passed to the host computer.

■ In the second option button group, select what the remote computer should receive when you press Backspace. For most systems, Ctrl+H is appropriate.

■ The Emulation drop-down list is set to Auto Detect. Unless you have trouble with your connection, keep this at the default setting. If you do have trouble, contact the host computer's support staff to find out what type of terminal the remote system needs to see at your end. (A *terminal* is a simple device—consisting of a monitor, a keyboard, and a physical connection—for communicating with a host computer. HyperTerminal can act like any of several different terminal models.)

■ Teletype-33 is the appropriate Telnet Terminal for most Telnet sites. Change this value only if required by the site you're connecting to.

■ The Backscroll Buffer Lines text box lets you specify how many lines of a communication session you can view by pressing the PgUp key. (A *buffer* is an area of memory used to store something temporarily.) While you're connected to another computer, everything you send and receive is stored in a buffer and displayed in HyperTerminal's window. The buffer gives you a way to review what you send and receive without capturing the "conversation" in a disk file or generating a printed transcript. As long as the buffer's capacity has not been exceeded, you can scroll up and down in the HyperTerminal window to reread everything that has passed back and forth over the telephone line. (There is one exception: Binary files that you send or receive are not recorded in the buffer.)

When the buffer reaches its capacity, each new line replaces the oldest line in the buffer. For example, if the buffer size is set at 500 lines, when the 501st line arrives, the first line is discarded.

You can set the buffer size at anywhere from 25 to 500 lines. If you have plenty of memory, reserve a full 500 lines; if memory is scarce, choose a smaller size. If you don't have enough memory for the buffer size you request, HyperTerminal gives you as much as it can.

TIP

> The buffer is convenient because it lets you reread material that has scrolled off your screen. But if you want a complete record of your communications session, consider sending a copy of it to your printer or recording it in a text file. For information about printing or recording to a text file, see "Creating a Transcript of Your Communications Session," page 499.

- If the check box labeled "Beep three times when connecting or disconnecting" is selected, HyperTerminal beeps to let you know whenever a connection to a remote system is made or broken, or if the remote system sends a "bell" character (Ctrl+G). Unless you object to the sound, it's probably best to leave this option selected.

- The ASCII Setup button displays a dialog box, shown in Figure 19-11 on the next page, that lets you control how text is transferred between your computer and the remote computer. You might need to adjust one of these options if your display is unreadable while you're connected, for example. The ASCII Setup dialog box offers the following options:

  - The check box labeled "Send line ends with line feeds," when selected, causes HyperTerminal to add a line feed character each time you press Enter. You won't need to change this setting when communicating with most online services, but if you're communicating with a live person who complains that everything on his or her screen is displayed on one line, select this check box.

  - If, after you've established connection with a remote computer, the characters you type are not displayed on your screen, select the Echo Typed Characters Locally check box. On the other hand, if every character you type appears twice on your screen, deselect this check box.

  - The check box labeled "Append line feeds to incoming line ends" provides a function similar to that of the "Send line ends

FIGURE 19-11.

The ASCII Setup dialog box sets options that control the display of transmitted text in your HyperTerminal window.

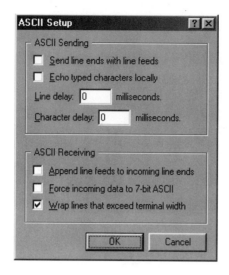

with line feeds" check box—except that it affects *your* display, not the remote system's. If everything sent by the host computer appears on a single line on your screen, select this check box. Conversely, if everything you receive is double spaced, deselect this option.

- The check box labeled "Force incoming data to 7-bit ASCII," when selected, ensures that you receive only standard letters, numbers, and punctuation—the original 128-character ASCII character set.

- The check box labeled "Wrap lines that exceed terminal width," when selected, causes HyperTerminal to start a new line when text you receive from the host computer reaches the right edge of the HyperTerminal window.

Transferring Files

Two common HyperTerminal tasks are sending *(uploading)* and receiving *(downloading)* files. For example, you might download new video drivers for your computer from the manufacturer's BBS, or you might need to upload an error log to a software publisher's support forum.

You can transfer two distinct types of files: text files and binary files.

Text files, sometimes called ASCII files, are human-readable, unformatted files that contain only letters, numbers, punctuation symbols, and basic control codes, such as line-ending codes. Text files don't require any special transfer protocols on the part of either the sending or receiving computer.

A binary file is any file that is not a text file. Formatted documents created in word processing, spreadsheet, or graphics programs, for example, are binary files. Programs, such as the ones to create word processing, spreadsheet, and graphics documents, are also binary files. When transferring binary files, you should use a file transfer protocol to ensure accurate transmission. (A *protocol* is a method for transferring files that provides error checking and, sometimes, data compression for faster transmissions.)

 NOTE

> You can also use a protocol to send or receive text files. To do so, follow the procedure for sending or receiving binary files.

Sending a Text File

To send a text file, follow these steps:

1   Open the connection you'll use for the transfer.

2   Log on to the host computer.
      Prior to sending a text file, you may need to alert the host computer to get ready for an incoming message. You can obtain the details you need from the help screens or the support staff at the remote service.

3   Choose Send Text File from the Transfer menu.
      The Select File To Send dialog box appears for you to enter the name and location of the text file you want to send.

4   Enter the name of the file to send, and then click the Open button.
      The text file appears in the HyperTerminal window. If it's a large file, the beginning of the file scrolls off the screen and you'll see the end of the file.

5   Press Enter to send the file.

TIP

When you use the method described above to send a text file, the host computer receives the file as a message incorporated in the other text of the communications session. If the text needs to be stored as a separate file, the users at the host computer will have to capture the session to a file, and then edit out the unwanted portions of the session.

To avoid causing the folks at the remote site these inconveniences, you can send the text file as a binary file—covered in the next section—so that it will be received as a separate file that's ready to use with no further fuss.

Sending a Binary File

To send a binary file, follow these steps:

1 Open the connection you'll use for the transfer.

2 Log on to the host computer.

As with sending text files, you might need to alert the operators of the host computer that you're about to send a file so they can prepare their system to receive the file. If you try to send the file before the remote system is ready, HyperTerminal waits for a ready signal from the host computer.

  3 Choose Send File from the Transfer menu.

4 In the Send File dialog box, enter the name of the file you want to send in the Filename text box. (Click the Browse button for point-and-click selection if you don't want to type the file's name and location.) Then select a file transfer protocol from the Protocol drop-down list.

The Protocol drop-down list, shown in Figure 19-12, offers a list of the available file transfer protocols.

The default protocol is Zmodem, which is a commonly used, fast, and very reliable protocol. If the host computer can use Zmodem, this is a good choice. Xmodem is even more widely used than Zmodem but is a slower protocol, so it should be a second choice. If the host computer doesn't like either of these protocols, check with its help screens or support staff to help you choose one of the other protocols.

The host computer often displays a list of available protocols when you initiate the transfer process. Just remember, the file transfer protocol on your computer and the host computer must match.

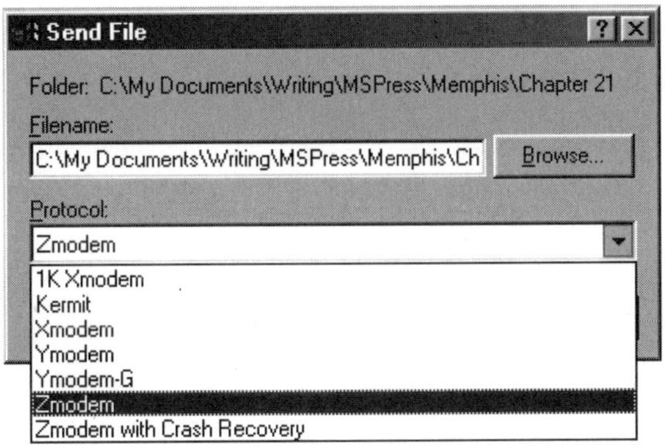

FIGURE 19-12.

The Send File dialog box displays the file transfer protocol options.

5 Click the Send button.

During the transfer, a dialog box keeps you informed about the progress of the transfer, as shown in Figure 19-13. The cps/bps button lets you change the displayed throughput—how fast data is being transferred—between characters per second (cps) and bits per second (bps). If you're sending multiple files, you can click the Skip File button to skip the current file. Use the Cancel button if you want to abort the transfer.

When the transfer is completed, the dialog box disappears.

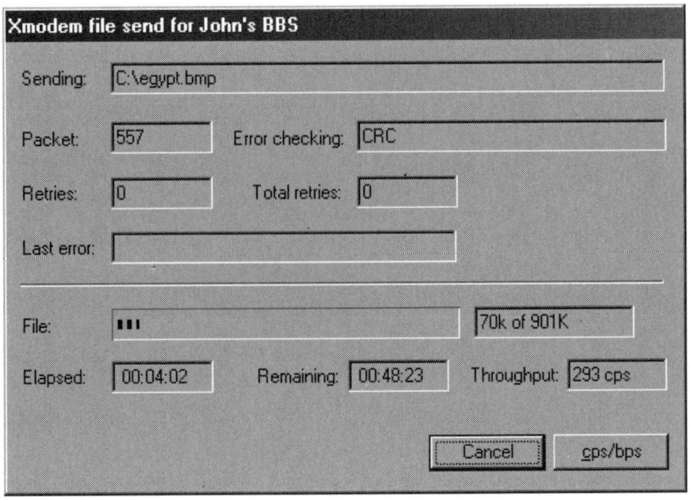

FIGURE 19-13.

You can monitor the progress of your file transfer with this dialog box.

Receiving a Binary File

To receive a binary file, follow these steps:

1 Open the connection you'll use for the transfer.

2 Log on to the host computer.

3 Use the appropriate procedures to request the file you want to receive from the host computer.

In most remote systems, you'll need to navigate to a special download or file library area before requesting a file to download. You'll also usually need to specify a transfer protocol before receiving the file. HyperTerminal's default protocol, Zmodem, is a good choice if it's available on the host computer.

 4 Choose Receive File from the Transfer menu.

The Receive File dialog box appears, as shown in Figure 19-14. If you want the downloaded file to be stored in a folder other than the default \Program Files\Accessories\HyperTerminal folder, change the entry in the Place Received File In The Following Folder box. Change the transfer protocol in the Protocol drop-down list to match the host computer's protocol if it doesn't support the default Zmodem protocol.

FIGURE 19-14.

The Receive File dialog box specifies where the received file is stored.

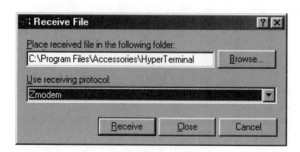

5 Click Receive and follow the on-screen directions to begin the transfer. With some protocols, such as Zmodem, the transfer begins automatically. Other protocols require you to specify a filename or otherwise signal your readiness to receive the file.

During the transfer, a dialog box similar to the one for sending files keeps you informed about the progress of the transfer. When the transfer is completed, the dialog box disappears.

Creating a Transcript of Your Communications Session

You can create a transcript of any communications session in either of two ways. You can capture (save) the session information to a text file on disk, or you can send it directly to the printer. With either method you can stop and restart the process to capture only the portion of the communications session you want.

To record your session in a text file, choose Capture Text from the Transfer menu. Enter a name for your file in the File text box of the Capture Text dialog box, and then click the Start button. Notice that the word *Capture* in the status bar is now black, indicating that capture mode is on.

You can temporarily pause capturing by choosing Pause from the Capture Text submenu. To resume capturing text, choose Resume from the Capture Text submenu. When you are finished capturing, choose Stop from the Capture Text submenu.

To create a printed transcript, choose Capture To Printer from the Transfer menu. A check mark will appear in front of the Capture To Printer command and all the session information you send or receive will be spooled to a print file in preparation for printing.

You can stop capturing to the printer—or start again—by choosing the Capture To Printer command again to toggle the check mark off and on. When you stop capturing, HyperTerminal prints the information.

As an alternative to capturing to the printer, you can print the contents of the backscroll buffer by choosing Print from the File menu. You can also print a selection of information from your online session by following this procedure:

1   In the HyperTerminal window, scroll to the information you want to print.

2   Select the information, using the standard Windows text-selection methods.

3   Choose Print from the File menu.

4   Select the Selection option button and click OK.

CHAPTER 20

Using the Multimedia Accessories

Using sound and video (which fall under the *multimedia* umbrella) can greatly enhance your computing experience. Some programs use multimedia to demonstrate concepts that aren't easily explained by words alone. Others use multimedia to provide realistic simulations of faraway places. And multimedia has more mundane uses too, such as chirping to let you know that a new e-mail message has arrived.

Most recent computers include at least the basic equipment necessary to take advantage of the multimedia capabilities in Windows. With the cost of multimedia hardware—primarily sound cards and CD-ROM drives—plummeting, it makes sense for most people to explore what multimedia can do for them.

If you haven't explored computer multimedia, or you associate the term with grade-school slide shows featuring musical accompaniment, you might find the scope of multimedia possibilities mind boggling. "Multimedia" encompasses everything from simple little beeps and dings that occur during the course of normal Windows operations to full-motion video (movies) with CD-quality sound that any Hollywood movie studio would be proud of.

Here are some of the things you can do with the multimedia tools provided by Windows:

- Add sounds to documents. For example, you can record spoken instructions for the users of a spreadsheet or a word processing document.

- Play DVD movies, games, or reference works on your DVD drive.

- Play audio CDs on your computer. You can certainly be more productive while listening to Beethoven or Pearl Jam.

The Sound of Music

When it comes to multimedia sound, there are two main varieties: wave (.WAV) and MIDI (.MID) files. The primary advantage of wave files is that they can be faithfully reproduced on any multimedia computer system. Like an audio CD, a wave file is a recording of the sound. Of course the quality of the playback is affected by the quality of the equipment, but a voice sounds pretty much like a voice and a piano like a piano, regardless of the equipment.

MIDI files are more like sheet music. Sheet music describes how the music should be played and which instruments should play which parts. If you give a piece of sheet music to two bands or orchestras, you'll get two different renditions. Because MIDI files only describe the music, they can be stored in a small fraction of the size of wave files. For this reason, many multimedia programs provide sounds in the MIDI format.

Fortunately, Windows supports the General MIDI standard that at least ensures that the correct instruments are used for playback of each part of the sound file. However, there is no guarantee that a voice or a piano will sound anything like a voice or a piano. That is determined by the MIDI capabilities on your computer's sound card.

MIDI files can be translated into real sounds by simulating the sounds with a process called FM (Frequency Modulation) synthesis, or by using samples of actual instruments. FM synthesis produces sounds that are, at best, low-quality facsimiles of what the creators of the sounds intended.

The route to realistic MIDI sounds is a sound card (or an add-on card) with wave-table sampling, which uses samples of actual musical instruments to play sounds. The results are much closer to recordings of real music and can greatly enhance the listening experience.

IV

- Attach custom sounds to various Windows events. For example, instead of the traditional "ta da" when you start Windows, you could have Windows say "Good morning" or "Time to get to work."

- See an electronic encyclopedia come to life with movies of Neil Armstrong stepping onto the moon or Martin Luther King giving his "I Have a Dream" speech. Or watch an animation of the workings of a CD player.

- Play interactive multimedia games with lifelike sound, video, and animation. Games can be a productivity tool if they help relieve stress—in case you needed an excuse.

Playing Audio CDs with CD Player

It's so simple to play audio CDs in Windows 98 that it hardly requires explanation. Insert any audio CD in your computer's CD-ROM drive. That's all there is to it. The CD Player program launches and starts playing the CD. A CD Player button appears on the taskbar, and all you have to do is listen and maybe adjust the volume.

There are a few features you can use to determine how the CD plays. Let's take a look at CD Player and its options. To open CD Player if it's already running, simply click the CD Player button on the taskbar. If CD Player isn't running, start it by clicking the Start button and then choosing Programs, Accessories, Entertainment, CD Player. The CD Player window appears, as shown in Figure 20-1.

FIGURE 20-1.

The CD Player window looks much like the front panel of a full-size CD player.

NOTE

If CD Player has not been set up on your computer, launch Add/Remove Programs in Control Panel, click the Windows Setup tab, select Multimedia, and click the Details button. Select CD Player and click OK. Click OK again in the Add/Remove Programs Properties dialog box.

Just like the CD player in your stereo system, CD Player has buttons to jump from track to track, skip forward or backward, pause, stop, start, and eject, as shown in Table 20-1.

TABLE 20-1.   CD Player Buttons

Button	Description
►	Plays the CD, beginning at the location shown in the track and time window
‖	Pauses CD playback; you can resume play by clicking the Play button or the Pause button
■	Stops playback and resets the track and time window to the beginning of the CD
⏮ ⏭	Moves to the beginning of the current track (subsequent clicks move to the previous track) or next track
◀◀ ▶▶	Skips backward (fast reverse) or forward (fast forward)
⏏	Ejects the CD from the drive

TIP

You can jump directly to a track by clicking the Track drop-down arrow and then selecting the track you want to jump to.

NOTE

The eject feature works only with CD-ROM drives that can respond to an eject command.

IV

Using the Windows Accessories

The upper left portion of the CD Player window displays track and time information. You can choose to display the track time elapsed, the track time remaining, or the time remaining for the entire disk by choosing the appropriate option from the View menu. You can also switch among these three display views by clicking in the time portion of the window.

To display a toolbar containing shortcut buttons for some of the more common features, choose Toolbar from the View menu. Table 20-2 describes the functions of the toolbar buttons. You can remove the default Disk/Track Info or Status Bar by choosing those commands from the View menu to remove their check marks.

TABLE 20-2.   CD Player Toolbar

Toolbar Icon	Description
	Allows you to edit information about the current CD, including the names of the artist, album, and tracks; also lets you select the tracks you want to hear and the order in which they play
	Changes the time and track window to display the elapsed time for the current track, the remaining time for the track, or the remaining time for the disc
	Plays tracks from the play list in random order
	Restarts the play list after the last track is played (continuous play)
	Plays only the beginning of each track (intro play)
	Includes all the audio CDs in a multidisc player if you select random, continuous, and/or intro play (multidisc play)

You can choose to play the tracks of the audio CD in random order (this is called "shuffle play" on some players), continuously (repeating the entire CD over and over), or just play a few seconds (the default is 10) of each track by choosing the option you want from the Options menu. And if you have a multidisc player (such as a CD changer), CD Player applies these playback options to all CDs if you choose Multidisc Play.

To change some of CD Player's default settings, choose Preferences from the Options menu. The Preferences dialog box appears, as shown in Figure 20-2.

FIGURE 20-2.

Choose Preferences from the Options menu to open CD Player's Preferences dialog box.

By default, CD Player stops playing the current CD when you close the CD Player program. If you want CDs to continue playing after CD Player is closed, deselect the Stop CD Playing On Exit check box. The CD continues to play until the end. Another useful option in the Preferences dialog box is Intro Play Length (Seconds). By changing this number, you can change the amount of each track that is played when the Intro Play option is chosen.

❓ SEE ALSO

For information about the Volume Control application, see "Controlling Sound Volume," page 514.

The one other item you might want to change is the volume level. To change the volume, choose Volume Control from the View menu. This command opens the Volume Control application.

Creating a Play List for an Audio CD

One of the really nice options available in the CD Player application is the capability to create a play list for each of your CDs. You can enter the title of the CD as well as the track titles. Once this information is added, CD Player recognizes the CD when you insert it, and, instead of displaying New Artist, New Title, and Track 1 or Track 2, CD Player displays the name of the disk, artist, and track.

To create a play list for the CD that's in the drive, follow these steps:

1 Choose Edit Play List from the Disc menu, or click the Edit Play List button if the toolbar is visible.

The Disc Settings dialog box appears with New Artist selected in the Artist text box, as shown in Figure 20-3.

FIGURE 20-3.

The Disc Settings dialog box lets you edit the names of titles and tracks as well as select which tracks you want to play and their order.

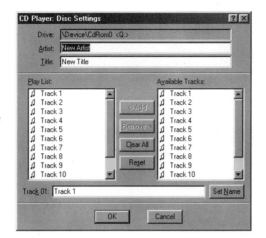

2 Type the artist's name in the Artist text box, and then press the Tab key to select New Title in the Title text box.

3 Type the name of the CD in the Title text box.

4 Click the first track you want to name in the Available Tracks list, and then type the name of the track in the Track box at the bottom of the dialog box. Press Enter or click the Set Name button to confirm the name change.

5 Repeat step 4 for all the tracks you want to name, and then click OK to close the Disc Settings dialog box.

After entering the titles, CD Player automatically recognizes the CD the next time you insert it. You'll also be able to choose tracks from the Track drop-down list by name instead of by track number, as shown in Figure 20-4, on the next page.

You can also use the Disc Settings dialog box to choose which tracks to play and in which order to play them. To remove a track, click the track you want to remove in the Play List, and then click the Remove button. To add a track, click the track in the Available Tracks list, and then click the Add button.

The easiest way to change the play order is to select the track (or tracks) you want to move in the Play List box, and then drag the selection up or down to the desired position.

FIGURE 20-4.

Once you enter information about a CD, CD Player thereafter recognizes the disk and displays the track names in the Track drop-down list.

If you want to restore the play list to the default setting, which is to play all tracks in order from first to last, click the Reset button.

Playing DVD Disks

If your system is equipped with a supported DVD drive and decoder, the Windows 98 Setup program automatically installs DVD Player. To play a DVD disk, insert the disk in your drive, open the Start menu, and choose Programs, Accessories, Entertainment, DVD Player. Your disk will start playing automatically.

Figure 20-5 shows an example of DVD Player's initial display. The readout on the left shows you what part of your disk is currently in play. To the right of this display is a set of controls that operate very much like the controls on your CD player or VCR. At the far right are some useful command buttons.

FIGURE 20-5.

DVD Player looks like a CD player with a few extra controls.

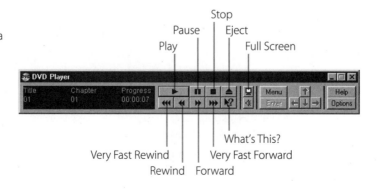

TIP

If you're unsure of what the controls do, right-click any of the controls and choose from the context menu that appears.

To make DVD Player use the full screen, click the Full Screen button, or right-click the Play button and choose Full Screen from the context menu. Once the player is using the full screen, you can click anywhere on the screen to get a menu of playback options. From this menu, you can return to a windowed display.

To see a menu of content options available on your DVD disk, click the Menu button. Once the menu appears, you can move between options by clicking the arrows to the right of the Menu button. To make a selection, click Enter.

To choose a playback language, click the Options button, choose Language, and then make your selection from the available languages. To choose a subtitle language, click Options, choose Subtitles from the Options menu, and then select from the available languages. You can use one language for sound and a different language for subtititles.

Playing Sounds, Video, and Animation with Media Player

What CD Player and DVD Player do for audio CDs and DVDs, Media Player does for other sound and video sources. If you want to play any multimedia sound or video file, start Media Player, open the file, and click the Play button.

 NOTE

You can play audio CDs from Media Player, but CD Player lets you play CDs using controls that are more like a standard CD player, and CD Player gives you more control over the way tracks are played. For information about CD Player, see "Playing Audio CDs with CD Player," page 503.

In most instances, multimedia files are part of a program, such as an encyclopedia or a game. Normally you'll access these files automatically as you explore the encyclopedia or play the game. However, Media

Player is often useful when you want to copy a multimedia file as a linked or embedded object into another document or for playing files that aren't played as part of another program.

You can learn about a media file by right-clicking that file's icon in a folder window or in Windows Explorer. Then choose Properties from the context menu. In addition to the usual file information available on the General tab in the properties dialog box, the Details tab often provides copyright, format, and length information. The Preview tab lets you play a sound or video file without involving Media Player.

To play a multimedia file using Media Player, follow these steps:

1 Start Media Player by clicking the Start button, and then choosing Programs, Accessories, Entertainment, Media Player. Media Player appears, as shown in Figure 20-6.

FIGURE 20-6.
Media Player's controls are similar to those of CD Player.

If Media Player has not been set up on your computer, launch Add/Remove Programs in Control Panel, click the Windows Setup tab, select Multimedia, and click the Details button. Select Media Player and click OK. Click OK again in the Add/Remove Programs Properties dialog box.

2 Choose Open from the File menu and use the Open dialog box to open the file you want to play.

If the file you open is a video clip, a window displaying the first frame of the video appears, as shown in Figure 20-7.

FIGURE 20-7.

Media Player opens a separate window to display .AVI (video clip) files.

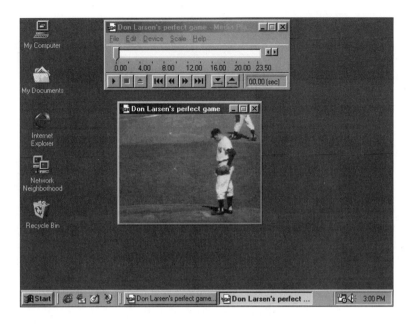

 TIP

You can also open Media Player and open a media file by right-clicking that file's icon in a folder window and choosing Open.

3 Click the Start button to begin playing the media file.

The Play button becomes a Pause button while the file is playing. You can use the other buttons to navigate through the file in much the same way as you use the buttons for CD Player. You can also use the slider and the scroll forward and scroll backward buttons to move to different positions in the file. Table 20-3, on the next page, describes each button.

 TIP

Two Windows or One

By default, when you open a video clip with Media Player, the clip is displayed in a separate window, as shown in Figure 20-7. You can combine the two windows into one with a simplified set of controls by double-clicking Media Player's title bar. Double-click the title bar again to restore the dual-window arrangement.

TABLE 20-3. Media Player Buttons

Button	Description
▶	Plays the current media file
❚❚	Pauses playback
■	Stops playback
⏏	Ejects the CD or video disc from the drive
◀◀ ▶▶	"Rewind" or "fast forward"; scrolls backward or forward through the media file
◀◀ ▶▶	Moves to the beginning of the previous or next track (if any), to the previous or next mark (if any), or to the beginning or end of the file
▼ ▲	Places a mark at the beginning and end of a selection; you can quickly jump to these marks (not available for all file types)

Media Player usually figures out which device to use to play your chosen media file. But, if it doesn't choose correctly, you can select a device from the Device menu.

The scale below the slider can be changed to Time, Frames, or Tracks, although not all of these options are available for all types of media. For example, video clip (.AVI) files allow only the Time and Frames scale options; video clips do not have "tracks." To change the scale, choose the command you want from the Scale menu.

Changing Media Options

You can change several of the options for the media clip by making choices in the Options dialog box. To open the Options dialog box, choose Options from the Edit menu. The Options dialog box appears, as shown in Figure 20-8.

FIGURE 20-8.
Media Player's Options dialog box lets you set playback and OLE options.

You can choose to have a media file automatically rewind or repeat by selecting the appropriate check boxes. The Options dialog box also lets you choose which OLE options to use for the file if you choose to link the file to or embed the file as an icon in a document you create with another program. You can, for example, choose a caption for the linked or embedded object, whether to place a border around the object, and whether to play the object in the destination document.

NOTE

The OLE options are relevant only if you intend to place the object (the media file or a portion of it) in another program. Otherwise, you don't need to bother with these items.

Linking and Embedding Media Files

SEE ALSO

For more information about linking and embedding, see Chapter 9, "Exchanging Information Using the Clipboard and OLE."

One of the primary uses for Media Player is to copy media files so they can be linked to or embedded in documents created in other programs. The procedures for linking and embedding media files are similar to those for linking and embedding any other files.

The first step to linking or embedding a media file is to open it with Media Player as described above. With the file open, choose Copy Object from the Edit menu. Then, open the program and document you want to link or embed the object in.

To embed the object, choose Paste (on the Edit menu) in the destination document. To link the object, choose Paste Special. Then select Paste Link in the Paste Special dialog box.

Controlling Sound Volume

The Volume Control program allows you to control the loudness of your computer's various sound sources. You can open the Volume Control program by itself or from either the CD Player or the Media Player program. To open Volume Control from CD Player, choose Volume Control from the View menu. To open it from Media Player, choose Volume Control from Media Player's Device menu.

> **NOTE**
>
> If Volume Control has not been set up on your computer, launch Add/Remove Programs in Control Panel, click the Windows Setup tab, select Multimedia, and click the Details button. Select Volume Control and click OK. Click OK again in the Add/Remove Programs Properties dialog box.

To open Volume Control by itself, click the Start button, and then choose Programs, Accessories, Entertainment, Volume Control. The Volume Control window appears, as shown in Figure 20-9.

> **TIP**
>
> You can also open Volume Control by double-clicking the volume icon in the taskbar's notification area.

> **NOTE**
>
> The sound sources available on your computer depend on what type of sound card you have and whether you have an internal modem. Your Volume Control window might have controls for sources different from the ones shown in Figure 20-9.

FIGURE 20-9.

The Volume Control window displays sliders for each sound source.

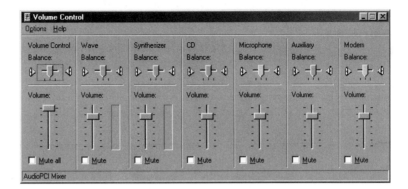

Use the sliders to adjust the balance and volume for each audio source. For example, use the CD balance and volume sliders to change the balance and volume of your CD-drive output.

The balance and volume controls marked "Volume Control" let you adjust the overall balance and volume. If the master volume is at its lowest level, it won't matter what the other levels are, you won't hear anything.

TIP

> A single click on the taskbar's volume icon brings up a slider that serves the same function as the Volume Control section of the Volume Control window—without opening the Volume Control program.

The Mute and Select check boxes let you turn off the volume for any of the audio sources. As with the master volume sliders, be careful with the Mute All check box. If Mute All is selected, all sound is turned off.

The Wave sliders control the wave (.WAV) files that are used in a number of multimedia applications. The Line-In sliders control the balance and volume of a device you might have connected to the line input of your sound card.

You can choose to display sliders for only the devices you want to control by choosing Properties from the Options menu. In the Properties dialog box, shown in Figure 20-10 on the next page, deselect the boxes for the devices you don't want to control.

FIGURE 20-10.

The Properties dialog box lets you select which sound sources you want to control.

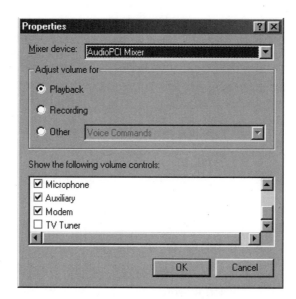

Recording Sounds with Sound Recorder

If you have a microphone attached to your sound card, you can use Sound Recorder to make your own voice recordings, which can then be added to other documents. And if your sound card has a Line In connector, you can connect a stereo receiver or other sound source to it and use Sound Recorder to make recordings from that source.

You can use voice recordings to annotate documents. For example, suppose you want to provide explicit instructions about how to interpret a particular portion of a spreadsheet—how you arrived at your assumptions, and so on. You could add those instructions to the spreadsheet so the person using it could hear the instructions in your own words—and in your own voice.

 NOTE

If Sound Recorder has not been set up on your computer, launch Add/Remove Programs in Control Panel, click the Windows Setup tab, select Multimedia, and click the Details button. Select Sound Recorder and click OK. Click OK again in the Add/Remove Programs Properties dialog box.

To make a sound recording, follow these steps:

1 Open Sound Recorder by clicking Start, and then choosing Programs, Accessories, Entertainment, Sound Recorder.

The Sound Recorder window appears, as shown in Figure 20-11.

FIGURE 20-11.
Sound Recorder lets you record your voice.

2 Choose Properties from the File menu. In the properties dialog box that appears, click Convert Now to display the Sound Selection dialog box shown in Figure 20-12.

Choose the file format and attributes you want. Higher sampling rates require more disk space but provide better quality. (Expressed in hertz, the sampling rate measures the number of times that a sound is recorded in each second.) If you find the sound quality unacceptably low, use the Attributes drop-down list to choose a higher sampling rate or 16-bit sound.

FIGURE 20-12.
The Sound Selection dialog box lets you select recording attributes and indicates the amount of disk space required for each combination of attributes.

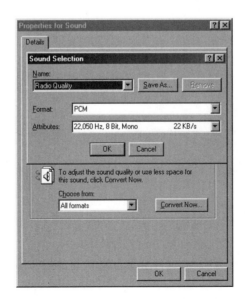

3 Turn on the microphone, if it has an on/off switch, and then click the Record button and start talking. (See Table 20-4 for a description of the buttons.)

As you record, the green line expands and contracts like an oscilloscope to indicate sound levels. You can see how much time has elapsed. The maximum recording length is 60 seconds.

4 When you finish the recording, click the Stop button.

5 Choose Save from the File menu, and then name the file if you haven't already.

Sound Recorder saves its documents as wave files and gives them the filename extension .WAV.

You can embed a sound file in any application that supports OLE linking and embedding. To do so, follow these steps:

1 Open or record the file you want to embed.

2 Use Sound Recorder's Copy command to put the sound data on the Clipboard.

3 Activate the application into which you want to embed the sound (the destination application).

TABLE 20-4.   Sound Recorder Buttons

Button	Description
◄◄	Moves to the beginning of the sound document
►►	Moves to the end of the sound document
►	Plays the sound
■	Stops playing or recording
●	Begins recording

IV

4   Put the cursor where you want the sound file to be embedded. Then use the destination program's Paste command.

In the destination document, the embedded sound file is displayed as a small microphone icon. To play the sound, double-click the icon.

Controlling Input Levels for Recording

② SEE ALSO

For more information about the Volume Control program, see "Controlling Sound Volume," page 514.

You can control the input volume level for the sounds that you record. To make volume adjustments, use the Volume Control program. With the Volume Control program running, choose Properties from the Options menu to display the Properties dialog box. Click the Recording option button and click OK. Balance and volume sliders let you adjust the recording volume level for each sound source.

Editing Sound Files

Sound Recorder's Edit menu has six editing commands, in addition to the Copy command.

The Insert File and Mix With File commands allow you to combine two or more sound files. To use either command, first position the slider at the point in the current file where you want the incoming file to appear. The Position indicator to the left of the oscilloscope display will help you find the appropriate spot.

The Insert File command adds a sound file at the current location and moves the remainder of the file forward. The Mix With File command superimposes the incoming sound file on whatever sound data is already at the current location.

The Paste Insert and Paste Mix commands combine sounds in a similar manner, except that they use the Clipboard as their source instead of a sound file.

The two Delete commands on the Edit menu simply delete data from the current location to the beginning or the end of the file.

You can also edit a sound file with commands on the Effects menu, shown in Figure 20-13, on the next page.

FIGURE 20-13.

The Effects menu commands let you distort sounds.

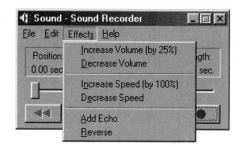

These commands actually change the sound data that makes up your file, not merely the playback mode. For example, if you increase the speed of a file and then use the Save command, the file plays at the increased speed each time you open it.

Playing Games with Windows

If you use only the business and productivity programs in Windows, you're missing a lot. Windows 98 is a terrific gaming environment, and playing games can be a great way to get some entertainment value from your computer investment.

What Windows 98 Brings to the Gaming Table

When it comes to playing games, Windows has finally come of age. If you are a computer-game enthusiast, you already know that early versions of Windows were not the best gaming platforms. For the most part, those versions were too slow for many non-Windows-based action games, and offered only limited multimedia capabilities.

Windows 95 changed everything. Almost all the multimedia advances that Windows 95 provided are as beneficial to complex multimedia games as they are to other multimedia programs. In fact, because games can be more demanding and resource intensive than any other software category, Windows is truly a blessing for avid gamers.

SEE ALSO

For information about multimedia, see Chapter 20, "Using the Multimedia Accessories." For information about Plug and Play, see "Plug and Play: The End of the Hardware Blues?," page 333.

Until the release of Windows 95, Windows-based games made up only a tiny fraction of the total game market. The vast majority of games were MS-DOS–based programs. The reason for this situation is that the layers of software that Windows added between the game and your computer exacted a tremendous performance penalty. Games that employ incredibly complex sound and video, such as the wildly popular DOOM from id Software, were originally written as MS-DOS–based games so they could have the maximum direct control of your computer's hardware.

Here's what Windows 98 brings to the gaming table:

- Built-in joystick support lets you just plug in a joystick, follow Windows through the calibration routine, and play. (Your computer must have a game port, which typically is included on a sound card or a multifunction I/O card.) Windows 98 also supports forced-feedback joysticks and USB game controllers.

- Plug and Play makes the installation and setup of the requisite gaming hardware—sound cards, joysticks, CD-ROM drives, and so on—nearly painless.

- Windows 98's support for DirectX allows game developers to deliver faster graphics and video performance, comparable to or better than what was possible with MS-DOS.

- Support for multiple monitors provides additional opportunities for game developers.

- Multiplayer support means more—and better—multiplayer games. The popularity of multiplayer games is evidenced by the number of network and modem DOOM players. To show off the multiplayer capabilities built into Windows, a multiplayer version of Hearts is included. (For information about the Hearts game, see "Playing Hearts," page 527.) For other kinds of multiplayer gaming experiences, point your browser to www.zone.com, Microsoft's online "gaming zone."

Games That Come with Windows 98

You don't have to rush right out and buy games to test your gaming ability. Windows includes several games that provide a nice diversion from the more business-oriented computing that you probably have to spend the bulk of your time on.

This chapter covers the basic concepts, rules, and strategies for playing the games that come with Windows. All the games are in the Games folder, so the procedure for starting any of them is the same. Open the Start menu, choose Programs, Accessories, Games, and then choose the game you want to play.

NOTE

If the games included with Windows have not been installed on your computer, launch Add/Remove Programs in Control Panel, click the Windows Setup tab, select Accessories, and click the Details button. Select Games and click OK.

TIP

Hiding a Game Window
Most of the games included with Windows have a "boss key." Simply press Esc to quickly reduce the game window to a taskbar icon—and not let onlookers know what you're *really* doing.

Playing Minesweeper

Minesweeper is a game of logic and deduction. The objective is to uncover all the squares in a minefield (presented as a grid of squares) that don't contain mines, and mark the squares that do, as quickly as possible—all without "stepping on" a mine.

When you start Minesweeper, a gridlike minefield appears, as shown in Figure 21-1.

FIGURE 21-1.

Minesweeper depicts a "minefield," where each square in the grid might be concealing a mine.

The game starts when you make your first move by clicking a square to uncover it. Each square contains a number or a mine, or it is blank. If the square contains a number, the number indicates how many mines are in the surrounding squares. If the square you reveal is blank, there are no mines in the adjacent squares, so the surrounding squares are uncovered automatically. If you click a square that contains a mine, you lose and all the mines are displayed.

If you win a game (no small feat), the smiley face between the counters appears with sunglasses. If you lose, the smiley face starts frowning. Figure 21-2 shows a winning game and a losing game.

To start a new game, choose New from the Game menu, or click the smiley face.

FIGURE 21-2.

A winner (left) and a loser. Notice that all the mines are displayed in the losing game.

The counter in the upper left portion of the Minesweeper window indicates the number of unmarked mines in the minefield. The counter in the upper right portion of the Minesweeper window displays the elapsed game time from the instant you uncover the first square. The clock stops when you finish the game—or when it finishes you.

You can mark squares that you think contain mines by right-clicking them. When you mark a square, the number in the counter displaying the total number of mines is decreased even if the square doesn't actually contain a mine. This can be misleading.

If you're not certain that a square contains a mine, right-click twice to mark it with a question mark. If you mark a square with a question mark, you can clear the question mark by right-clicking. You can then uncover the square by clicking the square or mark it as a mine square by right-clicking again. You can disable the feature that lets you mark squares with question marks by choosing Marks (?) from the Game menu to clear its check mark.

Customizing Minesweeper's Levels of Play

Minesweeper offers three levels of play—Beginner, Intermediate, and Expert. You can also specify custom levels. To specify the degree of difficulty, choose the level from the Game menu.

The Beginner level is the default and presents a grid of 8 rows by 8 columns with 10 mines. Intermediate uses a 16 by 16 grid with 40 mines. Expert uses a 16 by 30 grid with 99 mines.

You can set a custom level by choosing Custom from the Game menu. The Custom Field dialog box appears, as shown in Figure 21-3.

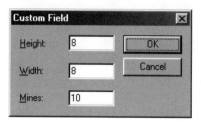

Enter the number of rows you want (up to a maximum of 24) in the Height box, the number of columns (up to 30) in the Width box, and the number of mines (from 10 to 667, depending on grid size). Then click the OK button.

NOTE

Whichever level you choose becomes the new default.

Keeping Score

You're playing against the clock, so you improve your score by winning as quickly as possible. As soon as you win (or lose), the timing counter stops so you can see how long the game lasted.

Minesweeper keeps track of the best winning times for each of the three predefined levels but not for custom levels. To display your best times, choose Best Times from the Game menu.

Strategies for Successful Minesweeping

Your first click in a new game is a "safe" one. You won't blow up with this first move, no matter where you make it. Your second click is another matter, however.

Once you've uncovered a few squares, you can start to deduce which squares are the most likely to be concealing mines. The following tips might help:

■ Remember that the number that is revealed in a square you click indicates the number of mines in the surrounding squares.

- If you uncover a square labeled 1, and there is only one covered square next to it, it must contain a mine. Mark the uncovered square by right-clicking it.

- If you're not sure about the contents of a square, mark it with a question mark (two right-clicks), and then clear it or mark it as a mine square later.

- If you point at an uncovered square that contains a number and press both mouse buttons, Minesweeper flashes the surrounding squares. If you have already marked the requisite number, Minesweeper uncovers the remaining surrounding squares, saving you the time and effort of clicking each one individually.

Playing Hearts

Yes, this is the same traditional card game you played with grandma. The only difference is that the other players can be anywhere in the world, connected only by a modem or a network. (To play Hearts via modem, players must connect to the network using Dial-Up Networking.) And if you can't rustle up anyone to play with, you can play against the computer.

When you start Hearts, the dialog box shown in Figure 21-4 is displayed. (Hearts bypasses this dialog box if your computer is not connected to a network.)

FIGURE 21-4.

When you start Hearts, you have a choice of joining someone else's game or starting your own.

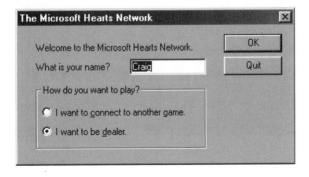

■ To join an existing game and play with others on a network, select the I Want To Connect To Another Game option button. If you select this option and click OK, Hearts then asks for the name of the dealer's computer. (Note that it's not looking for the dealer's name, but the name of the dealer's *computer.*)

■ To play a stand-alone game against the computer or to initiate a game with others, select I Want To Be Dealer.

To begin a new game, press F2 or choose New Game from the Game menu. (Only the dealer can start a new game, so if you chose the first option, you must wait for the dealer.)

Rules of the Game

The goal of Hearts is to end up with the lowest score. When you begin a new game, each player is dealt a hand of 13 cards. As shown in Figure 21-5, your cards are face up while the other players' cards are face down.

FIGURE 21-5.

An opening Hearts hand.

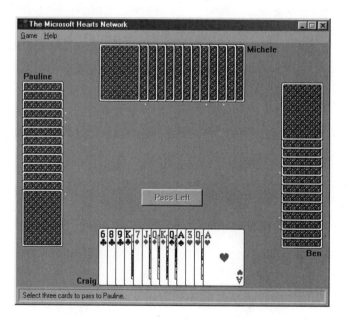

The game begins with each player selecting three cards to pass to another player. To pass cards, click each card you want to pass, and when you have selected three cards, click the Pass button.

After the cards have been passed, the player with the two of clubs begins play. Play moves in a clockwise direction—players must play a club if they have one; otherwise, they may play any card except a game card (the queen of spades or any heart). To play a card, you simply click the card when it's your turn.

Each round of play is called a *trick*, and the player with the highest card in the lead suit (the suit that began the trick) takes the trick. The player who takes the trick gets points for each heart or for the queen of spades; the same player then leads the next trick. The first trick is the only one that must begin with a specific suit. Players must always follow the lead suit unless they don't have a card in that suit; in that case, they may play any card.

Play continues until all cards are played. This is considered a *hand*. At the end of each hand, Hearts displays the scores and then begins the next hand. The game ends when one player accumulates 100 points or more. The player with the lowest score at that point is the winner.

You can check out the score of the current game by choosing Score from the Game menu. A Score Sheet dialog box appears with the scores for all the players.

The rules of hearts are pretty simple:

- The queen of spades counts as 13 points.

- Each heart counts as 1 point.

- No points are awarded for other cards.

- Aces are considered high cards.

- In order to end up with a low score, you want to avoid taking tricks that include the queen of spades or any hearts.

- You can't play a game card (the queen of spades or any heart) on the first trick.

- You can't lead with a heart until hearts have been "broken" (unless you have no other suits). Hearts are broken when a player uses a heart in a trick.

Shooting the Moon

This technique can be the fast track to winning at Hearts. If you can win all of the hearts and the queen of spades in one hand, you get 0 points and the other players each get 26 points. If you are dealt a hand with lots of high-value hearts and spades, consider trying this strategy. Be careful though! If any other player gets even one heart or the queen of spades, the strategy fails and you can end up with unwanted points.

Hearts Options

After you've played a few games of Hearts, you might want to customize certain options. Hearts provides a variety of options to suit you:

- By default, sounds are turned off. If you turn on sounds, Hearts uses sounds to proclaim when hearts are broken, when the queen of spades is played, and so on. You can turn on sounds, or turn them off again, by choosing Sounds from the Game menu.

- To change the animation speed, choose Options from the Game menu and select the Slow, Normal, or Fast option button.

- To change the names of the computer players—when you don't have four live players—choose Options from the Game menu and then enter the names you want to use in the Computer Player Names text boxes.

Strategies for Successful Hearts Play

The most obvious strategy is simply to try to get rid of your hearts, the queen of spades, and other high cards as quickly as possible. But there's more to it—if there weren't, where would the challenge be? The following tips and guidelines will help in your quest for that winning hand:

- If the cards you're dealt include the queen of spades, don't give away the ace or king of spades if you have them. You can often use these cards to take a trick when otherwise you would have to play the queen of spades.

- Unless you're trying to shoot the moon (or trying to prevent someone else from doing so), try not to take any tricks that include hearts or the queen of spades.

- Try to get rid of the queen of spades as quickly as possible. Until you get rid of it, don't worry too much about your hearts.

- Notice which player takes the queen of spades and try to determine whether that player may be trying to shoot the moon by taking all the hearts as well. If you see that happening, it's in your interest to win at least one heart, if possible, to thwart the attempt.

- Try to get rid of all the cards in one or more suits. When you have no more cards in any one suit, you can then play any card you like when another player leads with that suit.

Playing Solitaire

The Solitaire game that comes with Windows 98 is a computerized version of the addictive card game known as Klondike. If you've played solitaire with a deck of cards, you'll have no trouble adjusting to the program.

When the game is started, the deck appears in the upper left corner of the playing area with all the cards face down, and placeholders for four suit stacks appear in the upper right corner. Below the deck and the suit stack placeholders are seven row stacks, as shown in Figure 21-6.

FIGURE 21-6.

The opening Solitaire window.

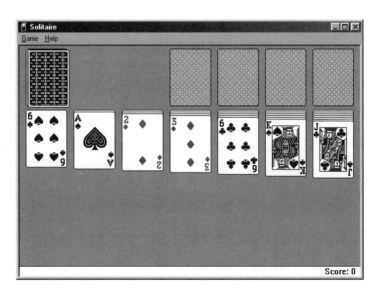

The seven row stacks below the deck and suit stacks have one face-up card each. The row stack on the left end has only one card. The number of cards in each row stack increases by one, so the row stack on the right has seven cards.

The objective of the game—just like the card game—is to build four complete suit stacks, each containing all the cards of one suit from ace through king.

Rules of the Game

You can add cards to the row stacks from the deck or from other row stacks in decreasing order and alternating color. For example, you can move a black three onto a red four.

You can add cards to the suit stacks only in consecutive, ascending order. You can move cards to the suit stack from the top of the deck or from the last card in a row stack.

To move cards from one place to another, drag them. As a shortcut for moving a card to the suit stacks, you can double-click the card. For example, if you double click an ace, it automatically jumps to an empty suit stack.

If you create an empty row stack by moving some cards, you must use a king to start that row stack.

When you move cards in the row stacks, you'll eventually uncover a face-down card. You can turn over a face-down card by clicking it.

After exhausting all the available moves, you can deal more cards from the deck by clicking the deck. By default, three cards are dealt when you click the deck, but you must use the top card first. If the top card is an ace, double-click it to move it to an empty suit stack. It the card is not an ace, but it can be used in a row stack or an existing suit stack, drag it there. If you can't move the card anywhere, click the deck again to deal another three cards. If you run through all the cards in the deck, you can turn over the dealt cards by clicking the circle that appears when the last card has been dealt.

Figure 21-7 shows a Solitaire game in progress with all four suit stacks under construction. Notice the circle to the left of the cards that have been dealt.

FIGURE 21-7.

Click the circle to turn over the dealt cards so you can go through the deck again.

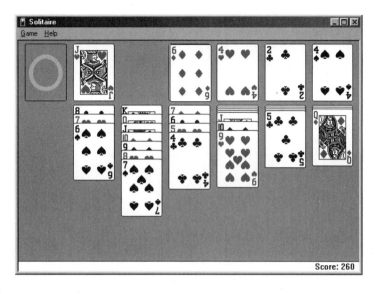

 NOTE

When you get to the point that you can run through all the cards in the deck without being able to make any additional moves, the game is over.

Changing Game Options

To change the game's options, choose Options from the Game menu. The Options dialog box appears, as shown in Figure 21-8.

FIGURE 21-8.

The Options dialog box lets you select dealing and scoring options.

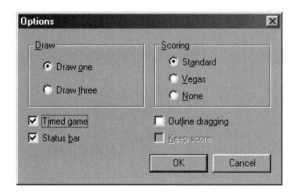

The Draw Three option specifies that three cards are dealt when you click the deck. You can select the Draw One option to have only one card presented each time you click the deck, which makes the game less challenging—purists might even call it cheating. (If you select Draw One while using Vegas-style scoring, however, you're allowed only one pass through the deck.)

The Timed Game option lets you choose whether to time the game or not. If you deselect the Status Bar check box, you won't be able to see your score or time.

 TIP

> If you're using a slower computer and you find that cards move in a jerky fashion when you drag them, select the Outline Dragging option. With this check box selected, you'll drag only an outline of the card, which puts less stress on your computer's processing power.

The scoring options, Standard, Vegas, and None, are described in the next section.

In addition to making functional changes to the game with the Options dialog box, you can change the design that appears on your face-down cards by choosing Deck from the Game menu to display the Select Card Back dialog box. Just click the design that strikes your fancy, and then click the OK button.

Scoring

Solitaire lets you choose one of two methods for scoring your games. Or you can choose not to keep score. You select scoring options in the Options dialog box, shown in Figure 21-8, on the previous page. (To display this dialog box, choose Options from the Game menu.) By default, Solitaire uses Standard scoring and game timing, which awards points for various moves and deducts points for other moves and for playing too slowly.

When using Standard scoring, you receive 10 points for every card you move to a suit stack, 5 points for every card you move to a row stack, and 5 points if you turn over a card in a row stack. You lose 15 points if you move a card from a suit stack to a row stack, 20 points each time you turn the deck after the third pass through the deck (if you're using the default Draw Three option), and you lose 100 points each time you turn over the deck (if you're using the Draw One option).

When the Timed Game option is on, you lose 2 points for every ten seconds of play, but you'll receive bonus points at the end of a fast game. The faster your game, the more bonus points you'll receive.

If you select Vegas scoring, you start the game by betting $52 and are awarded $5 for every card you move to a suit stack. The objective of the game when playing with Vegas scoring is to win back your $52 and more. Solitaire tracks your cumulative winnings if you also select the Keep Score check box.

With Vegas scoring, you're limited to three passes through the deck if you select the Draw Three option, or only one pass if you select Draw One.

Strategy Tips

Even though the objective of the game is to build up your suit stacks, you might find it useful to move a card from a suit stack to a row stack to make additional moves possible.

You can move a group of cards from one row stack to another by dragging the highest number card that you want to move and dropping it on the other row stack.

Pay attention to all the possible moves as you play. It's easy to be lulled into ignoring some possible moves as you focus on the most obvious. For example, after using one of the cards you were dealt, you might find that additional moves become possible between row stacks, or from row stacks to suit stacks.

TIP

You can undo any card move by choosing Undo from the Game menu.

Playing FreeCell

FreeCell is in some ways similar to Solitaire. The objective is to stack all of the cards in their respective suits, beginning with the ace. What's different about this game is that all of the cards are dealt face up—there's nothing hidden. Figure 21-9, on the next page, shows a FreeCell game in progress.

FIGURE 21-9.

The objective of FreeCell is to move cards to the home cells in the upper right corner.

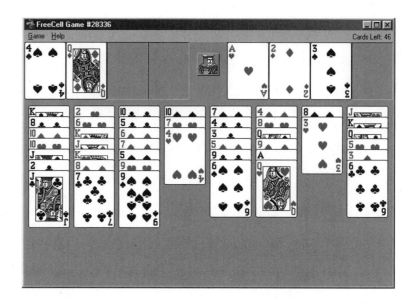

The four rectangles in the upper left are the free cells. During play, you move cards to the free cells to get them out of the way temporarily. Each free cell can hold only one card; you cannot stack cards in a cell. In Figure 21-9, several low-numbered cards were uncovered by moving the four of spades and the queen of diamonds from the deck to free cells.

The four rectangles in the upper right are the home cells. That's where you build stacks for each suit, beginning with the ace. In Figure 21-9, notice that the ace of hearts has been moved to a home cell, but the two of hearts is tucked away at the top of the second column. The trick is to somehow move the rest of the cards in the column out of the way in order to get the two of hearts stacked on its home cell.

To move a card, click to select it, and then click where you want the card moved. You can cancel a move by clicking the card again. As a shortcut, you can double-click a card in the columns to move it directly to an open free cell.

Rules of the Game

You win FreeCell by moving all the cards to the home cells. Following are the legal moves in FreeCell:

- Only the bottom card in each column and cards in the free cells can be moved.

- The bottom card in any column can be moved to any empty free cell.

- Cards can be moved to a home cell from the bottom of any column or from a free cell. You can move a card to a home cell, however, only if the card is the next highest in a suit. The bottom card on each home cell must be an ace. The next card must be the two of that same suit, and so on.

- Cards can be stacked within the deck as in a traditional solitaire game (cards of opposite colors in descending order). Using Figure 21-9 as an example, you could move the jack of clubs in the first column onto the queen of hearts in the sixth column. This would free the two of clubs. You can move cards back and forth between the deck and the free cells.

- Any card can be moved to an empty column.

NOTE

> The title bar flashes once if you have only one legal move available.

Strategy Tips

FreeCell can be extremely frustrating at first—don't expect to jump right in and win every game. Relax and scope out the situation—FreeCell becomes more interesting as you become more familiar with it. Here are some tips:

- Study the deck. Know where your aces and other low cards are and get a sense of what you have to do to get at them.

- Try to keep at least one free cell open. Don't move a card to a free cell just because you can—if you do, you won't have an empty free cell when you really need it.

- Empty columns can be even more useful than empty free cells, because you can stack more than one card in them.

 TIP

> Sometimes you can't tell the suit of a card that's partially covered by other cards. To see the covered card entirely, right-click it.

Changing Game Options

You can play 32,000 different hands of FreeCell. When you press F2 or choose New Game from the Game menu, FreeCell selects a game at random. To select a specific game, press F3 or choose Select Game from the Game menu, and enter the number of the game you want to play. If you want to play the same hand over, choose Restart Game.

Running MS-DOS–Based Games Under Windows 98

Along with making Windows a friendlier environment for Windows-based games, Windows 98 also goes a long way toward accommodating MS-DOS–based games that need most of the computer's resources.

? SEE ALSO

For more information about using MS-DOS–based programs in Windows 98, see Chapter 11, "Running MS-DOS–Based Programs."

Windows 98 gives MS-DOS–based programs more memory and better access to the computer's hardware than previous versions of Windows. You'll probably find that MS-DOS–based programs that simply refused to run under Windows 3.x run flawlessly under Windows 98 because of its improved management of memory and other resources.

Most MS-DOS–based games work with Windows and require no modification. However, if you do encounter difficulties running an MS-DOS–based game, here are some steps you can take to overcome the problems:

? SEE ALSO

For more information about memory settings, see "Options on the Memory Tab," page 293.

■ Windows automatically runs most graphics-oriented MS-DOS–based games in a full screen. However, if a particular game isn't running in a full screen, you can press Alt+Enter to enlarge the window to a full screen. This generally yields better and more stable performance.

? SEE ALSO

For more information about full-screen display, see "Full Screen or Window?," page 277.

■ You might need to increase the amount of memory available to the game. Open the program's property sheet by opening the folder that contains the program, right-clicking the program's icon, and choosing Properties from the context menu. When the Properties dialog box appears, click the Memory tab and modify the memory settings as necessary.

SEE ALSO

For more information about MS-DOS mode, see "Running a Program in MS-DOS Mode," page 291.

■ If all else fails, run the game in MS-DOS mode. To do this, right-click the program's icon and choose Properties from the context menu. When the Properties dialog box appears, click the Program tab, and then click the Advanced button to display the Advanced Program Settings dialog box. In the Advanced Program Settings dialog box, select the MS-DOS Mode check box. MS-DOS mode should be used as a last resort because all other programs must be closed before starting the game.

TIP

If you try everything you can think of and a game still refuses to run, try calling the manufacturer of the program. Perhaps they have a solution—or a later version—that allows the game to run under Windows 98.

CHAPTER 22

Using WebTV for Windows and WaveTop

If your computer is equipped with a sound card and television tuner capability, you can use WebTV for Windows to watch your favorite programs. WebTV can turn your entire monitor into a television set. Or you can display WebTV in one window while you do something useful in another. WebTV can also download program listings for your local broadcast or cable services, and you can search the resulting program guide by program title, category, or performer. You can even set up reminders so that a message appears on your screen shortly before a favorite program is about to begin.

Windows 98 also includes a program called WaveTop that brings Internet content to your system via broadcast or cable television signal. If you have a television tuner card, you can let WaveTop gather news, sports scores, market data, weather forecasts, and other information from selected Web sites all through the day—and night, if you leave your computer on. The information arrives unobtrusively through the tuner card and gets stored on your hard disk, waiting for the moment when you have time to read it.

Because WaveTop is advertiser-supported, it costs you nothing to use it. You don't need an account with an Internet service provider, and you don't even need a modem.

Running WebTV for the First Time

If you installed WebTV for Windows, you'll find a menu item for it on your Start menu. Choose Programs, Accessories, Entertainment. Windows also puts an icon for WebTV on the default Quick Launch toolbar.

 NOTE

> If WebTV has not been installed on your computer, launch Add/Remove Programs in Control Panel, click the Windows Setup tab, select WebTV For Windows, and click OK.

The first time you run WebTV, a wizard introduces you to the program and walks you through some simple configuration steps. The wizard asks whether you're watching on a desktop monitor, a large computer monitor to be seen from across the room, or a standard television set. Then it scans for available channels so that you don't have to flip the channel selector through a lot of white noise when you're cruising for content. Next it requests your ZIP Code so that it can get an initial set of program listings for your area.

You can download program listings in either of two ways—via the Internet or the vertical blanking interval (a portion of the television signal not used for programming). The Internet is quicker, but if you don't have an Internet connection you can still get your listings. Click the StarSight link to download from the Internet, or click the Get Now button to use the VBI (vertical blanking interval). If you opt for Internet download, you'll need to supply your ZIP Code again when you get to the StarSight download page. StarSight then displays a menu consisting of your local broadcast signals plus all cable services operating in your area. Click the appropriate link and the download begins. When the download is complete, close your browser and click the wizard's Next button.

After you finish the initial download, the configuration wizard offers to update your listings at a prescribed time every day. If you leave your computer on after hours, specify a regular update time and click Next.

On the following screen, you'll have the opportunity to specify which channel you want your VCR, DVD player, or game player to use. Finally, you'll get a quick tour of the program guide, and then you can click the Finish button and get on to watching TV.

Watching TV

WebTV for Windows normally devotes your entire screen—including the area occupied by your taskbar—to the television picture, but you can move the mouse pointer to the top of the screen or press F10 at any time to display the "TV Banner," an approximate equivalent to a normal window's title bar, and a toolbar. (See Figure 22-1.) A second press of F10 makes the TV Banner and toolbar go away, although they will do that of their own accord if you simply wait a few seconds. (Depending on the kind of system you're watching, you might also be able to display and hide the TV Banner and toolbar by clicking the Menu button on your remote control.)

FIGURE 22-1.
WebTV uses the full screen to display a program except when you display the TV Banner.

A channel selector appears at the left side of the TV Banner. You can click the up and down arrows to switch channels. Alternatively, you can press Page Up and Page Down (whether or not the TV Banner is visible) or simply type the number of the channel you want and then press the Enter key.

Provided you have downloaded the program listings for your area and service, the TV Banner also displays the name of the program you're watching—a feature you'll find helpful if you're merely surfing.

If a remote control is not available for your hardware setup, you'll need to turn your speaker system's volume knob or use the Volume Control program to make the sound louder or softer. (You probably have a Volume Control icon in the notification area of your task bar. If you don't, open the Start menu and choose Programs, Accessories, Entertainment, Volume Control.) WebTV does not provide a software control for this function, nor does it include a mute command.

At the right side of the TV Banner, you'll find close and restore buttons. Click restore if you want to see something else on screen while WebTV is running. Once you restore the window, you'll also have a minimize button at your disposal. Note, though, that minimizing WebTV does not turn the sound off.

 TIP

> You can also use keyboard shortcuts to switch programs: press Alt+Tab to switch to another open window, or press Ctrl+Esc to open the Start menu.

The toolbar includes a button that takes you to the program guide, a Settings button, and a Help button. The Settings button lets you remove channels from the channel selector (in case there are some you never want to watch) or add channels (in case the initial channel scan failed to find some that you do want to watch). You can also used the Settings command to turn closed captions on or off.

To the right of these three toolbar buttons, you'll find an additional button that says either Add or Remove. Add lets you designate the current channel as a "favorite." Once you've done this, that channel gets a toolbar button of its own, allowing you to reselect the channel with a single mouse click. You can display up to five favorites on the toolbar. If you've already made the current channel a favorite, the Add button becomes a Remove button—in case you change your mind.

Using the Program Guide

The program guide consists of two components—a listings grid (shown in Figure 22-2) and a search facility. To get to the guide, choose channel 99 or click the Guide icon on the toolbar.

FIGURE 22-2.

The program guide's Guide tab lets you see program listings by channel and time.

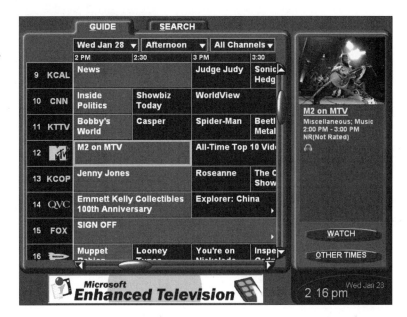

Programs that are currently running appear at the left side of the listings grid. As you scroll through channels in this column, a live preview of the selected channel appears in the thumbnail window at the upper right corner. To switch a current program to full-screen view, click either the thumbnail window or the Watch button.

If you select programs that are not currently running, you see only the WebTV logo in the thumbnail window, but you can read a description of the selected program below the window. If you plan to watch or record a program that's coming up, you can select it and click the Remind button. You'll see a dialog box similar to the one shown in Figure 22-3, on the next page. You can ask to be reminded on one occasion only or every time the show is about to run.

FIGURE 22-3.

WebTV can remind you of upcoming programs and switch the channel to facilitate recording.

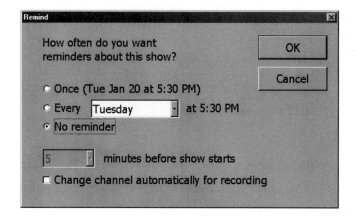

Drop-down lists at the top of the listings grid allow you to see listings for a different date or time of day. A third drop-down list, not shown in Figure 22-2 on the previous page, lets you filter the listings grid to show only those channels you've designated as favorites.

Searching for Programs

The program guide's Search tab, shown in Figure 22-4, gives you two different ways to find programs. You can select a programming category from the list at the left, or you can enter a search string in the Search For box. Either way, you get a grid of channels and program titles in the main part of the window. You can use the drop-down lists above the grid to change the time scope for your search or the sorting order of the grid. (You can sort by either time or title.)

When you select any program in the grid, text describing that program appears in the right side of the window. If the program is running now, a live preview appears in the thumbnail window.

In the Search For box, you can type a program's name, part of its name, the name of an actor, or anything else that might appear in the descriptive text at the right side of the window. It doesn't matter whether you use lowercase or uppercase letters, but you'll want to type enough characters to focus your search properly. Typing "win," for example, will produce a listing of all shows having to do with Oprah Winfrey, Kate Winslow, "growing pains," or "Windows 98." Typing "winf" will, in most cases, get you only Oprah.

FIGURE 22-4.
On the Search tab, you can find programs by category or by typing in the Search For box.

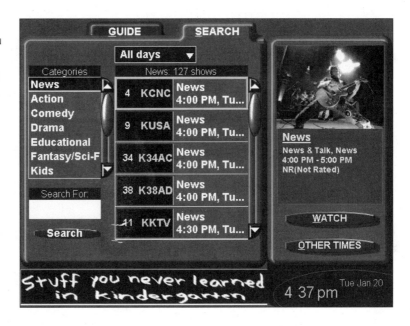

Like the Guide tab, the Search tab includes a Watch/Remind button. Clicking Watch takes you to a currently running program. Clicking Remind lets you set up a reminder.

Watching Interactive TV

Certain programs may offer various kinds of interactive enhancements—such as information about performers or sports statistics. If enhancements are available, a blue icon emblazoned with the letter *I* appears next to the program's entry in the program guide. When you're watching such a program, a similar icon appears in the TV Banner. (A red dot in the TV Banner means interactive TV is not available for this program.) To make the enhancements visible, click the icon in the TV Banner. (If a check mark appears beside the icon, enhancements are already turned on.)

Using WaveTop

WaveTop, shown in Figure 22-5 on the next page, was available only in a prerelease demo version at the time this book went to press. What follows is a brief overview, based on that demo version and accompanying fact sheets.

FIGURE 22-5.

With WaveTop, Internet content arrives all day long— free of charge— through your television tuner card.

Channel bar

Navigation bar

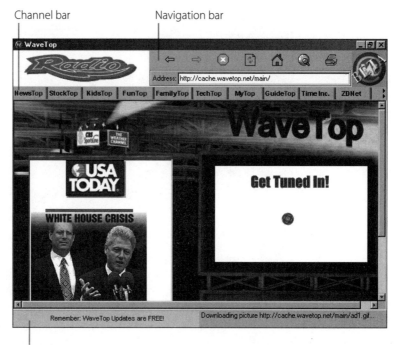

Flash panel

🛈 **SEE ALSO**

For information about Internet Explorer, see Chapter 25, "Using Internet Explorer."

WaveTop takes advantage of a portion of the television signal, called the *vertical blanking interval (VBI)*, that is not used for ordinary television transmission. The company behind WaveTop, WavePhore, Inc., contracts with providers of general-interest Internet content. These providers deliver information to WavePhore, which transmits it to Public Broadcasting Service (PBS) stations across the United States. The latter, in turn, deliver the Internet content to you via the VBI. Provided your computer has a television tuner and receives an acceptably strong PBS signal (via antenna or cable), you can set your system to receive the Internet content that interests you. Your tuner card simply takes in the VBI content whenever your computer is on and stores the material you want on your hard disk. The WaveTop viewer lets you peruse this material at your leisure, using an interface similar to that of Internet Explorer.

WaveTop requires a 90 MHz or faster Pentium processor and lots of hard disk space. You'll need only about 8 MB of disk space for the program itself (assuming you already have Internet Explorer installed; if you don't use Internet Explorer as your default Web browser, WaveTop installs it, and for that you need another 22 MB). But you should allow at least an additional 70 MB for downloaded content.

The first time you use WaveTop, the program scans your television signal to find PBS channels. This process can take up to ten minutes.

The WaveTop User Interface

At the top of the WaveTop window, you'll find two toolbars—a navigation bar and a channel bar. Buttons on the navigation bar work exactly like their counterparts in Internet Explorer. The Back and Forward buttons allow you to retrace your steps through a sequence of pages. The Stop button interrupts whatever page you're currently loading, and the Refresh button lets you reload the current page. The Home button takes you to WaveTop's "home" page—the page that WaveTop displays when you initially run it. The Search button lets you search for particular Internet content, and the Print button sends the current page to the printer of your choice.

The channel bar lets you move between categories of WaveTop content. It also includes a MyTop tool, which lets you select the content you want to receive, and a GuideTop tool, which presents a three-hour schedule of broadcast times and the content that will be available.

At the lower left corner of the WaveTop window is the flash panel. If the system has urgent information to display—such as a disaster alert in effect for your location—that information appears here. Otherwise what you'll see here, as well as in various other parts of the WaveTop window, are words from WaveTop's many sponsors.

Selecting WaveTop Content

To tell WaveTop what you want it to download, click the MyTop button on the channel bar. You will see a display somewhat like the one shown in Figure 22-6, on the next page.

Figure 22-6 shows offerings in the "NewsTop" category. Clicking buttons around the perimeter of the window (StockTop, KidsTop, and so on) lets you make selections in other categories. When you finish making your selections, WaveTop calculates the amount of disk space your selections require.

FIGURE 22-6.

You can use the MyTop tool to specify which Internet content you want WaveTop to download.

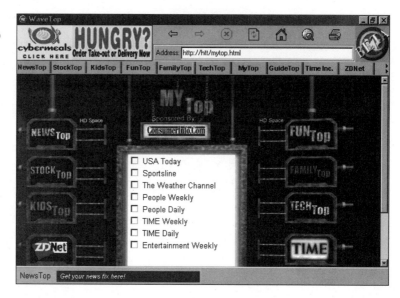

Using Imaging

I maging for Windows is a program that lets you view and annotate fax transmissions and other graphics images. With Imaging you can create multipage "scrapbook" files of images and faxes and use thumbnails to navigate between pages. You can also use the product to convert documents from one supported graphics file type to another. With three file types—.TIF, .AWD, and .BMP—you can add annotations, such as text boxes or freehand drawings, to your images. Imaging can also manage any Twain-compliant scanner, allowing you to scan photographs and other documents and save the resulting images in one of the program's native file formats.

Imaging includes a separate preview program that lets you view, rotate, size, and print images—but not annotate them or assemble them into multipage documents. By default, when you double-click a supported image file type in a Windows Explorer window, your file appears in the preview program. If you want to annotate the image, you can then open the full program by choosing Open Image For Editing from the preview program's File menu. (You can also change the program's default behavior, so that images open in the full program by default.)

Supplied by Eastman Software, Imaging for Windows is a scaled-down version of another Eastman product called Imaging Professional. To the feature set of Imaging for Windows, Imaging Professional adds such things as optical character recognition (allowing you, for example, to turn faxes into editable documents) and the ability to create hyperlinks that connect your local documents with documents on the World Wide Web. If you have an Internet connection, you can read about Imaging Professional by choosing the About command from the Help menu in Imaging for Windows, clicking Contact Info, and then clicking Visit Web Site.

File Types Supported by Imaging

Imaging has three "native" file types: .TIF, .AWD, and .BMP. When you work with any of these file types, Imaging can manage an annotation layer in addition to the underlying bitmap graphics data. You can add freehand drawing, "rubber stamps" (preset messages such as "approved" or "rejected"), and assorted other changes to the annotation layer, and then when you're satisfied with the result, merge the annotations into the underlying bitmap, making the annotations a permanent part of the document.

Imaging can save files in any of its three native file types. It can read files in the following formats (in addition to .TIF, .AWD, and .BMP): .JPG, .JPE, .JPEG,.PCX, .DCX, .XIF, .GIF, and .WIF. When you open a file in one of these types, Imaging's title bar displays the legend Read-Only. If you want to annotate one of these files, first save it in one of the three native formats.

Basic Options

To start Imaging, click its icon, which you can find on the Accessories menu within the Start menu's Programs submenu.

NOTE

If Imaging has not been installed on your computer, launch Add/Remove Programs in Control Panel, click the Windows Setup tab, select Accessories, and click the Details button. Select Imaging and click OK.

On Imaging's Tools menu, you'll find a command called General Options. The dialog box for this command, shown in Figure 23-1, lets you specify four settings that govern basic aspects of Imaging's behavior. You can tell the program how you want images to be sized initially (the default behavior enlarges or reduces image size so that their width fits the width of the main window), whether you want scroll bars, which folder you want Imaging to use by default, and whether you want image files associated with the full Imaging program or the preview program.

FIGURE 23-1.

Among other things, the General Options command lets you specify whether files you launch should open in the preview program or the full Imaging program.

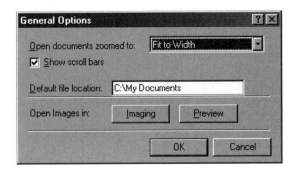

 TIP

If you choose to forego scroll bars, you can still move around a large image by using the Drag button on the Imaging toolbar. Click the hand (or choose Drag from the Edit menu), and then drag any part of the image.

Toolbar Options

 SEE ALSO

For information about the Annotation toolbar, see "Annotating Images," page 563.

Imaging offers four toolbars to simplify command selection. You can use the View menu's Toolbars command to tell the program which of these toolbars you want to see. Table 23-1, on the next page, describes the toolbars that appear at the top of the Imaging window: Standard, Imaging, and Scanning.

TABLE 23-1.   Imaging Toolbars

Toolbar Icon	Description
Standard Toolbar	
	Creates a new, blank document
	Opens an existing document
	Saves the current document to disk
	Prints the current document
	Cuts (deletes) the selection and places it on the Clipboard
	Copies the selection to the Clipboard
	Pastes (inserts) the Clipboard's contents in the upper left corner; drag to the location you want and then click outside the selection
	Undoes your most recent change
	Redoes the last action canceled by Undo
	Zooms in; doubles the current magnification level
	Zooms out; halves the current magnification level
	Fits the selection in the window
	Zooms to the "best fit," fitting either the image height or width in the window
	Fits the image width in the window width
100%	Changes the magnification (zoom) level to a predefined percentage or any value you type from 2 percent through 6500 percent
	Displays help

(continued)

TABLE 23-1. *continued*

Toolbar Icon	Description
Imaging Toolbar	
	Allows you to drag the image within the window instead of using scroll bars
	Allows you to select a rectangular area of the image
	Allows you to select annotations
	Hides or displays the Annotations toolbar
	Rotates the page 90 degrees to the left (counterclockwise) or right (clockwise)
	Displays the previous page, the next page, or the page corresponding to the number you type
	Changes to one-page view
	Changes to thumbnails view
	Changes to page-and-thumbnails view
Scanning Toolbar	
	Scans an image and creates a new document
	Scans an image and inserts it before the current page
	Scans an image and places it after the last page of the current document
	Scans an image and replaces the current page

Opening and Scanning Files

To open a document in Imaging, simply use the File menu's Open command. You can do this from either the preview program or the full program. The only point to note here is that the Files Of Type drop-down list, at the bottom of the File Open dialog box, always defaults to the last file type you used. If the file you opened or saved most recently used the .TIF format, for example, the File Open dialog box initially shows only .TIF files. To see another file type—or all supported file types—make your selection from the Files Of Type drop-down list.

To scan an image, you must be in the full program, and you must have a Twain-compliant scanner installed. If you have more than one such scanner, use the File menu's Select Scanner command to choose the one you want to use. Then choose Scan New from the File menu. This command activates your scanner driver, which will most likely ask you for further information—such as the nature of the source image and the resolution at which you want to scan. Once your scanner has finished its work, the image you scanned appears in Imaging's main window.

> The Scan New command creates a new document from the scanned image. You can also append or insert a scanned image as a new page in an existing document. See "Adding Pages to a Document," page 561.

Setting Compression Options

The Tools menu's Scan Options command, depicted in Figure 23-2, lets you specify the kind of compression that Imaging will apply to your scanned data. The default option, Best Display Quality, applies "loss-less" compression, which means that your scanned image retains as much color and resolution detail as the scanning operation supplies. The resulting file can be quite large, however. The Smallest File Size option performs a "lossy" compression that generates a dramatically smaller file, but one that may lack perfect fidelity to the source image. The Good Display Quality And Small File Size option is a compromise between these two extremes.

If you select Custom and click the Settings button, Imaging displays a second dialog box, shown in Figure 23-3. The various tabs in this dialog box show the method of compression that Imaging is currently set to apply to each of six document types—black and white, 16 shades of gray, 256 shades of gray, 16 colors, 256 colors, and true color. You can select alternative compression methods from the drop-down lists on each of these tabs.

FIGURE 23-2.
The Scan Options dialog box lets you change the mode of compression that Imaging applies to data supplied by your scanner.

FIGURE 23-3.
In the Custom Scan Settings dialog box, you can change the default compression method used for any of six document types.

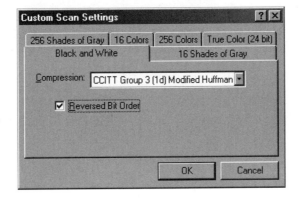

Transfer Mode Options

By clicking the Advanced button in the Scan Options dialog box (see Figure 23-2), you can specify the manner in which Imaging allocates memory to a scan operation. In the default mode, called Best Performance, Imaging allocates one large block of memory at the beginning of the scan. In the alternative mode, called Least Memory, Imaging allocates one block of memory at a time. While the default choice normally makes for a quicker scan (as its name suggests), it can cause Imaging to allocate more memory than is actually needed. If memory is not abundant on your system, you'll probably want to switch to the Least Memory option.

Selecting a View

The full Imaging program offers three views: one page, page and thumbnails, and thumbnails. You can switch between these via commands on the View menu. Figure 23-4 shows a multipage document in Imaging's page-and-thumbnails view.

FIGURE 23-4.

In page-and-thumbnails view, a thumbnail pane appears to the left of the main window. You can move between pages by clicking thumbnails.

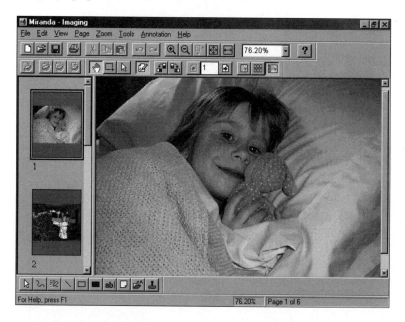

 TIP

In page-and-thumbnails view, you can change the width of the thumbnails pane by dragging the border between the two panes. Widening the thumbnails pane lets Imaging display two or more columns of thumbnails.

In any of these three modes, you can also switch to a full screen view, in which the title bar, toolbars, status bar, and window borders are all removed. To do this, choose Full Screen from the View menu or press Ctrl+F. In full screen view, a Full Screen button appears. Click this button to return to a normal windowed presentation.

TIP

If you prefer working in full screen view, you can display the toolbars. In full screen view, right-click the Full Screen button, and then choose the toolbar you want from the context menu. You can select several (or all) toolbars at once by choosing Toolbars from the context menu.

Changing Thumbnail Dimensions

To change the size of the thumbnails used by Imaging, choose Thumbnail Size from the Tools menu. As Figure 23-5 shows, a large black handle appears at the lower right corner of a sample thumbnail in the Thumbnail Size dialog box. You can drag that handle to change the dimensions of your thumbnails. Alternatively, you can select a different shape from the Aspect ratio drop-down list, or type numbers directly into the Width and Height boxes. Those boxes display the current dimensions, in pixels, of your thumbnails.

FIGURE 23-5.
You can drag the handle in the Thumbnail Size dialog box to change the dimensions of your thumbnails.

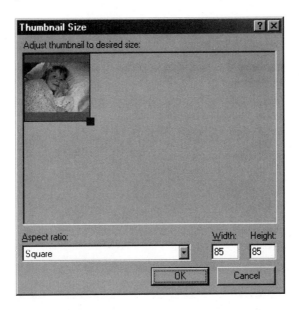

Navigating in a Multipage Document

Page-and-thumbnails view and thumbnails view are handy because they offer a simple way to navigate from one page to another in a multipage document. Clicking a thumbnail in page-and-thumbnails view changes the current page to that of the selected image. Double-clicking an image in thumbnails view presents the selected image in one-page view.

You can also get around without the thumbnails, however, by choosing commands from the Page menu. Next and Previous let you move forward or back a page at a time, First and Last take you to the first page and last page, respectively, and Go To lets you hop to a specific page. Go Back takes you to the page you were looking at last.

Ctrl+Page Down and Ctrl+Page Up are keyboard shortcuts for the Page menu's Next and Previous commands.

Rotating and Zooming

If you scan a picture taken in portrait orientation and it arrives in Imaging in landscape orientation, you can set matters aright by choosing the Rotate Page command from the Page menu. The submenu that appears lets you rotate the image 90 degrees to the left or right. You can also flip the image upside down by choosing 180 degrees.

Commands on the Zoom menu let you change the magnification of your image, from 2 percent of actual size to 6500 percent. (Actual size means the size the image would have if displayed as a bitmap on your desktop.) The Zoom In and Zoom Out commands (and their respective keyboard shortcuts, Ctrl+Up arrow and Ctrl+Down arrow) double and halve the current magnification. The commands at the bottom of the menu let you select a specific magnification value. Choose Custom to enter a value that doesn't have its own menu entry.

The Zoom drop-down list on the Standard toolbar shows you the current magnification. You can click the arrow to the right of this figure to choose a different magnification, or you can simply type in a different percentage.

Fit To Height and Fit To Width, in the middle of the Zoom menu, adjust the magnification of your image to fit the current dimensions of Imaging's main window. Best Fit performs either a fit-to-width or a fit-to-height, depending on which results in less unused space in the window.

Zooming to a Selected Area

If you want to focus on a particular portion of an image, follow these steps:

1 Click the Select Image button on the Imaging toolbar. (Alternatively, you can press Ctrl+Spacebar or choose Select Image from the Edit menu.)

2 Drag your mouse pointer across the area of the image that you're interested in.

3 Choose Zoom To Selection from the Zoom menu.

Imaging magnifies the selected portion of the image so that it fills the main window.

Adding Pages to a Document

To add a new page at the end of the current document, choose Append from the Page menu. To add a new page before the current page, choose Insert from the Page menu. In either case, a submenu appears, allowing you to specify whether the new page is to be scanned or read from an existing disk file. If you choose Existing Page, Imaging presents the equivalent of the File Open dialog box. If you choose Scan Page, Imaging awakens your scanner.

Be aware that while Imaging lets you assemble related source files into an image "scrapbook," the program lacks a convenient way to disassemble the resulting document. If you subsequently decide to extract a particular page, you're limited to copying that page to the Clipboard and then pasting it into another graphics program. There is no Delete Page command.

Getting and Setting Page Properties

The Page menu's Properties command, shown in Figure 23-6 on the next page, lets you see and change several properties of the current page. The dialog box has four tabs.

FIGURE 23-6.

The Page Properties dialog box lets you change the color depth, compression, and other properties of the current page.

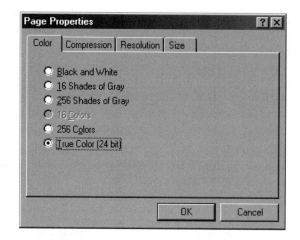

The Color tab lists the six color-depth options available in Imaging, in order of increasing depth. You can use this tab to switch to a lower color depth—for example, to change an image from true color to 256 shades of gray. You might want to reduce the color depth of an image if you plan to fax it (most fax machines are best at transmitting monochrome documents) or print it on a black-and-white printer.

Note the following points about color depth:

- You can decrease, but not increase, the color depth of an image. Once you have reduced an image, for example, from true color to 256 colors, you cannot restore the original 16 million colors.

- Compression is not available with the 16-color option.

- Black And White means literally that—two colors, black and white. To get the familiar look of a black-and-white photograph, select 256 Shades Of Gray.

- Certain color depths are not available with certain document types. For example, .AWD documents are restricted to black and white, and .TIF documents cannot be displayed at 16 colors.

The Compression tab lets you change the method that Imaging uses to reduce the amount of data required to store your image. The available options vary with the file type and color depth of your document. No compression is available for .BMP documents.

The Resolution tab provides another way to reduce the disk storage requirements for the current page. Switching to a lower resolution produces a smaller file, at the expense of image quality. You can use the drop-down list to select from the available resolutions, or you can enter values (expressed in dots per inch) directly into the X and Y boxes.

The Size tab lets you change the overall height and width of your page. Reducing the size of your page is the only method of cropping available in Imaging, and it can be used only to crop from the right or lower edge. Increasing the size of your page adds white space to the right of or below the image. As with reducing color depth, reducing page size is an irreversible action. Once cropped, an image cannot be restored to its original extent.

Annotating Images

 You can add nine types of annotations to documents saved in the .TIF, .AWD, or .BMP format. These annotations are available via the Annotation toolbar or the Annotation menu. Be aware that when you select an annotation tool by clicking an Annotation toolbar button or choosing an Annotation menu command, your selection remains in effect until you deselect it. For example, if you select the Attach-a-Note tool, each time you click your image, you get a new Attach-a-Note annotation. To deselect an annotation tool, choose Select Annotations from the Annotation menu or click the Annotation Selection button (the arrow) on the Annotation toolbar. You can also deselect an annotation tool by clicking the Drag button or the Select Image button (both on the Imaging toolbar), or choosing their Edit-menu equivalents.

After you create an annotation, you can change its appearance by right-clicking it and choosing Properties from the context menu. The options vary with the kind of annotation involved. With lines, for example, you can change thickness and color. With text, you can change font and color, and so on.

The annotation tools, and the Annotation toolbar buttons you use to select them, are described in Table 23-2, on the next page.

TABLE 23-2.   Imaging Annotation Tools

Toolbar Icon	Description
	The Freehand Line tool draws squiggly lines. Click where you want the line to begin, drag at will, and release the mouse button where you want the line to end.
	The Highlighter tool creates a filled rectangle that is, by default, yellow and transparent, providing a way to call a particular block of text to attention. Click where you want a corner of the rectangle to be, drag to the opposite corner, and release the mouse button. You can highlight graphics as well as text, but the Highlighter affects the color of the underlying graphics.
	The Straight Line tool adds straight lines. Click at one end point, drag to the other, and release the mouse button.
	The Hollow Rectangle tool lets you create a box around an area of interest. Click where you want a corner to appear, drag to the opposite corner, and release the mouse button.
	The Filled Rectangle tool works like the Hollow Rectangle tool, except that the resulting box is filled with an opaque background color. (You can use the Properties command to make the background transparent—but if that's what you want, you might as well use the Highlighter tool instead.)
	The Text tool allows you to add any amount of text to your document. Click and type.
	The Attach-a-Note tool creates a solid rectangle on which you may type. Click and drag to make the rectangle, and then type.
	The Text From File tool allows you to import the textual contents of a specified file. Click the image, and then specify the file you want to import.
	The Rubber Stamp tool adds a preset text block or image, including (optionally) the current date or time. Supplied stamps include Approved, DRAFT, Received, and Rejected. You can create your own as well; see the following section. Click where you want the stamp to appear, and then choose the stamp you want to use from the Rubber Stamp Properties menu.

⭐ **TIP**

If you don't like the annotation you just created, choose Undo Annotation from the Edit menu.

▶ **NOTE**

On a monochrome document, annotations might initially appear in color. They will be displayed in black and white as soon as you use the Save or Save As command.

Creating and Changing Rubber Stamps

Choosing Rubber Stamps from the Annotation menu generates the Rubber Stamp Properties dialog box, shown in Figure 23-7. Here you can select one of the supplied stamps or click the Create Text or Create Image button to make your own rubber stamp. To create a textual stamp, click Create Text. In the ensuing dialog box, you can specify the name and content of the stamp. Click the Date or Time button to add the current date or time to the content of your stamp. To create a graphic stamp, click the Create Image button. In the dialog box that appears next, specify the name of your stamp and the graphics file that you want to use as an image. If you don't know the name and path of your graphics file, click the Browse button to find it.

FIGURE 23-7.

Open the Annotation menu and choose Rubber Stamps to display this dialog box.

Back in the Rubber Stamp Properties dialog box, select the stamp you want from the list, and then click OK. Imaging then applies the selected stamp wherever you click the image.

 If you click the Rubber Stamp button on the Annotation toolbar rather than using the Annotation menu, Imaging bypasses the Rubber Stamp Properties dialog box. Instead, you get a pop-up menu of predefined stamps. (You can't create new stamps using this method.) Choose a rubber stamp from the menu, and then click the image to apply the stamp.

> Rubber stamps that include the date and time use the short date style and the time style from the Regional Settings Properties dialog box. Visit Control Panel if you want to change these styles.

Working with Annotations

 Annotations live initially in a separate layer of your document. Here they can be manipulated at will. You can copy and paste them, modify their properties, or delete them. To do any of these things with an annotation, first choose Select Annotations from the Annotation menu, or click the Annotation Selection tool on the Annotation toolbar or the Imaging toolbar. Then click the annotation you want to manipulate. (To select more than one annotation, hold down the Ctrl key as you click each one, or drag your mouse across the set of annotations you want to select.) To change an annotation's properties, right-click and choose Properties from the context menu. To cut, copy, or clear (delete), choose from the context menu or the Edit menu.

Once you have annotated your document to your satisfaction, you can use the Annotation menu's Make Annotations Permanent command to merge the annotation layer with the rest of your document. After you do that, you will not be able to manipulate the annotations.

> Annotations become permanent when you save your document, whether or not you have used the Make Annotations Permanent command.

Creating a New Document

You can use the New command on the File menu to create a new Imaging document from scratch. When you do this, Imaging displays a property sheet similar to the Page Properties dialog box. The only difference between this dialog box and the one shown in Figure 23-6, on page 562, is that this one includes a File Type tab. Here you can specify whether you want your document to be in the .TIF, .AWD, or .BMP format.

? SEE ALSO

For information about Paint, see Chapter 18, "Drawing with Paint."

Note that while you can use Imaging's annotations tools to build a new document, if the document you're creating consists primarily of graphics objects (lines, boxes, and other shapes), you will probably have an easier time working in Paint and then importing the resulting .BMP file into Imaging. Paint's tools are considerably more versatile than Imaging's.

Printing and Faxing

Once you've assembled and annotated your Imaging document, you can use the Print command on the File menu to print it or send it to a fax program. To print or fax, choose Print from the File menu, and then select the printer or fax driver you want to use from the Name drop-down list in the Print dialog box.

Windows to Go: Special Features for Mobile Computing

If your work requires you to travel, you know that computing on the road presents a number of challenges. You need to work in a physically scaled-down environment, you need to be able to get your electronic mail via modem, and you need to be able to access information stored on your home computer or on servers at the home office. In addition, there is the headache of synchronizing files that you carry with you on your laptop with versions of the same files stored at home.

Windows 98 can help reduce the trials and complexity of mobile computing. Using Dial-Up Networking (and a suitably equipped server at your home location), you can stay current with vital data stored at the office. Dial-Up Networking also makes it easy to send and receive electronic mail while you're away; you simply use the same procedures you would use at home, and the operating system makes the physical connections via modem. The Briefcase feature makes it easy to synchronize your traveling files with the files on your home system. You simply pack your briefcase when you're ready to travel and unpack it when you return.

Windows 98 provides a number of enhancements to the mobile-computing support that was introduced with Windows 95:

- **Improved power management.** Because Windows 98 supports Advanced Power Management (APM) 1.2, your portable computer can power down automatically, thereby conserving battery life. APM 1.2 also means that PC Card devices such as modems won't drain your battery excessively when they're not in use. Programs written to take advantage of APM 1.2, moreover, can respond to changes in power state for such purposes as warning you to save your work if loss of power appears imminent.

- **Better support for multifunction cards.** The separate functions in multifunction PC Card devices can now be configured and enabled independently.

- **IrDA 2.0 support.** The Infrared Data Association 2.0 standard provides support for Fast Infrared (FIR) and Serial Infrared (SIR) devices, allowing faster and easier wireless file transfer and LAN connectivity.

- **Better Dial-Up Networking.** You can now assign login scripts to your dial-up networking "connectoids."

- **Multilink Channel Aggregation.** With multilink channel aggregation, your dial-up networking "connectoids" can combine two or more modems and phone lines to achieve higher-bandwidth connectivity.

Monitoring and Conserving Power

Windows 98 supports the Advanced Power Management (APM) 1.2 standard for monitoring and conserving power. If your laptop or notebook computer is APM-enabled, you will probably see a power icon in the notification area of your taskbar, near the clock. If you don't see this icon, launch Power Management in Control Panel. Then, on the Advanced tab in the Power Management Properties dialog box, select the Show Power Meter On Taskbar check box.

The power icon takes various forms, depending on the power state of your computer. If you're running on battery power, it looks like a battery and the portion of it that's colored gives you a rough idea of how much juice you have left. If you're running on AC current and your battery is charging, the icon looks like a power cord with a lightning bolt passing through it. If you're running on AC with no battery installed, it looks like a power cord. In all cases, you can get more detailed information about the power state of your machine by double-clicking this icon. (Among other things, the detailed report provides separate information about each battery in your system, if you have more than one.)

TIP

You can also find out what percentage of your battery's power is still available by simply hovering your mouse pointer over the power icon.

Setting Power-Management Parameters

The Power Management Properties dialog box allows you to specify exactly when and how you want to use your computer's power-saving features. You can tell the system how much idle time it should allow before powering down the monitor or the disk drives or before putting the entire computer on standby. You can protect your privacy by specifying a password that must be entered to bring the computer out of standby mode, and you can create named schemes that encapsulate different groups of power-management settings. You might, for example, want to create one scheme to use when your laptop is docked and another to use when it's not.

Working with Power Schemes

To inspect or modify your power schemes, launch Power Management in Control Panel and select the Power Schemes tab. The default scheme for a typical late-model portable machine appears in Figure 24-1, on the next page. On a desktop system, of course, this screen does not show separate options for plugged-in and battery-powered states. And, depending on the capabilities of your computer, you might see only the Go On Standby option or only the Turn Off Monitor option.

V

Sharing and Communicating

FIGURE 24-1.

The Power Schemes tab in the Power Management Properties dialog box lets you create named combinations of power-down parameters.

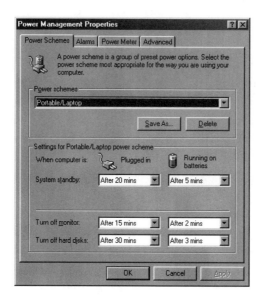

The Power Schemes tab in this dialog box lets you enter the amount of "idle time" (time during which you are not interacting with the computer) you want before the computer, the monitor, or the hard disks are switched to low-power states. To return your computer to its normal state after any part of it has been powered down, simply press a key (pressing Shift will do the job without affecting programs or data) and (if required) supply the appropriate password.

To change any of the power-down settings, click the associated drop-down arrow. You'll find a wide variety of options—including "never"—in the list that unfolds.

To save a group of settings as a power scheme, click Save As, and then enter a name for the scheme. To switch from one scheme to another, select a name from the Power Schemes drop-down list.

> **TIP**
>
> The quickest way to switch power schemes is to click the taskbar's power icon and then choose the scheme you want.

Setting Alarms for Low-Battery Conditions

The Alarms tab of the Power Management Properties dialog box, shown in Figure 24-2, lets you specify what should happen when your computer is running on nearly exhausted batteries. You can set two different alarms: one to serve as an initial warning and a second to alert you when power failure is imminent. Drag the sliders left or right to specify when the alarm should occur. To turn an alarm off altogether, deselect its associated check box.

FIGURE 24-2.

Use the sliders and buttons on the Alarms tab in the Power Management Properties dialog box to tell Windows when and how to warn you of low-battery conditions.

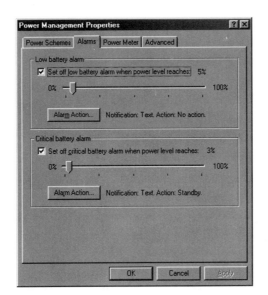

By default, the initial alarm generates a text warning. When the critical alarm goes off, you get another text warning, and then the computer goes into standby mode so you can take appropriate measures (such as plugging in the AC connection). You can change these defaults by clicking the Alarm Action buttons. Your choices are to have a text or audible warning (or both), and to shut the computer off altogether or put it in standby mode.

"Advanced" Settings

The Advanced tab of the Power Management Properties dialog box, like many other "advanced" options in Windows 98, simply gathers together options that don't fall neatly under other headings. Figure 24-3, on the next page, shows the Advanced tab in the Power Management Properties dialog box. Here you can tell the system whether you want to see the power meter icon on your taskbar, whether it should prompt for a password on emergence from slumber, and whether it should rouse itself from sleep to answer the phone. In addition, using the drop-down list at the bottom of the dialog box, you might (depending on the capabilities of your computer) be able to alter the behavior of your computer's power button, changing it from a shutdown switch to a standby switch.

Standby leaves the system running but dormant, allowing a quicker restart. You can leave your computer in a powered-down "standby" mode at the end of a day and then have it spring to life at the press of a key the following morning.

FIGURE 24-3.
On the Advanced tab in the Power Management Properties dialog box, the word *advanced* is a synonym for *miscellaneous.*

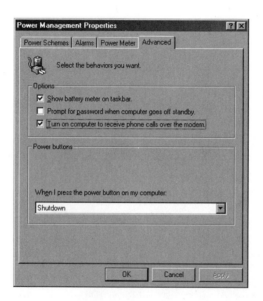

Setting Dialing Properties

If you travel regularly to particular locations and use your modem to initiate calls from those locations, you can simplify your life considerably by letting Windows know exactly how it should place a call in each location. When you arrive at one of your regular destinations, you can use a simple command to tell Windows where you are. Any Windows program that uses the Windows telephony interface (formally known as *TAPI,* which stands for telephony application programming interface) will then use the dialing information you've supplied.

To specify dialing information for a location, follow these steps:

1 Choose Settings from the Start menu.

2 Choose Control Panel from the Settings submenu.

3 In Control Panel, launch Modems.

4 On the General tab in the Modems Properties dialog box, click the Dialing Properties button.

Begin by filling out the Dialing Properties dialog box for your "default" location—the location from which you make the majority of your calls. Then click the New button, type the name of the next location you use, click OK, and fill out the properties dialog box for that location. You can repeat this process for as many locations as you need.

Figure 24-4 shows how the Dialing Properties dialog box would be filled out for a user whose Office location has the following characteristics:

- The area code is 303.

- Getting an outside dial tone, for both local and long-distance calls, requires 9 followed by a pause. (A comma in the dial string causes the modem to pause briefly.)

FIGURE 24-4.

The Dialing Properties dialog box lets you specify dialing requirements for as many locations as you need.

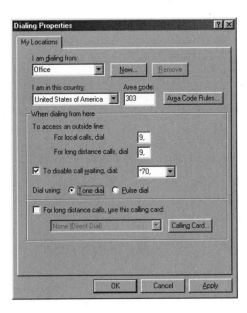

- The line has call-waiting service; the code to disable call waiting is *70 followed by a pause.

- The line uses tone dialing.

- Calls are not billed to a calling card.

Before leaving the Dialing Properties dialog box, be sure to click Area Code Rules and Calling Card and fill out the ensuing sections appropriately. TAPI-aware programs normally omit the prefix 1 and area code for any number within the area code from which a call is made and include these items for all out-of-area calls. But you can modify this behavior if needed. For example, you can prefix particular exchanges within your area code if necessary or omit the prefix for particular outside area codes. The Calling Card dialog box, meanwhile, lets you enter access codes and PINs for your long-distance and international calls that you want to bill to your calling card.

Using Dial-Up Networking

Dial-Up Networking allows you to connect to a remote computer by means of your modem and then access shared resources on the remote computer—as well as other network resources available to the remote computer. The computer to which you connect is known as a *remote-access server (RAS)*. The computer initiating the call is the *Dial-Up Networking (or remote-access) client*. The information that Windows 98 requires to execute the connection is stored in your Dial-Up Networking folder, which you can find by launching My Computer.

❓ SEE ALSO

For information about Network Neighborhood, using remote folders and files, and mapping folders to drive letters, see Chapter 5, "Using and Sharing Files on the Network."

If you've subscribed to a public information service, such as The Microsoft Network, that service may already have created one or more Dial-Up Networking connections for you. You can right-click one of these connections and choose Properties to see how the service has been set up. If you use a modem and an Internet service provider (ISP) for Internet access, chances are you have at least one connection for that service as well.

You or a system administrator can set up your own connections for communication with your company's remote-access services. Once you've connected, you can browse the remote network using Network

Neighborhood. You can also access remote folders and files using UNC path specifications and map remote folders to drive letters on your own computer. In other words, all the techniques you use to work with local-area network resources function the same way with a remote, or wide-area, network.

NOTE

If Dial-Up Networking has not been installed on your computer, launch Add/Remove Programs in Control Panel, click the Windows Setup tab, select Communications, and click the Details button. Select Dial-Up Networking and click OK.

Setting Up a Dial-Up Networking Connection

Before you can connect to a remote-access server the first time, you need to set up the connection. You do that as follows:

1 Open the Start menu and choose Programs, Accessories, Communications, Dial-Up Networking. Alternatively, open My Computer and open the Dial-Up Networking folder.

2 If you've never before set up a remote connection, step 1 takes you directly to the Make New Connection Wizard. Otherwise, launch the Make New Connection item in your Dial-Up Networking folder.

3 In the wizard's first dialog box, type a descriptive name for your new connection and tell the wizard which modem you plan to use (if you have more than one). Click Next to continue.

4 In the wizard's second dialog box, supply the dialing information required to connect to your remote-access server. Click Next to continue.

5 In the wizard's third dialog box, click Finish to store the new connection as an icon in your Dial-Up Networking folder.

Once you've created your connection with the help of the Make New Connection Wizard, you might need to visit the connection's properties dialog box to set additional options. To open the properties dialog box, right-click the connection in your Dial-Up Networking folder, and then choose Properties.

Specifying Server Types, Network Protocols, and Other Connection Options

Figure 24-5 shows the Server Types tab in the properties dialog box. Here you can specify the type of server you're connecting to, as well as various other options affecting the manner in which you connect.

FIGURE 24-5.

On the Server Types tab, you specify information about the server that you're going to dial into.

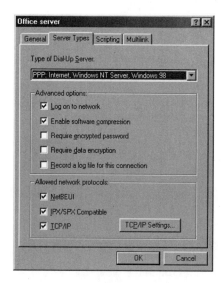

If you want the connection to attempt to log you on to the remote server using the login name and password that you use when connecting to your local-area network, select the Log On To Network check box. (Note that if your LAN login and password are not the ones you need for this remote connection, you can still automate the login process by means of a script.)

If your own computer and the remote-access server can use compatible data compression, you should select the Enable Software Compression check box. This will speed up the transfer of incoming and outgoing information.

If your remote-access server supports encrypted passwords, you can achieve enhanced security by checking the Require Encrypted Password check box. When you dial out with this option, you type your password in the normal manner and your computer encrypts it for you.

In the lower part of the Server Types tab, you can specify all the network protocols supported by your remote-access server. The options that appear here depend on settings established via the Network icon in Control Panel. To add a new protocol or remove an existing one, visit that section of Control Panel.

Specifying a Login Script

In the Scripting section of the connection's properties dialog box, you or a system administrator can specify a sequence of commands, encapsulated as a *script*, that will be executed automatically each time you connect. A script is simply a text file containing a series of instructions that will be passed to the remote computer. You can use Notepad to create such a file. To add the script to your connection, type the name of the file on the File Name line of the Scripting page, or click the Browse button and navigate to the file.

The scripting language is explained in a document called Script.doc, which you can read with WordPad or Microsoft Word. Use Find to locate this file on your hard disk.

Several sample scripts, which have a .SCP extension, are stored in the \Program Files\Accessories folder. You can use these scripts as models for your own.

Using Multilink Channel Aggregation

If you have two or more modems and phone lines and the service that you want to connect to offers a secondary phone number, you might be able to use multilink channel aggregation to achieve faster throughput. Windows 98 combines the aggregated channels, treating them as a single (relatively) high-bandwidth connection.

To set up channel aggregation, click the Multilink tab in the connection property sheet. On the Multilink page, select the Use Additional Devices option button. Then click the Add button and specify the name of the additional device (the modem name, as it appears in the Modems Properties dialog box) and the phone number that the added modem will be dialing. You can repeat this process for each additional device that you want to aggregate.

Connecting to a Remote-Access Server

Once you've set up a Dial-Up Networking connection, you can access the remote server by simply launching the connection in your Dial-Up Networking folder (or a shortcut to that connection anywhere in your system). The first time you do this, if you haven't automated the login process, you'll be asked to identify yourself, following whatever security methods are used by the remote server. If the dialog box in which you do this includes a Save Password check box, you can select this check box to save yourself the trouble of retyping your password each time you connect. If you're concerned that another user will try to connect to your remote-access account without your permission, do not select this check box.

After you've connected to the remote server, and after the server has authenticated your logon information, a small "Connected To" dialog box confirms your connection and displays the length of time you've been connected. You can also see the status of your connection by opening the Dial-Up Networking folder. In the notification area of your taskbar, you'll find a new icon with two lights, which (if all goes well) will flash on and off at irregular intervals. These lights indicate the transfer of data to and from the remote server. If the lights do not light, no data is moving. You can double-click this icon to see additional information about your current session.

To terminate the session, return to the Connected To dialog box and click Disconnect.

Reconnecting to a Remote Folder or File

? SEE ALSO

For information about shortcuts, see "Creating a Shortcut," page 83. For information about mapping a folder to a drive letter, see "Mapping a Network Folder to a Drive Letter," page 159.

To simplify reconnection to a particular remote folder or file, create a shortcut for it *while you're connected to the dial-up network*. Then, after you disconnect, you can reconnect by launching the shortcut. Alternatively, you can map a dial-up folder to a drive letter on your own system. Then you can reopen that "drive" just as you would reopen an ordinary local drive. If Windows determines that the mapped drive is not part of your local-area network, it presents a dialog box asking if you want to use a dial-up connection.

TIP

You can also reconnect to a remote-access server by choosing the Start menu's Run command and typing the server's name.

Allowing Others to Connect to Your Computer via Dial-Up Networking

SEE ALSO

For information about installing a network client, see "Changing Network Settings," page 262. For information about enabling sharing and sharing folders, see "Sharing Folders with Other Users," page 162.

You can make your computer a remote-access server, so that others can connect to it and share files on your local drives. To do this, you must have Dial-Up Networking and Dial-Up Server installed. You also must have a network client installed, with file sharing enabled. You'll need to share the folders to which you want to give remote users access, and, of course, you'll need to have a modem connected to your computer. Your modem should be set in "auto-answer" mode.

To enable others to dial into your computer, open My Computer, and then open the Dial-Up Networking folder. Choose Dial-Up Server from the Dial-Up Networking folder's Connections menu, and in the Dial-Up Server dialog box (see Figure 24-6), select Allow Caller Access.

NOTE

If Dial-Up Server has not been installed on your computer, launch Add/Remove Programs in Control Panel, click the Windows Setup tab, select Communications, and click the Details button. Select Dial-Up Server and click OK.

FIGURE 24-6.
Select Allow Caller Access in this dialog box to make your computer a remote-access server.

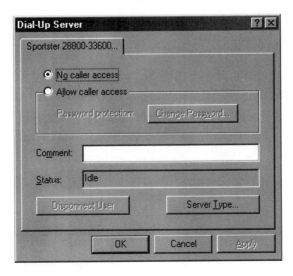

V

Sharing and Communicating

Setting or Changing a Password

To restrict access to authorized callers, you can assign a password to your system. To do this, click the Change Password button, enter a password in the New Password box, and reenter it in the Confirm New Password box. If you later want to change the password, return to the Dial-Up Server dialog box, click Change Password again, and enter the current password in the Old Password box. Then enter and confirm your new password.

Adding a Comment

When callers connect, your system becomes visible to the remote system via the remote system's Network Neighborhood folder. By filling out the Comment line in the Dial-Up Server dialog box, you can make descriptive information about your system visible in Network Neighborhood.

Setting the Server Type

For a remote-access session to work, the calling computer and your computer have to "speak" the same network protocol. To ensure a smooth connection, click the Server Type button in the Dial-Up Server dialog box. This takes you to the Server Types dialog box, shown in Figure 24-7.

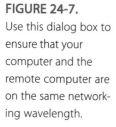

FIGURE 24-7.
Use this dialog box to ensure that your computer and the remote computer are on the same networking wavelength.

In the Type Of Dial-Up Server drop-down list, select Default to communicate with systems running Windows 98 or Windows 95. Select PPP:

Internet, Windows NT Server, Windows 98 to allow a connection from a system running Unix. Select Windows For Workgroups And Windows NT 3.1 to allow a connection from a system running either of those operating systems. In the Advanced Options section of the dialog box, you probably want to leave both check boxes selected. The first speeds up throughput by allowing data to be compressed before it moves across the ether. The second protects your privacy by allowing the remote computer to encrypt the logon password before sending it to your computer. Your computer then decodes the incoming password and authorizes or rejects the caller.

When the Remote System Connects

If everything is set up correctly and your modem is ready to answer the phone, a remote user can simply dial in and connect. If you have the Dial-Up Server dialog box open when the connection is made, you'll see evidence of the connection on the Status line. (See Figure 24-8.)

FIGURE 24-8.
When a remote system connects, the name of the caller and the time of connection appear on the Status line.

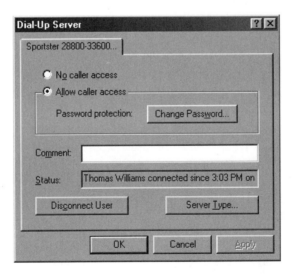

SEE ALSO

For information about Net Watcher, see "Monitoring the Use of Shared Resources," page 167.

You can use the Disconnect User button to do exactly what that button's name suggests. You can also use the Net Watcher utility to monitor the activities of the remote system.

Synchronizing Files with Briefcase

When you travel, you might need to take copies of documents stored on your desktop computer or network server. On return, you'll want to recopy any of those files that you've changed back to the desktop or server folders from which they originated. Sometimes synchronizing mobile and home-base document versions is a simple matter, but sometimes it's not. If you copy a great many files to your traveling machine, for example, it can be a nuisance to figure out which ones you really need to copy back to the desktop computer and which ones you don't. The matter becomes even more complex if you have one computer for home use and one for the office. If you regularly work at both computers, you probably have parallel copies of important documents on each, and you need to be careful not to overwrite a later version of a file with an earlier version.

The Briefcase utility takes care of these details for you. When you put a copy of a file in a Briefcase, Windows keeps track of where the file came from and always knows which version of the file—the one in the Briefcase or the one outside the Briefcase—is the more current. An Update command, available from Briefcase's menu bar or context menu, automatically updates the older version with the newer.

 NOTE

If you set up Windows 98 to include Briefcase, you might find an icon labeled My Briefcase on your desktop. If you do not see this icon, right-click the desktop (or within any folder), and choose New from the context menu. If Briefcase is installed on your system, you'll see a Briefcase item on the list of object types that can be created with the New command. If you don't find Briefcase on this list, you need to install the feature. Launch Add/Remove Programs in Control Panel, click the Windows Setup tab, select Accessories, and click Details. Then select Briefcase and click OK.

TIP

You can also use Briefcase to synchronize versions of documents stored on your desktop computer and a network server.

CAUTION

Do not move a Briefcase file out of the Briefcase. If you do, Windows can no longer keep track of which version of the file—the one you copied out of the Briefcase or the version that you copied into the Briefcase—is the current version.

TIP

The basic procedure for using Briefcase is as follows:

1 Open an existing or new Briefcase on your portable computer.

2 Copy into this Briefcase all documents that you need to travel with.

3 While traveling, work with your documents in the Briefcase.

4 On return, open the Briefcase and use either the Update All or the Update Selection command.

The details vary, however, depending on whether or not your portable computer can be connected (via network or Direct Cable Connection) to your desktop computer.

> If you right-drag a file into a Briefcase, the default option on the context menu is Make Sync Copy. This is the option you want. When you make a sync copy, Windows duplicates the file and at the same time records (in a hidden Briefcase file) information about the file's properties. It uses this information later to determine which version of the file is current.
>
> When you right-drag a folder into a Briefcase, the context menu includes the Make Sync Copy command as well as a Make Sync Copy Of Type command. Make Sync Copy copies the entire folder (including all files and subfolders) into the Briefcase. Make Sync Copy Of Type lets you make sync copies of particular file types only—for example, all Microsoft Excel spreadsheets.

Using Briefcase with a Network or Direct Cable Connection

You'll find it easiest to use Briefcase if you can first connect your laptop and desktop computers via the network or Direct Cable Connection. Then you can simply copy as many files as you need from your desktop computer to the Briefcase on your portable computer. When it comes time to synchronize, reconnect the two machines. Then you can use the Update All or Update Selection command from the Briefcase on the portable computer.

V

Sharing and Communicating

Using Briefcase with Floppy Disks

If your portable and desktop computers cannot be connected, you need to use floppy disks as intermediaries between the two machines. In this case, you need to be aware of one limitation: a Briefcase cannot span multiple disks. This doesn't mean you can take only one disk's worth of files on the road. Rather, it means you might need to take along multiple Briefcase folders. Here's the procedure:

1 Put a disk (preferably a freshly formatted one) in a floppy drive.

2 Open My Computer and launch the icon for your floppy drive.

3 In the floppy disk's folder, right-click, choose New, and then choose Briefcase.

    The first time you open a new Briefcase, a Briefcase Wizard appears. Simply click Finish to dismiss the wizard. When you do this, the wizard sets up your new Briefcase, creating the hidden files that Windows will use to track the status of your files.

4 Copy files into this new Briefcase until the floppy disk is somewhat less than full. Do not fill the disk, because you need to leave room for your files to grow as you work with them.

5 Insert the floppy disk in your portable computer and move or copy the Briefcase to your portable's hard disk.

6 Repeat steps 1 through 5 for as many floppy disks as you need, but give each Briefcase a unique name before moving it to your portable computer.

7 On return, copy each Briefcase to a floppy disk, transfer the disk to your desktop computer, and use the Update All or Update Selection command.

⊕ TIP

You can nearly double the capacity of your floppy disks by compressing them with DriveSpace. For details, see "Using DriveSpace 3 to Compress a FAT Disk," page 379.

Getting Status Information About Briefcase Files

In icon view, the inside of a Briefcase looks pretty much like the inside of any other folder window, except for the presence of a Briefcase menu. But if you switch to details view, Briefcase provides useful information about the provenance and status of your documents. As Figure 24-9 shows, the Status column in details view shows you which files are current and which need updating (in other words, which files have changed since you copied them into the Briefcase). The Sync Copy In column tells you where the original copy of each of your files is stored.

FIGURE 24-9.

By choosing details view in a Briefcase, you can see which of your files have changed since you copied them into the Briefcase.

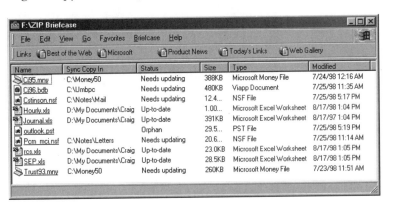

When your Briefcase is online with the computer on which it was created (for example, when your portable is connected to your desktop via direct cable or network, or when the Briefcase is on a floppy disk in the desktop computer's disk drive), you can also get status information about a particular file by right-clicking it and viewing the Update Status tab of its properties dialog box. Figure 24-10, on the next page, shows the Update Status tab for a file that has been changed in the Briefcase.

Updating Files

When you're ready to synchronize your Briefcase files with their sync copies, you can either work one file at a time or update the whole Briefcase at once. To update a single file, select it, and then choose

FIGURE 24-10.

The properties dialog box for a Briefcase file can tell you where the file's sync copy resides and which version of the file is more current.

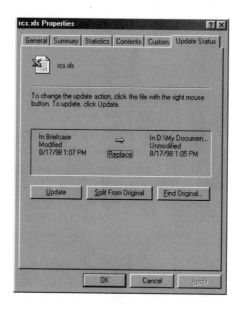

Update Selection from the Briefcase menu. (You can also update a group of selected files this way. Hold down the Ctrl key while you click each file you want to update. Then choose Update Selection.)

To update the entire Briefcase at once, right-click the Briefcase icon (in the folder where it resides) and choose Update All. You'll see a dialog box similar to the one shown in Figure 24-11.

Notice that the Replace arrows in the center of the dialog box can point either direction, depending on which version of a file is most current. When you click the Update button, Windows copies the newer version of each file, wherever it may reside, over the older version.

If the update action that Briefcase proposes for an item is not the action you want, right-click its entry in the Update New Briefcase dialog box. Then, from the context menu, choose the action you prefer. For example, in Figure 24-11, if you want to copy the Briefcase version of Pcm_mci.nsf over the version stored in C:\Notes\Letters, right-click the Pcm_mci.nsf icon and choose the Replace command with the right-pointing arrow. To prevent changes to either file, choose Skip.

FIGURE 24-11.

When you choose Update All, Windows uses left-pointing and right-pointing arrows to show which copy of each changed file is newer.

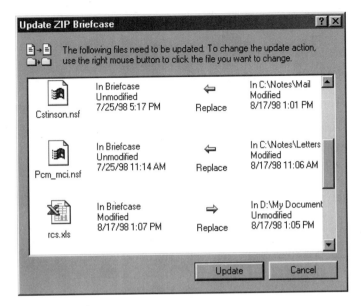

Divorcing a Briefcase File from Its Sync Copy

If you move a file from a Briefcase to any other folder, the link between that file and its sync copy is broken. The result is an ordinary copy. You can also sever the link between a file and its sync copy without removing it from the Briefcase. To do this, select the file and choose Split From Original from the Briefcase menu. In Briefcase's Status field, your file will then be listed as an *orphan*. You can carry as many orphans as you please in your Briefcase.

Creating New Files While Traveling

While you're on the road, you'll probably create new files as well as modify existing ones. Any such files that you store in your Briefcase will also enjoy orphan status. Briefcase's Update commands will not copy these files to your desktop machine for you (because Briefcase would not know where they should go), but you can do that manually by using the same techniques you would use to copy files between any two ordinary folders.

Using Deferred Printing While You're Away from the Office

If you've set up your portable computer to use one or more printers at the office, you can continue to print documents while you're away. With its normal printer(s) offline, Windows simply stores any print jobs you create on your portable's hard disk. When you return to the office, you can send all pending jobs to their printers. If your printers and portable computer support Plug and Play, Windows recognizes that the printers are back online and begins printing the pending jobs automatically. Otherwise, you can use a simple menu command to let Windows know the printers are back online:

1 Choose Settings from the Start menu.

2 Choose Printers from the Settings submenu.

3 In the Printers folder, select each offline printer in turn (the offline printers stand out because their icon is dimmed) and choose the File menu's Work Offline command again to remove its check mark.

TIP

Use the same procedure to resume printing on a network printer that has become available again after being unavailable. (This can happen, for example, if the server to which the network printer is attached gets turned off.)

Transferring Files with Direct Cable Connection

If your laptop can be connected to your network, you can easily copy files to it from your desktop computer. Simply share the folders that contain the files you want to copy, open Network Neighborhood on your laptop, open the folders containing the files you need, and then copy those files to folders on your laptop. (Or copy the files to a Briefcase on your laptop, if you want to keep the copies synchronized with the originals on your desktop. For information about Briefcase, see "Synchronizing Files with Briefcase," page 586.)

If your laptop cannot connect to your network, you can move files to and from it with the help of floppy disks. Or you can use a cable to connect your desktop and portable computers and then transfer files with the help of the Direct Cable Connection utility. Using Direct Cable Connection might be quicker than using floppy disks if you need to move a large number of files. Direct Cable Connection also has the advantage of letting you copy files that are too large to fit on a floppy disk.

NOTE

If you set up Windows to include Direct Cable Connection, you'll probably find an entry for it in the Accessories section of your Start menu. If Direct Cable Connection has not been installed on your computer, launch Add/ Remove Programs in Control Panel, click the Windows Setup tab, select Communications, and click the Details button. Select Direct Cable Connection and click OK.

What Kind of Cable to Use

Direct Cable Connection supports the following kinds of cables:

- Null-modem serial cables

- Basic four-bit parallel cables, including LapLink and InterLnk cables available before 1992

- Extended Capabilities Port (ECP) cables

- Universal Cable Module (UCM) cables

ECP cables provide faster performance than any of the other alternatives, but they require an ECP-enabled parallel port on both computers. A UCM cable can be used with different types of parallel ports.

Setting Up Direct Cable Connection

When two machines are hooked together via Direct Cable Connection, one acts as host and the other acts as guest. The host computer has the privilege of assigning a password to the connection (as well as separate passwords for any folders it chooses to share with the guest). The guest computer can access any folders shared by the host, but the host cannot access shared folders on the guest.

V

Sharing and Communicating

NOTE

You must have certain networking components installed for Dial-Up Networking to work properly. On both the host and guest systems, you need to have Client For Microsoft Networks, Dial-Up Adapter, and a protocol (the same one on both systems). In addition, on the host system, you must have the File And Printer Sharing For Microsoft Networks service. For information about installing network components, see "Changing Network Settings," page 262.

You need to set up Direct Cable Connection first on the host computer, and then on the guest computer. Begin by opening the Start menu and choosing Programs, Accessories, Communications, Direct Cable Connection. The Direct Cable Connection Wizard, shown in Figure 24-12, appears.

In the wizard's first dialog box, identify the current computer as host or guest. Then click Next. In the second dialog box, shown in Figure 24-13, you'll see a list of available ports. Choose the port you plan to use, connect your cable if it isn't already connected, and click Next again.

If you're setting up a host computer, the wizard's third dialog box gives you the opportunity to specify a password. After you've done this (or declined to do it) and clicked Next once more, your host will be ready. If you're setting up a guest computer, the password step is omitted.

FIGURE 24-12.

The first step in setting up Direct Cable Connection is to tell the wizard whether the current computer will act as host or guest.

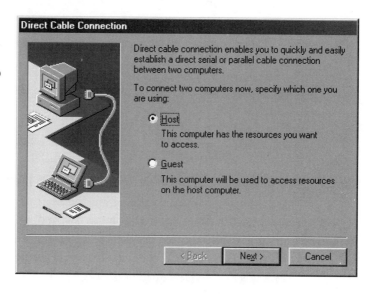

FIGURE 24-13.
The wizard's second dialog box presents a list of available ports.

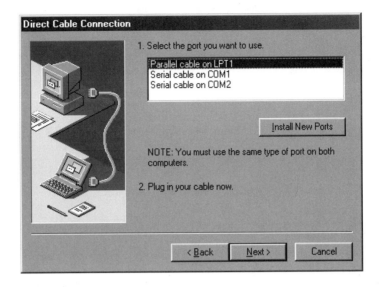

Once you've set up both computers, you can begin transferring files right away. Or you can click Close to leave the wizard for the time being. When you're ready to transfer files, simply run Direct Cable Connection again on both computers.

When you first establish a connection, your guest computer might be asked to enter the name of the host computer. Type that computer's name without any backslash characters. (That is, do not enter the host computer's UNC path; simply enter the name.)

Be sure to share any host computer folders that contain files you want to copy to the guest computer. For information about sharing folders, see "Sharing Folders with Other Users," page 162.

Using Internet Explorer

I nternet Explorer is Microsoft's tool for accessing Internet resources. You will undoubtedly use it mostly for browsing sites on the World Wide Web. But it also enables you to connect with FTP, Telnet, and Gopher sites. Internet Explorer is an extremely rich program, with a wealth of everyday conveniences and advanced features. We explore most of those features in this chapter.

This chapter assumes only that you have the means to access the Internet—that you've installed and set up a modem or that you participate in a local-area network that is connected directly to the Internet. If you're planning to connect using a modem and you do not yet have an account with an Internet Service Provider (ISP), you can use the Internet Connection Wizard to get a list of ISPs who serve your area, compare their offerings, and sign up with the provider of your choice. We'll begin our explorations with a discussion of the Internet Connection Wizard. If you already have an account with an ISP or you log on through your company's LAN, and you don't need to change any of the settings used to establish your connection, you can skip over the following several paragraphs.

Getting Started with the Internet Connection Wizard

The Internet Connection Wizard serves several purposes: it lets you establish a new account with an ISP, reestablish a Dial-Up Networking connection for an existing account, change some aspect of the way you connect to an existing account (such as the dial-up number), or connect or reconnect to an existing proxy server. If you're brand new to the Internet and need an ISP account, a visit to the wizard should be your first step. If you've just installed Windows 98 on a new computer and need to reconnect to the account you were using on your old machine,

---

A Smattering of Internet Jargon

Cache. Temporary local storage of Internet sites you visit.

Channel. A Web site that's been expressly designed for push technology.

Cookie. A file containing information about you that helps a Web site customize its offerings in accordance with your preferences or buying history.

Frame. A separately scrollable area of a Web page.

FTP. *File Transfer Protocol*, a protocol that lets you transfer files from one computer to another.

Home page. The Web page that appears automatically when you open Internet Explorer (unless you begin by launching a Web-page shortcut).

HTML. *Hypertext Markup Language*, the language used to encode Web pages. HTML settings tell Internet Explorer (and other Web browsers) how and where to render the typography, graphics, frames, and other elements that comprise a Web page.

HTTP. *Hypertext Transfer Protocol*, the protocol used by the World Wide Web component of the Internet. The prefix http:// at the beginning of an address identifies the associated site as part of the World Wide Web (or as part of an intranet).

Internet shortcut. An icon with an arrow in its lower-left corner that looks just any other kind of shortcut, except that it represents a link to an Internet site or to an electronic mail recipient.

Intranet. A network that uses the HTTP protocol to distribute information within an organization. An intranet may or may not be connected to the Internet.

ISP. *Internet Service Provider*, an agency that enables dial-up connections to the Internet.

the wizard will help with that task as well. If you want to reconfigure your connection to an existing account, you can use the wizard. (Alternatively, you can simply modify the properties of the Dial-Up Networking connection you're currently using.) You may also have occasion to use the Internet Connection Wizard if you grow dissatisfied with your current ISP and want to see what the competition has to offer.

A Smattering of Internet Jargon, *continued*

Link. An area on a Web page that, when clicked, either takes you to another Internet site or lets you send electronic mail to a particular recipient. Links can be portions of text, icons, pictures, or other graphic objects. They are often, but not always, highlighted or underlined. You can tell if an item is a link by putting the mouse pointer over it. If the pointer changes to a hand, the item under it is a link. A link may also appear in a non-HTML document (an Excel spreadsheet, for example, or an electronic mail message) or may be encapsulated in an Internet shortcut.

Push. A technology that brings requested Internet content to you, instead of making you retrieve it.

Secure Web site. A site that lets you transmit and receive encrypted data.

Security certificate. A statement, issued by a third-party certifying authority, that guarantees the identity of a Web site or person.

Subscription. A request to be notified of changes to a particular Web site or to have a site's content downloaded to your computer automatically at prescribed times.

Telnet. An Internet protocol that lets you log onto and issue commands to a remote computer.

URL. *Uniform Resource Locator,* an address that uniquely identifies a World Wide Web page or other Internet resource. For example, the URL for Microsoft Corporation's Web site is http://www.microsoft.com/. In this book, we use the more familiar term *address* as a synonym for URL.

Web browser. A program that, among other things, renders HTML documents and responds to links, allowing you to move from one Web page to another while either offline or connected to the Internet. Internet Explorer and Netscape Navigator are examples of Web browsers.

Web page. A document encoded in HTML. Web pages are commonly made accessible from other Web pages by means of links.

Web site. A location on the World Wide Web, consisting of one or more Web pages.

V

Sharing and Communicating

If you haven't yet set up a means of connecting to the Internet, launching Internet Explorer automatically takes you to the Internet Connection Wizard. Alternatively, you can get there by choosing Connection Wizard from the Internet Explorer section of your Programs menu or by launching the Connect To The Internet icon on your desktop.

By whatever means you arrive, a welcome screen is the first thing you'll see. Click Next and you'll come to the Setup Options screen, shown in Figure 25-1. Select the first option button if you're in need of a new ISP account or the second option button if you want to reconnect to or modify an existing account. You'll also want to select the second button if you need to set up a connection to a proxy server on your local-area network. If you've wandered by mistake into the wizard's den and you don't need to do any of the aforementioned things, select the third option button or click Cancel.

FIGURE 25-1.
Select the wizard's first option button to set up a new account, the second button to reconnect to an existing account, or the third to bail out.

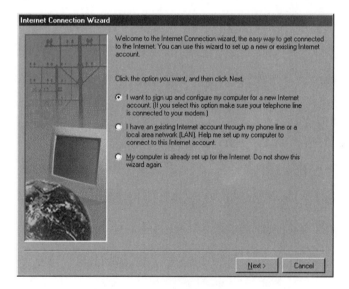

Creating a New ISP Account

If you select the first option button shown in Figure 25-1, the wizard makes a toll-free call over your modem to download a list of ISPs that serve your dialing location. If you make a selection from that list, you'll be asked to provide your name, address, and telephone number. Then the wizard will take you to the ISP, who will be happy to take your credit card number and open an account. Within minutes, you'll be ready to surf.

Reconnecting to an Existing ISP Account

To reestablish your relationship with an existing ISP account, select the second option button in the screen shown in Figure 25-1, and then click Next. In the ensuing dialog box, select the first option button if your ISP is not an online service such as The Microsoft Network. Select the second option button if your service provider is an online service. Then click Next. If you're using an ISP that is not an online service, select the first option button on the following screen. The wizard will then assist you in setting up a Dial-Up Networking connection to your existing ISP account. If your ISP is also an online service, the screen that appears when you click Next simply instructs you to double-click the icon for your online service, either on the desktop or in the Online Services folder.

Connecting or Reconnecting to a Proxy Server

You can use the Internet Connection Wizard to establish or reestablish a connection to the Internet via a proxy server on your local-area network. (A *proxy server* is a computer that serves as an intermediary between your computer and the Internet. On a local-area network, this provides a single, manageable gateway that allows administrators to control all users' access to the Internet and makes each computer more secure against attack by rogue programmers.) To do this, select the second option button in the screen shown in Figure 25-1. In the screen that follows, select the first option button. In the third screen, select Connect Using My Local Area Network (LAN). A Proxy Server screen appears, asking if your LAN uses a proxy server. Declare that it does, and click Next once more. Finally, you arrive at the screen shown in Figure 25-2, on the next page.

V

Sharing and Communicating

FIGURE 25-2.

You can use the Internet Connection Wizard to set up a connection to your network's proxy server.

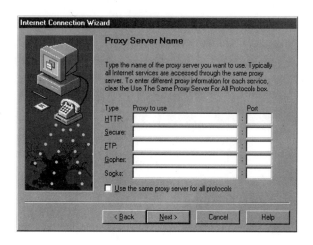

The wizard needs to know a server name and port number for each of five Internet protocols: HTTP, Secure, FTP, Gopher, and Socks. If you don't have the requisite information, consult your network administrator.

Because in a typical setup the answers for HTTP are the same as for the other four, the dialog box includes a handy Use The Same Proxy Server For All Protocols check box. If you select this box, you need only fill out the HTTP line.

Clicking Next then takes you to the Proxy Server Exceptions screen, where you can specify addresses that you can visit without going through the proxy server. Unless your network administrator tells you otherwise, leave the list box empty and select the Do Not Use Proxy Server For Local (Intranet) Addresses check box. With this setting, all Internet access goes through the proxy server, and all intranet access does not.

Modifying an Existing Dial-Up Networking Connection

If all you need to do is change the parameters for a Dial-Up Networking connection that you use to access an existing ISP account (for example, to switch to a different access number), you don't really need the Internet Connection Wizard. You can launch My Computer, open your Dial-Up Networking folder, right-click the connection, choose Properties from the context menu, and then make your changes. But the wizard stands ready to serve, if you don't prefer that route. Select the second option button in the screen shown in Figure 25-1, on page 600. Click Next, select Connect Using My Phone Line, and then click Next again. In the following screen, select Use An Existing Dial-Up Connection, and then select the connection you want to modify from the list that appears. After you click Next once more, the wizard gives you the opportunity to modify any of the properties associated with the selected connection.

Starting and Ending an Internet Explorer Session

 You can run Internet Explorer by double-clicking (or clicking) the Internet Explorer icon on the desktop or on your Quick Launch toolbar. You can also launch the program by opening the Start menu and choosing Programs, Internet Explorer, Internet Explorer.

Provided you have not made some other product your default Web browser, the following actions also start Internet Explorer:

- In a Windows Explorer window, type an Internet address in the Address Bar.

- Choose Run from the Start menu, and then type an Internet address.

- Click a link to an Internet site in an e-mail message or other document.

- Click a shortcut, on your desktop or elsewhere, to an Internet site.

- Choose an Internet site on your Favorites menu (on the Start menu, in Windows Explorer, or in Internet Explorer).

- Click an icon on the Channel Bar on your desktop.

- Choose a channel from the Channels section of your Favorites menu.

In response to any of these actions, Internet Explorer springs to life and attempts to display the selected Internet resource. (If you chose a channel from the Channel Bar or Favorites menu, Internet Explorer opens in its full screen view.) If you are not already connected to the Internet and have not asked to work offline, Internet Explorer activates the Dial-Up Networking connection with which it is associated, and that connection then dials the appointed telephone number. (More about working offline in a moment.)

NOTE

The dialog box that appears when your Dial-Up Networking connection attempts to dial might have a check box labeled Connect Automatically. If you want to the opportunity to confirm a dial-up operation before it begins, deselect this check box.

SEE ALSO

For information about Dial-Up Networking, see "Using Dial-Up Networking," page 578.

To end an Internet session, close all open Internet Explorer windows, or right-click the Dial-Up Networking icon in the taskbar's notification area and choose Disconnect from the context menu. (The latter method has the advantage of leaving Internet Explorer open, allowing you to continue reading the last Web page it displayed without tying up a phone line.)

Working Offline

Most of the time, you'll use Internet Explorer while you're connected to the Internet. But, like other Web browsers, Internet Explorer is perfectly capable of displaying HTML documents even when you're not connected—provided the documents themselves are available offline. There might be times when you'll find it more efficient to use Internet Explorer in its offline mode, reading Internet documents that are stored locally—on your own computer or on a LAN server to which you have access.

SEE ALSO

For more information about the cache, see "Controlling the Cache," page 655.

Internet Explorer stores pages that you have visited recently in folders contained within the folder named Temporary Internet Files. These stored pages are called a *cache*. One purpose of the cache is to make it possible for you to work with documents offline. (Another, as we'll see, is to speed up access to Web pages while you are online.) You can use offline mode to browse either a cached page or a document that you have saved by means of Internet Explorer's File Save command.

(If you use the Find command to look for documents with the extension .HTM, you'll probably find several thousand other HTML documents that Windows itself has stored on your hard disk, including all the help documents used by the Windows 98 help system. You can launch any of these documents from Windows Explorer and read them in Internet Explorer's offline mode.)

To switch Internet Explorer from online to offline mode, choose Work Offline from the File menu. This action does not terminate the current connection. Rather, it simply causes the File menu to display a check mark beside the Work Offline command. The next time you take an action that would ordinarily cause Internet Explorer to create a connection to the Internet, however, that connection does not take place. Instead, Internet Explorer searches local storage for the requested Internet resource.

To switch back to online mode, simply choose Work Offline a second time. This does not immediately connect you to the Internet, but it removes the check mark beside the command. The next time you ask Internet Explorer to fetch a Web page, it connects rather than searching locally.

If you use Dial-Up Networking to connect to the Internet, you can also begin an offline session by clicking the Cancel button when your connection is attempting to dial up. You may then see a dialog box similar to the one shown in Figure 25-3. Click Work Offline in this dialog box to confirm your intentions.

FIGURE 25-3.

You can work offline by canceling a dial-up action and then clicking the Work Offline button.

If Internet Explorer cannot find a document that you want to read offline, it displays the dialog box shown in Figure 25-4. You can then either click Connect to let the program search online, or you can click Stay Offline. If you click the latter button, Internet Explorer displays an HTML document called "Unable to Retrieve Webpage in Offline Mode." You can click the More Information link on this page to read about why Internet Explorer was unable to find your document. Alternatively, you can use the File Open command or type a different address in Internet Explorer's Address Bar to try fetching a different document.

FIGURE 25-4.

If Internet Explorer can't find your document in offline mode, you can click the Connect button to look for it online.

While reading an HTML document offline, you can click any of its links to hop to a different document. If the document to which you hop is also available offline, everything works in this mode exactly as it would online. If not, you see the dialog box shown in Figure 25-4.

 TIP

If a linked document is not available offline, the mouse pointer that appears when you point to the link changes from a hand to a hand plus barred circle.

Understanding the Internet Explorer User Interface

Figure 25-5 points out the most crucial landmarks of the Internet Explorer window.

FIGURE 25-5.

The Internet Explorer window has a set of tools and controls surrounding the document viewing area.

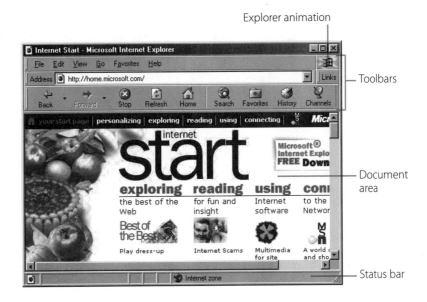

Explorer animation

Toolbars

Document area

Status bar

⑦ SEE ALSO

For information about displaying, arranging, and customizing the toolbars, see "Customizing the Toolbars," page 652.

■ The *toolbars* allow quick access to commands and Web pages that you use most often. Like the toolbar in Windows Explorer, the Internet Explorer toolbar can contain the Standard Buttons, Address Bar, and Links toolbars in any combination and arrangement you choose.

  The buttons on the Standard Buttons toolbar are described in Table 25-1, on the next page. The Address Bar displays the address of the page you're currently viewing. You can also use the Address Bar for navigation: type the address of a page you want to go to in the Address Bar and press Enter. The Links toolbar provides one-click access to your most frequently used pages.

■ The *Explorer animation* indicates when Internet Explorer is waiting to receive information from a computer on the Internet; the flag icon shimmers while Internet Explorer is waiting.

⑦ SEE ALSO

For details, see "Understanding the Status Bar," page 611.

■ The *status bar* gives you information about what Internet Explorer is currently doing.

■ The *document area* displays the Web page you are currently viewing. Any items that are highlighted (usually by underlining) are links, and clicking them takes you to the page they point to.

TABLE 25-1. **Standard Buttons Toolbar**

Toolbar Icon	Description
	Displays an earlier page in the list of previously viewed pages
	Displays a later page in the list of previously viewed pages
	Stops downloading the current page
	Downloads the current page again, ensuring that the latest version is displayed
	Displays your home page
	Displays (or hides) the Search Explorer Bar, which provides access to Internet search engines
	Displays (or hides) the Favorites Explorer Bar, which provides access to your favorite sites
	Displays (or hides) the History Explorer Bar, which provides access to sites you've visited recently
	Displays (or hides) the Channels Explorer Bar, which provides quick access to channels you select
	Switches to (or from) full screen view, which provides maximum viewing space for Internet Explorer's document area
	Launches your mail or newsreader program (by default, Outlook Express), and lets you send links and pages to others via e-mail
	Prints the current page
	Opens the current page in your HTML editor (by default, FrontPage Express)

Using Full Screen View

To increase the amount of screen real estate that you can use for viewing a Web page, Internet Explorer provides a special view called full screen. In some instances, Internet Explorer automatically switches to full screen view, but you can switch to this useful view at any time. To switch to full screen view, click the Fullscreen button on the Standard Buttons toolbar. In full screen view, Internet Explorer expands to fill the screen, the title bar and window borders disappear, the menu bar merges into the toolbar, and the toolbar shrinks down to a single row, leaving the majority of the screen to display a Web page, as shown in Figure 25-6.

FIGURE 25-6.

In full screen view, standard window elements disappear and Internet Explorer fills the screen.

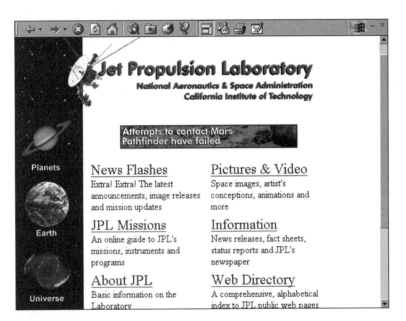

 TIP

Because Internet Explorer completely fills the screen in full screen view, the Windows taskbar isn't visible. However, it appears when you move the mouse pointer to the edge of the screen at the taskbar's usual location. Alternatively, you can use keyboard shortcuts to switch windows: press Alt+Tab to switch to another open window, or press Ctrl+Esc to open the Start menu and display the task bar.

In full screen view, the toolbar occupies a single row at the top of the screen, but you can specify which elements you want to include in the toolbar. Right-click the toolbar and choose Menu Bar, Address Bar, or Links. A check mark in the context menu identifies each element you've selected. (The Standard Buttons toolbar is always included in full screen view.) Within the limits of the single row, you can resize each of these elements by dragging the vertical line at the left edge of each toolbar element.

> **★ TIP**
>
> To completely maximize the viewing area, in full screen view right-click the toolbar and choose Auto Hide. The toolbar then retracts into the top of the screen; you can redisplay it by moving the mouse pointer to the top edge of the screen.

To switch from full screen view back to Internet Explorer's normal window, click the Fullscreen button.

Displaying and Hiding Explorer Bars

An *Explorer Bar* is a separate pane, displayed on the left side of the Internet Explorer window, that displays a specific kind of information. We've seen Explorer Bars already in connection with Windows Explorer. Four of the Explorer Bars available in that context—Search, Favorites, History, and Channels—are also available in Internet Explorer. (They were in fact designed for Internet Explorer and then incorporated into Windows Explorer.)

You display an Explorer Bar in one of two ways: click the toolbar button for a feature that uses the Explorer Bar, or open the View menu and choose Explorer Bar. To hide an Explorer Bar, click its toolbar button again; open the View menu and choose Explorer Bar, None; or click the X (the close button) in the Explorer Bar's upper right corner.

In full screen view, the Explorer Bar retracts into the left edge of the screen. To display it, move the mouse pointer to the left edge; when you move the mouse pointer away from the Explorer Bar, it again slides off the left edge. A small push pin button appears on the Explorer Bar, next to the close button. To prevent the Explorer Bar from sliding away, tack it down by clicking the push pin button. Click the push pin button again to restore the "auto hide" behavior.

TIP

You can make any Explorer Bar wider or narrower by dragging its right edge.

Understanding the Status Bar

The status bar provides information about the Web page you are viewing, as well as about the current state of the browser. The status bar is organized into sections, with each section providing a different type of information.

On the left is the current progress status. While you download a Web page, an icon and text in this area explain what the browser is currently doing. After the page has arrived, this area shows the address for any link you point to. To the right of the progress status text is the progress bar, which is active only while Internet Explorer downloads information. The bar fills up as data for the current page gets downloaded.

TIP

The complete text of the status bar's leftmost pane is often not visible, and you can't resize the panes. You can display the full text, however, simply by hovering the mouse pointer over the text.

SEE ALSO

For more information see "Working Offline," page 604; "Printing a Web Page," page 633; and "Working with Secure Sites," page 641.

The middle section of the status bar is split into three small panes. Each pane either displays an icon or is empty. The first pane displays an icon when you are working offline. The second displays an icon while Internet Explorer is printing. The third displays a lock icon if you have a secure connection to a Web site.

On the right end of the status bar is the security zones area. This displays the icon and name for the security zone that the current Web page is in.

Navigating on the World Wide Web

Internet Explorer offers several ways to navigate the World Wide Web. You can:

- Click a link to go to a page

- Enter an Internet address to go to a specific page

V

Sharing and Communicating

- Use the Forward and Back commands to revisit previously viewed pages

- Go farther back in your Web-browsing history using the History Explorer Bar

- Return to a favorite page by selecting it from the Favorites menu

- Use a search engine to find a page of interest

Using Links to Get to Other Pages

The World Wide Web works much like the HTML-based Windows 98 Help system. In Help, you can click any word that is underlined or highlighted to get more information. The Web works the same way; on the Web these underlined items are called *links*.

Keyboard Shortcuts	

You can use the following keyboard shortcuts as you work with Web pages in Internet Explorer:

Enter	Activates the selected link
Shift+F10	Displays the context menu for the current link
Ctrl+Tab	Cycles between frames (independently scrolling areas)
Tab	Selects the next link
Shift+Tab	Selects the previous link
Alt+Left Arrow	Returns to the previous page
Alt+Right Arrow	Moves to the next page
F5	Refreshes display of the current page
Esc	Stops display of the current page
Ctrl+O	Opens a document
Ctrl+N	Opens a new window
Ctrl+S	Saves the current page as a file
Ctrl+P	Prints the current page

Each page on the Web can have an unlimited number of links to other pages. You can identify a link by moving the mouse pointer over a text or graphic item on a page. If the pointer icon changes to a hand when you pass over the item, then the item is a link. Notice also that the status bar displays information about the link.

To use a link, all you have to do is click it. When you do this, Internet Explorer takes you to the Web page that the link points to.

? SEE ALSO

For information about setting the colors for links, see "Selecting Colors," page 653.

Once you click a link and go to its linked page, Internet Explorer remembers that you used that link. To let you know that you've already used a link, Internet Explorer changes the color of the text for that link.

Going to a Specific Web Page

If you know the address (that is, the URL) of the Web page you want, Internet Explorer's Address Bar provides an easy way to get there. The Address Bar always displays the address of the current Web page. However, you can also type the address of the Web page you want and press Enter, and Internet Explorer will take you there. Follow these steps to enter an address:

1 Click the Address Bar's text box to highlight the text currently in the box.

2 Type the address for the page you want to go to. The address should look something like this:

   http://www.microsoft.com/

3 Press Enter.

   Internet Explorer finds the page that you want. (It may take a few seconds for the Web page to respond to Internet Explorer's request for information.)

⭐ TIP

Internet Explorer Fills In the First Part . . .
For most Internet addresses, Internet Explorer can identify the correct protocol automatically. Therefore, you can shorten your typing for these addresses by omitting the protocol—the part of the address up to and including the two slashes, such as http:// or ftp://. So, for example, to enter the sample address in step 2 above, you could type just *www.microsoft.com*.

TIP

> **...and the Last Part**
>
> When you start typing an address, Internet Explorer attempts to complete the address by displaying any similar address that you've previously entered. If it completes correctly, just press Enter. Otherwise you can keep typing. (You can turn off this feature, called AutoComplete, by visiting the Advanced tab in the Internet Options dialog box.)

If the Address Bar is not visible, you can open the File menu and choose Open. The Open dialog box that appears contains a text box where you can type the address. You have other alternatives as well: you can enter an address in the Address Bar of any Windows Explorer window, in the Address toolbar that you can place on the desktop, or in the Run dialog box that appears when you choose Run from the Start menu.

> **The Anatomy of an Address**
>
> Internet addresses can be cryptic. But there is logic to their structure, and understanding the logic can help you to make reasonable guesses about a company's address or about what you'll find at a particular address.
>
> The first part of an address is the *protocol* (such as http or ftp), which is followed by a colon and two slashes. The part of the address between the two slashes after the protocol name and the next slash is the *domain name*. Domain names typically are made of two or three words separated by periods. If you read a domain name from right to left, each word more specifically identifies the site. You begin at the right with the *top-level domain*, a word such as .com (for a commercial site), .edu (educational institution), .gov (government), or .org (organization). The next word, the *second-level domain* name, typically identifies the name of the organization. The leftmost word tells you a little about the organization's site. For example, a domain name that begins with www indicates that the address is for a World Wide Web site (but not all World Wide Web sites start with www).
>
> By remembering this right-to-left order of importance, you'll be able to remember, for example, that The Microsoft Network's investment advice can be found at investor.msn.com, not msn.investor.com.

Each of the address-entry boxes is actually a drop-down list. You can click the drop-down arrow to display a list of previously entered addresses. (Note, however, that each address-entry box—the Address Bar and Open dialog box in Internet Explorer, the Address toolbar on the desktop, and the Run dialog box—maintains its own history of entries.)

Using Back and Forward

Internet Explorer keeps a list of the pages you've already viewed. The Back and Forward commands—or their toolbar equivalents—provide a simple way to move through that list so that you can easily return to places you have already seen. Try out the commands with this simple example:

1   On your home page, click any link to move to a new Web page.

2   When the new page appears, click the Back button on the Standard Buttons toolbar or choose the Back command from the Go menu to move back to your home page.

   Notice that the Forward toolbar button is now active.

3   Click the Forward button or use the Forward command on the Go menu. You will move forward to the page you visited in step 1.

TIP

Retrace Your Steps

You can easily move two or three pages at a time by clicking the drop-down arrow to the right of the Back or Forward button. Doing so displays a list of the last several pages in the back/forward list. Choose a page from this list to jump directly to that page. (You can also right-click the Back or Forward button to open its drop-down list.)

   You can also return to a recently visited site by choosing it from the File menu.

Revisiting the Past with History

The Back button provides a simple way to retrace your steps. But it only remembers where you've been during the current session. To return to a site you visited in a previous session, or to a site that's many steps back from your current location, you'll want to use Internet Explorer's history feature.

 To review your browsing history, display the History Explorer Bar by clicking the History button. A pane on the left side of the Internet Explorer window shows a list of pages you've visited, sorted by date and then by site. Figure 25-7 shows an example of the History Explorer Bar.

FIGURE 25-7.

The History Explorer Bar makes it easy to return to pages you've already visited.

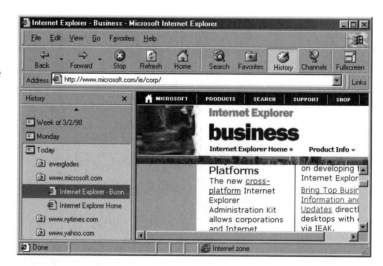

Returning to Previously Viewed Sites

The top of the History Explorer Bar hierarchy lists the beginning date of the past few weeks, and each day in the current week. When you click a date or day, the History Explorer Bar shows the sites, or domains, that you visited during that week or day, sorted alphabetically. Clicking a site name displays an alphabetically sorted list of all the pages you visited at that site. To revisit a page that's listed in the History Explorer Bar, click its title.

 TIP

To determine the precise time when you last visited a page that's listed in the History Explorer Bar, right-click the page title and choose Properties. Because some pages have similar (or identical) titles, you can sometimes use the time to determine which page you want to revisit.

Deleting Items from History

If you need to cover your tracks, you can remove any item from history. You can delete an individual page, a site (and all the pages it contains), or a date (and all the sites and pages it contains). Simply right-click the item you want to delete, and choose Delete.

You can obliterate your entire browsing history with a visit to the Internet Options dialog box. (Choose Internet Options from the View menu to display it.) On the General tab, shown in Figure 25-8, click the Clear History button to do the deed.

FIGURE 25-8.

On the General tab, you can set the number of days' history you want to keep. You can also delete all history items.

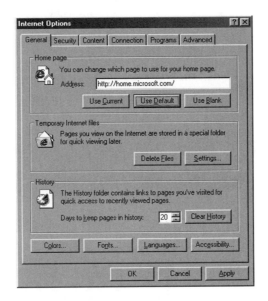

 NOTE

The History folder contains only pointers to the pages you've visited; the contents of those pages (that is, the page's text, graphics, and media files) are stored in the Temporary Internet Files folder. Therefore, if you're intent on hiding your past, you need to delete the files in that folder. The Delete Files button on the General tab does just that.

Internet Explorer automatically deletes items from the history list after a period of time that you can specify. On the General tab in the Internet Options dialog box, use the spinner to set the number of days' history you want to keep. The default is 20 days.

Keeping Track of Your Favorite Pages

As you surf the Web and discover pages that you like, you will probably want a way to get back to those pages easily. Internet Explorer provides a series of Favorites commands and a Favorites Explorer Bar for exactly this purpose. You can have as many favorite pages as you like.

Using Favorites commands, you can create a list of your favorite pages and organize them into folders. Then, to go to a favorite page, you simply select the page you want from the Favorites menu. The Favorites menu also appears on your Start menu and in Windows Explorer, so you can return to a favorite site easily, even if Internet Explorer isn't currently running.

The Favorites Explorer Bar places links to your favorite pages in a pane on the left side of the Internet Explorer window for even easier access. To display the Favorites Explorer Bar, click the Favorites button. Figure 25-9 shows a Favorites Explorer Bar.

FIGURE 25-9.

The Favorites Explorer Bar provides a convenient way to access sites that you've marked as important to you.

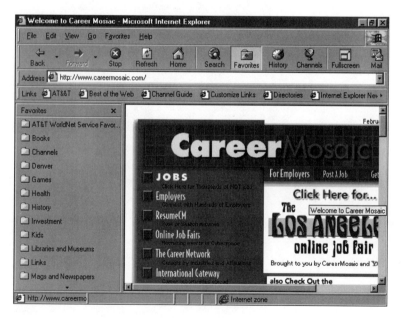

Adding an Item to Favorites

The Add To Favorites command allows you to create a favorite-page listing for the page you're currently viewing. To add the Web page you are currently viewing to your Favorites list, follow these steps:

1   Choose Add To Favorites from the Favorites menu, or right-click the page and choose Add To Favorites from the context menu. This opens the Add Favorite dialog box, shown in Figure 25-10.

FIGURE 25-10.
The Add Favorite dialog box creates a favorite-place listing for the current page.

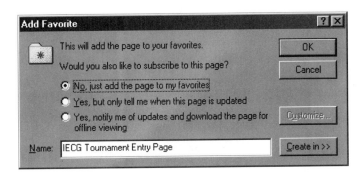

SEE ALSO

For more information about subscribing to a page, see "Using Subscriptions and Channels," page 624.

2   If you want to subscribe to the page—that is, have Internet Explorer automatically check the page periodically to see if it has changed and, optionally, download the updated page—select one of the Yes option buttons.

In the Name text box, make any changes you want to the name of the page.

3   Click the OK button. This creates a favorite-page listing for the current page.

 TIP

Adding Favorites with Drag and Drop
If the Favorites Explorer Bar is displayed, you can use drag and drop to add a page to your favorites. Drag the icon for the current page from the Address Bar to the Favorites Explorer Bar. A horizontal line indicates where the page will be added. (If you want to add the favorite to a folder, hover the mouse pointer over the folder momentarily and the folder opens.)

You can also drag a link from Internet Explorer's document area to the Favorites Explorer Bar.

Organizing Your Favorite Pages with Folders

After you've created a number of favorite pages, you might have difficulty finding the particular favorite page you're looking for. To help you organize your favorite pages, Internet Explorer allows you to create subfolders within your Favorites folder.

To create a subfolder, follow these steps:

1 Choose the Add To Favorites command from the Favorites menu. This brings up the Add Favorite dialog box shown in Figure 25-11, on the previous page.

2 Click the Create In button. The dialog box expands to display a folder hierarchy.

3 Click the New Folder button.

4 Type a name for your new folder and click OK.

5 Click OK to add the current page to your new folder.

The Favorites menu now includes a cascading item with a folder icon that has the name of the folder you created. Creating such a menu structure lets you group your favorite pages logically.

After you create a new folder, you can add favorites to it by selecting the folder you want in the expanded Add Favorite dialog box and then clicking OK.

Using the Organize Favorites Command

The Organize Favorites command allows you to view, organize, and return to your favorite places. When you choose the Organize Favorites command from the Favorites menu, you will be presented with a dialog box displaying the contents of the Favorites folder, as shown in Figure 25-11.

This dialog box functions much like Windows Explorer windows. You can drag files or folders to a folder icon to move them to that folder, and you can right-click files or folders to see the usual context menus. In addition, the dialog box's buttons provide a quick way to create new folders, rename items, and organize things as you see fit.

TIP

Organizing Favorites Using the Favorites Explorer Bar

The Favorites Explorer Bar provides an easy way to move, rename, or delete favorites. To move an item, simply drag it from one location in the Favorites Explorer Bar to another. To rename or delete a favorite, right-click it and choose Rename or Delete.

FIGURE 25-11.

The Organize Favorites dialog box provides a convenient way to move, rename, or delete items in your Favorites folder.

Click this button to create a new folder.

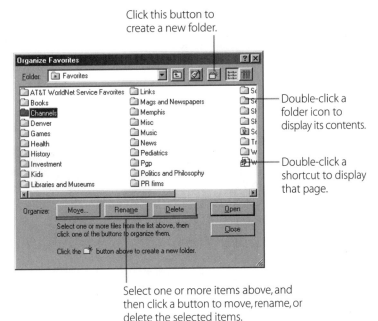

Double-click a folder icon to display its contents.

Double-click a shortcut to display that page.

Select one or more items above, and then click a button to move, rename, or delete the selected items.

Using Search to Find New Sites

The Internet is a vast repository of information, but sometimes it's difficult to find the information you need. The search feature in Internet Explorer provides easy access to search engines that comb the Internet for the words or topics that interest you.

To use the search feature, display the Search Explorer Bar by clicking the Search button. Figure 25-12, on the next page, shows the Search Explorer Bar. Search information appears in the Search Explorer Bar, leaving Internet Explorer's document area available to display a page that your search turns up.

When you want to find something on the Internet, follow these steps:

1 At the top of the Search Explorer Bar, click Choose A Search Engine and then select the search engine you want to use. (If you don't specify one, Internet Explorer uses the "provider-of-the-day." Until you know the strengths and weaknesses of the various providers, you might want to leave it as is.)

2 Click in the text box in the Search Explorer Bar, and type the words or topics you are trying to find.

FIGURE 25-12.

The Search Explorer Bar lets you select a search engine provider, enter a query, and view the results.

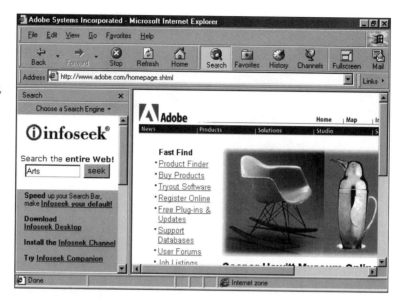

3 Click the Find or Search button. (The name of the button varies from one provider to another.)

In a moment, the results of your query appear in the bottom of the Search Explorer Bar.

> **TIP**
>
> Many search-engine providers offer categorized lists of links for locating the sites you're interested in. If you're using a provider of this type, instead of typing a query and clicking the Find button, click a link in the Search Explorer Bar.

4 Click one of the result links, and the page appears in Internet Explorer's document area.

> **TIP**
>
> For more details about a particular search result, hover the mouse pointer over the result link, and a small screen tip appears with information about that page. Most often, this information includes the page title, the first few sentences, and the address for the page. This helps you narrow down your search without having to navigate the browser to another page.

If you found the page you're interested in, you can close the Search Explorer Bar. But if you want to visit another page that appears in the results list, simply click the one you want to see. You can click links in the page you display or use other methods for navigating the Web, and your most recent search results remain available in the Search Explorer Bar; if at any time you want to try another result, you can click its link in the Search Explorer Bar.

Picking a Search Engine

Internet Explorer provides access to most of the popular Internet search-engine providers. Because each provider offers different features and maintains its own Web pages, you might get different results by trying the same search with different providers. To change the search engine that you are using, click the Choose A Search Engine link at the top of the Search Explorer Bar, and select the provider you want to use. This updates the Search Explorer Bar to show the user interface for the provider of your choice. If you choose List Of All Search Engines, Internet Explorer displays a list in the document area. To learn more about each search engine, hover the mouse pointer over its name.

Tips for Successful Searches

Searching on the Internet for information can be a tricky task. Here are some simple tips to help you find what you are looking for much easier and faster.

Be Specific

Whenever you type a query, use as many detailed words as possible. If you are searching for recipes for chocolate chip cookies, searching for "cookies" returns many results that are not useful. Instead search for "chocolate chip cookie recipes." The more words you use, the more likely you'll find good results.

Try Different Search Engines

Each search engine has its own algorithms and techniques for finding the best pages to match your query. The results you get from one engine might be completely different from another. So if you are having trouble with your favorite search engine, try a different one.

Using Subscriptions and Channels

If you grow weary of pulling down information from the Internet, you can have Internet Explorer push it to you instead. Internet Explorer implements "push" technology with three related features:

- Subscriptions

- Channels

- Active Desktop objects

There's not a huge amount of difference between these three features, but, unfortunately, the marketing jargon in which they've been clothed obscures what difference there is. Let's sort out the lingo first, and then we'll get down to procedures.

A *subscription* to a Web site is a request that Internet Explorer check that Web site periodically and report to you when it has changed. The notification takes the form of a red "gleam" attached to a Favorites-menu or Channel Bar icon, as shown in Figure 25-13. Additionally, you can have Internet Explorer notify you of the change via electronic mail.

FIGURE 25-13.

It's difficult to see here, but Internet Explorer uses a red "gleam" to mark the icons of subscription sites that have changed.

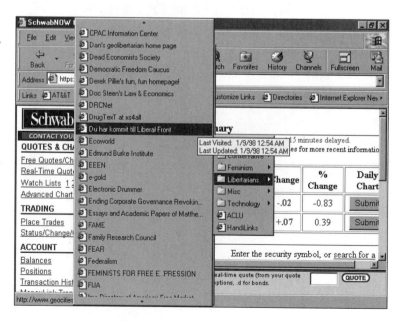

A subscription can also include an order to download some or all of the site's content, allowing you to peruse the downloaded data in offline mode. So, for example, if you're frustrated with the speed of your Internet connection, you can have Internet Explorer visit your favorite Web sites at night, and then deliver the goods for you to read offline the following morning.

> **NOTE**
>
> If your computer adheres to the OnNow specification, it can download subscribed Web content in its sleep. Only the parts of the system needed to carry out the download will be activated.

You can specify at what time of day and with what frequency Internet Explorer should visit the subscribed site. And if you choose to download, you can tell Internet Explorer whether it should download the site's first page only, or the first page plus linked pages. If you want the linked pages, you can choose how many levels deep into the subscribed site you want Internet Explorer to go.

A *channel* is a Web site that's been designed expressly for push technology. Such a site might offer news, weather reports, stock quotes, sports scores, or some other form of information that has widespread appeal and needs to be updated on a regular basis. Channel providers typically include a "publisher's recommended" update schedule in a special "channel definition" file (extension .CDF) that gets stored on your hard disk if you subscribe to the channel. Some channel providers also provide information in the .CDF that allows Windows to use their content in a special Channel screen saver.

SEE ALSO
For more information, see "Displaying the Channel Bar," page 73.

Internet Explorer includes a Channels Explorer Bar that provides easy access to selected channel sites. If you find a channel you like, you can add it to the Channels Explorer Bar (if it isn't already there), and then click the Channels Explorer Bar at any time for easy return to the site. If you've chosen to display your desktop as a Web page, you can also keep your Channel Bar visible on the desktop at all times, even when you're not connected to the Internet. Clicking a Channel Bar item when you're offline starts Internet Explorer in full screen view and initiates a connection (unless you've chosen to work offline). Thus the Channel Bar serves as a kind of graphical favorites menu.

V

Sharing and Communicating

TIP

Although the Channels Explorer Bar is ostensibly intended for channels, you can drag any link to it.

You can also subscribe to a channel, of course. Subscribing to a channel is exactly like subscribing to any other Web site, except that when setting up your schedule you have the option to choose the publisher's recommended schedule.

 SEE ALSO

For more information, see "Bringing The Internet to Your Active Desktop," page 69.

An *Active Desktop object* is a piece of Web content that you've elected to have pushed to your desktop. Such an object might be a stock ticker, a headline ticker, a weather map, or a stock graph—some kind of data that you want updated frequently and presented more or less in your face. As we saw in Chapter 3, "Using and Customizing the Desktop," Microsoft maintains an online gallery of Web sites that offer Active Desktop objects.

The Mechanics of Subscribing

Now let's look at the procedures for ordering a subscription. What follows applies to any subscription, whether it be to a channel or an ordinary Web site.

To subscribe to a Web page, visit that page and choose Add To Favorites from the Favorites menu. As Figure 25-10 on page 619 shows, the Add Favorite dialog box includes three option buttons. The first button merely adds the current page to your Favorites menu. The second and third buttons create a subscription—in addition to adding the page to your Favorites menu.

Ordering a "Notify Only" Subscription

To order a "notify only" subscription—that is, one that gets you a change notification without a download, select the second option button shown in Figure 25-10. If you click OK at this point, your subscription will have the following properties:

- Internet Explorer checks the page "daily," which means, by default, every day at 2:00 A.M. (If the site is a channel, you get the publisher's recommended schedule.)

- Internet Explorer alerts you to changes by adding the red gleam to the page's entry in your Favorites menu or on your Channel Bar, but not by e-mail.

- Internet Explorer assumes that you don't need to supply a name and password to access the subscribed page.

- In checking the page, Internet Explorer does not initiate a dial-up connection. If you are not already connected to the Internet, the page does not get checked.

- If you are working at your computer when Internet Explorer is scheduled to check the page, it does not check.

If you want e-mail notification in addition to the gleam, or if the page requires a logon procedure, click the Customize button to start the Subscription Wizard. The wizard's first screen is shown in Figure 25-14.

FIGURE 25-14.

Using the Subscription Wizard, you can request e-mail notification of changes to your favorite Web pages.

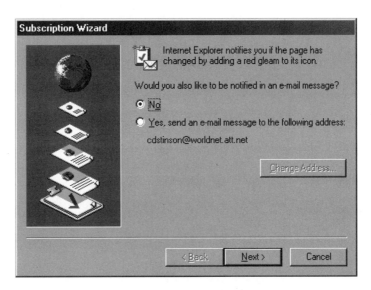

To change other properties of the subscription, including the definition of "Daily," go ahead and set up the subscription and then visit the subscription's properties dialog box. See "Changing Subscription Settings," page 630.

The second option button in shown Figure 25-14 lets you request e-mail notification, and when you select that option, the Change Address button becomes active. If the address that Internet Explorer proposes to use is not the one you want it to use, click Change Address and set matters straight. When you're ready, click Next. The wizard then gathers details about any logon procedure required by the subscribed page. After supplying that information, click Finish.

Ordering a "Notify and Download" Subscription

To order a "notify and download" subscription, click the third option button in the dialog box shown in Figure 25-10, on page 619. If you then click OK, your subscription will have the same properties listed above for a "notify only" subscription, including the schedule, notification method, logon parameters, and connection settings, plus the following properties:

- Pages linked to the subscribed page will not be downloaded.

- Images, ActiveX controls, and Java applets on the subscribed page will be downloaded.

- Sound and video on the subscribed page will not be downloaded.

- Disk space permitting, Internet Explorer will download the page (except for its sound and video), no matter how large it may be.

To change the download schedule, request e-mail notification, supply a logon name and password, or download linked pages, click Customize to start the Subscription Wizard. To change any other property associated with the subscription (for example, to suppress the downloading of images or limit the number of megabytes that Internet Explorer will download), go ahead and set up the subscription, and then visit the subscription's properties dialog box. See "Changing Subscription Settings," page 630.

When you click the Customize button, the Subscription Wizard begins by asking if you want to download pages linked to the subscribed page. If you say you do, the subsequent screen asks to what depth Internet Explorer should download the linked pages. The default here is one level, which means you get the subscribed page plus everything linked directly to that page. You can specify up to three levels, but you should be aware that the amount of material that Internet Explorer will have to download increases exponentially as you select deeper levels of links.

After you resolve the question of links, the wizard inquires whether you want e-mail notification when the page has changed, using the dialog box shown in Figure 25-14, on page 627. After you make that decision, it displays the dialog box shown in Figure 25-15. Here you can modify the downloading schedule.

FIGURE 25-15.

By default, Internet Explorer downloads subscribed pages at 2:00 A.M. daily. This dialog box lets you alter the schedule.

The two option buttons in this dialog box let you choose between a scheduled download time and manual downloading. If you opt for the latter, your subscribed page will not be downloaded until you choose the Update All Subscriptions command from Internet Explorer's Favorites menu. And when you do this, of course, all your subscriptions will be updated—including those for which you've chosen a scheduled update!

 TIP

> To update a single subscription, choose Manage Subscriptions from the Favorites menu, which opens the Subscriptions folder in Windows Explorer. Right-click the subscription you want to update and choose Update Now from the context menu.

If you select Scheduled in the dialog box shown in Figure 25-15, you can use the drop-down list to choose from the available predefined schedules. Initially, Internet Explorer gives you three:

■ Daily, defined as 2:00 A.M. every day of the week

■ Weekly, defined as 3:00 A.M. every Monday

V

Sharing and Communicating

■ Monthly, defined as midnight on the first day of every month

If you're subscribing to a channel, you'll find a fourth option, called Publisher's Recommended Schedule.

If none of these suits you, you can redefine one of the existing pre-defined schedules or create a new one. To redefine, first select the schedule you want to modify, and then click the Edit button. To create a new predefined schedule, click New. Either way, the next dialog box gives you plenty of control over your schedule. You can schedule your subscription's update for every other day, every Tuesday and Sunday, on the second Wednesday of every other month, or whatever meets your needs. You can even have the subscription updated at specified regular intervals between starting and ending hours—for example, every two hours between 8:00 A.M. and 5:00 P.M.

Changing Subscription Settings

The Manage Subscriptions command on Internet Explorer's Favorites menu opens Windows Explorer, which displays a system folder listing all your subscriptions. (See Figure 25-16.) You can inspect and modify the properties of any subscription—for example, change a notify-and-download subscription to a notify-only subscription—by right-clicking its entry in this folder and choosing Properties from the context menu.

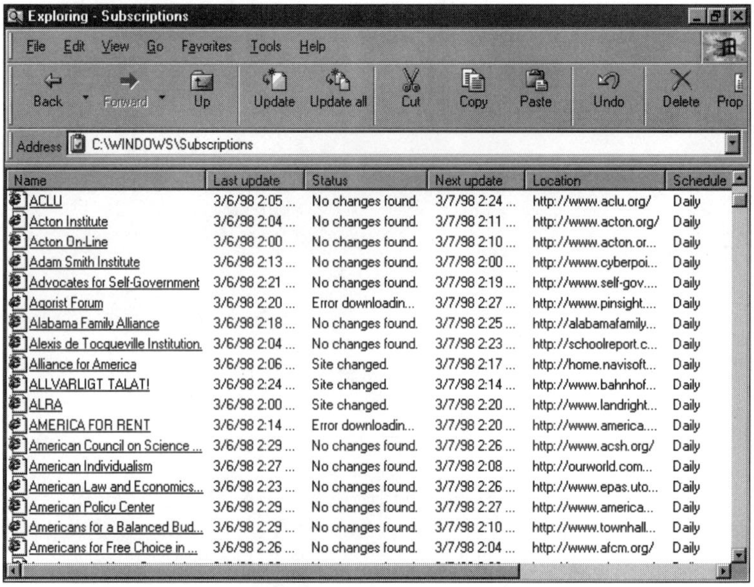

FIGURE 25-16.

The system folder C:\ Windows\Subscriptions lists all your subscriptions. If you display this folder in Details view, you can see the status and next scheduled update for each subscription.

You'll need to use the properties dialog box under any of the following circumstances:

- You want Internet Explorer to initiate a dial-up connection to the Internet (if necessary) when updating the subscription. (On the Schedule tab, select "Dial as needed if connected through a modem.")

- You want Internet Explorer to update the subscription even if you're working at your computer at the appointed time. (On the Schedule tab, deselect "Don't update this subscription when I'm using my computer.")

- You want to change the level to which Internet Explorer downloads linked pages. (On the Receiving tab, click Advanced and fill out the ensuing dialog box.)

- You want to change the kinds of items that Internet Explorer downloads—for example, to exclude images or add sound and video. (On the Receiving tab, click Advanced and fill out the ensuing dialog box.)

- You want to impose a maximum download size for the subscription. (On the Receiving tab, click Advanced and fill out the ensuing dialog box.)

- You want to modify the subscription's update schedule. (On the Schedule tab, choose a different predefined option from the Scheduled drop-down list. Or click New or Edit and fill out the ensuing dialog box.)

Updating Subscriptions Manually

You don't have to wait for the scheduled update time to check on the status of a favorite Web page. If you've created a subscription for that page, you can update it manually as follows:

1 Choose Manage Subscriptions from Internet Explorer's Favorites menu.

2 In the Subscriptions folder, right-click the subscription.

3 Choose Update Now from the context menu.

You can also perform a manual update of all your subscriptions at once by choosing Update All Subscriptions from the Favorites menu.

Canceling a Subscription

The simplest way to cancel a subscription is to remove it from your Subscriptions folder. Choose Manage Subscriptions from the Favorites menu, select the subscription in the Subscriptions folder, press the Delete key, and confirm. You can also delete a subscription by clicking Unsubscribe on the Subscription tab in its properties dialog box.

Finding Channels

The simplest way to scan for available channels is as follows:

1   Display the Channels Explorer Bar by clicking Channels on Internet Explorer's Standard Buttons toolbar.

2   Click Microsoft Channel Guide on the Channels Explorer Bar.

This takes you to a Web site maintained by Microsoft (the address is http://www.iechannelguide.com/). Here you'll find a categorized list of all the channels known to Microsoft. At the time of this writing, the categories were news and technology, sports, business, entertainment, and lifestyle and travel. Each category included more than 100 channels, so there were plenty to choose from. By the time you read this, there will likely be many more.

When you find a channel name or topic that looks appealing, click its entry in the Channel Guide to get a preview of its offerings. If you still like what you see, click the Add Active Channel button. This action adds the channel to your Channels Explorer Bar (if it isn't already there) and brings up a dialog box with which you can subscribe to the channel. Note that you're not obligated to subscribe! You might simply want the selected channel available to you via the Channel Bar.

Working with Web Pages

Surfing the Web with Internet Explorer is fine, but what can you do with the information you find? This section describes how to do the following:

■   Print a Web page

- Save a Web page as a document on your computer

- Create a shortcut to a page that you can reuse or share with others

- Send a Web page or a shortcut to someone else

- Use a displayed image as your desktop wallpaper

- Search for text within a page

- Edit a Web page

Printing a Web Page

Internet Explorer allows you to print any Web page; simply click the Print button or open the File menu and choose Print. If you choose the File-menu route, the Print dialog box shown in Figure 25-17 appears.

FIGURE 25-17.
Internet Explorer adds some unique features to the bottom of the Print dialog box.

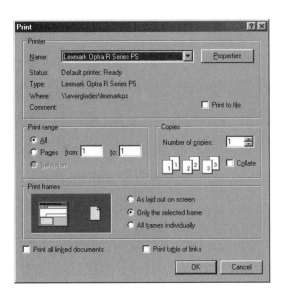

SEE ALSO

For more information about printing, see "Printing from a Program," page 188.

In addition to the usual print options, the Print dialog box provides some features specifically for printing Web pages:

- The Print Frames section lets you specify how you want to print a page's frames. Some Web pages are made up of multiple "frames," which are much like window panes—except that you usually can't see the divider between the frames. If you select the Only The Selected Frame option button, Internet Explorer prints the frame where you last clicked. The Print Frames option buttons are not available if the current page does not use frames.

■ If you select Print All Linked Documents, Internet Explorer prints the current page and also retrieves and prints all the pages that have links in the current page. Although this option can be very useful in some cases, use it with care or you might end up with a lot of unneeded printouts!

■ The Print Table Of Links check box lets you print a list of all the links in the current page along with their addresses.

By default, Internet Explorer prints the title of the Web page and the page number at the top of each printed page, and the address of the Web page and the date at the bottom. You can change these default headers and footers, as well as the page margins, by opening the File menu and choosing Page Setup. (See Figure 25-18.)

FIGURE 25-18.
To learn what the codes in the Header and Footer box do, click the What's This? button (in the title bar) and then click the Header or Footer box.

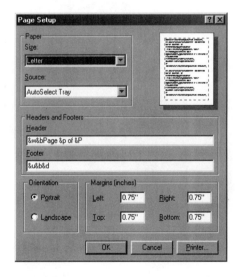

TIP

You don't have to wait for a page to arrive completely before using the Print command. If you click the Print button or choose the Print command while Internet Explorer is still downloading your page, the program waits until the entire page has arrived and then executes the command.

Saving a Web Page to Disk

With Internet Explorer you can save any Web page to a disk file on your computer. However, because most Web pages are created using HTML, you must consider what format to save them in. When you choose the Save As command from the File menu, you can save a Web page in either of two different formats: HTML or text.

If you save the page in HTML format, all the HTML formatting codes remain intact, but you need a Web browser (such as Internet Explorer) an HTML editor (such as FrontPage Express), or another program capable of rendering HTML (such as Microsoft Word) to view it properly. If you save the page in text format, you lose all the HTML formatting codes, but you can load the text in almost any program.

NOTE

> If the page you're saving includes both text and graphics, using the Save As command saves only the text, not the graphics images. If you want to save a graphics image, right-click the image and choose Save Picture As.

Creating Shortcuts to Web Pages

SEE ALSO

For more information about shortcuts, see "Adding Shortcuts to Your Desktop," page 83.

With Internet Explorer, you can create a shortcut to any Web page. Once you create an Internet shortcut, you can keep it on the desktop, send it in an e-mail message to your friends, or embed it within a document in another program.

To create a shortcut for the currently displayed Web page, right-click the page (except on a graphic or a link) and choose Create Shortcut. Alternatively, open the File menu and choose Send, Shortcut To Desktop. Either method creates a shortcut on your desktop.

Once the shortcut is created, you can move it, copy it, or rename it as you see fit. To use the shortcut, simply launch it like any other shortcut, and Internet Explorer will take you to that Web page. You can use the shortcut even when Internet Explorer is not running; like other document shortcuts, shortcuts to Internet destinations launch their associated program—in this case, Internet Explorer—if it's not already running.

TIP

> You can create a shortcut to a linked page by dragging the link to your desktop or to a folder.

Sending Web Pages to Others

With Internet Explorer, you can send a Web page (or a shortcut to a Web page) to someone else via e-mail. The Send submenu on the File menu offers two commands for this purpose. Choose Page By Email to send the complete page (the recipient must have an e-mail program that can display HTML files), or choose Link By Email to send a shortcut. If you send a shortcut, the recipient can launch it to download the Web page.

Choosing either command launches your mail program's new-message window. Specify the recipient's name or address in the To box, click Send, and the page or shortcut is on its way.

Turning a Web Image into Wallpaper

 SEE ALSO

For more information about wallpaper, see "Using Wallpaper," page 97.

If you see an image (or a Web page background) that you like on a Web page, Internet Explorer can save that image and install it as your desktop wallpaper. To do this, simply right-click any image in Internet Explorer. In the context menu that appears, choose Set As Wallpaper to use the image as your Windows wallpaper.

Finding Text on a Web Page

Many Web pages have large amounts of text. To find a specific phrase or word in a large Web page, you can use Internet Explorer's Find command. (See Figure 25-19.) Follow these steps to use this command:

1 Display the Web page on which you want to find a specific word or phrase. (The Find command works only on a single page at a time.)

2 Choose the Find (On This Page) command from the Edit menu.

3 Type the text you are looking for. You can type part of a word or the entire word.

4 Click the Find Next button, and Internet Explorer takes you to the next occurrence of your search text in the page.

FIGURE 25-19.
The Find command searches for text in the current Web page.

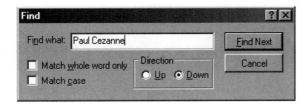

Editing a Web Page

You can edit the current Web page by opening the Edit menu and choosing Page or, more simply, by clicking the Edit button on the Standard Buttons toolbar. Doing so opens a copy of the Web page in your HTML editor (by default, FrontPage Express).

If a message ("This file does not have a program associated with it . . .") appears when you choose Edit Page, you need to install an HTML editor. To install FrontPage Express, the HTML editor that comes with Windows 98, launch Add/Remove Programs in Control Panel, click the Windows Setup tab, select Internet Tools and click Details, and then select FrontPage Express.

If you're conversant in HTML and you want to quickly view or modify a Web page's underlying HTML, right-click the page and choose View Source. This displays the HTML in a Notepad window.

Downloading Files from the Internet

On some Web sites, files are available for you to download to your computer. These files are usually shown in Internet Explorer as links. To download a file, click the link that represents the file. You will then see a dialog box like the one shown in Figure 25-20, on the next page.

Unless you're sure of a file's provenance, you should save it to disk, close other programs you have open, and scan the file for viruses before you launch it.

If the file you're downloading is a sound file or video clip that you want to play, a program that you want to run, or a document that you want to display immediately in a word processor or other program, select the first option (depending on the type of file, either "Open this file . . ." or "Run this program . . ."). Otherwise, select "Save this file (or program) to disk."

V

Sharing and Communicating

FIGURE 25-20.

When you download a file, Internet Explorer lets you launch the file immediately or save it to disk.

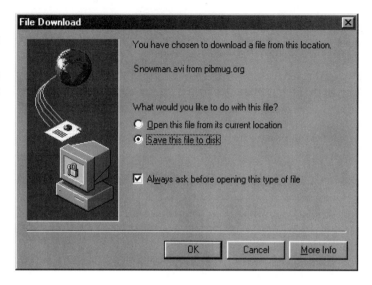

If you select the first option, Windows renders the data, just as it would if you launched an entry in a Windows Explorer window. If you select the save option, Internet Explorer presents a Save As dialog box before it begins downloading the data.

> If you select the open or run option, the only copy that Internet Explorer saves on your computer is in the Temporary Internet Files folder. As its name suggests, files in this folder soon disappear as they're replaced by others—so if you want a copy of the file to use in the future, select the save option.

Trusting Software Publishers

When you download a program or ActiveX control from a software publisher, you might see a security warning similar to the one shown in Figure 25-21. You can click Yes to go ahead with the download, No to cancel it, or More Info to read more about this publisher. If you find this kind of warning inconvenient and you trust that this publisher would never send you damaged goods, you can select the "Always trust content from . . ." check box. This action adds the publisher's name to a list of trusted publishers. You can view this list by following these steps:

1   Choose Internet Options from the View menu.

FIGURE 25-21.

A certificate like this appears whenever a publisher that is not on your "trusted" list tries to send an object that has a security certificate.

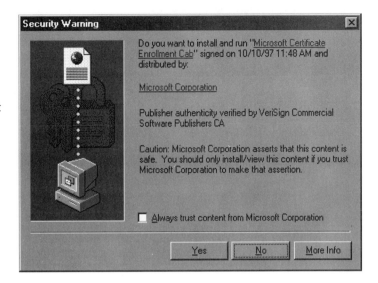

2 Click the Content tab.

3 Click the Publishers button.

To revoke your trust in a publisher, select that publisher's name from the list and click the Remove button.

Connecting to FTP, Gopher, and Telnet Sites

Some parts of the Internet are set up differently than the World Wide Web. Three such parts of the Internet are FTP (file transfer protocol), gopher, and Telnet sites. FTP and gopher sites usually consist of lists of documents and files for downloading. Internet Explorer provides the same interface for these Internet sites as it does for the World Wide Web, so you don't need to learn anything new to access information on Internet FTP or gopher sites. Telnet sites allow you to interact with a host computer in much the same way you would if you were dialing up a bulletin-board system (BBS). When you enter an address for a Telnet site, Internet Explorer "spawns" a terminal program—either HyperTerminal or another similar accessory—and you interact with your Telnet site using that program.

TIP

> One way to determine what type of site you are viewing is by checking the address: Internet addresses usually have the name of the service at the beginning. For example, the address for Microsoft's FTP server is ftp://ftp.microsoft.com; the address for the WELL gopher site is gopher://gopher.well.com.

To connect to an FTP or gopher site, enter the address for the site you want to connect to in the same way you would for a World Wide Web page. Just as with World Wide Web addresses, you can do this with the Address Bar or with the File Open command.

For example, an anonymous connection (one that doesn't require a password) to the Microsoft Corporation FTP site looks like this:

> ftp://ftp.microsoft.com

To connect to an FTP server that requires you to provide your username and password, use this format:

> ftp://name:password@ftp.microsoft.com

(Replace *name* and *password* with the logon information assigned by the server administrator.)

Using Security and Privacy Features

Security and privacy are related but somewhat distinct issues. Security means your ability to send sensitive data—your credit card numbers, for example—across the Internet without that data being intercepted by unauthorized parties. It also means your ability to screen out dangerous or objectionable content that may be coming toward you. Privacy means your ability to prevent Internet content providers and other parties from gathering information about you—demographic or marketing data, for example—that you'd rather they not have.

If you transact business over secure Web sites, you can be reasonably confident that third parties will not be able to intercept the information you send. In fact, thanks to encryption, you are almost certainly safer sending credit card information this way than you are sending it via fax or telephone. On the other hand, if you download a lot of material from the

Internet, you probably know that there is no such thing as perfect security. There is always a chance that you might someday become the unwitting target of a malicious or incompetent programmer. The only surefire way to eliminate this hazard is not to use the Internet. If that drastic solution doesn't appeal to you, you might want to become familiar with Internet Explorer's security-zone feature.

We'll explore the concepts of security zones and secure Web sites in this section. We'll also look at how you can prevent Internet sites from gathering information about you by downloading "cookies" to your hard disk.

Working with Secure Sites

Internet Explorer is a *secure browser*, which means it's capable of exchanging encrypted (secure) data with a *secure Web site*. A secure Web site is one that has been given a valid security certificate by a third-party agency such as RSA Data Security, Inc. When you're connected to a secure site, a padlock icon appears in the status bar, and whatever you upload to that site is automatically encrypted.

 SEE ALSO

For more information about security protocols and other security settings, see "Setting Advanced Options," page 656.

Internet Explorer supports two security protocols, called Secure Sockets Layer (SSL) and Private Communication Technology (PCT). SSL, a standard developed by Netscape, is used by most secure servers. PCT, developed by Microsoft, adds some additional features to SSL.

Internet Explorer automatically chooses the appropriate protocol for the secure site that you're using. But if you're interested in knowing what protocol a server supports, or any other details about its security, you can find out as follows:

1   Log on to the secure site.

2   Choose Properties from the File menu.

3   Click the Certificates button.

You'll see a dialog box similar to the one shown in Figure 25-22, on the next page. Here you can learn the name of the authority that issued your site's security certificate, the effective date and expiration date of that certificate, the protocol used, and so on.

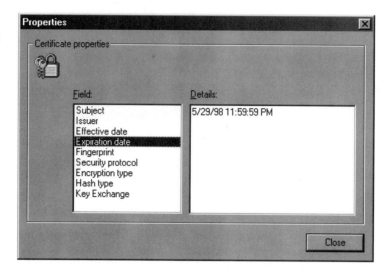

Security Zones and Security Levels

Internet Explorer lets you assign any Web site to one of four categories, depending upon the degree to which you trust the site. These four categories are called Trusted Sites zone, Local Intranet zone, Internet zone, and Restricted Sites zone. All sites initially are assigned to the Internet zone, with the exception of sites that you access via an intranet. Internet Explorer automatically detects intranet sites and assigns them to the Local Intranet zone.

Each security zone is associated with a particular "security level"—a default configuration of defensive measures that Internet Explorer's designers considered appropriate for that zone. The Internet and Local Intranet zones are given the medium security level, while the Restricted Sites and Trusted Sites zones are assigned the high and low security levels, respectively.

If you think that certain of the sites you use pose a higher than ordinary level of risk, you can move those sites to the Restricted Sites zone. On the other hand, if you find Internet Explorer's moderate safety measures intrusive with certain sites that you trust completely, you might want to assign these sites to the Trusted Sites zone.

Understanding Security Certificates

A *security certificate* is a statement issued by a third-party authority guaranteeing the identity of a Web site or person. Internet Explorer uses two kinds of certificates—site certificates and personal certificates. A personal certificate vouches for your identity. At this stage in the development of Internet commerce, a personal certificate's principal virtue is that it enables you to send encrypted e-mail. But you may at some time need to deal with a Web site that requires you to authenticate yourself by means of a personal certificate. You can read more about how to obtain and use a personal certificate; see "Working with Encryption," page 703.

A site certificate attests that a secure Web site is what it says it is—and not the work of an imposter. Site certificates, like personal certificates, have expiration dates. When you connect with a secure Web site, Internet Explorer makes sure that all the information on the site's certificate is valid and that the certificate has not expired. The program warns you if the certificate is invalid or not current.

On the Content tab in the Internet Options dialog box, you'll find two buttons relating to security certificates. The Personal button lets you inspect any personal certificates that have been installed on your computer. The Authorities button presents a list of certifying authorities that are currently trusted by Internet Explorer. You can deselect any that you do not want the program to trust.

A third button on the Content tab, Publishers, presents a list of software publishers that you have declared to be trustworthy. These publishers are not guaranteed by a certifying authority. They are simply software sources that you, for the sake of convenience, have asked Internet Explorer to trust. For more information about trusting publishers, see "Trusting Software Publishers," page 638.

To change a site's default zone assignment, choose Internet Options from the View menu and click the Security tab. (See Figure 25-23, on the next page.) From the Zone drop-down list, select the zone you want to assign the site to. Then click the Add Sites button (this button becomes active when you select any zone other than Internet zone). In the ensuing dialog box, you'll see a list of sites that you've already assigned to this zone, along with a text box where you can enter the address for the new site. Enter the site's address in this text box and click the Add button.

FIGURE 25-23.

Use this dialog box to assign particular sites to nondefault "security zones." Each security zone is associated with a particular "security level"—a default configuration of defensive measures.

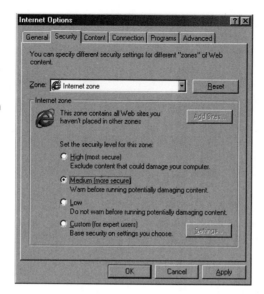

 **TIP**

To avoid typing errors when entering a site's address, first select the address in Internet Explorer's Address Bar. Press Ctrl+C to copy the address to the Clipboard. Then use Ctrl+V to paste the address into the security-zone dialog box.

Redefining Security Levels

Internet Explorer has three predefined security levels, called high, medium, and low. You can find out exactly what any of these security levels means, and, if none of the predefined security levels meets your requirements for a particular security zone, you can assign that security zone a custom security level. For example, to see what exactly constitutes Internet Explorer's high security level (the level it uses with Restricted Sites zone), follow these steps:

1 Choose Internet Options from the View menu and click the Security tab.

2 From the Zone drop-down list, select Restricted Sites Zone.

3 Select the Custom option button, and then click the Settings button.

Internet Explorer displays the dialog box shown in Figure 25-24. You can scroll through this dialog box to see exactly what potentially hazardous

FIGURE 25-24.

You can use this dialog box to fine-tune the security level associated with a security zone.

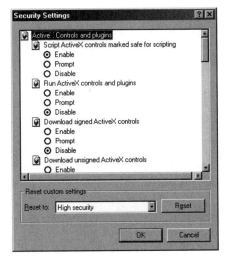

downloads are disabled by the high security level, what kinds of downloads require you to answer a confirmation prompt, and so on. If you don't like what you see, you can change any of these settings. Internet Explorer will then apply your custom settings, instead of its own predefined high security level, to the Restricted Sites zone.

Blocking Cookies

Don't ask how they got their name. A *cookie*, in Internet parlance, is a bit of information about you and your preferences, deposited on your hard disk by a Web site that you've visited. Web sites use cookies to customize their offerings for particular users. If you've ever wondered, for example, how that giant bookstore in the ether knows so much about your taste in reading matter, the answer is that it reads your cookie every time you log on. Cookies are stored in the Cookies folder, which is in your Windows folder. You can open your cookies in Notepad, but you'll find they're mostly indigestible—binary information that only a Web server can love.

In general, cookies are a convenience for end users. They make the Web sites you visit more responsive to your own needs and preferences. Nevertheless, some users do find them objectionable. If you want to keep Web sites from recording information about you on your own hard disk, you can either block cookies entirely or require Internet Explorer to display a confirmation prompt before downloading any cookie. To do either of these things, choose Internet Options from the View menu, click the Advanced tab, and scroll down the list of options until you come to the set of option buttons labeled Cookies. You'll find those option buttons self-explanatory.

If you decide to have Internet Explorer prompt before accepting any cookies, you will see a dialog box similar to the one shown in Figure 25-25 each time a site wants to send a cookie your way. If you tire of responding to these messages, you can always return to the Internet Options dialog box.

FIGURE 25-25.

You can ask Internet Explorer to prompt you before download-ing any cookies, but you might tire of seeing messages like these.

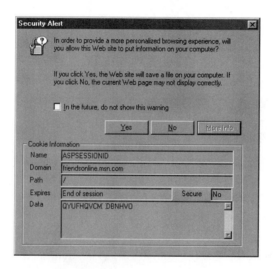

Blocking Pornography and Other Objectionable Content

Some Web sites provide information or pictures that you might find objectionable for you or your children. Internet Explorer provides a feature called Content Advisor to help you block the display of objection-able material. To take advantage of this capability, you supply a supervi-sor password and then specify the types of Web-page content you want to block. Users will then be unable to see the blocked material unless they can supply the supervisor password.

To set up Content Advisor, follow these steps:

1 Choose Internet Options from the View menu and click the Content tab.

2 Click Enable.

3 In the Create Supervisor Password dialog box that appears, supply and confirm your supervisor password, and then click OK.

The supervisor password is the master key that lets you change the Content Advisor settings or bypass the Content Advisor protections. Write this password down in a safe place so that if you forget it, you won't be locked out of Internet Explorer.

When you complete these steps, the Content Advisor dialog box appears, as shown in Figure 25-26. (After you enable Content Advisor, you can return to this dialog box by clicking Settings on the Content tab of the Internet Options dialog box.)

FIGURE 25-26.
Content Advisor allows you to specify what types of content are viewable in Internet Explorer.

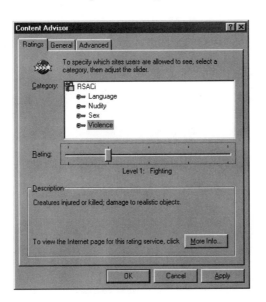

The Content Advisor dialog box contains a list of available rating systems and categories. By default, Internet Explorer comes with a system called RSACi, the Recreational Software Advisory Council's Internet rating system. The system has four categories: sex, violence, nudity, and language. Each category has five levels, numbered 0 through 4. A higher number indicates more explicit or intense content.

To set the level for a particular category, select the category, and then move the slider bar that appears to the maximum level of content that users will be allowed to see when Content Advisor is enabled. As you move the slider, a description of the current setting appears below the slider. When you've set a level for each category, click OK.

If a user tries to go to a Web page that is beyond the limits you set, Internet Explorer will not show the page, and instead displays a warning dialog box. Users who know the supervisor password can bypass the warning and view the page.

> Even if you use user profiles, the settings you make in Content Advisor apply to all users on your computer; you can't make separate settings for each user.

Blocking Unrated Sites

By default, Content Advisor blocks pages that do not have a rating, because Content Advisor has no way of knowing what types of content are on those pages. You can change this setting by clicking the General tab in the Content Advisor dialog box, shown in Figure 25-27, and selecting the check box labeled "Users can see sites that have no rating."

FIGURE 25-27.
The General tab lets you block unrated sites, bypass blocking, and change the supervisor password.

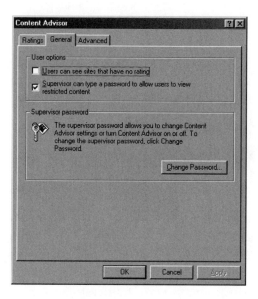

Allowing a User to Bypass Blocking

Normally, your supervisor password is used only to turn the entire blocking mechanism on or off. If you want, however, you can allow a user to see a blocked page by supplying the password when he or she attempts to access the blocked Web page. To do this, display the Content Advisor dialog box and click the General tab. On the General tab, shown in Figure 25-27, select the check box labeled "Supervisor can type a password to allow users to view restricted content."

Changing Your Supervisor Password

To change your supervisory password, display the Content Advisor dialog box and click the General tab. You will see the dialog box shown in Figure 25-27. Click the Change Password button.

Turning Off Blocking

If you change your mind about blocking offensive material, simply display the Internet Options dialog box and click the Content tab. Click the Disable button and enter your supervisor password.

Using Profile Assistant

SEE ALSO

For information about enabling or disabling Profile Assistant, see "Setting Advanced Options," page 656.

Many Web sites request personal information, purportedly to help them deliver useful information to you. Internet Explorer provides a feature called Profile Assistant, which allows you to enter all your information once, and then control which Web sites have access to which kinds of information. Using Profile Assistant saves you from having to reenter the same information, such as your name and e-mail address, and it provides privacy safeguards.

When you visit a Web site that requests information from Profile Assistant, the request shows you the address of the requesting site, what information the site is requesting, how the information will be used, and whether the site has a secure connection. Before granting the request, you can verify that the site is legitimate, and you can choose which information you want Profile Assistant to provide, or you can refuse to give the site any information.

To configure Profile Assistant, choose Internet Options from the View menu. Click the Content tab, and then click the Edit Profile button. In the dialog box that appears, fill in the fields on each tab. (Remember, Web sites do not have access to this information until you explicitly give them permission.) Click OK in the profile properties dialog box, and then click OK in the Internet Options dialog box.

V

Sharing and Communicating

If you allow one or more Web sites to access your profile information without further prompting (an option that's available when a Web site requests information from Profile Assistant), you can revoke that permission by clicking the Reset Sharing button on the Content tab in the Internet Options dialog box.

Using Microsoft Wallet

Microsoft Wallet is a timesaving feature that can securely transmit credit-card information to vendors that you do business with on the Internet. With Microsoft Wallet, you can store information about your billing and shipping addresses, as well as credit card numbers and expiration dates. You need to do this only once. Then, when a Wallet-enabled vendor requests payment information, you can select from the payment methods and addresses that you've already stored. The data that you supply to Microsoft Wallet is stored on your hard disk in encrypted form, and each payment method is protected by a password you supply. You'll be prompted for confirmation before Microsoft Wallet sends any address information across the Internet, and you'll be asked to supply a password before the system sends any credit card data.

Microsoft Wallet uses the SSL security protocol and, in addition, supports the Secure Electronic Transmission (SET) standard. The latter is a system whereby your credit card information is transmitted, in encrypted form, directly to the credit card issuer for validation, so that the vendor with whom you're shopping receives only a validation number, not your credit card data. It's safer to do business with a vendor that supports SET, because you don't need to worry that one of the vendor's employees might take advantage of your credit card number.

To use Microsoft Wallet, begin by choosing Internet Options from the View menu and clicking the Content tab. Near the bottom of the Content tab, you'll find buttons labeled Addresses and Payments. Use the Addresses button to enter billing and shipping information. Use the Payments tab to enter information about credit card accounts that you want to use while shopping on the Web.

> If the Addresses and Payments buttons are not available, Microsoft Wallet has not been installed on your computer. To install it, launch Add/Remove Programs in Control Panel, click the Windows Setup tab, select Internet Tools, and click the Details button. Select Microsoft Wallet and click OK.

Customizing Internet Explorer

If Internet Explorer's current setup is not to your liking, you can set a variety of options. For example, you can:

- Specify a different home page, the page that appears when you start Internet Explorer

- Select and arrange the toolbars you want

- Specify the pages that appear when you click an icon on the Links toolbar

- Select colors for text, the window background, and links

- Select a font for unformatted text

- Control how much hard disk space Internet Explorer uses

- Specify when pages that you've already viewed should be updated

- Set miscellaneous options that control Internet Explorer's appearance, browsing speed, security, compatibility, and other features

To change several of these options, you use the Internet Options dialog box. To display the Internet Options dialog box, use one of the following methods:

- Choose Internet Options from Internet Explorer's View menu.

- Right-click the Internet Explorer icon on your desktop and choose the Properties command.

- Launch Internet in Control Panel.

> **NOTE**
>
> Depending on how you get to it, the dialog box might be titled Internet Properties instead of Internet Options—but the content is the same.

Changing the Home Page

The home page is the one that appears automatically when you open Internet Explorer (unless you begin by launching an Internet shortcut). You can return to the home page at any time by clicking the Home button on the Standard Buttons toolbar or by choosing Home Page from the Go menu. You don't have to use the home page that Microsoft gives you; you can substitute any page you prefer.

To specify a different home page, follow these steps:

1 Display the page that you want to use as the new home page.

2 Display the Internet Options dialog box, and click the General tab.

3 Click Use Current, and then click OK.

Instead of displaying the page you want to use, you can type its address in the Address text box. If you use this method, do not click Use Current.

To restore Internet Explorer's original home page, return to this dialog box, and then click the Use Default button.

Customizing the Toolbars

Internet Explorer has three toolbars: Standard Buttons, Links, and Address Bar. The Standard Buttons toolbar includes Back, Forward, and Stop buttons, among others. The Links toolbar has buttons for quick access to a handful of favorite sites. The Address Bar toolbar displays the address of the current page. In addition, the menu bar is a "toolbar," and—except for the fact that you can't hide it altogether—you can move or resize it like any other toolbar.

You can display these toolbars in any combination. Open the View menu, choose Toolbars, and choose the toolbar's name from the submenu that appears. Choose the same command again to hide a toolbar. You can reduce the space occupied by the Standard Buttons toolbar by choosing the Text Labels command on the Toolbars submenu.

TIP

As a quicker way to display or hide a toolbar, right-click an unoccupied area of any toolbar, which displays the same commands as the View menu's Toolbars command.

You can also tailor the appearance of the toolbars in the following ways:

- To expand the toolbar, which can be displayed on one, two, three, or four lines, drag the lower boundary of the toolbar down. To collapse a multiline toolbar, drag the lower boundary of the toolbar up.

SEE ALSO

For information about other toolbar customization options, see "Setting Advanced Options," page 656.

- To change the location or size of any of the toolbars, drag the vertical line at the left end of the toolbar. With this capability, you can combine two or more toolbars on a single line, place each on a line of its own, change their order, and change their width.

Customizing the Links Toolbar

The Links toolbar provides convenient access to a handful of your very favorite pages. By default, buttons on the Links toolbar take you to Microsoft-favored sites—but you can supplement or replace these with your own most-needed links. To add a link to the Links toolbar, use any of these techniques:

- Drag the page icon from the Address Bar to the Links toolbar.

- Drag a link from a Web page to the Links toolbar.

- Display the Favorites Explorer Bar, and then drag a link to the Links folder on the Favorites Explorer Bar.

You can also change the order of the buttons on the Links toolbar. Simply drag a button to the desired location.

To remove a Links toolbar button, right-click it and choose Delete.

Selecting Colors

You can select the color used for ordinary text, links that you've already visited, links that you haven't visited, and the document area background. To change any of these color settings, display the Internet Options dialog box and click the General tab. Then click the Colors button to display the Colors dialog box, shown in Figure 25-28, on the next page.

V

Sharing and Communicating

FIGURE 25-28.

You can specify colors for text, background, and links in the Colors dialog box.

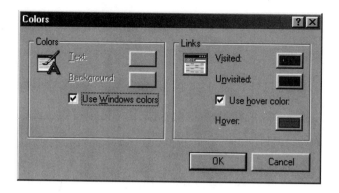

? SEE ALSO

For information about Windows desktop colors, see "Changing Colors, Fonts, and Sizes," page 91.

By default, Internet Explorer uses the colors you specify in Control Panel's Display Properties dialog box for ordinary text and for the window background. To override these defaults, deselect the Use Windows Colors check box.

Then, to specify the color for any of the four elements, click its button and then select a color in the palette that appears.

The Colors dialog box also lets you set the color to use for links that you hover the mouse pointer over. Select Use Hover Color, and then click the button and select a color in the palette that appears.

> NOTE

The colors you select in the Colors dialog box affect only documents that do not specify their own color settings, which override these settings.

★ TIP

If you find it difficult to read a Web page that sets its own colors, tell Internet Explorer to ignore those color commands and use your own color settings for all text and backgrounds. On the General tab in the Internet Options dialog box, click Accessibility and then select the check box labeled "Ignore colors specified on Web pages."

Selecting Fonts

Many Web pages include formatting codes that specify which fonts to use. Pages that do not include such codes display their text in one of two

SEE ALSO

For information about fonts, see Chapter 8, "Installing and Using Fonts."

fonts that you can specify—one proportionally spaced font and one fixed-width (monospaced) font. To specify the fonts, click the Fonts button on the General page in the Internet Options dialog box.

You cannot specify a particular font size for text display—but you can select among five predefined sizes. To change the size of unformatted text in the Internet Explorer document area, specify the size in the Fonts dialog box or choose the Fonts command from the View menu. A cascading submenu offers choices from Smallest to Largest.

 TIP

> If you find it difficult to read a Web page that sets its own fonts, tell Internet Explorer to ignore those font commands and use your own font and font size settings for all text. On the General tab in the Internet Options dialog box, click Accessibility and then select the check box labeled "Ignore font styles specified on Web pages," the check box labeled "Ignore font sizes specified on Web pages," or both.

Controlling the Cache

Internet Explorer stores pages that you visit in folders contained within the folder named Temporary Internet Files. These stored pages are called a *cache*, and Internet Explorer uses them to speed the display of pages you've already visited. By default, these cache folders use as much as 3 percent of capacity of the drive on which they reside. If that's too much space (or not enough), you can change the cache size by displaying the Internet Options dialog box. On the General tab, click the Settings button to display the dialog box shown in Figure 25-29, on the next page.

By default, if Internet Explorer finds a copy of the page you want in its cache, it uses the cached page instead of requesting another copy from the Web. Because Web pages change frequently, however, Internet Explorer checks once per session to see if the page on the Web is newer than the cached page. If the pages you're interested in never change (or you don't care if you see the latest version), you might want to override this behavior by selecting the Never option button.

V

Sharing and Communicating

FIGURE 25-29.

You control the cache size in the Settings dialog box for Temporary Internet Files.

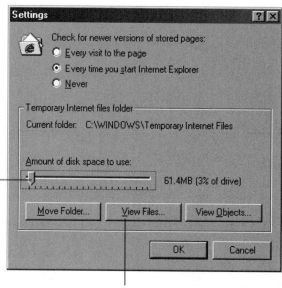

Move this slider to increase or decrease the allowable cache size.

Click View Files to display the Temporary Internet Files folder.

Setting Advanced Options

The Advanced tab in the Internet Options dialog box, shown in Figure 25-30, provides a number of options for customizing Internet Explorer. Table 25-2 describes these options.

FIGURE 25-30.

The Advanced tab is a compendium of miscellaneous settings.

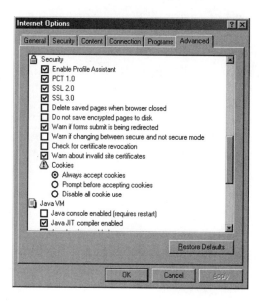

TABLE 25-2. Options on the Advanced Tab

Option	Description
Accessibility	
Move system caret with focus/selection changes	When selected, the "system caret" always follows the selection. This affects some screen magnifiers and screen readers, which focus on the area around the system caret.
Always expand alt text for images	If Show Pictures (in the Multimedia section) is deselected, Internet Explorer displays alternate text (usually a caption or description of the picture) in the space allocated for the picture. When this check box is selected, Internet Explorer expands the picture box if necessary to display all the alternate text.
Browsing	
Disable script debugging	Turns off debugging warnings for errors on Web pages.
Show channel bar at startup (if Active Desktop is off)	When selected, Windows displays the Channel Bar on your desktop when you start your computer—even if the Active Desktop's View As Web Page option is turned off.
Launch channels in full screen window	When selected, Internet Explorer uses full screen view whenever you launch a channel from the desktop Channel Bar.
Launch browser in full screen window	When selected, Internet Explorer opens in full screen view.
Use AutoComplete	When selected, AutoComplete attempts to complete an address when you type in the Address Bar, using addresses you've visited before.
Show friendly URLs	Determines the appearance of addresses in the status bar when you point to a link. A "friendly" address includes only the last part of a URL.
Use smooth scrolling	Uses extra processing time to smooth scrolling.

(continued)

TABLE 25-2. *continued*

Option	Description
Browsing	
Enable page transitions	Allows Web sites to use multimedia transitions from one page to another.
Browse in a new process	Allows Internet Explorer to get a separate share of processor time.
Enable page hit counting	When selected, Web sites can create a log of which pages you view, even when you work offline.
Enable scheduled subscription updates	When selected, Internet Explorer automatically updates subscribed pages using the schedule you set up.
Show welcome message each time I log on	When selected, Internet Explorer shows a welcome message on startup.
Show Internet Explorer on the Desktop (requires restart)	When selected, the Internet Explorer icon appears on the desktop; if you want to delete the icon, deselect this check box and restart your computer.
Underline links	Specifies whether you want text links to be underlined always, never, or only when you hover the mouse pointer over the link.
Multimedia	
Show pictures	When selected, Internet Explorer displays images and pictures, which can be slow. Deselect to display pages more quickly; you can still display an individual picture by right-clicking its icon and choosing Show Picture.
Play animations	Same comments as Show Pictures, except this setting affects animations.
Play videos	Same comments as Show Pictures, except this setting affects video clips.

(continued)

TABLE 25-2. *continued*

Option	Description
Multimedia	
Play sounds	When selected, Internet Explorer plays music and audio clips, which can be slow. Deselect to display pages more quickly, or if you don't have a sound card.
Smart image dithering	When selected, Internet Explorer uses additional processing time to smooth images.
Security	
Enable Profile Assistant	When selected, Internet Explorer responds to Web sites' requests for Profile Assistant information. (Internet Explorer always asks your permission before sending any information to a new site.)
PCT 1.0	When selected, you can send and receive secure information using PCT (Private Communications Technology), a Microsoft-proprietary protocol that's more secure than SSL 2.0.
SSL 2.0	When selected, you can send and receive secure information using SSL (Secured Sockets Layer) 2.0, the standard protocol for secure transmissions.
SSL 3.0	When selected, you can send and receive secure information using SSL 3.0, a newer protocol for secure transmissions that is not yet supported by many Web sites.
Delete saved pages when browser closed	When selected, Internet Explorer empties the Temporary Internet Files folder when you close the program.
Do not save encrypted pages to disk	When selected, pages from a secure or encrypted site are not stored on your hard disk.

(continued)

V

Sharing and Communicating

TABLE 25-2. *continued*

Option	Description
Security	
Warn if forms submit is being redirected	When selected, Internet Explorer displays a warning if you submit information via a Web-based form and the information is addressed to a Web site other than the one where you enter the information.
Warn if changing between secure and not secure mode	When selected, Internet Explorer displays a warning when you go from a secure site to an unsecure site.
Check for certificate revocation	When selected, Internet Explorer takes extra time before accepting a certificate to make sure that it is valid and has not been revoked.
Warn about invalid certificates	When selected, Internet Explorer warns you if the address in a certificate is not valid.
Cookies	Specifies how you want to handle *cookies*, information about you that a Web site can store on your hard disk. You can always accept cookies, have Internet Explorer prompt you before accepting cookies, or refuse all cookies.
Java VM	
Java console enabled (requires restart)	When selected, Internet Explorer uses the Java console.
Java JIT compiler enabled	When selected, Internet Explorer uses its internal just-in-time compiler to improve Java performance.
Java logging enabled	When selected, Internet Explorer keeps a log file for Java activity, which can be useful for security and troubleshooting.
Printing	
Print background colors and images	When selected, background images are included when you print the page.

(continued)

TABLE 25-2. *continued*

Option	Description
Search	
Autoscan common root domains	When selected, if you type an incorrect address (or if you omit the top-level domain), Internet Explorer automatically attempts to find the correct address by trying other common top-level domains (.com, .edu, and .org). For example, if you type www.auto.com and no such address exists, Internet Explorer tries www.auto.edu and www.auto.org.
Search when URL fails	Specifies what you want Internet Explorer to do if you type an incorrect address (or click a link with an incorrect address) and the address can't be found even after trying different top-level domains (see above). "Search" means to open an Internet search page.
Toolbar	
Show font button	When selected, the Font button (a shortcut to the Fonts command on the View menu) appears on the Standard Buttons toolbar.
Small icons	When selected, the Standard Buttons toolbar uses smaller icons, similar to the ones in Microsoft Office.
HTTP 1.1 settings	
Use HTTP 1.1	When selected, Internet Explorer attempts to use the enhanced features of the latest version of HTTP when connecting to Web sites. Many sites still use HTTP 1.0; if you have trouble connecting, try deselecting this check box.
Use HTTP 1.1 through proxy connections	Attempts to use HTTP 1.1 even when using a proxy connection.

Using Outlook Express

I n today's "wired world," electronic mail (e-mail) has become an essential communications medium. One of the most widely used features of the Internet is the ability it provides you to exchange messages and files with friends, business associates, and strangers.

Another popular method that many people use to exchange information is Internet news. Thousands of separate "newsgroups" on the Internet contain articles and messages about almost every imaginable topic, from particle physics to ragtime music.

Windows 98 includes a program called Outlook Express that handles mail and Internet news in a single "information store." Outlook Express includes a rich-text message editor and viewer, an address book, and a set of folders you can use to organize incoming and outgoing mail and news articles. It also gives you access to several on-line directories that you can use to find e-mail and postal addresses and telephone numbers.

Outlook Express can work with almost any mail or news service, including the protocols used by America Online; MSN, The Microsoft Network online service; and most other Internet service providers (ISPs). If you have accounts with more than one ISP, you can use Outlook Express to manage all your mail from a single window, and you can switch between news servers to participate in more newsgroups than you may be able to view from a single ISP.

Outlook Express is the news and mail client program supplied with Windows 98, but it's not an essential part of the operating system. If your computer does not have a network connection or a modem, or if you prefer to use a different news or mail program, it's a simple matter to disable or remove Outlook Express without any impact on the rest of Windows 98.

Outlook Express Versus Outlook

As the names suggest, Outlook Express provides some of the same functions that are provided in Microsoft Outlook, the communications component of the Microsoft Office suite, which is also available as a separate stand-alone application. Outlook offers many additional e-mail, scheduling, and contact management features that are not included in Outlook Express. If you install Outlook on your computer after you have been using Outlook Express, you can import the contents of your Outlook Express mailbox folders and address book into Outlook.

Outlook Express is designed to provide a basic, fast, and reliable Internet mail and news client program, whereas Outlook is a more complex product with many additional features and functions. If you use your computer in a home, school, or small-business environment, Outlook Express might be adequate to do everything you need in order to send and receive mail messages and news articles. On the other hand, if you want to integrate mail and news with other Microsoft Office applications, if you need the calendar and contact management functions in the larger program, or if you need to connect to a network mail server, you might want to consider using Outlook.

Installing and Running Outlook Express

If you installed Outlook Express when you installed Windows 98, you probably have an Outlook Express icon on your desktop and an item with the same name in the Programs section of your Start menu.

If you haven't already installed Outlook Express, follow these steps to install it:

1 Launch Add/Remove Programs in Control Panel.

2 Click the Windows Setup tab.

3 In the Components list, select Microsoft Outlook Express.

SEE ALSO

For information about setting up an account with an ISP, see "Getting Started with the Internet Connection Wizard," page 598.

4 If you plan to connect to the Internet through a modem, highlight Communications and click Details. Select Dial-Up Networking, and then click OK to close the Communications window.

5 If you plan to use America Online, AT&T WorldNet, CompuServe, Prodigy, or MSN, The Microsoft Network to connect to the Internet and you haven't already set up the service, highlight Online Services and click Details. Select the service you want to use and click OK.

6 Click OK in the Add/Remove Programs Properties dialog box to begin the installation.

7 If you plan to use America Online, AT&T WorldNet, CompuServe, Prodigy, or MSN, open the Start menu and choose Programs, Online Services, and the name of the service you want to set up.

After the installation is complete, you can start Outlook Express in any of the following ways:

■ Double-click (or click) the Outlook Express icon on the desktop.

■ Open the Start menu and choose Programs, Internet Explorer, Outlook Express.

 ■ Click the Launch Outlook Express button on the Quick Launch toolbar.

■ In Explorer, choose either Mail or News from the Go menu.

 TIP

Turning Off the Outlook Explorer Splash Screen
Like most other Windows-based programs, Outlook Express displays a "splash screen" every time you start the program. The splash screen doesn't contain any useful information, so you might want to configure Outlook Express to start without displaying the splash screen.

To disable the splash screen, use Registry Editor to create a new DWORD value in HKEY_CURRENT_USER\Software\Microsoft\Outlook Express. Name the new value NoSplash, and change the value data to 1. (For information about Registry Editor, see "Introducing Registry Editor," page 364.)

Outlook Express now opens without the splash screen. To turn the splash screen back on, change the NoSplash value data to 0.

V

Sharing and Communicating

How Outlook Express Is Organized

? SEE ALSO

For information about the optional sections, see "Changing the Appearance of Outlook Express," page 714.

Outlook Express uses an outline structure for folders, newsgroups, and messages that's similar to the structure that Windows Explorer uses for folders and files. Individual mail messages appear in mail folders. The program displays each news server where you have an account as a top-level folder, with each subscribed newsgroup as a subfolder. Newsgroup messages are stored in newsgroup folders. Figure 26-1 shows the structure of a typical Outlook Express installation. In this figure, the Outlook bar and other optional sections are visible.

FIGURE 26-1.

Outlook Express organizes messages and newsgroups in folders and subfolders.

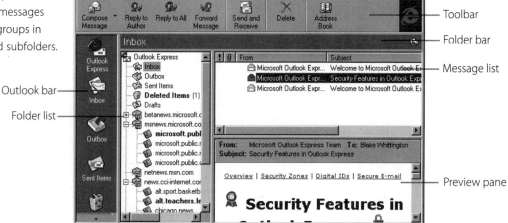

Navigating in Outlook Express

If you click the Outlook Express icon (at the top of the Outlook bar or at the top of the folder list), a window similar to the one shown in Figure 26-2 appears. This top-level window works like a Web page with graphic links to each Outlook Express function: mail, news, the address book, and other directory services. To jump directly to one of these areas, click its link.

The black bar at the top of the page includes links to Web sites for Outlook Express, Internet Explorer, and Microsoft Corporation.

FIGURE 26-2.

The top-level Outlook Express "folder" provides links to other folders and Web pages.

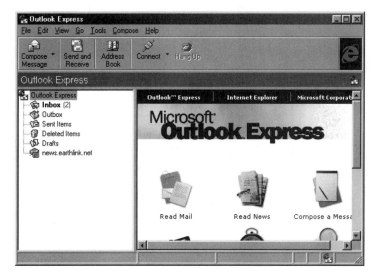

To move to any other location within Outlook Express, click its name in the Outlook bar or the folder list. If the folder list is not visible, you can open it by clicking the name of the current folder in the folder bar. You can also move to a specific location by choosing a command from the Go menu.

Mail Folders

SEE ALSO

For information about changing the displayed columns, see "Customizing the Message List," page 716.

When you install Outlook Express, the program sets up five standard mail folders: Inbox, Outbox, Sent Items, Deleted Items, and Drafts. Although you can't rename or delete these standard mail folders, you can create additional mail folders as either subfolders within an existing folder or as new top-level folders. Outlook Express displays messages in each mail folder in a list like the one shown in Figure 26-3, on the next page. To see the contents of a message, double-click the entry for that message.

TIP

Double-clicking an entry in the message list opens the message in a new window. The preview pane provides a quicker, albeit smaller, alternative: simply click a message entry to select it, and the message contents appear in the preview pane.

FIGURE 26-3.

The message list includes a line of information about each message in a folder.

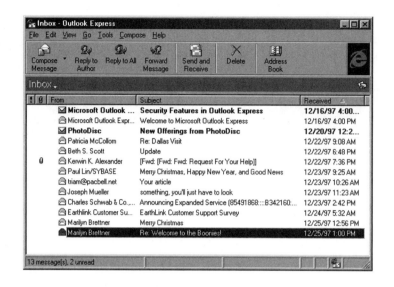

The following sections describe the purpose and use of the five standard mail folders.

Inbox

For information about the Inbox Assistant, see "Using the Inbox Assistant," page 698.

When Outlook Express receives a new message, it places that message in the Inbox folder—unless the Inbox Assistant includes an instruction to move the message to a different folder.

Outbox

The Outbox folder contains messages that have not yet been transmitted from Outlook Express to your post office server. After transmission is complete, Outlook Express moves the message from the Outbox folder to the Sent Items folder.

Sent Items

After Outlook Express transmits a message, it moves the message to the Sent Items folder. Depending on the filing system you use, you might want to retain messages in Sent Items, or move each message to another folder.

Deleted Items

When you delete a message from a folder, Outlook Express moves the message to the Deleted Items folder—the final storage place for messages that have been deleted from other folders. You can work with messages in the Deleted Items folder just as you can with messages in other folders; you can reply, forward, or edit messages, for example. There's one key difference: when you delete a message from the Deleted Items folder, it's gone for good, and you can't get it back.

As long as the message remains in the Deleted Items folder, you can restore a deleted message by moving it to another folder. You can do that by dragging the message from the Deleted Items folder to the name of the destination folder in the folder list, or by selecting the message and choosing the Move To Folder command from the Edit menu.

Drafts

The Drafts folder is a place to hold messages that you're not yet ready to send. When you use the Save command in the message editor, Outlook Express stores the saved message in the Drafts folder.

News Folders

Internet News is another system for distributing messages, but unlike mail, news messages, called *articles*, are public announcements that are posted in electronic bulletin boards devoted to a specific topic. These bulletin boards are called *newsgroups*. Along with mail, you can also use Outlook Express to send and receive news articles.

News Servers

Just as Outlook Express exchanges mail with a mail server, it obtains news articles from a news server. News servers exchange news articles with Outlook Express and other news client programs. When you set up an account with an Internet service provider (ISP), one of the things the ISP provides is access to their news server. Most news servers handle articles posted in the thousands of public newsgroups that are available to anybody who wants to read them. In addition, some servers use the same system for *private newsgroups* that are available only to people with accounts on those servers, but which are not distributed to other servers. Therefore, you might want to configure Outlook Express to use more than one server.

As Figure 26-4 on the next page shows, Outlook Express maintains a top-level folder for each news server where you have an account. When you subscribe to an individual newsgroup, it shows up as a folder under

V

Sharing and Communicating

FIGURE 26-4.

Newsgroups appear as
subfolders within a
news server folder.

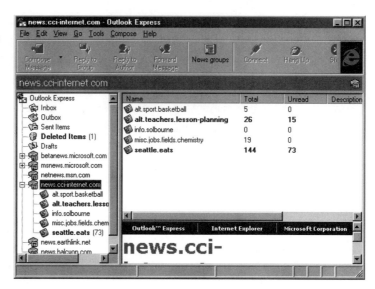

the server where you obtain that newsgroup. When you open a
newsgroup, the message list shows each article in that newsgroup.

Setting Up Mail and News Accounts

The standards for Internet mail specify separate servers for inbound and
outbound mail, so you must have accounts on both servers in order to
send and receive mail. Some ISPs, such as MSN and Prodigy Internet,
automatically configure Outlook Express when you install their software,
but many others require manual configuration. If your ISP gave you a list
of account codes and passwords when you opened your account, you'll
need that list now.

Follow these steps to set up a new Outlook Express mail account or
news account:

1 Start Outlook Express.

2 Open the Tools menu and choose Accounts. The Internet Accounts
dialog box appears.

3 Click the Add button and choose Mail to set up a mail account, or
choose News to set up an account with a news server.
The Internet Connection Wizard starts.

4 Use the information supplied by your ISP to fill in the blank fields in the wizard.

To see a list of your mail accounts, including the ones that you set up with the Internet Connection Wizard and those that were installed automatically, click the Mail tab in the Internet Accounts dialog box. If you have accounts on more than one mail server, Outlook Express checks for new mail on each of them unless you have specifically excluded one or more accounts, as explained in the following section.

SEE ALSO

For information about directories, see "Importing Addresses from Internet Directory Services," page 693.

You can view the names of your news accounts on the News tab in the Internet Accounts dialog box. The All tab shows your mail accounts, your news accounts, and your directory accounts.

Viewing and Changing Account Properties

To view or change the current configuration of a mail account, select the name of the account on the Mail tab and click the Properties button to open the Properties dialog box for the selected account, or double-click the name of the account.

Normally, Outlook Express checks all your mail accounts every time you enter a Send and Receive command. To exclude an account, click the General tab in the Properties dialog box and deselect the Include This Account When Doing A Full Send And Receive check box at the bottom of the screen.

Most of the other mail account properties should not change from the ones that were set when you established the account. There are a couple of possible exceptions:

■ It doesn't happen often, but if your ISP changes the name of its mail server, you must change the Server Information on the Servers tab.

■ Normally, Outlook Express instructs the mail server to discard each message after it delivers a copy to you. But if you're reading mail on a portable computer, or if you have computers both at work and at home, and you want to store all your mail in one place, even if you read it someplace else, you can keep copies of your messages on the mail server. To change this setting, click the Advanced tab and set the Leave A Copy Of Messages On Server check box accordingly.

V

Sharing and Communicating

Receiving and Sending Mail

Almost all electronic mail sent across the Internet and other networks uses a *store-and-forward* system: when somebody sends you a message, the message goes to a computer called a *mail server*, which holds it until your own computer comes looking for new mail. When Outlook Express connects to your mail server—either on a regular schedule or because you issued a specific command—it downloads all the messages that have arrived since the last connection. At the same time, it uploads any new messages from your Outbox folder to the server.

Messages you send follow a similar path. When you send a message, your mail client program (in this case, Outlook Express) transmits it to a program called a *post office server*, which reads the destination information in the message header and passes it across the Internet or some other network to the recipient's mail server, where it is held until the recipient's mail client program checks for new mail.

Before you can read your mail, you must download each message from your mail server. You can either check for new mail on a regular schedule or enter a manual "check for new mail" command. If you have mail accounts with more than one service provider, Outlook Express can automatically check for new mail from each server where you have an account. If you prefer, you can manually check for new mail on each individual server.

Setting Up an Automatic Download Schedule

To instruct Outlook Express to check for new mail on a regular schedule, follow these steps:

1 Open the Tools menu and choose Options.

2 On the General tab in the Options dialog box, select the Check For New Messages Every — Minute(s) check box.

3 Use the spinner to set the number of minutes between trips to the mail server.

4 If you want Outlook Express to issue an audible signal whenever a new message arrives, select the Play Sound check box.

Manually Downloading New Mail from Your Mail Server

When you want to check for new mail between scheduled downloads, or if you don't want to use a schedule at all, you can instruct Outlook Express to make an immediate connection to the server. Click the Send And Receive button on the toolbar, choose Send And Receive from the Tools menu, or press Ctrl+M.

Receiving Mail Through More Than One Account

If you have more than one mail account, the Send And Receive command on the Tools menu opens a submenu that lists each of your accounts. To check for mail everywhere, choose All Accounts from the submenu. To check only one account, select the name of that account from the submenu.

Reading Messages

After Outlook Express receives your new mail, it places each message in the Inbox folder (unless you have set up Inbox Assistant to move them to some other folder). The Inbox window, shown in Figure 26-5, contains a list of messages in your Inbox. New, unread messages appear in this and other folders in boldface type, with a closed envelope icon. After you read a message, its entry changes to normal type with an open envelope icon.

FIGURE 26-5.

Bold text makes it easy to identify new, unread messages.

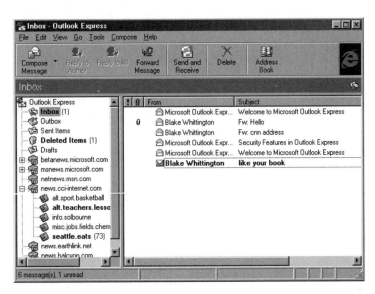

To read a message in a separate message window, either double-click its entry or select it and choose the Open command from the File menu. The message window, shown in Figure 26-6, includes a message header and the message body, in separate panes. The message header identifies the source, destination, and subject of a message and includes other useful information. The body of a message includes the text and can also include Web links and graphic images.

FIGURE 26-6.
Double-click a message entry to display the message in a separate window.

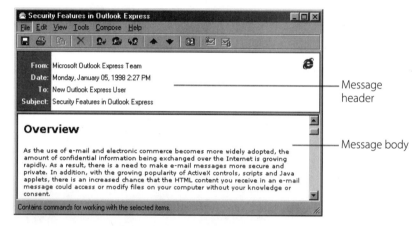

Message header

Message body

Seeing Messages in the Preview Pane

The preview pane is an optional section of the main Outlook Express window that displays the contents of the currently selected message. It can be a convenient way to scan the contents of messages and news articles without taking the time to open a separate message window. To display or hide the preview pane, choose Layout from the View menu. Select the Use Preview Pane check box and click OK.

> The Use Preview Pane check box is unavailable when the top-level Outlook Express folder is selected. Be sure you select another folder before choosing the Layout command.

Reading Messages Off Line

It's not necessary to have an active connection between your own computer and the mail server when you want to read your mail. Because Outlook Express downloads and stores a copy of each message, you see a local copy in the message window or preview pane. Therefore, you can read your mail (and compose new messages) at any time, even if you're away from a telephone line or other network link. For example, many people who travel with a portable computer download their new mail before leaving the office, and read it aboard an airplane or train.

Viewing Attached Files

Mail messages are not limited to text. It's also possible to send data files that are formatted for a word processor, spreadsheet, or other application; graphic images; programs; and other types of files as e-mail. A file included with a mail message is known as a *file attachment*. When a message has an attached file, the Outlook Express message list includes a paper clip icon in the Attachment column next to the description of that message.

SEE ALSO

For information about filename extensions, see "What Is a Filename Extension?," page 123.

In the preview pane, a message with attached files appears with a paper clip button in the message header area. To open or save the files, click the button and choose the name of the file you want to open or save to disk. In a message window, each attached file appears as an icon in a pane at the bottom of the message window. Windows 98 treats these file icons like the ones you see on your desktop or in Windows Explorer: you can open the file by double-clicking the icon. If Windows recognizes the filename extension, it loads the file into the program associated with that type of file. If the file is itself a program, double-clicking the icon runs the program.

In addition to the file icons, Outlook Express automatically displays certain picture files—those with a .BMP, .GIF, or .JPG filename extension—as fully rendered pictures at the bottom of the message. If you'd rather not be distracted, you can disable this feature by visiting the Read tab in the Options dialog box and deselecting the Automatically Show Picture Attachments In Messages check box.

Viewing Message Headers

In addition to the body of the message that carries text and attached files, every mail message also includes a *header*, which contains the information that mail servers use to deliver the message from its originator to its ultimate recipient. The familiar From, To, Date, and Subject lines are all parts of the header, but the header also includes several additional lines of data that the server uses to identify the message and figure out how to route the message to its recipient. Some message headers also contain formatting instructions that Outlook Express can use when it displays the message text.

Most of the time, you won't want to see the routing and message ID data in your message headers, but if you ever need to trace the source or delivery of a message, or if you're just curious to see what those computers are saying to one another, Outlook Express can display the entire header in a properties dialog box. To view a message header, follow these steps:

1 Select the message or display it in a window.

2 Open the File menu and choose Properties. The properties dialog box for the message appears.

3 Click the Details tab to see the full text of the message header.

You can also display the full source code of the current message (including the header) by typing Ctrl+F3 from the message window or clicking the Message Source button in the properties dialog box.

Reading Messages in Foreign Languages

Internet mail reaches users in almost every part of the world, and not all of them use the same alphabet that you do. In most cases, the message header includes information that identifies the language in which the message was written, so Outlook Express can display the proper alphabet. If Outlook Express does not automatically use the correct language, the text of the message will probably include a lot of peculiar characters that make it difficult or even impossible to read.

In order to display messages (and text in Web pages) in one or more foreign languages, you might have to use Add/Remove Programs in Control Panel to install a multilanguage support file from the Windows 98 CD.

To change the text of a message to use the alphabet for a different language, follow these steps:

1 Open the message in a message window.

2 Open the View menu and choose Language. A submenu with a list of supported languages appears.

3 Select the character set you want to use for this message.

Replying to a Message

You will probably want to write and send replies to many of the mail messages you receive. Replies to messages may contain quotes from the original message, along with additional text. A reply includes a normally hidden line in the header that identifies the original message, so Outlook Express and other mail client programs may organize a message and its replies (and the replies to *those* replies) into a message *thread*.

To reply to a message in Outlook Express, open the original message in either the message viewer or the Preview Pane, open the Compose menu, and choose one of the Reply To commands. Use Reply To Author if you want your reply to go only to the person who sent the original message; use Reply To All to also send copies to all the people who received copies of the original message.

When you choose a Reply command, Outlook Express opens a new message editor window, with the To field and the Subject field (and if it's a Reply To All, the Cc field) already filled in, and the text of the original message quoted in the body of the message.

 TIP

> If the original message contains more than just one or two lines, you might want to edit out the parts of the message that don't require an answer. There's not much point to sending unnecessary lines back to the person who wrote them.

Outlook Express treats a reply exactly the same way as it treats any other message you send. When you click the Send button, it stores the message in your Outbox folder until it is able to transfer it to your mail server. After the message has been sent, it moves your copy of the message to the Sent Items folder.

Creating a New Message

Sending a mail message may involve several steps:

- Composing the text

- Changing the appearance of the message

- Attaching files to the message

- Inserting hypertext links

- Using a spell checker

- Adding a signature block

- Sending the message to your mail server

? SEE ALSO

For information about stationery, see "Using Stationery," page 681.

To create a new message, click the Compose Message button on the toolbar, press Ctrl+N, or open the Compose menu and choose New Message. If you want to use "stationery" for your message, click the down-arrow next to the Compose Message button or choose the New Message Using command from the Compose menu.

Composing Messages

When you enter a Compose Message command, Outlook Express opens a message editor window. (See Figure 26-7.) Follow these steps to prepare your message:

FIGURE 26-7.

Start your message by filling in the address fields.

1 In the To field, type the e-mail address or addresses to which you want to send this message, or click the file-card icon to select one or more recipients from your address book. (Use a comma or a semicolon to separate addresses if you want to include more than one.)

2 If you want to send additional copies of the same message to other recipients, type their e-mail addresses in the Cc field or click the icon to select names from your address book.

3 If you want to send "blind copies" of this message to additional recipients, type or select the addresses in this field. The names of Bcc recipients won't appear in the copies of the message sent to other recipients.

4 Type a brief description of the subject of this message in the Subject field.

5 Type the text of your message in the work area at the bottom of the window.

Press the Tab key to move from the Subject field to the work area.

Changing the Appearance of Your Message

The original rules and protocols that control mail through the Internet were established in the days when most people using the Internet had character-based mail programs. In those days, mail messages were limited to plain text, which would work properly on just about any computer that received it.

Today, Outlook Express and other modern mail programs are more flexible—they can send and receive messages that include embedded pictures, special type faces, links to Web pages and other Internet resources, and other special features along with the text. Figure 26-8, on the next page, shows a sample. However, you can't automatically assume that everybody who receives your messages will be able to recognize all the fancy embellishments you have added to the text. Many computer users, especially those in schools and colleges and those outside of North America and western Europe, are still using older, less sophisticated mail programs. Messages that use rich text format are supposed to appear as plain text in mail programs that don't recognize formatting, but in practice, many mail reading programs add formatting commands and other distractions to the text. Therefore, it's a good idea to limit the number of graphic enhancements in your mail messages and news articles unless you know that your recipients have mail programs and newsreaders that will display them properly.

V

Sharing and Communicating

FIGURE 26-8.

Using stationery and fonts, you can quickly and easily create messages with flair.

Formatting toolbar

Outlook Express uses either of two text formats: Plain Text or Rich Text (HTML).

■ Plain Text format can be used for a message with no special typefaces, embedded graphics, or HTML codes. To select Plain Text format for a message you are composing, open the Format menu and choose Plain Text.

■ Rich Text (HTML) format must be used for messages that include graphics, Web links, or special typefaces. To use Rich Text format for a message you are currently composing, open the Format menu and choose Rich Text (HTML). If you select stationery when you open the message editor, the message editor automatically uses Rich Text. The message editor includes the formatting toolbar shown in Figure 26-8 when Rich Text format is active.

> **NOTE**
>
> You can add file attachments to either Plain Text or Rich Text format messages.

To change the default text format, choose the Options command from the Tools menu in the main Outlook Express window. Click the Send tab, and then select either HTML or Plain Text in the Mail Sending Format frame. You can change the settings for each format by clicking the Settings button next to each option.

Using Stationery

Outlook Express includes a folder full of special graphic backgrounds for more colorful mail messages. Just as you might use more festive paper stationery for an invitation to a birthday party than you would use in a business letter, you can use electronic stationery in your mail messages. To use stationery, either select it when you open the message editor, or choose Apply Stationery from the message editor's Format menu.

 TIP

> You can use any HTML file as stationery. Use FrontPage Express or another HTML editor to create your stationery.

Using a Background Graphic

If you prefer to use a solid color or a picture or graphic pattern as the background of your message, choose the Background command from the message editor's Format menu.

Choose Color and then choose a color if you want a solid background.

If you want to use a picture, choose Picture. In the Background Picture dialog box that appears, select the name of a picture file from the File drop-down list, type the name of a file (including its path and filename extension), or click Browse. You can use any .BMP, .GIF, or .JPG file as your background. Whatever image you choose, Outlook Express tiles (repeats) the picture to fill the entire page.

Formatting Your Text

When you use Plain Text format, the font in which your message appears is set by the recipient's mail program. But if you use Rich Text format, you can specify a font when you create the message, as shown in Figure 26-9, on the next page. (Note, however, that if the recipient doesn't have the same font available on their system, Windows—or whatever operating system the recipient uses—substitutes an available font.) To change the font in your message, select the text and use either the Font and Font Size drop-down lists in the formatting toolbar or the Font command on the Tools menu.

V

Sharing and Communicating

FIGURE 26-9.

Rich Text (HTML) format lets you use different fonts in your messages.

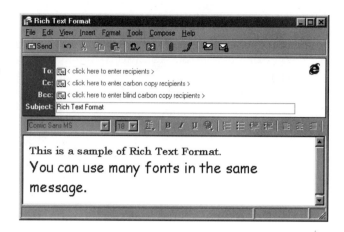

Other buttons on the formatting toolbar and commands on the Format menu control the size, color, style, and position of text in your message. (See Table 26-1.) To change the format of a block of text, select the text and then click a button on the formatting toolbar or choose a command from the Format menu.

Attaching Files and Pictures to Your Message

To attach a text file, data file, or program file to your message, click the Insert File button on the message editor toolbar or choose the File Attachment command from the Insert menu, and select the file you want to send from the file browser. Outlook Express opens a new pane at the bottom of the message editor window, and inserts the icon for the selected file in the attachment pane.

Another way to insert a file is to drag a file from your desktop or a Windows Explorer window to the message window.

Adding Web Links

You can easily add a hypertext link to a Web site or other Internet resource to your message. If you type an Internet address (one that starts with *http://* or *www*, such as http://www.microsoft.com/ or just www.microsoft.com), Outlook Express automatically converts the text to

TABLE 26-1.   Outlook Express Formatting Toolbar

Toolbar Icon	Description
	Applies a predefined paragraph style to the selection
B	Changes the selection to boldface (or, if the selection is already boldface, changes it back to normal)
I	Changes the selection to italic (or, if the selection is already italic, changes it back to normal)
U	Underlines the selection (or if the selection is already underlined, removes the underline)
	Changes the color of the selection
	Changes the selected paragraphs to a numbered list (or, if the selection is already numbered, removes the numbering)
	Changes the selected paragraphs to an indented, bulleted list (or, if the selection is already bulleted, removes the bullets and indents)
	Decreases the selected paragraphs' indent from the left margin
	Increases the selected paragraphs' indent from the left margin
	Left aligns the selected paragraphs
	Centers the selected paragraphs
	Right aligns the selected paragraphs
	Inserts a horizontal line; click the line and drag its handles to change its size
	Changes the selection to a hypertext link to an Internet address
	Inserts a picture

a link. But you can make any text or picture in your message into a clickable link by following these steps:

1 Select the text or picture that you want to be a link.

2 Click the Insert Hyperlink button on the formatting toolbar or choose Hyperlink from the Insert menu.

3 In the Hyperlink dialog box that appears, select the type of link you want (the most common types are http:, for Web addresses, and mailto:, for e-mail addresses) and the Internet address (URL).

> **NOTE**
>
> To insert hypertext links, you must use Rich Text (HTML) format.

If you want to modify a link after you create it, right-click it and choose Properties. This brings up the same Hyperlink dialog box, allowing you to change the type of link and the Internet address.

Using a Spell Checker

If you have installed Microsoft Office 95 or Office 97, or one or more of its component programs—Word, Excel, or PowerPoint—Outlook Express uses the Office spell checker. To run a spell check on the current message in the message editor, choose the Spelling command from the Tools menu. To automatically check the spelling of every message before you send it, in the main Outlook Express window, choose Options from the Tools menu, click the Spelling tab, and select the Always Check Spelling Before Sending check box.

> **NOTE**
>
> The Spelling tab appears only if you have installed a program that includes a compatible spell checker.

Troubleshooting Spell Checker Problems

If the spell checker does not work when you enter the Spelling command, you might have to do some additional setup. Try these steps to make your existing spell checker work with Outlook Express:

1 Make sure the program that includes your spell checker is a 32-bit program. If you're trying to use the spell checker from an older program created for use with MS-DOS or Windows 3.x, you probably won't be able to use it with Outlook Express.

2   Open Windows Explorer and look in the C:\Program Files\ Common Files\Microsoft Shared\Proof folder for these files:

- Mssp2_en.lex

- Mssp232.dll

- Custom.dic

If all three files are in the Proof folder, move on to the next step. If any of the files are missing, choose the Find command from the Tools menu to locate them and then make copies in the Proof folder.

3   If spell checking still doesn't work with Outlook Express after moving these files, try reinstalling the program that contains the spell checker.

Adding a Signature Block to a Message

A signature is a standard block of text that appears at the bottom of a mail message or news article. Signature blocks normally contain the name and e-mail address of the sender, along with other information that the sender wants to include in every message, such as the name and postal address of the sender's company or organization. Some people use large and elaborate signature blocks with pictures constructed from ASCII characters, political slogans, or attempts at humor, but this kind of signature is often unwelcome, especially by people who have seen them too often. As a general rule, a signature block should contain no more than four or five lines.

To create a signature block, follow these steps:

1   From the Tools menu, choose the Stationery command. The Stationery dialog box appears.

2   Click the Signature button.

3   In the Signature dialog box, shown in Figure 26-10 on the next page, either type the text of your signature block in the Text field, or select the File option button and use the Browse button to find a text file or HTML file.

V

Sharing and Communicating

FIGURE 26-10.

In the Signature dialog box, you specify the text you want to appear at the end of your messages.

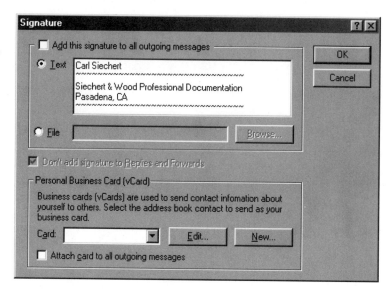

To automatically add your signature file to the bottom of every message you send, select the Add This Signature To All Outgoing Messages check box.

To insert your signature block to an individual message, either click the Insert Signature button on the message editor toolbar, or choose the Signature command from the Insert menu.

Creating and Using Business Cards

Electronic business cards (using a format called vCard) are a convenient way to exchange contact information with other people, and to add new names and addresses to your address book. You can attach your own vCard to outgoing messages to make it easy for the recipients of your messages to add you to their address books.

To create a business card for yourself, follow these steps:

For information about creating an address book entry, see "Adding and Changing Address Book Entries," page 689.

1 Create and save a new entry in your own address book for yourself, including all the information you want to include in your business card: your name, e-mail address, postal address, telephone and fax numbers, and so forth.

2 In the Address Book window, open the File menu and choose Export, Business Card (vCard).

3 Choose a folder where you want to store the card and click the Save button.

To send your business card as part of a mail message, choose Business Card from the message editor's Insert menu.

 TIP

> To automatically add your business card to every message you send, attach your business card to the stationery you use. In the Signature dialog box (see Figure 26-10), select your name from the Card list and select the check box labeled Attach Card To All Outgoing Messages.

Sending a Message

When you have finished composing, formatting, and checking your message, it's ready to send to the mail server. Click the Send button on the toolbar, and Outlook Express deposits the message in the Outbox to wait for the next visit to the mail server.

If you have more than one mail account set up and you want to send your message using an account other than the default account, choose Send Message Using from the File menu, and then choose the name of the mail account you want to use.

Managing Your Address Book

An address book is a list of names and e-mail addresses of people to whom you expect to send messages. Each entry in the Outlook Express address book can also include additional information about the subject of that listing, such as a postal address, voice and fax telephone numbers, and the address of their Web page. A single address book entry can also point to a group of names.

When you create a new message, you can select the name of an individual or group from your address book and automatically enter the correct e-mail address in the To or Cc field.

V

Sharing and Communicating

Working with Address Book

You can use any of several ways to open Address Book, shown in Figure 26-11:

- Click the Address Book link in the top-level Outlook Express window.

- Click the Address Book button on the toolbar.

- Choose Address Book from the Tools menu.

- Press Ctrl+Shift+B.

SEE ALSO

For information about the Find People command, see "Finding People," page 181.

You can also obtain access to address book listings by choosing the Find People command on the Windows Start menu, or by clicking one of the file-card icons in the address section of the Outlook Express message editor.

To see the detail of an address book entry, select the entry and click the Properties button, or double-click the entry. To locate an address book entry, type the first few letters of the name in the search field. (Begin typing the first name of the entry you want if entries are shown first name first, or begin typing the last name if entries are shown last name first.) To change the order in which listings appears, click one of the column headings.

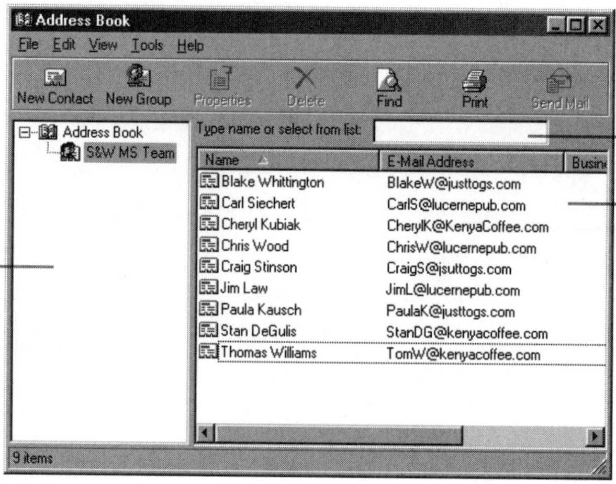

FIGURE 26-11.

Address Book shows the name, e-mail address, and phone numbers for each person in your address book.

Groups list ——

— Search field

— Address list

By clicking the Name column heading repeatedly, you can cycle through the four available orders for sorting by name: first name, ascending order; first name, descending order; last name, ascending order; last name, descending order.

Changing the Appearance of Address Book

The View menu contains commands for hiding or displaying the toolbar at the top of the Address Book window, the status bar at the bottom of the window, and the groups list, the outline-style pane on the left side of the window. To change the current status of one of these items, choose its command from the View menu.

Like Windows Explorer, Address Book can display the icons that represent address book listings as large or small icons, or as items in a list, with or without details. To change the icon display, choose the type of view you want from the View menu.

Adding and Changing Address Book Entries

To create a new Address Book entry, follow these steps:

New Contact

1   Click the New Contact button on the toolbar or press Ctrl+N. The Properties dialog box shown in Figure 26-12 appears.

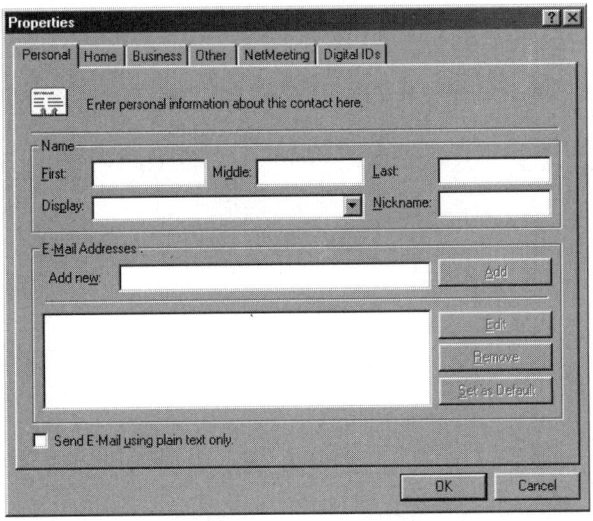

FIGURE 26-12.
The Properties dialog box for an address book entry includes spaces for all types of contact information, including multiple e-mail addresses, and phone numbers, fax numbers, and addresses for home and business.

V

Sharing and Communicating

2 On the Personal tab, type the name of the person or organization you want to add to your Address Book.

As you make entries in the First, Middle, and Last name text boxes, the Nickname text box, and the Company text box (on the Business tab), Address Book adds these entries to the Display drop-down list.

3 Select an item from the Display drop-down list, or type the text you want to use to identify this contact. The Display text you specify is used in the Name column (or as the icon name) in the Address Book window.

4 Type this person's e-mail address in the Add New text box and click the Add button. If this person has more than one e-mail address, type each one, click the Add button and select one as the default address. (To select a different address as the default, select it and then click Set As Default.) The default address is the one that Outlook Express uses when you send a message to this person if you don't specify a different address.

5 If you know that this person uses Outlook Express, Eudora, or some other mail program that can handle formatted text, leave the Send E-Mail Using Plain Text Only check box deselected. If they're using some other mail program, or if you don't know what kind of program they use, select this option.

6 Click the other tabs to add more information about this person, including postal address, voice, fax, and other telephone numbers.

7 If this person participates in electronic conferences with you, click the NetMeeting tab and type the person's conferencing address and the address of the directory server you use to contact them.

8 If this person has sent you a digitally signed e-mail message, or if they're listed with a secure directory service, you can import their digital ID code into your address book. The Digital IDs tab shows the security information for the current listing.

9 Click the OK button to save this address book entry and close the dialog box.

TIP

> **Adding Address Book Entries from Received Messages**
> After you open a message window, you can easily create an address book entry for the message sender or any of the message recipients. In the message header area, simply right-click the name you want to add and choose Add To Address Book from the context menu.

To revise an existing address book entry, double-click the entry. The Address Book Properties dialog box for that entry opens, and you can view or change the information.

Working with Groups

Groups are a convenient way to send the same message or file to more than one recipient. You might want to use groups to distribute a newsletter, send invitations to a meeting or party, or simply to send multiple copies of a message.

Creating a Group

To create a new group, follow these steps:

1 Click the New Group button on the toolbar or press Ctrl+G. The Group Properties dialog box appears. (See Figure 26-13.)

FIGURE 26-13.
Use the Group Properties dialog box to create a group, and to add or delete group members.

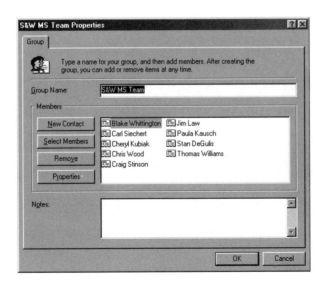

2 In the Group Name box, type the name that you want to appear in the address book list.

3 To add names to this group that are already in your address book, click the Select Members button and select the names you want from the Select Group Members dialog box. If you want to add all the members of an existing group to a new one, you can add the name of the other group to this one.

4 To add names for which you don't already have entries in your address book, click the New Contact button and fill in the information in the Properties dialog box, just as you would for an individual address book entry.

 TIP

To see the details for a name already in the group, select the name and click the Properties button.

5 If you want to save any additional information about this group (such as the type of information you normally send to its members), type the information in the Notes field.

6 Click the OK button to save the list and close the dialog box.

Editing a Group

To change the list of names in an existing group, double-click the name of the group. When the group's properties dialog box appears, click the New Contact and Select Members buttons to add more names, or the Remove button to delete names.

 TIP

Adding or Removing Single Names

To add a single new name to an existing group, select the group in the groups list and click the New Contact button on the toolbar. To remove a single name from a group, select the group in the groups list, select the name you want to remove, and click the Delete button on the toolbar.

Importing Information from Other Programs

If you used another mail program, such as Microsoft Exchange, before you installed Windows 98, you probably have an existing address book that you used with that program. Or perhaps you have a company directory, membership list, or other list of names and addresses in a text file, or in an address list on some other computer connected to yours through a LAN. Outlook Express includes a utility that you can use to import your old address book without the need to retype every entry.

To import an address book, follow these steps:

1 From the Outlook Express window or the Address Book window, choose Import Address Book from the File menu. The Address Book Import Tool window opens.

2 Select the type of address list you want to import into the Outlook Express address book and click the Import button.

3 When the import process is complete, click the Close button.

Depending on the type of address list you're importing, the program either automatically imports the list or asks you to specify the location of the "foreign" list. To confirm that the import has been completed successfully, open your Outlook Express address book and check to see if it includes the names that were previously in the other list.

Importing Addresses from Internet Directory Services

If you don't know the e-mail address of a person or company to whom you want to send a message, you might be able to find the address in an online directory that uses the standard LDAP (Lightweight Directory Access Protocol) format, such as Four11, InfoSpace, or Bigfoot. Outlook Express comes with links to several of the most widely used LDAP directories, and you can add others yourself.

V

Sharing and Communicating

To use a directory service, follow these steps:

1   Use any of these methods to display the Find People window, shown in Figure 26-14:

- In the top-level Outlook Express window, click the Find People link.

- In Outlook Express, choose Find People from the Edit menu.

- In Address Book, choose Find from the Edit menu or click the Find button on the toolbar.

- In the Select Recipients dialog box, click the Find button.

FIGURE 26-14.

Four11 is one of several directory services that help you find e-mail addresses and other information.

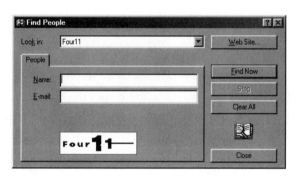

2   Select the directory service you want to use from the Look In drop-down list.

3   Type the name of the person whose address you want to find in the Name field and click the Find Now button.

> If you prefer to use the directory service's Web page, click the Web Site button to open Internet Explorer and load the Web page for the selected service. The service's Web page usually lets you provide more information to refine your search, and often returns more information about people you find.

4   The directory service lists all addresses in its database that match your request. To add a name and address from this list to your own local address book, select the listing and click the Add To Address Book button. To see more information about this listing, either double-click the listing or select it and click the Properties button.

Adding a New Directory Service

If your ISP operates its own directory service or you discover a new LDAP service, you can use it in Outlook Express along with the other, more widespread services. To add a directory service, follow these steps:

1 In the Outlook Express window, choose Accounts from the Tools menu. The Internet Accounts dialog box appears.

2 Click the Add button and choose Directory Service. The Internet Connection Wizard appears with a series of questions about the directory service you want to add to Outlook Express.

3 Use the information supplied by your ISP or directory service to answer the questions in the wizard.

Importing Names from a Business Card List

Many contact managers, personal digital assistants (PDAs), scanners, and other programs and devices store names and addresses in a standard file format that follows the vCard specification. To import a business card file into your Outlook Express address book, follow these steps:

1 Open Address Book.

2 Open the File menu and choose Import, Business Card (vCard). A file browser appears.

3 Use the file browser to locate the Business Card file you want to import, or type the full file path in the File Name field.

4 Click the Open button to import the file and close the file browser.

Exporting Information to Another Program

It's also possible to export an Outlook Express address book to certain other formats, but the list of export formats is not as extensive as the import list. (It's limited to formats used by other Microsoft programs, generic text format, and vCard format, but not those of competitive mail programs.)

To export your address book, choose Export from either the Outlook Express File menu or the Address Book File menu, and select the format you want the exported file to use.

Organizing Your Mail

Outlook Express includes five standard mail folders—Inbox, Outbox, Sent Items, Deleted Items and Drafts—but you can add as many additional folders and subfolders as you want in order to sort and store messages by topic, date, sender, or any other system. For example, you might create separate folders for sales reports, meeting agendas, and love letters.

> It's much easier to work with mailbox folders when the folder list is visible in the Outlook Express window. Use the Layout command on the View menu to display the folder list.

Creating and Using Folders

To create a new mail folder, follow these steps:

1 Open the File menu and choose Folder, New Folder, or right-click in the folder list and choose New Folder. The Create Folder dialog box appears, as shown in Figure 26-15.

FIGURE 26-15.

To create a subfolder of an existing folder, select the folder before you click OK.

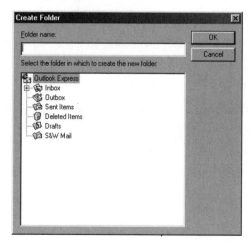

2 Type the name you want to assign to the new folder in the Folder Name text box.

3 In the folder outline, click the location where you want the new folder to appear. For a new top-level folder, select the Outlook Express folder; for a new subfolder, click the parent folder that should include the new folder.

4 Click OK to save your choice and close the dialog box.

You can't move, delete, or change the name of the five standard mail folders, but it is possible to change any mail folder that you add to the system yourself. To move a folder (including all the messages and subfolders inside the folder) to a different location within the Outlook Express folder structure, select the folder in the folder list and drag it to the new parent folder, or open the File menu and choose Folder, Move To. Outlook Express includes folders for both mail and news, but you can't move a folder from one type of folder to the other.

To rename or delete a folder, select the folder and choose a command from the File, Folder menu or from the context menu that appears when you right-click the folder.

You can also delete a folder by selecting it and clicking the Delete button on the toolbar or pressing the Delete key.

Moving, Copying, and Deleting Messages

To move an individual message to a different folder, open the folder that includes the message and either drag the message to the name of the destination folder, or choose Move To from the context menu that appears when you right-click the message. To place a duplicate copy of the message in a new folder, hold down the Ctrl key when you drag the message, or choose Copy To from the context menu.

To remove a message from a folder, select the message and press the Delete key or click the Delete button on the toolbar. Deleting a message from any folder except the Deleted Items folder actually moves the message to the Deleted Items folder. The "deleted" message resides there until you delete it from the Deleted Items folder or, if the Empty Messages From The 'Deleted Items' Folder On Exit check box (on the General tab in the Options dialog box) is selected, you close Outlook Express.

Using the Inbox Assistant

The Inbox Assistant is a tool that automatically examines new messages as Outlook Express receives them. You can use Inbox Assistant to store messages with a particular characteristic, such as a particular sender or subject line, in a different mailbox folder, or to automatically send a reply back to the sender, forward a copy of the message to another address, or discard the message without downloading it from your mail server. Inbox Assistant can be a real time-saver if you receive a lot of routine mail, or if you want to forward your mail to another address when you're not able to receive it.

To use Inbox Assistant, follow these steps:

1   Choose Inbox Assistant from the Tools menu. To create a new Inbox Assistant rule, click the Add button to open the Properties dialog box shown in Figure 26-16.

FIGURE 26-16.

In the top part of this dialog box, specify which incoming messages you want to affect. In the bottom part, specify what you want to do with those messages.

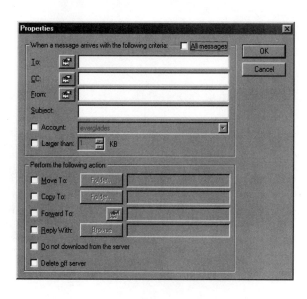

2 Select the All Messages check box to affect all incoming mail messages, or enter one or more criteria to specify which incoming messages you want to act on:

- To specify addresses that appear on messages you want to act on, in the To, Cc, or From boxes, type one or more e-mail addresses or click the file-card button. Separate multiple addresses with a space.

⭐ TIP

If you specify more than one address in a field, Inbox Assistant acts on an incoming message only if it contains all the addresses in the specified field. If you want to act on messages that come from any one of several addresses, set up a separate rule for each address.

- To act on messages that contain certain text anywhere in the subject field, in the Subject text box, type the text.

- To act only on messages that Outlook Express receives through a specific mail account, select the Account check box.

- To act only on large messages select the Larger Than option.

⊙ NOTE

If you specify multiple criteria, an incoming message must meet *all* the criteria in order for it to be considered a match.

3 Select one or more check boxes to specify the action Inbox Assistant takes when a message that matches the rule's criteria arrives:

- The Move To and Copy To options specify the mail folder where you want to store messages that match this rule. Click the Folder button to select a destination folder.

- The Forward To option instructs Outlook Express to forward a copy of each message that matches this rule to another address. Click the file-card button to select a forwarding address from your address book.

V

Sharing and Communicating

- The Reply With option instructs Outlook Express to send a copy of a message, a text file, or an HTML document back to the sender of each message that matches the rule. Click the Browse button to select a file to include in those automatic replies.

- The Do Not Download option instructs Outlook Express to leave any message on the server if it matches the rule criteria. Use this option if you want to save certain types of mail until you can download them to a different location. For example, if you are checking for new mail with your portable computer, you might want to save mail from certain senders until you get back to your own office.

- The Delete Off Server option instructs Outlook Express to discard certain messages without transferring them to your computer. If you expect to receive junk mail or other messages that you don't ever want to read, this is a good way to ignore them.

There's no limit to the number of rules you can create with Inbox Assistant. But remember that Inbox Assistant performs only the actions specified in the first rule in the Inbox Assistant list that applies to a particular message. If a message matches the criteria in more than one rule, only the first one in the list will work. To change the order, select an entry and click the Move Up or Move Down button.

 TIP

> You can disable a rule without deleting it altogether. In the Inbox Assistant dialog box, deselect the rule by clicking its check box. To reenable the rule, select the check box.

Using Inbox Assistant with Existing Messages

Ordinarily, Inbox Assistant monitors new messages as they arrive in your Inbox folder and acts according to the rules you set up. But you can also apply the rules to the existing messages in any mail folder. This can be a convenient way to clean out certain overburdened folders or send a standard reply to a large number of correspondents. To apply Inbox Assistant rules to existing messages:

1 Choose Inbox Assistant from the Tools menu.

2 Add, remove, select, deselect, and reorder rules to set up the criteria and actions you want to apply.

3 Click the Apply To button.

4 Select the folder that contains the messages you want to process, and then click OK.

Searching for a Message

After you have been using Outlook Express for a few months or more, your mail folders will undoubtedly contain lots of messages. As a result, it might become extremely difficult to locate an old piece of mail quickly. The Find Message command on the Edit menu provides an easy way to search for messages that contain a specified text string in the header or message body, messages that arrived during a specified period of time, or messages with attachments. To search for a message:

1 Choose Find Message from the Edit menu to display the Find Message dialog box, shown in Figure 26-17.

2 To search for messages that contain certain text, type the text that's contained in the header or body of the message you're looking for in one or more of the four text boxes at the top of the window.

FIGURE 26-17.

The Find Message window finds messages that contain the text you specify anywhere in a particular field.

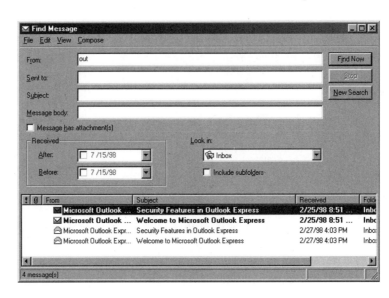

V

Sharing and Communicating

You don't need to type complete words; Find Message reports success if the text you type appears anywhere in the specified field. Text searches are not case sensitive.

3 If you want to find only messages that have file attachments, select Message Has Attachment(s).

4 To search by date range, click the down arrow at the right side of the After and Before boxes to display a calendar. Click the date you want.

5 Select a folder from the Look In drop-down list, and if you want to search folders contained within the folder you select, also select Include Subfolders.

6 Click Find Now. If any messages meet all the criteria you specify, they appear in a list at the bottom of the window. You can work with the messages in this window exactly as you do with messages in the main Outlook Express window.

Security Zones

 SEE ALSO

For information about security zones, see "Security Zones and Security Levels," page 642.

Outlook Express shares the settings for the two most restrictive security zones used in Internet Explorer, the Internet zone and the Restricted Sites zone. Therefore, for example, if you have set your Internet zone in Internet Explorer to reject Web pages with active content (such as ActiveX controls or Java applets), Outlook Express also rejects HTML messages with the same kind of active content.

NOTE

These security settings affect only the receipt of Rich Text (HTML) messages. Because of their limited capability, Plain Text messages can't contain any potentially harmful objects, such as Java applets.

To change your security zone settings, choose Options from the Tools menu, and click the Security tab. Select either Internet Zone or Restricted Sites Zone in the Zone drop-down list. If you want to review or change the settings for the selected zone, click Settings. Note that any changes you make here also determine how Internet Explorer handles Web sites in the selected zone.

Working with Encryption

Unless you take steps to protect it, every mail message you send or receive can be read by anybody who intercepts it. Obviously, this can be dangerous if you use e-mail to send confidential business information, credit card account numbers, or personal data such as medical records. The solution to this problem is to encrypt your message before you send it.

In order to exchange secure mail via Outlook Express, you need to follow these steps:

1   Obtain a digital ID.

A digital ID, also known as a security certificate, is a statement issued by a third-party certifying authority attesting to your identity. Your digital ID is good for a particular e-mail account, with mail sent from a particular computer. Thus, for example, if you want to send secure mail from two accounts, you will need a digital ID for each.

You can find a list of certifying authorities, with links to their Web sites, at Microsoft's Outlook Express Web site:

http://www.microsoft.com/ie/ie40/oe/certpage.htm

 TIP

After you have a digital ID, you should create a backup. This allows you to restore your digital ID if the copy on your computer is damaged, or if you want to move it to a different computer. To create a backup, launch Internet in Control Panel. Click the Content tab, and then click the Personal button. Select your digital ID and click Export to create a backup, or click Import to restore a previously backed-up digital ID.

2   Tell Outlook Express to use your digital ID.

To do this, choose Accounts from the Tools menu, and click the Mail tab. Select the account for which you want Outlook Express to use your ID, and then click Properties. In the Properties dialog box, click the Security tab. Select the Use A Digital ID check box, and then click the Digital ID button. Finally, select the certificate that you want to use and click OK.

3   Send your public key to anyone who wants to send you secure mail.

Outlook Express uses a public key/private key system to send and receive secure mail. To send encrypted mail to you, a correspondent must have your public key. A message sent to you is encrypted with your public key. When you receive the message, Outlook Express decodes it with your private key, which is stored on your hard disk.

To send your public key, choose Options from the Tools menu and click the Security tab. Select the Digitally Sign All Outgoing Messages check box. Then click the Advanced Settings button. In the next dialog box, select the check box labeled "Include my digital ID when sending signed messages." Click OK twice to get out of the dialog boxes, and then send a message to each of your correspondents.

When correspondents receive a digitally signed message from you, they need to add your public key to their address book entries for you. They do that by opening the signed message, choosing Properties from the File menu, clicking the Security tab, and then clicking Add Digital ID To Address Book.

4 Have your correspondents send you their public keys, and then add their public keys to their address book entries.

Once you have a digital ID and a correspondent's public key, you can send that person an encrypted message as follows:

1 Create your message in the normal way.

2 Before you click the Send button, click the Encrypt Message button on the message window's toolbar. (Alternatively, choose Encrypt from the Tools menu.)

You might also want to add a digital signature to your message. A digital signature provides verification to your recipient that the message is actually coming from you, not from someone pretending to be you. To add a digital signature, click the Digitally Sign Message button on the message window's toolbar, or choose Digitally Sign from the Tools menu.

To digitally sign all your outgoing messages, choose Options from the Tools menu, click the Security tab, and select the Digitally Sign All Outgoing Messages check box. To encrypt all your outbound messages, select the check box labeled "Encrypt contents and attachments for all outgoing messages." Note, however, that if you choose the latter option, Outlook Express displays an error message if you attempt to send mail to a recipient whose public key is not in your address book.

Working with Internet Newsgroups

News is one of the oldest methods of distributing public information through computer networks. Discussion groups (called *newsgroups*) about more than 15,000 different topics carry news articles across the Internet every day. In addition to its mail functions, Outlook Express can also send and receive Internet news articles.

How Internet News Is Organized

Many of the most popular newsgroups are part of the worldwide Usenet system, which has a formal conference structure and detailed rules for creating new topics. Other less formal newsgroups have fewer rules, and may be limited to a geographic region, a single business, or an institution such as a college or university.

Every newsgroup has a name that describes its topic. Each name has several words or abbreviations, separated by periods. The first part of the name is usually a broad general category, such as "sci" for newsgroups related to science and technology, or "umn" for newsgroups that originate at the University of Minnesota. Each additional word describes the topic of the newsgroup in more detail, such as sci.geo.earthquakes.

Many of the most popular newsgroups are in one of the seven Usenet hierarchies: comp (computers), news (news about Usenet), rec (hobbies, arts and recreation), sci (science and technology), soc (social issues and politics), talk (debates and controversies), and misc (topics that don't fit the other categories). Other important categories that are not part of the Usenet system include alt (a grab-bag category for "alternative" topics), bionet (biological science), biz (business topics), clari (news from the Associated Press and Reuters via the ClariNet service), and k12 (topics for primary and secondary students and teachers).

Still other newsgroups are operated by and for businesses and organizations, and are restricted to their employees, customers, and members. These private newsgroups are usually limited to a single server, which requires a restricted password for access. For example, The Microsoft Network uses private newsgroups for conferences that are accessible only to MSN subscribers.

? SEE ALSO

For information about setting up an account with a news server, see "Setting Up Mail and News Accounts," page 670.

Selecting a Newsgroup

In order to participate in a newsgroup through Outlook Express, you must set up an account with one or more news servers and select the individual newsgroups you want to see.

The Outlook Express folder list shows each server where you have an account as a folder.

The first step in reading articles in a newsgroup is to select the group from the list of newsgroups that are available from your news server. To view the list of newsgroups, follow these steps:

1   Choose News from the Go menu.

2   Click the Newsgroups button on the Outlook Express toolbar. The Newsgroups dialog box appears. (See Figure 26-18.)

3   If you have accounts on more than one news server, click the icon for the server you want to use in the News Servers box. If this is the first time you have used this server, the server transfers a list of newsgroups to Outlook Express.

4   To see a complete list of available news groups, click the All tab. For a list of new groups that have been added since your last visit to this news server, click the New tab.

FIGURE 26-18.

The Newsgroups dialog box lists all newsgroups on the selected server.

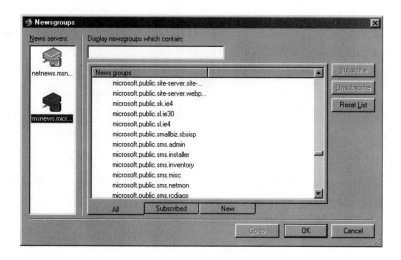

5   Select a newsgroup from the list. If you're looking for something specific, type one or more key words in the search field at the top of the window. This filters the list so that it includes only newsgroup names that contain the text you type.

6   If you expect to read the articles in a group often, double-click the name of the group, or select the name and click the Subscribe button. Outlook Express lists subscribed newsgroups under the news server folder in the folder list. To view a list of current articles in a newsgroup without subscribing, click the Go To button.

 TIP

If you have already subscribed to a newsgroup, you can go directly to a list of articles by selecting the newsgroup from the folder list in the main Outlook Express window.

Viewing Newsgroup Articles

When you select a newsgroup, Outlook Express connects to the server and obtains and displays a new list of articles in that group. To read an article in the Outlook Express preview pane (as shown in Figure 26-19), select the subject line in the article list. To view the article in a message window, double-click the subject line, or select it and choose Open from the File menu.

FIGURE 26-19.
Outlook Express displays a list of articles and, in the preview pane, the content of the selected article.

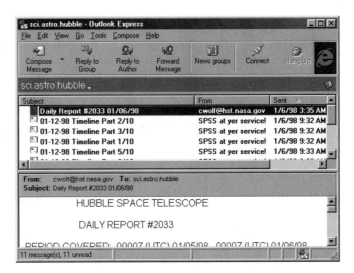

V

Sharing and Communicating

Outlook Express normally displays only the essential lines in the header of each article. But if you want to see the rest of the message header, open the article and press Ctrl+F3.

Reading News Offline

You need a connection to the Internet to download news articles to your computer, but it's not necessary to keep that connection alive while you read them. For example, if you're using a laptop computer, it might be convenient to download a handful of newsgroups before you leave your office, and read them on the train as you commute to work. Or if you use the same telephone line for both voice and data, reading news offline leaves the line free for incoming calls.

To configure Outlook Express for offline newsreading, follow these steps:

1   Select the name of the newsgroup you want to download in the folder list, the folder bar, or the main Outlook Express window.

2   Choose Properties from the File menu.

3   Click the Download tab.

4   Select the When Downloading This Newsgroup, Retrieve check box.

5   Select one of the retrieval options:

 • Select New Headers to download the headers from all new articles in this newsgroup, but not the messages themselves.

 • Select New Messages to download the full text (including headers) of all new articles in this newsgroup.

 • Select All Messages to download the full text of all the articles from this newgroup that are currently available on your news server.

6   Repeat the process for each additional newsgroup that you want to download.

Once you have selected newsgroups for offline reading, you can choose Download All from the Tools menu to transfer the articles you want from the news server to your computer. If you have accounts with more than one news server, you can choose Download This Account to limit the transfer to the articles on a single server.

Marking an Article for Download

If you download only the headers of new articles rather than the full text of all articles when you connect to the server, you can mark the articles that sound like they're worth reading for later download by following these steps:

1 Open the newsgroup in the main Outlook Express window.

2 Select the description of a message you want to read.

3 Choose one of the Mark For Retrieval commands from the Tools menu:

- Choose Mark Message to mark the currently selected message for downloading.

- Choose Mark Thread to mark the current article and all replies and replies-to-replies to that message.

- Choose Mark All Messages to mark all the articles in the current newsgroup for downloading.

- Choose Unmark to remove a mark from the currently selected article.

TIP

If you want to mark an individual article, right-click the article and choose Mark Message For Download. If the article you right-click has replies, and the thread is collapsed, choosing this command is equivalent to opening the Tools menu and choosing Mark For Retrieval, Mark Thread.

The next time your computer is connected to the Internet, you can retrieve the marked articles by choosing Download All from the Tools menu.

To read the articles you have downloaded, follow these steps:

1 Choose Current View from the View menu.

2 Select the Downloaded Messages option to display a list of all the articles currently available on your system.

3 Double-click the description of the article you want to read to load the article into a separate window, or select the header to view it in the Preview Pane of the main Outlook Express window.

Forwarding an Article

If you see an article in a newsgroup that would interest somebody who might not see it in the newsgroup, you can send them a copy of that article via e-mail. Click the Forward Message button on the toolbar, or choose Forward from the Compose menu. The message appears in an ordinary message editor window, ready for you to address and, if you like, add any comments.

Replying to an Article

Many people regularly read articles in newsgroups, but they never make any contributions to the ongoing conversations. These people are called *lurkers*. Almost everybody starts out as a lurker, but if you want to become an active participant in the community that grows around a good newsgroup, you will eventually want to write and post some articles of your own.

An article in a newsgroup can be either a reply to an earlier article, or the start of a completely new thread. Many news readers, including Outlook Express, can list replies directly under the original article, so a reader can follow the thread easily.

To reply to an article with a new article of your own, follow these steps:

1 Either select the original message in the Outlook Express window, or open the original in a separate message window.

2 Click the Reply To Group button on the toolbar, or choose Reply To Newsgroup from the Compose menu.

3 Type your reply.

4 Click the Post button.

Sometimes it makes more sense to send a reply to a public news article back to the sender as a private mail message. Because Outlook Express is both a news program and a mail program, you can send a private reply just as you would send any other mail. To send a private reply, click the

Reply To Author button on the toolbar, or choose Reply To Author from the Compose menu.

You can send the same reply to a newsgroup as an article and to an individual as a mail message. Choose the Reply To Newsgroup And Author command from the Compose menu to create a combined message. Because messages get deleted fairly quickly from some busy newsgroups, sending a copy of your reply directly to the author ensures that the author doesn't miss it.

 TIP

> To be sure you don't miss any replies to articles that you post, display the newsgroup where you posted, open the View menu and choose Current View, Replies To My Posts.

V

Sharing and Communicating

Posting a New Article

Not every article in a newsgroup is part of an existing thread. To create and send a new article, follow these steps:

1 Open the newsgroup to which you want to send an article.

2 Click the Compose Message button on the toolbar, or choose New Message from the Compose menu. The New Message editor window shown in Figure 26-20 appears.

3 To simultaneously post your message to other newsgroups, click the news icon and select the additional newsgroup names.

FIGURE 26-20.
The window for creating news articles is nearly identical to the one for creating mail messages.

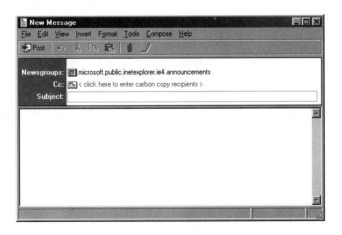

4 To simultaneously send your article to one or more mail recipients, type their e-mail addresses on the Cc line, or click the file-card icon to open your address book.

5 Type a brief description on the Subject line.

6 Compose the body of the message, as described below.

7 Click the Post button.

Composing an Article

SEE ALSO

For information about creating and formatting mail messages, see "Creating a New Message," page 677.

Writing a news article is just like creating a mail message. The message editor window is almost identical for both services, so you can add text, formatting, and attached files to a news article just as you would for a private message.

It's possible to use Rich Text (HTML) format in news articles, but many news reader programs will not recognize the formatting. Therefore, unless you're sending your article to a proprietary news server such as MSN, where you know that all recipients have sophisticated news readers, it's a good idea to stick with Plain Text.

Using Newsgroup Filters

Unfortunately, many newsgroups include articles from people who misuse the system by posting advertisements, abusive messages, and other irrelevancies. You can use Outlook Express newsgroup filters to hide articles that you don't want to view.

Newsgroup filters work on newsgroups in much the same way that Inbox Assistant monitors incoming mail; the biggest difference is that Inbox Assistant lets you specify any of several actions, whereas the only action that newsgroup filters performs is to not display filtered messages.

To set up a filter, follow these steps:

1 Choose Newsgroup Filters from the Tools menu.

2 Click the Add button to display the dialog box shown in Figure 26-21.

FIGURE 26-21.
Newsgroup filters
prevent articles you
don't want from
appearing in Outlook
Express.

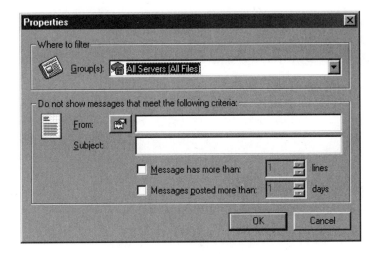

3 Select the server or newsgroup you want to filter from the
   Group(s) drop-down list.

4 Type the name of a sender whose articles you want to ignore, or
   type one or more key words that appear in the Subject header of
   the articles you want to filter.

5 If you want to suppress large or old messages, select one or both
   check boxes and adjust the spinners to the limits you want.

NOTE

Outlook Express filters out only those messages that meet all the criteria in a
particular filter.

6 Click OK to add this filter to your list and close the Properties dialog
   box.

7 Click the OK button in the Newsgroup Filters dialog box.

TIP

To display the filtered messages in the message list, open the View menu and
choose Current View, Filtered Messages. Filtered messages appear in blue.

V

Sharing and Communicating

Changing the Appearance of Outlook Express

With the single exception of the message list, all of the features of the Outlook Express window are optional. You can hide or display the Outlook bar, the folder list, the folder bar, the toolbar and the preview pane by choosing Layout from the View menu. Figure 26-22 shows the Window Layout Properties dialog box that appears.

FIGURE 26-22.

The Window Layout Properties dialog box lets you control which elements are included in the Outlook Express window.

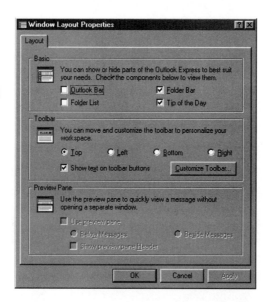

The top part of the Window Layout Properties dialog box controls the presence or absence of three different ways to display lists of Outlook Express folders:

■ The *Outlook bar* is a column of buttons—one for each mail folder and news server. Because the oversized buttons often necessitate scrolling the column of buttons, the Outlook bar is the most attractive and least useful of the lot.

■ The *folder list* shows all mail folders, news servers, and subscribed newsgroups in outline form, much like the All Folders Explorer Bar in Windows Explorer.

■ The *folder bar,* which displays the name of the selected folder near the top of the window, occupies the least screen space. When you click the folder bar, a folder list drops down to let you select another folder.

With any of these navigation tools, you simply click the name of a folder or news server and Outlook Express displays its contents in the message list. You probably won't want to make all three options visible at the same time, but you can experiment to find which ones you like best.

Changing the Toolbar

The Outlook Express Toolbar is a set of shortcut buttons that you can use to enter frequently used commands without opening a menu. At the right end of the toolbar, there's also an Internet Explorer icon, which is a link to www.microsoft.com.

In the Window Layout Properties dialog box, you can specify the location where you want the toolbar to appear, and turn text under each icon on or off.

The buttons on the toolbar change depending on what kind of folder you have selected: top-level Outlook Express, mail, or news. When you move between a mail folder and a newsgroup, for example, the toolbar changes to include commands that you're likely to use with that Outlook Express function. To add or remove buttons from the current toolbar, click the Customize Toolbar button in the Window Layout Properties dialog box, select the button you want to add or remove from one of the lists, and click the Add or Remove button. You can also change the order of the buttons on the current toolbar by selecting a button in the Customize Toolbar dialog box and clicking Move Up or Move Down.

Viewing or Hiding the Preview Pane

The preview pane is a section of the Outlook Express window that displays the contents of the currently selected message or article. When you're scanning mail messages or news articles rather than taking the time to read all of every one, it can save a lot of time to select items from the list and read the first few lines.

If you don't want to use the preview pane, use the Window Layout Properties dialog box to hide it, which allows more space for the message list. You can place the preview pane below the message list or arrange the message list and preview pane side-by-side.

Customizing the Message List

Outlook Express maintains a group of display settings for each folder. These settings let you decide which columns are displayed, the order and width of the columns, and the sort order. You can customize each of these settings.

Selecting Columns to Display

To specify which columns are displayed, or to change the order in which they appear, follow these steps:

1 Choose Columns from the View menu. The Columns dialog box appears, as shown in Figure 26-23.

FIGURE 26-23.

You can select which columns to display for each folder.

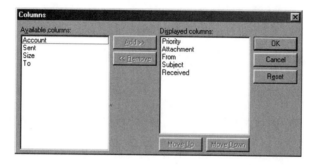

2 To add a new column, select the column heading in the Available Columns list and click the Add button.

3 To remove a column, select it in the Displayed Columns list and click Remove.

4 To change the order in which columns in the Displayed Columns field appear in the message list, select the item you want to move and click the Move Up or Move Down button.

5 Click OK.

You can change the width of any column by dragging the right border of the column heading. You can change the order of the columns by dragging a column heading to the new location; a blue line between column headings indicates where the column will go when you release the mouse button.

Sorting Messages

The column heading that Outlook Express currently uses to sort the items in the message list has an arrowhead in it. When the arrowhead points up, the messages appear in ascending order (A to Z, or earliest to latest); when the arrowhead points down, the messages appear in descending order (Z to A, or latest to earliest). To use a different field to sort the message list, click that column heading. To switch between ascending order and descending order, click the column heading again.

Setting Other Display Options

If your message list contains long chains of replies to replies to replies (called a *thread*), you might want to group the messages by thread. When you do so, only the first message in each thread appears in the message list, and it has a plus icon at the left end of the Subject column. Clicking the plus icon expands the thread so that replies to the original message are visible. To group messages by thread, open the View menu and choose Sort By, Group Messages By Subject.

If you receive a lot of mail messages or you frequent busy newsgroups, you might want to filter the display to show only the messages you haven't read. To do that, open the View menu and choose Current View, Unread Messages.

Reducing Wasted Disk Space

Every time Outlook Express adds a new message to a mail folder, it expands the size of the folder to make space for it. However, it doesn't automatically reduce the size of a folder if you delete a message. Therefore, your mail folders will eventually take up more hard drive space than necessary. To reclaim that wasted space, follow these steps:

1 Open any mail folder.

2 Open the File menu and choose Folder, Compact to reduce wasted space in the current folder, or Folder, Compact All Folders to reduce the wasted space in all of your mailbox folders.

V

Sharing and Communicating

You can also eliminate wasted space in your news folders. Follow these steps to compact your news folders:

1 Choose Clean Up Files from the File menu. The Local File Clean Up dialog box appears.

2 Select the news server or newsgroup that you want to clean up.

3 Click the Compact button to eliminate wasted space in your news folders.

Or click the Remove Messages button to delete the local copies of news articles, leaving only the message headers in place. If you want to see them again, you can download a new copy from the server later.

Or click the Delete button to remove all articles and headers.

How Outlook Express Relates to Internet Explorer

Outlook Express and Internet Explorer are separate programs, but each contains links to the other. If both programs are designated as defaults, you can open either one from within the other: when you click a link in an Outlook Express message or article, the destination of that link opens in Internet Explorer; when a Web page includes a "send mail to . . ." link, clicking that link in Internet Explorer opens the Outlook Express message editor with the address already filled in. In addition, both programs have commands in their respective Go menus that open the other program.

Making Outlook Express Your Default Mail and News Program

The default mail client or news reader program is the program that Internet Explorer automatically opens when you enter a command to send mail or read Internet news. If Outlook Express is the only mail or news program installed on your system, you don't have to worry about specifying a default, but if there's more than one program in place, you might have to change the default.

Follow these steps to change the default mail and news programs:

1 From the desktop, right-click the Internet Explorer icon and choose Properties. In the Internet Properties dialog box, click the Programs tab. The dialog box shown in Figure 26-24 appears.

FIGURE 26-24.

When you make Outlook Express the default mail and news program, Internet Explorer automatically launches Outlook Express when you click a mail or news link.

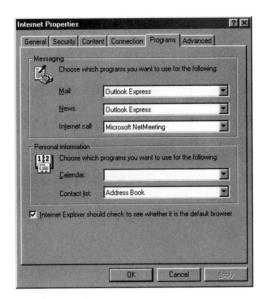

2 To change the default mail program, select Outlook Express from the Mail drop-down list.

3 To change the default news program, select Outlook Express from the News drop-down list.

4 Click OK to save your selections and close the dialog box.

When you open a mail or news program that is not the default, Windows asks if you want to make that program the new default. Click Yes to change the default or No to keep the old default.

Using NetMeeting

Microsoft NetMeeting is a program that lets you engage in a conference with one or many users across the Internet or a local-area network. If your computer has a sound card, a microphone, and speakers, you can talk to another person in something approximating real time. If you have a video camera connected to your computer's parallel port or to a video-capture card, you can exchange video images. With or without audio and video equipment, you can "chat" with others, exchange drawings and diagrams by means of a virtual whiteboard, send and receive files, and even work simultaneously in a shared program.

Getting Started with NetMeeting

The first time you run NetMeeting, a wizard greets you and introduces you to the program. Among other things, the wizard asks if you want to log onto a directory server whenever you start NetMeeting. If you answer in the affirmative, you'll be asked to select from a list of publicly available directory servers.

A *directory server*, also known as a *user location server (ULS)*, is a listing of people available for NetMeeting calls. If you log onto such a server, you make it easy for others to reach you via NetMeeting. The server keeps track of your whereabouts (your current IP address, if you're connected to the Internet), and, while you're logged on, someone who wants to call you can simply pick your name from the server listing and click the Call button. As Figure 27-1 shows, a directory server can also list your physical location (city, state, and country), and whether or not you have sound and video equipment. Not shown in the figure is a comments field where you can let people know a little more about you.

The wizard doesn't say so, but you have the option of logging onto one of the public directory servers but not listing yourself there. If you do that, the directory server can still help a caller find you. But the caller will need to know your e-mail address to do this. To take advantage of this option, go ahead and tell the wizard to log you on. Then, after you're in NetMeeting, choose Options from the Tools menu, click the Calling tab, and select the check box labeled "Do not list my name in the directory."

⚠ WARNING

> As you'll discover the first time you explore a directory server listing, not everyone who uses NetMeeting has business purposes in mind, and many people who list themselves on the servers are quite forthright about the type of communication they desire. NetMeeting does not offer a Content Advisor for its directory listings, so you might want to discourage underage family members from using this program.

After you tell the wizard whether you want to log onto a directory server when NetMeeting starts, you'll be asked to supply your name, e-mail address, location, and comments. Even if you don't plan to list yourself on a directory server, you need to give NetMeeting your first name, last name, and e-mail address. The other fields are optional.

FIGURE 27-1.

A directory server makes it easy for people to connect to you via NetMeeting.

Toolbar   Microphone volume control   Speaker volume control

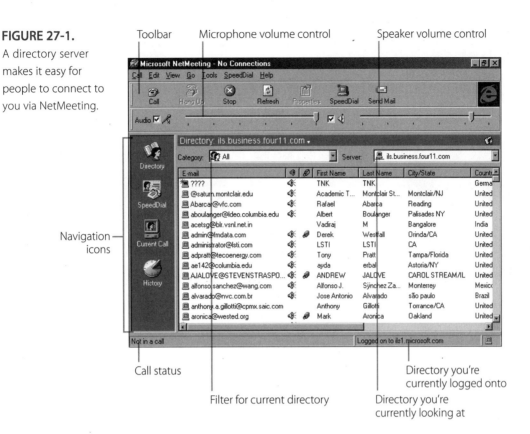

Navigation icons

Call status

Filter for current directory

Directory you're currently looking at

Directory you're currently logged onto

The screen that follows this one tells you that the information you just supplied will be available to users whenever you're logged onto a directory server. As noted, this assertion is not correct. But your information will be visible unless you visit the Options dialog box and suppress your listing. This screen also asks you to choose a category for your directory listing: personal use (suitable for all ages), business use (suitable for all ages), or adults-only use. Users can choose to display only a particular category of directory entries, so, if you say your listing is for business use, those who care only about adults-only entries won't see yours. But, practically speaking, you should assume that your listing is visible to one and all.

⭐ **TIP**

You can change your directory listing at any time. Choose Change My Information from the Call menu. Or choose Options from the Tools menu and click the My Information tab.

V

Sharing and Communicating

On the next screen, the wizard inquires about how you plan to make NetMeeting calls: via 14,400 bps modem, 28,800 bps or faster modem, ISDN, or local-area network. And, finally, this particular wizard hands you off to another wizard, which tests the volume levels of your microphone and speakers (assuming you have such equipment). Once you get past this second wizard, the program logs you onto the directory server you specified (if you did specify one), and you're ready for your first call.

 NOTE

NetMeeting does not work with IPX networks.

The NetMeeting User Interface

Figure 27-1, on the previous page, shows the most important landmarks of the NetMeeting window. The toolbar provides quick access to some of NetMeeting's commands. A few of the icons here change if you switch from Directory view to another view. Note that the Stop and Refresh buttons in Directory view control the current directory display; they have nothing to do with the calls you make. The sliders below the toolbar let you adjust your speaker and microphone volumes. Controls affecting video transmission and reception appear on the Video tab in the Options dialog box. (Choose Options from the Tools menu.)

The drop-down lists above the directory contents concern the directory you're looking at—which might not be the directory that you're logged onto. The name of the directory you're logged onto appears in the status bar.

The icons arrayed vertically to the left of the directory listing let you switch between NetMeeting's four main views: Directory, SpeedDial, Current Call, and History. If you're working with a low-resolution display, you might want to get rid of those icons to make more room for the directory. Choose Navigation Icons from the View menu to suppress or redisplay those icons. With the icons gone, you can still use View menu commands to move between views.

On the other hand, if screen space is abundant, you might opt to include NetMeeting's folder list in your display. To do this, choose Folder List from the View menu. The folder list provides an alternative way to switch from one directory server to another.

Working with the Directory Listings

Initially, Directory view shows a listing of the server you logged onto. The names that appear are those of all users who:

- are currently logged onto that server

- have chosen to have themselves listed, and

- meet the current display filter.

In Figure 27-1 on page 723, the current filter is All, but on your system a different filter might be in effect. The available filters are shown in Figure 27-2. Notice that NetMeeting uses icons to distinguish categories of users.

FIGURE 27-2.

You can filter the directory listing in a variety of ways. If you choose All, you can use the icons to the left of the E-mail column to distinguish different categories of users.

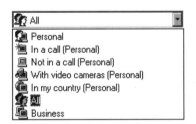

If someone you want to call is logged onto a directory server other than the one you're currently looking at, use the Server drop-down list above the directory listing to switch to the directory in which your party is listed. (Note that this action does not change the server that you are logged onto; it simply changes the server that's displayed.) Then scroll through the directory listing until you find the person you're looking for. If you know your party's e-mail address, you can speed up your search by typing the first character of that address.

NetMeeting initially displays its directory listings sorted in ascending order by e-mail address. You can reverse that sort order by clicking the E-mail heading. Or you can sort on a different column by clicking that column's heading.

If you don't find the party you're looking for, try switching the filter to All—if it isn't already set to All. If your party still doesn't appear, try clicking the Refresh button on the toolbar. The directory listing shows you who was logged onto the directory server when you logged on yourself—or when you last used the Refresh button. It's possible that your party logged on after you did, so it's always a good idea to click Refresh before deciding that your party isn't available.

Placing a Call

There are several ways to place a call in NetMeeting:

- If your party is logged on to a directory server and listed on the server, you can select his or her name in Directory view.

- If your party is logged onto a directory server but not listed, you can specify the server name plus your party's e-mail address.

- If your party is connected to the Internet and you know his or her IP address, you can specify the IP address. (The IP address consists of four numbers separated by periods, like this: 123.456.789.123.) Your party does not need to be logged onto a directory server.

- If you're calling someone on your own local-area network, you can enter the network name of your party's computer.

To initiate the call, choose New Call from the Call menu, or click the Call button on the toolbar. You'll see the New Call dialog box, shown in Figure 27-3.

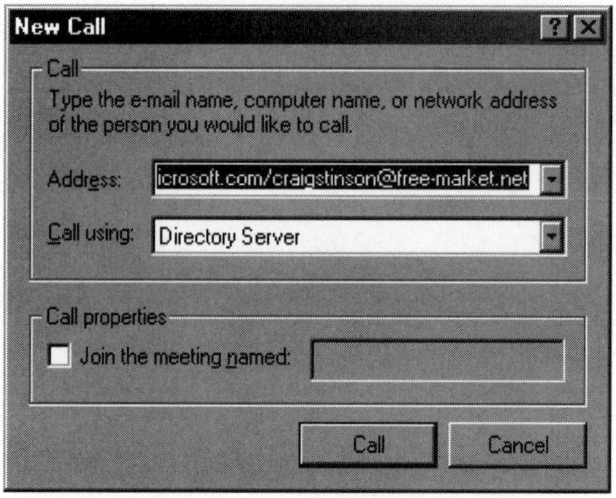

FIGURE 27-3.

When you select a name in a directory server listing and click the Call button, NetMeeting fills out this dialog box for you.

If you selected the party you want to call in a directory listing, this dialog box will already be filled out for you, so all you need to do is click OK. If you didn't select your party's name, but you know that he or she is logged onto a particular server, override whatever's on the Address line by typing information in the following format:

> servername\e-mail address

For example, if your party is logged onto ils2.microsoft.com and his e-mail address is Tjefferson@monticello.net, you would type

> ils2.microsoft.com\tjefferson@monticello.net

Leave the Call Using line set to Directory Server.

If you're using an IP address to reach your party, switch the Call Using line to Network (TCP/IP) and type the IP address on the Address line.

V

Sharing and Communicating

 TIP

You can find out your own IP address by choosing Run from the Start menu and typing *winipcfg*. Your party can do the same, if he or she is running Windows 98 or Windows 95. Be aware, though, that if you're using an ISP account to connect to the Internet, your IP address is probably different every time you connect.

TIP

The New Call dialog box maintains a drop-down list of recently used calling addresses. If you're calling someone again, you might be able to select that person's address from the drop-down list.

If you're calling someone on your own local-area network, type the network name of your party's computer on the Address line. (Type just the name of the computer; don't precede it with a backslash or domain name.) Set the Call Using line to Automatic.

In a moment, if all goes well, you'll hear a sound signaling that your party has answered the call, and NetMeeting switches from Directory view to Current Call view. In Current Call view you'll see your name, the name of the party you called, and the names of anyone else who is connected with the party you called.

If the person you call is already talking to someone else, you will see the following message:

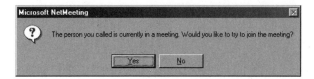

Click Yes to join the conversation. If the party you call does not answer the call, you might see the following message:

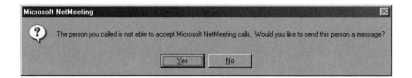

Clicking Yes here automatically transmits a "canned" message to your party's e-mail box, letting the person know that you tried to call.

Calling by SpeedDial

NetMeeting's SpeedDial view, shown in Figure 27-4, lets you create a list of people with whom you communicate. You can call someone from the SpeedDial list exactly as you would from the Directory list—by selecting a name and clicking the Call button. The advantage of working in SpeedDial view is simply that the list is, presumably, much shorter than Directory view's list, so it's easier to find the party you're trying to call. SpeedDial view also shows you at a glance whether a person you might want to call is connected to a directory server or not. To get this information in Directory view, you would need first to display the server your party uses, and then scroll through the list to see if your party is there.

By default, NetMeeting creates a new SpeedDial entry for each person you connect with, regardless of who initiates the call. You can change that behavior by choosing Options from the Tools menu and clicking the Calling tab. As Figure 27-5 shows, you can have NetMeeting prompt you before creating any new entries, or you can tell it never to create SpeedDial entries.

FIGURE 27-4.

SpeedDial view lets you see at a glance whether someone you've talked to is online and makes it easy to reconnect.

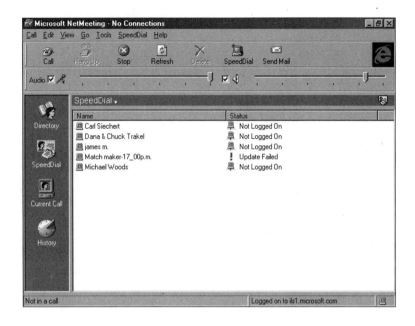

FIGURE 27-5.

By default, NetMeeting creates a new SpeedDial entry for everyone you talk to, regardless of who makes the call.

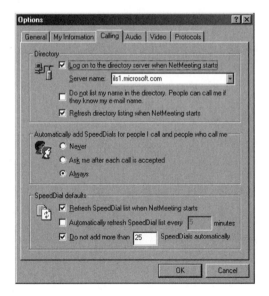

Other options on the Calling tab let you control the frequency with which NetMeeting refreshes the SpeedDial window. By default, the program checks at startup to see whether your SpeedDial comrades are online or not—and then does not check again unless you click the Refresh button in SpeedDial view. You can opt for a periodic automatic update by selecting the "Automatically refresh . . ." check box and entering a time value. Also, by default, NetMeeting stops adding people to the SpeedDial list after the list includes 25 entries. You can override this behavior by clearing the last check box in the dialog box or by entering a different maximum.

> **TIP**
>
> You can call a SpeedDial communicant in one step, without using the Call button or visiting the SpeedDial window. Simply select your party from the SpeedDial menu.

Creating SpeedDial Entries Manually

If you prefer not to have NetMeeting create SpeedDial entries automatically, you can create them manually. Select the name of the person you want in the Directory window and click the SpeedDial button on the toolbar.

Creating SpeedDial Shortcuts

You can turn a SpeedDial entry into a shortcut, suitable for storage on your desktop or elsewhere or for e-mailing to a friend. To do this, select the name in either the SpeedDial list or the Directory list, and choose Add SpeedDial from the SpeedDial menu. In the dialog box that appears, select Save On The Desktop or Send To Mail Recipient. (If you want your SpeedDial shortcut in a folder other than Desktop, you'll need to move it after it lands on the desktop.)

Calling from History View

NetMeeting's History view, shown in Figure 27-6, maintains a list of everyone you've talked to, regardless of who initiated the call. The list also includes callers whose calls you have chosen not to answer.

To place another call to someone in your History list, select a name and click the Call button on the toolbar.

FIGURE 27-6.

NetMeeting's History view keeps a log of those you've called and those who've called you.

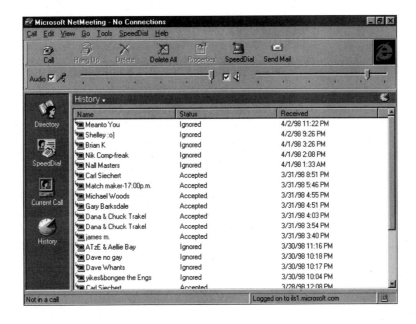

Answering a Call

To receive a call, you must be running NetMeeting. Unless you're communicating over your own local-area network, you must also be connected to the Internet. If the party calling you is planning to find you on a directory server, you must be logged onto that server. When the call comes in, you'll hear a sound like a telephone bell—assuming you have a sound card and speakers. A message window will appear, regardless of what program you're currently working in, informing you of the caller's identity and asking if you want to accept the call. The ringing will continue until you click Accept or Ignore, or until the caller clicks Hang Up.

Accepting Calls Automatically

You can have NetMeeting accept all incoming calls automatically. To do this, choose Options from the Tools menu. On the General tab, select the Automatically Accept Incoming Calls check box. If you choose this option, NetMeeting notifies you when a call arrives. It does not ask whether you want to accept.

Running NetMeeting Automatically at Startup

NetMeeting also includes an option that causes the program to run automatically when you start Windows. If you exercise this option, the program watches for incoming calls and notifies you if one arrives, but it remains out of sight until then. If you want to interact with NetMeeting after starting it in this way, you can double-click the NetMeeting icon that appears in the taskbar's notification area.

Note, however, that if you expect to receive calls over the Internet, your Internet connection must also be established automatically at startup for this background mode to work. Otherwise, NetMeeting reports an error when it tries to log onto your directory server.

To have NetMeeting run automatically at startup, choose Options from the Tools menu. On the General tab, select the check box labeled "Run when Windows starts and notify me of incoming calls."

Putting Out the Do Not Disturb Sign

To have NetMeeting automatically reject all incoming calls, choose Do Not Disturb from the Call menu. After you choose this option—and until you choose it a second time—anyone trying to call you receives a message saying that you're not currently available.

Note that NetMeeting always starts with Do Not Disturb turned off, even if the feature is turned on when you close NetMeeting.

Sending and Receiving Sound

If your computer is equipped with a sound card, microphone, and speakers, you can use NetMeeting for Internet telephony. Sound communication requires the TCP/IP protocol (which means that to use it on a local-area network, your network must be running on TCP/IP) and is limited to one pair of users at a time. (If you hold a conference with more than two users, you can still send and receive sound, but only with one other person at a time.)

Sound transmission can be either unidirectional or bidirectional. If you have full sound equipment, but the person you call has only a sound card and speakers (no microphone), that person can hear your voice, but there will be silence on your end.

Before you use sound for the first time, you need to run the Audio Tuning Wizard. This is a normal part of NetMeeting's initial startup procedure, so that detail has probably already been taken care of. If you change your sound card or upgrade its memory, however, you need to run the tuning wizard again. You can do that by choosing Audio Tuning Wizard from the Tools menu.

If you're communicating by voice with one person in a meeting with three or more participants, you can switch the sound communication to a different participant. To do that, choose Switch Audio And Video from the Tools menu, and choose the new person from the cascading submenu.

Figure 27-7 shows the Audio tab in the Options dialog box (choose Options from the Tools menu) with default settings. The full-duplex check box, selected by default, enables you to speak and listen at the same time, just as you would on a telephone. If you and the person you're calling find your sound breaking up to the point of unintelligibility, you might want to try deselecting this check box. The check box is gray if your modem does not support full-duplex communication.

FIGURE 27-7.
The default audio settings adjust your microphone's volume and sensitivity automatically as the volume of your voice and the level of background noise change.

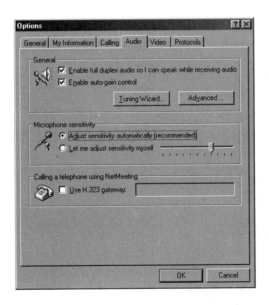

V

Sharing and Communicating

The Enable Auto-Gain Control and Adjust Sensitivity Automatically settings, both selected by default, allow NetMeeting to modify your microphone's volume level and sensitivity automatically as the volume of your voice and the level of background noise change. If there is a lot of background noise around your computer, you might want to try clearing the Enable Auto-Gain Control check box.

Sending and Receiving Video

Exchange of video information works much the same way as exchange of sound. You can do this with one other party at a time, and you must be communicating via TCP/IP. You can switch the video exchange to another meeting participant by choosing Switch Audio And Video from the Tools menu.

> **NOTE**
>
> Video might not work effectively on a computer with a processor slower than a Pentium.

As with sound, video communication can be unidirectional or bidirectional. While you're sending video, you can monitor what's going out by looking at the My Video window in the Current Call window. Video received appears in a similar window, labeled by the name of the person sending the video. Figure 27-8 shows how these two windows might appear.

You can detach either video window from its normal position by double-clicking its title bar. A detached video window normally floats on top of whatever window has the focus. You can make it a normal (not stay-on-top) window by right-clicking it and choosing Always On Top from the context menu. To reattach a detached video window, close it or double-click its title bar. Or right-click it and deselect Detach From NetMeeting.

Figure 27-9 shows the Video tab in the Options dialog box (choose Options from the Tools menu) with default settings. By default, NetMeeting receives video automatically at the start of a call, if the party on the other end of the connection has a camera. By default, video is sent automatically at the start of a call, if your computer has a camera.

FIGURE 27-8.

Video sent and received appears in two small windows, positioned by default at the right side of the Current Call window.

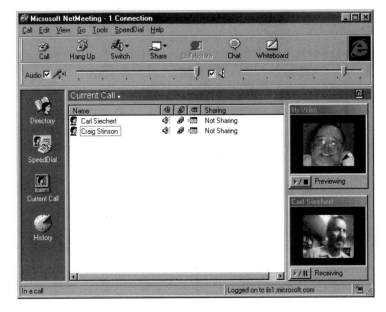

Because video transmission uses a lot of bandwidth and can degrade the performance of some of NetMeeting's other features (particularly shared programs), there might be times when you want to deselect either or both of the top two check boxes shown in Figure 27-9. You can also turn off video transmission in either direction after it has begun by clicking the stop button in the My Video or in the remote video window.

FIGURE 27-9.

By default, NetMeeting automatically uses video whenever possible at the start of a call.

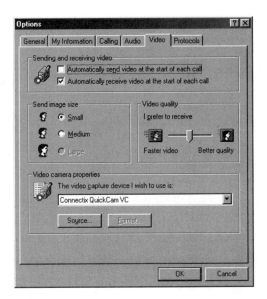

V

Sharing and Communicating

The Send Image Size and Video Quality sections of the dialog box allow you to trade quality for performance. NetMeeting sets the size to medium and the quality to middle-of-the-road by default. If you're working with a high-bandwidth connection (for example, if you're connecting with another user on your local-area network, or if your network is connected to the Internet through a high-speed T1 connection), you might want to move up to a larger image size and better quality.

If you're using a camera attached to a video-capture card, and you have more than one such card, the drop-down list at the bottom of the dialog box lets you specify the device you want to use.

> If you're considering buying hardware for use with NetMeeting, Microsoft says you'll get better performance from a camera connected to a video-capture card than from a camera connected to your parallel port.

Using Chat

The Chat window, shown in Figure 27-10, lets you send written messages to other call participants. You'll find this invaluable if you're not getting adequate sound quality from your connection or if you're communicating with more than one other user.

FIGURE 27-10.

The Chat window lets you send written messages to other call participants.

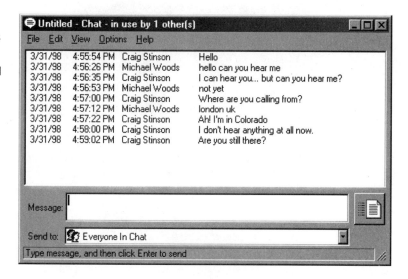

To use the Chat window, press Ctrl+T or choose Chat from the Tools menu. Then type whatever you want to send in the Message area of the window. When you press Enter, your message is transmitted, by default, to everyone else in the call. If you want to send it to one person only, select that person from the Send To drop-down list before you press Enter.

You can save or print a transcript of your chat session by choosing commands from the Chat window's File menu. You can change the font by choosing Font from the Options menu—but if the person receiving your messages doesn't have the font you choose, Chat substitutes a similar font on that person's display. Chat normally precedes each transmission with the date, time, and sender's name. You can suppress any of these header elements by choosing Format from the Options menu.

Using Whiteboard

Whiteboard, shown in Figure 27-11, is a drawing program that functions superficially like Paint, except that it's designed for sharing drawings, diagrams, screen shots, and other images with other users in a NetMeeting conference. Anything you create in the Whiteboard window is visible to all other parties in the conversation, and any participant can modify the whiteboard contents at any time. To run Whiteboard, choose Whiteboard from the Tools menu or press Ctrl+W.

FIGURE 27-11.
Whiteboard is a drawing program that lets you share images with other users in a NetMeeting conversation.

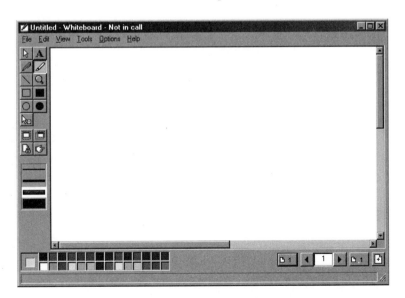

SEE ALSO

For information about Paint, see Chapter 18, "Drawing with Paint."

Like Paint, Whiteboard includes editing and line-width tools displayed to the left of the drawing window, and a color palette displayed below. You can enlarge the available drawing space by getting rid of the toolbar. (Choose Tool Bar from the View menu.) With the toolbar removed, you can use commands on the Tools menu to switch between editing tools and use the Options menu's Line Width command to change line width. Here's an overview of the available tools:

Use the Selector tool when you want to move, cut, copy, or recolor part of a drawing. Click the Selector tool, and then click anywhere on the object you want to manipulate. To select more than one object, drag a rectangle over the group of objects you want to manipulate.

The Text tool lets you add letters and words. Click the tool, and then click once wherever you want the text to go. Whiteboard displays a small rectangle for your text and expands the rectangle as you type. Words do not wrap. To begin a new line, press Enter. Whiteboard uses 8-point MS Sans Serif Regular in black as its default font. To change, choose Font from the Options menu or click a color in the color palette. Note that font and color changes always affect everything in the text rectangle. To emphasize part of your text, use the Highlighter tool.

The Pen tool lets you add freehand elements to your drawing. Click the tool, click the line width and color you desire, click a starting point in the drawing window, and hold down the mouse button while you move the mouse.

The Highlighter tool works just like the Pen tool, except that, if you choose an appropriate color, it creates transparent lines. Thus, for example, you can use yellow highlighting to emphasize particular words in a text object without obliterating the highlighted text. Note, however, that highlighting works best with light colors. You might want to experiment with highlighting colors before you use them in a presentation with your colleagues—particularly because Whiteboard does not include an Undo command.

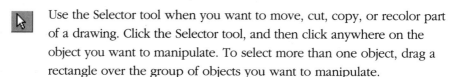 **TIP**

You can also use the Remote Pointer tool to call attention to a part of your drawing.

The Line tool creates straight lines in the current width and color. Note that Whiteboard's Line tool, unlike Paint's, does not constrain lines to particular angles when you hold down the Shift key. If you want perfect diagonals, horizontals, or verticals, you can do your work in Paint and then paste it into Whiteboard.

Clicking the Zoom tool enlarges your drawing. Clicking again returns it to normal size. If you're not displaying the toolbar, you can choose Zoom from the View menu.

The Unfilled Rectangle tool creates a rectangle in the current line width and color. Note that Whiteboard lacks Paint's ability to constrain rectangles into squares. If a perfect square is what you need, it's best to create it in Paint and paste it into Whiteboard.

The Filled Rectangle tool creates a solid rectangle in the current color. Note that Whiteboard has no counterpart to Paint's Fill With Color tool. If you want a rectangle filled with one color and outlined with another, use Paint and paste into Whiteboard.

The Unfilled Ellipse tool creates an ellipse in the current line width and color. If you need a perfect circle, use Paint and paste.

The Filled Ellipse tool creates a solid ellipse in the current color.

The Eraser tool works exactly like the Selector tool except that it deletes what you select. Click an object once, and the object is gone. Fortunately, although Whiteboard has no Undo command, it does have an Undelete command. Repair thereto if you zap the wrong object. After you have deleted something, the Undelete command stays active until you use it, even if you subsequently add new objects to your drawing.

TIP

> As an alternative to using the Eraser tool, you can select an object and press the Delete key.

The Select Window tool lets you paste an entire window into your drawing, making it easy to show the state of some program or document to your conference-mates. When you click the tool, Whiteboard displays a message saying that the next window you click will be pasted into your drawing. Then it gets out of the way and lets you click the window you

V

Sharing and Communicating

want to paste. Note that what you get is the client area of the window you click. If you click in a Word window, for example, you get the visible part of whatever Word document you're working in, along with Word's ruler (if displayed) and toolbar. You don't get the Word menu bar or title bar. Note also that if the window you click is displaying two or more document windows, you get only the active document window. After you paste your window, the window becomes a selected object. You can drag to reposition it.

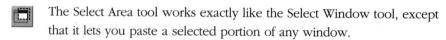 The Select Area tool works exactly like the Select Window tool, except that it lets you paste a selected portion of any window.

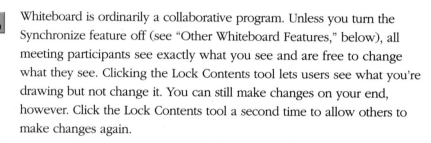 Whiteboard is ordinarily a collaborative program. Unless you turn the Synchronize feature off (see "Other Whiteboard Features," below), all meeting participants see exactly what you see and are free to change what they see. Clicking the Lock Contents tool lets users see what you're drawing but not change it. You can still make changes on your end, however. Click the Lock Contents tool a second time to allow others to make changes again.

Clicking the Remote Pointer tool displays a hand with outstretched index finger. You can move the hand to draw attention to a particular part of your drawing. Click the tool a second time to make the hand disappear.

Other Whiteboard Features

To work in Whiteboard without letting others see you at work, choose Synchronize from the Tools menu. Synchronize is normally on; choosing the command removes the check mark from its menu position and turns the feature off. When you're ready to show again, select the command a second time.

Whiteboard is object-oriented rather than pixel-oriented (as Paint is). When you create one object on top of another, they remain distinct objects. You can change the "z" (stacking) order of objects that lie atop one another by choosing Send To Back or Bring To Front from the Edit menu.

Whiteboard lets you create multipage documents. To insert a new page after the current page, click the Insert New Page button at the lower right corner of the Whiteboard window. To insert a new page before the current page, choose Insert Page Before from the Edit menu. To move between pages click the controls next to the Insert New Page button—or press Ctrl+Page Up or Ctrl+Page Down.

To save or print the current Whiteboard document, choose commands from the File menu. When you print, the Print dialog box lets you specify whether you want all pages or a selected page range.

Sending and Receiving Files

To send a file to all participants in your meeting, choose File Transfer from the Tools menu, and then choose Send File from the submenu. (Alternatively, press Ctrl+F.) To send a file only to a particular person, right-click that person's name in the Current Call window and choose Send File from the context menu.

Files that are sent to you are stored by default in the Received Files folder, a subfolder of your NetMeeting folder. You can change that location by choosing Options from the Tools menu and then clicking Change Folder on the General tab. You can use the View Files button, also on the General tab in the Options dialog box, to open your Received Files folder in Windows Explorer.

Sharing a Program

To share a program with other participants in your call, open the program you want to share. Then click the Share button on the Current Call window's toolbar. (If you're not displaying Current Call view, choose Share Application from the Tools menu.) From the list of running programs that appears, choose the one you want to share.

When you share a program, others can see what you see, but they can't work in the program. To enable others to work in the shared program, click the Collaborate button on the Current Call window's toolbar, or choose Start Collaborating from the Tools menu.

NOTE

When a program is shared amongst users with different screen resolutions, NetMeeting uses the highest available resolution. Users of lower-resolution displays might need to scroll to see the entire program.

V

Sharing and Communicating

When you collaborate on a program, only one user at a time can control the program. Other users then see that controlling user's mouse cursor, with that user's initials displayed beside it. To take control of the program away from the controlling user, click in the shared program.

If you share any Windows Explorer window, all the Windows Explorer windows you have open are shared. And once you have shared Windows Explorer, any program you start is also shared.

CHAPTER 28

Using Chat

Microsoft Chat is a program that lets you take advantage of an Internet service called Internet Relay Chat (IRC). IRC is the component of the Internet that lets you communicate with others all over the world in more-or-less real time by entering a "chat room" and typing at your keyboard. If you have an account with The Microsoft Network, America Online, or another similar service, you've probably found your way into one or more chat rooms already. But you don't have to be a member of an online service to use IRC. With Chat you can connect to an IRC server anywhere, get a list of available chat rooms, wander in, and start talking. You can even use Chat to create your own chat rooms.

Before you begin chatting, you should be aware of two things: not all chat-room content is suitable for children, and there are disreputable characters lurking on the Internet, particularly in IRC contexts. You can use Chat's content controls to screen out stuff that you don't want children (or others) to see. And to deal with the disreputable-character problem, you can choose a nickname that disguises your identity, gender, and age. Chat lets you attach "profile" information to your nickname, and you should avoid putting anything in the profile (your address, for example) that might be misused by your fellow chatters.

Comic Strip View Versus Plain Text View

One of the things that makes Chat different from most other IRC client programs is that it offers you the option of displaying the chat dialog as a comic strip. If you opt for Comic Strip view, you get to choose a comic character as your Chat persona, and whenever you say anything in the chat room, your words appear in a bubble above your character's head. Figure 28-1 shows an example of Chat's Comic Strip view.

FIGURE 28-1.
Chat's default view makes you a character in a comic strip.

If you're inclined to use your computer mainly for "serious" pursuits, the notion of becoming a comic-strip character may not have much immediate appeal. But Comic Strip view has one advantage over Plain Text view. In Comic Strip view, you can make the appearance of your character congruent with the feeling behind your words. If you say something you intend to be funny, for example, you can make your character laugh. If you are sad about something, have your character look sad. You don't need to add "emoticons" or other textual explanations to ensure that your fellow chatters understand what you're feeling.

On the other hand, in Plain Text view it's a little easier to tell who's talking. If several people in the chat room are using the same comic character, it's difficult to tell one from the other in Comic Strip view. In

Plain Text view, Chat displays the nickname of whoever is speaking. Figure 28-2 shows an example of Plain Text view.

Chat starts out in Comic Strip view. You can switch to Plain Text view by choosing Plain Text from the View menu. To switch back, choose Comic Strip from the View menu.

FIGURE 28-2.
In Plain Text view, it's easier to tell who's talking.

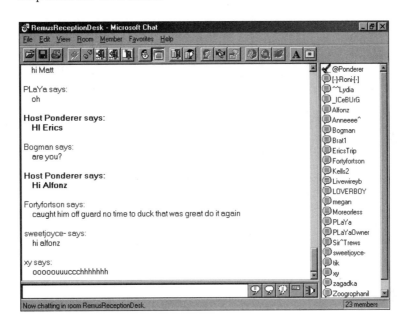

Getting Started with Chat

The first time you run Chat, you see the Chat Connection dialog box, shown in Figure 28-3, on the next page. On the Connect tab of this dialog box, you can choose the IRC server you want to connect to, as well as a particular chat room on that server. Before you make those choices, however, you'll want to visit the dialog box's other three tabs.

Entering Personal Information

Figure 28-4, on the next page, shows the Personal Info tab of the Chat Connection dialog box. Here you can enter as many or as few details about yourself as you want. Chat supplies some default entries for you. You should be aware that, while your nickname is the only identifier that appears above your utterances in Plain Text view (and in the user list that Chat displays in Comic Strip view), whatever entries you put in the

FIGURE 28-3.
This dialog box appears the first time you run Chat.

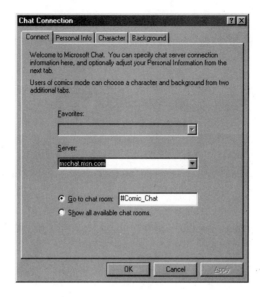

e-mail address, home page, and brief description areas are also available to anyone with whom you chat.

You can change your personal information at any time. To return to the dialog box shown in Figure 28-4, choose Options from the View menu and click the Personal Info tab.

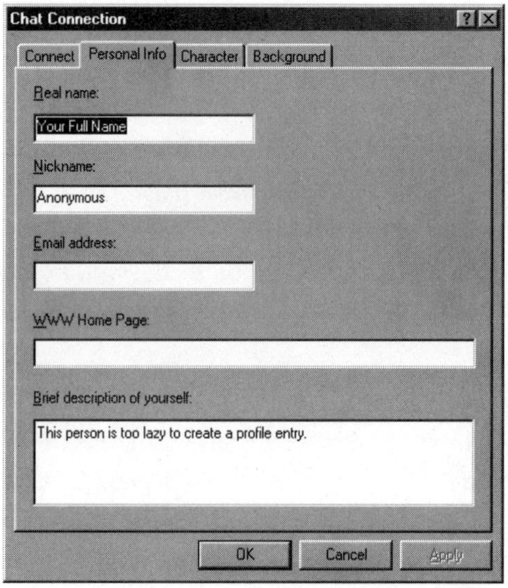

FIGURE 28-4.
Anything you enter in this dialog box (other than your real name) is visible to those with whom you chat.

Choosing a Comic Strip Character

If you're planning to use Comic Strip view, the next thing you'll want to do after entering your personal information is choose a character to represent you. Click the Character tab to arrive at the dialog box shown in Figure 28-5.

FIGURE 28-5.

Chat lets you choose from 11 comic strip characters.

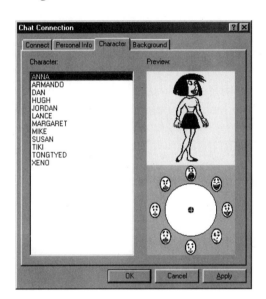

On the left side of the dialog box are the names of the 11 characters that Chat supplies. You can see what each one looks like by scrolling through the list. Initially, the characters are shown with a neutral affect. To see what moods are available, drag the black dot in the center of the emotion wheel, located in the lower right corner of the dialog box. As you move the dot toward the perimeter of the wheel, the emotion becomes more extreme. For example, if you select Anna in the character list and drag the dot from the center of the wheel toward the laughing face (at approximately one o'clock on the wheel), Anna moves from a mild chuckle to a hearty guffaw. (Note that not all degrees of all emotions are available for all characters.)

You don't have to commit to a particular emotion when you choose a character. You'll be able to change the character's affect at any time while you chat. But checking out the full range of each character's emotions in the Character dialog box might help you make a choice of character.

To switch characters later on, after you've begun using Chat, first be sure you're in Comic Strip view. Then choose Options from the View menu and click the Character tab.

Choosing a Background for Your Character

As your last setup step, you'll want to choose a background for your comic-strip character—provided, of course, that you plan to work in Comic Strip view. To do this, click the Background tab. Chat gives you three backgrounds to choose from. You can change your background later by choosing Options from the View menu and clicking the Background tab. You'll need to be in Comic Strip view when you do this.

Connecting to a Server and Entering a Chat Room

With your setup steps complete, it's time to log on to an IRC server and walk into a chat room. On the Connect tab in the Chat Connection dialog box (see Figure 28-3, on page 746), you'll find a Server drop-down list and a couple of option buttons. You can select one of the server names supplied in the drop-down list, or you can type the name of a server. (Some available servers not included in the drop-down list are comicsrv1.microsoft.com, comicsrv2.microsoft.com, and comicsrv3.microsoft.com.)

If you know the name of the chat room you want to enter, you can select Go To Chat Room and type that name. Alternatively, select Show All Available Chat Rooms and wait a moment or two while Chat gathers the room names from whatever server you've specified.

Once you've made your connections, you can switch to another chat room or another server at any time. Choose New Connection from the File menu, and you'll return to the Connect dialog box.

⭐ **TIP**

> If you find a chat room that you like so much you want to come back again and again, choose Add To Favorites from the Favorites menu. On subsequent visits to the Connect dialog box, you'll be able to select that room from the Favorites drop-down list.

Working with the Chat Room List

Figure 28-6 shows an example of the list that appears when you select Show All Available Chat Rooms on the Connect tab in the Chat Connection dialog box, shown in Figure 28-3, on page 746. (You can also display this list by choosing Room List from the Room menu.) Initially, the Chat Room List dialog box displays the names, the number of members present in, and the topic descriptions of all rooms on whatever server you're currently connected to.

FIGURE 28-6.

Chat's room list initially shows all rooms available on the current server. You can search for particular names and topics or limit the list to rooms that have a certain number of members.

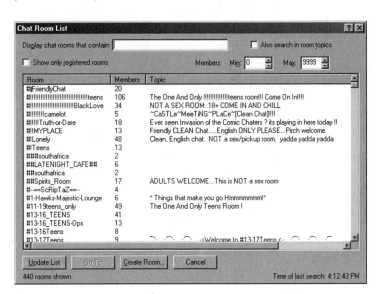

You can filter the list by entering a search string in the text box labeled Display Chat Rooms That Contain. Chat then searches through the Room column to find anything that matches your search string. If you want it to check the Topic column as well, select the Also Search In Room Topics check box.

If you're interested only in chat rooms that are currently populated by a certain number of users, enter values in the Min and Max boxes. Note that people come and go all the time in chat rooms. To make sure that the list has the correct population figures, click Update List before you enter values in the Min and Max boxes.

Conversing in the Chat Room

Whether you're in Comic Strip or Plain Text view, you talk in the chat room by typing in the text box at the bottom of the Chat window. As soon as you press Enter or click one of the buttons at the right side of the text box, your words are on their way.

Figure 28-7 shows the text box where you prepare your utterances, as well as the five icons associated with that text box. Note that after typing in the text box, you can express yourself in any of five ways.

FIGURE 28-7.

To express yourself, type in this text box and click one of the five icons at the right (or simply press Enter).

Type here.

To *say* something, type what you want to say and then click the Say button or press Enter. In Comic Strip view, your words appear within a balloon. In Plain Text view, Chat displays your nickname followed by the word *says*. Your words appear on the next line.

To *think* something, type in the text box and click the Think button. In Comic Strip view, your thoughts appear in a balloon, with bubbles connecting the balloon to your character. In Plain Text view, Chat displays your nickname followed by the word *thinks*. Your thoughts appear on the next line.

To *whisper* is to say something to a particular member or group of members only. First indicate who you want to whisper to by selecting one or more names in the member list that appears in the upper right corner of the Chat window. Then type in the text box and click the Whisper button.

 You can indicate an *action* by typing in the text box and clicking the Action button. In Comic Strip view, your action appears in a box across the most recent comic-strip pane, preceded by your nickname. For example, if your nickname is Zagadka and you type *pounds the table in frustration!*, Chat displays "Zagadka pounds the table in frustration!" In Plain Text view, Chat displays the same words in italics.

 You can play a sound to go along with your words. To do this, click the Play Sound button. Chat displays a dialog box that lists all the sound (.WAV) files in the current sound folder. In a text box in the same dialog box you can type the words that you want to accompany the sound. Select the sound you want to play, type the words that go with it, and then click OK. Any recipients who have the selected file in their own sound directories will hear the sound when your words appear.

Chat's default sound folder is C:\Windows\Media, assuming Windows is installed in C:\Windows. You can change that by choosing Options from the View menu, clicking the Settings tab, and typing in the Sound Search Path text box.

 TIP

In Comic Strip view, you can send an expression without saying anything. Simply right-click the emotion you want to send in the emotion wheel at the lower right corner of the Chat window. Then choose Send Expression from the context menu.

 TIP

If you get tired of hearing sounds sent by others, choose Options from the View menu and click the Settings tab. Then deselect the Play sounds check box.

V

Sharing and Communicating

Automatic Gestures in Comic Strip View

Chat supplies appropriate gestures for your character automatically when your text includes certain words. For example, if you say hello, your character holds a hand up to wave. If you type something in all capital letters, your character shouts. Table 28-1 provides a list of these automatic gestures.

Creating Message Macros

If you find yourself saying the same thing over and over again, you can encapsulate that utterance in a message macro. To do this, choose Options from the View menu and click the Automation tab. From the Key Combination drop-down list, select the keystroke combination you want to use to activate your macro. In the Name box, type a name for the macro. And in the large text box at the bottom of the dialog box, type the content of your macro. Finally, click the Add Macro button. You can create up to ten macros, assigned to the keystroke combinations Alt+0 through Alt+9.

Giving Someone the Cold Shoulder

You can tune out obnoxious members, so that their messages never arrive on your system. In the list of members that appears in the upper right corner of the Chat window, right-click the nickname of the party you don't want to hear from. Then choose Ignore from the context menu.

Saving, Opening, and Printing a Chat Session

If a particular chat-room conversation is so thrilling that you want to read it again and again, choose Save from the File menu and supply a filename. If you're in Plain Text view when you do this, Chat saves a rich-text-format (.RTF) file suitable for import into most word processors, including WordPad. If you're in Comic Strip view, Chat saves graphics and all. To read the transcript later, choose Open from the File menu.

To print a session, simply choose Print from the File menu. You can print a session as it's occurring, or you can save it and then open and print it later.

TABLE 28-1.   Automatic Gestures in Comic Strip View

When You Type	Your Character
are you	Points to the other person
will you	Points to the other person
did you	Points to the other person
aren't you	Points to the other person
don't you	Points to the other person
I am	Points to himself or herself
I'm	Points to himself or herself
I will	Points to himself or herself
I'll	Points to himself or herself
(All capital letters)	Displays shouting emotion
!!!	Displays shouting emotion
ROTFL	Displays laughing emotion (this is a chat abbreviation for "rolling on the floor laughing")
LOL	Displays laughing emotion (this is a chat abbreviation for "laughing out loud")
:) *or* :-)	Displays happy emotion
:(*or* :-(	Displays sad emotion
;-)	Displays coy emotion
At the beginning of a sentence	
I	Points to himself or herself
You	Points to the other person
Hello	Waves
Hi	Waves
Bye	Waves
Welcome	Waves
Howdy	Waves

V

Sharing and Communicating

Meeting Members Outside the Chat Room

Chat provides several means by which you can establish communication with a chat-room participant outside the chat room. You can send electronic mail to a member, invite the member to join you in another chat room, or invite the person to join you in a NetMeeting conference. You can also exchange files with a member or visit that person's Internet home page—provided one is listed in the member's personal information.

 There are two easy ways to invite someone into another chat room. You can simply whisper your invitation. (Select the member's name, type your message, and click the Whisper button.) Alternatively, you can go into the other room yourself and then choose Invite from the Member menu. In the ensuing dialog box, type the nickname of the person or persons you want to invite. If your party is connected to the same IRC server as you, he or she will see your invitation in a pop-up window.

To send electronic mail to a member, right-click the member's nickname in the member list and choose Send E-mail from the context menu. Chat activates your mail program, and, if the member has supplied an e-mail address with his or her personal information, sets up a message window for you.

To initiate a NetMeeting call to a member, right-click the member's name and choose NetMeeting from the context menu. Both you and that person must have NetMeeting installed for this to work.

 TIP

If you don't want to accept NetMeeting calls yourself, choose Options from the View menu and click the Settings tab. Then deselect the Receive NetMeeting Calls check box.

To send a file to someone, right-click the member's name, choose Send File from the context menu, and specify the file you want to send. The recipient will see a pop-up window asking whether he or she wants to accept the file.

 **TIP**

> If you don't want anyone to send files to you, choose Options from the View menu and click the Settings tab. Then deselect the Receive File Transfer Requests check box.

Hosting Your Own Chat Room

If there aren't chat rooms that focus on a topic of burning interest to you, you can set up your own room. As the host of a chat room, you get to define the room's properties—its topic, the number of members that it can accommodate, and various other matters. You can make the room invitation only, assign it a password, disallow whispered messages, or make the room a moderated chat room. In a moderated room, only the host and others designated by the host are allowed to speak. Everyone else is a spectator.

To create a new chat room, choose Create Room from the Room menu. You'll see the dialog box shown in Figure 28-8. Type a name for the room at the top of the dialog box and a topic below. Then select check boxes for the options that you want to apply to your room.

FIGURE 28-8.

If you host your own room, you get to set its properties.

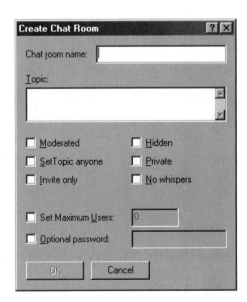

V

Sharing and Communicating

In addition to the aforementioned options, you can set up your room so that anyone is allowed to specify the room's topic. To do this, select the SetTopic Anyone check box.

After you've created your room, you can change its properties at any time. To do this, choose Room Properties from the Room menu.

Ejecting Unruly Participants from Your Room

As the host of a chat room, you get one other valuable privilege: you can give the heave-ho to anyone who doesn't meet your standards of decorum. You can eject members in either of two ways—by kicking them out or banning them. If you kick them out, they can come right back in. If you ban them, they're out until you "unban" them.

To kick a member out of your chat room, select the name of the person you want to eject. Choose Host, and then Kick, from the Member menu. A dialog box appears, in which you can type your reason for removing the person. A message box will then inform your ejectee of your decision.

To ban a member, select the member's name. From the Member menu, choose Host, Ban / UnBan. If you think you might later want to unban this person, write down the information that appears in the Ban / UnBan dialog box before you click OK.

Limiting Access to Unsavory Chat Rooms

SEE ALSO
For more information about using Content Advisor, see "Blocking Pornography and Other Objectionable Content," page 646.

You can use Internet Explorer's Content Advisor to control access to unacceptable chat-room content. The Content Advisor works exactly the same way in Chat as it does in Internet Explorer—and, in fact, your settings in either program are applied to the other. To get to the Content Advisor from Chat, choose Options from the View menu and click the Settings tab. Then click either Enable Ratings or Settings.

Publishing with Personal Web Server and FrontPage Express

Windows 98 provides several tools to help you publish information on the Internet or on an intranet. In this chapter, we'll explore two of these tools, Personal Web Server and FrontPage Express. Personal Web Server is a Web server that you can use on an intranet or as a test platform before you move your Web pages to the Internet. FrontPage Express provides an easy way to create, edit, and manage your Web pages.

The World Wide Web and Web Servers

In some respects, the World Wide Web works like the telephone system. When you pick up a telephone and dial a phone call, the phone company's network of switches routes the call to the number you dialed, the phone on the other end rings, and either a person or an answering machine answers. On the Web, when you try to connect to a Web site, Internet routers direct your request to the appropriate computer, and a computer on the other end then answers your request.

That computer on the other end and its related software is a *Web server* that is designed to deliver Web pages to Web browsers that request them. Every time you type an Internet address or click a link, your Web browser sends a request to the appropriate Web server, and the Web server figures out which Web page to send back to you. Each of these Web pages is written in a language called Hypertext Markup Language (HTML). Most Web server programs offer special features to help improve the speed at which pages are returned, but in general the function they provide is pretty simple. One of the most important aspects of Web servers is the number of simultaneous requests for documents they can handle. Web sites like www.microsoft.com receive thousands of page requests at any given moment. In contrast, personal Web sites, like the one you can set up with Personal Web Server, are designed to be set up quickly and easily, without worrying about the issues of concern to large-scale Web sites.

Some large Web servers, such as the ones used on Microsoft's Web site, provide the ability to use several different computers working together to support a large number of requests. Sometimes when a server is slow or takes a long time to respond to a link that you clicked, it is because the server is working through a large number of requests at the same time.

Using Personal Web Server

If you have a direct connection to the Internet (not a dial-up connection to an Internet Service Provider), or you work somewhere that provides an intranet (typically, a local-area network that uses the TCP/IP protocol), you can use Windows 98 to publish information, using a program called

Personal Web Server (PWS). Personal Web Server provides much of the functionality that commercial Web servers use, but it is simpler to set up and maintain.

Installing Personal Web Server

Personal Web Server is an optional component of Windows 98. If you launch Add/Remove Programs in Control Panel, you can find an entry for Personal Web Server amongst the Internet Tools options. You're welcome to select that option and "install" it, but you'll find that all this method really installs is a Start-menu shortcut and a Web page that explains how to *actually* install Personal Web Server. We'll save you the trouble and reproduce those instructions here, so you can bypass Add/Remove Programs.

To install Personal Web Server, follow these steps:

1 Insert your Windows 98 CD in a CD-ROM drive.

2 Choose Run from the Start menu.

3 In the Run dialog box, type *x:\add-ons\pws\setup.exe*, where *x* is the letter of your CD-ROM drive.

4 Click OK.

5 Follow the on-screen directions in Personal Web Server Setup.

Starting Personal Web Server

Personal Web Server, when installed, becomes an integral part of the Windows 98 operating system, and it starts automatically whenever your computer runs. As such, you don't need to do anything special to start Personal Web Server.

You might then wonder what Personal Web Server is up to; a utility called Personal Web Manager is available to answer that question. To start Personal Web Manager, open the Start menu and choose Programs, Internet Explorer, Personal Web Server, Personal Web Manager. Personal Web Manager, shown in Figure 29-1 on the next page, allows you to configure and use the Web server.

FIGURE 29-1.

Personal Web Manager lets you configure and customize Personal Web Server.

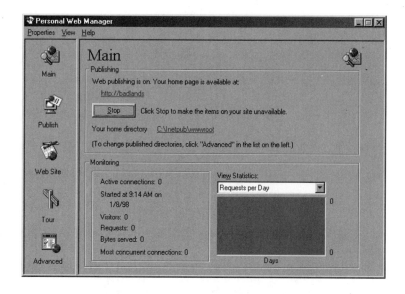

Setting Up Your First Web Site

Personal Web Server provides a wizard to help you get started. In Personal Web Manager, click the Web Site icon (in the navigation bar on the left side of the Personal Web Manager window) to start the Home Page Wizard. As you progress through the wizard's screens, you can set the following options:

- You can select a style for your home page. The style sets the fonts, colors, and images used on your Web pages. You can always change them later if you change your mind.

- You can set up a guest book, where visitors to your site can record their comments for subsequent visitors to see.

- You can provide a "drop box," a space for visitors to leave comments that only you can see.

In Personal Web Server and Personal Web Manager, "home page" refers to the first page that visitors to your site will see. Your home page normally provides introductory or "welcome" information and contains links to other pages at your Web site and at other Web sites. Be aware that Internet Explorer uses the same term to identify the first page you see when you launch Internet Explorer, which, despite the identical name, is not the same thing.

The wizard's final step opens your Web browser and allows you to enter the text that you want to appear on your home page. (See Figure 29-2.) When you're done, scroll down to the bottom and click the Enter New Changes button.

FIGURE 29-2.

The Home Page Wizard uses a Web-based form to help you set up your own home page.

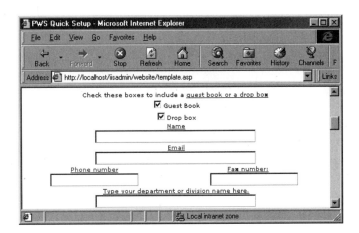

The wizard then takes you to a browser window that shows you what your site's home page looks like. Figure 29-3 shows an example. You can modify the settings for your page at any time by returning to Personal Web Manager and clicking the Web Site icon.

FIGURE 29-3.

Your first Web page might look something like this after the Home Page Wizard completes its work.

Using Personal Web Manager

With Personal Web Manager, you can configure everything you need to get Personal Web Server up and running, and you can customize your setup to match your needs. Personal Web Manager acts as both a status information area and a control station, allowing you to see how things are currently working and to make changes.

Personal Web Manager consists of five pages: Main, Publish, Web Site, Tour, and Advanced. Each page is represented by an icon in the navigation column at the left side of the window. Clicking any of these icons activates that page in Personal Web Manager.

- Main is the general-purpose control page. From here you can turn Personal Web Server on or off, and view status information.

- Publish launches the Publishing Wizard, which lets you "publish" (that is, make available to other users) files of any type on your Web site.

- Web Site launches the Home Page Wizard, which helps you create or customize your site's home page.

- Tour provides a quick overview of the features in Personal Web Server.

- Advanced lets you create a virtual hierarchy of folders (so you can organize folders in a logical way for visitors to your Web site) and place restrictions on what visitors can do with files in those folders.

 TIP

Many Personal Web Server settings can be changed only if Web publishing is turned on. To turn on Web publishing, open Personal Web Manager, click the Main icon, and click the Start button. If the only button is a Stop button, then Web publishing is already on.

Using the Main Page to Control and Monitor Your Server

The Main page, shown in Figure 29-4, displays the current state of Personal Web Server. From here you can see if Web publishing is currently active, the address of your site's home page, and the path to the folder where your home page is stored. The Main page also displays usage statistics for your site.

FIGURE 29-4.

The Main page is where you enable or disable Personal Web Server and view usage statistics.

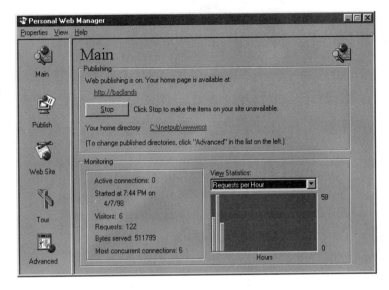

The Publishing section of the Main page displays information about the current state of your Web server, including whether Web publishing is on or off. When Web publishing is on, this area displays the address of your Web site's home page. You—or more importantly, others connected to your intranet—can view your home page by typing this address in Explorer's Address Bar.

The Stop button allows you to turn off the Web server. When Web publishing is turned off, nobody can visit your Web site; anybody who tries gets an error message in their browser. When Web publishing is turned off, the Stop button is replaced by a Start button that allows you to turn Web publishing back on.

TIP

You can turn Web publishing off or on without Personal Web Manager. Right-click the Personal Web Server icon in the taskbar's notification area and choose Stop Service to turn off Web publishing, or choose Start Service to turn it on again.

The path to your home directory appears below the Stop button. The home directory is the folder where Personal Web Server stores all your Web pages and related files. When a user connects to your server, Personal Web Server finds the appropriate page in this folder and delivers

V

Sharing and Communicating

SEE ALSO

For information about the Advanced page, see "Managing Folders with the Advanced Page," page 767.

it to the user. If you want to use a different folder as the home directory, you can change it by going to the Advanced page.

The bottom of the Main page displays statistics and status information about your Web server. The number of active connections tells you how many users are currently connected to your server. This area also tells you how many unique visitors have gone to your Web site and how many objects (such as HTML pages, graphics, and so on) have been requested since your computer was last started. If this is your first time using Personal Web Manager, most of these areas might be blank because no one has accessed your Web server yet.

 TIP

To see how the monitoring area responds to actual use of your server, open a Web browser and go to your home page. (The simplest way is to click the link to your home page near the top of the Main page.) If you then go back to Personal Web Manager, the monitoring area should report that someone has visited and requested a page.

The area to the right side of the monitoring section provides a graphical representation of some usage statistics. Select an item from the drop-down list to view the number of visitors to your Web site or the number of requested objects, broken down by hour or by day.

Using the Publish Page to Publish Other Files

Once your Web site is up and running, you might want to add files to your Web site that others can download to their computer. The Publish page lets you add all types of files to your Web site. This provides a way to post files you want to share with others, such as a document you want others to review, a shareware program, or a map to your office. You can do this easily by clicking the Publish icon, which launches the Publishing Wizard, shown in Figure 29-5.

You can publish any number of files. Simply follow these steps:

1 When you reach the wizard screen shown in Figure 29-5, type the path and filename of a file you want to publish (or click the Browse button to find it) and type a description of the file. (Visitors to your Web site will be able to see the filename and description, but not the path.)

FIGURE 29-5.
The Publish page lets you share files of any type on your Web site.

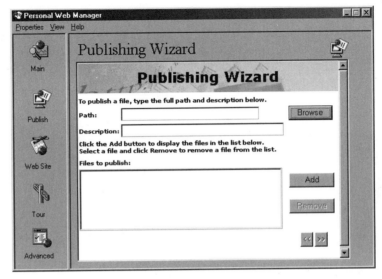

2 Click Add to place your entries in the Files To Publish list box.

3 Repeat steps 1 and 2 for any other files you want to publish.

4 Click the >> button to move to the next screen. Doing so publishes the files in your list.

Unlike most wizards, the Publishing Wizard doesn't have a Finish button. After it publishes your files, you can click the << button to make changes to your published files list, click another navigation bar icon to visit another Personal Web Manager page, or close Personal Web Manager.

To see what the Publishing Wizard has done, click the Main icon in Personal Web Manager, and then click the link to your site's home page.

The Publishing Wizard places a link on your home page that reads "View my published documents." When visitors to your home page click this link, they'll see a list of the files you've chosen to publish. Each entry includes a link to the file, the description you provided, and the size of the file. Visitors can download any of these files to their computer by clicking its link.

The next time you use the Publishing Wizard, it offers other choices: you can add or remove files from the list or change the file descriptions. In addition, you can "refresh published files from their originals." When you use the Publishing Wizard to publish a file, the wizard doesn't grant visitor

V

Sharing and Communicating

access to your original file. Instead, it makes a copy of your file in the webpub folder; it's this copy that visitors can retrieve from your Web site. If you make changes to your original file and you want those changes reflected in the copy that's on your Web site, you'll need to revisit the Publishing Wizard and refresh the files.

Using the Web Site Page to Manage Your Home Page

The Web Site page launches the Home Page Wizard. As you saw earlier in this chapter, the Home Page Wizard can create your first home page. After that page already exists, the Web Site button allows you to edit your home page, view your guest book, or view your drop box. (See Figure 29-6.)

FIGURE 29-6.

After you've created a home page, the Home Page Wizard lets you customize it and view messages from visitors to your Web site.

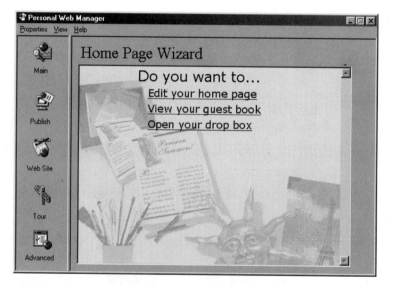

Clicking the "Edit your home page" link takes you to a page similar to the one you used to enter your personal information. (See Figure 29-2, on page 761.) With this option, you can select a different template and change any of the information that appears on your home page.

The link to your guest book allows you to find certain messages based on criteria you specify (such as date posted, author name, and subject); sort them by date, author, or subject; and view them. You can leave the messages in place or delete them when you're through viewing them.

The link to your drop box offers similar capabilities for reviewing its messages.

Managing Folders with the Advanced Page

The Advanced page, shown in Figure 29-7, lets you control which folders visitors to your Web site can see, and what visitors can do when they reach your site.

FIGURE 29-7.

On the Advanced page, you set up your virtual directories and set other advanced options.

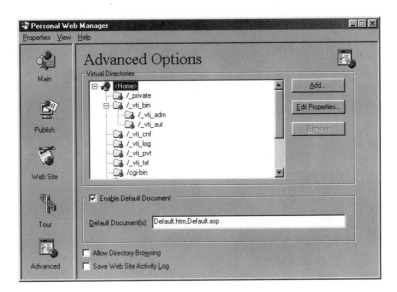

Virtual directories provide a way to make a connection between folders or directories on your hard drive and custom URLs that the Web server knows about. This is useful if you want to keep files organized one way on your computer, but have them appear to be organized differently when accessed through your Web server.

Before you add a new virtual directory, you should decide how you want to set the check-box options shown in Figure 29-7.

Selecting the Enable Default Document check box allows you to pick which Web page should be sent to visitors who try to connect directly to the root address of your Web site without specifying the name of a Web page. In the Default Document(s) box, type the name of the Web page that you want such visitors to see. (If you specify more than one page, Personal Web Server delivers the first listed page that it can find.)

Selecting Allow Directory Browsing enables users to navigate through your virtual directories.

Selecting Save Web Site Activity Log causes Personal Web Server to maintain log files of activity on your site. The log files are stored in the folder C:\Windows\System\Logfiles\W3svc1, assuming Windows is installed in C:\Windows. You can read the log files in WordPad. Personal Web Server opens a new log file at the beginning of each month.

To create a new virtual directory, follow these steps:

1 Click the Add button.

2 In the Add Virtual Directory dialog box, type the path on your computer of the folder that you want to add as a virtual directory.

3 Type the "alias" for the folder, which is the path you want to use to access the directory from the Web site. For example, if the address of your server is http://webserver and you specify *sneakers* as the alias, then the address for that virtual directory is http://webserver/sneakers/

4 In the Access section of the dialog box, select the check boxes for the access privileges you want to enable.

    By default, a new virtual directory has Read and Scripts privileges, but not Execute privileges. That means that users will be able to open or download files and run scripts. They will not be able to run ordinary executable program files (.EXE files, for example) in the virtual directory, but they will be able to download executables onto their own machines and run them there. For security purposes, it's a good idea not to enable the Execute privilege.

⭐ TIP

> With Personal Web Server running, the properties dialog box for a folder acquires a new Web Sharing tab. You can also create a virtual directory for a folder by right-clicking the folder in Windows Explorer, choosing Properties, and clicking the Web Sharing tab. Select Share This Folder, and then enter an alias and assign the appropriate access privileges.

Using FrontPage Express

Personal Web Manager provides tools to create a home page and a few related pages, but your design options are limited. (After all, Personal Web Manager's real purpose is to manage Personal Web Server.) If you want to go beyond those limitations, use FrontPage Express, an optional component of Windows 98. FrontPage Express helps you to design and create Web pages for the Internet or for your Personal Web Server, and to link an unlimited number of pages together. FrontPage Express allows you to work with Web pages without having to learn HTML. You simply use menu commands and toolbar buttons to add text, pictures, and links, and FrontPage Express does the rest.

To launch FrontPage Express, open the Start menu and choose Programs, Internet Explorer, FrontPage Express.

> If FrontPage Express has not been set up on your computer, launch Add/
> Remove Programs in Control Panel, click the Windows Setup tab, select Internet
> Tools, and click the Details button. Select FrontPage Express and click OK.

Exploring the FrontPage Express Window

The window you see when you start FrontPage Express looks much like that of WordPad or any other text-editing program: it includes a menu bar, a toolbar, and a work area. (See Figure 29-8, on the next page.) The toolbar has buttons for the common actions you take while editing a Web page, such as changing the selection to boldface or italic or inserting option buttons and check boxes. Clicking a button on the toolbar either modifies the selection or adds an item to your page. Table 29-1, on the next page, describes the tools in the FrontPage Express toolbars.

Using FrontPage Express to Customize Existing Web Pages

If you already have Web pages you have created, or if you want to modify the default pages provided by Personal Web Manager, choose Open from the File menu. If the file is on your computer, click Browse, and then navigate to the folder that has the file you want. If it's on the Internet or your intranet, type its address.

V

Sharing and Communicating

FIGURE 29-8.

FrontPage Express provides a familiar-looking window to help you edit your Web pages.

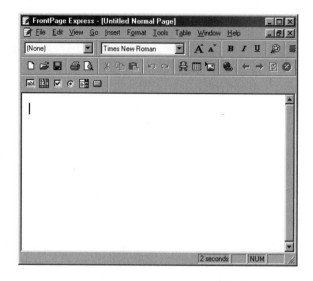

TABLE 29-1. **FrontPage Express Toolbars**

Toolbar Icon	Description
Standard Toolbar	
	Creates a new Web page, which can be blank or based on a template or wizard
	Opens an existing Web page
	Saves the current Web page
	Prints the current Web page
	Shows the page as it will look when printed
	Cuts (deletes) the selection and places it on the Clipboard
	Copies the selection to the Clipboard
	Pastes (inserts) the Clipboard contents at the insertion point
	Undoes your last editing or formatting action

(continued)

TABLE 29-1. *continued*

Toolbar Icon	Description
Standard Toolbar	
	Redoes the last action canceled by Undo
	Inserts a WebBot, a small program that runs when you save the page on a Web server or when a visitor views the page
	Inserts a table
	Inserts a picture
	Inserts a hyperlink to another location on the current page, another page, or another Internet address
	Displays an earlier page in the list of previously viewed pages
	Displays a later page in the list of previously viewed pages
	Downloads the current page again, ensuring that the latest saved version is displayed
	Stops downloading the current page
	Displays or hides paragraph marks and other formatting symbols
	Displays help
Format Toolbar	
[None]	Selects a style for the selected paragraph
Times New Roman	Changes the font (typeface) of the selection
A	Increases the size of the selected text

V

Sharing and Communicating

(continued)

TABLE 29-1. *continued*

Toolbar Icon	Description
Format Toolbar	
A	Decreases the size of the selected text
B	Changes the selection to boldface (or, if the selection is already boldface, changes it back to normal)
I	Changes the selection to italic (or, if the selection is already italic, changes it back to normal)
U	Underlines the selection (or, if the selection is already underlined, removes the underline)
A	Changes the color of the selection
≣	Left aligns the selected paragraphs
≣	Center aligns the selected paragraphs
≣	Right aligns the selected paragraphs
⅟≣	Changes the selected paragraphs to a numbered list (or, if the selection is already numbered, removes the numbering)
≔	Changes the selected paragraphs to an indented, bulleted list (or, if the selection is already bulleted, removes the bullets and indents)
⇤≣	Decreases the selected paragraphs' indent from the left margin
⇥≣	Increases the selected paragraphs' indent from the left margin

(continued)

TABLE 29-1. *continued*

Toolbar Icon	Description
Forms Toolbar	
	Inserts a one-line text box
	Inserts a multiline, or scrolling, text box
	Inserts a check box
	Inserts a radio button, or option button
	Inserts a drop-down list
	Inserts a push button, or command button

Creating a Hyperlink

You can insert hyperlinks—items on Web pages that, when clicked, take the user to another page—anywhere in your Web page. The address used for specifying where to take the user is called a *URL* (Uniform Resource Locator). To make a word or picture into a hyperlink, follow these steps:

1 Select the word, phrase, or picture that you want to make into a hyperlink.

2 Click the Insert Hyperlink button.

The Create Hyperlink dialog box appears, as shown in Figure 29-9 on the next page.

3 Click the appropriate tab for the type of link you want:

- Click the Open Pages tab if you want to create a link to another page in the current Web site.

FIGURE 29-9.

The Create Hyperlink dialog box allows you to specify where a given link will lead. You can specify local files or other Web sites.

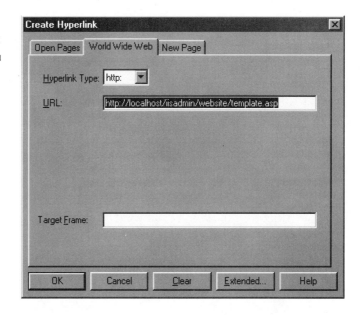

- Click the World Wide Web tab to create a link to another Web site.

- Click the New Page tab if you want to create a link to a new page in the current Web site. After you click OK, FrontPage Express creates a new page with the name you specify on this tab.

4   Type the URL for the Web page you want this link to take the user to. Then click the OK button to finish.

Creating a Table

It is common for a Web page to show information in a table format. Tables are useful not only for traditional table formats—such as tables of numbers—but also for aligning columns of text.

To add a table to your page, click the Insert Table button. The button expands to show a grid where you specify the number of cells in your table, as shown in Figure 29-10. Click in the upper left corner, and then drag to highlight the number of columns and rows you want.

After you release the mouse button, FrontPage Express inserts the table. You can move from cell to cell by pressing the Tab key.

FIGURE 29-10.
To insert a table, click the Insert Table button and drag to highlight the number of cells you want.

3 by 3 Table

X CAUTION

You can accidentally make changes to the HTML that can be difficult to correct. To be safe, click Cancel when you close the HTML viewer unless you are sure that the changes you made are safe.

Viewing the HTML for a Page

Sometimes you might want to make a very specific change to the HTML for your Web page, or you might just be curious about what the page looks like in raw HTML. To view your current page as HTML, open the View menu and choose HTML. This opens a dialog box that displays the HTML, and you can make changes and edits directly to the page's underlying HTML code. To see the effect of your changes and go back to WYSIWYG (What You See Is What You Get) editing, click OK in the View Or Edit HTML dialog box.

Publishing a New Page

If you've set up Personal Web Server as described earlier in this chapter, you can now publish your new page onto your Web site. Here's how:

1 Choose Save from the File menu. Give your page a title, and take note of the page location; you'll need it in the last step. Then click OK.

2 Start Personal Web Manager. Open the Start menu and choose Programs, Internet Explorer, Personal Web Server, Personal Web Manager.

3 To add the page to your list of published pages, click the Publish icon, select Add A New Page, and click the >> button. This takes you to the window shown in Figure 29-5, on page 765, where you can add your page to the list of published pages.

   If you want to create a link to your page on your home page (rather than requiring visitors to go to your list of published pages), click the Web Site icon. Then click the "Edit your home page" link. When the home-page editing page opens in Internet Explorer, type the address to your page (the page location) in the URL text box, type a description, and click Add Link.

V

Sharing and Communicating

Index

X

About the Author

Craig Stinson An industry journalist since 1981, Craig Stinson is a contributing editor of *PC Magazine* and was formerly editor of *Softalk for the IBM Personal Computer*. Craig is a coauthor of *Running Windows NT Workstation Version 4.0* and *Running Microsoft Excel 97*, both published by Microsoft Press. In addition to his numerous computer publications, Craig has written music reviews for *Billboard*, the *Boston Globe*, the *Christian Science Monitor, Musical America*, and other publications. He lives with his wife and children in Highlands Ranch, Colorado.

Craig can be reached at **craigstinson@free-market.net**

Colophon

The manuscript for this book was prepared using Microsoft Word 97 for Windows and submitted to Microsoft Press in electronic form. Pages were composed using Adobe PageMaker 6.5 for Windows, with text type in Garamond and display type in Myriad. Composed pages were sent to the printer as electronic prepress files.

Cover Graphic Designer
Tim Girvin Design

Interior Graphic Designer
designLab

Copy Editors
Carl Siechert
Stan DeGulis

Technical Editors
Blake Whittington
Thomas Williams

Layout Artist
Paula Kausch

Proofreader
Cheryl Kubiak

Indexer
Carl Siechert

Microsoft Press has titles to help everyone— from new users to seasoned developers—

Step by Step Series
Self-paced tutorials for classroom instruction or individualized study

Starts Here™ Series
Interactive instruction on CD-ROM that helps students learn by doing

Field Guide Series
Concise, task-oriented A–Z references for quick, easy answers— anywhere

Official Series
Timely books on a wide variety of Internet topics geared for advanced users

All User Training　　　All User Reference

Quick Course® Series
Fast, to-the-point instruction for new users

At a Glance Series
Quick visual guides for task-oriented instruction

Select Editions Series
A comprehensive curriculum alternative to standard documentation books

Microsoft Press® products are available worldwide wherever quality computer books are sold. For more information, contact your book or computer retailer, software reseller, or local Microsoft Sales Office, or visit our Web site at mspress.microsoft.com. To locate your nearest source for Microsoft Press products, or to order directly, call 1-800-MSPRESS in the U.S. (in Canada, call 1-800-268-2222).

Prices and availability dates are subject to change.

start faster and go farther!

The wide selection of books and CD-ROMs published by Microsoft Press contain something for every level of user and every area of interest, from just-in-time online training tools to development tools for professional programmers. Look for them at your bookstore or computer store today!

Professional Select Editions Series
Advanced titles geared for the system administrator or technical support career path

Microsoft Certified Professional Training
The Microsoft Official Curriculum for certification exams

Best Practices Series
Candid accounts of the new movement in software development

Microsoft Programming Series
The foundations of software development

Professional   Developers

Microsoft Press® Interactive
Integrated multimedia courseware for all levels

Strategic Technology Series
Easy-to-read overviews for decision makers

Microsoft Professional Editions
Technical information straight from the source

Solution Developer Series
Comprehensive titles for intermediate to advanced developers

Microsoft®*Press*

mspress.microsoft.com

Start something big!

U.S.A. $49.99
U.K. £46.99 [V.A.T. included]
Canada $71.99
ISBN 1-57231-874-0

If you seek the productivity power that comes with a thorough working knowledge of Microsoft® Word 97 and/or Microsoft Excel 97, this is the fast and effective way to get it. MICROSOFT WORD 97/EXCEL 97 IN-DEPTH TRAINING STARTS HERE™ is an interactive, task-based training program that teaches you through hands-on step-by-step lessons how to get the most out of Word 97 and Excel 97.

MICROSOFT WORD 97/EXCEL 97 IN-DEPTH TRAINING STARTS HERE is also the ideal preparation if you intend to pursue end-user certification. Word 97 training consists of two courses, one preparing you for the MOUS Proficient exam and one for the MOUS Expert exam. The same is true of the courses for Excel 97. There are 70 lessons in the combined courses, representing 20 hours of training.

Microsoft *Press*

In-depth reference and *inside tips* *from the* software experts.

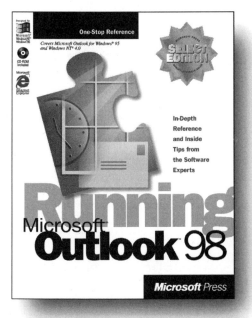

U.S.A. **$34.99**
U.K. £32.99 [V.A.T. included]
Canada $50.99
ISBN 1-57231-840-6

It's packed with everything from quick, clear instructions for new users to comprehensive answers for power users. And it's complete in one volume. In short, RUNNING MICROSOFT® OUTLOOK™ 98 is the authoritative handbook you'll keep by your computer and use every day.

CD loaded with must-have extras:
- Get fast on-screen answers from a searchable version of the book
- Cruise the Web using Microsoft Internet Explorer 4

Microsoft®*Press*

IMPORTANT—READ CAREFULLY BEFORE OPENING SOFTWARE PACKET(S). By opening the sealed packet(s) containing the software, you indicate your acceptance of the following Microsoft License Agreement.

MICROSOFT LICENSE AGREEMENT

(Book Companion CD)

This is a legal agreement between you (either an individual or an entity) and Microsoft Corporation. By opening the sealed software packet(s) you are agreeing to be bound by the terms of this agreement. If you do not agree to the terms of this agreement, promptly return the unopened software packet(s) and any accompanying written materials to the place you obtained them for a full refund.

MICROSOFT SOFTWARE LICENSE

1. GRANT OF LICENSE. Microsoft grants to you the right to use one copy of the Microsoft software program included with this book (the "SOFTWARE") on a single terminal connected to a single computer. The SOFTWARE is in "use" on a computer when it is loaded into the temporary memory (i.e., RAM) or installed into the permanent memory (e.g., hard disk, CD-ROM, or other storage device) of that computer. You may not network the SOFTWARE or otherwise use it on more than one computer or computer terminal at the same time.

2. COPYRIGHT. The SOFTWARE is owned by Microsoft or its suppliers and is protected by United States copyright laws and international treaty provisions. Therefore, you must treat the SOFTWARE like any other copyrighted material (e.g., a book or musical recording) except that you may either (a) make one copy of the SOFTWARE solely for backup or archival purposes, or (b) transfer the SOFTWARE to a single hard disk provided you keep the original solely for backup or archival purposes. You may not copy the written materials accompanying the SOFTWARE.

3. OTHER RESTRICTIONS. You may not rent or lease the SOFTWARE, but you may transfer the SOFTWARE and accompanying written materials on a permanent basis provided you retain no copies and the recipient agrees to the terms of this Agreement. You may not reverse engineer, decompile, or disassemble the SOFTWARE. If the SOFTWARE is an update or has been updated, any transfer must include the most recent update and all prior versions.

4. DUAL MEDIA SOFTWARE. If the SOFTWARE package contains more than one kind of disk (3.5", 5.25", and CD-ROM), then you may use only the disks appropriate for your single-user computer. You may not use the other disks on another computer or loan, rent, lease, or transfer them to another user except as part of the permanent transfer (as provided above) of all SOFTWARE and written materials.

5. SAMPLE CODE. If the SOFTWARE includes Sample Code, then Microsoft grants you a royalty-free right to reproduce and distribute the sample code of the SOFTWARE provided that you: (a) distribute the sample code only in conjunction with and as a part of your software product; (b) do not use Microsoft's or its authors' names, logos, or trademarks to market your software product; (c) include the copyright notice that appears on the SOFTWARE on your product label and as a part of the sign-on message for your software product; and (d) agree to indemnify, hold harmless, and defend Microsoft and its authors from and against any claims or lawsuits, including attorneys' fees, that arise or result from the use or distribution of your software product.

DISCLAIMER OF WARRANTY

THE SOFTWARE (INCLUDING INSTRUCTIONS FOR ITS USE) IS PROVIDED "AS IS" WITHOUT WARRANTY OF ANY KIND. MICROSOFT FURTHER DISCLAIMS ALL IMPLIED WARRANTIES INCLUDING WITHOUT LIMITATION ANY IMPLIED WARRANTIES OF MERCHANTABILITY OR OF FITNESS FOR A PARTICULAR PURPOSE. THE ENTIRE RISK ARISING OUT OF THE USE OR PERFORMANCE OF THE SOFTWARE AND DOCUMENTATION REMAINS WITH YOU.

IN NO EVENT SHALL MICROSOFT, ITS AUTHORS, OR ANYONE ELSE INVOLVED IN THE CREATION, PRODUCTION, OR DELIVERY OF THE SOFTWARE BE LIABLE FOR ANY DAMAGES WHATSOEVER (INCLUDING, WITHOUT LIMITATION, DAMAGES FOR LOSS OF BUSINESS PROFITS, BUSINESS INTERRUPTION, LOSS OF BUSINESS INFORMATION, OR OTHER PECUNIARY LOSS) ARISING OUT OF THE USE OF OR INABILITY TO USE THE SOFTWARE OR DOCUMENTATION, EVEN IF MICROSOFT HAS BEEN ADVISED OF THE POSSIBILITY OF SUCH DAMAGES. BECAUSE SOME STATES/COUNTRIES DO NOT ALLOW THE EXCLUSION OR LIMITATION OF LIABILITY FOR CONSEQUENTIAL OR INCIDENTAL DAMAGES, THE ABOVE LIMITATION MAY NOT APPLY TO YOU.

U.S. GOVERNMENT RESTRICTED RIGHTS

The SOFTWARE and documentation are provided with RESTRICTED RIGHTS. Use, duplication, or disclosure by the Government is subject to restrictions as set forth in subparagraph (c)(1)(ii) of The Rights in Technical Data and Computer Software clause at DFARS 252.227-7013 or subparagraphs (c)(1) and (2) of the Commercial Computer Software — Restricted Rights 48 CFR 52.227-19, as applicable. Manufacturer is Microsoft Corporation, One Microsoft Way, Redmond, WA 98052-6399.

If you acquired this product in the United States, this Agreement is governed by the laws of the State of Washington.

Should you have any questions concerning this Agreement, or if you desire to contact Microsoft Press for any reason, please write: Microsoft Press, One Microsoft Way, Redmond, WA 98052-6399.

Register Today!

Return this
Running Microsoft® Windows® 98
registration card for
a Microsoft Press® catalog

U.S. and Canada addresses only. Fill in information below and mail postage-free. Please mail only the bottom half of this page.

1-57231-681-0   *RUNNING MICROSOFT®*   *Owner Registration Card*
                         WINDOWS® 98

NAME

INSTITUTION OR COMPANY NAME

ADDRESS

CITY   STATE   ZIP

Microsoft®*Press*
Quality Computer Books

**For a free catalog of
Microsoft Press® products, call**
1-800-MSPRESS

**NO POSTAGE
NECESSARY
IF MAILED
IN THE
UNITED STATES**

BUSINESS REPLY MAIL
FIRST-CLASS MAIL   PERMIT NO. 53   BOTHELL, WA

POSTAGE WILL BE PAID BY ADDRESSEE

MICROSOFT PRESS REGISTRATION
RUNNING MICROSOFT® WINDOWS® 98
PO BOX 3019
BOTHELL   WA   98041-9946